Transitions, Environments, Translations

Transitions, Environments, Translations

Feminisms in International Politics

edited by

Joan W. Scott, Cora Kaplan, Debra Keates

ROUTLEDGE
New York and London

Published in 1997 by

Routledge
29 West 35th Street
New York, NY 10001

Published in Great Britain in 1997 by

Routledge
11 New Fetter Lane
London EC4P 4EE

Printed in the United States of America
Design: Jack Donner

Library of Congress Cataloging-in-Publication Data

Transistions, environments, translations : feminisms in international politics
edited by Cora Kaplan, Debra Keates, Joan W. Scott
Revised papers from a conference held April 1995 at Rutgers University
Includes bibliographical references and index.
ISBN 0–415–91540–6 (hb) — ISBN 0–415–91541–4 (pb)
1. Feminisms—Congresses. I. Kaplan, Cora. II. Keates, Debra. III. Scott, Joan Wallach.
Hq1106.T73   1997
305.42—dc20   96–41590
CIP

Contents

Acknowledgments

The Conference which produced these papers was funded by the American Council of Learned Societies, the Ford Foundation, the Rockefeller Foundation, and the Rutgers University Research Council. We would like to thank Jason Parker, Alison Bernstein, Sheila Biddle, Alberta Arthurs, and Lynn Szwaja for their encouragement and support. For their invaluable assistance in organizing the conference, we are grateful to Lisa Marcus, Beth Hutchison, and Arlene Nora at the Institute for Research on Women at Rutgers University, and to Deborah Koehler at the Institute for Advanced Study. Meg Gilbert did yeoman work preparing the manuscript for publication, Anne Hartman was tremendously helpful in the final stages of production, and Maureen MacGrogan was a terrific editor. We appreciate the quality of their work and the generous spirit with which it was carried out.

Introduction

The papers in this volume (with a few exceptions) were presented at a conference held in April 1995. Jointly organized by the Rutgers University Institute for Research on Women and the Institute for Advanced Study's School of Social Science, with funding from the Ford and Rockefeller Foundations and the American Council of Learned Societies, the conference was called "Transitions, Environments, Translations: The Meaning of Feminism in Contemporary Politics." In the course of three days, scholars and scholar-activists from many parts of the world presented information, compared their situations, and analyzed one another's premises—engaging in the kind of hard thinking and sustained debate that distinguishes academic work at its best.

After the conference, participants rewrote or revised their papers taking into account points made about their presentations as well as the issues that had become central to the discussions. We also solicited a few additional papers where they seemed particularly relevant. The organization of sections and chapters in the book departs somewhat from the conference format, for connections among papers often became apparent only when we had all the final drafts in hand. And the title has been adjusted to emphasize both the international dimensions of the project and the multiplicity of political and social movements that are referred to or refer to themselves as "feminist."

By pluralizing *feminism* we mean to signal the variety and complexity of women's movements throughout the world. The addition of *international* suggests both the importance of national differences among feminists and the fact that our movements transcend national boundaries. The new title captures the central preoccupation of the conference: the attempt to articulate the relationship between feminism as a universal movement for women's rights and feminism as a set of particular movements deeply rooted in national or regional histories.

The purpose of the conference was to explore the varied meanings of feminism in different political, cultural, and historical contexts and to ask whether all movements directed at women's interests were feminist movements. We wanted to examine in concrete detail the situation of women and women's movements in recent political and economic transitions in such places as Eastern Europe, the former Soviet Union, South Africa, China, and India, and to ask what these movements had in common with one another and with their Western counterparts. Instead of asking how these movements measured up to some ideal standard (which would have been a standard based on the history of feminism in Western Europe and the United States), we considered feminism to be a site of local, national, and international political and cultural conflict. We asked: What is at stake in various collective political efforts by women in different parts of the world? What meanings have women given to their efforts? What has been their connection to feminism, as a concept and as an international movement?

The relationships between the local and the international, the particular and the universal, are not easy to disentangle. In fact, their inextricable connection and the tension between them were evident in the conference discussions and are apparent in these papers. At least since the United Nations put women on the global agenda twenty years ago, it is impossible to address questions about women's needs, interests, and rights in purely local terms. And yet there is also no single standard, no essential meaning, no common language that "women" can be said to share. The originary, universalist status of Enlightenment traditions has been severely challenged, and in some instances displaced, by women who consider themselves feminists, but who reject the individual-rights claims that typified feminism in Western Europe and the United States in the nineteenth and early twentieth centuries. *Translation* in the sense of rendering more or less faithful copies of an original does not seem to capture the emergence of feminism outside of Western Europe. And yet, to the extent that there are recognizable similarities between concepts and actions in very different locations and languages, some kind of translation does seem to be taking place. Anna Tsing, in her paper in this volume, redefines translation as a continual negotiation, an irregular, haphazard process in which terms are appropriated from one context to another and then used to do different work. She urges us to attend to the process instead of trying to locate the original and analyze the faithfulness of the copies. "Faithless translation" is the term she uses to describe what is going on.

This volume provides a case study in "faithless translation." Its authors are engaged in a difficult process of negotiation around the terms *women* and *feminism*. Their papers analyze the negotiation historically and in contemporary politics and they are also part of the negotiation. The authors employ a number of strategies—structural analyses, historical comparisons, linguistic examinations, theoretical interpretations— to point up the differences in apparently similar situations. Their insistence on difference has the paradoxical effect of producing commonality—not, however, a commonality based on mutual recognition of the same, but a commonality based instead on an appreciation for difference and an awareness of the need to understand the operations and effects of difference in the arena of politics, even feminist politics.

The essays are organized topically and geographically. Part I, "Women and the State," is, as its title suggests, addressed to the political situation of women and to the ways in which women's movements develop in relation to state power. Most of the essays in this section deal with Eastern and Central Europe, although in the first section, "After State Socialism," we have included Lin Chun's piece on China both for its contrasting substantive material and for its theoretical analysis of state socialism. The essays by Margaret Watson and Susan Gal address the question of civil society and whether its emergence since 1989 has contributed to a "remasculinization" of politics in Eastern and Central Europe. Watson stresses the need to reconceptualize "civil society" if we are to understand why greater gender inequality seems to characterize the emergence of democracy and the introduction of market economies. Myra Marx Ferree compares the structures of patriarchy in East and West Germany as a way of understanding differences among women's movements before and after unification. And Hana Havelková pursues an argument she made eloquently at the conference, about Western misunderstandings of the experiences of women in Eastern Europe. "Nationalist Discourse" features three papers written by women from the former Yugoslavia (two are from Slovenia, one from Croatia). In different ways and with different takes on the situation, each discusses the relationships among ethnic mobilization, gender, and feminist political interventions in the current war. "Women's Movements" offers detailed information about and analyses of the structure, history, and substance of contemporary women's politics in a number of countries in Eastern and Central Europe. The authors are from Germany (both West and the former GDR), Poland, Slovenia, Hungary, and Bulgaria. The material they present at once permits generalizations to be drawn about women and politics in the post-Communist era and challenges the idea that Eastern Europe can be characterized as a single entity. The papers also provide important comparative information for pursuing the questions Sabine Lang raises about the effects of participation in state-supported organizations (whether parties or NGOs) on women's ability to press for fundamental reform in gendered structures of power.

Part II takes up issues of economic development and environmentalism. Two papers explore the effects of development projects on women in India and Ethiopia and women's responses to these projects. In the Indian case, as detailed by Bina Agarwal, the responses of women combine concern for the environment with concern for women's economic subsistence. The next two papers continue the exploration of links between feminism and environmentalism. They examine not only the gender dimensions of environmental movements in India and Indonesia, but also the ways in which local, national, and global interests intersect and conflict in the articulation of a politics aimed at protecting nature and natural resources. Both Yaakov Garb and Anna Tsing remind us that what counts as "nature" is as complex and open to contest and negotiation as what counts as "women" and "women's interests."

Part III addresses race in women's movements in the United States and South Africa. What have been the possibilities for and the limits of cooperation between black and white women in emancipatory and reform politics? How has difference been handled in these different political contexts? The papers—by an African-American and two South Africans, one black and one white—make clear that race is not a simple or transparent category that automatically structures lines of political affiliation, even though it has been central in organizing social life and individual experience. Each details the ways in which the recognition and repression of difference, within and across racial boundaries, has operated, sometimes to facilitate effective political engagement and sometimes to inhibit it. While Evelynn Hammonds and Jacklyn Cock provide historical perspective on these questions, Mamphela Ramphele offers a strategy for thinking about gender in the context of nonracialism in the postapartheid era.

Part IV takes up the question of women's studies—the production of new knowledge by and about women. In these papers questions about institutionalization and theoretical "translations" abound. The answers offered depend on the author's analysis of the context she describes. While Svetlana Kupryashkina and Anastasia Posadskaya-Vanderbeck stress the importance of developing what might be called "indigenous" women's studies in Ukraine and Russia, Zakia Pathak describes a pedagogy that employs Western theory ironically, to interrogate traditional values and practices in the interests of generating an Indian feminist politics. Kupryashkina and Posadskaya-Vanderbeck disagree, however, on the question of the location for women's studies, one arguing for the university as the appropriate base, the other for autonomous research institutes with no ties to the state. Afsaneh Najmabadi tracks Iranian feminists as they work (through journals and newspapers) within the terms of Islamic fundamentalism, looking to Western feminism not for theory, but for models of strategic intervention. And Rosi Braidotti complicates the notion of a "Western feminism" by looking at the ways in which Western theories have traveled and been transformed in multiple crossings of national borders within Europe and between Europe and the United States. The reports of these authors detail a variety of strategies for producing feminist knowledge; they describe different sites of activity and different modes of institutionalization. Their papers can be read as separate accounts of diverse national experiences; they can be read comparatively with an eye to identifying different structural, historical, and political constraints on feminist research and teaching; and they can be read in conversation with one another, as participants in the process of international negotiation that is the phenomenon we refer to as "global feminism."

All of the articles in this book should be read in conversation with one another. There are themes that carry over from section to section, despite ostensible differences in subject matter. There are arguments that reappear about women's movements and the state, whether it is women's studies or NGOs that are under consideration. We have tried as much as possible to preserve the atmosphere of the conference: multiple conversations, intense disagreements, sharp insights about the nature of difference, equally sharp observations about similarities, misunderstandings based on linguistic barriers, glimmers of understanding achieved by painstaking "translations." What we have here is not the raw materials out of which an international feminist movement will be built, but the movement itself—a contentious process in which difference is negotiated but never transcended or subsumed, in which women figure out how to cooperate in their particular strategic negotiations of the shifting grounds of gender politics.

< part one >

Women and the State

After State Socialism

< 1 >

Finding a Language

Feminism and Women's Movements in Contemporary China

Lin Chun

The pioneer literature bearing the new feminist consciousness produced by a few women scholars and novelists in China had a distinct voice in the general humanist and individualist turn of the country's political and cultural discourse immediately after the Cultural Revolution in the late 1970s. But it was not until the mid-1980s that a more or less autonomous wave of women's activities—organizational as well as intellectual—emerged.

There were, of course, existing government organs of "women's work," which were, however, never completely integrated into the state power structure. In fact, the first National Conference on Women's Issues (1984), which addressed the social impact of economic reforms on women's work and life, was jointly convened by the official All-China Women's Federation (ACWF) and several universities and research institutes. The new market-oriented environment not only directly affected women, but also posed a challenge to the established ideology of gender equality. Indeed, it was expected that the Women's Federation should side with its traditional constituency to resist, above all, the imminent threat of female unemployment. The next meeting with even more organizers and participants from nongovernment institutions or as independent individuals/collectives, was held in 1985. The first book series on women's studies appeared in 1986, and the first university research center was set up in 1987; it was soon followed by a number of others. The first feminist international conference in China outside the reach of ACWF occurred in 1990. By the early 1990s, many more women, mainly urban but also rural, had been involved in what might be now called nascent women's movements. These included self-organized discussion and support groups, training schools, conferences, telephone hotlines, radio talk shows, various cultural undertakings, oral history projects, professional associations, publication and translation initiatives, and the introduction of relevant college courses. Thanks to these developments, the government is now under greater pressure than ever before, since its reforms have been justified in terms of the interests of the entire population, including women.

Apart from the autonomous women's movements, feminist politics is now also visible especially in the People's Congress. Female deputies at both the national and local levels are in a stronger position to advocate prowomen policies and regulations. They make up 21 percent of the congress and, at the very least, are able to coordinate their efforts to speak on behalf of women in demanding realization of what the government has claimed or promised to do in various new laws and in commitments made to the international community to improve women's conditions and to protect children. Also remarkable is that some deputies have been actively involved in women's studies and other activities.[1]

The fourth United Nations Women's Conference, held in Beijing in 1995, was a far-reaching and unusual event for the Chinese. It was taken by the government as a matter of state, and the administrative and propaganda machines were duly mobilized to ensure its security and success (as seen by the authorities). This caused unexpected difficulties for those who were involved in the task of organizing, as well as distortions of the original intention and messages of the conference. But from a different perspective, the conference's scenes and themes enjoyed a high profile and immense publicity. Consequently the "women question," as it is customarily called in China, was further politicized and attracted attention from wide-ranging social circles throughout the country. Moreover, it was a rare chance for most Chinese participants (over five thousand) to exchange views with women from other parts of the globe. Another invaluable experience was to learn about NGOs: Although the word was familiar to the Chinese participants, both the literal meaning of the term and the discussion of NGO-type activities were introduced into China for the first time as a result of the conference. There were also other important gains at different levels, including increased legitimacy for women's studies and increased pressure on the government to improve conditions of female existence. Thus, despite all the clashes and setbacks evoked around the conference, the Chinese women's movements profited from it and, as a result, are continuing to advance with a greater sense of political and moral urgency.

How can we explain the emergence of autonomous women's movements? They were certainly enabled by two parallel processes: a significant retreat of the state and a rapid expansion of the market. The current women's movements would not have emerged without the post-1978 economic reform and its political and social consequences. The reform has had two basic effects: On the one hand, it has dismantled some of the actual policy arrangements for protecting women and thus also the ideology of universal emancipation, creating new barriers to liberation. On the other hand, the reform has also opened up unprecedented opportunities for women's self-organization and self-realization in the autonomous spheres outside the state's control. At first glance the negative side appears to be overwhelming. In the marketplace, women are more and more frequently turned into sexual objects, exploited, discriminated against, and abused. Dictates of "economic rationality" are beginning to prevail. Echoing the logical realities of the market, liberal intellectuals have emerged to attack the already diminished social commitment to egalitarianism. For them, the price of socialist gender equality has proven to be too high when measured by the efficiency principle, and henceforth gender inequality can and must be rejustified. On the grounds of a "natural" gender division of labor, these intellectuals suggest that women should happily return home "by choice"; that this is also the only way out of the now mounting umemployment predicament should be acknowledged.[2]

Women's movements rejected these views and resisted regression in female working and living conditions. It is here that the positive side of postreform social changes also manifests itself. In the space no longer occupied by the state and its ideologies, autonomous activities, fresh information, unfamiliar concepts, and, indeed, free thinking flourish. Women welcomed these changes because they brought new possibilities for action. Their position is necessarily contradictory: They lost preferential treatment by the state but gained freedom and independence in their relationship to the state. It is in this space of contradiction that women's movements in China have positioned themselves in order to explore and renovate the meaning of liberation.

"FEMINISM"

These developments, from the growth of women's studies in the universities and other research institutes to the wider political-social activities for women's rights and interests, are recent phenomena compared to what has taken place in Europe, the United States and many "third world" countries. The belated formation of women's movements in China, and many of their peculiarities, can be explained only by China's unique historical trajectory, which has precluded a separate feminist politics. Modern Chinese history was, at least in part, a history of simultaneous revolutionary struggles against both external imperialist powers and domestic "feudal" traditions. In these struggles women's emancipation was synonymous with national and social emancipation. Consequently male domination has not been a separate problem for universal nationalist or socialist agendas. The idea of "modernization" has inspired many different movements. Both the earlier Republican revolution, which involved the heroic participation of educated women, and the later Communist mobilization of women workers and peasants claimed to be "modern." The official postrevolutionary definition of women's work and the present women's movements for self-determination are also on the side of modernity. Modernization, without being linked with any particular theoretical or actual models in the West, has served the Chinese as a sign, signifying a just alternative to a traditional past when women were always at the bottom of society. The emancipation of women thus was an indicator of modernity. By this standard, the Communists can be seen as the most effective modernizers.

But surely "liberating women" differs from "women's (self)-liberation," and new research has revealed how "traditional" the Communists have actually been in their own gender politics.[3] But the point here is that the country accomplished an epic revolution, one that made a tremendous difference in women's lives. To begin with, there was a well-conceived unity but also a hidden tension between women's and universal liberation, and this has haunted modern Chinese reformers and revolutionaries from the outset. Chinese Communism in its embryonic stage chose the figure of a woman as the icon for all that needed to be saved in an imminent social crisis. The nation was engendered in political discourse as a raped and crippled female now ready to rebel. The revolution took Confucian ethics as its principal target and strongly aligned itself with a political critique of ancient patriarchalism. In this configuration, women's emancipation was to be essential to national salvation. A key step toward both was the abolition of a landlord system organized around clanship, which also formed the local regime allied with the imperialist power. Accordingly, overthrowing the oppression of women by clan authority and male domination in the family was an articulated goal of the revolution itself, in which vast numbers of women participated. [4] In this sense the Communist revolution was also intrinsically "feminist," although it was careful to distinguish its women's emancipation from the "bourgeois" feminism of the West.

There are two rather contradictory outcomes of such a Communist feminism. On the one hand, there was the development of a socialist state that was women-friendly, but on the other hand, because this state took responsibility for women's salvation, there also developed a dependence on the state that trapped the female population (along with the urban working class). After all, the postrevolutionary society did not achieve a democratic system capable of sustaining individual—either male or female—rights, civil liberties, or full citizenship. Thus, even if it is true that Chinese women enjoyed formal gender equality, they still shared with their fellow countrymen a place of dependency. The social consensus on equality expressed in official and popular rhetoric, as well as in legal and policy formulations, coexisted with the subordination of the people to the Party. As such, socialism was conceived in statist and paternalistic terms; women's liberation, and for that matter all social liberation, was fundamentally limited.

The lessons we may draw from the ambiguous experiences of Chinese women include this: Socialism ought to be analyzed not in terms of its suppression of any "genuine," essential female subject, but in terms of its core internal contradictions between the ideas of liberation and subordination, self-mastery and selfless submission, democratic participation and passive dependence. However, it is not the case that the twentieth-century trajectory of Chinese women through the revolutions and socialist experiments is a story of top-down "imposed" liberation, as some argue these days. It is fairer to acknowledge women's own contribution to the Party-led liberation process and its real achievements as well as its fundamental limits. To realize that voluntary and political participation does not necessarily imply empowerment is to see how the language and project of liberation got lost or hijacked by the ideology of "inevitable socialist advancement." This explains why a collective consciousness that might have been described as feminist did not arise in China until very recently. Feminism had little space to develop in a society where a monopolized political education embraced the principle of gender equality and deemed its female members to be already liberated. It is therefore understandable why all but a tiny minority of urban intellectuals under Western and/or Russian influence (mainly in the 1910s and the 1920s) found feminism an alien concept.

LIVING WITH CONTRADICTIONS

As mentioned earlier, the current women's movements in China are a product of the contradictory social conditions brought about by recent economic and political reforms. These reforms have changed the relationship between the project of women's liberation and the state, both of which are undergoing transformation. These conditions, in turn, shape and are reflected in the patterns of conflict within the movements.

The changing relationship between women and the state is best exemplified by the changes of and uncertainty felt among those who are involved in women's studies and gender politics. What is to be made of such government statements as "the All-China Women's Federation is a Chinese Communist Party mass organization. . . [and] is the largest women's NGO in China" (February 1995)? Historically the Women's Federation has been either powerless when it lacked official sponsorship or powerful when it had the backing of the state (as during the land reform campaigns) or served as its representative (as during the 1995 UN conference). The ACWF was never part of the state machinery, but could be an extension of it. Still, the process of having actually prepared the NGO forums for the UN conference began to transform the Women's Federation into an NGO. It seems possible that, coincident with a more general liberalization and decentralization process, the ACWF would become a more or less independent women's association on a par with other organized groups and NGOs. Indeed, compared with the still politically paralyzed All-China Federation of Trade Unions, another "Communist Party mass organization," the ACWF seems to be well on the track to autonomy and real empowerment.

Ever since the campaign for "protecting the rights and interests of women and children" was launched by the Women's Federation, the growing women's movements in China have benefited not only from the strong and devoted participation of their many members, but also from the institutional support that the Women's Federation and its nationwide network could supply. Yet the gap between a state-sponsored organization and those individuals and groups who seek political independence remains deep and inevitable. There are divisions, and at times also bitter disputes, between the ACWF's central office in Beijing and activists who collaborate with the provincial and local branches of the Women's Federation. Retaining their inherited ties with the official institutions whose support is often still crucial, the women's movements on the whole are no longer directed by the Party. They have created a space for independent thinking and communicating, for political initiatives and activity—a "public sphere" (the term is just beginning to make sense for the Chinese)—and hence for a truly democratic citizenship. In contrast to what is happening in Eastern Europe, these new public spheres in China appear to have, at least at this stage, a feminist rather than a masculinist character.

It is worth noting that women's studies in China has been for the most part oriented toward empirical research and aimed at the production of immediate policy formulations or reformulations in the People's Congress and the State Council. They have taken up issues such as discrimination in job recruiting; effects of village and township enterprises on the lives of rural women; conditions for women migrant workers and ethnic minority women; the dropout rate of schoolgirls; women's education, health and labor conditions; domestic violence and other forms of abuse that particularly affect women; women's human rights and legal reform; sexuality, marriage and the family (particularly questions of population and birth control); and the female image in the media and popular culture. So far this practical orientation represents the most valuable strength of the movements. Being directly engaged in politics and political debates, the women's movements are enlarging social concerns in public discourse to include the moral and ecological considerations that go into decision making.[5] Yet slowly, the importance of intellectual engagement in reconceptualization has also begun to be recognized, inspired by newly introduced ideas from the outside world, as well as by outstanding though still scattered theoretical works accomplished in China.[6]

It is promising that women are setting an example for others to follow. In alliance with other potential social movements and public actions involving workers (in their future organized union movements), peasants (ongoing village self-governing movements), intellectuals (with their traditional interest in civil rights and education), general citizens (who have an emerging ecological consciousness), and supporters within the government offices, the women's movements can and will reshape the social consequences of market expansion while regrounding the state in a more democratic way. A new kind of women-friendly state can be invented (as in the Nordic countries as well under different conditions) in a market environment. For we cannot avoid recognizing that such a state is in fact a necessary instrument for women's liberation. That is to say, rejecting political and psychological dependence while attaining autonomous citizenship by no means implies neoliberalist assumptions. It is interesting here to compare the feminist defense of the welfare state in the United States against charges that it promotes "dependency"[7] with feminist critiques of dependency in terms of the future of democracy in China. Both American and Chinese feminists share the conviction that a democratic citizenry and a state pursuing social welfare and justice are indispensable for one another.

REINTERPRETING FEMINISM

The term *feminism* was long ignored in China. And when, after a period of hesitation and deliberation, it began to be widely used in the 1990s (albeit with substantial modification) to refer to the Chinese movements, its original Chinese translation was abandoned and replaced. The wording turned out to be so important that for quite a while those who were involved were not able to choose from several possibilities or reach consensus. (Indeed, decades of Communist politics have only reinforced traditional wisdom about the sensitivity and constructive power of language.) Finally, instead of the translation used at the turn of the century, in which "-ism" was added to "women's empowerment" or "women's rights" *(nu-quan-zhuyi),* the new translation is *nu-xing-zhuyi,* or "womenism." Since the terms *power* and *rights* have the same written character and pronunciation in abbreviated Chinese, *quan* (in full expression they are each a two-character phrase with the identical first character but different second characters which, however, are pronounced the same), the original translation, *nu-quan-zhuyi,* does not distinguish between the two and can embrace both. Now, as the keyword *quan,* or "empowerment/rights" is dropped in the phrase and replaced with *xing,* or "sex," the term simply sounds modest and neutral, never mind how it might be interpreted otherwise.

It does not matter what the word *feminism* literally means in English; it has always had many interpretations anyway, possibly including something like "womenism" as well. What concerns us here is how and why there occurred this serious change in the Chinese translation; and moreover, what is conveyed when the old word *(nu-quan-zhuyi)* is resisted for the Chinese context, but still applied to women's studies and movements elsewhere especially in the West. Nowadays in writings from the Chinese women's studies we see references to "womenism" when Chinese ideas and movements are in question, and to "feminism" when what is referred to is non-Chinese. This deliberate distinction between Western feminism and Chinese womenism reflects an awareness of differences between the historical conditions of the West, where the term originated, and those of China, where the revolutionary and socialist experience created a different meaning for *feminism.* Following earlier Western Marxist teachings, "feminism" in China has been associated with the bourgeoisie and with so-called bourgeois feminist movements in Europe and North America, which are distinguished from Chinese national/social/women's liberation movements.

This distinction is not based on ignorance—although the impression in China, largely unexamined, is still that there is a single Western feminist tradition, which takes male dominance as its enemy and neglects the larger context of social relations. But *nu-xing-zhuyi* (womenism) is very unlikely to be replaced by the old *nu-quan-zhuyi* (feminism) in Chinese usage even though feminist literature from the West has begun to be translated and read. This is also not a matter of political caution: Well before *womenism* was invented, *feminism* was used and did not evoke official intervention or censorship. The innovative translation represents a specifically Chinese feminist consciousness, which recognizes the historical heritage of what I have named "Communist feminism" and the differences this heritage has produced. In addition, the new term avoids another possible linguistic confusion. In Chinese, *nan-quan-zhuyi* or "male dominance," is an alternative term for "patriarchalism." The early translation replaced *nan* or "men," with *nu* or "women," thus leaving open the possibility that the Chinese word for "feminism" could mean "women's dominance" or "matriarchalism." This is conceptually trivial but tactically sensitive. Contemporary women's liberation leaders do not want to be seen as simply reversing the gender hierarchy. For all these reasons, then, feminism as a concept that carries a Western set of concerns and conditions lost its chance to be revived in China. By way of retranslating, the Chinese women's movements discarded it once and for all.

Still, although Chinese scholars found feminism to be anachronistic and Occidental in character, they were not prevented from appreciating some feminist ideas and identifying with the more or less global cause of women's liberation. A basic background factor here is, of course, the market-oriented reforms. Hitherto unknown phrases and concepts are flowing into a society now open to the outside world, economically as well as intellectually. The potential impact of the introduction of the term *gender* provides an illustration. Gender as a social category and a concept central to feminist thinking was introduced for the first time to a group of Chinese women researchers meeting in Tianjin in July 1993. It generated an unexpected excitement.[8] Having no equivalent in the Chinese vocabulary, it could be used to denote the cultural construction or social organization of male and female subjects and subjectivity. Although the sociocultural aspect of sexual difference is not altogether missing in relevant Chinese writings from the classical age on, the absence of the notion of gender precluded any conceptual analysis of the mechanism and nature of gendered socialization. The concept of *gender* could help dismantle biological determinism which still entangled women in China, including many committed womenists. A Chinese translation was proposed: *shehui-xingbie*, or "social sex." To what extent the new word can be articulated in the Chinese language and context as a useful category remains to be seen.

It does not follow, however, that any feminist concept or movement, wherever it may occur, is necessarily a translation of something originally Western, nor the localization of a universal project. There are translations (which are historically specific) and there are indigenous traditions of women's efforts to achieve liberation. In the Chinese case, women's liberation has taken a unique route, one that selectively explored foreign influence. And the new Chinese womenism is taking shape by reading its differences from Western feminism.[9]

The task is therefore to rediscover or reinterpret or transplant key concepts. These concepts are crucial in struggles for ideological or cultural hegemony. But neither their meanings nor their political and social affiliations are the same in all times and places. They do not translate uniformly across these different contexts. Their meaning must be discovered; it cannot be assumed.

Returning to *gender* what is interesting is how the lack of a linguistic term could have actively affected our perspectives and analyses. In China, even within the women's movements, the idea that there are essential, fatally disadvantageous biological traits of "natural woman" is a commonplace. Women are seen as physiologically limited and nothing can change this, not even a liberation project. Epistemologically, this is a trap that not only justifies a patriarchal state treating women as a weaker and often also disabled sex, but also maintains the misleading dilemma of having to choose between equality or difference. Traditional socialist conceptions of liberating women by erasing sexual difference altogether have been widely criticized on the grounds that they universalize male desires and abilities. But the alternative—to recognize difference while still insisting that equality requires sameness—continues to pose a puzzle. Perhaps the substantial conceptual advance represented by *shehui-xingbie* (social sex) will enable women in China to pursue genuine equality while holding to notions of diversity and individuality as well as a collective identity of women and of humanity.

Behind the equality problematic lies the pressing question of whether there are not more universal tasks for women's movements in a society marked by state paternalism. In a society that lacks an independent exercise of citizenship for both men and women, it is not enough to oppose male dominance. Here one understands precisely why the term *feminism,* narrowly interpreted as "opposing male power," is rejected. The political potential of the women's movements goes beyond the issue of gender equality per se because the public patriarchy of the Chinese state means that citizenship is a general problem. Thus when the patriarchal state is challenged in the name of women's liberation, it is challenged to its root. Perhaps just a strategic reverse in the same liberation project of the earlier case of national/ social revolution embracing women's liberation—now women's studies and movements—in China can articulate a universal concept of emancipation. It is in turn the foundation of an equal and shared democratic citizenship.

NOTES

I am heavily indebted to Joan Scott for her insightful questions, suggestions and editorial help. I am also grateful to Rosi Braidotti and other participants of the Rutgers-Princeton Conference at which this paper was originally presented for their critical comments and discussions.

1. For example, Wu Qing is a deputy to the Beijing municipal People's Congress and a leading figure in women's studies. Cf. her account in Alida Brill (ed.), *A Rising Public Voice: Women in Politics Worldwide* (Feminist Press, 1995).
2. Cf. for example, articles by Zheng Yefu and Sun Liping in *Sociological Research* (a major publication of the Chinese Academy of Social Sciences) 2 (1994).
3. See, for example, Tani Barlow's introduction to Ding Ling, *I Myself am a Woman* (Boston: Beacon, 1989) and Christina Gilmartin, "Gender in the Formation of the Communist Body Politics," *Modern China* 19, no. 3 (July 1993).
4. See, especially, Mao Zedong on the four interdependent powers to be overthrown by the Chinese revolution: the regime kept by the imperialist forces, religious superstition, clan patriarchy, and husband-turned-master, in "Report on the Peasants Movement in Hunan" (1927), in *Selected Writings*, vol. 1 (Beijing: Foreign Language Publisher, 1970).
5. For example, since 1993 the Chinese Academy of Social Sciences has organized four large conferences on women's health and rights in relation to social ethics and population control, and formally proposed policy suggestions based on the results of the conference discussions to the State Commission for Family Planning.

6. For the Chinese scholarship, cf., for example, Li Xiaojiang, "Economic Reform and the Awakening of Chinese Women's Collective Consciousness," in C. K. Gilmartin et al. (eds.), *Engendering China: Women, Culture, and the State* (Cambridge, MA: Harvard University Press, 1994), and "Creating a Public Sphere: Women's Studies Movement—A Case in Self-Analysis" (unpublished manuscript), among her many writings. Also see the series *Women's Studies*, published by the People's Publishing House in Henan since 1986. For a brief survey of more recent developments, see Liu Bohong, "When Everybody Adds Fuel the Flames Rise High," *Views in Women's Studies* (1996), and Liu Bohong, Jin Yihong, and Lin Chun, "Women's Studies in China," in Alison Jaggar and Iris Young (eds.), *A Companion to Feminist Philosophy* (Oxford: Blackwell).

7. Cf., for example, Nancy Fraser and Linda Gordon, "Contract Versus Charity: Why Is There No Social Citizenship in the United States?" *Socialist Review* 12, no. 3 (July–Sept. 1992), and "A Genealogy of Dependency: Tracing a Keyword of the U.S. Welfare State," *Signs* 19, no. 2 (winter 1994).

8. Since then, a few key texts in this reconceptualization have been translated into Chinese, including Joan Scott, "Gender: A Useful Category of Historical Analysis," in *Gender and the Politics of History* (New York: Columbia University Press, 1988).

9. Also worth mentioning is a marginal but precious prerevolutionary literary tradition, completely native, that cherished the humanity and independence of women and was contributed to by both male and female authors.

< 2 >

Civil Society and the Politics of Difference in Eastern Europe

Peggy Watson

Exploration of the limits to mutual understanding, such as those that have become increasingly apparent in the dialogue between Western feminists and women in post-Communist Europe, offers the prospect of a better knowledge, not only of one's interlocutor, but also of oneself. In this vein, the present essay seeks to establish what is at issue in the "rejection" of feminism by women in post-Communist countries, and the surprise this reaction has occasioned in the West. Enikö Bollobás, an American studies specialist and from 1990 an official of the Hungarian Embassy in Washington, has written, for example, that she has "found more gaps between Western and Eastern views on women than exist on most other issues, such as democratic institution building, economic transformation, or environmental protection."[1] Nanette Funk has written, too, of how West German feminists perceive East German women as "backward" with respect to Western feminism, and as having "failed to appreciate" their new freedom, while East German women have resented West Germans theorizing about them, instead of reflecting on blind spots in their own thinking.[2] What lies behind this non-meeting of minds? I argue that it is the specifically *political* difference of women: an aspect of self-identification presupposed by Western feminists, yet by and large still repudiated by women in the East. The essay pursues this incongruence of collective identity by asking what the specific experience of competitive democracy, or of Communism, means subjectively for women, given that in objective terms, so much of that experience is shared. In seeking to address this question, I am thus also trying to define a comparative framework in which East and West can be seen as both relatively discontinuous (at least until 1989) *and* essentially indivisible (i.e., mutually constitutive and often materially similar) social formations. The idea of relative discontinuity is important if one wants to grasp the way in which Communism and competitive democracy provide separate and distinct fields of reference within which social phenomena that are essentially continuous over the East-West divide (for example, the sexual division of labor, the subordination of women, indeed the term *women* itself) gain political-regime-specific meaning. One way of characterizing these different fields of reference, of grasping the

quite different principles of collective/individual identity formation involved in each
case, is by reconsidering the implications for women of Western civil society as opposed
to the society that takes shape in the context of the prerogative state of Communism—
contrasting concrete (nonabstract) political and civil citizenship on each side. This
approach will, I think, make clear the extent to which a "transition to democracy" or a
"reconstruction of civil society" in Eastern Europe—its approximation to "European
civilization"—itself involves *the* politicization of difference, which is a prerequisite for
feminism as identity politics. As I shall argue below, such a conclusion is something
quite distinct from what is implied by the current use of "civil society" in the recent
feminist literature on transition in post-Communism, where the assumption is that civil
society offers freedom for the natural expression of unquestioned preexisting political
differences (of which gender is only one example), which Communism has simply suppressed.

POLITICAL IDENTITY AND IDENTITY POLITICS

The refusal of feminism that has been so widely noted in Eastern Europe, not only by
Westerners, but also by Eastern European activists themselves, represents more than
simply an allergy to a term contaminated by woman-emancipating Communism. After
all, six years of economic liberalism have acted as an effective antidote to such hyper-
sensitivity in the broader political arena—resulting, for example, in the recent electoral
successes of former Communist parties in a number of Eastern European countries.
Rather, Eastern European feminist reluctance, which emerges as a phenomenon of East-
West interchange, reflects an unexpected absence, from the Western point of view, of a
specifically political dimension to women's social identity as women—even though
women themselves may be dissatisfied with some aspects of what is implied by that
social identity.

For example, a large-scale survey of Polish women carried out in 1993 showed that
while most recognized that women had specific problems and saw the need for organizations dealing with these, very few in fact saw the need for organizations to fight discrimination and raise women's standing in society;[3] that is to say, despite widespread
recognition of women's particular problems, there was little support for organizations
with specifically political goals relating to the social inclusion of women. And although
women's magazines in Poland are full of letters from married women complaining that
their life is not easy, that they are rushed off their feet and have nothing to show for their
efforts,[4] it is also true that, according to the director of the Women's Studies Center in
Łódź, "almost any Polish woman would accept the principle of equality, [but] the concept of 'women's rights' is met with enmity."[5] Only 3 percent of the two hundred or so
Polish women in local government canvassed by Regulska in 1994 perceived a need for
women's organizations at the local level. Czech women, too, tend not to see the status
of women as a public issue.[6] "Some Czech women," writes Snitow, "have explained that
they don't want cultural discussions to be developed along gender lines because then

women lose their majority, their human status, and become like a 'minority.' To mention the group 'women' is to demote individual women to a subset of society. . . . Essentialism, rather than seeming like a reductionist definition of a woman, is often equated with finally letting women flower as particular beings."[7]

Thus the first difficulty in East-West "dialogue across minority discourses"—that is, between Western feminism, on the one hand, and Eastern European women, on the other—lies, I argue, in present limits to mutual recognition. With whom and how can (any) Western feminism engage, if the other voice does not identify itself as a minority voice?[8] And from the other side, who are the Western feminists—do they convey clear messages about their own identity (even if this means clarity about ambivalence and ambiguity)? Or do mistaken feminist assumptions concerning Eastern Europe also signal limits to Western self-understanding? At what point do the overwork, low pay, and ultimate deference of women become experienced as the oppression of this group and constitutive of a marginal political identity? My way of approaching these questions is to hold them together and address them in terms of a comparative framework that relativizes Communism and competitive democracy with respect to each other, rather than confining itself to the legacy of Communism as a single and overstretched explanatory variable. For the elasticity required of the concept of "legacy of Communism" is to some extent a measure of the degree to which a number of expectations generated on the basis of an undefined but fixed and asocial idea of civil society have been confounded by Eastern European post-Communist reality. Feminism is one of these unfulfilled expectations, and because it is, we are offered a new opportunity of reflecting on what it is we are in fact saying and doing when we conceptualize the transformation of Eastern Europe in terms of a transition to a genuine civil society.[9]

CIVIL SOCIETY AS POLITICAL SPACE

Perhaps the best way of illustrating what is misleading about the way the term *civil society* is deployed in the rhetoric of transition in Eastern Europe is by considering what is entailed in its representation as political space. It is this metaphor that, more than any other, resonates throughout the recent literature on the subject. "The words 'civil society,'" writes Michael Walzer, "name the space of uncoerced human association and also the set of relational networks—formed for the sake of family, faith, interest and ideology—that fill this space";[10] the sphere within which Eastern European dissidents were operating under Communism represents, for him, "a highly restricted version" of this space. Charles Taylor talks of civil society under Communism as serving to articulate "the hopes of those fighting to open spaces of freedom";[11] Cohen and Arato speak of new social movements in the West serving to democratize public spaces,[12] while Seligman says that such groups are "predicated on the definition of public space as one of instrumental interaction between autonomously constituted individual moral agents."[13] A recent example of the metaphor as it often appears in the feminist literature is provided by Waylen, who uses it freely in her attempt to explain the relative absence of women's movements in transition politics in Central and Eastern Europe in comparison with the role such groups played in Latin America. The reason for this difference, she surmises, lies in the fact that the "more concerted suppression of civil society by the state meant that the same degree of political space did not exist in Eastern Europe."[14]

It is not that the concept of space cannot convey some useful meaning to us in the context of the discourse of civil society; on the contrary, it can. What I would like to suggest, rather, is that what often continues to be invoked in this discourse is an obsolete Newtonian notion of absolute space—one that was discarded by physics long ago. This is a space that can be posited independently of the actors that exist within it and often regardless of historical circumstance. It is an idea, in fact, that renders well the power-free social medium within which the theory of liberal pluralism seeks to suspend itself, and it is one that seriously needs to be recast if it is to become useful for our analytical purposes. In contrast, the more legitimate physical metaphor would draw on the Einsteinian understanding that there is no absolute space, that the very existence, and particular quality, of any space depends on the existence of actors, in that it is the presence of these actors, and not others, that gives rise to specific forces that "bend" it. All space is "curved." That is to say, we are not entitled to conceive of civil society—if we wish to conceive of it in properly spatial terms—as a realm devoid of social power. It cannot be legitimately envisioned as, for example, a parceled-off sphere of basic equality inhabited by the free citizen, or a level playing field set aside for the pursuit of individual or group interests. Instead, it is better understood in strictly analogous metaphorical terms as a domain of fluctuating yet stable power relations constituted by, yet also existing beyond, the interactions of specific social actors. Furthermore, it is a sphere where the identities of the actors concerned are simultaneously shaped by these immanent fields of power relations. The metaphor, then, bids us think of liberal civil society as only one of many possible versions of politically "curved space."

STATE SOCIALISM AND THE DEPOLITICIZATION OF DIFFERENCE

Under Communism, the state abrogated all prerogative in the public sphere, and society became a "private society." The monopoly achieved by the "prerogative state"[15] over the public sphere corresponded to the comprehensive curtailment of any real rights of political, and to some extent also civil, citizenship. This is usually what is referred to when it is said that under Communism there was no civil society. What is important to note for the purposes of the present argument is that in this state-dominated "curved space," both abstract and concrete rights of citizenship were universal: All of society was equally deprived of these rights, and hence excluded from social power. That is not to argue there was equality under state socialism; there was not. It is to say, rather, that political/civil citizenship in both its formal, abstract, positive sense and its real, everyday, negative sense was impervious to social difference. That is, whatever the effect in daily life of social factors such as gender, level of wealth, ethnicity, or age, in terms of political identity, participation, and voice, they made no difference. It is for this reason that the "'male subject,' so scorned in the West, did not have a chance to develop . . . or existed only as a pathetic caricature."[16] And if the male subject was absent, so, one should note, were women as the other side of this subject. That is why Jiřina Šiklová was able, in spite of everything, to write that under Communism, "women were not exploited by men."[17] For under state socialism, society was excluded *as a whole,* and citizens, far from feeling excluded relative to each other, were held together in a form of political unity. It was this essential unity that made possible the idea of Solidarity.

From a vantage point within a political "curved space" characterized by negative but equal citizenship, one might be forgiven for envisioning democratization as an absolute and universal gain, one that would involve nothing more disruptive of existing social identities than a new measure of empowerment for all—the transcendence of the sham of Communism by the switching of the sign against (real, effective) rights from negative to positive, so to speak; living in truth, as opposed to living a lie. Charter 77's manifesto, it will be recalled, stated that its "principal concern [was] to achieve genuine democracy, i.e., democracy for all."[18] Slavenka Drakulic echoes this when she says that "democracy is about citizens', human, and women's rights."[19] Current disillusion with "really existing democracy" probably has something to do with this kind of expectation, as Sabine Berghahn suggests when she writes that "with regard to the hopes and desires arising in the beginning of the East German revolution, the political structure of the Federal Republic now seems to be merely disappointing."[20] In this connection, it is interesting also to see how often the readily-deconstructed phrase "male democracy" or "masculine democracy" has recently been used by Eastern European women.[21] What is less immediately apparent is why the term should be construed by Eastern and Western writers alike as a specifically Eastern European phenomenon.[22] After all, masculine democracy is what unites us now; it is, in itself, a fundamental aspect of Western civilization and what it means to rejoin Europe. This fact should be enough to signal to us that it is time to release our grip on the legacy of Communism a little and look to the rendering of democracy, civil society, and feminism that is counterposed to it, if we are to understand current transformations, and each other, better.

DEMOCRATIZATION AS THE MOBILIZATION OF DIFFERENCE

Democratization and the construction of civil society in Eastern Europe represents the reconfiguration of political curved space, involving the implementation of certain rights of citizenship, on the one hand, and the political project of the marketization of the economy on the other.[23] The political and civil rights of democratic citizenship that support civil society (such as exist in the West currently, and are only partially present in the East)[24] represent universal capacities or opportunities, some of which (such as the right to vote) are more genuinely universal than others.[25] "A property right (for example) is not a right to possess property, but a right to acquire it *if you can,* and to protect it *if you can get it.*"[26] Similarly, the right to free speech is not a legally guaran-

teed equal right to voice, but a conditional capacity that is dependent on the outcome
of the complex interplay of a variety of social factors. Consider, for example, the gap
noted by Heinen between the outlook of the unemployed in Poland and the confident
national and international press accounts of successful economic transition in that
country (a gap that in fact currently separates the national/international press and a
successful minority from the rest of the population). Or consider again the way in
which Solidarity 80 union representatives were (informally but effectively) banned by
management from expressing their views to the press during the high-profile privatization of the Szczecin shipyard.[27]

Thus, insofar as new rights of citizenship are dependent for their realization on external social resources, democratization and civil society in Eastern Europe may be said to
entail the mobilization of the very differences that under Communism had been a
matter of political irrelevance. Ethnic strife in Eastern Europe is thus understandable in
part as a consequence of democratic citizenship. For under adequate historical circumstances, ethnicity can be invoked as the key difference by means of which access to
the benefits of citizenship is to be defined. For this reason, nationalism cannot, in itself,
be blamed for "constructing a definition of autonomy and citizenship which is male,"
as Einhorn for example, seeks to do.[28] Similarly, the claim that in East-Central Europe
"the continued existence of strong ethnic and group solidarities . . . have . . . thwarted
the very emergence of those legal, economic, and moral individual identities upon
which civil society is envisioned"[29] needs to be substantially revised, for civil society
itself *mobilizes* those selfsame differences that subvert its universal ideal.

Within this new "curved space," then, gender takes on a new and specifically political meaning, because it begins to matter with respect to how individuals come to be differentially included within the new political community created by democratic
citizenship. Traditional ideas of gender difference, reinforced under Communism,[30] are
integral to the realization of the new rights of citizenship, and it is this new fusion of the
social with the political that produces the "male subject" or "political man." In this sense
the construction of civil society in Eastern Europe is the construction of a man's world.
It is important to be clear about what is at stake for women in these changes. It has
recently been written, for example, that under Communism, "the felt absence of collective political voice" was part of the powerlessness "directly evident in the experience
of *women's* subordination by collective . . . male power."[31] The argument I am making
here is that precisely the opposite is true: The felt absence of collective political voice,
or powerlessness, is just what is *not* part of the subordination of *women* under
Communism, since voicelessness/powerlessness in this political "curved space" is a
genuine universal. It is only when this space becomes reconfigured as civil society that
absence of political voice and powerlessness can become meaningful aspects of the
subordination of women (as what is there to be voiced also changes). That is because
within liberal civil society, citizens are excluded *relative to each other* in a way that was
impossible under Communism. It is democratization itself that brings a new, essentially

divisive, political force to gender relations. Consider, for example, what it does to the meaning of the sexual division of labor. Under Communism, the time devoted by women to domestic labor may save the time of men, but neither this saved time nor higher earnings in the public sphere can be translated into the political advantage of men—it cannot contribute to their constitution as individuals. Women's work thus represents neither a political loss for women nor a political gain for men. There is no private sphere that is constructed in *gender-political* opposition to the public sphere. In liberal civil society, the situation is quite different. Time, money, and labor all become politically relevant resources (i.e., they have implications for how a person belongs within the political community). Because they are also transferable resources, the same objective sexual division of labor becomes an arrangement whereby, frequently, the political disadvantage of women is the political advantage of men. This illustrates how, as the male subject emerges, so women are constructed as a politically marginal grouping. It is within the context of the universal political emancipation offered by Western-type democracy, then, the creation of a specific political community, that women acquire their minority identity, and within this context, too, that differences among women acquire political significance. This is the cue for the emergence of feminism as identity politics. However, there are good reasons—current difficulties in reconfiguring political "curved space" according to plan, that is, in installing liberal civil society, and the availability of memories of Communism among them—to be wary of supposing outcomes identical with those that currently prevail in the West.

CONCLUSION

It is the representation of civil society as an absolute political space rather than a socially specific domain of power relations, I argue, that underlies the limits to mutual understanding of East and West, since what it means is the unwarranted universalization of the identities inherent in liberal civil society. Each political "curved space" is constituted by and creates the particular identities of the players within it—paradoxically, it is liberal civil society itself that constitutes women as a minority as it also offers freedom for feminism. Feminism is thus both the failure and the achievement of this civil society. Contrary to the tenor of much of the post-Communist literature, feminism is "not a sign of the benign and progressive operations of liberal individualism, but rather a symptom of its constitutive contradictions."[32] And so, for example, if it has been written of the Eastern side that the "'personal is political' slogan of Western feminists had little salience,"[33] the reason lay, as I hope I have shown, not so much in the fact that "there was no public discourse through which such issues could be aired and reflected upon"[34] but rather in the fact that discourse becoming possible and the personal becoming political are two sides of the same process of transition to liberal civil society. That is to say, the absence of public discourse *was* the absence of these issues. Similarly, it is not that "the lack of democratization and democratic discourse prevented the subjective realization of liberation" in Eastern Europe;[35] rather, it is democratization itself that creates the need for this subjective liberation. Finally, if it has been suggested that this is "a time of *discovery* of [women's] otherness" in Eastern Europe,[36] then I suggest instead that it is the time of its creation. And from the point of view of the Western side of the exchange, there is a need to be clear that to uphold an idea of civil society as a (physically unknown) "absolute space" for feminism in Eastern Europe is to acquiesce in what has been identified as the false universalism of democratic citizenship at home; that is to say, it is to acquiesce in the very conditions of political exclusion that give rise to feminism in the first place. For the limits to East-West feminist communication make plain that the oppression of women does not primarily inhere in the objective/concrete aspects of daily experience, but is crucially bound up with the subjective/ social meaning that experience acquires within a specific political context—meaning that contributes to and derives substance from the strikingly gendered polarization of symbolic and material advantage currently taking place in Eastern Europe.

NOTES

1. E. Bollobás, "'Totalitarian Lib': The Legacy of Communism for Hungarian Women," in N. Funk and M. Mueller, (eds.), *Gender Politics and Post-Communism* (New York: Routledge, 1993), p. 202.
2. N. Funk, "The Fate of Feminism in Eastern Europe," *The Chronicle of Higher Education*, February 2, 1994.
3. CBOS, *Reprezentacja Interesów Kobiet: Komunikat z Badań* (Warszawa: CBOS, 1993).
4. B. Chołuj, "Matka Połka i Zmysly," *Res Publica Nowa* 1, no. 64, pp. 31–33.
5. E. Oleksy, *Selected Proceedings of the Women's Studies Conference*, Łódz, Poland, May 17–21, 1993, p. 6.
6. Council of Europe, "Women's Participation in Political and Public Life," background document for the conference "Equality and Democracy: Utopia or Challenge?" (Strasbourg: Council of Europe, 1995).
7. A. Snitow, "Feminist Futures in the Former East Bloc," *Peace and Democracy News* VII, no. 1, (summer 1993), p. 42.
8. The formulation of this question was provoked by the title of Paula Ebron and Anna Tsing's (forthcoming) paper: "In Dialogue: Writing Across Minority Discourses."
9. A term used by J. Gray in "From Post-Communism to Civil Society: The Reemergence of History and the Decline of the Western Model," *Social Philosophy and Policy* 10, no. 2 (1993), pp. 26–50. Gail Kligman speaks similarly of a transition to a "fully-fledged" civil society in "Reclaiming the Public: A Reflection on Creating Civil Society in Romania," *Eastern European Politics and Societies* 4, no. 3 (1991), pp. 393–438.
10. M. Walzer, "The Civil Society Question," in C. Mouffe (ed.), *Dimensions of Radical Democracy: Pluralism, Citizenship, Community* (London: Verso, 1992), p. 89.
11. C. Taylor, "Modes of Civil Society," *Public Culture* 3, no. 1 (1990), p. 95.
12. A. Arato and J. Cohen "Social Movements, Civil Society, and the Problem of Sovereignty," *Praxis International* 4, (1984), p. 269.
13. A. Seligman, *The Idea of Civil Society* (New York: Free Press, 1992), p. 164.
14. G. Waylen, "Women and Democratization: Conceptualizing Gender Relations in Transition Politics," *World Politics* 46 (April 1994), p. 352.

15. A. Arato, "Civil Society Against the State: Poland 1980–1981," *Telos* 47 (1981), pp. 23–47.

16. Smejkalova-Strickland, quoted by M. Grünell in "Feminism Meets Scepticism: Women's Studies in the Czech Republic," *European Journal of Women's Studies* 15, no. 1, (1995), p. 108.

17. Ibid., p. 106.

18. J. Fleischman, *Toward Civil Society: Independent Initiatives in Czechoslovakia* (New York: Helsinki Watch, 1989), p. 53.

19. S. Drakulic, "Women and Democracy in the Former Yugoslavia," in N. Funk and M. Mueller (eds.), *Gender Politics and Post-Communism: Reflections from Eastern Europe and the Former Soviet Union* (New York: Routledge, 1993), p. 128.

20. S. Berghahn, "Gender in the Legal Discourse in Post-Unification Germany: Old and New Lines of Conflict," *Social Politics* 2, no. 1 (1995), p. 46.

21. A term coined by Sonja Licht of the Belgrade Women's Lobby and subsequently used by Jiřina Šiklová and others. See B. Einhorn, *Cinderella Goes to Market: Citizenship, Gender and Women's Movements in East Central Europe* (London: Verso, 1993), p. 148.

22. See, for example, J. Heinen, "Polish Democracy Is a Masculine Democracy," *Women's Studies International Forum* 15, no. 1 (1992), pp. 129–138; A. Posadskaya, "The Women's Dimension of the Social Formation: From Forum to Forum," *From Problems to Strategy*, Materials of the Second Independent Women's Forum, Dubna, 27–29 November 1992, (Moscow: Hilversum, 1992), p. 15; R. Rosen, "Male Democracies, Female Dissidents," *Tikkun* 5, no. 6 (1990); M. Molyneux, "Women's Rights and the International Context: Some Reflections on the Post-Communist States," *Millenium: Journal of International Studies* 23 no. 2 (1994), p. 306.

23. See C. Offe, "Capitalism by Democratic Design? Democratic Theory Facing the Triple Transition in East Central Europe," *Social Research* 48, no. 4 (1991) pp. 865–901.

24. See I. Bialecki, "Obywatel we Mgle Liberalizmu," *Res Publica Nowa* 3, no. 51 (1992), pp. 19–20; J. Szacki, *Liberalizm po Komunizmie* (Kraków: Społeczny Instytut Wydawniczy Znak, (1994).

25. J. M. Barbalet, *Citizenship* (Milton Keynes: Open University Press, 1988), p. 17.

26. Marshall, quoted in Barbalet, op. cit., my emphasis.

27. Author's interview with Union representatives in Szczecin Shipyard, September 1994.

28. Einhorn, op. cit., p. 257.

29. Seligman, op. cit., p. 164.

30. P. Watson, "Eastern Europe's Silent Revolution: Gender," *Sociology* 27, no. 3, (1993), pp. 471–87.

31. M. Ferree, "Patriarchies and Feminisms: The Two Women's Movements of Post-Unification Germany," *Social Politics* 2, no. 1, (1995), p. 16, my emphasis.

32. Joan W. Scott, "Introduction," in *Only Paradoxes to Offer: French Feminists and the Rights of Man* (Cambridge: Harvard University Press, 1996).

33. P. Chamberlayne, "Gender and the Private Sphere: A Touchstone of Misunderstanding between Eastern and Western Germany," *Social Politics* 2, no. 1, (1995), p. 29.

34. Ibid.

35. Weller, in Chamberlayne, op. cit., p. 30.

36. Siklova, quoted in Grünell, op. cit., p. 109.

<< 3 >>

Feminism and Civil Society

Susan Gal

Most observers of social change in Eastern Europe have pinned their hopes on civil society as the key to creating democratic politics after the demise of one-party states. The idea and ideal of civil society itself are rarely questioned. My aim, in contrast, is to argue that the analysis of gender relations and feminist politics in the region provides a necessary, critical perspective on the concept of "civil society." The countries discussed in this collection are historically distinct and their current trajectories show increasing differences. Comparison among them is nonetheless instructive because they share structural similarities produced by their state-socialist past. I focus my discussion around two related questions.

First, how should we conceptualize civil society so that it contributes to an understanding of changing relations between men and women in Eastern Europe? In the Western tradition, the definition of "civil society" has changed repeatedly since its meaning in antiquity, when it was synonymous with the state. Amid considerable debate in the late eighteenth century, civil society was reconceptualized as not only separate from, but even opposed to, the state and its laws, on the one hand, and economic (market) relations, on the other. In some versions of this idea, the myriad organizations of civil society—voluntary associations, professional guilds, political parties, churches—take on an idealized, revolutionary, even utopian twist: They are conceived as a protection against despotism. It is this eighteenth-century concept of civil society as a safeguard against the state that has recommended its use as an interpretive frame for opposition to the one-party states of Eastern Europe.

Note, however, that in all of these meanings, the "civil" or "civilized" society of public action—whether equated with or opposed to the state—is already implicitly contrasted to a "natural" and domestic, "private" realm of family life and procreation, to which women are assigned. Indeed, feminist political theorists have argued that in the West, the "public," the "private," and "nature" are ideas that have been variously linked together in a dynamic discourse about political power and the relation of men and women to it.[1] In American anthropology, second-wave feminist theorizing about women and politics has also been deeply influenced by the idea of a public/private opposition. Rejecting earlier universalist claims, recent analyses show that the public/private dichotomy is constructed differently across cultures and historical periods, as is the definition of what counts as nature.[2] Such comparative evidence suggests that if we are to understand the relationship between civil society, gender relations, and feminism in Eastern Europe, it is crucial to examine current conceptualizations of the private, the public, and the way nature has been used as a political category in the region. These terms are not entirely new to the lexicon of formerly state-socialist societies, but their current use does not match the patterns familiar before the fall of state socialism in 1989. Thus, the first task at hand is to specify the complex transformations of these terms in discourse and practice in relation to changing social structures.

My second question is about the relation of civil society to feminism: What kind of conversation, cooperation, and political action is possible among U.S. women, Western European women, and Eastern European women? Although such regional contrasts are often reduced to "East vs. West," it is important to remember that there are multiple centers involved. Furthermore, each region varies widely within itself, and the definition of regions is itself problematic. Indeed, these essays serve as exemplars of such diversity, differing markedly in the kinds of cross-regional understandings they imagine and advocate.

Nonetheless, the papers share a common starting point. In 1989, when the end of state socialism provided the context for increased contact between women in different regions, the result was profound surprise and dismay on the part of all the participants at the expectations voiced from the "other side." Eastern European women often saw Western feminists as proselytizers whose behavior and work were messianic, implicitly universalizing, and thus imperialistic. On the other hand, Eastern European women were often seen by Western feminists as disappointingly underdeveloped politically, backward and ignorant in their rejection of Western feminism, and sometimes as simply apolitical. The disappointment was made particularly sharp by the widespread expectation in the West that once the establishment of civil society gave women the liberty and opportunity to organize on their own behalf, feminist movements would easily and "naturally" emerge, given the obvious and much recognized wage differentials and other economic disadvantages of women vis-à-vis men in Eastern Europe.[3]

Significantly, scholarly commentary has moved beyond simply noting the genuine difficulty of dialogue: There are now systematic analyses of what expectations existed as well as the structural reasons for their disappointment. One salutary result, aided by similar work on non-Western feminisms, has been a growing understanding that feminism is not an automatic reflex of gender identity, nor a necessary outgrowth of women's opportunity to organize in response to economic and political oppression. Indeed, we cannot assume that "woman" denotes an unproblematic, self-evident, *political* category, or that such a political category is stable across social formations. Feminism itself refers to political movements that emerge in specific historical conjunctures, and we may expect various forms of feminism to bear the mark of their particular political, cultural, and historical context.[4]

To put it more generally, how we understand the possibility for communication among women across these regions is linked to how we conceptualize the difference between gender relations in postsocialist states when compared to parliamentary (welfare) states. Specifically, the current widespread rejection of feminism in Eastern Europe depends on the kind of political subjectivity that versions of "civil society" in the region allow and encourage for women. Furthermore, we must not expect that concepts with similar names will always describe similar things. Communication across regions and social formations always depends on the decontextualization of political terms taken from one local, political situation and recontextualized into often quite differently constructed discourses, gender regimes, and historical political economies. Feminism is no exception to this general semiotic process.[5] Careful attention to this intertextual aspect of political and social activity—which can produce gaps, slippages, and differences, as well as the invention of unities and common origins—is useful for understanding the ways in which political mobilization and cooperation become possible.

CIVIL SOCIETY

The checkered history of the term "civil society" has been well documented. Once civil society had been firmly distinguished from the state in the course of the eighteenth century, it could be thought of as a bulwark against state power. But because of this independence, civil society itself was often seen as the threat to social order that had to be controlled and regulated by the state. In one line of reasoning, the separation of market, state, and civil society has been seen as the definitive mark of "modernity" that allowed for the emergence of a "public sphere" of opinion and debate, thus forming the basis of liberal, democratic politics. For instance, Habermas argues that the category of the "public" was the product of an emerging bourgeois society.[6] It was a realm separate from the state and market in which private persons, formed as individuals within bourgeois families, could come together for reasoned debate, at first about literature but eventually about politics. Other analysts include the capitalist market as one aspect of civil society—or of the public sphere. Still others suppose that the complex labyrinth of voluntary, professional, and cultural organizations that they define as civil society protects the state apparatus insofar as worker outrage during economic crises is directed at civil society rather than the state.[7] Finally, as Lang (this volume) reminds us, civil society is not uniform across social formations. It makes sense to distinguish among liberal and other (for instance, more corporatist) versions of civil society.

Debate over its meaning has never kept "civil society" from being part of everyday usage. Nor has it ever been a politically neutral concept. Indeed, it served as the rallying cry of Eastern European dissidents in the 1970s and 1980s. Borrowing from postwar American and Western European political science, dissidents often figured their opposition to Communism as the brave fight for the reinstatement of civil society and hence of democracy. At the same time, it was the term with which Western commentators hailed the supposed superiority of the West to Communism. It was therefore not surprising that it became, after 1989, the prescription for societal health offered to Eastern Europe by these same Western advisors and political theorists.

This critical, anti-Communist use of the idea of civil society was linked in Eastern Europe to a particular and compelling analysis of state socialism. The argument, briefly, was that the "spoiler state" of state socialism, in attempting to construct its own power, tried to destroy those institutions and organizations that mediated between the state and the family. It arrogated their functions to itself, and by atomizing society weakened popular resistance. Direct interaction between the state and individuals was encouraged in the form of political denunciations. It was not so much that the socialist state was powerful in itself, but rather that it systematically tried to eliminate any potential competition for central power. Institutions independent of the state and family were undermined, outlawed, infiltrated by the state and Party, co-opted, or otherwise diminished.[8] Accordingly, one common and important critique of state socialism was that it allowed no "space" for civil society.[9]

But these analyses have sometimes been interpreted too literally to mean that there was no other organizational structure in state socialism besides the family and the state. On the contrary, although they lacked a legitimating ideology, there was nevertheless a whole range of informal but essential nonstate organizations related to the state bureaucracy, medical care, and industrial production. These were social structures through which much of the business of everyday life was actually accomplished. Such "black" or "gray" organizatons had varying degrees of legality and importance in the different countries of the region. But, as many analysts have argued, they were not deviations or anomalies of state socialism, but rather were produced by the logic of shortage and reform within the system itself.[10]

In Hungary, for instance (the country in which I do ethnographic work), such social forms were called the "second economy" and were studied in detail by social scientists. By the 1970s and 1980s there was also a "second society" of meetings among artists and social thinkers, or simply among music fans, folk dancers, or families building houses for each other. Even the famous atomization of society into fearful, cynical, amoral individuals was double-edged. In villages, the outward appearance of atomization could provide a means of united if hidden resistance to state surveillance and the demands made by production plans from the center.[11] Control was not totally centralized during the 1970s and 1980s, even in the realm of public debate. Instead, a kind of complicitous development was evident in which the reform Communists not only allowed the existence of a variety of non-Communist political networks, but actually courted them, and even worked together on an implicit agreement about which issues could be discussed.[12] Outside observers as well as some insiders often saw parts of these interstitial networks not only as a second economy, but also as evidence of moral lapse and societal "corruption." They lamented the special payments the networks extracted in return for the smoother operation of the official medical, legal, or production systems; they criticized the theft from state firms that was routinely ignored and even condoned. Nevertheless, whatever they were called, we may as well recognize in these social structures a well-developed, though stigmatized, form of organization situated between state and family. Thus, the distinctive quality of the state-socialist past, in contrast to the present scene, is not the sheer lack of organization between family and state but the way such organizations were conceptualized, evaluated, and elaborated.

Since interstitial structures are not new, I argue that we should understand civil society in the region not primarily as a determinate set of institutions and organizations, which it also is, but as an ideological formation that produces the quite real social effect of newly perceptible boundaries between "politics," "economics," and "family," or, more simply, between a "public" that refers to market and political organizations and a "private" that refers to household domesticity. Such redefinition makes newly visible a range of what can now be called nonstate organizations. But it is important simultaneously to pay close attention to the still existing links that such newly valorized organizations, now seen as part of civil society, maintain with the state and market, while simultaneously seeing the practices and ideas that produce the appearance of separation between them.

This boundary-creating process has two effects: First, it increases the value, prestige, number, and financial rewards of these interstitial organizations, which are now no longer merely necessary but clandestine ways to survive. Renamed, reconceptualized, somewhat reorganized, burgeoning in size and number, supported not only by ideology but also by foreign capital, they are now seen as the right way to run the world. Second, the creation of conceptual boundaries between civil society, the state, and the market— enacted in legal and administrative practices—permits the democratic claim of universal inclusion in public activity, especially in politics, while accomplishing the exclusion of various categories of person. It is this aspect of civil society that has been addressed by a large critical literature in the West: While claiming the equality of individuals in the political realm, the idea of civil society obscures the economic and other social differences that, in practice, fundamentally constrain political participation.[13] First-wave feminism in the West had to challenge this hidden exclusion while simultaneously appealing to the explicit promise of universal political inclusion. But even beyond this contradiction between idea and practice, feminist critics have pointed to even more fundamental exclusions. They have shown how the "individual," "civil society," and "the public" have in fact been "constituted as patriarchal categories in opposition to womanly nature and the 'private' sphere," at least since the theories of the eighteenth-century British and French philosophers of democracy.[14]

By all accounts, the newly emerging civil societies of Eastern Europe are also being defined as the site of male action. It is indicative that, according to a report by the Associated Press, the first free elections in the region systematically produced legislatures with drastically smaller numbers of women members. Szalai argues that in

Hungary, the new political parties are not seen as representatives of particular political interests or of alternative visions of a future society, but as instrumental channels for the correction of patterns of stalled upward mobility for men.[15] Men who could not be socially mobile in the earlier regime are now able to move up through new party ties. In contrast to earlier attitudes toward women's activity in politics, such upward movement is now seen as inappropriate for women, and is so seen by most women themselves. Similarly, Watson has shown that in the newly valorized civil society in Poland, men have taken the lead in private enterprise and in various civil organizations,[16] often with the argument that women are inherently ill-suited to such work.[17]

It would be difficult to understand these patterns if civil society were merely the opening up of a neutral social space heretofore occupied by the state. Rather, we must see the gendered aspects of post-1989 organizational change in Eastern Europe as the ideological effect of shifting boundaries in a social field that was not only already occupied, as I have argued, but also already structured by discourses and practices developed during state socialism and already focused on ideas about privacy, sexual difference, and nature. There is a parallel here with the category of ethnicity, another supposedly natural difference. Like ethnicity, sexual inequality was supposed to be erased under socialism, but in fact it operated as an important if officially unacknowledged part of the system's logic.[18]

Current reconceptualizations of private and public occur through arguments about what kind of person is best suited to engage in political action or in market activity, and in discussion about what kind of social support the state should provide. They occur, too, in battles over laws that regulate employment, reproduction, and sexual harassment in the workplace, and in the practical responses to the often gendered requirements of foreign capital and international organizations. These new conceptions gain their coercive force, however, through their juxtaposition with earlier conceptions and long-standing strategies. It is therefore necessary to review not only the dual use of the public/private distinction in official state socialism, but also its underground life in oppositional discourse.

Throughout the region, the ideology of state socialism stressed the unity of state and society, the unity of "social space," an image that Lefort has aptly called the "people-as-one."[19] To maintain this unity, and in the interests of eliminating social inequality, the bourgeois division of public/private was to be erased, and with it all other social differences. Eventually everyone would be part of the category of "worker." Women's social equality in particular was to be accomplished by their entry into production; compensatory legislation, establishing maternity leaves and day care, would allow women to accomplish their secondary social duty of reproduction. While production was in principle more important, both were considered essential in the 1950s and 1960s when the state-socialist systems were hungry for labor.[20]

In practice, the timing, intensity, and consistency with which these ideas were enacted differed considerably from country to country. But it seems clear that throughout the region, the gender regime of state socialism "broke open the nuclear family, socialized significant elements of reproduction even while leaving women responsible for the rest, and usurped certain patriarchal functions and responsibilities."[21] In Hungary during the 1950s, through directives to women about matters as intimate as housework, clothing, and makeup, the state actively attempted to produce a homogenization of social differences and a degree of gender equality. In some cases, women could even appeal to the legal system if husbands refused to help in washing floors.[22] In Romania during the Ceaușescu era (1970s–1989), the state brought even reproduction under its direct control by identifying childbirth as equivalent to all other forms of labor, namely a service to the state. Contraception and abortion were disallowed and women's bodies were routinely subjected to surveillance to ensure only "productive" sexual activity. The aim was to produce the "new socialist person" by forcibly attempting to make social differences insignificant. To this end, "race, gender, and ethnicity were all homogenized. Each body was to be moulded into a productive member of the socialist masses."[23]

The crisis of this system in Hungary during the 1950s led to the Kadarist compromise, in which the state withdrew from many areas of family life in return for silent complicity in politics and the workplace. "Private" became the designation for that aspect of life that the state tacitly ignored. It was the realm in which families, along with informal networks of friends and kin, worked extraordinarily hard so as to be able to consume more. The informal economy produced by this partial withdrawal of the state occupied a disproportionately large part of the country's economy and of the workers' energy and productivity. Men and women invested the bulk of their time, energy, pride, and self-respect in this officially ignored private sphere. Minutely imbricated with the official, socialized economy, the informal sector may have been experienced by some workers as a form of resistance, but it also became part of the logic of the centralized, planned, command economy, enabling the latter to survive.[24]

Similarly, while the official line of equality and homogenization remained in place, a second discourse of naturalized sexual difference began to emerge in many of the officially sanctioned media in the countries of the region, starting as early as the 1960s. Just as the centralized economy ignored, controlled, depended on, and reproduced the informal sector, these two discourses on sexuality were similarly intertwined. In the Hungarian case, when the birthrate declined, or when the hoarding of labor ("overemployment") characteristic of later state-socialist economies became acute, official newspapers and magazines would mount campaigns chastising women for competing with men in the workplace and urging women to be more nurturing toward men, to be less selfish and less masculine workers, to retreat from the labor force, and to bear more children. Again, this was less a move against the socialist system than a way of dealing with its internal logic, which reliably produced overemployment and slack labor discipline. In the 1980s, a wave of press activity and advice books blamed women for the extremely high levels of male alcoholism, suicide, early mortality, and juvenile crime. Women, it seemed, were being too much like men in the workforce. As a result, men had become feeble, frightened, and feminized. This unnatural reversal, allegedly perpetrated by women themselves, supposedly caused the many social ills of Communism.[25] Furthermore, it was this unnatural reversal, and not persistently low pay, the double day, or overwork, that was also said to cause women's ubiquitous complaints about anxiety, fatigue, and frustration. As sociologist Zsuza Ferge wryly noted, in these state-controlled media campaigns, the dictates of nature and the needs of the failing socialist economy came harmoniously together.[26]

But such arguments about nature were not limited to state-sponsored discourse. The charge that the "socialist person" was an unnatural creation was, by this time, also a familiar claim made by opponents of Communism. In Hungary, "nature" was part of a widespread discourse that questioned the fundamental homogenization advocated by the official line. Like its avatars in eighteenth-century debates about the legitimacy of absolute monarchy,[27] this critique of relations between men and women argued that gender was natural, and it used gender relations to question broader social arrangements, implicitly charging that Communism was illegitimate since it violated laws more fundamental than those of any society. This opinion was also expressed in a growing nostalgia for an imagined nineteenth-century, male-dominated, bourgeois family in which everyone had a natural place, and in which women could responsibly and lovingly perform the domestic nurturance denied them under socialism. In Hungary, this was enacted in consumer fads for old furniture, antique lace, elaborately decorated porcelain, and even busts of Franz Josef. Such commodities contrasted with the spartan, uniform, and cheap designs of socialist realism and thus carried a tinge of subversion, a sort of tolerated, symbolic dissent. In this way, the nineteenth-century bourgeois family became a paradigm for oppositional discourse, enthusiastically espoused by women as well as men. In sum, active discussion of natural gender difference was conducted by both the regime and its opponents, which suggests that such ideas had gained hegemonic force.

A third use of this group of concepts was, however, more explicitly dissident and thus less easily tolerated by the state. Artists and social thinkers of the 1970s and 1980s romanticized and elevated the "private" to sacred status as the sphere where Vaclav Havel could claim to live in truth and where Konrad Gyorgy could practice an "antipolitics" of silent subversion. It was conceptualized as a zone of genuine opinion and sentiment in contrast to the usual cynical pretense of political life. In direct contradistinction to the antipolitical bourgeois private sphere, it was theorized as a place for significant political action that provided the opportunity to resist the state by acting *as though* there were a civil society. In practice, women remained responsible for housework and a double day even in dissident circles, but in cultural imagination this private sphere was as male as it was female.

The political changes of 1989 took place in the context of this complex and shifting discursive field. Despite their inclusion in state-sponsored discourses, the private, the natural, and the ideal of the bourgeois family became firmly associated with anti-Communism, courageousness, and dissent against an oppressive system. As such, these terms were often championed most, as a source of legitimacy, by those who had not dissented at all. At the same time, the compensatory legislation around maternity leave, child care, divorce, and housing that allowed women to be workers was redefined as a symptom of the unnatural alliance between aggressive women and the socialist state. Political figures on the nationalist right could portray themselves as forward-looking by invoking both ethnicity and sexual difference because these two supposedly natural categories had allegedly been disallowed by an unnatural, unhealthy Communism. While the income of two wage earners was ever more necessary to the maintainance of a family, and women's domestic labor had become even more burdensome because of cuts in state support of child care and other services, the nationalist right provided counterimages of considerable evocative power. By calling for the sacralization of motherhood, higher birthrates, and the family wage, they simultaneously promised to relieve women of the double day, to enable them to nurture (as they had been told even by state ideologues that they should), to strengthen the nation numerically, and to return the country to a bourgeois system that was the obvious expression of human nature.[28]

On the other side of the political spectrum, neoliberal and (neo)socialist parties in search of legitimacy were just as eager, at first, to distance themselves from those aspects of the earlier system that had been figured as homogenizing and thus unnatural. As we have seen, their ideal that all citizens should be treated equally in a civil society also relied, but less obviously than the nationalist view, on the establishment of a zone of private domesticity, coded as female, where natural difference does exist. But privacy and natural gender difference now operated in a changed political economy. When international lending agencies and Western economic advisors started pressuring Eastern European states to cut social services, it was the boundary-making of civil society that legitimated this move. Such support services have been redefined by neoliberal and even the new socialist governments as no longer the business of the state. There has thus emerged an odd but important convergence in the gender politics of otherwise contrasting positions in political life: Nationalists, neoliberals, and socialists all rely on the history of the public/private discourse in the socialist period, and all, for different reasons (and with different levels of explicitness), have espoused a newly valorized private sphere, coded as a place for women, children, and the natural, where—at least ideally—men rest from the exertions of politics.

It is perhaps through a brief example concerning employment that we can best see the way in which the shifting definitions of public and private have interacted with the desires, ideals, and life strategies shaped in an earlier period. The increasing need for women's wages for family survival coincided with massive unemployment among women in the region, who had been disproportionately employed in the very institutions—schools, clerical support, day care, hospitals—that the state has shed. Women's response has been to deploy those strategies used by families under state socialism: They have taken on multiple part-time jobs. This pattern holds even in Hungary, where women's unemployment has not outstripped that of men. Part-time jobs have often been all that is available, but, just as in the socialist period, this strategy also allows women to intertwine wage work with the domestic work that they, no less than men, believe to be their rightful, natural responsibility. In a horrible parody of Marx's ideal, they may well do typing in the morning, cleaning of an office building in the afternoon, phone service for a laywer while cooking dinner, and bookkeeping in the evening. Under state socialism this meant overtime work or clandestine work in the informal economy while they enjoyed the benefits and security of nominal state employment. Its necessity was perceived as the unfortunate, even immoral result of the irrationality and inefficiency of socialist production. In the new order, the security and benefits of nominal state employment are gone. And the ideology of boundaries between spheres makes such strategies appear no longer as systemic problems of society, but rather as the necessary behavior of "flexible" labor in a competitive capitalist economy or, more popularly, as the dilemmas of individual women trying to coordinate their private lives with wage work.

This review of the changing definitions and boundaries of public and private, in the context of the immediate past, allows some understanding of the often paradoxical relations between gender relations and civil society in Eastern Europe. Relying on this for background, I now turn to the question of feminism in the region.

WOMEN'S MOVEMENTS

The difficulties of communication between Eastern European women and American or Western European feminists have pointed up a painful irony. Even as American feminism is engaged in extensive self-examination about its understanding of diverse feminisms and culturally different women's movements, it still seems hard for it to recognize and to respect the specific stands of Eastern European women when they say they are *not* feminists, at least not in the ways that Americans expect. A reverse racism seems to operate. Many American feminists particularly interested in Eastern Europe are the daughters and granddaughters of European immigrants. More broadly, U.S. immigration patterns in the late nineteenth and early twentieth centuries have led many white Americans, even social scientists, to think of Eastern European women as "like us." Indeed, in a tropological move that renders the past as another country, the women of Eastern Europe are seen as "our grandmothers," and thus as part of an imaginary genealogy of European feminism, even if temporarily dislocated.[29] Perhaps this is what makes it more difficult to acknowledge their differences than those of women whose cultures and genealogies are routinely viewed as more racially different and more distant.

But this misperception only adds to the urgency of understanding why feminism remains a dirty word in Eastern Europe, even an object of ridicule, at the very moment when the introduction of civil society supposedly made voluntary organizations, interest groups, and lobbies of every kind possible. Before looking more closely at several lines of explanation for this phenomenon, it is important to note that this attitude does not indicate a general political apathy or lack of social and political consciousness on the part of women in the region. An ethnographic example will illustrate my point.

In the town in southern Hungary where I have been conducting fieldwork since 1987, three women and twenty men ran for office in the first multiparty local election in 1990. All three women were elected to a council of ten. The women, like the men, were already leaders in the community: a bank vice president, an accountant, a language teacher. Like the men who were elected, each of the women represented a form of expertise, but note that in no case was this the stereotyped feminine expertise of nurturing found in professions such as nursing or early-childhood education.

One of the first acts of the local government, now working with a very limited budget, was to close the town's day care center. There were very few children in it, most mothers were home on maternity leave anyway, and the center was expensive to maintain. Although the women elected to the local government did not oppose this move, the five women working in the day care center did. They organized and marched into a council meeting, arguing vociferously. They had heard that a foreign entrepreneur was being lured to this small town and would establish a biscuit factory there. Indeed, they had heard that the council was considering renting the day care center's building to the new entrepreneur. The women proposed that in exchange for their government-funded day care jobs they be guaranteed jobs in this new factory.

The five women got what they demanded, but the sad end of the story is that the entrepreneur could not make a quick profit and a few months after his arrival he closed shop and left town. My point is not the outcome, however, but the organizing itself. The women acted politically, and in concert with free-market changes in which they wanted their share. They justified their demands, however, in terms of socialist as well as gendered values: They had a right to work, and so the provision by the government of a replacement job was seen as part of their entitlement; this particular solution would allow them to keep working close to home, for the sake of their own children. These women, along with the ones elected to the council, are part of a much larger pattern in Hungary in which women are active in newly formed local governments. Indeed, women often represent over 50 percent of nonelected, part-time members of local policy commissions. More significant, a comparison of per capita social spending by local governments since 1990 shows significantly higher spending on child care, day care, homes for elderly, and other social support services in that minority of localities where women are a majority on the decision-making body (see note 15).

This kind of evidence suggests that general political apathy is not the issue. We should look elsewhere for explanations of Eastern European women's current neglect of various forms of Western feminism. Recent scholarly literature points to two kinds of factors, the first broadly structural, the second discursive. Because the gender regime of state socialism was differently configured than that of various parliamentary (welfare) states, women in the East and West experienced the difficulties of their lives in distinct ways. As several astute analyses of the German case have argued, while both East German and West German women before 1989 developed grassroots feminist movements, these created quite different diagnoses about the sources of women's oppression.[30] East German women's deep involvement in the labor force prevented them from seeing wage work as the solution to gender inequality that it was taken to be in the West. Rather, they analyzed their problem as the extensive intrusion of the state into their lives and bodies, and as a usurpation by the state of men's role in families. The paternalist state of state socialism provided benefits such as generous maternity leaves for women, but it also infantilized the entire population, taking over the "paternal role" of men directly through support of children and the socialization of some household functions.

In contrast, the gender regimes of parliamentary welfare states tend to delegate power over women to individual men in families. These states support the relative power of men by indirect involvement in families through tax law, property and family law, and by allowing or encouraging differential bargaining power for men and women in labor markets. In these kinds of systems, women experience gender inequality as arising from the actions of individual men, from whom they want to gain independence, autonomy, and noninterference. Indeed, women often turn to the state to protect them, thereby seeking legislative and other help in gaining leverage against individual men. The juxtaposition of the two German cases provides a particularly clear example of the way in which feminisms are political movements that are perforce embedded in the particular gender regime and historical moment from which they emerge.

Despite the lack of any large, popular feminist movement in Hungary,[31] my ethnographic work in urban and rural contexts reveals that the everyday analysis women developed about their own problems during and immediately after state socialism took just the form one would predict: It neatly matched that of East German feminists, while contrasting with that of West German feminists. This became clear in conversations around the abortion issue in the 1990s, when the lenient law of the socialist period was challenged, and a more restrictive one proposed in Parliament. Hungarian women were appalled that restriction of abortion ever became a political issue because they had come to see relatively liberal abortion regulation as an entitlement. Given the dearth of alternative contraceptive techniques, most saw it as a necessity in planning their lives and in doing right by those children they did have. But unlike supporters of legal abortion in the United States, for instance, they did not see this as a matter of women's privacy, control over their own bodies, or independence. Far from wanting sexual or social autonomy for such a decision, Hungarian women wanted men to be more involved in decisions to abort. Indeed, in public opinion polls, a large percentage of women were willing to support the idea that men of the family must be legally obligated to participate. What they strongly rejected, on the other hand, was the state's involvement in abortion decisions. One woman voiced to me the opinion of many: "If the state makes me have the baby, the state ought to pay for its upbringing." Another said: "Who is going to provide the extra seat at the kitchen table for this extra child?" Both statements implied that since the postsocialist state was not about to take economic responsibility for children, it should stay out of the decision to abort.[32]

These structural analyses help to explain why East and West German feminists famously clashed about a variety of issues, although in some sense both sides believed that the "personal is political." Similarly, if American abortion rights activists were to sit down to discuss abortion with some among the vast majority of Hungarian women, their understandings of the issues would surely differ fundamentally, even though on the face of it they share the same goal of safe, cheap, and easily accessible abortions for women who want them. In precisely this kind of situation it is important to remember that the meaning of key terms such as "private," "public," "rights," and "needs" are hardly self-evident, stable, or transparent; debate about their meaning makes politics.[33] By focusing on the contextualized, historically embedded way in which political issues are framed and understood, these examples provide insight into the structural sources of misunderstanding.

But the cases I have discussed so far do not address the question of why feminism as a social movement (with varying issues and arguments) is currently rejected in so many countries in Eastern Europe. For this it is helpful to turn to discursive factors. Recall my earlier argument that civil society in Eastern Europe is not a neutral space, vacated by the state, in which any kind of organization can flourish. Rather, it is the ideological or discursive formation of boundaries between the economic and political public sphere, on the one hand, and the domestic private sphere, on the other—categories that, as we have seen, are far from new in Eastern Europe. What can be legitimately political depends neither on people's perception of inequality nor on the wherewithal to organize, important though these are. It depends on what identities and activities can count as part of the public in various historical versions of a civil society. And at the moment, as I have suggested, all colors of political activity in Eastern Europe—the national, the neoliberal, and the neosocialist—implicitly or explicitly support a naturalized gender order in which, by various convergent logics, women as a social category are depoliticized.

In the current configuration, no political subjectivity for women is readily available that is neither the homogenized worker-with-reproductive-responsibilities of the state-socialist era, nor the privatized, sexualized, naturalized, and thus unpolitical woman of nationalist discourse and neoliberal civil society. In other words, as Watson (this volume) shrewdly points out, in Poland and other parts of Eastern Europe today there is "an absence of a specifically political dimension to women's social identity as women." Havelková's (this volume) descriptions of public issues in the Czech Republic provide important corroboration and expansion of this point. For women as well as men, social problems such as increased prostitution and violence against women, which would perhaps be framed as "women's issues" in Western Europe and the United States, are understood in the Czech Republic in gender-neutral terms as problems of increased border traffic and the disorder unhappily but inevitably produced by rapid economic changes. Havelková argues that women feel a sense of equality with men *as workers* that has been retained from the official ideology of state socialism. Relying on this, and being as eager as anyone else to be part of a capitalist democracy, women too want to think of themselves not as some special category of person but primarily as "individuals" and equal "citizens" of a new society. Thus, what has not been discursively constructed, at least for the moment, is the political category of "woman" seen not as a worker-recipient of Communist entitlements, nor as the naturalized, sexualized private being of civil society, nor as the sacred and inert mother of nationhood, but as an independent subject whose interests and issues can be publicly defined and debated.

The case of Eastern Europe provides striking illustration for a number of general propositions. Far from being an essential and ahistorical reflex of women's identity or of gender inequality, feminism is a social movement marked by the particular historical contexts in which it emerges, and it is predicated on a specifically political identity for women that must be discursively constructed. As feminist political theorists in the West have argued, this construction of political identity for women itself depends on challenging neoclassical notions of civil society. In particular, it requires the questioning of assumptions about the linkage of maleness with the public, femaleness with the private; about the coding of the public as political and politics as a masculine endeavor.

When analyzed from the perspective of feminist theory, civil society in the West is hardly a neutral space in which women can organize. Nor has it been so in Eastern Europe. Even before the withdrawal of the state, there were myriad informal organizations and a discourse about persistent natural sexual difference that, intertwined with and counterposed to the official line asserting homogenization, organized and legitimated gender relations in socialism. The optimistic expectation that civil society would provide a neutral social space in Eastern Europe was made possible not only by omitting feminist critiques from the discussion of civil society, but also by ignoring how this quite active, but unofficial, set of ideas and practices around sex, nature, and the private, which had enabled state socialism, could have new political effects in a changed political economy.

NOTES

1. E.g., Carol Pateman, "The Fraternal Social Contract," in J. Keane (ed.), *Civil Society and the State* (London: Verso, 1988), pp. 101–28; Norbert Elias, *The History of Manners* (New York: Pantheon, 1978) provides illuminating discussion of the opposition between "civilization" and "nature" in European political consciousness; Keith Tester in *Civil Society* (London: Routledge, 1992), among others, has linked this explicitly with ideas about civil society.
2. Carol MacCormack and Marilyn Strathern (eds.), *Nature, Culture, and Gender* (Cambridge: Cambridge University Press, 1980); Jane F. Collier and Sylvia J. Yanagisako (eds.), *Gender and Kinship* (Stanford: Stanford University Press, 1987).

3. As with Western popular images of "resurgent" ethnic conflict in Eastern Europe, this expectation for feminist social movements owed much to the dubious view that Communism put a lid on otherwise seething social tensions. Note that Western ideals of civil society are only rarely realized in the West itself. See Gail Kligman, "Reclaiming the Public: A Reflection on Reclaiming Civil Society in Romania," *East European Politics and Societies* 4, no. 3 (1990), pp. 393–438.

4. The sociopolitical "embeddedness" of feminism is cogently argued by Micaela diLeonardo in "Gender, Culture and Political Economy: Feminist Anthropology in Historical Perspective," in M. diLeonardo (ed.), *Gender at the Crossroads of Knowledge* (Berkeley: University of California Press, 1991). Whether or not feminism is a Western export, and what definitions of it are legitimate for whom, are questions raised recently by non-Western feminist movements, as well as nonwhite women's movements in the United States. See, for instance, Kumari Jayawardena, *Feminism and Nationalism in the Third World* (London: Zed Books, 1986); Chandra T. Mohanty et al. (eds.), *Third World Women and the Politics of Feminism* (Bloomington: Indiana University Press, 1991). For a discussion of the constructedness of categories such as "woman," and the implications of this for feminist activism, see, among many others, Judith Butler, "Contingent Foundations: Feminism and the Question of 'Postmodernism,'" in J. Butler and J. Scott (eds.), *Feminists Theorize the Political* (New York: Routledge, 1992).

5. This process was one of the themes of the conference and was discussed as a form of "translation." Recent work in semiotics provides empirical approaches to analyzing such phenomena.

6. Jürgen Habermas, *The Structural Transformation of the Public Sphere* (Cambridge: MIT Press, 1989 [1962]).

7. John Keane, "Introduction," in J. Keane (ed.), *Civil Society and the State* (London: Verso, 1988), pp. 19–20.

8. Jan T. Gross, *Revolution from Abroad* (Princeton: Princeton University Press, 1988); Katherine Verdery, *National Ideology Under Socialism* (Berkeley: University of California Press, 1991).

9. E.g., Jean L. Cohen and Andrew Arato, *Civil Society and Political Theory* (Cambridge: MIT Press, 1992); Claude Lefort, *The Political Forms of Modern Society* (Cambridge: MIT Press, 1986); John Keane, *Civil Society and the State* (London: Verso, 1988).

10. E.g., Janos Kornai, "The Hungarian Reform Process: Visions, Hopes and Reality," in Victor Nee and David Stark (eds.), *Remaking the Economic Institutions of Socialism* (Stanford: Stanford University Press, 1989), pp. 32–94.

11. Istvan Rev, "The Advantages of Being Atomized," *Dissent* 34, no. 3 (1987) pp. 335–350.

12. Elemer Hankiss, personal communication.

13. More broadly, the negative logic inscribed in notions of "civil society" and "public sphere" is well known. For example, sociolinguistic analyses have recently argued that the category of the "public" should be seen as a form of language-based political legitimation. It celebrates a form of verbal interaction—open, reasoned debate—that gains authority from being, in a sense, anonymous. Publics (and civil societies) supposedly include "everyone," but they abstract from each person's interest-bearing and privately defined characteristics. By this reasoning, publics can claim to represent everyone because they are no one in particular. See Susan Gal and Kathryn Woolard, "Constructing Languages and Publics: Authority and Representation," *Pragmatics* 5, no. 2 (1995), pp. 129–139.

14. Carol Pateman, "The Fraternal Social Contract," in J. Keane (ed.), *Civil Society and the State* (London: Verso, 1988), p. 20.

15. Julia Szalai, "Women and Democratization: Some Notes on Recent Changes in Hungary," unpublished manuscript, 1995.

16. Peggy Watson, "The Rise of Masculinism in Eastern Europe," *New Left Review* 198 (1993), pp. 71–82.

17. Cf. Nanette Funk and Magda Mueller (eds.), *Gender Politics and Post-Communism* (London: Routledge, 1993) for further evidence.

18. The argument about the crucial role of ethnicity and nationalism in the logic and workings of state socialism, despite official denials of its importance, is most cogently made by Verdery, op. cit. She shows that in a shortage economy, appeals for resources made to redistributors at every level (including the political center) often relied on ethnic categories, even as official discourse asserted the imperative of homogenization.

19. Lefort, op. cit., p. 287.

20. Barbara Einhorn, "Ironies of History: Citizenship Issues in the New Market Economies of East Central Europe," in B. Einhorn and E. J. Yeo (eds.), *Women and Market Societies: Crisis and Opportunity* (Aldershot: Edward Elgar, 1995), pp. 217–33.

21. Katherine Verdery, "From Parent-State to Family Patriarchs: Gender and Nation in Contemporary Eastern Europe," *East European Politics and Societies* 8, no. 2 (1994), p. 232.

22. Joanna Goven, "The Anti-politics of Anti-feminism: Gender, State and Civil Society in Hungary, 1949–1990." (Ph.D. dissertation, University of California, Berkeley, 1992), chapter 2.

23. Gail Kligman, "The Politics of Reproduction in Ceauşescu's Romania," *East European Politics and Societies* 6, no. 3, p. 367.

24. David Stark, "Coexisting Organizational Forms in Hungary's Emerging Mixed Economy," in David Stark and Victor Nee (eds.), *Remaking the Economic Institutions of Socialism* (Stanford: Stanford University Press, 1989), pp. 137–68.

25. Joanna Goven, "Gender Politics in Hungary: Autonomy and Antifeminism," in N. Funk and M. Mueller (eds.), *Gender Politics and Post-Communism* (London: Routledge, 1993), pp. 224–40; for an example, see Judit B. Gaspar and Zsuzsa E. Várkonyi, "Ket masodik nem" [Two second sexes], *Valosag* 7 (1985), pp. 67–76.

26. Szuzsa Ferge, "Kell-e Magyarorszagon feminizmus?" [Do we need feminism in Hungary?], *Ifjusagi Szemle* 2 (1987), pp. 3–8.

27. Maurice Bloch and Jean H. Bloch, "Women and the Dialectics of Nature in Eighteenth-Century French Thought," in C. MacCormack and M. Strathern (eds.), *Nature, Culture and Gender* (Cambridge: Cambridge University Press, 1980), pp. 25–41.

28. The interaction of religious organizations and religious ideals with nationalist positions varied greatly from country to country but was everywhere a factor.

29. Thanks to Cora Kaplan for this phrasing.

30. Myra Marx Ferree, "Patriarchies and Feminisms: The Two Womens Movement's of Post-Unification Germany," *Social Politics* 2 (1995), pp. 10–24; Dorothy Rosenberg, "Shock Therapy: GDR Women in Transition from a Socialist Welfare State to a Social Market Economy," *Signs* 17 (1991), pp. 129–51.

31. Note there are several small but important feminist organizations in the capital: one of entrepreneurial women, another of university women, another mobilized around the abortion issue, and an organization of nationalist right-wing women called Mothers for the Nation.

32. Susan Gal, "Gender in the Post-Socialist Transition: The Abortion Debate in Hungary," *East European Politics and Societies* 8, no. 2 (1994), pp. 256–86.

33. Nancy Fraser, "Talking About Needs: Interpretive Contests as Political Conflicts in Welfare-State Societies," in C. Sunstein (ed.), *Feminism and Political Theory* (Chicago: University of Chicago Press, 1990), pp. 159–84.

< 4 >

German Unification and Feminist Identity

Myra Marx Ferree

Identities are in transition all over Europe. The focus of this paper is the process of German unification and what consequences for women's identities the creation of a partly new, partly old Federal Republic of Germany (FRG) is having on both sides of the former border. It is particularly concerned with the implications of these identity issues for feminism, both as an organized social movement and as an aspiration for a better life for women, however expressed, in the population at large.

The German case is, of course, unique among the transitions in Eastern Europe. The FRG absorbed its East German counterpart without changing so much as its name. The former German Democratic Republic (GDR) existed only briefly as a separate state after the domination of its Communist Party, the SED (Socialist Unity Party), was broken. One year after the wall to the West was broken down in November 1989, the citizens of the GDR had become citizens of the FRG and the SED had renamed itself the Party of Democratic Socialism (PDS). The nation itself disappeared. But its history was not thereby erased or made meaningless. Some of the features that the abrupt transition makes obvious in Germany may also be found in other transitions from socialism.[1] But the German case has always been far from typical, and the issues and tensions described in this instance are not necessarily characteristic of these other translations.

In Germany in the early 1990s it is not uncommon to hear concern expressed that women are "the victims of unification."[2] Victims, indeed, they are. Many of the costs women bear come as a result of the collapse of socialism, especially the loss of child care subsidies and the disappearance of a state commitment to women's labor force participation. These problems are being experienced throughout East-Central Europe, but the speed of the transition in Germany has accelerated their impact.

The rapid shift to a market economy was accompanied by conversion to a hard German currency that immediately priced GDR goods out of their markets, made factories unprofitable, and produced massive employment losses: Between December 1989 and December 1992 the number of jobs dropped nearly 40 percent, even though the unemployment rate was officially only 15 percent.[3] The difference was made up by pushing people out of the labor force entirely, and women, particularly older women, were especially targeted for such exclusion.[4] Unemployment rates for women have averaged twice those of men, and losses of better-qualified positions have been especially severe. While East German men have lost over half the jobs they held in upper management, the number of women in these jobs has dropped from about 100,000 in 1989 to fewer than 1,000 in 1992.[5]

The disappearance of policies that facilitated the combination of child care and a paid job, the fierce competition for jobs, and the absence of any serious antidiscrimination measures in West German employment law have imposed tremendous costs on young women as well. Their desire to remain employable under these conditions has led to a drop of more than 50 percent in the birthrate in just a few years; rather than the 200,000 babies born in 1989, there were only 88,000 born in 1992. This drop is so extreme that, as one demographer comments, they "have come as close to a temporary suspension of childbearing as any such population in the human experience."[6]

But women are not only passive victims. Women are also actors who are struggling to define and articulate their interests politically. This struggle is shaped in Germany by the specific problems that unification has brought to the country, by creating a single nation out of two profoundly different and unequal parts. There is now a cleavage running through all political institutions and organizations, a division known as the "wall in the head" that separates the perceptions and aspirations of those raised in the former GDR from those who grew up in the old West Germany.

The women's movement is no exception to this. The different understandings of what feminism is and should be that are brought into the women's movement from the East and the West make the formation of a common agenda extraordinarily difficult. For women in the former West, for example, paid employment has been structurally inconsistent with motherhood, and most women have had to renounce one or the other, if not permanently, at least for a period. In such a context, policies that facilitate continued employment or reentry into paid employment after an extended period out of the labor force for child rearing can look like progress for women.[7] Yet for women in the GDR, who grew up expecting to combine paid employment and child rearing, the assumption that paid employment is equivalent to women's liberation seems to miss the point of the double day that women carry as a result.[8] Many efforts are being made by feminist groups to bridge these differences, to understand each other, and to cooperate in finding common ground.

This process of mutual discovery is complicated by the reality that in the overall politics of unification the West has been established as the norm, even the ideal, and the East as the lesser partner. The unification process has been largely one of absorption of the GDR into a fundamentally unchanged Federal Republic. Because West Germany successfully resisted the adoption of policies and institutions that were part of the GDR, the creation of a single state was also the creation of two classes of citizens. The citizen of the ex-GDR, or, as one now says, of the "new federal states," was defined from the outset as inferior and in need of remediation. This was explicit in policies that, for example, set different wage rates for East and West Germans who are working for the same company in exactly the same job. The ex-Communist Party, the PDS, has a considerable number of supporters in the new federal states, yet is a pariah in the West, its political supporters dismissed out of hand.

Another example of the disparate political impact of unification is the changing status of abortion law. Initially confronted with resistance to imposing the restrictive West German law on the East, the issue was set aside for two years for resolution. The reformed abortion law that was then passed in the unified but majority-West legislature was far less liberal than the right to abortion in the first trimester that women in the ex-GDR had known, yet even this compromise was rejected by the constitutional court as insufficiently respecting the fetus's right to life.[9] For many in the new federal states, such experiences produce a palpable "deficit in democracy," expressed in the frequent use of the term *colonization* to describe what unification has accomplished. Ex-GDR citizens are increasingly aware that they do not have a nation, that they are now a minority voice in all political organizations and institutions, and that their perspectives will not be automatically heard or respected, even though the new rules give them greater freedom to participate.

Overall, therefore, unification has meant not one but many national transitions, each of which has special meaning for women. There is an economic transition that has been especially brutal and costly for women in the ex-GDR, creating an acute need for resistance, and hence for an active women's movement. There is a social transition that has thrown together two societies with very different experiences of work, family, and community. As such, women with markedly different backgrounds and aspirations are now in the same national arena and must work together to be politically effective, yet their differences in experience and perspective seriously complicate their efforts to build a common movement. And there is a political transition that has introduced a new dimension of inequality into the nation as a whole and overlays issues of gender inequality with the inequality of East and West. The dynamics of inequality, such as resentment and condescension, that poison the relationships between ethnic or religious subcommunities in other nations pose additional problems for articulating any overall feminist agenda. What is a small gain for women in the West may be a great loss for women in the East, as was the case with abortion reform.

In this context, my concern is to understand the tensions between feminism, as women in the old West Germany had come to understand it, and the new expectations and demands that women in the former GDR raise. I see these as partly rooted in the concrete experiences women of both preunification Germanies had, experiences that were strongly shaped by the respective gender policies of each country, and partly reflecting the specific strains that the unification process as such has produced.

I want to make clear that I am not arguing for a simplistic translation of women's experience into the politics of feminism in either portion of the country. In both East and West, there is a complex process of debate among feminists and between feminists and others that shapes the understanding of what goals the women's movement stands for and what means it wishes to employ. From this debate arises what I call a "collective self-representation" of feminism, that is, a sense of what a collective identity as a feminist means.[10] Such a collective identity links an interpretation of the past (what are women's experiences?) to an interpretation of the future (what are women's aspirations?). Collective identity is thus neither just a reflection of past experience nor independent of it.[11]

The collective self-representation of feminism differed in important ways in each portion of Germany because each system was organized around a fundamentally different sort of patriarchy.[12] Here, I wish to draw on the important work of Scandinavian feminists in distinguishing between public and private patriarchy.[13] In this formulation, the state is seen as organizing gender relations, as it also organizes class interests. The activities of the state support the relative dominance of men over women, but this power may be organized and expressed either collectively (public patriarchy) or in the state's support for the interests of individual men in maintaining domination over individual households (private patriarchy). The state socialism of the GDR embodied principles of public patriarchy; the state policies undergirding the social market economy of the FRG are, in contrast, strongly oriented to sustaining private patriarchy. The issue here is *not* whether the state is more or less influential in women's lives, but rather the nature of the effects that the state attempts to produce.

In the GDR, state policy tended to diminish the dependence of women on individual husbands and fathers but to enhance the dependence of women as mothers directly on the state. In the FRG, state policy follows the principle of subsidiarity and actively encourages private dependences. In particular, it has a mandate to preserve "the" family, which it understands primarily to be the husband-wife relationship as a context in which children can be raised. Thus, overall, the nature of the state's role in public patriarchy is to emphasize the direct relationship of mothers to the state, and the nature of the state's role in private patriarchy is to encourage the dependence of wives on husbands and of children on parents. In turn, this means that in public patriarchy, women experience their oppression as *mothers,* and as more directly connected to the activities of the state as patriarch; in private patriarchy, women experience their oppression as *wives,* and as more directly connected to their individual dependence on their spouses.

To make these abstractions more concrete, compare the nature of women's ordinary life experiences in the two systems. In the former GDR, approximately a third of all babies were born out of wedlock; virtually all women were in the labor force and worked essentially full-time jobs, earning on average 40 percent of the family income. Out-of-home child care for children under three and kindergartens for older children were universally available at low cost (which, one should note, is an exception among socialist as well as nonsocialist countries). Subsidies from the state for child care, rent, and other basic necessities reduced differences in standard of living between single mothers and two-parent, two-income families. Divorce was easy to obtain, women were primarily the ones who petitioned for divorce, and the divorce rate was the highest in the world. Dependence on an individual husband was reduced to a minimum.[14]

By contrast, in the FRG, 90 percent of babies are born within marriages. Living together is not uncommon, but when the baby comes, so does marriage (87 percent of cohabiting relationships are childless compared to 18 percent of marriages). Having a child is structurally inconsistent with having a full-time job, given the short and irregular school hours and the scarcity of child care for preschool children. There are child care places for fewer than 5 percent of children under three years old. Of all women aged 30 to 50, the prime child-rearing years, only a third have full-time jobs. Because of this incompatibility also, a substantal percentage of women are childless (23 percent of those born in 1960). Given their restricted labor force participation, it is not surprising that West German women provide on average only 18 percent of the family income and that the majority of employed women do not earn enough to support themselves independently, let alone raise a child. Tax subsidies such as income splitting further widen the gulf between the standard of living of two-parent families and single mothers; if a mother is confronted with the choice of keeping her job or keeping her marriage, the economic incentives strongly favor the latter. Dependence on an individual husband is strongly institutionalized.[15]

These differences work themselves out in feminist identity in several different ways. First, there is a difference in women's own identity that arises in relation to the dominant form of patriarchy in general and how it has been institutionalized. In the West, there is a conceptual package invoked by the phrase "wife-mother"; these two roles are treated as bundled together and virtually inseparable. This conceptualization does not carry over easily to the East, where motherhood is not so structurally bound to wifehood. Thinking about mothers in the FRG shades easily into imagining them only as wives; one needs to specify "single mother," and in doing so, one invokes the image of mothers who are politically and culturally deviant as well as impoverished. In the East, the imagery of single mother was not so necessary: women were mothers and workers and they may or may not have chosen to be or stay married. It was not an identity that carried a connotation of victimhood, deviance, or struggle.

The imagery of "woman" is more shaped by the wife role in the West as well, whether as housewife or as the woman who devotes herself to the job of attracting an individual man on whom she can then economically depend.[16] For ex-GDR women, the conventional woman was not at the disposal of an individual man but instrumentalized by the state as patriarch. The image of woman is thus the "mother-worker" who contributes both reproductive and productive labor to a collectively male-defined state. Her femininity was conceptualized in relation to the workplace.[17] In the conventional image of the GDR woman, her wifeness is much less salient than the fact that she is a mother; her constant and exhausting work takes precedence over her sexuality, and her motherhood is the basis on which the state had offered her special rights.[18]

The exaggerations and stereotypes of each version of women's "normal life" are reflections of these differently organized patriarchal demands. The East sees the West either as a wife, with money and leisure to work on her appearance and wait for her husband to come home, or as a feminist who has inexplicably rejected husband, home, and children; the West sees the East as a single mother with a career who has the help and support of the state to do it all.[19] Note that from each side, the dependency of the other is idealized: husbands support their wives, the state supports "its" mothers, and neither patriarch supposedly asks anything in return. From the outside, it is a "grass is greener on the other side of the fence" phenomenon. From inside either public or private patriarchy, it was never so simple, of course.

In reality, neither public nor private patriarchy constitutes liberation for women, but each does tend to shift the focus of women's attention to different aspects of their oppression. In the context of private patriarchy, the family and relations between husbands and wives are initially at the forefront of theorizing.[20] Feminists suggest that if relationships between individual men and individual women could be put on a different footing, this would lead to structural change and vice versa—the structural changes that are most avidly sought are those that would change the balance of power within familial relationships. Power relationships within the family are often problematized and are seen as "spilling over" into the rest of social organization. Rejecting marriage and seeking full-time employment, in the context of private patriarchy, are in fact ways for women to live out a challenge to the status quo.

In the context of public patriarchy, the role of public policy and the state is more immediately central. The male domination of political decision making in all areas, the role of the state as "guardian," one who speaks for women rather than allowing them to speak for themselves, the felt absence of collective political voice: These are all aspects of the sense of powerlessness that are central to the experience of women's subordination by collective rather than individual male power.[21] Power relations within the family, if problematized at all, are seen as stemming from the more fundamental policies and decisions taken at the public political level. Private relationships—whether lesbian or heterosexual—are experienced as irrelevant or secondary in comparison. To live out a challenge to the status quo was to find a way to raise children outside of the tutelage of the state: keeping kids out of state child care and military training, finding ways to work part time and rely less on state caregivers. It was also an ongoing struggle to organize political activites of which the state disapproved, to meet and discuss alternative politics. Freedom from the state and its demands, not from the family, was the critical issue. Family relations were more likely to be experienced as supports for resistance than as sources of oppression.[22]

I am not arguing that either of these experientially grounded perceptions is wholly wrong. At a more abstract level, I suspect we would all agree that patriarchal power is both public and private and that both intrafamilial relations and state politics are arenas in which women's subordination is constructed and male domination exercised on a daily basis. However, each form of organization of patriarchy tends to encourage one distinctively one-sided form of analysis or the other because each "fits" and explains certain gut-level experiences of oppression better. What is particularly interesting and instructive, albeit painful, is the collision between these two understandings.[23] Refusal of private patriarchy as Western feminists had practiced it is not something that Eastern feminists readily recognized as a form of resistance at all, but the five years of unification and experience of FRG social pressures are teaching them about the trade-off "your baby or your job." Most younger women are in fact choosing the latter. Because unification has taken place on FRG terms, there has been less pressure on Western feminists to rethink their assumption that women with husbands and children are nonemancipated "mommies."

Because of German unification, the two differently grounded feminist identities that arose in different contexts now have to share the same political space. Both sides have a tendency to disparage the degree of feminist understanding of the other: backward, hypocritical, arrogant, atheoretical, insensitive, hypersensitive—the charges and countercharges go on and on, unfortunately cast primarily in terms of the individual or collective personalities of the Other. The attempt to define "better" and "worse" feminists, and in the process to defend one's own version of feminism as "more true," is exacerbated by the tensions that the unequal relations of unification have also introduced into the relationship.[24] For feminists in the West, the patterns of interaction and relationships between women's-movement organizations and other social groups remain institutionalized and routine, although they are facing serious cutbacks in levels of state support that are attributed to the "costs of unification." For feminists in the East, a rapid and extreme deinstitutionalization has occurred on both individual and organizational levels. All the social and political organizations of the GDR have been swept away and replaced with those of the FRG. As one woman put it, "I feel like an immigrant in my own land." The gender policies and political practices of the FRG now provide the structure of opportunity for the entire country, and the institutionalized feminism of the West is perceived as defining "feminism" as such. In this context, it can hardly be surprising that some women in the former GDR look to this alien feminism and say, "If that is feminism, perhaps I'm not a feminist after all."

Yet at the same time, the feminism that was emerging in the old GDR before the fall of the wall has become irrelevant to the new conditions facing women in the unified FRG. The Independent Women's Association (UFV) had established itself as the feminist umbrella organization in the GDR in 1989; its initial struggles were to establish women's centers and media that would allow women to develop and express their own political perspectives and to participate in reforming the GDR.[25] Many of the demands they initially articulated assumed that the basic practices of the GDR—such as generous maternity leave, virtually free public child care, and affirmative action on the job—would be kept and improved to make them more gender-inclusive, less authoritarian, and more respectful of women.[26] Instead, not only have these benefits disappeared, but even once-unquestioned entitlements such as abortion on demand in the first trimester have been wiped away as well.

It thus remains important, therefore, to look at the persistence of the small but organized feminist movement in the new federal states and its continuing struggle to claim an identity that expresses its own perspective and aspirations.[27] The UFV and other political mobilizations of Eastern women, such as so-called women's political round-tables at the local level, attempt to define what feminism is, to articulate a feminist identity that "feels true" and resonates with ex-GDR women's experience of oppression both then and now. Such a feminism needs to confront the two differing structures of patriarchy that women have experienced within their lifetimes, but it perhaps stands in a unique position to be able to grasp the costs and benefits of each. Repressed and reviled in the old GDR as bourgeois, feminism in the new federal states now stands under the suspicion of being too socialist and too close to the old regime. The feminist identity that women in the new federal states are attempting to develop will have to arise as a collective self-representation of their needs and aspirations under these transformed conditions.

NOTES

1. Cf., Nanette Funk and Magda Mueller, *Gender Politics and Post-Communism* (New York: Routledge, 1993); Barbara Einhorn, *Cinderella Goes to Market: Citizenship, Gender and Women's Movements in East Central Europe* (New York: Verso, 1993).
2. E.g., Bettina Musall, "Viele dachten, die spinnen," *Der Spiegel*, March 18, 1991, pp. 68–84; Annemarie Engelhardt, "Verliererinnen der Wende?" *Die Frau in unserer Zeit* 22, no. 2 (1993), pp. 27–28.
3. Christiane Bialas and Wilfried Ettl, "Wirtschaftliche Lage, soziale Differenzierung und Probleme der Interesseorganisation in den neuen Bundesländern," *Soziale Welt* 44, no. 1 (1993), pp. 52–75.
4. Elke Holst and Jürgen Schupp, "Frauenerwerbstätigkeit in den neuen und alten Bundesländern: Befunde des Sozio-ökonomischen Panels," DIW (German Institute for Economic Research) discussion paper, 1992.
5. Friederike Maier, "Frauenerwerbstätigkeit in der DDR und BRD: Gemeinsamkeiten und Unterschiede," in Gudrun-Axeli Knapp and Ursula Müller (eds.), *Ein Deutschland—Zwei Patriarchate?* (Bielefeld: University of Bielefeld Press, 1992), p. 38.
6. Nicholas Eberstadt "Demographic Shocks After Communism: Eastern Germany, 1989–1993," *Population and Development Review* 20, no. 1 (1994), p. 139.
7. Ilona Ostner, "Ideas, Institutions, Traditions: West German Women's Experiences Since 1945." *German Politics and Society* 24–5 (1991–92), pp. 87–99.
8. Myra Marx Ferree, "The Rise and Fall of 'Mommy Politics': Feminism and Unification in (East) Germany," *Feminist Studies* 19 (1993), pp. 89–115.
9. For additional details, see Jeremiah Riemer, "Reproduction and Reunification: The Politics of Abortion in United Germany," in Michael Huelshoff and Andrei Markovits (eds.), *The New Germany in the New Europe* (Ann Arbor: University of Michigan Press, 1992); Eva Maleck-Lewy, "Between Self-Determination and State Supervision: Women and the Abortion Law in Post-unification Germany," *Social Politics* 2, no. 1(1995), pp. 62–75.
10. Jane Mansbridge, "What Is Feminism?" in Myra Marx Ferree and Patricia Yancey Martin

(eds.), *Feminist Organizations: Harvest of the New Women's Movement* (Philadelphia: Temple University Press, 1995).

11. Verta Taylor and Nancy Whittier, "Collective Identity in Social Movement Communities: Lesbian Feminist Mobilization," in Aldon Morris and Carol McClurg Mueller (eds.), *Frontiers of Social Movement Theory* (New Haven: Yale University Press, 1992); Barbara Hobson and Marika Lindholm, "Collective Identities, Women's Power Resources and the Making of Welfare States," paper presented at the Tenth International Conference of Europeanists, Chicago, March 1996.

12. Some of the following summarizes an argument that I have advanced and developed elsewhere in greater detail. See Myra Marx Ferree, "Patriarchies and Feminisms: The Two Women's Movements of Unified Germany," *Social Politics* 2 no., 1 (1995), pp. 10–24.

13. Birte Siim, "The Scandinavian Welfare States: Toward Sexual Equality or a New Kind of Male Domination," *Acta Sociologica* 3–4 (1987), pp. 255–70.

14. For details and statistics on the status of women in the GDR, see Barbara Einhorn, op. cit.; Gisela Helwig and Maria Nickel Hildegard (eds.), *Frauen in Deutschland, 1945–1992.* Band 318, Studien zur Geschichte und Politik (Bonn: Bundeszentrale für politische Bildung, 1993); and Friederike Maier "Frauenerwerbstätigkeit in der DDR and BRD: Gemeinsamkeiten und Unterschiede," in Gudrun-Axeli Knapp and Ursula Müller (eds.), *Ein Deutschland—Zwei Patriarchate?* (Bielefeld: University of Bielefeld Press, 1992). For a history of policy that discusses its objectives and how it has secured these outcomes, see Virginia Penrose, "Vierzig Jahre SED-Frauenpolitik: Ziele, Strategiem, Ergebnisse," *IFG: Frauenforschung* 4, pp. 60–77.

15. For more extensive and detailed data on the status of women in the preunification Federal Republic of Germany, see Helwig and Nickel, op. cit.; Maier op. cit.; Eva Kolinsky, *Women in West Germany: Life, Work and Politics* (Oxford: Berg, 1989); Jürgen Dorbritz, "Bericht 1994 über die demographische Lage in Deutschland," *Zeitschrift für Bevölkerungswissenschaft* 19, no. 4 (1994), pp. 393–473. For a history of policy that suggests how these outcomes were sought and institutionalized, see Robert Moeller, *Protecting Motherhood: Women and the Family in the Politics of Postwar West Germany* (Berkeley: University of California Press, 1993); and Ostner op. cit.

16. Waltraud Cornelissen, "Traditionelle Rollenmuster: Frauen- und Männerbilder in den westdeutschen Medien," in Gisela Helwig and Hildegard Maria Nickel (eds.), *Frauen in Deutschland, 1945–1992,* (Bonn: Bundeszentrale für politische Bildung, 1993).

17. Irene Dölling, "Frauen- und Männerbilder: Eine Analyse von Fotos in DDR-Zeitschriften," *Feministische Studien* 8 (1990), pp. 35–49.

18. Ferree, "The Rise and Fall of 'Mommy Politics.'"

19. Katrin Rohnstock, *Stiefschwestern: Was Ost-Frauen und West-Frauen voneinander denken* (Frankfurt am Main: Fischer, 1994); Ulrike Helwerth and Gislinde Schwarz, *Von Muttis und Emanzen: Feministinnen in Ost- und Westdeutschland* (Frankfurt am Main: Fischer, 1995).

20. See, for example, Marielouise Janssen-Jurreit, *Sexismus* (München: Frauenoffensive, 1976); Kate Millet, *Sexual Politics* (Garden City: Doubleday, 1970); Betty Friedan, *The Feminine Mystique* (New York: Dell, 1963).

21. See GDR feminist materials from the period of the *Wende* such as Ina Merkel, et al. (eds.), *Ohne Frauen ist kein Staat zu machen* (Hamburg: Argument Verlag, 1990); Cordula Kahlau (ed.), *Aufbruch! Frauenbewegung in der DDR* (München: Frauenoffensive, 1990).

22. Many of these arguments are based on interviews I conducted during 1990–92 with feminist activists in the former GDR; see also discussions of East German women's history, experiences, and identity in Birgit Bülow and Heidi Stecker, *EigenArtige Ostfrauen* (Bielefeld: Kleine Verlag, 1994).

23. See, e.g., Helwerth and Schwarz op. cit.; Rohnstock op. cit.

24. See critiques also in Christina Schenk and Christiane Schindler, "Frauenbewegung in Ostdeutschland—eine kleine Einführung," *Beiträge zur feministische Theorie und Praxis* 35 (1993), pp. 131–145; Helwerth and Schwarz, op. cit.; Bülow and Stecker op. cit.

25. Anne Hampele, "Der unabhängige Frauenverband" in Helmut Müller-Enbergs, Marianne Schulz, and Jan Wielgohs (eds.), *Von der Illegalität ins Parlament* (Berlin: LinksDruck Verlag, 1991).

26. Myra Marx Ferree, "'The Time of Chaos was Best': Feminist Mobilization and Demobilization in East Germany," *Gender and Society* 8, no. 4 (1994), pp. 597–623.

27. E.g., Schenk and Schindler op. cit.; articles in *WeibBlick*, the UFV's magazine.

< 5 >

Transitory and Persistent Differences

Feminism East and West

Hana Havelková

As compared to other postsocialist countries in Central Europe, there have been since 1989 in the Czech Republic no big social issues that specifically concern women. Unlike in Poland, the Czech abortion law remained fully liberal; unlike in East Germany, there is no massive unemployment of women; unlike in Hungary, there is a different kind of ideological pressure on women to return to the home. The issue in the Czech Republic turned out to be political; it was the low number of women in top political positions that, as compared to the numbers in the other countries I've mentioned (and including Slovakia), is the most striking "retreat" we've seen. Only 9.5 percent of members of parliament and only 16 percent of members of the local boards of representatives are women; there are no women ministers, and only two out of the fifty-one deputy ministers are women. In other words, women's political absence can be regarded as precisely the Czech problem.

For many Western feminists, this picture evokes a direct evaluation: Czech women are second-class citizens. But this formulation misses the core of my story. At the very least it fails to ask the question of whether the low number of women in politics can be interpreted as a decline, since the higher number under Communism represented sheer tokenism and was irrelevant with respect to power or decision making. In this paper I will briefly reflect on the different positions in the dialogue between women in the East and the West.

My claim is that this dialogue has thus far been one-dimensional and has failed to distinguish between transitory and persistent phenomena. The fault is on both sides. In order to assert the difference of their position, women from the East often absolutized it without distinguishing between its different levels. Women from the West supported this fixed image by not taking seriously the possibility that women's issues are contingent and change with a changing political situation. In my country, women and politics (and women in politics) is a topic that is strongly determined by the character of social transformation, meaning that the specificities of inherited patterns are mingled with new features. Their destination is not comparable with stable Western societies. This does not mean we cannot address the issue of women and politics, but our analysis must address the current context as well as deeper and more persisting structures that may decide the course of the current situation. The core of the misunderstanding in the dialogue between Eastern and Western European feminists is, in my opinion, that we were assuming that a focus on women must necessarily mean the same thing in all contexts. But I want to argue that the difference does not lie in specific problems as such, but in their relative political and social status. We will not be able to name the real differences unless we acknowledge the practical and theoretical relevance of their status, be it a topical one (the task for Western women) or the separation of the topical from the persisting phenomena (the task for Eastern women). By status I mean the location of the problems in the general context of each country, their proportion, their perception, and, generally speaking, their framing.

I will give concrete examples. When I said that there is no big women's issue in Czech society at present, I was far from claiming that there are no women's problems at all. There are women's problems, but they are not yet defined in terms of women's interests. For example, the problem of prostitution, which is concentrated mostly around the Czech-German border, is regarded primarily as a problem posed by the abruptly opened border and the disproportion between the Czech and German currencies. The customers are German, the prostitutes Czech. Prostitutes report that they earn in one night more than their mothers earn in a whole month in the factory. So this problem is framed by the broader problem of the relative economic position of the country (an issue I will address later on). Another example: Violence against women (especially rape) is, by and large, dealt with in the context of the previously neglected care of crime victims and is therefore only a part of a more general attempt to provide assistance. It is seen as a part of the dramatic rise in the overall crime rate after 1989 and as an example of the general decay of morals. The statistically lower remuneration of women has not yet become a political issue; the situation in the labor market is very much in flux at the moment. By entering new and attractive jobs in the service sector and in private enterprises, women often improve their financial situation, and the statistics about them are, in any case, inexact. In short, the situation here is not transparent enough for gender issues to emerge.

Of course, I want to avoid another kind of one-dimensional argument that says everything is shaped by current politics. Any analysis of women's situation must take into account at least three different levels. The first is cultural and deals with questions common to East and West, which follow from our participation in a single civilization. Second, there are the modifications of this culture, which result from our different histories during the modern period—these concern differences in institutions, social patterns, and mentalities. Third is the process of transformation, which we are undergoing now.

I will focus on the topic of women and/in politics during the time of transformation. Most of my theoretical claims are supported by data gathered in extensive interviews with women during the autumn of 1995. But let me first distinguish which phenomena are characteristic of the transformation as a whole and which are bound only to certain stages. Let me remind you that it is the very foundations of society that are being changed; we are rebuilding basic democratic institutions and learning to live in them. To understand this situation better, I suggest the working concepts of abstract and concrete citizenship. By *abstract citizenship* I mean an imaginary system-in-process into which certain ideals are projected. By *concrete citizenship* I mean the attitudes that are rooted in the concrete knowledge and experiences of the individual within a social or political system. During the process of transformation, citizens encounter unknown conditions onto which they project their concrete experiences of the past and their abstract ideals concerning the future.

With the help of these two concepts, the present attitude of Czech women toward their representation in politics can be explained. Since there is yet no spark that mobilizes them on the basis of their identity as women, their reluctant relationship to power can only express their abstract relation to it. This does not imply a lack of interest in politics, but rather that women have thus far preferred to watch or to be indirectly useful (to be active in local politics, NGOs, charities, etc.). This may be a transitory attitude. Nonetheless, it has a more persistent component that always seems to modify women's political strategies whenever they begin to be more involved. What persists are the real conditions, different from those in the West. These include the awareness of the irreplaceable role the family played under socialism, a role continued and reproduced at present and which is a key part of women's concrete citizenship. Because the economic transformation of the Czech Republic was made possible by the inherited family-strategy skills of women, the context of Czech politics has appeared to apply fully and directly to them. Women do not feel any need to create women's lobbies; they do not regard political engagement as attractive or prestigious when compared to their more creative jobs, which allow them to combine their familial and professional duties. Nonetheless there is another underlying factor that conflicts with this sense of universal representation, and that is the importance of employment outside the home and women's financial independence. The tension between these two equally strong values is the key to understanding women's political presence. For the most part, women have voted for right-wing parties because they share with men the belief in the absolute priority of economic reform, the success of which could improve their difficult financial situations and liberate them. Hence gender issues remain subordinated to the economic problems of the country as a whole. Although this is largely an abstract belief, it converges with what actually bothers people most: the decision about what the future geopolitical status of the country will be.

It seems pertinent here to consider what Nanette Funk said in her reflections on the East-West dialogue. She drew a parallel between Eastern European women and black women in the United States, a comparison that ignores many of the problems that seem central to the issues that concern me. As Laura Busheikin, a Canadian employee of the Prague Gender Studies Center, put it in 1993: "Now it has become fashionable in the West to talk of race, class, and gender as intersecting lines of oppression, but this doesn't offer a framework which can fully account for East European women's experience." But let me ask what are we, Czech women, with respect to the categories race, class, and gender? We experience neither race nor class oppression, and we still do not consider gender oppression a priority. Both white middle-class and socialist women's identities were articulated long ago (in the 1920s) in this country and need only be updated once the time of transformation is over. The frameworks of identity remain the country and the family. The point is that any individual position is extremely dependent on the development of the country in a way an American citizen cannot imagine. The geopolitical situation is a designation that must be included in any consideration of the categories of class, race, and gender, for belonging to a country in Eastern or Central Europe makes second-class citizens of all of us when we are compared to the West.

Is the term "national identity" correct in this connection? In the Czech case, nationalism is closely connected with a sense of individual responsibility for the success of the whole. This formula is confirmed repeatedly by sociological polls. Individualism has been the ethos of the first-stage transformation in Czech lands. It would be a big mistake to think that women are passive or politically apathetic, as some Western observers have put it. Women do not wait for their husbands to be successful in the labor market; they themselves enter it. If we want to describe this situation in relation to Simone de Beauvoir's dichotomy between transcendence and immanence, we could say that Czech women were long ago included in the "realm of transcendence." To put it more strongly, the subordination of women's issues to general civic issues can be regarded as a form of citizenship that proves that women do not feel confined to immanence. One effect of the totalitarian experience is that both women and men think politically rather than psychologically. On the one hand, this leads to a lesser degree of sensitivity on gender issues, but on the other, it also makes women feel politically equal. And this effect will probably persist in that when women do start to see the political relevance of the gender difference, they will most likely see it in the context of and in proportion to other political realities.

If we want to put this question in Carole Pateman's terms, my claim is that socialism was a peculiar combination of traditional patriarchy, in which women and men were in the same position, and a very weak fraternal patriarchy (insofar as it concerned the relation between the sexes). The reaction after 1989 was, therefore, very interesting: Men eagerly entered their "lost" but traditional public domain, while women did not fear male dominance in either the private or the public sphere. Nor do women regard political power, as such, as prestigious or attractive, but this does not mean they are inactive; they comprise about 70 percent of all the activists in the emerging NGOs. There are no signs that women intend to retreat from the workforce. Women's employment has declined only from 47 percent of the total working force in 1989 to about 45 percent today. And the qualitative changes in the structure of women's employment testify to the fact that women are not about to leave the public sphere.

Now I come to the way the topic of women and/in politics is affected by this very phase of the transformation, which is characterized by the incompleteness of the politics itself. Up to now, politics has not been a politics in the full sense of the word. It has been reduced almost entirely to the economic program. The last elections were in fact a referendum about radical economic reform. Social reform began only after a long delay, when the first drafts of new social political arrangements were published. So what would typically be the domain of women politicians has been so far more or less absent. The new social structures have not yet been settled, and the status of women in them is not clear. Therefore, for women, as well as for men, this is a time to test one's individual professional abilities in the new conditions of competition.

The value of individualism in the Czech experience is a special topic. When women acquired an improved social status under Communism, principally through employment outside the family and consequent financial independence, they were prepared to enter capitalist competition precisely *as individuals*. This is a considerably different starting point from the situation in which the Western women's movement began in the 1960s.

In my research, I discovered that none of the women interviewed thought that women's representation in politics was an irrelevant question, but on the whole they preferred pragmatic strategies, i.e., solutions to concrete problems when they emerge. They also often speak about a "natural" way. This preference is due to their suspicions whenever ideology seems to precede reality, an opinion that I do not think is only temporary. The failure of the leftist intelligentsia in post-Communist countries should be taken very seriously. So-called ordinary women are obviously very well aware of gender problems, but they are used to thinking "strategically," a kind of thinking that is typical of Czech women's citizenship. Women start from a position of strength in Czech society, and their pressing issue now is the problem of men's irresponsibility. Whereas the typically post-Communist phenomenon that Cris Corrin called a "superwoman" has been amply described, its counterpart, namely men's lessened responsibility in the family in these countries, has as yet been virtually ignored in feminist reflections. And yet it is the reason why women often regard their own empowerment as less urgent than a rebuilding of responsibility in men.

Now I will take up the question of whether the experience of Czech women calls for a reconsideration of "civil society." I do not think so. Civil society consists of many components, which in different times have different meanings and relevance. I think much stronger emphasis needs to be placed on the factors of time and space when considering who participates in civil society and in what ways. We also need to pay more attention to continuities and discontinuities in the way the "new" democracies are being (re)constructed, and to accept that there are historically and geopolitically determined modes of Central and Eastern European democractic organization. It seems to me that Czech women fear that women's collective action will be counterproductive; their skepticism concerns the premature introduction of projects that run ahead of everyday understandings and culture.

Articulation in local terms is important, but I am afraid that women from the East will not articulate their experience in their own terms, because the Western feminist theoretical discourse has taken up the task of translation. For them, translation is a one-way project from West to East. This really means that those from the East speak two languages: their own and that of Western feminism. What is needed is awareness by Western feminists that they speak in a contextually bound way, too. They must be willing to learn our language and to grant it validity.

There is an additional reason for doing so. Whereas the political mainstream (dominated by men) in my country willingly accepts Western patterns, Czech women, by rejecting an automatic adoption of Western feminism, actually defend the value of their world. As soon as men enter positions of power, they must bargain with their Western counterparts. So they are deprived of autonomy. Women retain an autonomy that men lose. Unless this kind of cultural understanding is achieved, the East-West feminist dialogue will not succeed.

There are other dimensions of this dialogue that need further study. First, the question of the status of feminism. Initial reports about feminism being "a dirty word" in the East need to be reexamined. There is a history of feminism in the Czech Republic; it needs to be understood in its own terms and in its changing relation to Western feminism.

Second, the level of concrete historical experience needs further attention. Two basic mistakes about this history have been repeated: First, the socialist modernization of women's status has not been regarded as something to learn from, for it has been imposed from above. But the analysis of the socialist era is far from finished. It must include, besides state policy, the concrete experiences of women as they acted in accord with or resistance to that policy. The absence of public discourse under Communism must not be taken literally, either. There was discussion of changing gender relations for a long time—among friends, in the workplace. Only an elaborated feminist theory was missing. History must take into account women's experience with lifelong financial independence and with the growing problem (since 1989) of men's irresponsibility. There are other issues, too: the backlash against affirmative action and deep skepticism about ideas of liberation.

The second mistake about history underestimates the impact of long-term persisting structures, those from the pre-Communist past, which influenced Communist society and those acquired under socialism that also affect the face of the present societal transformation.

Democracy has taken many forms in the West and the East. There once was, and now again is, a Czech democracy—whose shape will differ from others and from its own past. The different timing of the development of Czech democracy has repeatedly favored women's goals. Since the nineteenth century, we can speak about a continuity of a liberal approach to the "women question" in this country, which has never been interrupted. The Communist era can be regarded as continuing the "traditional" liberal trend. As a result, women in the Czech lands are not attracted by the idea of a change in status. They long for a refinement of gender relations, not for revolution. A big plurality of identities is at stake for women and men in the Czech Republic today, and the situation is dialectical, full of paradoxes, which indeed are not easy to reveal, but must be grasped.

Nationalist Discourse
in the Former Yugoslavia

< 6 >

Affective Nationalism

Djurdja Knezevic

Although it may seem that nationalism does not have a gender, this is not entirely true. Even the most recent example, the war in the former Yugoslavia, shows it clearly, although it has been evident many times before in history. The problem of rape in this war can be seen as a paradigm since all three warring sides basically agree that the nation has been raped. Of course, each side has its own nation in mind, but when we look at the words of the publicly declared strategy of the Serbian warlords, that rape is a strategy of humiliation and contamination of the nation. It is clear that the nation is a female body or a woman. Women are not considered as "only women" but as the personification of and symbol for the nation. When this is the case, women are not human beings or individuals. Male discourse denotes women as a group imbued with (imagined) characteristics similar to those of the nation. Phrases such as "mother nation" or "mother homeland" are examples of this point of view.

Since nationalism also offers a concept of community, it has a great and particular attraction for women. There are different reasons for this. First of all, within the women's and feminist movement and ideology, a feeling of "belonging to" was consciously and systematically developed. This process was almost "natural": as individualism was never a woman's privilege, it could not be an obstacle to the development of group feelings. There are certain similarities here with nationalism, and even though there are also some significant differences, the sense of belonging sometimes gets transferred to the nation anyway. Women's groups tend to be egalitarian, without leaders, and often have a sort of fear of power (especially of powerful women, because women have learned to accept and respect powerful men but not women). They are uneasy about making decisions and reluctant to take an active role in any form of public life, especially in politics. This is so because none of these fields of human activity is made for women; the public sphere in modern societies (and in liberal theory) is designed for men. For example, when we do not talk about citizenship but about men and women, these notions immediately imply gendered bodies, not just bodies with rights. And it is easy to recognize that male bodies are those that fit into certain codes of privileges and responsibility etc., thanks to the sociopolitical practice expressed through liberal theory. Whenever women want to fit into the same codes, it is at expense of their particularity. Nationalism, however, seemed to offer a kind of inclusion that did not exclude women.

As a second point, we could say that exactly this feeling of "belonging to" makes the whole process of acceptance of nationalism far easier because it offers the only exclusive opportunity for women to enter the public sphere or politics, and to be (to some extent) on an equal level with men, and/or to be recognized as active participants in social life—but only as a group, and rather limited in social and political respects.

There are two aspects of entering the public sphere for women. One gives women the role of being men's supporters, and the other gives them recognition through an idea of a "safe space." First let us say something about the role of women as supporters of men. It appears almost as a rule in history that whenever deep social changes take place and whenever a whole society seems threatened, women are "invited" to participate actively in public life. The power of women has always been welcomed to help establish male domination, and women have always been very pleased to take part. Of course, women were not usually aware of what was going to happen because they never had a clear idea about how to introduce a social project that would include women as equal partners. This scenario is clearly visible in the example of the interaction of nationalism and several of the women's feminist groups in Croatia. After the elections in 1990 in Croatia an impressive number of women's groups emerged almost overnight and took part in public life. This was also frightening since many of these groups were strongly and clearly nationalistic and sometimes, in public discourse, tougher than men. Women's groups were attracted by nationalism because the public space under the Communist regime was too narrow for them. As long as Communist regimes and their ideologies were able to rule, and although their rule was based on military and police power, it is paradoxically the case that citizens felt a certain safety. The whole system and its rules were quite clear in the peculiar sense that everybody knew how political decisions were made within closed circles. Therefore it was relatively easy to relate oneself politically to the system; you were either in opposition, or a supporter, or—the majority—a part of an unconscious and/or indifferent mass. If you wanted to pursue a private project of your own and be left alone by the regime, you simply had to respect the political taboos. Lack of democracy was compensated for by a relatively good standard of living (social security, security of jobs, etc.).

In the present time, since the former ideological legitimacy of the political system has disappeared, a new, widely accepted ideology—nationalism—has emerged as a way of legitimating the new rule. Strangely, though, the idea of the national state as the supreme value seems to work surprisingly well as a legitimation for an almost unchanged power structure. And there is one more point that confuses people, mostly Westerners: How could it happen that nationalism appeared so quickly and it was accepted so easily in the countries that had been under the strong pressure of Communist regimes for half of the century, where any sort of expression of nationalism had been strongly punished? There is something that is rooted more deeply in the education and ideology of all the countries of the former Communist regimes. As we know, the problem of "belated nations" in Eastern Europe and Russia was "solved" by establishing Communist regimes, which declared that nationalism no longer existed. But since they could not offer a different ideological system with comparable appeal, they took over the whole set of nationalistic ideas (devotion to the charismatic leaders to one-state ideology mother Russia, the placement of collective interests above private interests, the need to sacrifice for the bright future, the fear of external and internal enemies, etc.). The problem was that nationalism was reserved for the nomenklatura's use only, and was forbidden to the common people. Thus, on the one hand, nationalism was suppressed as a movement from below, and on the other, the Communist leaders claimed the position of champions of the "national cause." Not having any rational way to organize themselves, the societies under Communist regimes preserved nationalism as the most articulate expression of an irrational sense of belonging to a community.

After the elections in 1990, and with the beginning of the war, this narrow public space was (and still is) in danger of disappearing entirely. At first sight this does not seem logical, since these were democratic elections that followed decades of Communist one-party rule. But the newly elected parties were strongly nationalistic, and after the elections in 1990, Croatia entered into a kind of pluralism that was strictly reduced to a specific framework designed to allow as legitimate only that which can be identified or considered as acceptable. This means that pluralism is possible only within a framework of nationalistic exclusiveness. Any opinion that falls outside of this framework is considered a betrayal of the nation. Under these circumstances, endorsement of nationalism appears merely as an opening to a much wider space for women's activism. Within this space women are provided with the widest social recognition. It does not matter what kind of society it is, nor does it matter what role they play in this society; women can participate in the public sphere as long as they support or advocate things that fit within mainstream politics. In the Croatian case this was one reason for women's engagement in the argument that only Croatian and Muslim women were raped and that the whole Serbian nation had raped those women. This claim was immediately accepted by the government through a regime-controlled media and used in political power games. Women's groups, such as Bedem Ljubavi (literally, "Fortress of Love," but they also call themselves "Chain of Love" or other similar names), Kareta, Tresnjevka (both self-declared feminist groups), and some others, were immediately presented in the media as "patriotic feminists" and praised for their heroic work for women. But groups that wanted to raise some social and political problems with the government could not reach the public sphere and, moreover, were fiercely attacked by the regime-controlled media, which never made it clear what exactly those groups wanted. These nonsanctioned groups were also attacked by one woman M.P. during a regular session of the Croatian parliament, who warned her male colleagues that "these feminist groups are dangerous and, even though they are women, they should be taken seriously by my male colleagues." In Croatia, "dangerous" means "Yugo-nostalgic," "Communist," even "pacifist," and any other stance construed as critical of the regime. The accusation actually can endanger the people who are "dangerous." They could have trouble at their jobs or even lose them; they could be harassed in many different ways, physically attacked (one journalist was beaten in the middle of a big city in Croatia because of his opinion), and so on. Of course, this woman M.P. made it clear exactly which groups she meant. The culminating point in her accusations was reached during the end of 1992 and the beginning of 1993. First, a lengthy article appeared in Zagreb's weekly, *Globus*, under the significant headline "Croatia's Feminists Rape Croatia!" Five women were accused of being traitors of the Croatian nation and of "hiding the truth about sexual violence as the instrument of Serbian racist and imperialistic politics." It was stated that "the Croatian and even the world's feminist movement died morally in the Balkan wars of the nineties." These women were described as belonging to the "feminist 'movement' that appeared in the early seventies in Zagreb and Belgrade" and as having "discovered American and French feminist literature, which preached the necessity of not only class struggle but of the struggle between the sexes as well. As most of these ladies had serious problems finding a partner of the male sex and an area of interest, they chose feminism as their own 'destiny,' ideology and profession." The author(s) gave further information: "The small number among them who, in spite of their theoretical position and physical appearance, did succeed in finding a partner for marriage, chose according to official Yugoslav standards: one, a Serb from Belgrade, was married twice, each time to a Serb from Croatia." This is, in the view of the author(s) "a matter of systematic political choice rather than an accidental choice made from love!" This chauvinistic crescendo had a grand finale: These women were making a "political quadrangle of the feminism-Marxism-Communist-Yugoslav idea" and were, in fact, the "little girls of Communism." At the end of the unsigned article was a list of their names and detailed information about them, such as their place of birth, nationality, marital status, number of children, husband, property, etc. After a while the campaign became international. A message distributed through electronic conferences, made in close cooperation with the office of Catherine McKinnon, fiercely attacked two of these women, using the same repertoire of accusations: traitors to the Croatian nation, Communist, pro-Serbian, attempting to conceal information about victims (raped women in particular), equating the victims with perpetrators, etc. This time the letter was signed by four groups: the feminist group Kareta, the International Initiative of Women of Bosnia and Herzegovina (BISER), the Bosnia-Herzegovina Refugee Women's Group (Zene Bi), and Bedem Ljubari (Fortress of Love, or Chain of Love). There were other attacks, but these last two were the most severe and the most dangerous. They have in common that they operate with a typical mixture of "information" and commentary, very often lies; they label people politically and accuse them of sins they did not commit or of "sins" that are not sins at all.

Those women's groups that accepted a nationalist framework (strongly supported by the government) came to the point of protecting the behavior of the Croatian government by explaining that although it is nondemocratic, "we" are at war and "we" should give the government space to finish it (the war) and to work in general. This also means giving the government free rein to bring about very bad laws for women.

It is clear that the groups who accepted state ideology, based on nationalism, were allowed to participate in the public sphere, while the others were brutally expelled. But this participation in the public sphere was and is also strictly limited to certain women's issues as defined by strongly traditional, patriarchal tradition. (A clear signal to women that they are not welcome in the public sphere is the number of M.P.'s in the Croatian parliament. Before the 1990 elections, 17 percent of M.P.'s were women; in the newly elected parliament, that number has dropped to only 3 percent.) This "ticket to the political arena" was false. Instead of an opportunity to raise genuine women's issues as political issues, these women were given only an opportunity to play again the very same roles that have always been allocated to them in the male-dominated political sphere. They appear again as advocates of a transcendental collectivity of Croats, or Muslims, or Serbs, thereby replaying the roles of wives, mothers, sisters, nurses. The positive response they have received from nationalist-dominated public opinion and the recognition they have gotten from male authoritarian leaders offer them a "proof" that they were "right." Women appear as supporters, as participants in social changes, only within and under strict rules of male ideologies, as an addition to the male society.

The second form of recognition open to women is the offer of a "safe space." How are we to understand this? When the situation in the country is getting worse, why are masses of women attracted by a growing nationalism and neopatriarchalism, especially when it is clear that problems such as the fragmented state, anxiety, apathy, social insecurity, etc., burden women more then men? Why should this be so when it is women who are the first to be fired from their jobs, whose health insurance and other welfare benefits are always and everywhere first to be reduced, and who alone are affected by restrictive neopatriarchal values?

Since nothing else, no rational economic or political program, was offered to women (nor to the society and citizens of Croatia), several of the old-new traditional, patriarchal images of women appeared wrapped in ethnic and national decorations. Croatia became Mother and women became Homeland. This was repeated in almost every speech by almost every Croatian politician. This simple combination of Croatia and women was finally sanctioned in the state's "Project of Spiritual Restoration," announced in the spring of 1992 by none other than the president of the state. Among other things, the project includes laws and conditions to ensure that the most sublime profession in Croatia will be that of Mother Educator, that employed mothers with children will be taken from the factories, that marriage will be encouraged and any other kind of relationship suppressed. There are also some other ideas included, such as the "rejection of the atheist/materialist tendency in public and family life, the need to emphasize that the father of a Croatian family is the fundamental linchpin of the demographic restoration of Croatia and therefore responsible for the prosperity and happiness of the family, and that the quiet exodus of young Croatian women must be stopped." In every part of this document warnings about abortion are repeated, such as the reminder that "as far as abortion goes, we are still living in the time of Serbo-communism."

Given the difficult position of women, the government answer was to limit their space to the role of mother, simultaneously closing workplaces and firing women first. This kind of policy works on two levels. First, state power is employed to strictly and clearly limit women's space and define it as separate, next to or outside of the (male) public space, which makes it difficult for any possible women's struggle for a different position in society to operate. Secondly, by ascribing to this same space certain mystical qualities such as respect, importance, and recognition, it is very possible that it will be seen as the only escape from misery and will therefore be attractive to the majority of women.

Nationalism and neopatriarchal pressure are firmly closing off the way to the public sphere, to equality and participation in all fields of social life. Instead, it offers women an "easier," but actually misleading, way to solve their problems. The Project of Demographic Restoration repeatedly argues that women should be protected from hard work and that their lives should be without men's problems. Nationalism and neopatriarchal ideology offer women group security and a "safe space" in family life, and they show women that all their troubles were caused by "the others." Women are offered their own identity as wives and mothers, once again the supporters of men in general.

There are women and women's groups still working and struggling for the real equality of both sexes; these groups are nonnationalistic, clearly antiwar, and internationally, multiethnically oriented. Their influence, despite incredible difficulties and obstacles, cannot be ignored.

But instead of drawing any conclusions that might seem to summarize the problems I've discussed, I will just describe what happened a few days ago [October 31, 1995]. At the initiative of the Women's Infoteka from Zagreb and the Group for Women's Human Rights, a group of women from all parts of Croatia, representing different women's groups and organizations, established an ad hoc coalition for monitoring the elections in Croatia. They organized a public hearing and talked with women candidates from the different party lists. The room where this event took place was full of women and candidates from different parties (only opposition representatives came; members of the ruling party, HDZ, either did not appear or excused themselves). In the middle of the event, four self-declared representatives of the right-wing group called the New Croatian Right Party, three men and one woman, entered the room shouting and yelling that the women should stop the session and go back to their homes. They claimed that democracy was rotten and called for a fascist regime. The women were called "Yugo-communist whores" and, as an insult, "feminist lesbians." These four also began giving the Nazi/fascist salute. When their interruption was protested, one of the intruders slapped a woman's face. Finally, the police came and order was restored. Two days later, this right-wing group was registered as a regular political party. Even before registration, their leader was given a large block of time on the television network, which is entirely under the control of the government, to express their fascist ideas freely, and no one made any attempt to stop it.

This happened two days ago [November 2, 1995] and today, as I finish this article, is election day in Croatia. The question is, what will tomorrow bring?

It is not easy to explain what happened after the elections because, paradoxically, nothing happened. The elections were complicated by the fact that they were held not only to elect representatives, but also to allow the ruling party to effect a change in the constitution so that its president could stand for election. The leader of the Hrvatska Demokratska Zajednica (HDZ—Croatian Democratic Union), Franjo Tudjman, wanted a second term, but reelection to the presidency was illegal under the existing constitution. To change the constitution, Tudjman and the HDZ needed to end up with a two-thirds majority in the parliament. To try to influence the voting, the election was moved forward so that the memory of the HDZ's successful military actions in Krajina would be fresh in the voters' minds. Not only did they not win the two-thirds majority, they lost in important areas such as Zagreb, a city in which one fourth of the citizens of Croatia live and where the opposition parties took 60 percent of the vote. Tudjman had to confirm the candidate(s) for the presidency of the city parliament before they could be admitted, but he refused to sanction three of the proposed opposition candidates. Even pressure from the international community, whose agreement is necessary if Croatia is to be admitted to the Council of Europe, has not helped to resolve this issue. The ruling party, with its nomenklatura, is governing in a way that is very like the previous regime (if there is any difference, it is that the former governments were more sophisticated and liberal). In our current society there are no basic democratic rights nor any available means to fight for them. Citizens are afraid to demonstrate or to strike because these actions would brand them as "public enemies" more dangerous than the Serbs. The government uses the excuse of the war to justify everything from censorship of the media to the destruction of the economy. It is rather easy to maintain control in these circumstances, for so long as this government can seem to provide a kind of peace for the region, it will have the support of other world governments. Dissidents will not be able to find the kind of international support they would need to allow them to develop a significant counter-politics which could affect internal problems. The most scary thing is that this state affairs can last for a long, long time. For decades. Actually, this is what tomorrow brought.

< 7 >

Nationalist and Women's Discourse in Post-Yugoslavia

Svetlana Slapsak

In recent academic and journalistic writing on the former Yugoslavia and its dissolution, nationalism, cited as the main motivation, pretext, or even highly theorized justification for its war, is usually presented as a nongendered concept, something that victimizes both men and women, who are equally responsible for and equally immersed in it. There is hardly any reflection on differences between Yugoslav men's and women's cultures and discourses. The main topic concerning women that comes up is the loss of women's legal and social rights and privileges, a feature said to be common to all post-socialist Eastern and Central European societies. But socialist Yugoslavia did not quite fit the pattern of pre-1989 Warsaw Pact countries, either politically, historically, or culturally. Therefore, even while the loss of rights and the diminution of public and political representation has occurred, there are different reasons that this has happened.

Another common problem with writings on Yugoslavia is the consistent failure to mention women's groups, actions and feminism/feminisms/feminists. Two authors recognized by American feminists as relevant sources of information, Slavenka Drakulic and Renata Salecl, never provided information about feminism and its changing agendas before the war, either inside or outside academia. Nor do they talk about the names of feminists past and present, about radical changes that evolve from the war, or even about women's actions that visibly changed the war.

Yugoslavia does have an interesting feminist tradition that developed shortly after World War II, which distinguished it from the Eastern and Central European paradigm. If women in post-Yugoslavia are now presented as women without feminism, this corresponds to stereotypes shared, surprisingly enough, by Western public opinion and by Western feminist academia. As far as the academy is concerned, women's position in post-Yugoslavia is thereby reduced to "raw material" for research, classification, and theorizing by others. What interests me is not to provide such raw material, but to open a different kind of discussion.

I would ask first of all that we explore the relationship between nationalist and women's discourse in post-Yugoslavia. Only by understanding that women's culture, and therefore women's discourse, in Yugoslavia had some distinctive gendered features may we be able to connect and compare women and nationalism. The starting point of this connection is the fact that in the public discourse of post-Yugoslavia, women's discourse found itself openly opposed to nationalist speech. Considering the importance and the power of such speech in conceptualizing the war in Yugoslavia, and the role of academia and intellectuals in this process, and given the apparent lack of effective criticism, we simply must emphasize the critical energy that is emerging from various women's groups and women authors who are politically and socially disconnected, marginalized, and denigrated but who have begun to appear in unexpected grassroots movements and peripheral places.

If the choice and the construction of a genre is a political decision, then nationalist discourse could be defined as a genre. Since its very beginnings, nationalist discourse has had a tendency to monopolize the space of communication, moving between the academy and the media, philosophy and populism, pragmatics and rhetorics, poetry and politics. It has taken on flaws from all of these fields, from the scientific thinking of the past century to the most extravagant and avant-garde ideas of this century. It has also adapted traits from different grand ideological projects, some clearly nationalist, such as National socialism and fascism, and some suspiciously inclined to embrace nationalism, such as Communism. Even when it is subject to elaborate aesthetic procedures and linked to highbrow literary projects, nationalist discourse always has a message to deliver, a "truth" to disclose that is universal, collective, and undeniable. This prophetic context places it somewhere between political, poetic, scientific, and religious discourse. It can indeed be observed to be a hybrid genre, with a collagelike structure in which each and every element is recognizable and refers clearly to its original context. The message, however, emerges from the disposition of the elements and cannot be mistaken.

Nationalist discourse indifferently addresses both large audiences and the elites who would perceive themselves as representatives of the "masses." Its rhetoric therefore is popular and commonsensical, and does not venture into complicated, multidimensional criticism. Popular myths, which assume the function of biblical parables, are chosen from a cultural range that spreads from oral tradition to pop culture. Nationalist narrative is not choosy; it will willfully mix and deliberately blur distinctions and go on to mold new forms. The former Yugoslavia's nationalist discourses of the prewar and war periods reveal a vast panorama of forms that the genre has taken on while reviving old and inventing new genre clusters: nationalist memoirs, new mystifications of oral poetry, belligerent homily, fascist essay and manifesto, propagandistic drama, etc. Orthodox church rhetoric, social realist propaganda, and decadent aestheticism mix freely and employ a thesaurus of motives, metaphors, images, and allusions.

For all that it must constantly repeat basic truths, nationalist discourse is a resourceful genre, vital and inventive. This invention depends mainly on the force, capacity and will of the creative intelligentsia to indulge in its production; nationalist discourse cannot survive in half-educated narratives, and so it must find innovative force in intellectual feedback. Certainly, in the long run, nationalist rhetoric proves lethal for the intelligentsia itself, not just in terms of its intellectual integrity, but also in terms of the stability of its social and professional environment. Nationalist power games can cause dramatic changes in academic populations; it can lead to the loss of positions, the forced generation of change, the dismemberment of institutions, and their emigration. But this instability makes it difficult in turn for the nationalist narrative maker to maintain a steady level of persuasiveness. Torn between the constant search for originality (and new authors), on the one hand, and the need for a stable stereotype on the other, the competitive field of nationalist narrative production will exploit any set of motives.

In order to understand what the structural elements of women's discourse in post-Yugoslavia could be, it is necessary to give a very short outline of the history and present situation of feminism.

Feminism in the Yugoslav countries started among socialist intellectuals in Serbia in the late 1870s in contact with Central European feminism in Slovenia and Croatia. Between the two world wars several women's organizations and movements emerged, composed mostly of literary and academic women, some supported by the government or even by the royal family. During World War II, the Communist partisan movement proclaimed equality of the sexes and attracted large masses of peasant women to fight in the resistance. Along with the emancipated women inside and outside the Communist Party, this huge population of women was organized into the Antifascist Women's Front (AFZ). At the end of the war it continued to engage in a range of activities such as the rehabilitation of ruins, education, aid for the handicapped, territorial defense, the propagation of the new socialist ideology, and other kinds of voluntary work. They also celebrated newly acquired rights: suffrage, equal pay, easy divorce, free and universal medical and child care, easy access to abortion, and political representation. After the 1948 split with Stalin, politics gradually changed, and the AFZ was dissolved by 1954. Although the separation of women remained a rule for all electoral procedures, none of their previous rights were denied. By 1960, access to gynecological treatment was made even easier, as no specific documents were required for service and no records were kept. Women could choose and change their doctor at any time. But the position of women was heavily manipulated: The Communist Party, wavering between the Western way of life and a one-party system with some liberal features, controlled the population of women by imposing patriarchally defined behavior, attributes, and ideas through the media, and by maintaining a certain ideological disdain for feminism inside Party circles. Many devoted women Communists and feminists from the old generation felt betrayed by their comrades, a feeling they articulated during feminist underground meetings in the 1970s. The students', and later the dissidents', movement, which began in 1968 and was intellectually based in a more liberal Marxist approach, considered feminism a "not serious" topic in debates over the future of socialist Yugoslavia.

A new interest in feminism developed among women academics in Croatia and grew into the network that during the 1980s organized congresses on the subject of women's writing and feminism in Dubrovnik, engaging women from all over Yugoslavia. It coincided with, but also contributed to, the public appearance of feminist and women's groups in Slovenia and in Serbia. Women's studies courses were organized at the universities of Zagreb and Ljubljana. In the three years preceding the Yugoslav war, feminist networks linked all of Yugoslavia, some of them clearly organized as women's response to the emerging conflicts. Modern Yugoslav feminism, based both on American feminist traditions and on French theoretical discourse, demanded a free field for philosophical, social, and political discussions, distancing themselves from the sterility of official Marxist theory, from the growing nationalist discourse inside the dissident population, and even from the nonnationalist left wing of the dissident movement that was feminism-resistant and which radically changed their position only shortly before the war began.

When the war broke out in Yugoslavia, feminist positions took on explicit political goals, such as pacifism, the reestablishment of communications, women's solidarity to aid and support women in other regions, the fight for endangered rights, the lobbying of Parliament and the parties, and the creation of new women's movements. In the post-Yugoslav context, it is difficult to establish any valid parallels between these feminists and other movements in the rest of Central and Eastern Europe, although there are some comparative features. Among these, the general attitude toward diminishing women's rights and the visible absence of women from the new parliaments could not be avoided. But while most feminist and women's movements in the former socialist Eastern European countries have to deal with many challenges in establishing dialogue with Western (especially American) feminism and in articulating a program for which "feminism" is an occasionally uncomfortable tag, the post-Yugoslav feminisms have, because of the war, had much clearer goals and few inside problems with the definition of their own position and their role in politics. In fact, it is because of the war that post-Yugoslav feminism grew so quickly and so determinedly; in Serbia, for instance, the military draft shut men in their homes or made them leave the country, while women could circulate freely, so they organized most of the resistance activities that took place. The Women's Center in Zagreb, Croatia, leads one of the most important research efforts concerning rape in war areas, and has programs that actually help the victims. They face both the suspicion of the local government and the problems caused by exaggerated and ill-informed Western views on this sensitive topic.

The issue of family life and women's role in the family also presents more contrasts than similarities with features of other Central and Eastern European countries. Women in post-Yugoslavia have had to deal with radical splits in the texture of the family. There are, for instance, no more dispersed families. A family must be mono-ethnic and reside in one state if it is to be socially functional. Members who do not fit the new nationalist standards come up against the denial of citizenship, unemployment, and other kinds of state-imposed harassment at the workplace and elsewhere. Depending on the region, many young men prefer to emigrate or to desert the army rather than be forced to kill their former cocitizens. The elderly, incapable of traveling in war conditions, have to stay where they happened to be before the war, and are often denied not only social and medical protection, but also the retirement money they are due. Real estate in other, unfriendly states cannot be recuperated; jobs, possessions, and trade are sacrificed to the new state and national ideals. Therefore, family life must now be sanctioned by the state, which controls even the emotional life of the citizens: Attempts have been made all over post-Yugoslavia to publicly debase, defame, or even forbid so-called mixed marriages. Inflammatory statements by wives and husbands of different ethnicities have been used by all the national media in the crucial political moments before or during this war. Children are exposed to the new schoolbooks and media programs, which freely develop hate speech and even racism. In education and in private life, the question of national "identity" is deprived of any personal freedom of choice, a freedom guaranteed by the previous state. And all of this is just the lighter side of the destruction imposed on the population in the war zones. One very specific problem imposed on the survivors and refugees is their treatment in the neighboring states and in the rest of the world. Croatia and Slovenia closed their borders to Bosnian refugees as early as August 1992. Refugee camps in Croatia and Slovenia, which consist mainly of women, children, and a few elderly men, do have the basics, but they lack resources to help younger women to work, educate themselves, or communicate in any way with the culture and the society. They have no freedom of movement in the country that was formerly their own. Most European countries replicate these limitations, which are sometimes based on totally uninformed political views about the new enforced ethnicities and the citizenships obtained by chance. The misunderstandings that follow from the lack of information throughout Europe and the rest of the world inflict a deterioration of the quality of life mainly on women and their families.

Let me give just one crucial example of this. Western media and even some Western feminists blindly followed Croatian propaganda on war rapes as a genocidal project. The hidden message was that Muslim women were raped in large numbers, but only a few Croatian women suffered. The feminist critics inside Croatia, who pointed out that victims of rape were, first of all, women, no matter what their nationality, provoked such rage in the Croatian media that five Croatian women authors and journalists were proclaimed "witches," accused of "raping Croatia," and harassed publicly—after their addresses, phone numbers, and other family data were published. All five of these women lost their jobs, and most of them left the country. But the Western media, and some feminists, never paid any attention to the fact that only a few years ago the Serbian media accused Albanians of raping Serbian women in Kosovo, thus starting the whole nationalist and racist hysteria that eventually led to the Yugoslav war. My own public (and very lonely) position in Serbia at that time was that the Serbians should stop raping Serbian women in order to see what the Albanians really were doing. The official Serbian state statistics showed, a year later, that the number of rapes in which the perpetrator was an Albanian man and the victim a Serbian woman diminished almost to zero, while the number of rapes of Serbian women by Serb men only increased. Because the question involves a mixture of rape as a male fantasy, its political use, and its real expansion in different patriarchal ethnic and social groups, the problem is almost impenetrable for an uninformed Western observer. This is one field of research in which the approach should be tailored to the particular circumstances, and it may yield an analysis very different from other Central and Eastern European patterns. Anthropological, historical, and cultural research that pertains to the specific qualities of the areas studied should never be omitted.

Another example of the misunderstanding of local specificities is the program that sends presumed "Muslim" refugee families to conservative Muslim social settings such as Pakistan. Bosnian families, which only a short while ago had Yugoslav and local Muslim identities, are forced to obey rules that have nothing to do with their way of life and live through this enforced Islamization as through their worst nightmare. The Western media still call the Bosnian army the "Bosnian Muslim army," although the chief commander of this army is a Serb and the soldiers have different ethnicities. At the level of representation, the Western media would always prefer to show an old village woman rather than a modern, emancipated woman from an urban setting. This choice displays a preference for prefabricated images and stereotypes, which are not wanting in basic racism and misogyny.

To counter these stereotypes, what ought to be represented is the vibrant example of feminism in the former Yugoslavia, which has the character of a social revolution. This revolution goes farther than opposition to the war; it is one in which feminists and academics and women generally have become opposed to intellectuals as a group being the bearer of nationalist discourse. They have had the privilege both of being pacifists and of reconstructing the lost knowledge that is being destroyed in this place and time. This destruction has not only been material, as in the case of the destruction of the Sarajevo library, but also includes the less visible acts of the new state in destroying Yugoslavia bibliography as an institution and disconnecting the scientific and humanist networks of learning. In all the centers of the former Yugoslavia, women have been reconstructing these knowledges, and doing so, of necessity, exclusively outside of academia.

The most fascinating case is perhaps Slovenia, in which the formation of centers of women's studies or (gender studies, which is the more neutral form adopted to make things go there), has been backed by the liberal coalition of the government but is, at the same time, denied by academia. In this revolutionary situation you have this double play in which everything is unbelievably difficult and easy at the same time. My aim, therefore, is first of all to incite more interest in an area in which in one year centers for women's studies have been set up, new generations of feminists are being formed, and feminist activists and feminist academics are not only communicating but also organizing in the most improbable, unbelievable circumstances. This phenomenon is well worth studying, but it is not being done. We have a real feminist revolution in one small portion of this world, but it isn't being recognized elsewhere.

But my point can be generalized if we inquire into some of the reasons and remedies for this neglect. Although in the United States everyone would insist on multiculturalism as a kind of ideal, multiculturalism can't really be put into practice without speaking (at least) three languages. So we are once again in the space of translation, one that affects both the production and reception of information. It is crucial that multiple sides of a situation be represented and asked for. In this respect I mean to criticize not only myself and my context, as well as other women who produce information about it, but also the rest of the world, which remains too easily satisfied with single sources that can yield only a solitary, one-sided representation of a complex reality.

< 8 >

The Postsocialist Moral Majority

Renata Salecl

The present outbursts of nationalism in Eastern European postsocialist countries are a reaction to the fact that long years of (Communist) Party rule, by destroying the traditional fabric of society, have dismantled most of the traditional points of social identification. When people now attempt to assume a kind of distance toward the official ideological universe, the only positive reference point at their disposal is their national identity. In the new struggles for ideological hegemony, national identification is used by the ex-opposition as well as by the old Party forces. On the one hand, national identity serves as a support for the formation of a specific version of the "moral majority" (in Poland, Slovenia, and Croatia, etc.) that conceives Christian values as the ideological "cement" holding together the "Nation," demands the prohibition of abortion, etc. On the other hand, the Communist Party in some countries (Serbia, for example) has assumed an authoritarian populist-nationalist discourse, thus producing a specific mixture of orthodox Communist elements with elements usually associated with fascism. Both national movements—the right-wing moral majority and the authoritarian populism of the Communist Party—have built their power by creating similar fantasies of a threat to the nation and so put themselves forward as the protector of "what is in us more than ourselves"—our being a part of the nation.

NATIONALISM THROUGH PSYCHOANALYSIS

Psychoanalysis enables us to avoid both the simple condemnation of nationalism as well as the false solution of dividing it into "good" (progressive, anti-imperialist) versus "bad" (chauvinist, colonizing) elements. It enables us to articulate the fantasy structure that serves as a support for ethnic hatred.

It is necessary to emphasize that with all nationalism, national identification with the nation ("our kind") is based on the fantasy of the enemy, an alien who has insinuated himself into our society and constantly threatens us with habits, discourse, and rituals that are not of "our kind." No matter what this Other "does," he threatens us with his existence. The fantasy of how the Other lives on our account, is lazy, and exploits us, etc., is repeatedly recreated in accordance with our desire. For example, there is the common notion that immigrants are lazy, they lack good working habits, etc., which goes along with the simultaneous accusation that they industriously steal our jobs. The Other who works enthusiastically is especially dangerous—it is only his way of deceiving us and becoming incorporated into "our" community. Similarly with immigrants who assimilate: They are usually accused of retaining their strange habits, of being uncivilized, etc. If they adopt our customs, though, then we assume that they want to steal from us "our thing"—the nation.

We are disturbed precisely by the fact that the Other is Other and that he has his own customs, by which we feel threatened. As Jacques-Alain Miller says, hatred of the Other is hatred of the Other's enjoyment,[1] of the particular way the Other enjoys. For example, when Croats are irritated by the Albanian "mafia-type" businesses, or when the Slovenes find the way "Southerners" (Bosnians, Serbs, Montenegroes, etc.) enjoy themselves unbearable, what they are identifying is the threat in how the Other does not find enjoyment in the same way we do. As Miller says:

> I am willing to see my neighbor in the Other but only on condition that he is not my neighbor. I am prepared to love him as myself only if he is far away, if he is removed. . . . When the Other comes too near, when it mingles with you, as Lacan says, new fantasies merge which concern above all the surplus of enjoyment of the Other. . . . What is at stake is of course the imputation of an excessive enjoyment. Something of that kind could consist, for example, in the fact that we ascribe to the Other an enjoyment in money exceeding every limit.
>
> The question of tolerance or intolerance is not at all concerned with the subject of science and its human rights. It is located on the level of tolerance or intolerance toward the enjoyment of the Other, the Other as he who essentially steals my own enjoyment. . . . When we are considering whether the Other will have to abandon his language, his convictions, his way of dressing and talking, we would actually like to know the extent to which he is willing to abandon or not abandon his Other enjoyment.[2]

The conservative English writer John Casey says of West Indians: "They simply cannot form part of 'our' group or belong to 'our' kind, for their behavior outrages 'our' sense of what English life should be like and how the English should behave towards a duly constituted authority."[3] But the Other who outrages "our" sense of the kind of nation ours should be, the Other who steals our enjoyment is always the Other in our own interior; i.e., our hatred of the Other is really the hatred of the part (the surplus) of our own enjoyment that we find unbearable and cannot acknowledge, and which we transpose ("project") onto the Other via a fantasy of the "Other's" enjoyment." Therefore hatred of the Other, in the final analysis, is hatred of one's own enjoyment. Intolerance of the Other's enjoyment produces fantasies by which members of particular nations organize their own enjoyment.

A clear example of this "theft of enjoyment" is Serbian authoritarian populism, which has produced an entire mythology about the struggle against internal and external enemies. The primary enemies are Albanians, who are perceived as threatening to cut off the Serbian autonomous province of Kosovo and thereby stealing Serbian land and culture. The secondary enemy is an alienated bureaucracy, which threatens the power of the people: alienated from the nation, it is said to be devouring the Serbian national identity from within. And the third enemy has become the Croats, who with their politics of "genocide" are outlawing the Serbian population from "historically" Serbian territories in Croatia. Nowadays the enemies are primarily Muslims who are pictured as Islamic fundamentalists threatening the Serbs living in Bosnia and Herzegovina.

All images of the enemy are based on specific fantasies. In Serbian mythology, the Albanians are understood as pure Evil, the unimaginable, which cannot be subjectivized; they are beings who cannot be made into people, because they are so radically Other. The Serbs describe their conflict with the Albanians as a struggle of "people with nonpeople." The second enemy—the bureaucrat—is presented as a non-Serb, a traitor to his own nation who is also effeminate. The Croats are portrayed as the heirs of Goebbels, i.e., as brutal Ustashi butchers who torment the suffering Serbian nation, whose fate is compared to that of Kurds in Iraq. And the Muslims are named religious extremists who would like to expand their religion all over the world.

However, along with Albanians, at the end of the 1980s Slovenes have also emerged as the enemies of Serbian nationalism; they are supposed to share with the Albanian separatists the wish to constrict the political hegemony of Serbia. What do we get when we combine these two enemies? Remember that in Serbian mythology Albanians are presented as dirty, fornicating, rapacious, violent, primitive, etc., while the Slovenes are presented as unpatriotic, anti-Yugoslav intellectuals, and as nonproductive merchants who exploit the hard work of the Serbs, etc. If we simply put the two pictures together, we get the typical anti-Semitic portrait of the Jew: dirty, fornicating, but at the same time the intellectual, nonproductive, profiteering merchant. So, add an Albanian to a Slovene and you get a Jew.[4]

In Serbian mythology the enemy is revealed to be impotent. How is this demonstrated? Just as English conservatives describe the threat to Britain from immigrants, especially blacks, as "the rape of the English race,"[5] so the Serbs portray Albanians as rapists of the Serbian nation, who steal the Serbian national identity in order to install their own culture. Reinforcing this figure of rape are allegations about actual attempts by Albanians to rape Serbian girls. What is important here is that the rape is always only an attempted one. A picture of the enemy thus takes shape as an Albanian who tries to rape Serbian girls but is actually unable to do so. This portrait is based on the fantasy of the enemy's impotence—the enemy tries to attack, to rape, but is confounded, is impotent, in absolute contrast to the macho Serb.[6]

The mythology of the new Serbian populism constantly stresses the difference between real men—workers, men of the people—and bureaucrats. In this mythology the bureaucrat is portrayed as a middle-class feudal master, a kid-gloved capitalist with a top hat and a tie, "clean outside and dirty within," in real contrast to the worker, the man of the nation, "dirty on the outside but pure within."[7] The essence of the argument is that the bureaucrat is not a real man—he is effeminate, sluglike, fat; he drinks whisky and eats pineapples—as opposed to the macho worker, who eats traditional national food and dresses in worker's dungarees or national costume. Bureaucrats are not men because of their alienation from tradition and their betrayal of the heroic Serbian people.

To demonstrate its ties to the nation, Serbian populism invokes the heroic dead—not just their names, but also their actual bodies. In the new Serbian populist mythology, current fighters for Serbian sovereignty are constantly compared to the Serbian heroes who fought the Turks six hundred years ago. Bones play a special role in this dramatic identification with the heroic past. Serbian populism has rediscovered the old Orthodox custom by which the mortal remains of a ruler were carried through all the monasteries of the country before burial. The restoration of the Serbian identity was confirmed in 1989 by the transfer to Kosovo, after more than six hundred years, of the bones of the famous Serbian hero King Lazar, who died in battle with the Turks. When the old Orthodox ritual of carrying the bones around the monasteries was reinstituted for Lazar's remains, it designated the new birth of the Serbian symbolic community. The bones can be seen here in Lacanian terms as the Real, that "something more" which designates the symbolic community of the Serbian nation—the national "Thing" comes out precisely in the bones. Thus Lazar's bones function as the Real that has returned—as it always does—to its place. Lazar's return to Kosovo constitutes symbolic confirmation of the "fact" that Kosovo has always been the cradle of "that which is Serbian."

As Lacan says, race becomes established according to how a particular discourse preserves the symbolic order. The same can also be said of the concept of a national community. In the case of Serbia, the ridiculous ritual of transferring bones functions both to reinstitute and preserve the symbolic order. On the actual level, what we have here amounts to no more than a pile of trivial bones, which may or may not be the king's, which may have some archaeological or anthropological value. Yet within the Serbian ideological discourse, these bones also represent that which "the enemy has always wanted to deprive us of, that which we must guard with special care." The national conflict between the Serbs and the Albanians, as well as the struggle between Serbs and Macedonians, has always exploited the symbolism of bones stolen from Serbian graves. For example, one myth has grown up around the claim that Albanians have supposedly dug up the graves of Serbian children; another myth claims that Macedonians supposedly used the bones of Serbian soldiers who fell in the First World War for anatomic studies in their medical faculties. Furthermore, during the war in Croatia the bones of the Serbs killed by the Ustashi in the Second World War acquired a special meaning, and once again the rituals of transferring bones and ceremonial reburials with ideological speeches started to appear.

THE POSTSOCIAL MORAL MAJORITY

National identity serves as the basis upon which the specific ideology of the moral majority depends. This is the moral majority we encounter both in Slovenia and Croatia, as well as in other Eastern European countries. However, it does not have the same significance as the moral majority in the West. In view of its structural role, the moral majority in socialism was democratic and antitotalitarian—its voice was an oppositional one. Moral revolt against a real socialist regime predominated in its criticism of the authorities.[8] It thus articulated the distinction between civil society (in the name of which it spoke) and the totalitarian state as a distinction between morality and corruption. A return to Christian values, the family, the "right to life," etc. was presented as a rebellion against immoral socialist authority which, in the name of the concept of Communism, permitted all sorts of state intervention into the privacy of the citizen.

Paradoxically, the moral majority in the East, in spite of its oppositional role, is comparatively more socialist than conservative in relation to its Western counterpart. Where the latter is characterized by an antisocialist market ideology in which people answer for themselves first and the state is not the guardian of their well-being, the new postsocialist moral majority, in the name of an organic national ideology, reforges a link with the socialist heritage. When it calls for the reinforcement of national affiliation and Christian values, this moral majority simultaneously stresses that we must not surrender to soulless capitalism—that we must create a state-supported national program.

The difference between Western and postsocialist moral majorities can also be seen in their different perspectives on the issue of abortion. First we must point out that in the former Yugoslavia, as in the majority of other Eastern European countries, abortion was legalized and within easy reach of every woman. Indeed, it has often been the only available form of birth control. But during socialism, abortion was perceived more as a necessary evil than as the right of women to control their own bodies. The state made abortion legal because it wanted to prevent illegal abortions. It also wanted to keep women in the labor force. At the same time, the state retained the power to regulate abortion in the interests of its population policy. For example, special committees were established to approve abortions. Although obtaining permission from the committees amounted to a mere formality, the state's aim was to humiliate women and to remind them who really had the power over their bodies. Similar humiliation was encountered in the hospitals where abortions were performed: women waited for hours for abortions, the medical staff were rude to them, women sometimes would not get anesthetics, etc. As Lawrence H. Tribe points out, people who opposed abortion in socialism also "argued not in terms of the right to life of the unborn child but in terms of the duty of the mother to perform her 'natural' role in society, that of bearing children. The socialist state, they believed, had a right to the 'natural' increase of the labor force occasioned by this role."[9]

On two well-known occasions, the socialist state prohibited abortion. In 1936 Joseph Stalin outlawed abortion in the Soviet Union for two decades, and in 1966 Ceauçescu strongly prohibited abortion in Romania. Stalin's opposition to abortion was based on his opinion that socialism had solved the problems causing abortion. For Stalin it was necessary for Soviet women to "fulfill their natural role and 'give the nation a new group of heroes.' In Stalin's words, woman 'is mother . . . she gives life, and this is certainly *not* a private matter but one of great social importance.'"[10] Ceauçescu's prohibition of abortion turned on his efforts to increase the population and thereby to strengthen the Romanian state. In socialism, therefore, prohibiting and legalizing abortion were both part of the Communist tendency to exert control over people. Abortion was allowed primarily to control "public hygiene" by preventing illegal abortions, while abortion was prohibited in attempts to control the population.

In this regard, women received special attention from the state, but only because of their capability to bear children. Mothers, however, were limited in their roles; the socialist state had reserved for itself the "duty" to educate children and to form them into devoted Communists. The state did not trust parents, which is why it constantly interfered in family life, took charge of organizing children's spare time, etc.

As we can see, in socialism the state-control process of socialization and the mistrust of the family as the agent of socialization paradoxically coincided with elements of traditional patriarchal ideology (glorification of the role of the mother, etc.). What was actually the status of these elements of patriarchal ideology? As with nationalism, which officially did not exist, but nevertheless remained at work in a concealed way,[11] patriarchal domination, although officially overcome, remained a surmise of political discourse. Thus, it was not difficult for the post-socialist moral majority to articulate patriarchy in a new way and present the return to "natural" sexual roles as an attempt to introduce morality into a previously "immoral" social regime.

The question raised by this call for a "new" postsocialist morality is, to what extent is this demand supported by women? Are women in the front lines of the nationalist and antiabortion movement? Actually, women in postsocialism are much less involved with the antiabortion movement and nationalist parties than men. Few women are preaching the need for more morality and less abortion. This lack of women's involvement in the moral majority movement is, of course, linked to the marginal role women play in postsocialist societies. But the question is also, does not the success of postsocialist regressive ideologies rely on this non-presence of women in public life? In response to this question, Julia Kristeva makes a puzzling claim:

> The very recent studies that are beginning to be published on the underlying logic
> of Soviet society and of the transition period (that is already bitterly being called
> "catastroika") show to what extent a society based on the rudimentary satisfaction
> of survival *needs*, to the detriment of the *desire* for freedom, could encourage the
> regressive sado-masochist leanings of women and, without emancipating them at

all, rely on them to create a stagnation, a parareligious support of the status quo crushing the elementary rights of the human person.[12]

In my opinion, the Communist society did not encourage a special kind of "sado-masochist leaning" of women, but only relied on the entrenched patriarchy of the society. The shortage of goods, of course, forced women to spend endless hours shopping around, and the lack of men's involvement with housework and early child rearing required women to do a double job, one in the workplace and one at home. But in this regard women in socialist countries did not differ so much from women in the West. In fact, consumerism also pressures Western women to spend most of their free time shopping, and housework remains a burden for women even in the most democratic societies. The difference between Eastern European and Western societies lies in the Eastern European refusal to acknowledge the problem of patriarchal domination. Just as Communist ideology erased the problem of patriarchal domination, today's post-socialist societies also erase the problem of sexual inequality. The postsocialists act as if the emancipation of women is not an issue for them at all. The only political force addressing the status of women is the nationalist right, although its major concern is, of course, to help women rediscover their "natural" mission.

In the 1980s, it was the Catholic nationalist opposition that first raised the possibility of restricting abortion, but it did so in terms unfamiliar to Western antiabortion movements. The traditional "moral majority," as known in Western countries, does not oppose abortion on the grounds of the threat it poses to the nation, but in the name of the Christian values of the sanctity of life, the sacred significance of conception, etc., from which it derives the claim that abortion is murder.[13] Objections to abortion by the moral majority in Slovenia and in Croatia are connected to their claim that abortion poses a threat to the nation. Linking images of abortion as a crime against humanity to images of abortion as a threat to the nation produces an ideology through which support for Slovenes or Croats becomes synonymous with opposition to abortion. When the former Croatian opposition asserts that "a fetus is also Croat," it clearly demonstrates that an opinion about abortion is also going to be an opinion about the future of the nation. The production of these kind of fantasies of a national threat must of course be seen in terms of the political struggle they engender. The strategy is to transform the internal political threat of totalitarianism into an external national menace which can only be averted by an increase in the birthrate—in other words, by limiting the right to abortion. Thus emerges the hypothesis that to be a good Slovene or a good Croat means primarily being a good Christian, since the national menace can be averted only by adhering to Christian morals.

The postsocialist moral majority has reinterpreted the relation between "foetus" and "life" on which the Western moral majority has built its ideology. The idea that the fetus is a human being who is being "murdered" during abortion is, in the case of the postsocialist moral majority, linked to the image of the "death of the nation." Behind this is the idea of the importance of national identification: The life of a human being has special meaning because he or she belongs to a national community. By allowing abortion, we not only kill a human being, but also erode our national substance—in the long term we kill the nation.[14]

In the ideology of the Western moral majority, abortion is similarly presented as an attack on "personhood." As Kristin Luker points out, the moral majority asserts "that personhood *is a 'natural,' inborn, inherited right, rather than a social, contingent, and assigned right*" (emphasis in original).[15] When the fetus is presented as a person, one can produce an image whereby the rights of our own personhood are endangered by abortion. And the postsocialist moral majority plays precisely on this image when it links abortion to the threat to the nation; because in their ideology national identity fully determines us, our own identity and personhood are endangered when abortion is allowed.

The postsocialist moral majority also opposes the role women had under the socialist regime. The ideology of the postsocialist moral majority, on the one hand, plays on the hard life women had under socialism,[16] and, on the other hand, it touches the problem of motherhood. The postsocialist moral majority regards socialism as a system that downgraded motherhood and did not allow "woman to be a woman," meaning that a woman, to be a woman, can choose only to be a housewife and a mother. Here the postsocialist moral majority plays the same card as its Western counterpart and establishes sexual roles as natural.[17] Linked to this also is the idea that abortion is something utterly "unnatural," because it opposes the "natural" consequence of marriage and sex: procreation.

The moral majority produces a special kind of "imaginary identification with the fetus" when it presents the fetus as a human being, and uses pictures of babylike fetuses suffering when they are torn from the mother's body. The idea behind this is that the human being, a being like ourselves, has been killed by the abortion. As Mark Bracher says:

> Through such representations of abortion, many people come to experience the assault on the fetus as a threat to their own integrity at the level of the body ego . . . images of dismemberment assault them at the bodily core of their identity. In the image of the fetus being aborted, these people thus encounter a deep sense of their own radical lack, a sense grounded in the earliest mnemic traces laid down by their infant body's experience of chaos and dismemberment, which, Lacan maintains, constitutes the ultimate (Imaginary) referent of one's notion of death.[18]

The postsocialist moral majority goes further in following the same logic when it presents abortion as an attack on our national identity and as something that contributes to the possible death of the nation. Here a link could be made with the theft of enjoyment, which I have tied to our perception of national identity. The prochoice movement is perceived by the moral majority as the enemy within, the enemy who steals our national substance by aborting potential members of our nation.[19]

In this ideology of national threat, women are pronounced both culprits and victims. The strongest former opposition party in Croatia, the Croatian Democratic Community (which came to power after the first free election in 1990), has gone so far in this that it has publicly blamed the tragedy of the Croatian nation on women, pornography, and abortion.[20] "This trinity murders, or rather hinders, the birth of little Croats, that 'sacred thing which God has given society and the homeland.'" The Croatian moral majority regard women who have not given birth to at last four children as "female exhibitionists" since they have not fulfilled "their unique sacred duty." Women who, for whatever reason, decide on abortion have been proclaimed murderers and mortal enemies of the nation, while gynecologists who have assisted them in this "murderous" act are pronounced butchers and traitors.

Women, then, are pronounced guilty; yet at the same time, they are depicted as the victims of overly liberal abortion laws. Ideologists of the postsocialist moral majority take as their starting point the notion that a free decision about how many children a person will have is an inalienable human right, and that society is obliged to maintain population policies that enable people to have the desired number of children. These ideologists believe therefore that a state that prioritizes the right to abortion is refusing its citizens access to this second right—that of having a desired number of children. Here the real victims are women.[21] This fantasy about the woman is based on the belief that the woman and the nation share the same desire: to give birth. Opposed to this "fundamental" feminine desire is the idea of excessive feminine enjoyment (*jouissance*): while mothers are glorified, women who forget their "natural" mission are perceived as an excess. The enjoyment of the latter group of women has to be regulated through the prohibition of abortion.[22] If a woman is defined by maternity, then abortion is an attack on her very essence; yet it is also an attack on the essence of the nation, since the national community, according to this ideology, is defined by the national maternal wish for an increased population.

The ideologists of national threat invoke the same logic used by Ceauçescu when a journalist asked him whether the ban on Romanians traveling abroad was not a violation of human rights. Ceauçesu's answer was that since the most important human right is to be able to live in one's own country, the ban on traveling abroad simply guarantees this right. So, too, the ideologists of national threat represent their desire to limit the right to free abortion as simply reinforcing the human right to have the desired number of children.

The ideology of national threat also produces in Croatia a specific form of anti-Semitism that is linked to the national conflict between Croats and Serbs. It is first necessary to stress that serbs see themselves in their mythology as "Jews," the chosen nation of Yugoslavia. According to the Serbian philosopher Jovan Rašković, the "Serbian nation has always been a nation of tragic destiny, some sort of God's nation," which lost in Kosovo its "sacred country." So the Serbs understand the Kosovo problem in terms of a struggle of their holy land, i.e., the cradle of the Serbian community. The Albanian population is thus constantly presented as immigrant, although this immigration took place in the Middle Ages and the Albanians are arguably the descendants of much earlier Illyrian inhabitants of the region. It is precisely this Serbian self-depiction as the Jews of Yugoslavia that reinforces Croat anti-Semitism. In Croatian mythology, the Jews and Serbs together are involved in a conspiracy against the Croat nation. The traditional anti-Semitic fantasy of the Jew as Shylock, the sly cheat who lives on the labor of others, unites in the image of the Serb as the national enemy who threatens Croatian sovereignty. That this anti-Semitism is used entirely arbitrarily in the national struggle is confirmed by the Serbs themselves. On the one hand they proclaim themselves to be the Jews of Yugoslavia and thus reinforce Croat anti-Semitism, while on the other hand, it is actually the Serbs themselves who construct "Jews" as enemies (as has been already shown, if you put together the images of their two enemies, the Albanians and the Slovenes, you get a Jew.)[23]

The common point between the two ideologies presented—Serbian "authoritarian populism" and the postsocialist nationalistic moral majority—is that both offer a collective fantasy whose between-the-lines message is "We are the only defenders of the nation." But to understand the new mixture of nationalism and Communism emerging in postsocialist countries, one has to take into account that under Communist regimes, especially under Stalinism, nationalism always existed, although in a concealed way. It was only with the advent of more liberal types of Communism, in the 1970s and 1980s, that nationalism was less present as a surmise of political discourse. That is why contemporary nationalists find Stalinists more appealing than the Brezhnev or Gorbachev types of Communists. The conclusion one can draw from the success of the new coalition of Communists and nationalists (in Serbia and Russia, for example) is that when people identify within a certain political discourse, fantasy plays a greater role than ideological meaning.

At this point we have to return to the theoretical question of how to separate the two levels of political discourse: its ideological meaning, and the fantasy that functions as its surmise. When people identify with a certain political discourse they identify with its surmise, with the level of unsaid fantasies that determine their economy of enjoyment. The two discourses presented—authoritarian populist and moral majority—offer a possibility to explore the logic of this identification even further. In this exploration of the subtle process of political identification, I shall rely on contemporary French linguistics and its criticism of the speech act theory.

MEANING AND FANTASY IN POLITICAL DISCOURSE

In his early seminars, Lacan articulated the performative dimension of speech; what he called the "founding word" corresponds clearly to what was later conceptualized as a "speech act"—the word that, through its very enunciation, establishes a new intersubjective network that redefines the places of the speaker and the receiver. It looks, then, as if speech act theory did nothing but elaborate this early Lacanian intuition about the creative, structuring role of speech. There is, however, a crucial aspect to speech act theory that makes it incompatible with Lacan's theory. In speech act theory, a speech act is conceived as a closed totality where the intention corresponds to the act itself. I "do things with words" insofar as I mean what I say. In other words, a successful speech act presupposes a whole set of fulfilled conditions: the sincerity of my intention, the truth of the propositional content, respect for the rules of authority that ensure that my word will achieve its performative aim. (For example, to proclaim a couple husband and wife, I must be in a position to do so, they must not be married already, etc.)

It was probably this closed aspect of speech act theory that prevented it from further "communication" with Lacanian theory. How can we unite speech act theory—with its notion of the unique and nondivided subject (i.e., of the speaker fully responsible for what she says and for what she does by saying it)—with the fundamental Lacanian notion of the split subject, the subject who by definition cannot control the intersubjective effects of what she says, and whose words find their meaning determined in another, decentered place? Recent developments in French linguistics and semantics have revised speech act theory so that we can finally establish a link between it and Lacanian theory. In his book *Le dire et le dit* (1984), Oswald Ducrot attacked the basic notion underlying classical speech act theory, the thesis of the subject as the unitary, self-centered author of the act, responsible for its effects.

The starting point of Ducrot's criticism is his dismissal of the psychological level, i.e., the irrelevance of the speaker's sincerity for the utterance's illocutionary effect. For example, if I say "I promise to come," the illocutionary force of this proposition is in no way diminished if I think, while pronouncing it, "But I probably won't come because nothing really obliges me to do so." According to Ducrot, it is contradictory (i.e., it is a pragmatic paradox) only if one says expressly "I promise to come, although I don't intend to do so." Such considerations have brought Ducrot to split the apparently unique entity of the speaker as the empirical person and author of the speech act into three distinct agencies: *speaking subject* as an empirical individual, and a *speaker* and an *enunciator* as two discursive agencies. The individual who speaks is empirically responsible for the utterance, but she is totally irrelevant to its semantic structure. On the level of semantic structure, Ducrot introduces the further split between speaker (the abstract entity responsible for the enunciation) and the enunciator (the entity whose point of view is supposed to be expressed in an utterance, the central point of perspective of an utterance). Ducrot's accent falls on how the same speaker can—in the course of a continuous series of utterances—assume different enunciator positions. This is the main point of his "polyphonic" theory of meaning. The clearest case of this distinction between speaker and enunciator is irony: In the ironic speech, the speaker mockingly presents or imitates the position or the point of view of some other enunciator with whom she clearly does not identify. For example, if, after a disastrous party, I say to the host "Thank you for a marvelous evening," it is clear that I mockingly assume the perspective of a delighted guest.

It is also clear that Ducrot's distinction between speaker and enunciator, corresponds to the Lacanian distinction between the *sujet de l'énonciation* (subject of the enunciation) and the *sujet de l'énonce* (subject of the utterance). The speaker, the subject of the enunciation, is an empty place, a vanishing point without any positive identity, which can subsequently assume a series of positions (i.e., which subsequently identifies with some definite figure determining the perspective of her enunciation). But the crucial factor here is that Ducrot introduces a homologous split also on the other, receiving end. His thesis is that the illocutionary act always refers to a strictly determined and defined hearer, to the addressee as a discursive figure and not to some empirical embodiment of the addressee (i.e., the empirical person of a hearer). The addressee is a certain discursive position constructed by the illocutionary act, and a given empirical person (hearer) becomes the addressee only upon recognizing herself as such, i.e., when she assumes the obligation forced upon her by the illocutionary act. For example, the order "Give me back my money" establishes a certain intersubjective space where the addressee is put into the position of the debtor. It is up to the empirical hearer to either recognize herself in this position (and then to obey the order or to refuse to obey it, inventing excuses, and so forth) or simply to ignore the order (i.e., behave as if she is not the addressee of the order). The crucial point is that obligation exists only in the discursive universe; it concerns the addressee, the figure created by the discourse itself, not the empirical hearer. The discourse does not address a given individual, it creates the place of the addressee by itself and it is up to the receiver to recognize herself in this place.

We can now see how Ducrot's modified version of speech act theory implies a split or divided subject, an empty point striving to achieve positive identity by identifying itself with different enunciator figures. And in this implied split subject Ducrot's relevance for the analysis of the political discourse is found: This conceptual apparatus enables us to approach the question of how a subject recognizes herself as the addressee of a political discourse and thereby comes to identify with a certain political position. Answering this question requires reference to two further notions elaborated by Ducrot: that of the *later discourse* and that of the *surmise* of the speech act. The later discourse constructs the place of subject's identification, while the surmise functions as a place for fantasy.

According to Ducrot, a given utterance must always be described with regard to its ideal continuation (i.e., it always constructs an ideal space of its possible continuation which, retroactively, confers on it its signification). The most elementary case of this later discourse is a question. A question obliges the addressee to answer it in a certain way; it delineates in advance the ideal, fictional place of the response to come. The later discourse is thus a symbolic fiction, a network by means of which the present discourse self-referentially establishes the link between itself and what is to follow. If I ask somebody a question, I not only determine the type of speech I expect from the addressee, but at the same time I establish a certain discursive relationship between myself and the other; I locate my own discourse in relation to the other. In this sense, we could say that the notion of the later discourse points in the same direction as the notion of the "founding word" in Lacan's early seminars. This is the word that establishes a new symbolic reality, a new intersubjective network between the speaker and the addressee: "Thou art that, my wife, my master and a thousand other things. As soon as I accept this 'thou art that,' it makes out of me in the word something other than what I elsewhere am."[24]

In political discourse, it is precisely this later discourse that designates the place of identification: Political discourse succeeds when we recognize ourselves as its addressee. What is crucial here is the distinction between present and later discourse. The trick of a successful political discourse is not to directly offer us images with which to identify—to flatter us with an idealized image, an ideal ego, to portray us the way we would like to appear to ourselves—but to construct a *symbolic space*, a point of view, *from which* we could appear likeable to ourselves; in other words, to construct the "later discourse" in such a way that it leaves the space open to be filled out by images of our ideal ego.

Such a discourse is well exemplified by the success of Thatcherism in Great Britain in the 1970s and 1980s. When Stuart Hall (1988) analyzed the causes of the Labor Party's defeat in the 1987 election, he pointed out that the Labor politicians were directly addressing the voters' so-called real, effective interests and needs (such as unemployment, health, education, and housing policies). Thatcher, on the other hand, perceived very well that the crucial point is not the actual needs and problems themselves but the way their meaning is perceived, so her first step was not to offer better solutions to existing problems but to radically redefine the status of these problems. Thus her telling statement at the 1975 Conservative Party conference: "serious as the economic challenge is, the political and moral challenge is just as grave, and perhaps more so, because economic problems never start with economics."[25] What matters is not economics as such but the way it is symbolized through ideology; pure economics does not exist. Unemployment and poverty are of course hard facts, but what matters in political battles is how they are perceived, how they are symbolically mediated or structured.

From the Labor perspective, such things as poverty and unemployment are clearly the responsibility of society, so the Labor Party offered improvements in the welfare state, more state control, state-directed investments in depressed areas, and so forth. Thatcherism, on the other hand, inverted this perspective and took as its motto "There is no such thing as society"; there are only individuals and their families, fully responsible for their fate, which is why state intervention is not the remedy but the cause of the illness. It undermines the aggressive, active, competition spirit of individuals, and saps their belief that they themselves can fight for their success and must not rely on the state for support. If this constitutes Thatcherism's symbolic reinterpretation of social reality and of the causes of the economic crisis, once we accept it, once we symbolically identify with it, what imaginary identification does it offer us?

It is an essential part of the ideological efficiency of Thatcherism that a handful of people did succeed in getting rich through individual entrepreneurship. These successes function as a "little piece of reality" that gives everyone else the hope that, someday, they too will succeed.

> Mrs. Thatcher's symbolic majority includes all who identify with the enterprise cul-
> ture as the way of the future, who see themselves in their political imaginations as
> likely to be lucky in the next round. They form an "imaginary community" around
> Thatcherism's political project.[26]

This hope "to be lucky in the next round" is the precise locus of the imaginary identification constructed by the later discourse, the place at which the subject would like to be seen.

Similarly, the success of the moral majority relies on constructing the image of community, family, and tradition. When the moral majority preaches that the woman's place is at home and opposes abortion, it does so in terms of morality, involving the image of an ideal traditional community in which people do not put their economic interests above all else. As Kristin Luker points out, for prolife people in America "the private world of family as traditionally experienced is the only place in society where none of us has a price tag."[27] The family is supposedly the place where the social worth criteria are not at work and where "love is unconditional." In this regard the moral majority opposition to abortion takes on a special meaning:

> Protecting the life of the embryo, which is by definition an entity whose social worth
> is all yet to come, means protecting others who feel that they may be defined as
> having low social worth; more broadly, it means protecting a legal view of person-
> hood that emphatically rejects social worth criteria.[28]

When people identify with moral majority ideology, they do so because they want to see themselves in the image of the community "where love and morality reign" constructed by the moral majority discourse.

This ideal image offered by the neoconservative discourse is, however, not enough for it to succeed. The effect of signification of an ideological discourse must always be supported by some fantasy frame, by some unspoken fantasy scenario that stages its economy of enjoyment. The place of this fantasy is not constructed by the later discourse; to locate it, we should turn to another distinction elaborated by Ducrot, the distinction between *presupposition* and *surmise*. Presupposition is an integral part of the speech act; responsibility for it rests with the speaker (i.e., it is the speaker who, by pronouncing a certain proposition, guarantees its presuppositions). For example, if I say "I promise to avenge your father's death," I assume thereby a whole network of symbolic, intersubjective relations and my place within it. I accept as a fact that the father's death was the result of an injustice, I assume that I am in a position to compensate for it, and so forth. The surmise is, on the other hand, the place of the inscription of the addressee in the enunciation; it is the addressee who assumes responsibility for the surmise, who has to derive it from what was said. The surmise emerges as an answer to the question that the addressee necessarily poses herself: "Why did the speaker speak that way? Why did she or he say that?" The surmise concerns the way the addressee must decipher the meaning of what was said, which is why the surmise necessarily touches upon fantasy. In Lacan's graph of desire,[29] fantasy is specified as an answer to the famous "Che vuoi?", to the question "What did she mean by saying that?"

In the political discourse, this split between proposition and surmise assumes the form of a necessary distance between the *field of meaning of an ideological discourse* and the *level of fantasy functioning as its surmise.* To exemplify it, let us again recall the Serbian political scene at the end of the 1980s. Already on the level of ideological meaning, Milošević's achievement was considerable, because he succeeded in uniting in the same discourse elements which were hitherto regarded as incompatible: a return to the old Stalinist Communist Party rhetoric, a proto-fascist nationalist movement, economic liberalism, and so forth. But the key to the success of this authoritarian populism is the delicate balance between what he said and what he left unspoken. On the level of ideological meaning, Milošević, in the time of his ascent to power, spoke for a strong, unified Yugoslavia where all nations would live in equality and brotherhood. He presented his movement as a new, "antibureaucratic revoltuion," as a broad democratic populist movement of rebellion against he corrupted bureaucracy of the Party and the state, and as an attempt to save Tito's legacy. Behind this, however, there was another level, another message that was easily deciphered by his supporters as the answer to the question "Why is he telling us this?" He aimed at crushing the Albanians by turning them into second-rate citizens; he aimed at unifying Yugoslavia under Serbian domination by abolishing the autonomy of other republics. He presented Serbia as the only really sovereign nation in Yugoslavia, as the only nation capable of assuring state sovereignty, and he promised to the Serbian masses revenge for the supposed exploitation of Serbia by the more developed republics of Croatia and Slovenia. So we find as a surmise of his discourse a *bricolage* of heterogeneous elements, each of which ignites the desire of Serbs: the revival of old Serbian nationalist myths, glorification of the Orthodox church as opposed to the intriguing, anti-Serbian Catholic church, sexual myths of the dirty Albanians fornicating all the time and raping innocent Serbian girls. In sort, we find the whole domain of fantasies on which racist enjoyment feeds. The crucial thing is that this fantasy-support of Milošević's populism, although unmentioned, although outside the scope of ideological meaning, was easily recognized as the *surmise* of the discourse.

The same can be said of all other successful neoconservative populist ideologies, from Thatcherism to Reaganism, etc. Their very success rests upon the distance between ideological meaning (return to the old moral values of the family, of the self-made man, etc.) and the level of (racist, sexual, etc.,) fantasies, which, although unmentioned, function as surmise and determine the way the addressee deciphers the signification of ideological statements. But far from being something to deplore, this very distance is perhaps that which marks the difference between neoconservative populist ideologies, still attached to democratic space, and so-called totalitarianism. "Totalitarianism"—at least in its radical version—can be said to state directly and openly what other ideologies only imply as a surmise. Hitler, for example, appealed directly to racist, sexual, and other anti-Semitic fantasies. One of the common self-designations of fascist discourse is precisely that fascists say openly that to which others (their fellows on the moderate right) only allude. Hitler thus openly said that it is necessary to eliminate the enemy (Jews, for example). But what remained as a surmise of the fascist discourse was the fantasy scenario of the forms of torture by which the enemy had to be eliminated.

An example of the neofascist logic of the surmise could be the slogan of the Slovene National Party (SNP), the extreme right-wing party in Slovenia, which proclaims: "Let's make this country Slovene again. "This statement alludes to Hitler's famous speech from 1941 when, during the occupation of Slovenia, Hitler demanded: "Let's make this country German." As a variation on Hitler's statement, the SNP's slogan implies as its surmise a whole set of fascist fantasies: Every addressee will recognize in it the need to close the borders to refugees, to expel foreigners, etc.

But the discourse of the SNP becomes even more interesting in terms of our analysis if we take seriously their leader's claim that the "Slovene National Party openly says what other parties think." This thesis is actually true. The fact is that among the right-wing parties in Slovenia, it is only the SNP that openly utters extreme nationalist demands (to expel foreigners and refugees), which other right-wing parties only imply as a surmise of their discourse. Such outspokenness is possible for the SNP because it has a declared nationalistic stand while other right-wing parties cloak their nationalism in Catholic or populist ideology. But the real paradox is that, on another level, the SNP openly says what the left is unable to say. Declared nationalism enables the SNP to object to the return of the confiscated forest to the Church on grounds that the first is a Slovenian national treasure, to cherish the past partisan struggle against fascism while criticizing fascist collaborators among the Slovenes, etc. The left, which is represented by the former Communist Party, because of its unclear identity and historical burden, remains silent in regard to these questions. The left is neither for nor against returning the forests; it no longer pays tribute to the partisans, and it constantly stresses that things have to be seen in their context. Because national interest is the ultimate priority for the SNP, it can openly utter the surmises that neither the right nor the left dares to.

The question remains, what is left unspoken in the discourse of the SNP? Significantly, the Party leader projects a kind of "Rambo image"; the Party openly advocates the right to possess arms; it has unclear connections with the secret police and presumably has access to a fair amount of arms and munitions. All this constructs an unspeakable surmise of their discourse that the national interest has to be defended by force. In the SNP's discourse, the fantasy at work is that society will attain prosperity (and that the nation will survive) only after the "enemy" is removed. But the means of removing the enemy in the discourse of the SNP remains unspoken.

Returning to the problem of the new mixture of nationalism and Communism emerging in postsocialism, it has to be pointed out that nothing connects Communists and nationalists on the level of the ideological meaning of their discourse. Communists are, in their own words, internationalists who condemn nationalism, while nationalists are usually anti-Communists. But one can easily find a link between Communism and nationalism on the level of fantasy: both discourses have as a surmise all kind of hatreds of other nations and races. They are driven by the submerged energy of sexism, homophobia, and anti-Semitism. That is why these discourses have so easily coalesced in postsocialist societies.

There is no politics without fantasy. As long as there is some hidden surmise that organizes enjoyment, the aim of democratic politics is not how to replace one type of fantasy with another, more democratic fantasy or how to prevent racist fantasies from being articulated. The goal of democratic politics should be to create a political space in which racist fantasies would not have any real effect. Only a society that "believes" in democratic institutions and has mechanisms of "self-binding" of power is able to stand having such fantasies articulated without fearing that the democratic order will consequently collapse.

A real democratic advance in the post-socialist countries can be expected only when the driving force becomes "to each their fantasy. "This does not mean a refusal to admit national identity; it means the removal of the Subject presented as its sole protector, as the only one who acts in the name of "our kind."

NOTES

1. As many translators have noted, the term enjoyment does not adequately translate *jouissance* because it lacks the connotation of displeasure, the pain linked to the pleasure.
2. Miller, Jacques-Alain, *Extimité*, unpublished seminar, (1985/6).
3. Parekh, Bhikhu, "The 'New Right' and the Politics of Nationhood," in *The New Right*, (London: Runnymede Trust, 1986).
4. See Mladen Dolar, "Kdo je danes Žid?", *Mladina* (3 November 1988).
5. *Ibid*. Foucault, Michel (1980), *The History of Sexuality, Volume 1*, trans. R. Hurley, New York, Vintage Books.
6. This macho ideology of the Serbs was most clearly at work when the Serbs used rape of Muslim women as one of the "weapons" to eliminate their enemy during the war in Bosnia and Herzegovina.
7. Ivo Žanić, "Bukvar 'antibirokratske revolucije,'" *Start* (30 September 1989). Minson, Jeffrey (1985) *Genealogies of Morals: Nietzsche, Foucault, Donzelot and the Eccentricity of Ethics*, London, Macmillan.

8. The first postsocialist (Christian Democratic) government in Slovenia tried to inject more morality into schools by promoting the need for religious education. Although this effort failed, the Minister of Education went so far as to propose an "*hora legalis*" for youngsters and the extension of school to Saturdays. To support his proposal, the Minister cited some biorhythmological study which found that a long weekend break "interrupts students' efficiency, lowers their efforts and forces them into laziness" (interview with Minister Peter Vencelj, *Dnevnik*, 30 March 1991). This citation of biorhythmology seems to be a reference to an objective knowledge. But from Michel Foucault's work we know that appealing to some neutral knowledge always serves to legitimate the power itself. In fact, the power produces this neutral knowledge so that it can legitimate its own actions. Foucault confirmed this thesis by analyzing the relation between power and sexuality. In its relation to sexuality, power does not strive to repress some natural sexuality; actually it is power itself that produces sexuality as such. As Foucault says, the discourse of sexuality was produced in the seventeenth and eighteenth centuries when sex became the object of scientific and medical analysis and when society tried to impose control over sexual reproduction. And the same goes for biorhythmology. Biorhythms are not something produced by science when the body became the object of its research. The government reference to biorhythmology in support of its efforts to change school hours thus parallels earlier references to the discourse of sexuality. Behind each lies a motive of social control.

    Significantly and disturbingly, in its efforts to impose new forms of morality—through religious education in schools, *hora legalis*, Saturday schools, etc.—the government assumed certain aspects of the previous socialist regime. The socialist government had always been worried about how people were spending their spare time, especially given the kind of immoral activities they could become interested in. To prevent children from doing "deviant" things in their spare time, the socialist regime formed special Komsomol youth organizations, political discussing groups and working camps. When the postsocialist regime started talking about the need to extend school hours into spare time, it revealed that it shared the previous regime's mistrust of parents, thinking them too incompetent to raise and educate children, just as the Communists had done.

9. Tribe, Lawrence H. *Abortion: The ClASh of Absolutes* (New York and London: Norton, 1990), p. 56.

10. *Ibid.*

11. It is well known how nationalist the Romanian and Albanian Communist regimes were. But elements of nationalism were, in a specific way, incorporated into the official ideology in other Eastern European regimes, too.

12. Kristeva, Julia, *Nations without Nationalism*, trans. L. S. Roudiez (New York: Columbia University Press, 1993), p. 34.

13. When the Western moral majority opposes abortion it implies that the "right to life" is an absolute, transhistorical concept. But as Jeffrey Minson argues, Christianity did not confront the question of abortion until the seventeenth century, when it became concerned with controlling sexuality and reproduction. When the Church first addressed the question of abortion it regarded the fetus as having no soul (like any child who died before being baptized)—the "right to life" was not an issue at all. In the nineteenth century, when the Church began propounding marriage, it did so as a means of population control. The idea was that marriage would prevent people from having illegitimate children and make them more responsible to their families and thus less dependent on state support. The contemporary moral majority shares with its religious predecessors the desire to control people's sexual behavior. The same nineteenth-century antiwelfare ideology is also present in the current moral majority's ideology. The contemporary moral majority cares a lot about the unborn child, but the quality of the born child's life is not its concern.

14. The Slovenian moral majority found some "scientific" studies showing that the Slovene nation will die out by 2050 if the birth rate continues to decrease. To reverse this process, in the opinion of the Slovenian moral majority, the society has to prohibit abortion.

15. Luker, Kristin, *Abortion and the Politics of Motherhood* (Berkeley: University of California Press, 1984), p. 157.

16. During the socialist era almost every woman was employed. Apart from ideological reasons (linked to the Marxist theory of emancipation through work), the high employment rate among women was also the result of the economic hardship that forced families to need a double income. Žižek, Slavoj (1989), *The Sublime Object of Ideology*, London, Verso.

17. The moral majority ideologues in Slovenia proposed the idea of establishing special schools for housewives, where women would be taught cooking, cleaning, serving meals, etc.

18. Bracher, Mark, *Lacan, Discourse, and social Change: A Psychoanalytic Cultural Criticism* (Ithaca: Cornell University Press, 1993), p. 114.

19. Moral majority ideologues similarly perceive homosexuals as enemies of the nation. In this way, the postsocial moral majority acts in the same way as Communists. In almost all Communist countries, homosexuality was considered deviant and thus punished by the law or treated as an illness in need of a cure. For that reason, in Slovenia homosexual organizations were one of the cornerstones of the oppositional "new social movements." But with the end of Communism, there has not been any great advance in the public tolerance of homosexuality. In its attempt to encourage a rise in the birth rate, the Slovenian moral majority began to attack homosexuals also. For example, one of the independent organizations that disseminates moral majority ideas has called homosexuals "people who are the degenerates of society, since, with their form of sexuality, they are in no way able to have children. They are therefore already in the first generation doomed to extinction and present a dead branch on the living tree of life" (*Delo*, 29 May 1993).

20. *Dnevnik* (26 February 1990).

21. See Ante Vukasović, "Zavaravanje žena," *Danas* (27 March 1990).

22. The antiabortionists construct women who have abortions as unfeminine, upper-class, ambitious professionals who care only about their career and hate children. The reality is that the majority of women having abortions are women from the lower classes who already have two or three children and whose major reason for abortion is economic hardship.

23. The thesis about the Judaic nature of the Serbian nation also attempts to substantiate the image of Albanians as terrorists. Since peaceful demonstrations of Albanians crying "We want democracy" are difficult to characterize as classical terrorism, the Serbian media has to produce the fantasy of a secret terrorist organization which uses the struggle for democracy only as a veil. Notably, the Serbs have been calling the Albanians terrorists only since the disintegration of socialism in Eastern Europe; prior to this they had been using the term counterrevolutionary. Talk about terrorists is much more effective: it tries to create the impression that the Serbian struggle against the Albanians means, for example, the same as the Western struggle against Gadhafi's terrorism or the Jewish struggle against Arab terrorism.

24. Lacan, Jacques, *Le seminaire, livre III: Les psychoses* (Paris: Editions du Seuil, 1981), p. 315.

25. Hall, Stuart, *The Hard Road to Renewal* (London: Verso, 1988), p. 85.

26. *Ibid.*, p. 262.

27. *Op. cit.*, p. 207.

28. *Op. cit.*

29. For the analysis of Lacan's graph of desire, see Žižek (1989).

Women's Movements
in Eastern and Central Europe

< 9 >

The NGOization of Feminism

Institutionalization and Institution Building within the German Women's Movements[1]

Sabine Lang

The creation of a more "women-friendly" civil society was one of the myths associated with the peaceful revolution of 1989 in East Germany. Many East German women therefore watched the rising public demand for unification with suspicion: "Do we want to reunite with the men in Bonn and replace the dictatorship of the politburo with that of the chancellor's office?" was a rhetorical question frequently asked by the newly founded women's movement in the GDR.[2] Apprehension about the gendered structure of the West German state and skepticism about distributions of power and social influence were widespread among East German feminists. And indeed, while West German women hoped that with unification some of the progressive women's policies of the GDR state would find their way into new legislation, the outcome of the unification treaty and subsequent German policy decisions have disappointed such hopes.

Why didn't the overhaul of the East German political system and its social and economic foundations bring about considerable improvement in the status of women? And why didn't this in turn result in large-scale mobilization? Have women indeed become a silent majority? Why was neither of the women's movements in East or West Germany visible in public discourse? And why did they seem to be disillusioned with each other as much as with their impact in the transformation period?

Recent feminist literature on German unification has offered a number of explanations for the fact that mobilization along feminist lines did not acquire momentum during the transition process. Myra Marx Ferree has pointed to the irritation East German women felt when their desire to preserve measures of socialist "mommy politics" collided with a new movement ideology that stressed women's autonomy.[3] Irene Dölling reminds us of the fact that a relevant spectrum of East German women during the transition period held on to or were eager to revive traditional gender roles.[4] Peggy Watson and Birgit Sauer have analysed structural and symbolic features of "remasculinization" within the democratization process.[5] Anne Hampele and Brigitte Young have offered interpretations of the differences or asymmetries between the two women's movements as a way of understanding their marginalization.[6] And in her latest work

Brigitte Young has explored the role of the German state in regard to the marginalization of women during and after unification.[7]

These different approaches suggest the complexity of ideological, historical, and structural rifts that prevented stronger mobilization around gender issues. This essay adds yet another dimension to the problem. My interpretation will focus on the feminist politics of building organizations and institutions within civil society and on the causes and effects of institutionalization in the German political system. This point of departure shifts the critical perspective from ideology and strategy to the effects of specific forms of institution building and institution structure.[8] It analyzes how decisions on conduct and agency lead to specific group processes, organizations, and forms of institutionalization, which in turn shape agency and conduct.

I argue that beyond economic insecurity and life-management priorities, beyond the different histories and ideologies of the two women's movements, lies a topical taboo: an area that is hardly ever discussed, although it is related to the question of politicization and mobilization around gender issues. This area concerns the forces of feminist organization building and institutionalization that have replaced movement activism and have decisively altered, if not abolished, women's movements in their traditional forms. The primary mobilizing forces for women's issues in Germany—the "new" women's movement of the West, created in the 1970s, and the women's movement of the East, with its organization, UFV (Unabhängiger Frauenverband [Independent Women's Union]), formed in 1989—have been separately engaged in similar processes of organization building and institutionalization. As a result, both put less emphasis on traditional movement goals such as the politicization and mobilization of a feminist public. In effect, both German women's movements have metamorphosed from overarching movements into small-scale professionalized organizations. They no longer focus on mobilizing feminists for the rebuilding of a democratic public sphere but have turned into women's nongovernmental organizations (NGOs) with strong ties to the state. This change has had ambivalent consequences.

The effects of this radical reorientation are visible in structure, ideology, program, and strategy. The transition from movement to NGO brought with it a structural emphasis on professionalized but decentralized small-scale organizations and a turn from antihierarchical to more-hierarchical structures. Ideologically, there is a tendency to translate the "traditionally" complex feminist agenda of emancipation and equality into specific single issues and a form of politics with a predominantly state-oriented focus. While feminist movement building was once about the establishment of new democratic counterculture, feminist organizations today are about issue-specific intervention and pragmatic strategies that have a strong employment focus.

To be more specific about the indicators and effects of this organizational transformation, I will look at the role of the two feminist movements in German civil society in and after unification. Specifically, I will address feminist organization and intervention strategies within civil society during the transformation period and try to extract their definitions of political mobilization and agency. While the argument is based on the specific German context, it might ultimately contribute to a broader discussion about options and barriers for feminist NGOs in gendered societies.

FEMINIST DISCOURSE ON CIVIL SOCIETY

Debates about the potential revival of democratic culture through and within civil society have been as vivid in Germany as they have been throughout the rest of Europe and the United States.[9] At the same time, there are remarkably few feminist interventions in this debate.[10] Instead, German feminist discourse and gender studies tend to frame their political agenda around concepts such as citizenship, equality, and difference, with a strong focus on participation and representation.[11] One reason for this feminist intellectual distance from the concept of civil society is the experience of German society as a corporatist and gendered space that has not lived up to the promises offered by civil society discourses, namely self-defense against and relative autonomy from the state and the capitalist market economy.[12] From this perspective the general attractiveness of the term *civil society* in social analysis and politics might reflect on the experience of increasing violence in day-to-day life.[13] Civility appears as an intellectual projection onto realities of exclusion, marginalization, and opposition, a projection that is likely to be less vivid for the excluded and marginalized than for those in the centers of social and political power. That feminists from East and West Germany hesitate to attribute to the concept of civil society normative value and inherent democratic strength indicates their wariness of a social setting in which the "civilizing of the male warrior"[14] has not yet occurred.

Depending on whether one posits an abstract-normative, an institutional, or an anti-institutional definition of civil society,[15] the term entails either a modification of current social organization, a mere broadening of institutions such as schools, churches, and trade unions, or an attempt to institute alternative modes of political organization specifically through new social or civic movements. In most literature, civil society is treated as a space or arena other than the market that stands between the household and the state and that makes concerted action and social self-organization possible.[16] However, issues of the allocation of institutional power, resources, and, more specifically, gender-specific access and influence remain blind spots in these definitions. Civil society has no "natural innocence."[17] It is not free of power and is not an open location for rational argument and forceless decision-making processes, as some civil society literature suggests.[18] While it may refer to a public space that provides the possibility for democratizing communication, and the development of agendas and strategies that take account of positional differences, it is also a concept with specific traditions marked by political and economic power struggles. Critical feminist perspectives on German civil society therefore will have to focus on the engendering of its

concepts and will have to juxtapose its political rhetoric with actual gendered and corporatist structures. In what way, then, does such a critical concept of civil society
acquire meaning in the social formation processes after German unification?

GERMAN UNIFICATION: THE (RE)PRODUCTION OF GENDERED SOCIETY

Whether East Germans took to the streets or left the country in 1989, the impulse for
democratic reform was not voiced in gender-specific terms.[19] Mobilization occurred as
a response to the lack of civil society under state socialism, where organized political
resistance or dissidence had been sanctioned by the state. Yet the revolutionary establishment of a functioning democratic public sphere occurred within the context of an
accelerating influx of West German political culture and its institutions as well as the
breakdown of the East German economy.

   With unification, East Germans entered a liberal democracy and a market economy
with its promise of individual and pluralist participation, on the one hand, and its
structural, economic, and corporatist restraints on the other. Within this seemingly
wider civic space lurked the discovery that the freedoms acquired were, in Isaiah Berlin's
distinction, negative freedoms, that is, *freedoms from,* rather than substantial positive
and creative freedoms, *freedoms to.*[20] Freedom from repression, which permitted public
speaking, or even the "afforded possibilities of concerted action and social self-organization,"[21] did not necessarily translate into the creation of new opportunity structures,
new itineraries for participation, or new jobs. Nor did it entail the freedom to decide
which features of the socialist system's women's policies would be worth transporting
into the newly unified German society. Instead, the rising democratic order instigated
stratification processes along gender lines, which insinuated themselves quickly, deeply,
and with almost no resistance into the newly created unified German social and political sphere. In the former GDR, women lost their jobs disproportionately. While in 1989
there were 4.3 million women in the GDR with jobs, by November 1994 only 59 percent
of those were still employed, as compared to 70 percent of the men.[22] Women were
specifically pushed out of high-income and comparatively high-status positions in areas
such as public management or the universities.[23] Without much overt public discour-
agement, the rates of women applying for traditional male jobs in, for example, the
building sector or certain technical sciences decreased rapidly. The advent of Western
capitalist democracy successfully promoted a transition to a Western liberal model of
the public and private spheres: The market economy came to be considered private and
is therefore experienced "privately," with all the ramifications of individualization, anxiety, paralysis, and shame about unemployment. Women were by and large the first to
lose jobs and the first to adopt more family-centered roles as an immediately available
option. The primary, visible actors in the civil public sphere of the former East Germany
turned out to be men, thus mirroring the Western political public and its predominantly male actors.

But women in the former West Germany also feel the costs of this transformation, primarily in the experience of having to share those public resources that, until 1989, had been allocated for women's centers and special programs by federal and state agencies. To take one example out of many: The West Berlin Parliament established a program in 1990, the C1 Program, which enabled West Berlin universities to hire sixty-four women assistant professors and qualify them for full professorships as part of state affirmative action policy. Now that the united city has three universities in West Berlin and four more universities in East Berlin (not including the professional training colleges and private colleges), the same resources have to be divided among a much larger number of institutions, which leads to increasing competition and provokes fear among West German feminists that their advances—achieved under prosperous economic conditions and a stable social welfare system—are in danger.

Yet beyond what one might subsume under the topic of distributive struggles, West German feminists were wary of the transformation because their "feminisms" were criticized by East German women as ideologically rigid, essentialist, and ahistorical. As compared to other Eastern European societies, where feminism has been a "no-word" for some time,[24] East German women claimed an independent version of feminism for themselves. In this sense, the divisions between East and West German women were more than rhetorical digressions or definitional quarrels. They represented power struggles over agendas and strategies in the public sphere. West German feminists insisted on the need for East and West German women to adopt a common voice, underestimating the problem of hegemony within this commonality. Ultimately, they were disappointed with the reluctance of Eastern women to adopt the language and the terminology of Western feminisms.

There were, of course, other reasons for the lack of a public presence for a women's agenda during unification. The Eastern civic public needed women's voices at exactly a time when individual life management and the demands of the new market economy had priority for most. Developments in the university system put enormous strain on women intellectuals in the arts and sciences, who were about to be marginalized by being forced either into limited contracts or, if they wanted to qualify for the academic market, into doing research in mainstream areas that by definition excluded feminist approaches and topics. An audible civic voice for women would also have required media and other communication resources, but a strong feminist journalistic tradition was missing in Germany.[25]

Yet while such structural, economic, and psychological constraints do account for the lack of broad and massive mobilization among women, they do not sufficiently explain the two movements' overarching invisibility or the paralysis of their public voice. There seems to have been a set of impediments that added to the quietude of the movements and their activists and which ultimately fostered overall civic silence during the transformation period.

FEMINIST MOVEMENTS AND THE POLITICS OF ORGANIZATION

Both West and East German feminist movements lacked the means to counteract discriminatory policies invoked and regenerated during unification. One of the central obstacles to mobilization was a rising trend in the East and West German movements alike toward a new politics of organization. That politics at first took on different shapes in the East and the West, yet ultimately it seems as though sisterhood has converged in what I call the establishment of NGOs instead of political movements.

Feminists and Civil Society After State Socialism

While the GDR had carved out semiprivate niches for women's groups within the church and academia, most political organizing around women's issues was channeled through the official state women's organization, the Demokratische Frauenbund Deutschlands (DFD). Representation of women in Parliament was granted through a prescribed number of seats for the DFD, which defined its agenda strictly according to party doctrine.[26] Analyzing these East German niches as bastions for women within a Gramscian understanding of civil society[27] underestimates the regime's effective strategy of appeasement in these small and highly state-infiltrated spaces and the official repression against critical public discourse. Even within the broadest possible definition put forward earlier—treating civil society as a space for concerted action and social self-organization—East German society allowed neither for the evolution of such a sphere nor for a political public to sustain it.

In 1989, however, there was a surprisingly quick turnaround when compared to women's presence in other Eastern European revolutions. Some of these semiprivate circles began to use the momentum of the civil rights agenda to organize and to push for feminist claims.[28] In contrast to the situation in countries such as Poland and Czechoslovakia, East German women had infrequent contact with West German feminist groups and their literature. East Germany itself had produced, if not a "feminist literature" according to Western definitions, gender-conscious and gender-concerned women writers such as Christa Wolf, Irmtraud Morgner, and Maxie Wander. Additionally, East German feminists did not have to make their claims in opposition to established civil rights movements such as the Catholic Solidarity movement or Charta 77. Thus they became, by far, the most visible force for feminist mobilization within the Eastern European revolutions.

When on December 3, 1989, approximately a thousand women gathered in an old theater in East Berlin to found the UFV, the focus of its interventionist politics was the reform of state socialism. There was at first little discussion about how to broaden the organization. Participants were well aware that the majority of Eastern women might perceive their customary style and political rhetoric as alienating and that most women in the GDR did not identify with feminism in its Western form.[29] Besides, the acceleration of political change demanded concentration on interventionist strategies and a feminist agenda within the existing state. The "immediate demands" (Sofortforderungen) presented by the UFV on this founding day did not include reflections on its feminist framework or its ideological substance, nor an invitation for GDR women to join debates and open a new feminist public forum. Instead, the eleven articles of the document were pointedly geared toward government and SED party institutions, demanding among other things the establishment of an affirmative action fund administered by the GDR ministers' cabinet—but with "guaranteed access for the independent women's movement."[30] This reality focus was appropriate at the time, taking into account the political power structure a few weeks after the breaking down of the wall. An equally strong institutional focus occurred in the demand that the UFV be represented in the first alternative central policy-making institution, the Central Roundtable in East Berlin, where negotiations among the protagonists of the old system, the church, and the civil movements took place. The UFV was at first not admitted and acquired a seat at this central policy-formation institution only after intense negotiations. Birgit Sauer has pointed out how the quest for representation by the UFV at the Roundtable might serve as a gender-sensitive indicator for the political distribution of power within the emergent GDR civil society. In her analysis, the Roundtable was "the ritualized passage from old forms of exclusive publicity to new forms of public exclusiveness."[31] Even though the political space had been widened substantially, the terms of trade between representatives of the old regime and actors from the civil rights movements had remained gender-exclusive. Roundtable negotiations would have been held without feminist input had not the UFV insisted on being included among the participants. Roundtable participants, while invoking participatory and democratic ideals, did not question its representational basis and were not fundamentally concerned with the problems of representation, legitimacy, and communication with the larger public. In Sauer's interpretation, therefore, the Roundtable was "less a metaphor for democratic and equal participation than a symbol for the exclusiveness of civil society."[32]

The UFV served (with others) as a catalyst for establishing civil society. Yet what it initially set out to achieve was political participation and representation *within* the existing and then reformed socialist political system through a feminist expansion or redefinition of its institutions. Its political agenda thus was largely directed toward state policies and their implementation. Central for policy implementation became the Women's Equality Offices, which, under pressure from the UFV, were established in every community with a population over ten thousand.[33] Their efforts were primarily directed at the acquisition of state resources for women's centers, shelters, and job-creation programs. What impact these Equality Offices had, or could have had, on mobilizing and politicizing gender consciousness has not yet been analyzed, especially since the implosion of East German society began under the auspices of a neosocialist state that still guaranteed basic social rights such as the right to paid labor, cheap rents, child care, and abortion. UFV politics shared this orientation toward state reform, and this in turn had repercussions for its own organizational structure. The decision whether to aim at parliamentary representation in coalition with the Green Party or to remain committed to grassroots organization and politics was fought out vividly among UFV members and affiliates.[34]

Only after its devastating loss in the March 1990 elections to the East German parliament—the UFV, in an alliance with the Greens, won only 2 percent of the vote and, because of distribution mistakes, received none of the eight parliamentary seats it had helped to earn—did the movement turn from its state focus to a renewed emphasis on autonomous organization.[35] But neither inclusion in the traditional political arena nor project orientation proved to be a sustainable strategy. A combination of factors, including the acceleration of the political process largely dominated by state and party agencies, and policy making by directive and economic hardships, put the UFV in crisis by the end of 1990. "For women it has become an absolute necessity to concentrate on one's profession, one's life, and on the struggle for identity with one's work, rather than accommodate oneself on the parliamentary level to man-made structures. It is also the experience of women that within parliament they can achieve practically nothing," said activist Petra Streit in 1991.[36] The individualizing forces of rising unemployment, changing gender relations under pressure from a new economic system, declining child care facilities, and other issues proved more consuming than the newly created feminist alliances. The lack of individual time commitment, of presence in public-sphere arenas such as the media and local or regional political spaces, and last but not least, a tremendous lack of funds for broader mobilization and issue-oriented campaigns turned out to be insurmountable difficulties on the way to form a viable movement.

When the UFV held its fifth congress, called "Against Individualization," in 1993, it had no more than three hundred members in all of the new states. After two years of separatism, West German women were allowed to participate.[37] By December 1994, the UFV orchestrated a symbolic funeral for its old claim "Without women you cannot make a state" and coined the more realistic phrase, "Yes, without women there can be a state!"[38] The state of affairs was summarized by this disillusioned statement: "The women's movement [of the] East has ended up where it never wanted to be: in a societal and political niche without influence. In this it caught up with the West German movement in no time."[39] Thus the primary focus of the UFV—to foster women's participation within established institutions such as parties, unions, foundations, and corporatist representative bodies—had failed. Ironically, it had been a similar experience, namely that existing social institutions and options for political participation were male-centered, that had turned the West German feminist movement into a quest for autonomy and a separatist women's culture in the 1970s.

West German Corporatism and the Women's Movement

West German society rests on an institutional political system that features corporatism, consensus, and cooperative federalism[40] and thus is, in comparison to less corporate social structures, more resistant to challenges from the political margins. By corporatism I refer to a "web of institutional linkages between state and society,"[41] which, in contrast to pluralist lobbying as a political strategy, is confined to a limited number of institutions. These institutions have a history as corporatist partners of the state and have developed hierarchical structures, specific representational bodies, and functionally differentiated agendas. Through these special links centralized and powerful interest groups such as the German unions and economic chambers are incorporated on a regular basis in the process of policy formulation. State decision making and its implementation relies on consensual agenda formulation with these corporatist actors, who in turn assume their role as civil society actors via the media and via fostering consent in the public sphere.[42]

The politics of the West German feminist movement have been developing in opposition to this patriarchal web of centralized and powerful interest groups and parapublic institutions.[43] It is within this corporatist political paradigm that the ideological focus of women's mobilization in West Germany during the 1970s and into the 1980s, namely the insistence on "autonomy," becomes meaningful. Women articulated their refusal to be subsumed and co-opted by structures that allowed for neither easy access to nor the active incorporation of a feminist agenda. Instead, the gender-specific distribution of power was at first challenged not in the institutional realm of society and state but within the structures of family and personal gender relations. Feminist culture thus served as a source of identity production in and against existing repressive social structures, prevalent cultural codes, and patriarchal symbols.

Teresa Kulawik identifies three phases in the process of identity formation and mobilization of the West German feminist movement.[44] The first phase represents the struggle against the classic German model of a gendered division of labor and "body politics," symbolized in the struggle against existing abortion legislation. The second phase she describes with Melucci's term as a phase of "latency,"[45] in which new cultural codes were created and public visibility strongly decreased. The third phase, beginning around the mid-1980s, saw a "considerable shift toward visibility, challenging political power and decision structures."[46] A major carrier for this institution-oriented feminism were the "Realo" (realistic) women in the Green Party, most of whom were based inside the autonomous movement but changed strategies so as to introduce feminist issues into the parliamentary process on local, regional, and federal levels. A first wave of institutionalization of women's claims happened—again instigated by the Green Party—when specific women's equality issues were taken up by the Social Democrats and other established political parties. The most visible result of the equality debates in the labor force are the Women's Equality Offices which have since become compulsory for many public institutions and executive bodies, again from the local to the federal level. But the establishment of these offices also provoked skepticism within the autonomous movement. Not only did the movement have little influence on the establishment, structure, and agenda of these equality offices, but it had not opted for their creation in the first place.[47] Instead, the offices were mostly perceived as products of the selective incorporation of feminist issues into the corporatist structures of the political system, and wariness existed concerning their role within state bureaucracies.

There has been widespread consent among German feminists about the functional relevance and legitimacy of this "division of labor" within feminism. Yet while institutional feminism and femocracy blossomed in the early 1990s, resulting in the establishment of women's ministries or, at least, the establishment of state secretaries in all German states, and women's offices and affirmative action plans in most of the larger institutions, the visibility of women's movement politics in East and West Germany declined.

The public silence that accompanied the legislative process of reshaping the abortion law after unification is a striking example of an issue in which the feminist movements were almost invisible while actors in corporatist civil society, Parliament, and the constitutional court remained the uncontested central policy makers. After a progressive parliamentary initiative sponsored by Social Democrats, Liberals, Democratic Socialists, and even a few Conservatives succeeded, an abortion law was approved that guaranteed a general right to abortion during the first twelve weeks of pregnancy. The German constitutional court overruled this law in May 1993 and required a stronger prolife focus from the legislature. The court ruling stated that abortion in the first twelve weeks would not have to be punished but would nonetheless have to be considered unlawful. This established a moral bind for women, counselors, and doctors by claiming that abortion as such would be against the moral code of society and law. The constitutional court's judges also required that counseling have a strong prolife orientation and that health insurance could not be required to pay for an abortion.[48]

The ruling turned out to be a paradigmatic text for the backlash against women in the transformation period—and yet there was very little protest by feminist activists. A week before the official decision, the basic outlines of the verdict had already been leaked by the media. But it was mostly Social Democratic women's ministries of the state legislatures and members of the Green and Social Democratic women's caucuses who called for protests and demonstrations on the day of the ruling. Nearly a thousand women protested in Berlin; three hundred protested in Cologne, and four hundred in Hamburg and Munich. Compared to the big prochoice rallies of the mid-1970s, this was a clear and traumatic defeat for feminist mobilization. The movements were almost invisible—feminist civil society had turned a central political and symbolic issue over to medical associations, the churches, prolife organizations, Parliament, and, ultimately, the courts.[49] "We were infuriated, but we did not know where to go to protest" was a phrase frequently heard in Berlin in the month following the court's ruling.

But in terms of feminist politics there was more at stake here than the defeat of feminist positions on abortion. The institutionally absorbed policy formulation in the abortion issue reflects not just on the individual political abstention of women, but also on a lack of organization and mobilization of movement structures. While there are decentralized networks of women's projects and centers, organized decision-making processes for interventionist strategies do not seem to exist within the movement.

Beyond the organizational problems that both German feminist movements face in setting up specific agendas and developing policy strategies, there are also conflicts bound up with membership and ideology. In terms of membership, many women, but especially young German women, do not want to be labeled "feminists" or be identified with the claims made by their mothers. In respect to Albert Hirschman's thesis of generational cycles of engagement and disappointment, the majority of the young female generation in Germany (ages eighteen to twenty-eight) has indeed replaced political engagement with disappointment, but compensates by strong individual ambition and a rather pragmatic attitude toward labor market options and career tracks. In effect, the women's movement appears to be aging without young successors. The age cohort in Berlin feminist centers and projects is at present between thirty and fifty. Ideological rifts are bound up with the realization that the feminist principle of antihierarchical and decentralized organizational structures has not been effective in mobilizing resources for such crucial issues as abortion, the constitutional debate, or the National Women's Strike Day in March 1994. The West German women's movement has also put a strong emphasis on autonomy, creating a separatist culture of feminist projects, health and educational centers, shelters, etc. This quest for and insistence on autonomy is, as I will point out below, a fragile construct and is undermined by the effects of an increasing financial dependence on the state.

Thus the apparent political apathy among East and West German women toward such crucial issues as abortion cannot be simply attributed to economic individualism and distance from established politics, but must be seen in relation to the general lack of feminist mobilization strategies. The lack of mobilization is in turn the result of specific forms of institutionalization in the women's movements. We have arrived at what I would call the fourth and present phase of the West German feminist movement, a phase in which the two women's movements move from their asymmetric histories and converge in similar processes. We witness at present the "NGOization" of the feminist movements. NGOization occurs, I will argue, in response to developments within German social and political institutions and tends to reduce feminist NGOs to marginalized forces within corporatist civil society. Before I go into greater detail about the specific form that NGOization takes, I will take a quick and, for the purpose of this argument, selective look at the relationship between the German state and feminist organizations.

THE GERMAN STATE AND FEMINIST ORGANIZATION

The internal dynamics that changed feminist movement politics into organizational politics were the result of several factors, among the most important of which were the selective regulation practices of German state agencies. Ironically, the *institutionalization of the feminist movement* is the unwanted and also unintended consequence of a core demand of the West German feminist movement during its successful fight against unpaid labor and the campaign to convince state institutions to support socially important women's work (such as in shelters, women's centers, and feminist job training institutions). The Berlin Senate financed some 250 women's projects in 1994. The approximately 120 initiatives that received funds directly from the State Ministry for Women were subsidized with approximately US$20 million in 1994.[50] Others are state or federally funded through intermediate institutions such as the Federal Agency for Employment or by state-specific labor market programs.

Since unification, in East Berlin alone, some ninety women's projects with about 1,500 jobs were financed with federal and/or Berlin state funds. Considering rent, salaries, maintenance, or jobs through federal work creation and retraining programs (ABM and FuU), the women's infrastructure and the feminist job market are at this point thoroughly dependent on state financing. What I describe for East and West Berlin is equally relevant for all five new states of the ex-GDR. Women's shelters, centers, developmental training programs, etc., have been almost exclusively financed by the Federal Ministry for Women and Youth and the Federal Agency for Employment, and a considerable amount of Federal funds were distributed through the oldest institutional and politically centrist-conservative organization of women in Germany, the German Women's Council (Deutscher Frauenrat).

What must be interpreted, on the one hand, as a strong state focus on supporting women's issues and antidiscrimination policies, must, on the other hand, also be analyzed in relation to questions of power allocation, dependency, and regulatory force. The most active parts of the autonomous women's movement are at this point highly dependent on those structures and institutions that feminism has identified as thresholds against gender equality and which, feminists claim, should be targets of subversion and change. This dependency goes beyond a functional relationship based on finances. It includes state decisions about which initiative does or does not get financed.[51] And in times of fiscal crisis it might spur increasing competition and friction among projects instead of coordinated efforts to influence distributive decision making by state agencies.

This specific German observation might be generalized to a certain degree: Western governments have suddenly over the course of the past few years discovered NGOs as central organizations of civil society. At the World Social Summit, which took place in March 1995 in Copenhagen, there were about 120 references in the official declaration to either NGOs directly or to the important role of civil society in counteracting social injustice, creating jobs, etc.[52] NGOs are more and more called upon to replace state activities in the social sector and function as repair networks for economic and political disintegration processes. But is it not more accurate to describe NGOs as SGOs, that is, semigovernmental organizations, in that they are thoroughly dependent on the distributive influence of state agencies and that their politics and their policies will have to correspond with the specific agenda setting of respective state politics? To put the problem differently, if NGOs don't want only to engage in social repair work, but actually want to change structural features of a certain political agenda, how successful can they be when they are dependent on exactly the structures that need to be transformed? Insofar as public funding excludes public discourse about this funding and thus excludes the public from the details of the state-society relationship, public funding also tends to preclude public voice.

The consequence should by no means be to renounce public funding. But the present weakness of the movement lies in its inability to articulate and expose these dependences. Instead, each project and initiative tends to adopt the premise of secrecy and tends to deal with those dependences rather defensively. The structural mechanisms of such dependences might prove especially problematic in times of fiscal crisis, when cutbacks in the social sector cause distribution fights among these "benefit recipients."[53] Some of the effects are already visible. Segmentation and competition within the movement inhibit the focus on a common agenda; internal lobbying takes the place of joint public pressure and public lobbying. This means, in effect, too little presence in the public discourses of civil society; instead, energy is put into private lobbying strategies to secure jobs and finances.

I am aware that the point I'm raising might easily be misunderstood in that it ignores other gatekeepers of the public sphere, like the selectivity of the media, in deciding on public topics. Nor do I intend that my argument put into question the legitimacy and necessity of state funding for feminist initiatives. Quite the contrary: I would argue that these financial involvements have to be exposed more by feminists and turned into a collective and public bargaining power for feminist claims so as to prevent them from becoming strongly individualist dependences. Additionally, I want to point to the dangers that are built into a feminist strategy that focuses primarily, or even solely, on the stabilization of initiatives and centers and as such loses the impetus to develop larger feminist publics, stronger voices, and more interventionist means. If we put this dependency in the larger context of the decline of welfare states in Western Europe,[54] then the question is where future resources will be accumulated for critical state gender politics and for social mobilization against the divisions that discriminate anew against women (social security reforms, etc.).

THE FEMINIST MOVEMENTS AS NGOS

German feminist project advocate Renate Rieger has recently published a collection of essays on the state of the feminist movement, ironically entitled *The Laming of the Shrew.*[55] The authors included in this collection all share a sense of disillusionment and crisis. To explain this common perception, Rieger identifies four major shifts within project culture. One is that women now look to feminist projects more for jobs than for feminist political ideas. Many women dropped out of the UFV and went—as state-financed workers—into women's projects. The dependence on state-financed work creation programs (ABM) has resulted in a high rate of fluctuation because these programs only run for up to two years per person. This in turn prevents continuity within the project agenda. Second, cutbacks in social policies are anticipated and produce high levels of insecurity. Third, as women look for traditional recognition for their work and tend to become more conscious about pay, projects become less attractive. Fourth, project women are disillusioned because work conditions have not substantially differed from nonfeminist work contexts.[56] In sum, the utopia of feminist havens in heartless societies has vanished.

These shifts, which, on the one hand, are structural and, on the other hand, are ideological and "personal," have encouraged a stronger focus on organization building and professionalization. This entails a conviction that voluntary work and engagement should be replaced by paid labor. It implies a commitment to effectiveness and the reemployment of hierarchical structures.[57] It means negotiating money and contracts with local, regional, and federal bureaucracies, and carving up projects so that they fulfill the logic and meet the standards of funders such as the European Community. It gives a new weight to public relations and the search for funding for such jobs in women's projects. In short, project organization is oriented toward internal project consolidation, lobbying power, and public relations rather than public mobilization. Professionalization refers to the projects' attitude toward their work, which shifts from the creation of feminist spaces for "alternative" modes of life and work to "job" attitudes and to an identification with being a part of the formal tertiary sector.

NGOization may well be more effective in issue-oriented politics, cooperation with the media, and state institutions. But the question to be kept in mind is the degree to which this effectiveness will be paid for by dependency and the translation or relocation of political agendas. Dependence on femocratic structures within the state, that is, on women's offices and ministries on the local, state, and federal level, work so long as these institutions have strong positions and bargaining power within state decision making processes. Yet, as I will point out below, there are indications that this femocratic strength can no longer be taken for granted. What may also be lost in this development is the possibility of forming broader networks and institutions that may indeed have the power to mobilize along central feminist issues and challenge the gendered structure of civil society within the established organizations and parties. Feminist NGOs are in danger of adapting to the vertical structure of current political life, even if their ideological focus remains a participatory and horizontally oriented political structure in which gender-conscious policies have become part of every level of decision making.

As women's movements professionalize and as their dependence on the state increases, unification has resulted in decreasing participation by women in the institutions of the political system. There is a noticeable downward trend: Engagement in feminist issues is becoming less popular in the 1990s. In the 1994 elections to the German parliament, all parties except the Liberals (FDP) and the Party of Democratic Socialism (PDS) put forward considerably fewer women candidates than in 1990. The number of female direct candidates[58] for parliamentary seats went down in the Conservative Party

(CDU) from 15.2 percent to 13.4 percent, the Social Democratic Party (SPD) from 31.2 percent to 23.2 percent, and the Green Party from 34.6 percent to 28.3 percent.[59] Even in the Green Party there is an increasing reluctance among women to specialize in women's issues,[60] because this concentration is said to reduce the chances of achieving higher office and visibility in all parties. This development is mirrored by a decline in young women's interest in politics. During the first elections in united Germany in 1990, only 60.4 percent of young West German women between twenty-one and twenty-five voted, as compared to 82 percent of women between forty-five and fifty and 84.2 percent of women ages fifty to sixty.[61] And in the first elections to the European Parliament in the united Germany less than half of young women between eighteen and twenty-four even went to vote.[62] Whereas political interest among young men ages twenty to thirty increased, it decreased in the same age cohort of young women.[63] Generally, German women express considerably less interest in politics than German men do: In 1992, in a representative study, 66 percent of the women claimed to have very little or no interest in politics, as opposed to only 41 percent of the men.[64]

In the light of these developments, the feminist turn from collective mobilization to NGOs becomes understandable and at the same time even more problematic. Where there is a decreasing constituency and demand for mobilization, institutions must learn and change. But, as Mary Douglas has pointed out, institutions are "cognitive communities" that do not simply respond to societal trends but have a stake in generating social and self knowledge themselves.[65] Feminist institution building would have to refocus on engendering civil society and specifically its corporatist German version, not by reproducing its secretive structures and hierarchical bonds with the state, but by generating more public voice and knowledge and by working hard at alternative institution building.

CIVIL SOCIETY AS GENDERED SPACE—
CHANCES FOR FEMINIST INTERVENTIONS?

Feminist activist and writer Mechtild Jansen titled one of her recent articles about the present state of the German women's movement "Democracy in the Fog."[66] If the feminist impact on democratization is in the fog, so too is its impact on civil society. What we associate with civil society—democratization, participation, public sphere and voluntary associations—are essential for feminist political theory and practice. But at the same time the reality of feminist political organization and organizing has shifted with NGOization toward limited participatory venues and equally narrow options to gain a public voice within German civil society. Institutionalization and organization building describe two sides of a coin. On the one side, there is the professionalization and internal cohesion of feminist projects and, on the other, the danger of trading relative autonomy for increasing dependence on the state and the possible reduction of feminist constituencies to professional "expert publics."

This process results in the exclusion of a larger public and in the controlled and restrictive appropriation of a feminist agenda for state policies. The present institutions of corporatist civil society and state are not so much challenged by a radical feminist critique and by strong feminist public voices as they are confronted with particularized feminist NGO politics. Certainly, cooperation and collaboration have led to legislative action on some feminist claims such as the current parliamentary proposal for legislation on marital rape. Yet without the public visibility of feminism as a movement, what becomes an issue and how it will be phrased is turned over to an institutionalized process that is dominated by professional politics.

Counting on the "obvious permeability of political and economic institutions to societal norms" and on the "development of egalitarian and democratic institutions" through the feminist movements' "challenge to the male standards behind the allegedly neutral structure of these domains"[67] won't be enough. German institutions within state and civil society employ criteria of selectivity that are male-biased, and because feminists are forced increasingly into constant networking with state agencies they are less able to challenge those agencies' structures and policy-making processes.

NGOization entails a shift away from experience-oriented movement politics toward goal- and intervention-oriented strategies. In that sense it might be also interpreted as a reply and statement about the "grounding of feminist politics once the existence of women as women is put into question."[68] Yet the focus on difference and the politicization along multiple issues in diversified arenas pulls attention and impact away from exactly those political spaces where "women" as a gender group are needed as a strategic and political force. The German abortion law is just one example of these issues. Feminist agency is in danger of leaving political agenda-setting on issues of broad public relevance to corporatist civil society and state actors; it also risks being reduced and reducing itself to local contexts, the tertiary sector and the feminist social service and job market. Such a division of labor is prone to leave feminist NGOs on the margins of civil society and political agenda setting.

While five years ago the "de-institutionalization of the hermetic public sphere" and "de-professionalization of established forms of politics" was on the future agenda of the German feminist movement,[69] much of feminist practice has pointed in the opposite direction, toward adaptation to the existing pillars of society and politics. As the women's movements in East and West Germany were forced to employ specific strategies in relation to state agencies and to participate in the distribution fights that came with scarce resources and the declining social sector engagement of the state, not much discussion about the corollaries of these developments has occurred. Yet these conflicting interests need to be at the core of feminist debates again. NGOization is not the result of extensive and democratic discussion among feminists, but it is embedded in a general and yet subtle redefinition of feminist politics as state-oriented action. It responds to the specific rationale of institutionalization within the German state and, for that reason, might be seen as a reflection of the regulatory practices that are inscribed into the societal structure. Therefore it poses questions about democracy, participation and gender bias within civil society.

One possible future line of thinking and strategy should take into account the possibility of more-powerful institution building set against NGOization. Institution building, in the language of the social sciences, refers to the "creation of relationships of meaning by fitting together the action-oriented perspectives of individual actors."[70] This definition entails above all a focus on the creation of shared meaning among a diversity of individual feminist claims, and also an orientation toward action and intervention. Institution building within the feminist movement would then be characterized by what Roland Roth calls the "production of disagreement and protest,"[71] the development of means for mobilizing, yet also the achievement of a balance between latency and visibility.[72] Institution building could channel single-issue claims and individual agendas into a politicized, strategically oriented framework. Feminist institution building would temporarily reduce complexity and difference among feminisms for the purpose of developing a common agenda, strategy and intervention. Yet institution building would, I claim, not abolish these differences, but relocate their space within feminist discourse and use a feminist presence within corporatist civil society more effectively than single strong NGOs as expert publics can. Corporatist German society would need stronger feminist institutions, drawn from a larger feminist public, to counteract male dominance in established organizations and to add a distinctive voice to public discourse.[73]

Ultimately the question is whether feminist notions of civil society and participation will be developed in the narrow framework of liberal representative democracies[74] or whether feminist initiatives will find ways to move beyond NGOization and use existing public spaces for a broader repoliticization of gender issues—as a critique of the corporatist political system and as a framework for a new gender contract with concrete options for female participation, democratization, transparency, institutionalized communication venues, and decision-making processes. We should be reminded that Germany in the nineteenth century already was aiming for civil society—a society in which a strong state and economic independence guaranteed by male agents would support and legitimate the interests of the male bourgeois citizen.

NOTES

1. I would like to thank Margit Mayer, Birgit Sauer, Roscha Schmidt, and Brigitte Young for their stimulating discussions and references on the topic.
2. Ina Merkel, "Manifest für eine autonome Frauenbewegung," *Tageszeitung*, December 5, 1989.
3. Myra Marx Ferree, "The Rise and Fall of 'Mommy Politics': Feminism and Unification in (East) Germany," *Feminist Studies* 19, no. 1, (1993), pp. 89–115.
4. Irene Dölling, "Aufschwung nach der Wende—Frauenforschung in der DDR und in den neuen Bundesländern," in Gisela Helwig and Hildegard Maria Nickel (eds.), *Frauen in Deutschland 1945–1992* (Bonn: Bundeszentrale für politische Bildung, 1993), pp. 397–407.

5. Peggy Watson, "Osteuropa: Die lautlose Revolution der Geschlechterverhältnisse," *Das Argument* 202 (1993), pp. 859–874; Birgit Sauer, "Der 'Runde Tisch' und die Raumaufteilung der Demokratie. Eine politische Institution des Übergangs?" in Birgitta Nedelmann (ed.), *Politische Institutionen im Wandel. Sonderheft der Kölner Zeitschrift für Soziologie und Sozialpsychologie* (Opladen: Westdeutscher Verlag, 1995), pp. 108–125.

6. Hampele, Anne, "Der Unabhängige Frauenverband," in Helmut Müller-Enbergs, Marianne Schulz, and Jan Wielgohs (eds.), *Von der Illegalität ins Parlament. Werdegang und Konzept der neuen Bürgerbewegungen* (Berlin: Verlaf Werstfälisches Dampfboot, 1991), pp. 221–82; Brigitte Young, "Asynchronitäten der deutsch-deutschen Frauenbewegung," *Prokla* 24, no. 94/1 (1993), pp. 49–64.

7. Brigitte Young, *German Unification, the State, and Gender* (New Haven: Yale University Press, 1996).

8. Ibid. This is an extensive and excellent study using such an approach.

9. Ulrich Rödel, Günter Frankenberg, and Helmut Dubiel, *Die demokratische Frage* (Frankfurt: Links-Verlag, 1989); Rainer Schmalz-Bruns, "Civil Society—ein postmodernes Kunstprodukt?" *PVS* 33, no. 2 (1992), pp. 243–55; Volker Heins, "Ambivalenzen der Zivilgesellschaft," *PVS* 33, no. 2 (1992), pp. 235–42.

10. The first visible public discussion among feminists on the concept of civil society occurred at a conference in Berlin in October 1994 with the title "Democracy and Difference." A feminist critique of the concept of civil society has been put forward in the discussion in *Links* nos. 257 to 259 (1991), with comments by Andrea Maihofer, Sylvia Kontos, and Irmgard Schultz.

11. See for example Elke Biester, Barbara Holland-Cunz and Birgit Sauer (eds.), *Demokratie oder Androkratie? Theorie und Praxis demokratischer Herrschaft in der feministischen Diskussion* (Frankfurt: Campus Verlag, 1994); Ute Gerhard, et al., *Differenz und Gleichheit. Menschenrechte haben (k)ein Geschlecht* (Darmstadt: Ulrike Helmer Verlag, 1990); Eva Kreisky and Birgit Sauer, (eds.), *Feministische Standpunkte in der Politikwissenschaft* (Frankfurt: Campus Verlag, 1995).

12. Jean L. Cohen and Andrew Arato, *Civil Society and Political Theory* (Cambridge: The MIT Press, 1992), p. 492.

13. Irmgard Schultz, "Demokratie und Gewaltfrage. Feministische Kritik an der Idee der Zivilgesellschaft," *Links* 257 (1991), p. 18.

14. Andrea Maihofer, "Noch immer bedarf es der Zivilisierung männlicher Krieger. Einige kritische Anmerkungen aus feministischer Sicht zu Demokratie und Öffentlichkeit," *links* 258 (1991) p. 22.

15. Anna Schwarz, "Gramscis Zivilgesellschaft und die Analyse der Umbruchprozesse in der DDR," *Das Argument* 193 (1992), p. 415.

16. Christopher G. A. Bryant, "Social Self-Organisation, Civility and Sociology: A Comment on Kumar's 'Civil Society,'" *British Journal of Sociology* 44, no. 3 (1993), p. 399.

17. John Keane, *Democracy and Civil Society* (London: Verso, 1988), p. 14.

18. Rödel, Frankenberg, and Dubiel, op. cit.

19. While gender-specific issues did come up occasionally within the GDR literary semipublic (see, for example, Irmtraud Morgner, *Leben und Abenteuer der Trobadora Beatriz nach Zeugnissen ihrer Spiel frau Laura* [Darmstadt: Leucterhand Verlag, 1976]) and were the focus of a few semiclandestine academic women's groups, the dominant political, academic and media discourses did not give voice to feminist standpoints and debates.

20. Isaiah Berlin, "Two Concepts of Freedom," *Deutsche Zeitschrift für Philosophie* 41, no. 4 (1992), pp. 741–55.

21. Bryant, op. cit.

22. Bundesanstalt für Arbeit, Abt. Statistik, Eckwerte des Arbeitsmarktes Bundesrepublik Deutschland, 1995.

23. Brigitte Young, "Asynchronitäten der deutsch-deutschen Frauenbewegung."

24. See Peggy Watson's article in this volume.

25. The same holds true for women's presence in the media professions in general. While in 1970 women made up 29 percent of German journalists, they account for only 31 percent in 1994. This figure also indicates how massive numbers of women from the former East German media sector—where they held about 50 percent of the posts—were forced into unemployment during the transformation. At present only three out of ten journalists at daily newspapers in Germany are women. In the political sections of the media women journalists still hold only 25 percent of the jobs (IG Medien/Forschungsgruppe Journalismus, *Frauen in Journalismus* (Dortmund: I.G. Medien Verlag, 1995).

26. Myra Marx Ferree, "Institutionalizing Gender Equality: Feminist Politics and Equality Offices," *German Politics and Society* 24/25 (1991), p. 58.

27. Schwarz, op. cit., p. 418.

28. Irene Dölling, "Between Hope and Hopelessness: Women in the GDR after the 'Turning Point,'" *Feminist Review* 39 (1991), p. 3.

29. Ibid.

30. *Tageszeitung-taz,* Berlin (daily newspaper), December 3, 1989.

31. Birgit Sauer, op. cit., p. 123.

32. Ibid.

33. The purpose of these offices as part of the executive branch is mainly to implement and coordinate women's policies. In doing so the Women's Equality Offices are supposed to evaluate legislation, to cooperate with women's groups and organizations, and to regularly inform central government agencies on womens' concerns.

34. Anne Hampele, "Frauenbewegung in den Ländern der ehemaligen DDR" *Forschungsjournal Neue Soziale Bewegungen* 1 (1992), pp. 34–41.

35. Hampele, "Der Unabhängige Frauenverband," p. 252.

36. Petra Streit, "Raising Consciousness," *German Politics and Society* 24/25 (1991), p. 13.

37. *Tageszeitung*-taz, Berlin (daily newspaper) June 7, 1993.

38. Ulrike Helwerth, "Ohne Frauen ist ein Staat zu machen," *Freitag* 51, (December 16, 1994), p. 14.

39. Ibid.; translation by author.

40. Simon Bulmer, (ed.), *The Changing Agenda of West German Public Policy* (Dartmouth, 1989).

41. Peter Katzenstein, *Policy and Politics in West Germany: The Growth of a Semi-Sovereign State* (Philadelphia, 1987).

42. Roland Czada, "Korporatismus" in Dieter Nohlen (ed.), *Wörterbuch Staat und Politik* (München, 1991), p. 322.

43. Brigitte Young, *German Unification, the State, and Gender.*

44. Teresa Kulawik, "Autonomous Mothers? West German Feminism Reconsidered," *German Politics and Society* 24/25 (1991), p. 70.

45. Ibid.

46. Ibid.

47. Clarissa Rudolph, "Die Institutionalisierung von Frauenpolitik im Parteienstaat," in Elke Biester, Barbara Holland-Cunz, Eva Maleck-Lewy, Anja Ruf, and Birgit Sauer (eds.), *Gleichstellungspolitik—Totem und Tabus* (Frankfurt, 1994), p. 70.

48. This turns the right to abortion into a socially stratified right, since abortions in Germany are very expensive. In addition, in almost all other European countries health insurance is required to pay for abortions.

49. In June 1995 a revised version of the abortion law was voted on in Parliament and accepted.

50. Fiscal plan Senatsverwaltung für Arbeit und Frauen, 18 02, 1994.

51. Do state agencies think public relations jobs necessary in feminist projects? Or are they the

first to be cut in times of recession? How much public opposition by their "benefit recipients" (*Zuwendungsempfänger* is the official term for German state funding of projects) do state agencies tolerate?

52. *Tageszeitung-taz*, Berlin (daily newspaper), March 10, 1995.
53. Brigitte Young, "Asynchronitäten der deutsch-deutschen Frauenbewegung."
54. Ibid.
55. Renate Rieger, (ed.), *Der Widerspenstigen Lähmung? Frauenprojekte zwischen Autonomie und Anpassung* (Frankfurt, 1993).
56. Ibid., p. 16.
57. Ibid.
58. Direct candidates campaign to gain a mandate in a specific voting district *(Direktmandat)*. Other candidates are put up through party lists.
59. *Frankfurter Allgemeine Zeitung*, Frankfurt (daily newspaper), October 8, 1994.
60. *Freitag*, Berlin (weekly magazine), September 30, 1994.
61. *Tagesspiegel*, Berlin (daily newspaper), January 9, 1994.
62. *Frankfurter Rundschau*, Frankfurt (daily newspaper), October 14, 1994.
63. *Tagesspiegel*, Berlin (daily newspaper), January 9, 1994.
64. Institut für Demoskopie Allensbach (ed.), *Frauen in Deutschland. Lebensverhältnisse, Lebensstile und Zukunftserwartungen. Die Schering-Frauenstudie '93* (Köln, 1993).
65. Mary Douglas, *How Institutions Think* (Syracuse: Syracuse University Press, 1986), p. 127.
66. *Tageszeitung*, October 20, 1994.
67. Cohen and Arato, op. cit., p. 549.
68. Chantal Mouffe, "Feminism, Citizenship, and Radical Democratic Politics," in Judith Butler and Joan W. Scott (eds.), *Feminists Theorize the Political* (New York: Routledge, 1992), p. 381.
69. Barbara Holland-Cunz, "Perspektiven der Ent-Institutionalisierung," in Ute Gerhard, Meredith Jansen, et. al. (eds.), *Differenz und Gleichheit: Menschenrechte haben (k)ein Geschlecht* (Frankfurt, 1990), p. 309.
70. Gerhard Göhler (ed.), *Grundfragen der Theorie politischer Institutionen* (Opladen, 1987) p. 39; translation by author.
71. Roland Roth, *Demokratie von unten. Neue soziale Bewegungen auf dem Wege zur politischen Institution* (Köln, 1994), p. 183.
72. Ibid.
73. Feminist institution building is not to be confused with the establishment of a "Women's Party," which was formed in Germany in June 1995.
74. Anne Phillips, *Democracy and Difference* (University Park, Pennsylvania, 1993), p. 104.

< 10 >

The East German Women's Movement After Unification

Eva Maleck-Lewy

In this essay I focus on the East German women's movement. Five years after German unification, it now seems the right moment to look back at what the present position of the East German women's movement is, what its achievements are, and what stage of its historical development it has arrived at.

BACKGROUND

German unification and the subsequent social transformation has been a contradictory process that has produced an ambivalent situation. This is particularly evident in the changes in the situation of women. No other social group was more radically affected by these contradictions, either with serious losses or with new opportunities. The struggle over the redistribution of wealth and power between East and West has grown in viciousness. There is an increasing indifference toward the situation in East Germany, which obviously privileges West German vested interests, and at the same time a growing denunciation of East Germans for bleeding the West Germans dry. Efforts to integrate East German women into political and academic institutions, in accordance with their qualifications and a proportional balance of their numbers, have waned.[1]

In this contribution, I intend to concentrate on the new East German women's movement in three distinct periods. The first period is the final years of the existence of the GDR, a period I will call the incubation of a modern women's movement. This period paved the way for the emergence of an independent women's movement that was not yet able to constitute itself because of the political situation. The second period covers the time from the dissolution of the GDR to its consolidation with the Federal Republic in October 1990. In this phase the women's movement established itself as a politically active factor. It was characterized by an intensive search for effective methods of political action and by the emergence and development of concepts and strategies for their implementation. The third period of development occurs with German unity. At this point, the East German women's movement began a process of differentiation and reorientation. It took up many traditions from the women's movement in West

Germany but transformed their meaning, adapting them to the different requirements and interests of East German women.[2] At the same time, it had to come to grips with the loss of its own political power.

PREPARING FOR A MODERN EAST GERMAN WOMEN'S MOVEMENT DURING THE FINAL YEARS OF GDR EXISTENCE

The GDR officialdom ignored the term *feminism*. It was used only exceptionally and was generally understood as a pejorative term. This has led West German feminists, particularly those from academic backgrounds, to believe that modern feminism had no roots in East Germany. To this day renowned West German feminists and experts in women's studies talk about the German women's movement after unification without ever mentioning the preunification East German women's organization with its specificities and potential.

The official policy of the GDR ruling party aimed at formal equality. Women's emancipation was part and parcel of socialism. Official policy with regard to women was subjected to the state's labor market program. State socialism could not forgo the creative labor of women, whether on the labor market generally or in the particular fields of academic, cultural, or political life. The policy of the ruling party was therefore always ambivalent. The government refused women a say in important areas of political decision making and took advantage of their work commitment for its own purposes. At the same time, opportunities were provided for women to develop their professional or trade skills, which enabled them to combine their professional lives with their responsibilities as mothers. The family code of the GDR provided for women's rights to self-determination, underwritten by abortion legislation. One third of all East German women were single parents and raised their children outside marriage but free from basic financial fears. Far more East German than West German women had full time gainful employment, and far more engaged in political activities. Although the professional careers of women were officially promoted, the emergence and development of an independent women's consciousness took place below the level of official policy.[3] Cultural activities, especially literature, played a key role in this. East German women writers in the mid-1970s—such as Brigitte Reimann, Maxie Wander, and Christa Wolf—took up the autonomous personality of woman and her chances for individual happiness and self-determination. Their writings offered a critique of political and social reality in the GDR, in terms of concepts of democracy and human rights. They were read outside of the GDR and constituted a link between East German women and international feminism.

In the last years of the GDR, women social scientists (who met in discussion groups), women in the civil rights movement, and lesbians developed a feminist consciousness and an awareness of the limits of women's lives in the GDR.[4] In the early eighties, these women established independent groups, frequently under the umbrella of various Protestant coalitions. One of these groups was made up of members of the ruling party. It was to play an important role in the establishment of an independent women's policy in the GDR from 1990 forward. Because of their specific living conditions and socialization, when GDR women freed themselves from the political fetters of state socialism, they did not simply call for the right to participate in all fields of public life or for self-determination. Instead they called for the democratization of the conditions under which they lived, aware that they needed equal political opportunities and power to achieve this.

THE NEW WOMEN'S MOVEMENT DURING THE *WENDE*

The independent women's movement in East Germany seemed to become a rallying point for a considerable number of women. The most important event was the founding of the independent Women's Organization (UFV), which became the leading voice of East German women in the brief period of the Velvet Revolution in East Germany. The UFV criticized the lack of democracy in the GDR and its paternalistic and patriarchal policies with regard to women and their needs. They also criticized the civil rights movements for ignoring the interests of women. They appealed to women to take their concerns into their own hands. Such slogans as "No state without women sharing in the decision making of the country," "Democracy without women is no democracy," and "Resist or you'll be back at the kitchen sink" illustrate not only women's demands, but also their premonition of future developments that were in no way desirable.[5]

The period from the fall of 1989 to the summer of 1990 was the glorious heyday of the East German women's movement. Women activists spared neither time nor effort in participating in national, regional, and local roundtables, discussions, and parliamentary committees. They shared fully in political decision making and insisted on the establishment of institutional means for safeguarding the equal opportunities of women and men. The participation of women in these political activities provided a platform from which to publicize their ideas and demands, and women activists were appointed to important posts at various levels of the establishment.

Taking advantage of their specific GDR socialization, women were active in three fields: They built up their own women's infrastructure (projects, clubs, publishing); they were involved in elections and parliamentary activities; and they took part in ventures outside the legislative bodies. During this period they successfully established the foundation for an effective structure for an independent women's movement. On the political stage, they achieved results that are still important today. In particular, they developed a new concept of equal-opportunities policy and political instruments for its implementation. They passed a law that provided for the appointment of full-time equal-opportunities officers in communities of more than ten thousand inhabitants.

By the spring of l990, the situation of the women's movement had changed radically. As West German political structures and parties took over, the East German women's movement lost its political importance and prominence; its organizational cohesion declined. Its offensive for women's equal opportunities and its efforts to replace formal with real equality and to reform gender relations gave way to the defense of jeopardized social, economic, and domestic rights for women and to the fight against the increasing erosion of democratic rights for everyone. From that time, women were fighting on two fronts: first, to prevent a further loss of their traditional GDR independence in regard especially to their social rights, and second, to exercise their newly acquired democratic opportunities, achieved in the process of the *Wende*.

THE WOMEN'S MOVEMENT AFTER UNIFICATION:
DIFFERENTIATION AND REORIENTATION

Already by 1990 it had become obvious that the East German women's movement was not the monolithic body that certain observers and many feminist activists thought it to be. The controversy that illuminated its divisions was the question of which strategy to pursue under the conditions of the newly adopted West German parliamentary democracy. Women aligned themselves on the basis of the answer they gave to this question. They rallied around different political parties, government institutions, equal-opportunity officers, and women's projects or they remained close to the Independent Women's Organization.

Mass unemployment was one of the major problems confronting East German women. By turning professional, women's organizers and many other women who had been feminist activists managed to solve the redundancy problem successfully. A considerable number of former activists found new jobs in political administration, in government institution, and as equal-opportunity officers, and so retained their financial independence; naturally they were well satisfied. Others have been disappointed with the official women's policy pursued by the federal German government and the various state governments and consider it deficient in respect to women's interests.

An independent women's infrastructure was one of the leading demands of the women's movement. East German women were able to build an infrastructure that was in no way inferior to that in the West by cleverly taking advantage of the decisions made during the GDR era and of the complicated finance system of the Federal Republic. They established women's centers, battered women's shelters, antiviolence centers, women's archives, periodical projects, and cultural centers. Much of what is done in the women's centers falls under the category of social services, for which state funds are easier to get. These services include counseling for unemployed women, psychological consultations, training courses, and sensitivity groups. They also provide a meeting place for lesbians, prose or poetry readings, and political education groups. Some of these centers have lost their interest in politics. This development resulted from a broadening of the women's projects; it was also caused by activists withdrawing from women's projects in order to find better-paid jobs.

Reorientation of the women's movement changed the character of their work. In conforming to established traditions of the West German women's movement, the different aims and priorities that characterize the work of the East German women's movement are hidden. East German women speak a much simpler language, they are more pragmatic, though not necessarily politically indifferent. Gainful employment is still considered the essential prerequisite of emancipation by East German women; thus their efforts are directed toward an improved labor market situation for women. To this end, many activities are geared toward strengthening women's self-confidence.[6] Activists try to encourage women to act independently by organizing activities that relate back to familiar women's experiences or women's symbols from the GDR period. The successful revival of International Women's Day on the eighth of March is a case in point. In the federal state of Brandenburg this date is deliberately chosen as the beginning of a women's week. Such state-organized, politically oriented women's weeks are unknown in the West German federal states.

But the most interesting experiment within the East German women's movement was the UFV. To establish a modern feminist political organization was a truly creative act on the part of East German women. While the contribution of the East German movement toward a new women's structure is acknowledged, little attention is given to the political ideas on which this structure is based. From its foundation in December 1989, the UFV called itself a feminist organization, indicating that its program and basic concepts differed from those incorporated by the former GDR women's organization. UFV women considered it necessary to rally women who held different viewpoints and to organize them as a political network, thereby connecting support for differing interests from different levels of political activity, i.e., from different legislative bodies, projects, and institutions. The UFV was politically successful inasmuch as it was able to organize a cooperative network of nonparty women. Women from different organizations and political parties agreed to organize joint demonstrations and to coordinate other kinds of events or initiatives. Some of the women's roundtables in East Germany, initiated by the UFV, continue to this day. In contrast to the original roundtables, these continuing efforts are largely invisible in the mass media and deal with a wider range of issues, only some of which concern formal, institutionalized politics.

After unification, the political influence of the UFV declined dramatically. There were many reasons for this. Because it was an organization outside the orbit of the established political parties and therefore without secure financial support, it lost the bulk of its activists to organizations, political parties, and institutions that were able to offer the chance of gainful employment or political careers. Moreover, the UFV concept of an organization of women, be they politicians or activists, irrespective of their allegiance to any particular political party, proved unrealistic under the new conditions of a party-dominated political system.[7]

Since 1991, countless UFV debates centered on the question of how to proceed. In an official paper published in the summer of 1993,[8] the UFV named some of the causes of its decline; these included the pluralistic political system of West Germany with its specific organization of political power and influence, which made the UFV's concept of organization inadequate. As the paper put it: "We organized demonstrations, published letters and manifestos and organized networks. But all our activities were defensive. We lost every important issue, e.g., our job policy, our fight to defend the liberal abortion law of the GDR granting women the right of self-determination, and the struggle to amend the Constitution so that it included women's rights." It is a fact that from 1991 to 1993 all political battles and campaigns were or seemed to be lost. Grassroots UFV members found the feminist demands suggested by their leaders very far from their everyday chores and problems.

The response by UFV members has differed. A large section of the membership left the UFV but are committed to other political contexts. Others found that their work or their domestic obligations left them no leisure for the women's organization. At present, the UFV is rebuilding its structures and reformulating its constitution. Most of the remaining membership have acquired a new understanding of what can be called "feminist politics." The new slogan announces "The UFV is what its members make of it." Members meet to enjoy each other's company. Whatever women do to resist their isolation and discrimination, is, after all, politics. UFV members, however, also believe that a feminized society would be a desirable nonpatriarchal, nonhierarchical option oriented toward peace and ecology. But that vision must not obscure the pursuit of the day-to-day tasks of politics that can help women discover their own interests.

This reorientation and internal differentiation in the East German women's movement also goes along with women's efforts to interpret their own experiences historically and theoretically. The first studies done by activists and movement-inspired researchers are now coming out. Further advances in the theoretical understanding of the history of the East German women's movement are hampered now by the extreme scarcity of East German women academics in universities and research institutions.

Because of the differential distribution of resources in general and the marginalization of East German women academics in particular, West German feminist research has the power to define the theoretical questions and shape the discourse about the meaning of the transformation. Although shared research and common understanding of the women's movement is constantly called for, it is unlikely to occur unless and until the differences in experience of both movements are acknowledged and taken into account. The inclusion of East German perspectives and research findings is a prerequisite for a successful interpretation of the transformation as well as for a productive future for feminist research in Germany.

NOTES

1. Hanna Behrend, "Keeping a Foot in the Door: East German Women's Academic, Political, Cultural and Social Projects" in *Women and the Wende: Social Effects and Cultural Reflections of the German Unification Process* (Amsterdam and Atlanta: Rodopi, 1994).

2. Myra Marx Ferree, "'The Time of Chaos Was the Best': Feminist Mobilization and Demobilization in East Germany," in *Gender and Society* 8, no. 4 (1994), pp. 597–623.

3. Giselinde Schwarz and Christine Zenner (eds.), *Wir wollen mehr als ein "Vaterland": DDR-Frauen im Aufbruch* (Hamburg: Rowohlt Taschenbuch Verlag, 1990).

4. Ursula Sillge, *Un-Sichtbare Frauen: Lesben und ihre Emanzipation in der DDR* (Berlin: LinksDruck Verlag, 1991).

5. Cordula Kahlau (ed.), *Aufbruch! Frauenbewegung in der DDR. Dokumentation* (München: Frauenoffensive, 1990).

6. Ulrike and Schwarz Helwerth, Gislinde *Von Muttis und Emanzen. Feministinnen in Ost- und Westdeutschland* (Frankfurt am Main: Fischer, 1995).

7. Eva Maleck-Lewy, "Die Wende in der DDR und der Aufbruch der Frauenbewegung" in Hanna Behrend and Eva Maleck-Lewy, *Entmännlichung der Utopie* (Berlin: Humboldt Universität, 1992).

8. Ulrike Bagger, Sybill Klotz, Eva Maleck-Lewy et al., "Die Ostdeutsch Frauenbewegung: Zwischen JetztErstRecht und NieWieder," paper presented at the Fifth Independent Women's Association Congress, Berlin, June 4–6, 1993.

< 11 >

Women's Movements in Poland

Malgorzata Fuszara

An author attempting to describe women's movements faces all the problems inherent in the analysis of social movements. Such problems first arise because studies in different disciplines, such as sociology and political science, define social movements in a variety of different ways. The definitional confusion is caused not only by the researchers' changing approach to social movements, but also by the fact that diversity and variability are the inherent features of a social movement.[1] D. Dahlerup, in her study of women's movements in Denmark, suggests that a "social movement is defined as a conscious, collective activity to promote social change, with some degree of organization and with the commitment and active participation of members or activists as its main resource."[2] In accordance with her definition, women's movements would be only those acting toward change, and all movements for the preservation of the status quo (which often arise in response to the prochange movements) would lie beyond the scope of analysis.

Analyses of women's movements in Poland, however, should for many reasons embrace women's movements, organizations, and initiatives in the broadest possible interpretation. This need results from the hitherto small number of such analyses and from the fact that nearly all of the Polish women's organizations are to some extent new (even those that revert to traditions that predate World War II were forcibly prevented from acting in the intervening years by the Communist regime). The new women's movements, like other new social movements, arise already in dialogue with the movements organized by a previous generation; they therefore draw from the latter's achievements and to some extent formulate their own goals in specific discussion with them. It is thus difficult in many cases to say with any certainty whether or not these movements act toward social change.

The analysis of women's movements in Poland must therefore consider both their sociopolitical background and their history and pose the following kinds of questions: In what societal types does the movement occur? What continuities or discontinuities exist vis-à-vis the past? Which institutions are the issue? What are the general political stakes of the contestations? And what are the developmental possibilities culturally available to collective actors?[3] The hope of such analyses is to answer such questions as: To what needs of women does the activity of women's organizations, movements, and informal initiatives respond? What steps toward change are suggested? What changes are desired? Finally, I will try to answer the question of whether the Polish women's movement can be called a social movement and whether it bears the traits of a traditional or a new women's movement.

One more factor needs to be mentioned. The international diffusion of ideas acquires special importance in the analysis of women's movements in post-Communist countries. Women from post-Communist countries now have contacts with women's movements and organizations from Scandinavia, France, Great Britain, and the United States. As a result, we can see clearly the difference between those movements as regards their fragmentary aims or current achievements. The great progress made in Scandinavia in the area of women's participation in power stands in contrast with the extremely low rate of women's participation in the United States whereas the emphasis on fighting sexual harassment is particularly great in the United States and found less often elsewhere. As a result, it is difficult to compare the Polish women's movement in the making and its mature counterparts in Western Europe and the United States; one can hardly choose one women's movement from one Western country to serve as a model with which to compare women's movements in post-Communist countries.

Difficulties in comparing women's movements result also, or perhaps chiefly, from the different situation of women at the moment of emergence of such movements in Eastern Europe and that of analogous movements in the West. The experiences of Eastern European women differ greatly in many respects from those of Western women, both at the moment of emergence of women's movements and today. A great many aims of Western women's movements were for many decades of no immediate interest to the women in Poland and the rest of Central and Eastern Europe. This is true of issues such as abortion or women's employment. Several generations of Polish women took a high level of education and employment for granted. Access to abortion was in fact quite easy; although not defined this way by legal provisions, it bore many traits of abortion on demand. As for phenomena such as pornography, they were prohibited by Communist censors. That the regime politicized them in this way still affects society's attitude toward them today. The Communist state also offered paid maternity leaves and leaves to care for a small child, where the woman's job remained secure until after the leave. Therefore, before suggesting answers to the question of the shape of the women's movement in Poland today, and in what respects it is similar to the movements operating in the West, and to the many other questions formulated above, a brief discussion of the history of that movement in Poland has to be provided in the context of the social situation of women which influences its fragmentary as well as its far-reaching aims.

The peculiar aspect of the women's movement in Poland from its very beginnings in the nineteenth century was its connection with the struggle for independence. At the time, that struggle was so important that no group, including the women's movement, could avoid expressing an opinion about it. The first organized group whose aim was the improvement of women's status and education was formed by writer Narcyza Zmichowska in Warsaw in the years between 1840 and 1850. The "enthusiasts," as they called themselves, were also engaged in an underground struggle for the independence of Poland from Russia. Most of the activists were imprisoned or exiled by Russian authorities, and this put a stop to the group's operation.

Despite the division into male and female roles, the struggle for independence was a common national experience. Women took part in that struggle, joined underground movements, and suffered as much as the men who struggled against the authorities. The division into countrymen and enemies mattered much more than the one into men and women.

And yet the first signs of progress toward equal rights for women could be seen in the latter part of the nineteenth century. The first women's congresses were held in Lwów in 1894, in Zakopane in 1899, and in Kraków in 1900 and 1905 to discuss the role and tasks of women. The first women's professional self-help organizations emerged (e.g., the Working Women's Professional Association, formed in 1897), as did the first Catholic women's professional organizations (e.g., the Catholic Female Employees' Association, formed at the Kraków Cigar Factory in 1900). In 1904, the Women's Union was established in Kraków, followed in 1907 by the Polish Society for Equal Rights for Women which struggled, among other things, for women's right to vote. As opposed to countries such as France or England, the Polish struggle for women's electoral rights never assumed bloody and violent forms. Because they shared common political aims and attitudes toward the partitioning powers, and suffered together the costs involved in the struggle for independence, it was not likely that women who fought for their rights and who were bound to end up in prison or be killed in the struggle would be opposed by men. An example of their common cause appears in women's struggle for electoral rights in the Austrian sector of partitioned Poland, which was obstructed by the Hapsburgs' 1867 associations act stating that "no foreigner, woman, or minor shall be admitted to membership of political associations."

Another interesting campaign was launched in 1896 by female inhabitants of the town of Biala, in Polish territory, who claimed to have actually met the requirements of the 1866 municipal government act (under which a voter had to be a citizen of age, living in the commune for at least one year, and paying a specified amount of direct taxes). The women first approached the municipal authorities about having been left out from the voters list; when this proved ineffective, they appealed to the Supreme Tribunal of State. The tribunal was to decide whether the term "every person" meant both men and women or men only. The tribunal's judgment was to the women's advantage, but the electoral regulations were implemented in a most peculiar way: In elections to the town council and the national Diet, female voters could vote only through a proxy. Under the general provisions of the civil code, it was the husband who superseded his wife, acting as her proxy in elections. Also, convents had to vote by proxy. There was no possibility whatever of checking whether the proxy respected the wish of the woman he superseded.[4]

When Poland regained independence in 1918, women acquired the right to vote on the same terms as men. But this is not to say that this right was automatic and required no special endeavors on the part of the women themselves. Initially there was no plan to grant electoral rights to women. Activists of the women's movement organized a congress on the issue in 1917 that resulted in a petition submitted to Marshal Pilsudski by a delegation of women headed by Zofie Budzyńska-Tylicka, M.D., who was to become deputy to the Diet herself in subsequent years.[5] When women were finally granted the right to vote, in 1918, they not only voted but also ran for and were elected to seats in the first elections to the Polish parliament.

In the years between the two world wars over eighty different women's organizations were established in Poland. They varied in type from professional groups to religious organizations. In addition, women's journals and books intended for a female audience were published. Women had their own Parliamentary Group; there were women's funds, scholarships, and women's clubs such as the Peasant Women's Clubs, organized by the Farmers' Society. At the same time, in the Polish tradition, there was little segregation of the sexes. This can be illustrated by the absence of clubs that banned women. It is something of a paradox that such clubs are emerging only now in response to Western influence.

A number of different classifications for women's organizations can be found in the literature of the period. Thus, from the viewpoint of political orientations, there were progovernment, neutral, and antigovernment organizations. For a social program, the organizations could be divided into conservative, moderate, and radical. From the perspective of the circles in which they operated, there were women's organizations of the gentry, intelligentsia, workers, and peasants. Depending on the members' religion, organizations could be divided into Catholic, other Christian, and Jewish. Finally, in the multinational Poland of those days, there were nationalistic women's organizations such as the Union of Ukrainian Women and the Union of German Women.[6]

As it is impossible to describe all those organizations in the present study, only several will be discussed. Distinguished among the organizations that aimed generally at raising women's status in society was the Women's Union. Established in 1904, its goal was the "defense and promotion of women's moral and economic interests." Also distinguished by its achievements among the professional organizations at this time was the Female Post-Office Clerks Association, formed in Kraków in 1905. The glaringly inferior situation of female clerks induced women to unite and to struggle for their rights. Beside organizing assistance and support, the association also demanded a hostel for single female employees.[7]

Another important type of women's organization, which tended to have large memberships, were Catholic women's organizations and girls' associations. The Catholic Girls' Association numbered 180,000 girls in 1937, of which most (70 to 75 percent) were peasants. In contrast, women's participation in leftist peasant organizations was minimal; for example, women constituted a mere 10 to 30 percent of the members of the peasant unions Wici and Siew, which then had a membership of about 200,000.[8] Other organizations that operated in rural areas included the Peasant Women's Clubs, which were initially established at the initiative of Ladies' Clubs and later at the Central Farming Society. In 1933, the Central Organization of Peasant Women's Clubs was established. By 1938, the organization had 2,852 member clubs with a total membership of 52,658 women. The organization aimed broadly at the education of peasant women, effected through a variety of forms (reading rooms, lectures, discussions, courses, scholarships for peasant girls, etc.), and at assistance to mothers (through, among other things, the organization of creches and kindergartens). Paradoxically, such organizations—established in some regions of Poland before the Second World War by landed proprietesses—were taken over in the Communist period and merged into a single women's organization, the Women's League, which was closely related to the ruling Communist Party.

The situation changed radically after World War II. The grassroots movements were replaced with institutions imposed from without. "Equal rights for women" was a slogan of the new sociopolitical system. A single mass women's organization, the Women's League, was set up in 1945. Its aims included the promotion of women's employment, assistance for the problems of everyday life, and educational activities. The league's first bylaws spoke of the need for Polish women to contribute to the fulfillment of the Party's and the government's tasks. At the first congress of the Women's League, in 1951, a program was adopted that foregrounded a struggle for peace and contributions to the fulfillment of the six-year economic plan. The means to this latter aim were a planned increase of women's employment; women were to make up one third of all employees by the end of the six-year period. After the democratic transformations of 1956, the second congress of the Women's League was staged. Its participants stressed the need for changing the principles of the League, so that instead of playing its previous role as a political organization carrying out the Party's instructions it was to become a genuine women's organization acting toward the resolution of women's problems. Several years later, in 1966, still another institution was established by order of the authorities: The National Polish Women's Council was designed as a specific representation of women before political authorities and the international women's movement. Regional councils were also set up.[9] Yet like the Women's League, the councils also were inauthentic organizations imposed from above with which women never identified themselves and of whose existence they were seldom even aware.

Because the Women's League in all its forms was an organization established by the authorities, it came into being without the involvement of women themselves. Like many other organizations set up in those days by the new authorities, it was treated as part of the imposed rule, and therefore it failed to promote the interests of the group it was originally supposed to represent. Such an organization could hope for no social backing whatsoever. This was reflected even in the pronouncements of Women's League activists at the league's extraordinary congress in 1981, during the period of democratization initiated by Solidarity. The speeches contained formulations such as: "The corset with which they once laced us keeps disabling us"; "Why are we so weak and helpless?"; and "Democracy is impossible without women's involvement."[10]

Despite all the slogans about equal rights, a great many indices of discrimination against women can be found in the period of Communist rule in Poland. In 1989, women constituted 46 percent of employees. Although their level of education was not inferior to that of men (women being even better-educated, if we take secondary and higher education only into account), they held a mere 28.1 percent of managerial positions, and almost all of these were of a lower or medium rank and were mostly in strongly feminized occupations.[11] Despite propaganda about how the division of "male" and "female" occupations had been overcome, the actual labor market was strongly divided during the Communist period. The most feminized branches were finance and social insurance (proportion of female employees: 84 percent), health protection and social welfare (80 percent), education (76 percent), and trade (72 percent).[12] Although men's and women's wages were not differentiated by force of legal provision, the actual differences were very big indeed. Women's wages were about 30 to 40 percent lower than those of men.[13] While more than 20 percent of parliamentary deputies in the Communist period were women, the parliament had no real power in those days. Characteristically, in periods when the parliament acquired real power (after 1956 and 1989), the proportion of women deputies declined rapidly.[14] Centers that exercised genuine power under Communist rule, especially the Central Committee of the (Communist) Polish United Workers' Party, had one woman at most among their members, as a manifestation of nondiscrimination on account of gender.

It is true that a model of the professionally active woman became widespread in the Communist period. This was a woman who worked full time, had the same educational level as men, but was additionally burdened with all the duties of a housewife and mother. Polish law introduced gender-neutral regulations in many spheres and declared equality and nondiscrimination in others (constitution, family code, labor code, etc.). The liberal abortion law of 1956, and especially its application, led in fact to accessibility of abortion on demand.[15] Penal law definitions of rape made it possible to prosecute all rapists, irrespective of their relation to the victim, that is, also those who were guilty of rape in marriage. At the same time, however, society had a highly traditional view of the role and position of men and women, which often made the actual application of law much more conservative and disadvantageous for women. As state control over all manifestations of social life made it impossible to establish associations and organizations, women's organizations included, women were unable to oppose this situation. The energy of men and women in illicit, underground organizations focused on joint struggle against the totalitarian regime and moved gender-based inequality to the background. This was the heritage with which we started the building of a democratic state in 1989.

In many respects, 1989 was the beginning of a new era. Among other things, a draft of an abortion act was submitted to the Diet. The most interesting effect of its submission was the activation of women's groups, the emergence of women's organizations, and other attempts at the articulation of women's needs. The trend is interesting because it was initiated by the rank and file rather than imposed upon women. Some of the actions organized during a campaign against the draft of the abortion act gave rise to more permanent movements representing women's interests. The *Directory of Women's Organizations and Initiatives in Poland,* published in 1993 by the Center for the Advancement of Women, provides information on more than forty women's organizations and initiatives. A second directory will embrace an even larger groups, including associations, federations, clubs, foundations, charity organizations, religious groups, sections of political parties and trade unions, and women's studies centers. The second directory, published by that same center, will include information on more than seventy women's organizations and on institutions that, not being such organizations themselves, nevertheless act on behalf of women and have special programs devoted to women.

Let me describe some of those organizations and their recent initiatives. One of the oldest of the grassroots organizations is the Polish Feminist Association. Informally operating since 1980, it was registered only in 1989. Among its objectives, the association mentions promotion of the idea of feminism, propagation of the principles of equal rights for women, activation of and support for women's initiatives, and dissemination of research findings on women's problems. The association organizes seminars, conferences, and courses of instruction. It also published a Polish translation of the Norwegian act on equal status of men and women.

One of the association's recent initiatives, which enjoys great popularity, is the organization of monthly seminars—"feminist meetings"—to present and discuss a variety of issues pertaining to women. Topics have included the future of feminism and the situation of women in the former Communist bloc; sexual identity; feminist history, art, literature, and theology; and legal regulations that pertain to women. The seminars seem a great success: The lecture rooms are invariably overcrowded, and ever more women apply to attend. What is particularly important is that many of the persons who take part in the seminars are "unfamiliar faces"—persons not connected so far, at least formally, with women's movements and organizations in Poland.

The Polish Feminist Association is one of the organizations that make up the Federation for Women and Family Planning. Other member organizations include Polish Women's League, Pro Femina, Association for a Nonideological State (Neutrum), the Polish YWCA, the Democratic Union of Women—EWA Group, the Movement for

Women's Rights Defense, the Association for Family Development, and the Polish Sexologist Association. The federation's objectives are, first and foremost, to secure access to information and services in the area of family planning, to propagate the various means and methods of family planning, to defend women's right to choose maternity, and to disseminate knowledge on human sexuality and demography.

The federation runs an emergency call-in service. In 1994 it also published two extremely influential reports. The first, prepared by Wanda Nowicka, dealt with the effects of the antiabortion act, which had been in force for over a year. The report was based on data gathered by the federation, provided chiefly by the women who had approached the federation for help. It criticized reports prepared by the Ministries of Health, Education, Justice, and Labor and Social Welfare—the agencies responsible for implementation of the act—and argued that state agencies actually implemented only the restrictive portion of the act, that is, they limited access to abortion such that the degree of restriction was at times even greater than what followed from legal regulation. The agencies failed to implement the "positive" portion of the act, which would have provided social assistance to persons in need, removed real obstacles to access to contraception (in particular financial obstacles), and provided sexual education.

The second report, prepared by Beata Fiszer, concerned violence against women in Poland and was the first study to venture an analysis of all the different forms of violence that have been experienced by Polish women: physical violence, rape, sexual molestation, compulsory maternity, prostitution, and mental violence, as well as a follow-up of what happened to female victims of violence. The report recommended the implementation of a national educational campaign to make the society at large, the prosecuting agencies, and the judiciary aware of the extent of this phenomenon. They hoped that this program would produce further research into violence against women and encourage the effective enforcement of existing provisions of Polish and international law. They hoped to organize courses on violence for the staff of law enforcement agencies and physicians and develop procedures to protect the victims of violence, a development that would bring about a system of cooperation between state agencies and nongovernmental organizations and result in a network of crisis phone services and hostels. Finally, they hoped to provide an education that would change people's attitude toward violence.

Domestic violence is a problem that went unnoticed in the Communist period, and little was done to help its victims. Too little is still done in this sphere today, for that matter. However, many foundations, centers, and initiatives have recently emerged to organize assistance to the victims of domestic violence. The most interesting of these seems to be the Beaten Wives Association, set up in Bydgoszcz. Numerous women's organizations and state institutions became involved in its activity, along with the local university, a senator and an M.P. from the region (both women), and—a fact of great importance for popularization of the initiative—the local daily, *Gazeta Pomorska*. An analogous organization was established in Warsaw. They organize, integrate, and propagate activities on behalf of ill-treated women. They offer legal assistance in cases for divorce, maintenance, and eviction, and aim at creating a network of guidance and assistance centers for ill-treated women. It is their aim to set up crisis intervention centers.

Shelters and hostels are also organized for single mothers; frequently these are set up and run by institutions related to the Catholic Church. Examples include the Assistance to Single Mothers Foundation, in Poznań, or the St. Joseph Foundation for Assistance to Single Mothers, which runs a hostel for single mothers, a guidance center, and crisis telephone services.

Some Polish women's organizations focus chiefly on providing assistance to women in the labor market, an area of concern that is becoming more important as growing unemployment and segmentation of the labor market have resulted in a deteriorating situation for women. There are a variety of such organizations; some are foundations established by women's initiatives and financed by sources other than the treasury (e.g., the Center for Advancement of Women); others, also established by women's initiatives, operate within the structure of communes and receive a considerable portion of their finances from local authorities (e.g., the Żoliborz District Women's Center). Both of these groups organize vocational training courses and other market-related counseling; they run women's labor exchanges and organize self-help groups.

Some organizations originated from an ad hoc campaign that eventually developed into a more permanent initiative. One example is a group called Women As Well, organized spontaneously during the last local elections to generate support for female candidates. The group includes members of various women's organizations, female university workers and journalists, women who were on the staff of local authorities, and female candidates running for positions in those authorities. The group began by organizing support for female candidates, and as part of that process it arranged media events with the local press that helped to propagate the idea that increasing numbers of women were participating in power. They arranged for courses to train female candidates in the techniques of self-presentation and public speaking, particularly in methods designed to defuse the domination techniques used against women who make public appearances. After the elections, this initiative developed into a more permanent series of seminars that offered assistance to female office-holders in local authorities. The group's interesting trait is its informal character: It has never been formally registered.

The youngest women's organization is the Center for Women's Rights, established late in 1994 by Urszula Nowakowska. Its objectives include monitoring and analyzing legislation and other draft acts to ascertain whether they contribute to the equal status of men and women. The center also reviews Polish laws to see if they are consistent with international agreements ratified by Poland, sponsors programs designed to increase the legal consciousness of women, and organizes legal assistance for and gathers data about female victims of violence and discrimination. Although the center's chief objectives do not include intervention in individual cases, it has to devote a great deal of time in its everyday operation to precisely those individual cases where assistance must be given to women. Victims of violence, divorced women who face the threat of being evicted from their flats by their former husbands, and those who are helpless in their confrontation with the courts or the machinery of the administration of justice but who are unable to pay for legal assistance frequently approach the center for help. The first several months of the center's operation have clearly demonstrated that there is a great and urgent need for an organization that can provide such legal assistance to women.

In 1996 we introduced gender studies as a two-year postgraduate program at Warsaw University. The project has been jointly prepared by a group of more than twenty women from over a dozen faculties within the university. Before 1996, gender studies have not been offered by any of the Polish universities. Under the plan for Warsaw University, gender studies would evolve gradually, and many faculties would begin to offer courses on gender, women, or equality of the sexes. Earlier this academic year, together with Eleonora Zielinska from the Faculty of Law, I conducted a seminar entitled "Equality of Men and Women in Law and Social Reality." Although designed chiefly for students of the Faculty of Law and Institute of Applied Social Sciences, it was nevertheless open to students of other faculties. We received over one hundred applications from students in a great variety of faculties—the business school, biology and computer science included. We not only received extensive feedback telling us how popular the course was, but also were asked to extend the course to two semesters. This gives us grounds for our belief that gender studies are likely to arouse the students' interest if we manage to develop the program.

It should also be mentioned that the longer-established organizations, the Women's League and the Peasant Women's Clubs, still continue their activity. And in recent years, organizations and initiatives with a religious background or organizationally related to the Church have emerged. The largest is the Catholic Women's Forum, which has about five thousand members. Another such organization is the Polish Catholic Woman's Union, which aims at defense of the Christian model of education and woman's comprehensive development in society. This latter organization promotes a rather traditional vision of woman in society; one of its statutory aims is "the postulation of freedom of choice for women so as to prevent situations where employment is an economic necessity but actually paralyzes family life." Nor are all new religious groups Christian: a Committee for Women and the Family was established attached to the local Baha'i assembly of Warsaw.

Of course, it is impossible to discuss in a short essay the entire multitude of women's groups, movements, and initiatives that emerged in Poland after the fall of Communism. It would also be difficult to formulate their general characteristics. Indeed, among the greatest advantages of women's movements in today's Poland is their great diversity. I have described women's movements on the basis of their aims and types of activity. Many movements and organizations deal with the professional work of women. Their attention seems focused on two extremes: unemployed women and women who set up or run a private business. Another group of organizations assist women in diffi-cult family situations. Still another group of organizations and initiatives act on behalf of women's rights, particularly the rights involved in procreation; they emerged from the aggravation of abortion regulations. Other organizations focus on women's participa-tion in public life, especially on increasing the proportion of women in institutions of power. Finally, there are organizations and initiatives that aim at a radical change of the status of women in society.

This analysis of women's organizations and initiatives shows that they tend to emerge in spheres in which a problem pertaining to women has been noticed and defined. For example, in the Communist period, a low proportion of women participated in orga-nizations involved in the running of society. After 1989, the proportion of women in the parliament went down even further. In response, initiatives and organizations have emerged that aim at increasing that participation. As another example, the differences between men's and women's wages did not decrease after 1989, and the new problem of unemployment affected women to a greater extent than men. In response, a number of organizations and initiatives emerged that act on behalf of professionally active women. Yet another example involves the change of legal regulations that greatly limited the access to abortion resulted in the emergence of groups that organize guidance in family planning and birth conrol. And so forth.

What is symptomatic, however, is not only the fact that in specific spheres a relatively large number of women's organizations have been established, but also that in other spheres few such organizations exist. In particular, there are extremely few women's organizations and institutions acting in the area of culture and sports.

To conclude, I would like to return to the question about the similarities and differ-ences between the women's movement in Poland and its counterparts in Western Europe and the United States, and to ask whether the Polish women's movement bears the traits of a traditional or a new social movement.

The women's movements that exist in Poland seem to operate in a situation approx-imating that of Western, including American, women's movements in periods of a turn to the right. The rights attacked during the Reagan administration were similar to those impaired in Poland after 1989. And the different governments apply similar strategies: Either they refrain from appointing women to high office or they promote women who cannot see the need for a change in the situation of women.[16] It was therefore not by chance that both the Founding Fathers and President Reagan were quoted in the Polish Senate during discussions on abortion issues; the American example is most often cited by those who represent rightist views. This was all the more surprising for Polish women, as nobody in Poland had had the chance to voice rightist opinions for many decades. Polish women's movements are emerging in a situation where women face new problems. Problems pertaining to women have now been disclosed that were kept secret before, and this has coincided with the encounter with rightist ideologies that promote a traditional definition of women's role and field of activity. The women's movements that emerge in this specific situation seem to have quite a lot in common with the traditional rather than the new social and women's movements. Their ideology is equality rather than liberation. It is worth stressing, though, that American literature describes the struggle for women's rights as a possible means toward further changes.[17] But this is not to say that the Polish women's movement lacks any traits attributed to new movements. Although often based on registered institutions, its actual scope is much broader than merely formal membership in organizations. The women who act in such organizations are most susceptible to attempts to manipulate a genuine movement for some other private purpose. Therefore, many organizations are spontaneous and have little hierarchy, a characteristic of new social movements. What also results from the diversity of movements and their fear of being manipulated is a reluctance to form broader structures. They do unite, however, toward a common aim whenever the need arises. Although they strive to influence the existing structure in an organized way and thus follow the rules of the game, a trait of traditional women's movements in many countries,[18] they sometimes also resort to actions that are inconsistent with those rules. An example is a recent campaign in which copies of an extremely sexist poster advertising an engine oil were coated with paint.

We can notice the similarity in goals of the Polish women's organizations and the Scandinavian movements. In particular, what they share is the stress on women's participation in the agencies of power and on equality of rights. On the other hand, Polish women's organization are like their American counterparts as regards the recurrent problem of freedom of procreation and the need to contend with rightist advocacy of the reduction of women's field of activity to a traditional definition of the role of women in society.

To end, there is one trait characteristic of many women's movements and organizations in post-Communist countries: Many such groups fear that they might be identified with feminism. (This fear, for that matter, is also shared by many activists in Western women's organizations.) As is well known and has been frequently repeated, feminism used to be effectively derided in countries under Communist rule; it was associated with irrational campaigns in defense of sham problems and was at the same time completely unknown, reminiscent of Communist propaganda about the equality of men and women whose purpose was to conceal their actual inequality. The effects of this situation can still be noticed in today's Poland. It has become practically a rule that female journalists from the press, radio, or TV who interview us or invite us to take part in programs for women immediately point out that they are not feminists themselves and that the program will have nothing in common with feminism. Yet when asked what they actually mean, or what they imagine to be the thing with which the program is to have nothing in common, they are at a loss because the only thing they really know is the term *feminism.* During a TV interview I gave to Hungarian television at a conference held by the Network of East-West Women, a young female journalist asked me whether I did not fear that feminism might go too far in our region. This was a most symptomatic question—one of the signs of the phenomenon called "backlash" by participants of a feminist seminar to discuss Faludi's work *Backlash*. This is a phenomenon that is taking place in Poland even before any "lash" of feminism could happen.

The fear of being identified with feminism can also be seen among certain female activists of organizations that work on behalf of women. This is the more interesting case study for a researcher, as it sometimes happens that two women who are organizing the same activity on behalf of women, and who are most similar to each other with respect to statements, attitudes, and actions, will differ greatly precisely on this question. One of them renounces feminism and stresses—even before she is asked—that she has nothing in common with it, while the other one seems to have nothing against being identified with feminism. Among other things, this demonstrates not only a defective knowledge of feminism, but also the fact that many women may find such an identification dangerous and may even subconsciously treat it as a threat to their career, position, or image. This is one of the most important problems facing to women's movements in Poland.

More promising, however, is the growing number of female students, journalists, scientific workers, and rock singers who take interest in the problems of feminism and admit it quite openly. Sociological studies have also shown that most women in Poland are aware of the inequality of opportunities and the greater threats and burdens faced by a woman. Most women are also for the emergence of organizations that will represent their specific interests. It is quite difficult to say whether women's consciousness has undergone any significant changes in this respect; in the days of the Communist slogans about the equality of men and women, such questions were never asked. It seems, however, that ever fewer women in Poland tend to believe in their own equal opportunities or in the promotion of their interests. Instead, this kind of belief—as to actual equality of the sexes and a proper promotion of women's interests in today's Poland—is quite widespread among men. The present differences between the views of men and women are considerable and operate in a great many spheres, such as the model of family and attitudes toward money, values, and norms. This demonstrates the need for the representation of women's actual points of view in a variety of organizations, groups, and centers of power.

The women's movement in Poland also faces a number of threats of a different nature. These threats concern the entire sphere of NGOs, not just the women's movements. A great many women's organizations in Poland have the legal form of foundations, which is the most advantageous one for them as it offers tax reductions and permits both easy reception of financing from abroad and pursuit of advantageously taxed economic activity. The public criticism with which the activities of foundations today are met—criticism that is based on individual but real cases in which this type of foundation has been used to further individual economic interests through the misappropriation of public funds—is likely to result in legal provisions. Such changes may in turn have a deleterious effect on the conditions of operation of all foundations, including those working on behalf of women. Not long ago, an attempt was made to tax specific types of foundations. The idea was eventually abandoned, but disadvantageous changes can still be expected. Moreover, in a situation where the state seeks additional sources of income in all spheres, one can hardly hope for a friendly attitude toward initiatives that might greatly help women and that operate only through the efforts of volunteers and external financial assistance. Such initiatives depend on tax reductions, which we fought to obtain for persons defending the interests of female victims of violence free of charge, or direct funding from the state for projects such as hostels.

It appears once again that the existence and development of women's movements depends to a great extent on the country's general situation. Admittedly, we no longer are subject to a lack of independence, as we were back in the nineteenth century, nor do we need to struggle against the regime, as was the case under martial law; what women's movements depend on nowadays is the economic and political forces that define the importance and hierarchy of the needs to be granted or refused state support. The areas I've discussed can hardly expect to receive state support at this time. And it follows from the experiences we've had so far that while women's organizations have developed most vividly and interestingly, the activities of the state have moved in the opposite direction. The office of the government's Plenipotentiary for Women and the Family was for many years vacant in Poland despite the fact that we have had a series of leftist cabinets, which (as usual) promise to solve this problem and (also as usual) fail to keep their promises. The office functioned at its best under liberal rule. The office remains vacant; no official was competent enough to prepare, in the name of the government of Poland, a report for the 1995 United Nations conference in Beijing. Instead, as opposed to the nonexistent government report, a report on women's NGOs had been prepared by a number of organizations and activists associated with women's movements. One might find comfort in the fact that things have always turned out better in Poland when problems were solved by independent organizations and not by the state. However, this situation burdens NGOs, already lacking state support for their activities, with an immense amount of work. It is perhaps for this reason that, after a period in which organizing street manifestations and petition campaigns was popular (as during the days of discussion on the abortion act), the activity of Polish women's movements has now entered a stage of less spectacular "basic work," hard but interesting, conducted by a variety of movements, organizations, and initiatives on behalf of women.

NOTES

1. This fact is something about which much of the topical literature can seem to agree. Blumer, for example, defines a social movement as a "collective enterprise to establish a new order of social life" (see H. Blumer, "Collective behaviour," in A. M. Lee (ed.), *A New Outline of the Principles of Sociology* [New York: Barnes and Noble, 1946], p. 3); Wilson stresses the tendency of social movements to cause changes in the social order by noninstitutionalized means (see J. Wilson, *Introduction to Social Movements* [New York: Basic Books, 1973]); Smelser calls social movements "collective attempts to restore, protect or create values or norms in the name of a

generalized belief" (see N. Smelser, *Theory of Collective Behaviour* [London: Routledge and Kegan Paul, 1962], p. 313); and Pakulski offers a more precise definition of social movements as "recurrent patterns of collective activities which are partially institutionalized, value oriented and anti-systematic in their form and symbolism" (see J. Pakulski, *Social Movements: The Politics of Moral Protest* [Melbourne: Longman Cheshire, 1991], p. xiv). In contrast, Pakulski says that *new* social movements are characterized by their transfunctional, innovative, and fluid nature; their inclusive, nondoctrinal, and nonideological orientations; an absence of formal membership; a sociocultural character that is self-limiting; and non-violent means. I will return to the distinction between old and new social movements at the end of this paper.

2. D. Dahlerup, "Is the New Women's Movement Dead? Decline or Change of the Danish Movement," in D. Dahlerup (ed.), *The New Women's Movement: Feminism and Political Power in Europe and the USA* (London: Sage, 1986), p. 218.

3. J. L. Cohen, "Strategy or Identity: New Theoretical Paradigms and Contemporary Social Movements," *Social Research* 52, no. 4 (Winter 1985) pp. 663–716.

4. Walentyna Najdus, "O Prawa obywatelskie kobiet w zaborze austriackim," in A. Żarnowska, A. Szwarc (eds.), *Kobieta i swiat polityki* (Warsaw: 1994), pp. 101–102.

5. Cited in S. Walczewska, "Cy kobietom w Polsce potrzobny jest feminizm?" in A. Titkow and H. Domański (eds.), *Co to znaczy byc kobieta w Polsce?*, Warszawa, 1995.

6. Z. Chyra-Rolicz, "Kościółkatolicki a ruch kobiecy przed 1939 rokiem," in *Społeczna i kulturaina działalnosć kościoła katolickiego w Polsce* XIX i XX wieku. (Kielce, 1994).

7. Ibid.

8. H. Brodowska, "Dziewczęta wiejskie w ruchu oświałowy w Polsce międzywojonnej," in A. Zarnowska and A. Szwarc (eds.), *Kobieta i edukacja* (Warsaw: 1992).

9. I. Ratman-Liwerska, *Edukacja poza konwencja* (Bialystok: 1993).

10. Ibid., p. 124.

11. Report of the Government of Poland, 1990.

12. M. Fuszara, "Market Economy and Consumer Rights: The Impact on Women's Everyday Lives and Employment," *Economic and Industrial Democracy* 15, no. 1 (1994).

13. H. Domanski, *Zadowolony niewolnik?* (Warsaw: 1992).

14. M. Fuszara, "O równiosci i demokracji rozważań ciag dąlszy," in J. Kurczewski (ed.) *Demokracja po polsku* (Warsaw: 1995).

15. E. Zielińska, *Przerywanie ciaży. Warunki legalnośsci w Polsce i na Świecie*, (Warsaw: 1990).

16. V. Sapiro, "The Women's Movement, Politics and Policy in the Reagan Era," in D. Dahlerup (ed.), *The New Women's Movement: Feminism and Political Power in Europe and the USA* (Sage: 1986).

17. E. M. Schneider, "The Dialectic of Rights and Politics: Perspectives from the Women's Movements," in L. Gordon (ed.), *Women, the State, and Welfare* (Madison: University of Wisconsin Press, 1990).

18. D. Dahlerup, op. cit.

< 12 >

Politics in Transition

Milica Antić Gaber

When old institutions are replaced by new ones, it is useful to draw attention to issues that have been, in the *ancien régime,* taken for granted—especially the many problems concerning women's lives and women's rights. Speaking of women's rights in the context of socialism may seem curious enough, but during socialism, full-time (eight hours per day) employment and social benefits (health care, legal and social protection of motherhood, liberal legislation governing abortion and family planning, and a network of public kindergartens) were considered rights that, once achieved, could never have been lost. Unfortunately, this belief proved to be wrong: many rights granted by the state were endangered by the new circumstances.

What we have had to acknowledge is that in the era of parliamentary democracy, private property, and a more aggressively political Catholic Church (to mention only the most important factors), women need to be more politically active or aggressive both to preserve the formal and substantive rights already achieved in the time of the old regime and to gain new ones. The question that immediately arises is, How we will do this? Which forms of activity and organization will lead to the assertion of old rights and the achievement of new ones?

WOMEN IN THE PERIOD OF THE SO-CALLED SELF-MANAGEMENT SOCIALISM

When we talk about the political organization of women in contemporary Slovenia (and in the former Yugoslavia), we must notice that there has been no massive women's movement like those seen in the history of some Western European countries or in the United States. Looking back at the recent history of Slovenia, when it was still part of Yugoslavia—the period of so-called self-management socialism—we can say that we did not engage in political organization in the modern sense of the term. Our lives were entirely occupied by the self-management system, which gave the false impression that it was the people (which also included women) who decided everything. Clearly, the society as such was not the place where real decisions occurred; the real decisions were made earlier and in much narrower circles.

The involvement of women in the self-management system had no specific features that would distinguish their activity from the rest. Women were involved primarily as members of the League of Communists. Women who found themselves in various political structures were there because of their membership in the league or in the Socialist Alliance of Working People or the League of Socialist Youth. It was not until the end of 1970s that the first critical analyses of women's participation in sociopolitical life showed that women were not represented in that sector of life to the same extent as they were in the sphere of labor,[1] where they represented 45 percent of the entire workforce.

In spite of the now prevalent belief that at the time, the assembly was really a front for the League of Communists, the participation of women in the three chambers of the assembly in the period from 1976 to 1982 varied from 22 percent to 29.5 percent. The research project that published the study "Women Establishing Themselves in the Delegate System" showed, among other things, that employed and educated women between the ages of twenty-five and forty were far more active than the rest.[2] There were some women who were involved in the party machine itself, since the party took care to have some women and young members participating in it. Several of these were even active in the area of women's questions, which, however, represented only a part of the class question. Vida Tomsic, for example, represented the position of working mothers inside the party.[3] She demanded the protection of motherhood in the fields of work and health care, abortion rights, the right to divorce, equal pay for equal work, and political equality. Following the arguments of theorists such as Zillah Eisenstein, she advocated "protective legislation" that created special forms of assistance (such as maternity leave and free day care) as a means "to assist women in their gender roles rather than to reorganize gender responsibilities between men and women."[4] We could agree that protectionist measures were necessary at a time when caring for the needs of the family was still considered to be women's business. But socialist "protective legislation" had already given women rights in other fields, such as abortion and consensual divorce. But Vida Tomsic was an exception to the rule. The majority of women politicians at that time did not primarily deal with questions that were important to them as women.

There were many reasons for this. Under socialism, the women question was considered to have been solved by the fact that women formally had the same rights as men. There was also an official position known as "state feminism," a situation in which the state guaranteed the fundamental social rights of women in the sphere of work. However, these rights were given to women on the basis of collective rights and not as special civil rights. The state itself, instead of its female (and male) citizens, managed the position of women in society and took measures of so-called positive discrimination, by means of which the position of women was supposed to become equal to the position of men. The advocacy of special rights for women would have been regarded as feminist and feminism was still labeled as a bourgeois ideology. We cannot, therefore, talk of a specific political commitment of women as women for women in that period. Nor were there any special women's organizations at the level of sociopolitical organizations at that time; there was only the Section for Sociopolitical Activity of Women, which could be (and from time to time even was) led by a man. The political power of women, as one of the social groups, was minimal.

We could conclude that the "emancipation" of women was given to them from above by the socialist state and was not the result of organized activities of the women's movement for their rights.

THE LIBERAL PERIOD OF COMMUNIST RULE AND THE INTERESTS OF WOMEN

The second half of the 1980s is widely recognized as the liberal period of Communist rule. It was a time when the League of Communists' decreasing power allowed civil society groups to blossom. Nostalgic people will refer to those years as "the best years of our lives." There seemed at last to come a time when different needs and interests were able to express themselves and the fragrance of democracy was in the air. We could even say that the "Slovenian spring" did not begin with the military trial of "The Four" (1989), but rather several years earlier, when the Slovenian League of Communists, under pressure from various organized groups, was forced to consider views that were quite different from the views of the Yugoslav Communist Party on some contemporary movements and phenomena. The punk music scene, the student radio, and the weekly *Mladina*, all united under the name of "alternative culture," and the cultural scene, which was gathered around the journal *Nova Revija* and the Slovenian Writers' Society, played a large role in this period.

There were also various women's groups that saw an opportunity for the realization of their specific interests in the upsurge of "small stories." The organization of women as a specific social group in Slovenia began six years later than the earliest such organizations elsewhere in Yugoslavia, an interesting piece of information that still has not been studied. The first organized women's group in Slovenia, the Women's Section of the Sociological Society, was established in 1984 and caused considerable discontent amongst the rest of the society's membership. The first feminist group, Lilith, was founded a year later; it intensified the discontent in society and caused some "macho" reactions in theoretical circles and in the mass media in reaction to its discussions of female sexuality, violence against women, and the question of women's identity. The authorities, however, did not persecute those groups; rather, they tolerated them.

With the emergence of special women's groups based on feminist principles, or so their representatives claimed, the attitude toward the very notion of feminism was liberalized and gradually gained ground. Newly freed from its association with the so-called bourgeois women's movement (which was supposed to be in contradiction with the so-called labor women's movement), feminism began to articulate its own area of research on the social position of women in Slovenia. In the second half of the 1980s, there were several publications in which one could find writings that were no longer tied to Marxist theory but instead flirted with psychoanalysis, structuralism, or other contemporary trends found in so-called Western feminism.

The period of "state feminism"[5] seemed to be definitely over. The time came for the liberalization of social relations, for the dissolution of many former fetters, for the abatement of tensions between ethnic relations, for the "marketization" of economic relations, and for the pluralization of political ones. The process of the so-called democratization of the life of the society required necessary changes in the political organization of the society and in many of its social subsystems. The political elite no longer had any illusions that it could take care of all the different interests, and it became more and more clear that specific interests "would have to take care of themselves." More, if smaller, women's groups were founded,[6] and they took as their sphere of activity the dissemination of feminist ideology, which meant that they provided aid to the victims of violence and sexual abuse, and support for the organization of self-help groups. Most of those groups followed the example of feminist groups in Western European countries such as Germany and England. Other groups paid more attention to the central problem of women's politics: the possibility of the participation of women in politics. The Women for Politics group played an important role, first by making political space for women and later on by opposing the conservative circles' campaign against abortion rights.[7] The discussion about the right to abortion was, as in many other post-Communist countries, an important part of the attempt to create a "new woman" who wouldn't be a working woman but a mother and wife. Those who wanted to create this new woman failed, and Slovenia is one of the few countries where the right to abortion is written in the constitution.[8] The credit for this resolution of this long debate during the adoption of the new constitution goes to a well-organized pro choice movement, which mounted a well-organized demonstration that included the participation of thirteen women's groups, women's initiatives inside trade unions, and ten parliamentary and nonparliamentary parties.[9] The final success was also largely due to the fact that all women deputies, a mere 11 percent of all the deputies in Parliament, were unanimous in their decision to preserve the existing rights to abortion. The whole course of events around the abortion debate demonstrated the state of women's organization in Slovenia: Women were prepared to organize themselves primarily, or only, when one of their customary rights was threatened. It should also be noted that women were visible participants in other civil society movements, especially the ecological and peace movements. But what is important in all this is that a network of women's organizations that were not party-oriented began to develop. This network determined and established the field of women's politics in Slovenia. The period of "state feminism" was followed by the period of "movements feminism," but these new structures were still located within the *ancien régime.*

SPECIAL POLITICAL INTERESTS OF WOMEN

After the fall of the Berlin Wall, political parties typical of classical representative democracy started to form in Slovenia as well. 1990 was marked by the first democratic election; in 1991, Slovenia declared independence. During this period, the political interests of women were recognized as the legitimate interests of one social group, but little attention was paid to their implementation. "Great issues" were, once again, in the forefront. In the place of the previous all-embracing subject, the "working class," there emerged the "Slovenian nation." The problem of the creation of the sovereign state of the Slovenian nation was the central issue to which all others had to be subordinated, including the question of the position of women in society.

In part this subordination seemed to stem from the popular assumption that once women had gained the right to vote, men and women were legally and politically equal, and therefore it was individuals' free choice as to if and how they would exercise those rights. Such a persuasion glorifies the importance of the formal equality of women and ignores their fact that social inequalities have an important impact on their politically unequal position.[10] The inferior socioeconomic starting point of women, together with the traditional, gender-specific division of labor around household needs and the education and care of children, hinders the more balanced passing of men and women from the private to the public sphere and politics. The warning that democracy in the home and the family was the foundation for a democratic society had already been given by J. S. Mill when he argued that marriage had to be a partnership of free and equal individuals.[11] Or, as C. Pateman argued, "Neither the equal opportunity of liberalism nor the active, participatory democratic citizenship of *all* the people can be achieved without radical changes in personal and domestic life."[12]

The question often raised in feminist circles was whether a democracy that did not care about the political equality of women was a democracy in the strict sense of the word. Such a democracy was called "unfinished democracy" by some feminists and "male democracy" by others.[13] Regardless of the fact that both designations can be theoretically debated, it was agreed that there was something wrong with a democracy that did not care about the political representation of women and was satisfied merely with formal legal equality. To solve the problem, feminist theory insisted that either the concept of democracy or the concept of politics had to be reconsidered. Either focus had to concentrate on the creation of a democracy that would consider gender as one of the main social categories and as a central—not peripheral—issue. This democracy would have to reconfigure what Z. Eisenstein, for example, describes as the situation in most of the former socialist systems: "someplace between [a] liberal and socialist vision of patriarchal society, where the tension between individual freedom and gender equality has not been resolved."[14]

POLITICAL PARTIES AND WOMEN'S INTERESTS

Political parties, formed at the end of the 1980s, did not at first think of women as political subjects but rather as a more or less important part of the national voting body to which the parties had to turn for support on certain occasions. The first parties' platforms paid no attention to so-called women's politics with the exception of the former League of Socialist Youth—now the Liberal Democracy of Slovenia—which accepted the demand for a "ministry of women" in their congress.

The run-up to the first multiparty election in 1990 already showed that few women would be elected to the new parliament, since they were poorly represented on the lists of candidates. *Women were the losers of the first democratic election.* Their percentage in the parliament was half of what it had been at the time of socialism, falling from 24 percent to 11 percent. The outcome would have been even worse were it not for the proportional electoral system. There were 26 women and 214 men elected to the first Slovenian parliament as deputies. After the second national election in 1992, the proportion of women increased a little, so that there are 12 women deputies (13 percent) in the present-day National Assembly. Such a result ranks somewhere in the middle on the scale of European states.

The relatively low participation of women in politics is the result of several factors. In modern—representative—democracies, apart from a *favorable, positive political atmosphere* (where mass media play a key role), the participation of women is primarily influenced by the *electoral system* together with structurally imposed conditions. It is well known that the proportional system offers more opportunities for women to be elected. In countries where the critical limit of the participation of women in politics (one third) has been exceeded, use has been made of special strategies by means of which a certain number of places on parties' lists of candidates is ensured. A well-known strategy is the *quota system.* For the majority of parties in Slovenia, though, the relatively low level of participation of women in politics seems to present no serious problem, and therefore no special actions have been taken. However, one begins to detect some changes.

Besides the eight parties whose representatives were elected to the Slovenian parliament in 1992, there are many more nonparliamentary parties. The ideological spectrum of the parliamentary parties is heterogeneous—it varies from the strong nationalistic ideology of the Slovene National Party (SNS) to the promotion of traditional and Christian values advocated by the Slovenian Christian Democrats (SKD), the Slovenian Popular Party (SLS), and—to some extent—the Social Democratic Party of Slovenia (SDSS). There is also a spread from the centrist orientation of Liberal Democracy of Slovenia (LDS), with its strong emphasis on the concept of an individual citizen's rights, to a strong emphasis on collective rights by the left-wing United List of Social Democrats (ZLSD).[15]

The objectives and principles of party programs regarding the situation of women differ from each other. They range from the programs that do not mention women at all (SNS, SDSS) to the one that expresses the equality of men and women (SLS), and the one that declares it is the duty of the state to enable women to pass from the private to the public sphere on equal terms with men (LDS). There is also the program that advocates that the status of a woman as a mother and a housewife be equal to the status of an employed woman (SKD).

On the level of the use of language, these parties are even less sensitive to women's expectations. All the parties (except LDS, which consistently uses both male and female gender forms) use only male forms. Even women's groups within or connected to some parties either use male and female forms inconsistently or use only male forms (SDSS, SKD). Statistics shows that the membership of women in parliamentary parties ranges from 61 percent (SKD), which is an extremely high percentage, through a number of parties where women represent a third of their membership (SLS, 33.3 percent; ZLSD, 37.3 percent; LDS, 28.2 percent), to some parties that have 20 percent or less of women members (SDSS, 20.3 percent; SNS, 18.5 percent). However, the participation of women in important bodies of a party is not in proportion to their membership percentage; it is lower in all the parties. There is only one party in which the participation of women in the highest bodies of the party approaches one third (26.6 percent in LDS), whereas in other parties the percentage varies from 22 percent (SLS) to 10 percent (SDSS). At the highest level, there is no woman president of a party; three parties have a woman vice president, and recently one party got a woman secretary-general. But in no party is the percentage of women less than 10 percent of its entire membership. One parliamentary party has no women among their Members of Parliament (SDSS). The others have one, two, or three women Members of Parliament, which means that the percentage varies from 9 percent in larger parties to 20 percent in smaller ones.

It is the rhetorical strategy of supporting women's interests that prevail in the policies of the Slovenian political parties. Perhaps this is because verbal support has not been followed by the admission of women to the important bodies of the various parties. Only two parliamentary parties in Slovenia now have no special women's "suborganization"; all the others have women's associations, clubs, committees, or forums, which are linked to the activity of the party as a whole but have formed their own aims and methods of work.[16] Women have a stronger impact on a party's policies through the demands of their own policies, at least in the areas that are important to them.

As we have mentioned before, feminist groups formed in the 1980s (Women's Section of the Sociological Association, Lilith, Women for Politics, the Initiative Association, the Women's Initiative from Koper) "triggered a set of burning issues": the right of sexual freedom; the distinction between the private, the public, and the political; violence within the family and against women; the image of women in media and in schoolbooks; and the need for women to enter politics. They also suggested many solutions regarding the status of women.[17] Despite the fact that these groups were small and had no possibility of directly changing reality, they have accomplished a lot. They have served as the "guilty conscience" of the society, alerted the press and other media to possible adverse effects of parliamentary decisions on the status of women, and offered help to women however they needed it, either as victims or as underprivileged but outstanding women. They did not claim to be political groups, they preferred to be recognized as pressure groups. Their organizational forms were loose, nonhierarchical, and without strong membership.

The newly formed women's groups connected to political parties are different. They proclaim themselves political groups, and their political activities are oriented toward greater gains in political power for women. They do have a formal organizational structure, with membership and leadership, programs, and statutes. One cannot identify them as feminist groups, nor as women's groups with a feminist orientation. In some cases they are very patriarchally oriented, with a strong emphasis on traditional values (women as mothers, the demand to treat employed women and mothers equally in terms of legislation), which could be said of the Slovenian Women's Alliance (connected to SKD).

Other new women's groups modeled more on feminist groups have recently appeared. They are rather small and their field of work is offering help to those who need it. Some whose work has had a particularly strong impact have established hotlines that deal with the sexual abuse of women and young girls. But these groups are not connected to or coordinated with one another; there are no joint projects and good work often does not bring desired results. They tend to have unfriendly and hostile attitudes toward politics and toward women who work in politics or for the state.

CONCLUSION

At least for the time being, it is the parties that dominate the political sphere in Slovenia. It is for this reason that it is important for women to occupy prominent positions in the highest levels of parties. It also seems that the necessity of breaking through the "voting machinery" has gained ground in women's considerations of politics. The negative attitude of women (especially Western feminists) toward official parties—which caused the formation of separate or autonomous women's organizations through which women tried to influence political changes from the outside—seems to have changed, too, possibly because of the inefficiency of such a policy. Now there is much more talk about "taking advantage" of the institutions of the political system in order to change the position of women. This does not mean that the activities of the "nonpolitical" women's groups or the civil society activities in general are unimportant. On the contrary, from the point of view of women who are becoming more and more aware of their own position, these groups have developed a whole network of women's organizations and laid the foundation for the articulation of the women question. But these groups are different and they cannot always cooperate. One example of the problem is the previously mentioned debate about abortion rights, where an alliance of civil society organizations (among which there were also women's groups) opposed constitutional abortion rights. Another recent example is the proposed introduction of a three-year maternity leave, supposedly due to concern over population growth. This proposal has been put forward by some M.P.'s of the SKD and supported by some women's groups. But it is not difficult to see that this proposal cannot be considered a part of feminist cultural politics. On the contrary, the prolongation of maternity leave from the existing one year to the proposed three years, without a provision in the law that would make it mandatory for a child's father to take half of the parental leave (which is not at all what the bill's proposer had in mind), would have serious consequences: In a society in which a majority of women were employed in the time of socialism, women would now be forced back home and would become, to a great extent, merely mothers and wives.

What is interesting for Slovenia is the fact that, through the mechanisms of official policy, there is a growing awareness of the importance of the coexistence of the elements of civil society, on the one hand, and politics in the narrow sense, on the other. Especially in a time when a new social order is beginning to take shape, it is of the utmost importance for women—in order to preserve the rights already achieved as well as gain new ones—to combine the mechanisms of both civil society and politics. There are too many serious issues at stake for women to leave politics to men. In order to build a women-friendly state and democratize everyday life, it is necessary that the civil society movements, nongovernmental organizations, and "femocrats" each work in their own fields without fierce jealousy and cooperate as efficiently as they possibly can on certain questions that are important to all of them.[18]

NOTES

1. Maca Jogan, "Women on the Way from Partial Familial to Entire Social Emancipation," in Maca Jogan et al., *Women and Discrimination* (Ljubljana: Delavska Enotnost, 1986), p. 32.
2. Tanja Rener, "Women Establishing Themselves in the Delegate System," in Jogan et al., op. cit., p. 127.
3. Vida Tomsic was one of the Communist politicians who had been actively engaged in sociopolitical work for a long time. Among other things she was a president of the Federal Council for Family Planning.
4. Zillah Eisenstein, "Eastern European Male Democracies: A Problem of Unequal Equality," in N. Funk and M. Mueller (eds.), *Gender Politics and Post-Communism* (New York: Routledge 1993), p. 308.
5. Similar understandings can be found in the works of some other authors as well. Z. Eisenstein, for example, speaks of "state-enforced feminism"; D. Dahlerup uses the term *statefeminism* to designate the institutionalization of the politics of equal opportunities and the tenure of important functions in particular sections by the "femocrats," that is, women officials who used to be members of women's movements.
6. Here we should mention the lesbian section of Lilith, established in 1987, which published its own journal *Lesbosin*, organized lesbian film festivals, and worked on the question of the socialization of homosexuality; also the first SOS Telephone for Women and Children Victims of Violence, founded in 1989, from which there later developed other groups, such as the Women's Self-Help Group and the Women's Consultancy.
7. Women for Politics also published a book on abortion: Eva D. Bahovec (ed.), *Abortion—A Right to Choose?! Legal, Medical, Sociological, Moral, and Political Aspects* (Ljubljana 1991).
8. See the Constitution of the Republic of Slovenia, article 55 (Ljubljana, 1992): "Persons shall be free to decide whether to bear children. The state shall ensure that persons have every opportunity to exercise this freedom and shall create such conditions as enable parents to freely choose whether or not to bear children."
9. The demonstration around Parliament took place on December 11, 1991. There were a few thousand participants, from different generations, both men and women.
10. Carole Pateman, *The Disorder of Women* (Cambridge: Polity Press, 1989), p. 214.
11. John Stuart Mill, "The Subjection of Women," in J. S. Mill and H. Taylor Mill, *Essays on Sex and Equality* (Chicago and London: University of Chicago Press, 1970 [1869]), p. 235.

12. Pateman, op. cit., p. 222.

13. The concept of "unfinished democracy" can be found in the works of Scandinavian feminist authors (see, for example, E. Haavio-Mannila [eds.], trans. C. Badcock, *Unfinished Democracy* [Oxford: Pergamon Press, 1985]). The term "male democracy" is also quite current; it can be found in the works of many authors from the socialist camp (see N. Funk and M. Mueller [eds.], *Gender Politics and Post-Communism* [New York: Routledge 1993]).

14. Eisenstein, op. cit., p. 305.

15. All the data about parties and their women's activities has been taken from Governmental Office for Women's Politics, *Women in the Political Parties* (Ljubljana, 1994).

16. These are the Minerva Club of the Liberal-Democratic Party, the Women's Committee of Social Democrats of the Social Democratic Party of Slovenia, the Slovenian Women's Association of the Slovenian Christian Democratic Party, and the Women's Fraction of the United List of Social Democrats.

17. "Action for Equality, Development and Peace, National Report for the Fourth World Conference on Women, Government of the Republic of Slovenia," Office for Women's Politics (Ljubljana, 1995), p. 12.

18. Although, as we can see, many women in politics and women's groups are not committed to feminist issues and perspectives.

< 13 >

Hungarian Women in Politics

Andrea Petö

In the past, women have been used as soldiers and activists, only to be pushed back later into their "traditional places." When power was redistributed in times of transition, women also took their place in the queue, but it turned out that there was nothing for sale. And after each of the transitions in Hungary—in 1918, 1945, and 1989—the same questions were raised: Why are women so weak in the field of politics? Why are they so tragically and continuously underrepresented in politics?[1] Political scientists often use the red carpet as a symbol for Communism, saying that it covered the whole society and masked its heterogeneity. After the collapse of Communism, the red carpet was rolled back and, surprisingly, what has been found is what was previously there. If we want to examine the roots of the so-called underrepresentation of women in politics, we should briefly explore the case study of Hungary.

"GRÜNDENZEIT": THE BEGINNINGS

By 1914 there was in existence a network of women's societies. Along with trade unions, charity, professional, educational, and religious groups also became an integral part of society. On the level of "great politics," women's particular interest appeared with the fight for suffrage. Hungarian women's right to representation in politics was based on two different claims. The first was the claim for *equality*. A new type of paid employment, clerical jobs in offices, had been opened for women in Hungary, enabling them to leave their secure, traditional workplace—the home. As they were doing the same type of job and paying the same pension contribution as their male colleagues, they demanded equal rights for the same work. The Association of Female Clerks, founded in 1890, nourished the future leaders of the Feminist Association. Their monthly journal, founded in 1904, was entitled *Woman and Society*. It argued that if, in the framework of bourgeois society, women were granted the same liberal individual rights as men, then women would one day have the same status as men.

The second type of women's movement was based on *difference.* These were moderate movements that tried to improve the status of women in society using available cultural means. They defined the key problem as unpaid domestic labor. In this framework there were two types of solution: a *utopian* solution, in which the burden of domestic labor would be taken away from women by society (this solution usually implied the necessity of state intervention and depended on the availability of central financial sources), and a *traditional* one, which claimed that women were the center of the family and that the point of a women's movement was to help them to perform this role better. Neither of these movements was political; they did not organize rallies or mass demonstrations in the pre-1914 period.

THE INTERWAR YEARS

In the interwar period there were two important changes affecting Hungarian women's participation in politics. The first was a new limited women's suffrage, and the other was the foundation of mass women's associations, some of which had an explicitly political character.

Universal suffrage was a product of the revolutions of 1918–1919. After the fall of the Hungarian Bolshevik revolution, the Horthy regime introduced women's suffrage with some restrictions on who qualified: women had to be thirty years old and have their own income, three children, and four grades of elementary education or a degree from a higher educational institution. The election laws of 1922, 1925, and 1938 retained these restrictions on women's access to politics. Complete universal suffrage was introduced only in 1945.[2] The first female M.P. in the Hungarian parliament, Margit Slachta, was elected in 1922. In 1925 Anna Kéthly, a Social Democrat, joined the exclusive club of female M.P.s, the membership of which did not exceed two until after 1945. There were two active paradigms for women's participation, a Catholic family-centered model and an emancipatory social democratic model. Both urged an increase in state legislation that would protect families, mothers, and children (see table 1).

Mass women's associations developed during the 1920s and 1930s. The total number of associations in Budapest in 1932 was 2,236, and, of these, the number of women's associations was 114.[3] The registers of these associations indicate that the average membership in women's associations was between 150 and 300. In this period, women's societies provided services that were later taken over by the state (hospitals, nurseries, insurance companies). The membership of the National Association of Employed Women grew to 183,636 because it ran an efficient employment office. The National Association of War Invalids, Widows, and Orphans Foundations had massive membership. Working-class women were unionized, either by the Catholic Church or by the Social Democrats. Peasant women filled out the membership of religious girls' and women's circles. The religious women's associations strengthened the values of the conservative, right-wing women's societies. Political parties also sought women's votes, though not their active leadership.[4] A few influential patriotic women's associations, such as the National Association of Hungarian Women, were also formed after 1918.[5]

Table 1 Women's Participation in the Hungarian Parliament and Governments
(1922 and 1994)[a]

Year of Election	Number of Women Deputies in the Parliament (and percent of total)	Woman Serving as President of the Parliament	Woman Serving as a Minister	Name of the Ministry
1922	1			
1931	1			
1935	2			
1939	2			
1944	12 (2.4%)			
1945	14 (3.3%)			
1947	22 (5.3%)			
1949	71 (17.6%)		1949–1951, Anna Ratkó	Minister of Welfare
1953	52 (17.4%)		1956, Anna Kéthly	State Minister
1958	62 (18%)		1958–1961, Valéria Benke	Minister of Culture
1963	62 (18.2%)	1963–1967, Istvánné Vass	1955–1971, Józsefné Vass	Minister of Light Industry
1967	69 (19.7%)			
1971	84 (23.8%)		1971–1980, Keserü Jánosné	Minister of Light Industry
1975	101 (28.6%)			
1980	106 (30.1%)			
1985	80 (20.7%)		1987–1990, Judit Csehák	Minister of Welfare and Health
1990	27 (7%)		1990, Katalin Botos	Minister Without Portfolio
1994	43 (11.1%)		1994–95, Kósáné Kovács Magda	Minister of Labor

a. Jónás Károly, *Pártpanoptikum 1948–1990* (Budapest, 1990).

The goal of protecting the nation brought together the conservative upper-middle-class and the religious and fascist lower-middle-class women's movements on the eve of World War II. Subordination to German war aims meant that conservative upper-middle-class women joined in supporting the fascist hierarchical women's movements on the common ground of anti-Semitism.

After 1945 a new option opened because the National Association of Hungarian Women was banned, but the other women's societies were too weak to use this moment to renew their activity. The place of the National Association of Hungarian Women was filled by the Communist mass women's organization, the Democratic Association of Hungarian Women, which absorbed all existing Hungarian women's movements.

HUNGARIAN WOMEN AND THE RED CARPET

After World War II, because of the extension of universal suffrage, women's branches of the different political parties became more important. Hungary suffered considerable war damage, so the years after the war brought state intervention in social welfare politics. It was the Communist Party that first recognized the importance of the welfare system in building up a stable electorate. The number of female deputies increased considerably in the election of 1949, the first election orchestrated by the Hungarian Communists. The private view of the Communists about the role of women in society remained as traditional as that of any other "traditional" political party,[6] but after the shock of the 1945 elections, in which the new women voters were generally blamed for the electoral success of the conservative Smallholders Party, their public strategy changed. As Mátyás Rákosi, the general secretary of the Hungarian Communist Party, put it: "These are women who have become used to fastidious, slow and unrewarding work, and we can rely on this."[7] But more cynically, this new interest by the Party in women weakened the women's societies.[8] The state intervened in areas that had been the province of the charity societies. Religious societies also fell victim to the Kulturkampf between the Communist Party and the churches.

In a sense, Hungarian women's societies participated in their appropriation by the state insofar as they maintained a traditional definition of their spheres of activity. Hungarian women's societies were not interested in helping women to break out of their private domain into the public sphere; they actually preserved the public-private dichotomy by clearly delimiting the scope of women's activities. The heterogeneity of civil organizations may seem to produce a colorful picture, but it obscures the fact that the one task that was out of question for women was politics. When, after the storm of World War II, women's associations renewed their activity, they all denied that they had been dealing with politics before the war. As the leader of the Lutheran Girls Society declared during a secret police investigation in Orosháza in June 1947, "Our association never took a position in a political matter, it is even truer since the members are young girls."[9] Women's societies by and large claimed to be harmless in the realm of politics and thereby abdicated the right to directly influence policy.

This trap could have been avoided in two possible ways. Women could have either joined already-existing political parties or created a new, independent movement. The latter course had been pursued by the Feminist Association in 1904, but with limited success, due in part to their elitist attitude and their wish to remain independent of any political party. The former course was taken by the Democratic Association of Hungarian Women, founded by Communist women in 1945 as part of the Communist Party's response to the first round of elections, which voted in representatives of the Smallholders. Women were "backward, unpolitical, and undeveloped," declared the secretariat responsible for women's issues in the Communist Party: "Women are not at the proper political level, they have not realized who is responsible for the present situation. The voters did not know what they were doing. We have to get back the votes of women.

Women should go to agitate among women."[10] But as members of the Communist Party, the leaders of the Democratic Association of Hungarian Women aimed to destroy other women's societies and incorporate them into a mass organization of the entire female population of Hungary, which would serve the Communist transformation of the country. This hierarchically organized mass group successfully implemented the Party's decision to force the emancipation of women by mobilizing them into the labor force. But in 1956, when a Stalinist politics that tried to destroy traditional families proved not to be a viable alternative, a conceptual change in gender politics in Hungary occurred. Patriarchal family values were embraced, and it was agreed that the state, meaning the Party, should not involve itself with the family.[11]

HUNGARIAN WOMEN WITHOUT A RED CARPET

The end of Communism, in 1989, saw the emergence of a new and highly fragmented women's movement. The large, centrally controlled women's organization was shattered by the collapse of the Party state. But the division of interest and activity between society and politics remained. The Alliance of Hungarian Women was the successor organization to the Democratic Association of Hungarian Women. The Women's Committee of the National Alliance of Hungarian Trade Unions claimed to be able to mobilize women in mass numbers. Religious organizations such as the Christian Female Union, the Female Board of the Hungarian Evangelic Church, the Hungarian Calvinist Female Alliance, the Association of Social Fraternity (Hungarian Catholic Church), and the Alliance of Hungarian Jewish Communities are continuing the rich Hungarian tradition of women's participation in clerical life. Religious women have also formed NGOs, such as the Society of Girl Scouts.

The phenomenon of NGOs has been important since 1989. These can be divided into professional and political groups. Professional NGOs include the Association of Enterprising Women, the Alliance of Graduate Women, the Science for Women Foundation, the Association of Policewomen, and the Association of Nurses. Political NGOs exist in the form of foundations or offices that offer comprehensive programs. These include the MONA Foundation and the Ombudswomen's Program Office. Other NGOs aim to help women in their traditional roles: the Alliance of Households, the Association of Larger Families, and the Society for Equal Opportunities. Women Together for Women Against Violence Association and the Esther Society operate hotlines for those women who are victims of violence. The Feminist Network is a successor organization to the Feminist Association and is closer to the Western concept of women's movement; it also publishes a feminist quarterly. The Gypsy Mothers of Hungary is one of the few organizations that serves the interest of one of the most powerful minorities in Hungary. In fact, women's issues are often handled in the framework of minority groups. The Hungarian dissent movement developed closely with environmental groups and this explains the larger number of women's societies active in environmental questions. Astonishingly small is the number of local women's clubs, given their role as pioneering institutions in the nineteenth century. At the moment, there are two Women's Clubs, in Veszprém and in Sopron.[12]

POLITICS

After 1989, with the end of "socialist affirmative action," the number of women deputies in the parliament decreased dramatically to 7 percent. The high percentage of women's representation in the pre-1989 parliament was secured not only by government quotas, but also by the influence of corporate bodies such as parties, trade unions, and state-organized women's associations. But this greater number of women representatives under Communism did not fundamentally matter, since the parliaments were show-cases for the Communist Party, which really decided all the issues outside of the system of representative government.

Since 1990, there has been a gradual shift in the way women deputies are elected. Initially, they were most likely to gain seats if they ran on national party lists. Recently, the number of women deputies elected from individual constituencies has increased, which shows that women slowly but surely are becoming acceptable as politicians (see table 2). While fewer than one fifth of the deputies elected directly in individual constituencies were women, women were more than one third of those who received the most votes as individual candidates.[13] As was the case under Communism, female M.P.'s now have a strong presence in the parliamentary committees on social, family and educational issues. As a result, a joint subcommittee on women's issues has been convened as part of the Committee on Human Rights, Religious, and Minority Issues. It remains, however, standard for women to subordinate their demands to the main political discourse.[14]

The recent foundation of the Secretariat on Women's Policy at the Ministry of Culture as a possible call for a future independent governmental institution on women's issues has already raised the doubts of some NGOs as to the efficiency of the reconstruction of centrally organized governmental bureaucracy on implementing substantial changes in this field.

GENDER AND FEMINISM

Since 1989, women researchers have taken up such fundamental issues as housing, employment, economic and sexual rights, subjectivity, body image, sexuality, and media

Table 2 Breakdown of Female M.P.'s by Route to Parliament in 1990 and 1994 (%)[a]

Route to Parliament	1990	1994
From Individual Constituencies	18.5	34.6
From Regional Party Lists	29.6	37.2
From National Party Lists	51.5	27.9

[a.] National Report of the Republic of Hungary for the United Nations Fourth World Conference on Women (1995), Table I.5/3.

representation from a gendered point of view. Geographically, the interest in gender studies centers is exclusively based in the main university towns, and it comes from women intellectuals in the fields of sociology, economics, journalism, and, to a lesser extent, history.

The current situation contrasts with the 1970s. Then, emphasis was on sociology and economics, since research on women's employment was of interest to the state. These fields nurtured many of the women academics who became sensitive to gender issues. In the Communist era, research institutes affiliated with the Hungarian Academy of Sciences enjoyed relative independence in comparison with the faculty of the universities. But their influence was also small.

Post-1989 Hungarian feminism has many possibilities, but it also confronts new problems. Some advocates for women are imprisoned in the socialist emancipatory paradigm that linked women's status to their economic roles. Rejecting state-sponsored economic emancipation and still continuing to advocate women's full employment in a situation of major economic restructuring is not a promising standpoint. The challenge for a new feminist economics is to address the new and disturbing trends in women's employment. What can Hungarian women do to diminsh their increasingly unfavorable situation during modernization?

Another issue is the status of feminism itself. Feminism in Hungary has always been, with the exception of the turn of the century, an isolated stream. Feminists were considered aliens by conservative Christians, and bourgeois by the labor movement. Unfortunately, not too much research has been done on the roots of this antifeminism, which continued into the post-1989 era. The image of a feminist in the contemporary Eastern European press is of a masculine, man-hating lesbian. Not only has there been no research on the sources of these myths, but much current research has introduced some myths of its own. One of these new myths is that everything that has some relationship to women is good, modern, democratic, etc.; what is evil and bad is traditional patriarchy. The term *gender*, partly because of translation problems, refers only to women. The new researchers blame the media for perpetuating patriarchy through pornography and its endorsement of misogynist ideas. But the media only reflects long-standing views about the political incapacity of women.

One question never raised in the women's movement is related to legitimacy. Are women better able to represent their own political interests? Who decides what are women's interests? Although there are some attempts to form independent, alternative women's groups or parties, so far they have not been successful. In the long run, however, that is the only chance. Women's political movements have a chance for revival if their leaders realize that discrimination has social and historical roots that are fixed by power structures. Additionally, mass public support is needed. But how to mobilize it? Women politicians must define women's problems within the terms of the dominant political discourse. Academics must attend to questions of citizenship instead of arguing about the meaning of the past. In East-Central Europe the democratic system is new and fragile, so the redefinition of political and social citizenship to include women as individuals is a difficult task. We need to reconsider and rethink these concepts of citizenship in their specific Hungarian historical and political contexts. For it is within the specific Hungarian context that the meanings of citizenship, democracy, and feminism will be defined.

NOTES

1. Mária Neményi, "Miért nincs Magyarországon nõmozgalom?" [Why Is There No Women's Movement in Hungary?] in Hadas Miklós (ed.), *Férfiuralom* [Patriarchy] (Replika, 1994), pp. 235–I 245.
2. For more on this see Irén Simándy, "A nök választójoga a századfordulótól 1938-ig Magyarországon." [Female Suffrage in Hungary from the Turn of the Century till 1938]. Unpublished MA thesis, ELTE, Budapest, 1995.
3. Dobrovits Sándor, "Budapest egyesületei" [Associations of Budapest], *Statisztikai Közlemények* 74 (1936), pp. 119–66. The registration documents of the Hungarian associations were destroyed during the siege of Budapest in 1944–45. These statistics are the only available source; however, we have to consider two methodological problems. The first is virtual membership; in the submitted documents the associations indicate the highest possible membership figures. The second is the problem of multiple membership, for respectable members of the society were members of several associations and societies.
4. From the statutes of the National Association of Hungarian Women: "The Association incorporates all Hungarian women, Catholic or Protestant, who insist on Christian belief and love the Hungarian nation. Nothing else was required from the members, but that they should not be influenced by demagogic agitators, but to demand courageously and persistently that their representative should be a good Christian Hungarian person and a member of that party which is fighting for Christian ideas." (Budapest, 1930).
5. Patriotic associations such as the National Association of Hungarian Women had 490,000 members countrywide. The Pro-Hungary World Association of Hungarian Women had 7,000 members, and the Sacred Crown Association of Hungarian Women had 1,790 members; these were not formed in the traditional framework and aims of women's associations.
6. See Andrea Petö, "As He Saw Her: Gender Politics in Secret Party Documents," in Andrea Petö and Mark Pittaway (eds.), *Women in History—Women's History* CEU History Department Working Paper Series, no. 1 (Budapest: Central European University, 1994), pp. 107–121.
7. Speech of Mátyás Rákosi at a general meeting on women, Budapest, October 21, 1945, protecting women who were accused of being so obsolete that the Smallholders Party could easily win the elections of 1945. Politikatörténeti Intézet Levéltára [Archives of Institute for Political History] 276.f. 19. cs. 1. öe., p. 100.
8. See Andrea Petö, "As the Storm Approached: The Last Years of the Hungarian Women's Societies Before the Stalinist Takeover," in Andrea Petö (ed.), *CEU History Department Yearbook 1994–1995* (Budapest: Central European University, 1995), pp. 181–204.
9. Uj Magyar Levéltár [New Hungarian Archive], XIX-B-1-h. 563.15.
10. Politikatörténeti Intézet Levéltára [Archives of Institute for Political History], 276.f. 19. cs. 1. öe. p. 105.
11. For more on this, see Joanna Goven, "Anti-politics of Anti-feminism," unpublished Ph.D. thesis, University of California, Berkeley, (1994), pp. 115–21.
12. For two differing lists of Hungarian women's organizations, NGOs, and party sections, see the *National Report of Republic of Hungary* for the United Nations Fourth World Conference on Women (1995) Appendixes II and III. See also "*A nök szerepe a pártok politikai programjában*"

[The Role of Women in Party Programs], conference paper organized by Friedrich Ebert Stiftung and MONA (Budapest, 1994), pp. 131–133.

13. National Report of Republic of Hungary for the United Nations Fourth World Conference on Women (1995).

14. On the pro-abortion campaign, see, for example, Mária Adamik, "Feminism and Hungary," in Nanette Funk and Magda Müller (eds.), *Gender Politics and Post-Communism* (New York: Routledge, 1993), pp. 207–212, esp. p. 208.

< 14 >

The Women's Movement in Bulgaria After Communism

Krassimira Daskalova

What follows is an overview of the state of the women's "movement" in Bulgaria several years after the celebrated changes in Eastern Europe that began in 1989. I am interested in how women's organizations formulate and pursue their goals, which obstacles they typically encounter, and the character and prospects of the movement in general.

Women's organizations proliferated in Bulgaria after 1989 (their number reached thirty-five in 1995), quite in tune with the burgeoning of political life in general. They are of different types. Some of the most important exist within, or are closely connected with, the existing political parties and the major parliamentary parties in particular. But the price of being linked to political parties is high, as women's claims are often subjugated to party interests and party discipline (especially since women activists enter the National Assembly on party lists). This does not bother the activists of such organizations very much, as they conceive of themselves as party activists in the first place, trying to capture women's votes for the party by addressing audiences of women. In the case of the party that is the heir of the former official Women's Union, this mimicry is hardly surprising, but the same pattern is observed in the case of women's organizations attached to other parties as well. One hesitates to define this type of party-dependent women's organization as part of a "women's movement" proper, as their scope of autonomous action is very limited and their agenda—which seems to serve party propaganda purposes in the first place—changes on a notice from the party leadership.

One organization of this type is the Democratic Union of Women, the abovementioned heir of the official Women's Union from the Communist period, which has, of course, duly renamed itself to make an emphatic verbal demarcation from the past.[1] The platform of the Union abounds in declarations of good intentions, phrased in very general terms reminiscent of the former resounding and hollow style: The organization undertakes to express the interests and to defend the rights of Bulgarian women, and of the family and children; it undertakes to work for the attainment of real equality and to support women's striving for self-fulfillment and spiritual uplifting; a concern is voiced for the dignity, rights, and freedoms of women. The Union undertakes, furthermore, to campaign for economically "justifiable" social protection of the Bulgarian family and women under the conditions of a market economy, for the participation of women in all power structures, for reduction of unemployment and the removal of all obstacles to the professional self-fulfillment of women, for the support of newly formed families and families with many children, and for the protection of women against violence (and crimes against the person in particular). The Union also purports to work for "recognition in the laws" of the social utility and significance of motherhood (and of the domestic work of women) and of parenthood in general as well as for the strengthening of the family and the observation of children's rights.[2]

This is at best a welfare agenda, aimed at the "protection" of women (and, in the same breath, of the family); at worst, it is a conservative stance aimed at preservation of traditional gender roles. It reveals a patronizing attitude toward women, viewed "from above" by a condescending and caring agency. The long patriarchal tradition of the party transpires behind the thin veil of women's activism. Besides being so general as to be meaningless, such declarations are unrealistic and thus, in the present situation, clearly demagogic.[3] Another document of the same Union states that the participation of women in earning the family income "substantially limits the time that women can devote to the rearing and the instruction of children," which in turn presents "one of the factors for the upsurge of a host of undesirable phenomena, of which most difficult to overcome are juvenile delinquency, underage prostitution, drug addiction, adherence to religious sects that are foreign to our traditions and restrict personal freedoms, etc."[4] As is to be expected from the leaders of this organization, who inherited the socialist concept of women's emancipation, *feminism* and *feminist* are bad words that signify a threat to the normal relationships between men and women and an impingement upon the "traditional Bulgarian values" of love, marriage, and family.[5] If I have devoted so much space to this particular organization, it is not only because of its ties with the strongest political party in Bulgaria but also as a way of describing other women's organizations in Bulgaria of similar persuasion and rhetoric.[6]

There are women's organizations (or women's "clubs") affiliated with other political parties such as the Bulgarian Agrarian People's Union, the Bulgarian Social Democratic Party (the Federation of Women's Clubs), the Bulgarian Green Parliament (Women for Pure, Natural Habitat), and the National Ecology Club. Their public activities are very much dependent on the views and instructions of their respective party leadership; while intentions and programs are always in good supply, resources remain meager and organizations, especially local organizations, remain underdeveloped; activities are accordingly severely handicapped. The women activists from the Social Democrats in particular are convinced that the fact that their party is not represented in Parliament constitutes a grave obstacle to the wider propagation of their views and the promotion of their initiatives.[7]

The so-called Christian Women's Movement presents a curious mixture of nationalism and Christian patriarchalism.[8] Thus it postures as a speaker for women "who consider their situation as mothers and wives to be honorable enough, and conceive of it as a supreme fulfillment of their duties as citizens," and for whom "biology is destiny." It professes to be for the recognition of the right of women to choose between "bearing many children and a professional career." But, as the first alternative leads, in its view, to economic and social inequality, the organization favors the recognition of "the social utility of the mother's work" and the restoration of family traditions as a means to the "humanization of the society." At the same time, this Christian organization takes a liberal view on abortion and on pornography (provided it is restricted to "special zones").[9]

Something needs to be said about the links between women's initiatives and the ecological movement in particular. The Bulgarian ecological movement originated in the late 1980s in the town of Russe (exposed to heavy air pollution from a Rumanian plant across the Danube) as a protest movement and a genuine civic initiative. Since many women were active in it, it acquired ecofeminist traits. In the events immediately preceding and following November 10, 1989 (when the long-term Bulgarian Communist ruler Todor Zhivkov was replaced in a palace revolt), the ecological movement became politicized with a manifestly anti-Communist profile. Subsequent developments led to the glaring but quite understandable failure of the ecological agenda in Bulgaria, especially after the anti-Communist opposition (which promoted it) won the elections of October 1991 and formed a government. Since the ecological organizations no longer served directly political (anti-Communist) goals, they lost their original raison d'être, and the present economic collapse makes any ecological initiatives seem entirely utopian. The NGOs that now parade under the sign of feminist ecology lack grassroots support and are actually geared toward the possibility of receiving financial support from the institutions of the European Union (some NGOs seem to be organized solely for this purpose).[10] In any case, these groups are not to be mistaken for ecological feminism of a Western type. The two biggest trade unions in Bulgaria—the Labor Confederation (Podkrepa) and KNSB (Confederation of Independent Trade Unions in Bulgaria)[11] also have women's organizations, called "women's sections," attached to them. These are oriented toward social protection of the unionized women. While they could perhaps exert greater influence, commensurate with the influence of the trade union headquarters, the representatives of these women's organizations are not particularly active or engaged in specific initiatives for the time being. Still, trade union representatives are sometimes present at the meetings of other women's organizations (and especially of the coordinating National Women's Forum) and express support for some of their initiatives.

There exist a number of women's organizations not affiliated with parties. Perhaps most influential among these is the Bulgarian Women's Association (BWA), set up on December 18, 1993, which claimed to be heir of the biggest pre-Communist ("bourgeois") Women's Association.[12] This association claims 2,500 members and is organized on a territorial basis; it has nineteen groups in Sofia and thirty-two groups in other communities all over the country.[13] Although not affiliated with a particular political party, the Association leans toward anti-Communist or antisocialist forces. Most of the women M.P.'s of the Union of Democratic Forces—the backbone of the initial anti-Communist opposition—are at the same time members of the Bulgarian Women's Association. Through its representatives in the parliament, the BWA is trying to realize its idea of setting up a special parliamentary committee, entrusted with control over the observance of the constitutional rights of women in Bulgaria. The BWA is perhaps the most active of the women's organizations and is engaged in the widest range of activities, from the organization of free retraining courses for unemployed women to free legal counseling and free medical advice for women. The Association initiated a program that assists orphans, who must leave the homes for orphans at the age of eighteen, adapt to life "outside." The program envisions, among other things, that these orphans could be trained as social workers. The BWA also actively supports (e.g., with milk and baby food) socially weak young families and members of the Gypsy minority; it also has an educational program against drug addiction. With Dutch financial support, the BWA organized a center with "telephones of confidence," free counseling, and temporary shelter for women who had become subject to violence (the center is called Nadia, after a woman who was physically and psychically victimized).

As one may see, the bulk of this organization's activities fall within an older charity tradition so badly needed in the traumatic times of the transition. While the BWA wants to promote legislation and policies in favor of women, this is meant in a traditional projectionist and welfarist (and pronatalist) sense. Leaving general and fuzzy formulations aside, the BWA wants preferential treatment for women in some laws, e.g., the recognition of women's and mothers' work by lowering the age of retirement for the rearing of children, a tax reduction for employers who employ mothers with children below age ten or young people from the orphanages, remuneration for mothers looking after their children up to a certain age (this work being treated as employment), etc.[14] Without commenting upon the utopian element of such proposals, the fact that there is no mention of the possibility that the father may undertake care for the child(ren) is revealing of a traditional concept of women's roles. The problems of pornography and prostitution are not the focus of attention of this organization.[15]

As for feminism proper, the leaders admit their desire to learn more. In any case, this organization exemplifies the approach of nonsocialist and nonparty women's organizations to women's issues: While making sincere efforts with the very inadequate means at its disposal to help individual women and to do some charity work, it operates within traditional and widely held concepts of women's roles and identities.

Representative of a women's organization with a specific goal is the association Single Mothers (registered in 1991). It has about three hundred members: single mothers (whether divorced or unmarried), adoptive mothers, and even some single fathers. The activities of the organization are geared toward the problems of this specific group and include the struggle for social benefits, legal counseling, and financial support for the socially weak. For example, the association lodged a petition with the presidency that argued for lowering the interest rate on loans taken by single mothers for the purposes of housing; another petition, lodged with the parliament, argued for a prolongation of the retirement age for mothers who have given birth at an older age or adopted a child late in life, so that they may work and provide for their children until the latter become of age (instead of having to rely on the meager state pensions).[16]

There are, furthermore, various women's organizations along professional lines, such as the Bulgarian Association of Women in Law, Eterna (a businesswomen's club), Zherika, Women in Science (affiliated with the Union of Scholars in Bulgaria), the Association of Clubs of Women in Business and the Liberal Professions, the Club of Women Inventors, Women in the Information Technologies, etc.—all centered upon the particular professional problems of their women members. While most of these undertake restricted activities in defense of the interests of their members and some hardly do anything, others have an established international status. A case in point is the Bulgarian Association of Women in Law, set up in 1991 and receiving financial aid from the European Union. The organization undertakes to assist the parliamentary parties in the drawing up of bills that concern women, children, and the family, via participation of its members in working groups of the National Assembly. Its basic goal is the improvement of the Bulgarian legislature's record on social practice in the area of the protection of women's, children's, and family rights, and seeks to bring them into harmony with international instruments (such as the United Nations Convention on Children's Rights).[17]

Another professional women's organization, Women in Science (set up in 1993), regards as its central task the creation of more favorable conditions for the professional realization of women in science. Among the priorities of the organization is the representation of women in positions of authority in science. However, its leaders feel obliged to stress (as if in anticipated defense) that the promotion of women in science should not go against the criterion of professionalism and the priority of scholarly qualities; taking these into consideration will, according to them, actually guarantee higher positions for women in science. As one may infer from this rather defensive stance, there is a basic lack of awareness about unequal conditions between men and women in the academy. In particular, they do not address the fact that specific problems encountered by women in their scholarly careers (such as tensions about family versus career, domestic work versus professional work) place women scholars in an unfavorable situation from the outset and interfere with their professional goals, often confronting them with dramatic choices.[18] One may say that the position of this organization reflects an older, turn-of-the-century stance in the women's movement, when feminists wanted to prove the worth of women in professional life and the public sphere on male terms, without questioning the traditional division of labor between the sexes. This left women with a hard choice between work, on the one hand, and marriage and motherhood, on the other hand; or else it created the heroic (and quite unattainable) ideal of a woman combining both roles with equal success.[19]

The Association named Zherika (zheni—razvitie i kariera, risk i kriza, "women—development and career, risk and crisis") was set up in December 1994 with the ambitious goal of working for the reduction of risk among women and supporting women under stress and in psychological crisis. It assumes that the rapid social change in Bulgaria affects the lives of women much more than those of men, and that the feminization of poverty and the growing social risk place a bigger percentage of women in a crisis situation. The association envisions the establishment of a special center for risk prevention; it also purports to offer information services and medical, social, and educational counseling to its members, and to work for the better "integration of women in society."[20] Apart from the very common disease of inflated general statements and lofty-sounding but actually meaningless words (a style of expression in no way restricted to this particular organization), a somewhat technological approach to the problems of women is perceivable.

The Bulgarian Association of University Women (BAUW) was set up in 1991, restoring a historical tradition of academic women organizations of the pre-Communist period.[21] It is a women's organization of a more intellectual orientation as far as membership and goals are concerned. Because it is a member of the International Association of University Women, it recognizes the IAUW's goals as defined in its program: to support the personal, professional, and social self-fulfillment of highly educated women. The association is broadly democratic and "progressivist" but not exactly feminist.[22] On the other hand, there are among its members women who are well-read in feminist literature and some who share feminist views of one sort or another; in this sense, one can say that the organization has a profeminist bent. Besides academic representation of its members, it is currently engaged in a project for the introduction of women's studies in Bulgaria.[23]

In fact, feminist voices are rare in the present Bulgarian public space. Occasionally one may read articles by women feminists in central intellectual newspapers on literature and culture in general, such as *Literaturen Forum*, *Kultura*, and *Literaturen Vestnik*.[24] In such materials, various occasions are used to pose questions and reflect on the power relations involved in gendering and on women's roles and identities, and to criticize stereotypes about women in the Bulgarian society. But feminist sensitivity is rather the exception, even among the leaders of women's organizations. In fact, most of them emphatically disclaim feminism or, to be more precise, some caricature of it.[25] On the contrary, one can hear many of them speak in a lofty manner about motherhood, childbearing, and child-rearing and implore for the protection of women and for benefits in particular.[26]

To conclude the presentation of the various women's organizations in Bulgaria according to type, I would like to mention the National Women's Forum, a formation that purports to unite and coordinate the efforts of all existing women's organizations in Bulgaria, thus forming a sort of umbrella organization, a forum for meetings and discussion. It is on this common ground that representatives of the various women's organizations in Bulgaria meet to debate their activities, try to coordinate them, and unite their efforts on particular initiatives while preserving their own profile and organizational autonomy. In fact, the National Women's Forum was conceived as a sort of interest association to lobby the legislative and executive branches of government, the Church, and various public bodies on behalf of the interests of women on particular issues.[27] It also provides representation for Bulgarian women at various international conferences and meetings. However, as one may expect given the different profiles of the constitutive women's organizations and the links of some of them with competing political parties, the formation of unified opinion and action is extremely difficult. This is not to say that the existence of this organization is superfluous, as it provides a neutral place for debate on women's issues and for deploying various approaches to them, even if accord is hard to achieve.

Insofar as this short discussion of various women's organizations in Bulgaria may give a glimpse of the present condition of the women's movement in Bulgaria, one may point to the following characteristics. To begin with, affiliation with political parties is strong, and for many women activists it is a preferred pattern. While this situation is clearly continuous with a time when women's goals and aspirations were chained to Communist objectives and party organization, the tradition of direct party affiliation predates Communist rule (and was then shared with most of Western Europe). Not that political parties cannot serve as an instrument for the attainment of some specifically women's purposes, especially as far as the legislature is concerned. But the danger is that women's issues become demagogically exploited for party propaganda purposes and are not really taken seriously.[28] In fact, the parties often include women's objectives in their programs (usually formulated as paternalistic measures for "social protection" of women), only to forget them as soon as the electoral campaign is over. Moreover, parties in office are extremely reluctant to have women's issues pressed upon them by independent organizations and through public initiative; it is actually to preempt such action and monopolize the right to speak for the women—in order to be able to ignore them—that they set up their own women's sections.

Sharp political polarization during the Bulgarian transition subverts women's solidarity by crosscutting it with supposedly more "basic" political divisions on supposedly more important political issues. Even women activists are prone to give priority to the dominant political interpretations of reality and to consider their own aims as secondary to, and conditional upon, other and (allegedly more pressing) issues. But there is never an end to supposedly more pressing needs. This is true not only for the present over politicized situation; in the (pre-Communist) past, "unresolved" national and social issues have habitually taken precedence over women's issues, and women have viewed themselves as subordinated to the wider national community.[29] In a nationalistic milieu, to act in favor of their own objectives would expose women to reproach for being selfish. Women themselves accept this understanding of the situation more often than not, thus interiorizing the blame of being "unpatriotic." It is as if the problems of women do not form part and parcel of the community's pressing concerns. Unless women learn to view their own aims as a priority (or at least as important as other tasks), it is not clear how women may come to matter politically at all. The priority of political issues is not determined beforehand, but rather in social contests where social actors press certain issues as politically important, and there is no chance for those who fail to take part in the contest and at least try to make their voices heard on the political arena.

The women's organizations are generally rather weak, and the discrepancy between resources and professed purposes is striking. In fact, behind the general phrases, purposes are not clearly defined, are too broad and sweeping to be realistic, or, again, are pursued via inadequate means (thus, lodging petitions with state bureaucracies or with a dismissive National Assembly hardly impresses anybody). Less ambitious but better-circumscribed and better-directed action can be more effective. Referring the issues directly to the authorities, without first mobilizing support in a broader public campaign, is reminiscent of the recent past: It puts too much faith in administrative intervention, which in this case is not likely to occur at all, as the authorities can safely ignore the demands. Regrettably, the present-day Bulgarian women's movement is rather invisible to the public eye; it has not yet managed to seriously occupy public attention and present its issues more authoritatively. It is here that one comes to the general weakness of civil society in post-Communist Bulgaria, expressed in the underdevelopment of genuine (as opposed to sham) civic voluntary organizations of various sorts and around various causes, and in the ineffectiveness of public opinion and social protest in particular. Not that public space is lacking wherein to debate various issues and to voice protests; meetings and assemblies are held, the mass media are relatively free, etc. But public opinion, indeed very volatile and contradictory, does not find appropriate channels through which to translate itself into effective pressure and is therefore easily disregarded by the authorities. In the general chaos of the present times, with the struggle of atomized individuals for survival, women's voices are simply not attended to; in fact, even parties do not serve their proper function as aggregates of interests in their representation and mediation.

I have already remarked upon the regrettable propensity of women's organizations to use vague and imprecise language in formulating women's goals. Phrases such as "work for the promotion of the welfare of Bulgarian women," "professional development and self-realization of women," and the like pay tribute to the well-known rhetoric of the former socialist regime. They do not further particular women's demands, which should be defined more precisely in order to be effective. In general, the language of women activists sounds more like a plea than a claim. The idiom itself invites a patronizing, condescending attitude toward women, one that treats them as an "object" of social protection (owed to the "weaker sex," as the old cliché had it).[30] Pleas for social benefits and for the granting of special protections take the place of more-resolute claims and the affirmation of rights. While this is understandable under the pre-

sent conditions where severe economic crises expose women to special threats, it may
be self-subverting in the long run.

In accounting for the present state of the women's movement in Bulgaria, it is useful
to look for ideological links with Communist and pre-Communist times. One cannot
help noticing the strong influence of older socialist ideas about women's equality in the
current women's movement.[31] Earlier and cruder notions of gender equality and
women's rights prevail; the problem of "emancipation" is mechanistically perceived as
solved by employment; the presence of individual women in political bodies (as representatives of parties) is seen as the success of women entering the political arena.[32] This
is complemented with newer (social welfarist) ideas about benefits and social protection
for women. There is little place in this conceptual world for the "finer" aspects of
women's self-awareness, such as professional self-fulfillment, varieties of individual
experience, and reflection on the forging of women's identities (and the ways they determine women's lives).

In the Bulgarian historical tradition, such concerns were developed by the "bourgeois" women's movement—a movement of middle-class women and especially of
women in the liberal professions.[33] Both the socialist and the bourgeois feminist movements were predated by a proto-movement for women's education around the middle
of the nineteenth century.[34] After ascending to power, the Communists did away with
the "bourgeois" women's movement (outlawing the word feminism as connected with
it) and established a monopoly for the socialist understanding of women's equality,
identified with full employment, social benefits, and "representation" in some political
bodies (e.g., a quota for women in Parliament).[35] As noted above, the continuity with
this intellectual current is obvious in the discourses of women activists today. While this
is not necessarily a bad thing, there are other women's concerns that cannot be voiced
within this framework and in these terms. Thus sensibilities about gender inequalities
deriving from domestic patriarchal domination and the various everyday forms of
women's subjugation are underdeveloped. "Milder" forms of domination that are
deeply ingrained through socialization in attitudes, habits, opinions, evaluations, etc.,
and which for that reason are even more difficult to perceive and change, remain undis-
covered, and women thus become complicit in the domination. Theoretical reasoning
that explores the various forms of subjugation and digs deeper into gender inequalities
is almost lacking.

It would be perhaps interesting to attempt to situate the Bulgarian women's movement in the Western tradition and "measure" it against the development of Western
feminism. Thus plotted against Nancy Fraser's scheme of the development of American
feminism,[36] it would occupy the initial stage of fighting for gender equality (in the economic and social dimension), rather than the insistence on difference (in the cultural
sense of identities)[37] or the third stage of (deconstructionist) antiessentialism and multiculturalism, still less a fourth stage of mediation between all of these (implicitly
claimed by the author). Within the tradition of struggles for equality, which began as

struggles for civil rights, equal rights claims still constitute a dominant discourse in Bulgaria. And again, the Bulgarian women's movement seems to be in a phase of making more general claims that have been superseded in the West by the quest for specific rights such as the right to be free from sexual harassment and legal protection against the battering of women.[38] On the other hand, most of these earlier rights have been already attained or granted to Bulgarian women, including reproductive rights with a liberal abortion law. Discourses for rights, on the one hand, and for social benefits and entitlements, on the other hand, are curiously intermingled in the statements of Bulgarian women activists, and it is rarely noticed that the overriding concern with social benefits and social protection of women exists in a relationship of some strain with the equality discourses, as it is a differential treatment of women (as mothers) that is being claimed.

Or, if we take a culturally and historically more encompassing and perhaps better-suited view of historical feminisms, the Bulgarian women's movement can be defined as "relational," as against "individualist," feminism, though signs of the latter may also be found.[39] Relational feminism was the dominant line of argument prior to the twentieth century throughout the Western world and dominated the European continental debate until recently; it emphasized women's rights as women (defined by their childbearing capacities) in relation to men and insisted on women's distinctive contributions (in the traditional women's roles) to the broader society, making claims on the commonwealth on the basis of these contributions.[40] The Bulgarian national(ist) tradition explains very well the primacy of this kind of "feminism" until the present day. Even the rather traditional-sounding emphasis of some Bulgarian women activists on the motherly function have a parallel in Ellen Key's sort of motherly love "feminism" (and the demand for state subsidies for mothers) in turn-of-the-century Sweden, which influenced subsequent feminist developments.[41] If I am quite reluctant to designate this style of argument—a very strong one in present-day Bulgaria—as feminism, it is because it does not follow a critical phase of contesting inequalities and male dominance but seems rather to be a natural outgrowth of traditional representations and come close to the position of patronizing patriarchalism.

Now, I wonder how much sense there is in seeing the Bulgarian women's movement as a stage of the feminist movement elsewhere, though it certainly imitates and bears close resemblance to other feminisms (historically, with the one under the influence of German social democracy).[42] Even in the West the varieties of feminism seem not to be neat stages to be "superseded," but rather to be ideas driven to marginality at certain times but which may recur one way or another. The Bulgarian women's movement may better be regarded as having a value of its own and interacting with the society within which it exists; thus it may never pass through all the stages it is expected to, nor develop all varieties of feminism, especially if the respective concerns fail to make their appearance, and if, furthermore, they are not adequately perceived and conceptualized or fail to serve as foci of mobilization. The Bulgarian women's movement, then, should be evaluated not so much for what it is not (especially while the respective concerns are not present) but on its own terms, and should eventually be criticized for its intrinsic deficiencies and contradictions. This is what I attempted to do when I mentioned its existence in the shadow of political parties, its rather naive belief in laws and authorities (still more naive in a society where the legal order is unreliable), its fuzziness of aims, its exclusive concern with social protection, etc.

The women's movement in Bulgaria has arrived at a critical juncture of its development; already free from (Communist) party subjugation and domestication (but still clinging to political parties), it has yet to acquire its own profile. In order to do that, new ideas and conceptual tools are needed; those of the older "bourgeois" feminism have also been superseded in the meantime, as problems and concerns have changed. The focus on gender equality need not be confined to women's rights, and the women's movement should regard itself more openly as a political movement in its own right for the social restructuring of gender relations; within the women's rights movement, a concretization of claims is needed, as well as a constant effort to make rights effective. An understanding of the ambiguous nature of welfare provisions and protections is also overdue; while vitally necessary, especially in the present situation, it may reinforce traditional gender notions and gender roles to the detriment of women's autonomy (and dignity).[43] More fundamentally, gender equality and difference should be conceived as standing in a more dialectical relationship, if logical discrepancies between claims for equality and claims for social protection are to be evaded.

NOTES

1. However, the continuity can be traced at the level of organization and membership; the present vitality of the DUW is largely due to the preservation of its former ties and organization at the local level. Its leader, Ms. Emiliia Maslarova, entered the first democratically elected National Assembly on the Communist ticket (and eventually became a member of one of the Communist-dominated coalition cabinets), even if she claimed the "independence" of the organization.

2. See *Platforma na Demokratichniia suluz na zhenite. Ustav na Demokratichnlia suluz na zhenite* (Sofia, 1992), pp. 2–3.

3. This is evident in the addition of caveats that emasculate the whole statement. For example, the social protection of the Bulgarian family and women under market conditions has to be "economically justifiable." Decoded, this means that the realization will depend upon available financial resources, and that it is to the party in office to decide what is financially feasible (women's claims will be given free rein only while the Socialist Party is in opposition). One might consider this to be only realistic (and perhaps honestly so), were it not masked behind the seemingly "objective" and hence demagogical formula of "economic justifiability."

4. "Sotsialniiat status na bulgarskata zhena v perioda na prekhoda kum pazarna ikonomika," in *Za ravni prava i vuzmozhnosti na zhenite v Bulgariia* (Sofia, 1994), p. 14.

5. In an interview, shown on the national TV channel on March 8, 1995 (International Women's Day), Emiliia Maslarova gave to the question "Are you a feminist?" the following characteristic answer: "No, no, no, a hundred times no, because we love men, we believe in love and in life in couples." While popular opinion may well define feminism in this way after the Communist

eclipse of the problematic, such understanding hardly credits a leader of perhaps the largest women's organization in Bulgaria. One would be tempted to attribute this statement to calculated political demagogy on the part of an activist of the Bulgarian Socialist Party, but I have reasons to believe in the ignorant sincerity of Emiliia Maslarova (and she reiterated her opinion of feminism in several interviews).

6. A similar socialist formation is the so-called Women and Mothers Against Violence movement set up by the Communist Party at the beginning of the transition. "Violence" here stands for the anti-Communist opposition. The "movement," which became known for organizing rallies of shouting women around the buildings of the national TV and radio stations in 1991, lost its raison d'être afterward.

7. This opinion was communicated in an interview by the president of this organization, Ms. Teodora Moskova.

8. It is mentioned here separately just because it succeeded in returning some of its candidates to the parliament (in coalition with the Bulgarian Socialists) in the elections of December 1994.

9. Publication of the Christian Women's Union, *Pressluzhba "Kurier"* 237 (512), 3 dekemvri 1991, pp. 11–12. Interview with Elisaveta Milenova, current president of the union.

10. Activists of one of these organizations (Zheni za chista prfroda, in translation "Women for Pure Habitat") collected signatures in favor of an ecological Marshall Plan—an initiative of German intellectuals and statesmen. See *Natsionalen Zhenski Forum. Informatsionen Biuletin*, N2 (1995), p. 13.

11. In post-Communist conditions names such as "independent" characteristically signify their opposite—former state-Communist affiliation. In the case of trade unions, one should not attribute too much significance to former ties with the Communist government, discounting the somewhat smaller initial militancy.

12. The issue of property restitution blocks the formal recognition of the BWA as heir of the older Women's Association (1901–1944). The property of this organization was actually confiscated by the Communist state after 1945.

13. The data was supplied by Darlia Vladikova, deputy chairwoman of the Bulgarian Women's Association. The association is currently chaired by Lullia Berberian, mother and coach of the internationally known Bulgarian tennis players, Manuela, Magdalena, and Katerina Maleevi.

14. See *Bulgarian Women's Association. Our Strength Is in Action*, p. 1.

15. On the other hand, quite like every post-Communist party, the organization has views (and, in fact, programs) on Bulgaria's international policies, on Bulgarians abroad, and on the development of Bulgarian culture.

16. See Lidia Ivanova, "Kurazh samotni maiki" [Courage, single mothers], *Obshtestvo i pravo* n 6 (1992) p. 26.

17. Thus in the working out of the Children's Law, the association consulted the treatment of children's rights and of the parent-child relations in current foreign legislature and practice. It also looked at the role of courts in cases of child abuse and the possibility of entrusting children to alternative care, etc. (Interview with the president of the Bulgarian Association of Women in Law, Ms. Genoveva Tisheva.)

18. See the sensitive treatment of the problems of women in the scholarly world by Nadya Aisenberg and Mona Harrington, *Women of Academe: Outsiders in the Sacred Grove* (Amherst: University of Massachusetts Press, 1988).

19. About an older expression of this understanding in the Bulgarian women's movement see Ravnopravie?" in *v. Ravnopravie*, 4, (10 fevruari, 1909), p. 3; Maria Dhzidrova, *Iskanliata na bulgarkata. Skazka* (Sofia: Pechatnitsa "Grazhdanin," 1912); Dimitrana Ivanova, "Bulgarkata pred subitliata, in *Dneshnliat dulg na bulgarkata*' (Sofia: Zhenski glas, 1923), pp. 9–16; Dimitrana Ivanova, "Strachut ot feminizma," in *v. Zhenski glas* 11, (1 mart, 1926), pp. 1–2.

20. Interview with the president of this association, Associate Professor Pavlina Dragomirova.

21. The Society of Bulgarian Women with Higher Education was created in 1924 and existed until 1953, when it was abolished by the Communist authorities. The argument for its dissolution was the existence of similar organs working toward the same goals.

22. Interview with the president of the association, Ms. Ralitsa Mukharska.

23. Organization members translated into Bulgarian and edited texts on gender issues to be published by Sofia University Press. It is perhaps interesting to note that while the Bulgarian language, like English, has a separate word for (grammatical) gender, "rod," alongside the biologically connoted word for men and women as "sexes," "pol," it is the biological word that is habitually used, while the other one sounds very awkward, no doubt because of a lack of feminist tradition of the type that regards the "sexes" as social and cultural constructs.

24. Thus in 1995 interviews with Julia Kristeva and Ida Blom (then president of the International Federation for Research on Women in History [IFRWH]) were published in Kultura. One may also mention the organization of a group of Bulgarian women historians (a member of the IFRWH since the summer of 1995) and their contribution to a special issue of the journal Obshta i prilozhna kulturologia [General and applied culturology], dedicated to the field of women's history, to be published by Sofia University Press in 1996. Problems of feminism and of women's history are also treated in a special issue of the academic journal Sotsiologicheski pregled no. 1, (1996) as well as in a special issue of the newspaper Kultura (March 8, 1996).

25. Vulgar notions commonly associated with feminism are: "hate for men," living single ("an old spinster"), or being lesbian. As Nancy Cott writes about the situation in the United States in the beginning of the century, feminism and "militance" are not the same thing, "but common parlance linked them." See Nancy Cott, The Grounding of Modern Feminism (New Haven and London: Yale University Press, 1987), p. 53. Tatyana Mamonova explains the negative image of feminism in Russian society with the "silencing" of ("bourgeois" but also of postrevolutionary) feminism by the Communist partocracy. See Tatyana Mamonova, Russian Women's Studies: Essays on Sexism in Soviet Culture (Pergamon Press, 1989), pp. 163–64.

26. I admit that even "motherly" identities (or the appeal to chivalrous generosity of the "stronger sex") may have strategic use in a "politics of identity" and may serve immediate feminist goals (e.g., protection of women in a crisis) but I doubt that this is meant as strategy in the Bulgarian case; besides, playing with the most traditional notions is self-defeating, as it actually reinforces them.

27. This was written down in the Constitutive Charter of the National Women's Forum, signed on May 17, 1994.

28. Besides, parliamentary party discipline stands in the way of lobbying across parties in favor of issues on which women activists in different parties otherwise agree; some Bulgarian women activists (and M.P.s) complained about the subversion of agreements reached beforehand when it comes to actual voting, at which time party lines show up again.

29. About this tendency, see Sharon L. Wolchik, "Introduction," in Sharon L. Wolchik and Alfred G. Meyer (eds.), Women, State and Party in Eastern Europe (Durham: Duke University Press, 1985), p. 49.

30. The frequent use of the singular ("the Bulgarian woman") when speaking about the problems of women is especially degrading and subjugating not only because it is typifying and essentialist, but also because it reveals a patronizing attitude. The program documents of women's organizations in Bulgaria often use the singular, revealing a total lack of sensibility on the issue.

31. About the history of socialist ideas on women's equality, see Alfred G. Meyer, "Feminism, Socialism, and Nationalism in Eastern Europe," in Sharon L. Wolchik and Alfred G. Meyer (eds.), Women. State. and Party in Eastern Europe. (Durham: Duke University Press, 1985), pp. 13–30.

32. The socialist notion of "women's emancipation" actually amounted to the drawing of women into the labor force (as "builders of socialism") and demanding public activism (of a strictly prescribed type). But the Communist regime treated women (and men) as subjects of a quasi-patriarchal state while leaving domestic patriarchalism untouched. Earlier (pre-1945) "feminists" in Bulgaria fought for equality in education, voting rights, access to the professions, etc. Since that time new concerns have come to the forefront of the women's struggles.

33. See Krassimira Daskalova, "Diskursite po 'zhenskiia vupros' i Miastoto na zhenite v bulgarskoto obshtestvo 1878-1944," *Obshta i prilozhna kulturologliaz* (1995).

34. See Krassimira Daskalova, "Obrazovanieto na zhenite i zhenite v obrazovanieto na vuzrozhdenska Bulgaria," *Godishnik na Sofiiskiia Universitet—Tsentur po kulturoznanie* 85 (1992).

35. During this period women's education was substantially extended, and women made a more massive entry into some prestigious professions.

36. Nancy Fraser, "Ravestvo, razlichie i demokratsia: Suvremennliat feministki debat v Suedinenite Shtati" [original title: "Equality, Difference and Democracy: Recent Feminist Debates in the United States"], *Obshta i prilozhna kulturologlia* 2 (1995).

37. Of this there is only a modest beginning in the Bulgarian conditions, and the affirmation of women's identities is all the time in danger of relapsing into traditional essentialism (or of being intentionally misunderstood in this way).

38. See Elizabeth Schneider, "The Dialectic of Rights and Politics: Perspectives from the Women's Movement," in Katharine Bartlett and Rosanne Kennedy (eds.), *Feminist Legal Theory*, (Boulder: Westview Press, 1991), pp. 318–32.

39. In the description of Karen Offen, individual feminism "emphasized more abstract concepts of individual human rights and celebrated the quest for personal independence (or autonomy) in all aspects of life, while downplaying, deprecating, or dismissing as insignificant all socially defined roles and minimizing discussion of sex-linked qualities or contributions, including childbearing and its attendant responsibilities," (Karen Offen, "Defining Feminism: A Comparative Historical Approach," *Signs* 14, no. 11 [1988], p. 136). As has perhaps become clear, my own sympathies lie here.

40. Ibid., esp. pp. 135–37.

41. See Cheryl Register, "Motherhood at Center: Ellen Key's Social Vision," *Women's Studies International Forum* 5, 6 (1982); Torborg Lundell, "Ellen Key and Swedish Feminist Views on Motherhood," *Scandinavian Studies* 56, no. 4 (Autumn 1984), pp. 351–69.

42. As described by Karen Honeycutt, "Socialism and Feminism in Imperial Germany," *Signs* 5, no. 11 (1979), pp. 30–41.

43. As pointed out by Jennifer Nedelsky, "Reconceiving Autonomy: Sources, Thoughts and Possibilities," *Yale Journal of Law and Feminism* 1, no. 7 (1989), pp. 7–37. In the present crisis in Bulgaria, such concerns may sound vain, if not an outright mockery; still, the contradiction between dependence (on the state) and autonomy is real enough to warrant one to reason beyond this particular unhappy situation.

< 15 >

Response

Ann Snitow

Because life goes on, and because the writers here—Fuszara, Maleck-Lewy, Gaber, Lang, and Petö—show grace under pressure as they play the extraordinary hand history has recently dealt them, one perhaps obvious point seems understated in these texts: Since 1989, the pace and scale of change in East-Central Europe and the former Soviet Union are, taken together, simply unprecedented. And unlooked for. No one now immersed in the drama inadequately summed up in the inert term *post-Communism* expected changes this fundamental in their lifetimes. On the contrary, life was (for some grievously, for some more happily) static, insulated, predictable. When Western feminists speak of what is happening to women in the former Communist countries, the women in question can easily feel belittled—or grossly misunderstood—by a formulation so narrow, dry, and neat. If it weren't for the common Eastern allergies to self-pity and rhetorical flights, surely women in the East would speak far more extravagantly than they do of the failure of Western imagination. The incalculability of such enormous changes can sometimes make "the women question" seem a relic of an innocent past, when categories of identity seemed relatively permanent and power struggles had a local habitation and a name.

Instead, now, in the East, one barely knows what new challenge will confront one, minute by minute, day by day. Since Westerners of all classes are used to the constant surface flux of consumer societies, they can easily miss this strangeness, the depth of the change, for Easterners. In the precipitous transformation, one must figure out—and in a hurry—completely new ways of doing things, from where one buys food, to how one will afford it; from where one will learn the news of the day, to how one will describe one's life to oneself and to others. How will one adjust one's expectations and take advantage of opportunity (now seemingly everywhere on offer) without becoming lost if one goes too far afield or disappointed if one can't seem to reach the new, promised lands? Now it is supposed to be oneself and not the state one blames for failure. This can be bracing (the much-trumpeted end to paternalism) or it can be terrifying (new responsibilities and burdens with no old-style dependency allowed.) In this context, what does it feel like to suggest gender as a new systemic cause of one's failure? Like sour grapes? Or a return to Communism's protectionism, which privileged women but also thereby controlled them and their families?

As one Czech friend described these dynamics during the Velvet Revolution in Prague, first there was mass euphoria; then came a mass depression, because people were disoriented, unclear about who they were going to become in the still unknowable new order; then began the rush apart, as each one began to develop further what Milica Antić Gaber reminds us the first women's movements of the region called "the little stories," the development of new, separate subjectivities. If in this individuation men and women had stereotypically gendered social fates, this hard fact of group membership was obscured by the excitement and novelty of separation, of having to find independent, personal solutions. The air of freedom was so delicious that only secondarily did people remark that this new race was to the swift. Everyone had to move fast and to hope his or her choices would turn out to make personal and historical sense.

The new marketplace is a challenge and a test that divides people along fault lines that were always there during Communism but that are now widening out into major, visible differences—by no means only of gender. (See Peggy Watson's disturbing description in this volume of how the new democracies create and require these increasing stratifications.) Now it is the old who are in the dustbin of history, and also the poor, the rural, the less-educated and less-skilled. And, of course, post-1989 opportunities are complexly gendered, a fact Fuszara tells us is much more likely to be noticed by women than by men but which may not be the most striking point to anyone feeling for a foothold in this melee.

Gender discourses in the East have been dead meat a long time, overdone rhetorically while often neglected and obscured in both politics and daily life. Given the tired familiarity of gender equality rhetoric in the East, and given gender's weakness as an explanatory paradigm for current, major social realignments, gender is rarely one of the first categories by which people sort out their new experiences. Elsewhere in this volume, Hana Havelková gives the example of what in the West is called the issue of "prostitution." On the Czech border with Germany, this issue gets called either another instance of East-West currency wars or another instance of the invasion of Western immorality. In such formulations, women do not appear. And even if both Western and Eastern feminist observers agree that the category of gender difference will soon become useful and politically necessary as new power relationships emerge and women fall to the bottom of new capitalist hierarchies, just *how* can new political demands for women be successfully framed? Prostitution is but one example of this enormous conceptual challenge. Should it be separated out (as it is sometimes in the West) from other issues of women's lack of power in the marketplace? Each issue in isolation, often borrowed from the West, can become abstract or grotesque and be easily dismissed unless it is linked meaningfully with others in a string, a local analysis, that holds. (Just such a piece of feminist grotesquerie appeared recently in Romania, where liberal divorce laws and new antibattering laws can't be used by women because women are entirely dependent on the family for socially acceptable and economically viable lives. Instead, according to Judge Daniela Lupas, these laws are currently being used almost exclusively by men.)

As Andrea Pető observes in this section, there are violently distinct phases in each country: before Communism, during Communism, after Communism; and in each country the pattern of women's second-class citizenship has its own continuities and discontinuities. Which past is useable, if any, in the formation of a contemporary feminism? Pető warns us against answering too fast, against assuming that past feminisms or Western ones will serve Eastern women well. She offers a disturbing history of Hungarian feminisms, some profoundly conservative, nationalistic, and class bound, and some (under Communism) driven by instrumental labor policies and organized from the top down. In a germinal piece, "Ambiguities of Emancipation: Women and the Ethnic Question in Hungary," Maria Kovács gives a related account of some of the early-twentieth-century feminist groups in Hungary. They organized a brilliant campaign to save bourgeois women's access to the university—but at the expense of the Jews, who were banned instead. Kovács adds weight to Pető's warning when she concludes, "This . . . was . . . not the last time that a major step in women's emancipation . . . happened simultaneously with a reverse process of partial deemancipation of some other social group." Such cautionary tales raise questions: How will the problem of women's often dramatic losses in post-Communism get connected to other group losses and to other ways in which post-Communist states are introducing new (or revived) forms of inequality and injustice in general? In the current chaos, how separable are women's problems, conceptually and practically? And, strategically, how separate should they become? What alliances can—and should—women form? And, finally, which women will define "women's interests "?

All the writers in this section of *Transitions, Environments, Translations* express frustration at how hard it currently is to know just how gender will play as a political issue in the development of their new national cultures. Questions of framing are urgent—never academic—for them, since the boundaries of politics are being hotly contested, and quickly redrawn. Nancy Leys Stepan and Mindy Roseman recently expressed the anxiety that haunts these pieces by posing a founding question for a productive East-West dialogue of feminist scholars at the Central European University: "What is the political?"

Each writer here is offering or building on a historical account of which sort of politics has been possible for women in the region in the past. Their speculations about what women's groups are doing now arise out of this sense of women's political culture and its shifting context. The group "women," they generally observe, has been particularly vulnerable to instrumental manipulation by a wide range of politicians, while women have only sporadically seen themselves as sharing a group interest. Before Communism, feminism seems to have been a discourse of relative privilege with little organizing across class and ethnic lines, though class and ethnic considerations are not much mentioned by our writers here, perhaps because they are used to the homogenization of the category of "women" established by fiat, if not in fact, under Communism.

In the post-1989 transformation of their societies, these writers identify major difficulties in the development of women's resistance to their current losses—of social services, of jobs, and more intangibly of the sexism of respect, now replaced by a more rapacious variety. In passing, they record a number of reasons why "women" don't become a meaningful political bloc. For example, several observe that women in the transformation are often swamped with the daily work of reconstructing personal life and of reknitting connections among social institutions, work that helps structure all societies but is rarely counted as politics.

Explanations like these ring true, but at the same time, some of the writing here points to changes for women that are so swift and dramatic that such explanations also feel inadequate. When all the good reasons for women's losses are lined up and taken into account, a sentence like Sabine Lang's can still shock: "The rising democratic order instigated stratification processes along gender lines, which insinuated themselves quickly, deeply, and with almost no resistance into the newly created unified German social and political sphere." Lang is speaking of the Eastern bloc country that had the most developed and genuinely realized "state feminism" in the region. It is chastening to realize as one reads Maleck-Lewy's piece about the three post-1989 periods of East German women's activism that one is reading of a decline that took only a matter of months.

Each writer here faces into the wind of these new difficulties for women. Worried, but with the enduring hopefulness of activists, they confront the enormousness of the task of constructing an indigenous feminism. While Maleck-Lewy records the disappearance of the initial mass feminist surge in East Germany, Malgorzata Fuszara greets the same disappearance of feminist demonstrations in Poland as a sign that women organizers are digging in for the long haul, building groups of varied kinds, and beginning on the basic work of institutional reform, which is not visible or glamorous but is absolutely essential given the complex new configurations of Polish state power structures. (Joanna Regulska of the Rutgers program Local Democracy in Poland would agree and has documented that Polish women's political clout is growing at the local level, in locations that may prove key if they manage to wrest some control and funds from the entrenched centralism of the Communist past.) Fuszara points out that women must struggle over seemingly trivial bureaucratic details; these micro decisions will underpin all that is to follow. Will the foundations in which many new Polish women's groups have organized themselves be prohibitively taxed to feed a government that no longer offers women protections or services out of that tax money? Should women's groups lobby—or sue—for their share of the changing national purse? Alternatively, what will be the fate of the still rare and unfamiliar nonregistered groups with no standing in the state? Will they lose too much through their marginality and the consequent lack of funds, or will they ultimately gain by their institutional loose-ness, their reliance not on professional staffs but on a new volunteer political energy still mostly unknown in the region?

Writing of related questions in Slovenia, Milica Antić Gaber suspects that independence may be a source of weakness for women's groups. They may succeed in reminding society of its "bad conscience," but, she argues, they are situated too far from government to have any direct effect. Gaber sees the state as the place where most new political capital is collecting and defines the "political" in opposition to the role of "pressure group," a location she sees as outside "politics." Similarly, she defines women's groups such as SOS hotlines, which offer "help," as uncoordinated locations of antipolitics. Their organizers, she says, are hostile toward those who work in political parties or for the state. Gaber is ambivalent, since she sees such small, rogue groups as more likely to criticize patriarchy than women's party caucuses ever do, but she also believes the state still holds the key to all substantial change.

Here we confront a possible East-West misunderstanding. Is Gaber's narrow use of the word *political* partly a matter of semantics? Western women's movements, operating in societies with layers and layers of nongovernment activity, have defined the term broadly and have constantly sought to multiply the locations that matter when social decisions are made—in institutions, in daily social practices, and, too, but less confidently, in governments. Particularly in the United States, rather than trying to enter the conventional sphere of "the public," women's movements have often tried to haul "the private" into public space, to politicize private experience in ways Eastern Europeans would rarely consider, given their recent history with invasive states. Western movements have had a stake in blurring public and private, in seeing change as coming from many contested sites. But they have varied widely in their ability—and in their interest—in gaining state power for their groups or for individual feminist activists. In spite of big differences due to race and class, many U.S. activists have had the luxury of avoiding confrontation with the enormousness of U.S. state power. They have designed projects or published critiques that did not depend directly on the support or approval of government. For Easterners too, politics may indeed have often developed in the private realm—but defensively, in opposition to state colonization of all aspects of life. Coming up from underground, Easterners have a healthy respect for the centrality of the state to all they do. They see it as a battleground they cannot avoid.

This respect for the power of the state is a valuable theoretical and political resource in Eastern feminist thinking, no doubt born in part from living in societies where the state was everything, and lobbying, pressure groups, and other nongovernmental powers were unknown. (Lobbying is a concept that often requires a long explanation in East-West conversations.)

Yet recent Eastern and Central European tradition also includes the antipolitics of dissidents. Reading Gaber, I wondered why, given the still often romanticized record of marginal oppositional culture, she showed so little confidence in the potential power of outsiders. Sociologist Jeffrey Goldfarb suggests that former dissidents are now often seen as dreamers, utopians, people of principle who never expected, and therefore never planned for power. The new men (and, rarely, women) see that oppositional time as happily over and those who look back to the absolutist social values of that period as "nostalgic," a very pejorative word just now in the region. Jiřina Šiklová, a leading Czech dissident and founder of the Prague Gender Center, agrees in her current pieces that the period of undergrounds and "creative improvization" is past; now political life is located in the system of political parties. To Šiklová, most of these new political actors are spoilers; she calls them "the gray zone." Goldfarb also sees this side of the instrumental new politicians, but adds that many of them have their own species of idealism: They want to be involved in the real at last, to accept the responsibility, the dirty hands, of politics. The new, practical generation is willing to make bureaucracies, and to try for the brass ring of political power, which the (usually older) dissidents disdained. Their romance revolves around economic miracles and the high promises of the European Enlightenment. In Goldfarb's scenario, they are statist by default, because civil society is so underdeveloped. Or as Nanette Funk, philosopher and expert about the region, puts it: No wonder a new generation of both insiders and outsiders are interested in the state. Before, governmental power was writ in stone; now, the young have reason to hope that at last they can be part of democracy. Gaber is the Slovenian translator of Wollstonecraft and shares Wollstonecraft's yearning to be included as an insider at last.

Perhaps, then, one element buried in Gaber is generational warfare. Ironically, old-style dissidents and old-style Communists were locked in the embrace of their shared history. Again the question: What, now, will be the political? And will the new mundane world of government be a place where women will participate? Or will the new politics of dirty hands, structural readjustments, hardball, and all those other tough-guy metaphors now in vogue turn out to be a world the new men (of whatever party) inhabit happily and most women disdain?

An irritated Anna Tsing gave these questions of the future of political culture another turn at the "Transitions" conference when she asked from the floor why the dream of both these political generations was always and only to join Europe. Once again: Which narrative of the past, which plan for the future, and chosen by whom? Tsing implied that the failure to see the South as a source of models for the East's liberation struggles and for ways to resist economic colonization was a disturbing blindness, a refusal of identification that might well be the founding taboo of a newly repressive, exclusionary and racist political class.

Gaber expresses a paradox she cannot resolve. The new governments are as patriarchal as the old. They include few women and even fewer feminists, and as yet they show little interest in public opinion. Hence there are few women inside. But, for the same reasons, women outside are also unlikely to be heard. Gaber wants the new order to maintain the best social welfare policies of the old, but this balance between old entitlements and new capitalist cost-cutting is being negotiated now, and quickly, in a stream of parliamentary decisions. Given this pace, Gaber writes from a state of emergency and can't identify where to place women's political lever, how to hold the line against women's losses. Only time will tell if significant numbers of women will become parliamentary insiders, as she thinks they must to achieve anything solid and lasting. And only time will tell if those little groups that now seem so hopelessly marginal to Gaber will turn out to have more effect than she expects, as social organizing expands and citizens seek a variety of ways to make demands on their new governments.

Sabine Lang agrees with Gaber in part that party politics and government agencies are proving to be key places where, at least in the new Germany she is writing about, women are already consolidating new powers and holding on to social benefits. However she is worried about this very fact, since without women's movement outsiders to point out the "bad conscience" of a now "corporate" state feminism, Lang fears feminist politics will have all its teeth drawn. Programs for women will become professional hierarchies, each with its own little power niche, none with a general criticism of the state, the hand that feeds it. Lang wants the outsiders who seem to have disappeared to revive, to keep insiders awake, and to orient the larger societal debate to basic questions about the systemic causes of women's oppression. Only from an independent women's movement does she expect the kind of feminist vision that can fundamentally change the depth structure of women's disadvantages. Her description of the atomization of women's projects inside state bureaucracies is a disturbing portrait of state co-optation of women's issues. Lang makes explicit what Gaber implies about the current troubled relationship between women and states: the unspoken, patriarchal continuities between the periods before and after Communism; the paternalism of even quite femocratic governments; the lack of general social debate about women, which leaves the field open for divisive manipulation by politicians. In an ecumenical, liberal voice, Gaber concludes by calling for a future world where outsiders and insiders will both be at work on the social fabric. In a harsher, more radical, and more desperate voice, Lang puts this point differently. In her view, without a critical, independent women's movement, there will be no real political insider position for women, only governmental crumbs doled out for them to fight over.

For European readers, these discussions of different public sectors will be quite familiar. European parliamentary traditions include small parties and can, at times, empower individuals on national party lists in ways quite unfamiliar in U.S. politics. Most Europeans assume certain publicly funded social services and are familiar with the issues of control that arise in welfare states. In contrast, on first contact, U.S. feminists often find Eastern feminists' focus on the state and on political parties hard to understand. Arising in the rebellious sixties, the U.S. women's movement began with mostly outsider strategies. Even now, after a quarter of a century of growth and diversification, when many U.S. women's groups have developed insider aspirations, U.S. feminism has had little success at electing women, or at passing women's movement legislation, or even at institutionalizing basic social welfare benefits at either the national or local level. Hence the U.S. lens view: because of a passionate anxiety about, and a love-hate relationship to state power, it may need some careful adjusting if any useful dialogue is to follow.

The state, its ethnic, spiritual, and geographical formation, its legitimation, and its ways of redistributing wealth and authority are all central questions for feminist activists living through the fundamental changes of post-Communism. The U.S. movements tendency to move from the local to the global has less immediate resonance in the East, where, until the day before yesterday, "the local" was powerless and "the global" a universalist fiction of a political unity that, in fact, empowered very few. In spite of the totalitarian past, and perhaps also because of it, the state, that middle realm between the dreams of an internationale and the reality of a corrupt local boss remains a central generator of identity, a potential source of security from being overrun—by global economics, and by neocolonial moves from outside. The writers here have many historical reasons for seeing their fledgling, post-totalitarian governments as protectors of local culture, of the "nation," with its (sometimes romantic, sometimes also racist) promise of coherent community.

The new aggressive nationalisms are one face of this yearning for self-determination. But antinationalists, too, recognize the new states as potentially liberating. Feminist friends in Poland wait for the last Russian army unit to leave Warsaw. Thought they are in that still quite small minority that speaks of gender, and also of new race and class conflicts at home, they recognize that most of the people around them will avoid such discussions until the outer boundary is secure.

The pieces here, then, are part of a mass activity, the reframing of everything. These theorists differ in their definitions of just how nongovernmental a nongovernmental organization is; just how much the concept "civil society" includes; just how far-reaching state regulation of groups will be or should be; just how much leadership hierarchy, coordination, and legal accountability a group must have to become a political force. And they all know that independence does not eliminate opportunities for tyranny. Control has been a bad habit, but in the breakup of old patterns of control come new problems, among them what the early U.S. women's movement activist Jo Freeman called "the tyranny of structurelessness." Finding a balance between structure and flexibility—a problem in all movements—is particularly pressing where control was so one-sided for so long. Feminist activists in the East will have to nerve themselves to demand regulation of the new markets at the very moment when others in their societies see such controls as poisonous "nostalgia" or naive innocence about economic necessity. Since organized women's call for "control" is often mapped in the public mind onto "Communist control," women's groups will have trouble positioning themselves so as to get out beyond these old terms of discourse.

In this situation, feminism will have to seek its subject—in every sense of that word. If we accept (as I do) Peggy Watson's argument elsewhere in this volume and Sabine Lang's similar insight that women's political powerlessness is central to—and not a mere by-product of—the new order, we need to see at the last, too, the brilliant, confrontational verve implied in these pieces. Fuszara's descriptions of the proliferating levels of practical politics, Gaber's claim that old and new supports and rights may not inevitably be on a collision course, Maleck-Lewy's description of the willingness of the East German women's movement to start over and continue to search for a new definition of the political, and Petö's call for a new theory to place, define, and legitimate feminist activity—all suggest a new political involvement born of the momentum of this kinetic period. The shape of a feminist politics in the East is still indistinct, ragged, sometimes far to seek. But the writers here offer open, antidogmatic speculation. They are among the fast-growing group of feminist theorists in the East who are thinking while running. They record vivid change in which women's political energies are on the loose, seeking new pathways, shaping new feminisms, and suggesting—to all feminists—new tricks.

< part two >

Economics and Environments

The Politics of Development

< 16 >

Gender Perspectives on Environmental Action

Issues of Equity, Agency, and Participation

Bina Agarwal

Forests and village commons (VCs) have always been important sources of livelihood and basic necessities for rural households in developing countries. For many poor households and especially for women, who own little private land, they have been crucial for survival. However, in India, as in many other regions, first under colonial rule and then after independence, the availability of these resources to rural communities has been declining rapidly. This is due both to degradation and to reduced access to what is available, the latter resulting particularly from the twin processes of statization (appropriation by the State) and privatization (appropriation by individuals). This has had a range of negative consequences for poor households in general and for women in particular. For the latter, among other things, it has meant ever-lengthening journeys to collect fuel, fodder, and water, and a sharpening of the crisis of subsistence. How have rural communities responded to these processes and effects? Are there gender differences in the responses? If so, what underlies the differences, and what are their implications?

A growing literature on ecofeminism in the West and its third world variants[1] argues that women have a special relationship with nature, which gives them a particular stake in environmental protection and regeneration. Although ecofeminist discourse embodies several strands, most characteristically emphasize that the domination of women and the exploitation of nature are interrelated and have historically emerged together from a common worldview, giving women a special interest in ending the domination of nature and by implication their own subordination. The connection between the two forms of domination (of women and of nature) is typically traced to ideology—to the identification within patriarchal thought of women with nature (= inferior) and men with culture (= superior).[2] To change this, ecofeminism calls upon women and men to reconceptualize themselves as well as their relationships to one another and to the non-human world in nonhierarchical ways.[3]

Elsewhere I have critiqued the ecofeminist position on various counts that cannot be detailed here.[4] But the central points relevant to the present discussion need mention.

To begin with, by locating the relationship between women and nature mainly or solely in ideology, ecofeminism neglects women's (and men's) lived material relationship with nature and their specific forms of interaction with and dependence on natural resources. It also ignores differences between women stemming from class, race, location, and so on. Not all women need have the same stake in environmental protection, nor need women alone have such a stake. Further, ecofeminist discourse typically does not take account of a possible gap between the interest women may have in environmental protection and regeneration and their ability to translate that interest into effective action. Such a gap may arise, for instance, due to gender differences in public decision-making power, private property ownership (and other economic means), social norms, and so on. Indeed, some significant environmental initiatives to protect forests and village commons in India have been catalyzed and controlled largely or solely by men. Clearly we need a more complex and nuanced understanding of environmental action.

The concept of feminist environmentalism provides an alternative. People's relationship with nature is centrally rooted in and shaped by their material reality. Ideological constructions of women and nature impinge on this relationship but cannot be seen as the whole of it.[5] People's *responses* to environmental degradation thus also need to be understood in the context of their material reality, their everyday interactions with nature, and their dependence on it for survival. To the extent that both women and men of poor peasant and tribal households are dependent on natural resources for their livelihoods or for particular needs, *both* are likely to have a stake in environmental protection and regeneration. However, whether this leads to their initiating or participating in environmental action would, among other things, be contingent on the extent and nature of their dependence and their ability to act in their own interests. Gender-specific responses can typically be traced to a given (unequal) gender division of labor, property, and power,[6] rather than primarily or solely to the notion of women being closer to nature than men, or to women's biology, as is suggested by the ecofeminist perspective.

In this essay I seek to extend and further concretize the idea of feminist environmentalism by examining several different forms of environmental action that are ongoing in India today. I also seek to throw light on some issues concerning women's agency. Recent literature on women's resistance, for instance, has insightfully demonstrated that even under severely oppressive conditions women often resist their subordinate position in various (typically individual, covert) ways.[7] Examples of this resistance have been used by many to represent women as "agents," a representation counterposed against the depiction of women as victims. The unqualified celebration of such resistance can, however, be problematic. It sometimes obscures the fact that women, even if not passive, may still be victims of larger processes and structures of dominance.[8] More commonly, the inherent limitations of particular forms of resistance in undermining material and ideological dominance, as well as the possible constraints on women's ability to exercise agency (or what Sen terms "agency-freedom") are seldom examined.[9]

Elsewhere I have suggested that women's resistance can take various forms, ranging from individual-covert to group-overt (with individual-overt and group-covert resistance coming in between), and that individual-covert resistance is the least likely and group-overt the most likely to be effective in seriously challenging structures of male dominance.[10] But women's ability to move from one form of resistance to another— from covert to overt, individual to group, informal to formal—is not unconstrained. In the present context, I would like to argue that women (especially of poor peasant and tribal households) are indeed victims of environmental degradation, although they are usually not "passive" victims in that they often recognize the need for environmental protection, and many seek to take action in various, typically informal, ways. To be effective agents of change, however, requires also the ability to challenge and change in their own interest the formal structures that control natural resource use and abuse. This begs the question of what factors might constrain women's exercise of agency in terms of environmental action and how these constraints might be overcome.

The context for examining these issues is provided by a range of initiatives for environmental management that have emerged in India in recent years. In particular, numerous micro-level forest protection groups have been formed. Some are state-initiated under what is termed the Joint Forest Management (JFM) program, in which village communities and the government share the responsibility and benefits of protecting and regenerating degraded forest land; others are self-initiated by village communities; yet others are catalyzed by nongovernmental organizations (NGOs). A common feature of these initiatives, however, is that most are dominated by village men. This suggests that a new system of property rights is being created in communal land and that these rights, like existing rights in privatized land, are strongly male-centered. This raises critical questions about gender equity in the sharing of benefits and costs from environmental action, about women's participation (or its lack) in these new initiatives, and about what restricts or facilitates women's exercise of agency.

This essay is based on field visits (especially during 1993–1995) to several sites of environmental action, discussion with villagers and NGOs, and emerging case studies. To set the context, before outlining the features and implications of the new initiatives I first examine below the class-gender impact of environmental degradation.

CLASS-GENDER EFFECTS OF ENVIRONMENTAL DECLINE

Class and Gender Specificity

Rural households have always depended on VCs and forests for a wide variety of items essential to personal use or offered for sale. Fuel, fodder, fiber, food items, small timber, manure, bamboo, medicinal herbs, oils, materials for house building and handicrafts, resin, and gum are just a few of the products obtainable from such sources.[11] In particular, firewood—the single most important source of domestic fuel in rural South Asia (providing 65 percent or more of the domestic energy in large parts of north India, and 95 percent in Nepal)—is mostly gathered and not purchased.[12] Moreover, several million people in India (estimated at thirty million a decade and a half ago) depend wholly or substantially on nontimber forest products for a livelihood.[13] These sources prove especially critical during lean agricultural seasons and acute food shortage contexts such as drought.[14]

Although all rural households use VCs in some degree, for the poor they are crucially important because of the unequal distribution of private land in the country.[15] In Jodha's[16] study of twelve semiarid districts in seven states in the 1980s,[17] VCs accounted for between 9 and 26 percent of total income among poor rural households but only 1 to 4 percent of total income among the nonpoor. The landless and land-poor are especially dependent on the commons for fuel and fodder: VCs provide over 90 percent of their firewood and 69 to 89 percent (varying by region) of their grazing needs, compared with the relative self-sufficiency (from private land) of landed households.[18]

Within poor households, however, there are important gender differences in both the extent of and the nature of dependence on forests and VCs. To begin with, direct access to resources (private or communal) is especially important for women because of a systematic antifemale bias in the intrahousehold distribution of subsistence income controlled by men, including that used for health care and food. These differences are markedly acute in northwest India but are found in some degree in most parts of the country.[19] Hence resources in the hands of male household heads cannot be assumed to benefit women and children in equal degree.

However, women are much more dependent on common property resources because of their lesser access to private property resources and fewer other avenues for livelihood. For instance, the most important productive resource in rural economies—agricultural land and associated technology—is concentrated largely in male hands.[20] Women are also systematically disadvantaged in the labor market, with fewer employment opportunities, lesser occupational mobility, lower levels of training, and lower payments for the same or similar work. Due to the greater task-specificity of their agricultural work, they face sharper fluctuations in employment and earnings and have less chance of finding work in the slack seasons.[21] Common property resources, such as VCs, have therefore been for rural women and children (especially those of tribal, landless, or land-poor households) one of the few independent sources of subsistence available to them. Rights in VCs were customarily linked to residence in the village community, so that women were not excluded, as they typically were from the ownership of individualized private land.

Communal resources acquire additional importance for women in regions with strong norms of female seclusion (as in northwest India), where women's access to the cash economy, to markets, and to the marketplace itself is restricted and dependent on the mediation of male relatives. While these constraints leave women of poor households particularly vulnerable, those in well-off households are also not immune, since in the absence of personal assets they too face the risk of impoverishment in case of widowhood or marital breakdown.[22]

Apart from the *extent* of dependence, the *nature* of men's and women's dependence on communal resources is also different because of the existing gender division of labor. In poor peasant and tribal households, it is women who do most of the gathering and fetching from forests and VCs, and they also bear a major responsibility for family subsistence, not uncommonly being the primary or (in most female-headed households) sole economic providers. Women, especially tribal women, are the main gatherers of nontimber forest products for consumption or sale. An estimated 70 percent of such products are collected in the tribal belts of five states: Bihar, Maharashtra, Madhya Pradesh, Orissa, and Andhra Pradesh.[23] Men's direct dependence on forests and VCs in these communities is much more in terms of timber, especially small timber for agricultural implements, and materials for house building. (Indirectly, of course, men too depend on the products women gather for home use.)

Their importance to rural communities notwithstanding, the availability of forests and VCs in India has been declining rapidly. Both under British colonial rule and in postcolonial policies, at least up to the late 1970s, forests were viewed primarily as a resource for commercial exploitation. Large tracts were cut for timber, cleared for agriculture, or (especially under colonialism) cleared for tea and coffee plantations. The state monopoly over forests established under colonial rule persisted after independence, as did the practice of forestry for profit, with local villagers and forest dwellers being treated as transgressors by the Forest Department. In 1987–89 only sixty-four million hectares, or 19.5 percent of India's geographic area, was forested. Much of this land was highly degraded, with poor tree cover, and the remaining forests were disappearing rapidly. Today the good forest land is mostly concentrated in a few states of central, eastern, and northeastern India.

The process of statization of forest land has been accompanied by the privatization of VCs. Between 1950 and 1984, for instance, VCs declined by 26 to 63 percent across seven states. Population pressure apart, this can be attributed mainly to government actions that benefited selected groups, such as the legalization of illegal encroachments by influential farmers, the auctioning of parts of VCs to private contractors for commercial exploitation, and the distribution of common land to individuals under various land reform and antipoverty schemes that were intended to benefit the poor but in practice benefitted the well-off.[24] For sixteen of the nineteen districts in the seven states studied by Jodha, the share of land received by the poor was less than that received by the nonpoor.

The statization and privatization of communal resources have not only altered the distribution of available resources in favor of a few. They have also systematically undermined the traditional institutional arrangements of resource use and management that existed in many areas. Under these community institutions, responsibility for resource management was linked to resource use; many traditional methods of gathering firewood and fodder were typically not destructive of nature.[25] When control over the resources passed from the community to the State or to individuals, this link was effectively broken. In turn, the shift in control increased environmental degradation.[26]

Aggravating these trends toward deforestation and VC decline are other factors, including population pressure, the expansion of agriculture at the expense of forests and pastures, large hydroelectric schemes, and so on.

These processes, however, have had different implications for women and men because of preexisting gender inequalities and differences in dependence on these resources. Women have borne the main burden of deforestation and declining VCs.

Implications for Poor Rural Women

First, as the main gatherers of fuel, fodder, and water, it is primarily women's working day (already averaging ten to twelve hours) that lengthens with declining forests and VCs. In recent years, there has been a notable increase in firewood collection time, to a small degree in some regions, dramatically in others (see table 1).[27] Fodder shortages

Table 1: Time Taken and Distance Travelled for Firewood Collection in Different Regions

State/Region	Year of Data	Firewood collection[a]		Data Source
		Time taken	Distance travelled	
Bihar (plains)	c.1972	NA	1–2 km/day	Bhaduri & Surin (1980)
	1980	NA	8–10 km/day	
Gujarat (plains)				
(a) forested		once every 4 days	NA	
(b) depleted	1980	once every 2 days	4–5 km	Nagbrahman &
(c) severely depleted		4–5 hr/day	NA	Sambrani (1983)
Karnataka (plains)	NA	1 hr/day	5.4 km/trip	Batliwala (1983)
Madhya Pradesh (plains)	1980	1–2 times/week	5 km	Chand & Bezboruah (1980)
Rajasthan				
Alwar plains	1986	5 hr/day (winter)	4 km	Author's observation in 1988
Ajmer plains	1970s	1.9 hr/journey	1.9 km	Survey by author in 1993
(average: all seasons)	1990s	2.1 hr/journey	2.1 km	
Uttar Pradesh				
Chamoli (hills)				
(a) Dwing	1982	5 hr/day[b]	over 5 km	Swaminathan (1984)
(b) Pakhi		4 hr/day }		
Garhwal (hills)	NA	5 hr/day	10 km	Agarwal (1983)
Kumaon (hills)	1982	3 days/week	5–7 km	Folger and Dewan (1983)
Kumaon (hills)	1970s	1.6 hrs/journey	1.6 km	Survey by author in
(average: all seasons)	1990s	3–4 hrs/journey	4.5 km	1993

NA: Information not available.

[a] Firewood collected mainly by women and children.

[b] Average computed from information given in the study.

are even more acute. My survey in Rajasthan, Gujarat, and the Kumaon region of the Uttar Pradesh hills in 1993–94, indicates not only an increase in fodder collection time, but also a growing dependence on market purchase. Moreover, in regions where grazing is still possible, twenty years ago it was boys and/or men who usually took the animals out; now (as in the Kumaon village) girls are more often sent for grazing while their brothers attend school. Over time this shift could widen the gender gap in literacy in such areas.

Second, the decline in items gathered from forests and VCs has reduced incomes both directly and indirectly, the latter because the extra time spent in gathering reduces time available to women for crop production. This can adversely affect crop incomes,[28] especially in hill communities where, due to high male outmigration, women are the primary cultivators. Similar negative implications for women's income arise with the decline in grazing land and associated fodder shortage.

Third, as the area and productivity of VCs and forests fall, so do the contributions of gathered food in the diets of the rural poor. In addition, nutrition suffers with fuelwood shortages, as households economize on fuel by shifting to less nutritious foods that can be eaten raw or need less fuel to cook; by eating partially cooked food, which could prove toxic, or eating leftovers, which could rot in a tropical climate; or by missing some meals altogether, as observed in Bangladesh in the early 1980s.[29] A trade-off between the time spent in fuel gathering rather than cooking can also reduce the meal's nutritional quality. Although these nutritional consequences impinge in some degree on all household members, women and female children bear the greater burden because of the noted gender biases in intrafamily distribution of food. Nutritional inadequacies in turn have health consequences.

Fourth, large-scale deforestation disrupts social support networks involving kin and other villagers, networks built up primarily by women and important in sustaining poor households during scarcity. Such support can include reciprocal labor-sharing arrangements during peak agricultural seasons and loans in cash or kind (small amounts of food, fuel, fodder, etc.), on which many poor women depend.[30]

Fifth, gathering food and medicinal items helps build up knowledge of the nutritional and medicinal properties of plants, roots, and trees, including edible plants not normally consumed but critical for surviving prolonged food shortages.[31] Such "famine foods" are gathered mainly by women and children. The degradation of forests and VCs and their appropriation by a minority is destroying the material basis on which such indigenous knowledge of natural resources is founded and kept alive, leading to its gradual eclipse. This, in turn, further undermines the ability of poor households, and especially women, to cope with any subsistence crises.

Of course, the implications outlined above vary in strength across India, since there are distinct regional differences in the extent of environmental vulnerability, incidence of poverty, and gender bias. Rural women are worst off in regions where all three forms of disadvantage are strong and reinforce each other, as in parts of northern India.

Women are less badly off where all three forms of disadvantage are weak, as in much of southern and northeastern India. But the effects are likely to be felt to some degree in most parts of the country.[32]

Against this backdrop it becomes especially important to examine the gender implications of recent initiatives for protecting and regenerating forests and VCs.

EMERGENT COMMUNITY INSTITUTIONS FOR FOREST MANAGEMENT

In recent years, many forest management groups have emerged, some initiated by the state, others self-initiated by village communities, yet others catalyzed by nongovernmental organizations (NGOs) or charismatic individuals, including forest protection movements such as Chipko and Appiko. These initiatives can broadly be classified into four categories: the government-initiated Joint Forest Management (JFM) program; autonomous forest management initiatives; mixed forest management initiatives (State-cum-autonomous); and people's movements. The main features of each are outlined below.

Government-Initiated Joint Forest Management Program

The basic idea behind the JFM program is to establish a partnership between the state Forest Department and village communities, with a sharing of responsibilities and benefits. Although the earliest such initiatives were catalyzed by two district forest officers in West Bengal in the early 1970s, these remained isolated cases until the late 1980s, when there was rapid informal expansion.[33] A formal policy was finally approved by the West Bengal government in 1989 and subsequently by the central government, which in 1990 announced a new national policy for involving village communities across the country for reviving degraded forest lands.

JFM represents a notable departure from the government's earlier attempts to deal with deforestation, which by the 1970s had reached crisis proportions in many regions. At that time, the alarm sounded by grassroots activists, journalists, and some academics led the government to initiate tree-planting schemes under the banner of "social forestry." Undertaken in a top-down manner, most such schemes succeeded neither in regenerating degraded commons and forests nor in meeting everyday village needs. In particular, they raised serious doubts about the ability of the State or of individuals to develop, without some form of action involving local communities, what was a communal resource. In contrast were emerging success stories of some forest officials involving villagers in degraded-forest management as a "joint" venture. As a result of the lessons learned, the JFM program was launched.

To date, sixteen states have passed JFM resolutions; nonparticipating states are Kerala in the south and all the states, except Tripura, in the northeast. The resolutions allow the participating villagers free access to most nontimber forest products and to 25 to 50 percent (varying by state) of the mature timber when finally harvested. On their part, villagers are responsible for protecting the forests by forming an organization, typically

Table 2: Forest Protection Committees Under JFM:[a]
Membership Conditions by State

Membership Conditions	States
One person per household	Bihar, Jammu and Kashmir, Karnataka, Madhya Pradesh, Maharashtra, Tripura
One adult per household	Jammu and Kashmir, Uttar Pradesh
One adult male and one adult female per household	Andhra Pradesh, Himachal Pradesh, Orissa, West Bengal[b]
One male and one female per household	Tamil Nadu
All village adults	Haryana
All village residents	Rajasthan and Gujarat
Not clear	Punjab

[a] In some states, the Forest Protection Committees also take the form of cooperative societies or general bodies.

[b] In West Bengal, if the husband is a member, the wife automatically becomes a member.

Sources: SPWD (1994), *Wastelands News* (1993–94), and personal communication from Sushil Saigal (SPWD Staff) on Uttar Pradesh.

a Forest Protection Committee (FPC). However, eligibility rules for membership in the FPCs vary considerably: some states allow all village residents to be members, others allow membership to only one person per household, and so on (table 2); this has important gender implications that are traced later. From among the FPC members a few are elected to an executive committee (or managing committee) which also usually includes the village council head and some others (varying by state).

There are no comprehensive figures for the area under JFM, but data for five states (Gujarat, Haryana, Jammu,[34] Orissa, and West Bengal) indicate that in 1992, .6 million hectares of forest land were being protected by 4,486 FPCs. In some cases, state governments have worked in conjunction with NGOs (or vice versa) in catalyzing the formation of these committees.

Autonomous Forest Management Initiatives

Parallel to and often prior to the JFM initiatives, numerous self-initiated forest management groups have been constituted in several states, catalyzed by local leaders or NGOs. Enormously diverse in form and structure, these autonomous groups have emerged primarily in areas where people are still strongly dependent on forests and have a long-standing tradition of community resource management.[35] The groups are present in largest numbers in Bihar and Orissa and to a lesser extent elsewhere, as in Gujarat, Rajasthan, Karnataka, and Madhya Pradesh. Their organizational setup varies, taking the form of groups of village elders, village councils, Forest Protection Committees, village-based voluntary organizations, youth clubs, and so on.[36] Over time, some of these groups have registered with the Forest Department, but most remain autonomous, without official standing but with tacit village sanction to punish offenders, including by imposing fines.

There are no exact figures on the number and coverage of such groups. But some close observers estimate that in mid-1992 there were about ten thousand community institutions (including both JFM and autonomous groups) protecting some 1.5 million hectares of forest land in ten states.[37]

Mixed Forest Management Initiatives

A diversity of initiatives that are operating in conjunction with the State or as autonomous units could be classified under this category. In particular, I have in mind cases in which formal State initiatives have become effectively defunct for various reasons, and a range of protection groups in the form of Mahila Mandal Dals (women's associations) have emerged instead.[38] A good example is *van panchayats* (VPs), or forest councils, established by the colonial government around 1931, some of which were revived in the 1980s by local NGOs. In 1985 there were an estimated 4,058 VPs covering about .4 million hectares (or 14 percent) of forest area in five districts of the Uttar Pradesh hills.[39]

Typically consisting of from five to nine members elected from the village (or villages) falling in the *van panchayat* jurisdiction, the VPs are responsible for preventing encroachments and devising rules for forest use.[40] Most hire watchmen to keep guard. The VP committees are authorized to collect fees from users and levy fines on offenders. But this structure is subject to the administrative and technical control of the Revenue and Forest Departments.

Most VP committees are constituted entirely of men. In recent years, however, Mahila Mandal Dals have emerged in some regions as independent bodies that are often neither answerable to nor integrated with the VPs, but which are doing the effective work of protection and reporting offenders to the formal VP body. In rare instances all-women VPs can be found.[41]

People's Movements

More loosely structured than any of the above are people's movements for forest protection, the most publicized being the Chipko movement initiated in 1973 in the hills of Garhwal (Uttar Pradesh). The movement began as an attempt by local people to stop indiscriminate commercial exploitation of the regions' forests, 95 percent of which are owned by the government and managed by the Forest Department. The specific incident that sparked the movement was when the people of Chamoli district successfully resisted the auctioning of three hundred ash trees to a sports goods manufacturer, while the local labor cooperative had been refused government permission to harvest even a few trees for making agricultural implements. Since its inception the movement has spread within the region, and its methods and message have reached many parts of the country and outside, in some cases inspiring less well-known movements such as Appiko in Karnataka.

Although in most states the emergent community initiatives are too new to make generalizations possible, in broad terms, they appear to have typically arisen in communities that are highly dependent on forest resources and which are facing considerable scarcities, sometimes due to acute degradation. Most involve tribal or hill populations that are relatively less socially and economically differentiated.[42] And while some groups, as noted, are formally registered with or formed through the Forest Department, others have no official standing.

In terms of regeneration, there have been some notable successes. Where the tree rootstock is undamaged, natural regeneration begins at an encouraging pace, often yielding a good harvest of grass within the first year of protection, and fuelwood through cutback operations within a few years. Several protected tracts I visited in March 1995 showed impressive natural regeneration. For instance, when Malekpur village (Sabarkantha district, Gujarat) began community forest management in 1990, with the encouragement of an NGO, VIKSAT (Vikram Sarabhai Center for Science and Technology), and registered their Tree Grower's Cooperative Society, the protected area consisted of little more than barren hillsides, from which it was difficult to obtain much except dry twigs and monsoon grass. However, given the strong rootstock, by 1995 there was a young teak forest there, with trees ten to twelve feet tall interspersed with other species. In the 1994 monsoon season there had also been a substantial harvest of grass. And in early 1995, thinning and pruning operations yielded enough firewood for domestic use to last every participating village household some five months. Similarly, in Baruch district of Gujarat, where another NGO, AKRSP (Agha Khan Rural Support Group), has served as a catalyst, several protected forest tracts that I visited in 1995 showed impressive natural regeneration.[43] Biodiversity was also reported to have increased. A number of other case studies report similar encouraging returns after protection, and a decline in seasonal migration.[44]

Undeniably there are also cases of serious conflict (especially intervillage) and failure, and the factors that account for success or failure need more probing. But a study of some forty-two FPCs in West Bengal indicate that "the most effective FPC is when a single village is involved in the management of the forest, its ethnic composition is tribal, a majority of the households in the village become members of the FPC and . . . forest land is allowed to regenerate rather than afforested with plantations."[45]

THE GENDER GAP IN EMERGENT INSTITUTIONS

The question, however, remains: Have the communities that have displayed impressive results in protection and "greening" been as successful in ensuring gender equity in control over common property resources and in the sharing of benefits? To answer this, we need to examine women's participation in the decision-making forums of the emergent community initiatives—for instance, women's presence and voice in FPCs and executive councils, which make the rules about responsibility and benefit sharing. We also need to consider the implications of such participation (or its lack) for the effectiveness of protection and regeneration activities, for the distribution of burdens and benefits from them, and for women's empowerment.

Effective participation would involve women's formal membership in management committees, their attending meetings where they are members, and their views being given weight in the meetings they attend.

In terms of women's formal membership, whether in JFM schemes, autonomous initiatives, or VPs, the overall picture to date is discouraging, with some notable exceptions, discussed later. In several JFM states that allow membership in FPCs to only one person per household, women are effectively excluded since inevitably a man is the member. But even where they are not so excluded, women's numbers are low. In West Bengal, out of 8,158 members in 72 FPCs in Midnapore district, only 241 (3 percent) are women, mostly widows.[46] In Barsole and Lekhiasole villages (also in Midnapore district), where the FPCs have 44 and 303 members respectively, the first has only 2 women and the second 17, most of them again being widowed heads of household.[47] In Tamil Nadu, of the 22,561 members in 2,594 FPCs, only 7 percent are women.[48] Orissa's self-initiated groups also typically exclude women,[49] and most VPs in Uttar Pradesh have few or no women members.[50]

Membership apart, to participate in decision making women need to attend and be heard in committee meetings. For the reasons discussed further below, usually few women attend; those who do rarely speak out, and when they do speak their views are seldom taken seriously.

Within this rather negative scenario, there are also cases of vocal women being present in notable numbers in some forest protection initiatives. These cases (described later) can provide pointers on how women's participation could be increased. But consider first why it is important that women participate in their own right.

Women's membership in forest protection institutions and their effective participation (or its lack) in the decision making forums impinge on at least three crucial aspects: entitlements, efficiency, and empowerment.

Entitlements and Welfare Considerations

A household's entitlement to a share in the benefits from protection is linked to membership in the forest protection initiatives. To be sure, women could benefit in some degree by virtue of belonging to households where men are members. For instance, where degradation is not acute, member households continue to enjoy the rights of collecting dry wood or leaves from the protected area.[51] Also, some FPCs under JFM have given very poor women special consideration in allowing them to collect leaves for making plates.[52] But for several reasons, benefits mediated through male membership have welfare disadvantages compared with women's direct membership and participation in the decision-making processes.

First, in many villages in Gujarat, West Bengal, Bihar, and Orissa, when protection began women were barred from any form of collection, even of dry twigs. Where the land was barren anyway this caused no extra hardship. But where women were previously able to fulfill at least a part of their needs from the protected area, the ban on entry imposed by all-male forest protection groups has made it necessary for women to travel to neighboring unprotected areas, spending many extra hours and also risking humiliation as intruders.[53] In some protected sites in Gujarat in 1993 and West Bengal in 1994, Sarin found that women who prior to protection spent one to two hours for a headload of firewood now spend four to five hours, and journeys of half a kilometer have in some cases lengthened to eight or nine kilometers.[54]

Similarly, during my field visit to Gujarat's Sabarkantha district, several women said that they were not allowed even to walk through the protected area to the neighboring one for fuelwood collection, on the grounds that they would break the rules. They were thus forced to skirt the area and spend several additional hours on their journeys (see box). In Pingot village (Baruch district, Gujarat), Shah and Shah found that since protection began women are compelled to take their daughters along to help with collection, spending over six hours a day to walk five times farther, for the same quantity of fuelwood.[55] Over time this could negatively affect the girls' education. When asked to comment on a recent award for environmental conservation conferred on the village, the women expressed only resentment: "What forest? We don't know anything about it now. We used to go to the forest to pick fuelwood, but ever since the men have started protecting it they don't even allow us to look at it!"[56]

These gender-specific hardships have typically surfaced where women are not members of protection committees and therefore did not participate in the initial formulation of rules. The household's everyday requirement of fuel and fodder, which is women's relentless responsibility, was therefore bypassed; what received attention was the sporadic need for small timber to construct and repair houses or make implements (which are men's responsibilities) and the potential cash returns from large timber.

In some instances, interventions by NGOs remedied the situation once women brought it to their notice, leading to cutback operations that yielded considerable firewood per household. For instance, in Malekpur village (Sabarkantha district, Gujarat), where some women say their headload collection time has increased from an hour or two to a whole day, a meeting organized by VIKSAT with the Tree Grower's Cooperative Society (which was doing the protection) led to cutback operations in 1995 that yielded both firewood and fodder. Some households that could afford it also switched to biogas. But the hardship in the interim years was borne solely by women.

Also in some of the autonomous initiatives, all-male youth clubs that are protecting the forests not only have banned entry completely, they have also been selling (rather than distributing) the forest products obtained from thinning and cleaning operations.

---

*Extracts from the author's interviews with village women
from Sabarkantha district (Gujarat), 25th March 1995*

Q: On what issues do women and men differ in FPC meetings?

A: Women face the problem of firewood. Because women protect the forest they
    should get some benefit from it. Men can afford to wait for a while because
    their main concern is timber. But women need fuelwood daily. When we ask for
    permission to take dry twigs, men say: What is the guarantee that you won't cut
    green branches? You might cut more. The men don't listen to us. We can get
    some fallen twigs and leaves for only ten days. The forest is closed for the rest of
    the year.

Q: What do you do then?

A: At the moment it is closed, so we use crop stalks, cattle dung, kerosene. Some
    have biogas.

Q: What did you do before the closure?

A: We used to go to the Rajasthan border for fuelwood. The route was through our
    own forest. On the return journey we would pick up dry wood from our forest.

Q: Do you go to Rajasthan now?

A: No, we can't now, because the route through our forest is blocked. From our
    forest, we are only allowed to get dry wood for ten days in the winter. That's all.
    We collect enough for two to three months. But in the monsoon we don't know
    what we will do. Last year they gave us special permission to collect for ten
    additional days. This year we are hoping for permission again.

Q: Will you get permission?

A: At the last *parishad* meeting they told us they won't give us permission.

Q: If you don't get permission, what will you do?

A: We can only call a women's meeting and talk to the men and put forward our
    problem. We will say: We have to cook, we have no wood. So what now?

Poor households that cannot afford to buy firewood and other forest products are the
worst sufferers under this policy, with the burden again falling disproportionately on
women. As one woman commented: "Earlier it was the Forest Department which controlled the forest, now it is the youth clubs."[57]

Second, cash benefits from protection, generated, say, through the sale of timber or
grass, are often put into a collective fund rather than being distributed to member
households. How that fund gets spent again depends on the male representatives in the
protection committees. In the late 1980s some youth clubs undertaking protection in
Orissa made substantial gains (in some cases up to Rs. 25,000) from selling forest products obtained during cleaning-up operations in the protected areas. Although in one
case the money was reportedly used for a school building, in some others it was spent
on clubhouse construction or for club functions.[58]

Even if such money were distributed to the participating households through the
male members, cash given to men does not guarantee equal sharing within the family.

In West Bengal, for instance, the daily wages paid by the Forest Department during the period of planting and the income from the subsequent sale of trees are usually given to the male household head even where the family works as a group. Guhathakurata and Bhatia found that the men in one village had used the money from timber sales to buy additional land, and in another village for gambling and liquor, rather than for pressing household needs.[59]

When the question of benefit sharing was discussed in a meeting of FPCs from three villages of West Bengal in which both women and men were present, all the women unequivocally said that shares should be equal and separate for husbands and wives: "There was no vote for 'joint accounts' or the husband being more eligible as the 'head of the household.' These women are responsible for a major share of household sustenance and they wanted control over their share of the income."[60] Indeed, benefits reaching the women would improve the welfare of the whole household, since poor rural women are noted to spend money mostly on family needs.[61]

Third, "needs" are only one criterion for the distribution of intrahousehold benefits. Entitlements within the household are also linked to perceptions about women's contribution and notions about rights.[62] Insofar as "perceived contribution" is an important criterion for the distribution of benefits, women seen to be participating in forest management would be better placed to claim equal benefits. Membership would give women a formal independent right in the new resource and not merely indirect benefits mediated through male members.

Fourth, membership in FPCs could lead to additional financial gains. In the villages where AKRSP works, for instance, a part of the daily wage earnings from tree planting goes into savings funds. Where women are not members, the savings have gone into a family account (which is effectively controlled by the male household head). But in recent initiatives where, as a result of AKRSP's specific attempts to involve women, female membership is high, savings go into separate accounts for women and men, and women often make their own decisions about how they will spend this money.[63]

EFFICIENCY CONSIDERATIONS

Women's active involvement also appears necessary for the effective functioning and long-term sustainability of these initiatives. For instance, to prevent infractions, women as the main collectors of firewood and other nontimber forest products need to adhere to the rules. In some cases, male FPC members have threatened their wives with beatings if they break the rules, thus reinforcing existing positions of male power.[64] Its reprehensibility apart, this is hardly an enforceable form of control in the long run, given that women's collection activities fulfill a basic household need and thus benefit men as well.

Oftentimes both women and men are aware of the importance of women's involvement in the protection programs. Britt's interviews in two villages in Nainital district (Uttar Pradesh hills) in 1992, although dealing with VP experience, also have relevance for JFM and other contexts.[65] In both villages the VP committee includes only one woman. Britt notes:

> Males and females generally concur . . . that if more women were to attend meetings, the workings of the forest committee would be improved. When prompted, the majority of the villagers thought that some kind of mechanism necessitating attendance by greater numbers of women, such as a 50 percent reservation policy, would provide for greater information dissemination and better implementation of forest committee rules.[66]

In women's own words:

> It would be good if women went [to forest committee meetings]. . . The men don't seem to realize where fodder and fuelwood come from.[67]

> Women often don't even know what rules the forest committee has decided upon. If more women were on the forest committee then they could pass on the information to other women and the forest would be better protected.[68]

> The male members of the forest committee have difficulties implementing the rules. Women could discuss these problems with the men. Perhaps more "mid-way" rules would be, in the long run, more effective . . . more viable.[69]

Despite this recognition, typically few women participate in the VPs, or in the FPCs under JFM. But it is not uncommon for them to form informal patrol groups where men's groups are ineffective (as elaborated later).

Also, women's knowledge as well as preference for certain plant species often differ from men's. Involving women in decisions about planting and silviculture practices in the protected areas would be an effective way of ensuring that a larger proportion of household needs from the forest are taken into account, and that women's particular knowledge of plants and species enriches the selections made, thus enhancing biodiversity. In Panchmahals district (Gujarat), women's rich knowledge of medicinal herbs was important in promoting such plants in the protected area.[70] In the same region, in Muvasa village, a woman's group, when replanting a part of the village common land, resisted pressure from the men to plant eucalyptus for cash benefits. The women used their considerable knowledge about local trees and shrubs, and their suitability for different uses, to select diverse species instead.

EMPOWERMENT CONSIDERATIONS

The absence of women's formal participation in the new community initiatives will reinforce preexisting gender inequalities and further reduce women's bargaining power within and outside the household. In contrast, participation in public decision making forums such as FPCs, would help reverse rural women's traditional exclusion from such forums, and also increase their self-confidence in asserting their rights in relation to public bodies in general.

In Navagaon village (Gujarat), for instance, where women constitute 50 percent of the members in village development associations and are entitled to hold separate savings accounts, they now feel they are treated more respectfully by the village men, not least because they deal with institutions such as banks themselves.[71] Similarly, in the Chipko struggle it is notable that, over time, as participation enhanced women's confidence they began to demand membership in the village councils and a greater say in their decision-making process.

More generally, numerous case studies have noted the empowering effect on women of greater control over economic resources, especially land, and of participation in the forums that control these resources, especially via collectivities.[72]

CONSTRAINTS ON WOMEN'S FORMAL PARTICIPATION

What, then, constrains women from formal participation and a more effective exercise of agency in many of these emergent institutional initiatives? Broadly the constraints are of five types: rules governing membership; traditional norms of membership in public bodies; social barriers; logistical factors; and attitudes of Forest Department personnel.

First, as noted earlier, in several states the JFM resolutions allow only one member per household. This is inevitably a man, except in widow-headed households. Even where the rules allow one man and one woman per household (as in Andhra Pradesh, Himachal Pradesh, Orissa, and West Bengal), other household adults remain excluded (including dependent widows and unmarried daughters). The most equitable situation would be to allow JFM membership to all village adults, as is the case in Haryana and Gujarat.

Second, traditional village assemblies and councils customarily excluded women, even among tribal (including matrilineal) communities.[73] In many autonomous forest-management initiatives, as in parts of Bihar and Orissa, this long-standing tradition has been replicated in the new institutions. Women are not called to meetings for conflict resolution even when the dispute directly involves them.[74]

Third, women face social constraints that need probing. Most studies attribute women's low attendance in FPCs and executive committees and their not speaking up in JFM and VP meetings to "cultural barriers," but few explore what these might be.[75] Given that a large majority of the community initiatives we have been discussing involve tribal or hill communities where there is no female seclusion, and where women's participation in economic activities is visibly high, clearly the constraints have little to do with explicit norms of seclusion, and much to do with gender ideology, viz. the social constructions of acceptable female behavior, notions about male and female spaces, and assumptions about men's and women's capabilities and appropriate roles in society.

For instance, although many of the women Britt interviewed in 1992 in the two VP villages recognized that their presence in meetings would improve VP functioning, they felt they could not attend unless the men invited them, and that the men were not seriously interested in doing so:[76]

> The meetings are considered for men only. Women are never called. The men attend and their opinions or consent are taken as representative of the whole family—it's understood.[77]

> Male committee members are not interested in calling women to meetings even though women . . . are the ones who go to the forest and do the cutting.[78]

Women's effectiveness is also restricted by their limited experience in public speaking, illiteracy, a lack of recognized authority, or the absence of a "critical mass" of women. As one woman in the VP area said:

> Only I alone cannot change procedures. If I tried to change the rules, people would think what sort of woman is she, that she has these ideas. . . . I am not in the habit of speaking publicly, not like other women who have worked with CHIRAG [a local NGO].[79]

In Katuual village the sole woman member, although elected to the VP several months prior to Britt's visit, had yet to attend a meeting. She was interested in going to the next one but felt that as the only woman member and without the acquiescence of other village women, she would be ineffective:

> I discuss the forest with other women. Many times I have told outsiders not to go to the forest and cut leaves or trees. I warn them that they will be fined. Sometimes I have lied, telling them that a government officer is coming and that if they are fined in front of him then they must pay a deposit in Nainital. But all this has very little effect on the women. If they intend to collect, then they will.[80]

Women also feel discouraged from attending meetings because their opinions are disregarded. One woman member of a VP committee commented as follows on the attitude of her male colleagues:

> I went to three or four meetings. . . . No one ever listened to my suggestions. I marked my signature in the register. I'm illiterate so I couldn't tell what was written

in the meeting minutes. I was told that my recommendations would be considered, but first that the register had to be signed. They were uninterested.[81]

There are similar complaints about the functioning of FPCs under JFM from parts of West Bengal.[82] Even women who are executive committee members and attend meetings regularly usually sit at the back as mere observers, while the points raised by male members who sit in front receive priority.

Fourth, age and marital status affect women's participation in meetings. In many of West Bengal's FPCs, the few women members are mostly widows.[83] Sharma et al. similarly note for Chipko women: "When one looks at the profiles of a few of these women who have taken active part earlier in the prohibition movement, and later in the 'Chipko' movement on a more sustained basis, they are older women or widows or single women" and that "young married women are more constrained by their family responsibilities and kin-based authority patterns."[84] The burden of work is also usually greater on young married women, especially daughters-in-law.[85]

Fifth, women's participation is often impeded by logistical constraints and double work burdens. The timings of meetings (which are often called when women are busy with other work) and women's heavy workload (child care, housework, agricultural activities, and other responsibilities) can be serious barriers:

> Women are very busy with household work. If they go to the meetings who would watch the children? It is impossible for all women to attend.[86]

Most hill women in VP villages told Mansingh that they did not have time to "sit around for [the] four hours that it took to have a meeting in the middle of the day."[87] As a result, women's attendance tended to thin out over time.

Sixth, many male Forest Department personnel involved with JFM are known to call only men to meetings,[88] while there are few women among the department's personnel. In the Haryana Forest Department only fifteen village forest workers were appointed, as against an official provision for three hundred.[89] In four divisions of Tamil Nadu only 6 percent of total social forestry workers are women.[90] Women in parts of West Bengal report that male officers rarely consult them in preparing the village-level microplans for forest development, and some had heard about the plan only through their husbands, or had been consulted initially but not for revisions or updates, nor on choice of tree species.[91] Women interviewed by Narain in two West Bengal villages complained that male officials discouraged them from coming to the forest office and rebuked them if they came in the evening even on an urgent matter.[92]

Elsewhere in West Bengal women complain that:

> the forest officers put very little value on what they say and always crosscheck with the men to verify the truth of their words. And if ever there is any conflict or con-

tradition between the women and the men, the foresters always settle the disputes in favor of the men.[93]

Many Forest Department personnel see women's involvement in JFM activities as useful mainly for keeping out other women "offenders," rather than for reasons of gender equity or to take advantage of women's knowledge of plants and trees. Women are seen as better able to catch female culprits, since men doing so are susceptible to being charged with molestation.

These constraints underline the fact that while rural women have particularly strong reasons for participating in environmental action, their ability to exercise agency (their "agency-freedom") is strongly circumscribed.

CONTRASTING EXAMPLES AND WOMEN'S INITIATIVES

Despite these constraints there are contrasting examples where women's presence in forest protection groups is high, sometimes in the formal forums, more commonly in informal ones. These cases suggest that the "cultural" barriers to women's participation, especially in tribal or hill communities, are not insurmountable.

First consider the formal groups. In parts of Gujarat, 30 percent of the members in the village general body are women, and their presence in the JFM executive committees ranges between 14 and 50 percent.[94] In a number of other recent initiatives in Gujarat, under AKRSP encouragement female membership in the FPCs has risen to 50 percent. In parts of West Bengal's Bankura district, women are doing most of the protection work. For instance, in Chiligarah village women are the members and men their nominees;[95] Korapara village initially had only male members, but now twenty-two out of thirty-five FPC members are women.[96] There are also several all-women FPCs in Bankura district.[97] Likewise, in a Bihar village in Ranchi district with a mixed population of Muslims, Hindus, and Scheduled Tribes, women took the initiative of forming a FPC in 1991 when the all-male committee was ineffective in resolving conflicts and in saving the forest. The committee has four hundred to five hundred women members drawn from all sections of the village, covers about 490 hectares of forest land, and has since been given formal recognition by the Forest Department.[98] In Orissa, women in two villages approached a young forester in charge of the range to help them form an all-women FPC.[99]

More commonly, though, it is women's informal groups that are in effect undertaking forest protection and wasteland development. In some villages it was the failure of men's committees that led women to form their own. In Machipada village (Baruch district, Gujarat), which falls in AKRSP's ambit, in 1994 the women started their own protection group, even though an all-male group already existed. They now patrol the area in rotation with the men. My conversation with some of the women during a field visit in March 1995 threw light on this:

Q: Why don't you leave forest protection to the men?

A: We protect the forest for our children. We have an old relationship with the forest.

Q: Don't men also have such a relationship? Do women have a special relationship?

A: Yes, women do. We go there for firewood, nuts, berries, and many other items.

Q: Don't men protect well?

A: Men don't check carefully for illegal cuttings. Women keep a more careful lookout.

Q: Is there any other advantage of your forming a separate patrol group?

A: Our patrolling leads to the feeling that there is continuous protection. Now people feel everyone is taking responsibility for protection.

Q: Since you formed your own patrolling group are you treated better at home?

A: Yes, it makes a difference. Now women can explain why the forest is important. Men listen better. Now it feels like our forest.

In Rajasthan, with the help of PEDO (People's Education and Development Organization), women in several villages have established plantations and employed watchmen to guard them.[100] There are also numerous success stories of women's groups reclaiming village wastelands from across India.[101]

Again, in the Uttar Pradesh hills, where, as noted, most formal VPs have few women, there are numerous cases of women's informal groups guarding the forest. In Buribana village (Nainital district), which I visited in 1993, the Mahila Mandal Dal (the women's association) devised its own rules for the collection of forest produce, kept a lookout for offenders, and reported infractions to the VP head. Now women are also invited to VP meetings (although formally the VP members are all men). Elsewhere, women either guard the VP forest themselves or employ a guard.[102] It is notable that in Sharma and Sinha's study of twelve VPs, the four they deem "robust" and successful all have active Mahila Mandal Dals.[103] In general they attribute the success of many VPs to the presence of active Mahila Mandal Dals, even though these women's associations have no formal authority for forest protection. The associations spread awareness among women of the need to conserve forests, exert social pressure on women who violate usage rules, and monitor forest use. The importance of a Mahila Mandal Dal cooperating with the VP lies especially in the fact that women in this region not only do most of the fuel and fodder collection, they also play a critical and highly visible role in agriculture. If they refuse to follow the rules, the men are unable to effectively enforce them. Moreover, women are in the best position to apprehend transgressors.

Here Vieges and Menon's observations for FPCs in West Bengal have wider relevance:

> In complete contrast to their [typically low] representation in the committees, the active contribution of the women to the aims and objectives of the FPCs is . . . much more than that of the male members. This seems to be the irony . . . that recognition is given through official membership to the males whose contribution is much less than that of the women. . . . There is no time in the day when a few women are not present in the forest. Hence, in most areas no need is even felt to appoint special patrols to guard the forests from offenders. The women invariably take on this role. Whenever they spot an offender it is they who apprehend him/her directly.[104]

Women's participation in movements such as Chipko is again illustrative. Although mobilization and protest in the movement have been typically situation-specific, in some Chipko areas women have formed vigilance teams against illegal felling and are monitoring the use of the local forest. Moreover, Chipko women have protested against the commercial exploitation of the Himalayan forests not only jointly with the men of their community, but also on occasion even in opposition to the men, revealing different priorities in resource use. On one occasion, women successfully resisted the axing of a tract of the Dongri-Paintoli oak forest for establishing a potato seed farm that the men supported. Cutting the forest would have added five miles to women's fuelwood journeys, while they felt cash earned from the project would stay mainly in the men's hands. Again, in tree-planting schemes, Chipko women have typically favored trees that provide fuel and fodder rather than the commercially profitable varieties often favored by the men.[105]

The above examples clearly highlight women's concerns and organizing abilities. At the same time, the examples are not unambiguously positive since forming informal groups adds to women's responsibilities and burdens without vesting them with additional authority. Improving women's participation and authority in the *formal* forums therefore remains vital.

OVERCOMING THE CONSTRAINTS

What accounts for women's participation in some initiatives and not in others? What factors could make the emergent community institutions for resource management more gender-equal and in particular strengthen women's formal involvement in the groups? These questions warrant more in-depth probing, but some pointers are provided below.

Gender-Progressive NGO Presence

Typically a major factor facilitating women's participation and also effectiveness in FPC meetings is the presence of a gender-progressive organization. We have noted several examples where such an NGO has explicitly brought women's concerns to the fore and led to those concerns being addressed to some degree. In Malekpur village in Gujarat we noted how, at a community meeting, VIKSAT's focus on the hardships women were facing in fuelwood collection led to cutback operations that yielded substantial fuelwood. In Navagaon village (Gujarat), AKRSP was able to considerably increase women's membership in FPCs as well as their attendance at meetings. Similarly in Rajasthan, explicit dialogue with the community's men through the intermediation of PEDO reduced male hostility toward women's efforts at reclaiming village common lands. All the three NGOs in question, VIKSAT, AKRSP, and PEDO, were not exclusively women's organizations.

All-women organizations, however, can make a particular difference. The contrast between north and southwest Bengal in Mukerjee and Roy's study is revealing.[106] While in southwest Bengal (Midnapore district) only 3 percent of the 8,158 FPC members are women, in north Bengal female presence in FPCs is marked. There almost all the women members in FPCs are also members of the local woman's organization, the Ganatantrik Mahila Samity. In parts of West Bengal's Bankura district where women's NGO presence is strong, there is also a notable female presence in FPCs. In Korapara village the shift from an initial all-male membership to 63 percent female membership is attributable to the active encouragement of the local women's associations, the *mahila samitis* of the Nari Bikas Sangh. This organization was initially formed under the leadership of the Centre for Women's Development Studies (Delhi) to enable women to develop degraded village lands as an income-generating activity. In 1980 a group of women reclaimed wasteland within their village and planted trees for sericulture. By 1988 some 1,500 women in thirty-six villages were members of such groups.[107] Today Nari Bikas Sangh is a registered body and its members are also among the most active members of FPCs in Bankura district.

The fact that these initiatives primarily involve tribal or hill communities makes it easier to overcome social barriers than would be the case in settings that are more class- and caste-differentiated, and especially where norms of female seclusion are strong. However, the problem of women's opinions not being given much weight in mixed forums, even when they speak out, is part of a larger issue of the cultural construction of gender, and social perceptions about women's capabilities and place in society, from which even hill and tribal communities are not immune. Changing these perceptions will not be easy since many institutions contribute to the creation of gender ideology, including educational establishments, the media, and religious bodies. At the same time, it is encouraging that many aspects of women's situation are amenable to change over time when women begin to speak out collectively through the facilitating presence of a gender-progressive NGO.

In two meetings that I attended in March 1995 in Gujarat, one convened by AKRSP, the other by VIKSAT, the personnel from these NGOs helped both in soliciting the opinions of women who were present and in ensuring that those opinions were given due weight. Of course, if the NGO is itself male-biased, it can reinforce existing bias within village communities. The gender awareness now being displayed by AKRSP and VIKSAT is reported by them to be of relatively recent origin—a result both of field experience and of discussions initiated especially by some of their women office holders.

Gender-Sensitive Forest Officials

A gender-sensitive forest officer can also make a marked difference. Women labeled as "offenders" who became "defenders" of forests through the intervention and support of forest personnel are cases in point. In Brindabanpur village (West Bengal), for instance, women were forced to trespass into the neighboring village for fuelwood and other necessary forest produce, since they had no forest of their own. But when a sympathetic forest officer examined the complaints against the women and assured them that they would be allotted some forest land if they formed a FPC and followed its rules, they constituted an all-women protection group. It is reported that these women now monitor the space carefully, sell saplings from a nursery they have developed, and operate a savings account.[108] Some of them who earlier had depended solely on illicit felling now have part-time employment. Mansingh recounts a similar case in a VP area where the matter was similarly resolved by discussions between the villagers, the village government functionary, and a local NGO.[109]

Involvement in the Initial Stages

Experiences in several areas suggest that if women are involved from the inception of the organization, the chances of their sustained participation is greater, probably because they are then more motivated and their presence has greater legitimacy. Mansingh, in her study of women's attendance at VP meetings, found that

> women were involved substantially in the voluntary work and always seemed well informed about what had happened. This was in my opinion because they had been present in vast numbers in the first meeting and had understood, agreed to, and participated in the concept of the *van suraksha samiti* [forest protection committee].[110]

Further:

> It was in the first few meetings that the basic protecting resolutions of imposing a moratorium on the cutting of green wood and [of] leaves for fodder, and stopping the grazing of animals were passed. Women being the main collectors of wood and fodder needed to agree to this unanimously, either themselves, or through their husbands. Though the latter were often the means by which the outcomes of later meetings were communicated to them, it didn't always work with the initial agreements to change their use pattern.[111]

AKRSP's experience in Gujarat leads to a similar conclusion. In villages where from the start an attempt was made to recruit women as members in the village development associations (which also undertake forest protection), both membership rates and attendance at meetings are high. In some of these villages, 50 percent of those attending are women.[112] An AKRSP project officer told me that sometimes even the way the idea of membership is introduced can make a difference. Earlier when forming a FPC committee, they had said "there should be at least two women" (since that was the stipulated minimum for the working committee in the Gujarat JFM resolution). Now they say, "Anyone who wants to can become a member," leading to larger numbers of women joining.

Critical Mass

The presence of a critical mass of vocal women also appears necessary to give women an effective voice in mixed forums. Some women Britt interviewed in VP villages emphasized that "without a good majority of women present it is impossible to express opinions," and that men would find it difficult to ignore larger numbers of women.[113] The women I interviewed from the Gujarat villages where VIKSAT is working were clear that "more women should be involved; that will help." I do believe that even in the Chipko movement women's high participation has been an important factor, enabling them on occasion to take independent initiatives without the men's support, and at times even in opposition to the men.

Nevertheless the question of whether or not women should organize separately by forming all-women groups remains a vexed one.

All-Women Groups

In general it is noted that village women are more comfortable and vocal in all-women groups than in mixed ones. Women village leaders also argue that separate groups will enhance women's participation. For instance, in West Bengal's Midnapore district, the woman *panchayat pradhan* (council head) of Kesiary block said that women's participation in JFM would increase only if separate meetings were convened and women's special constraints dealt with. She recommended that there be an equal number of women and men in the FPCs and executive councils.[114] Similarly, in Durgala village (Sambalpur district, Orissa), Mohini Naik, the local woman activist who started a women's association in 1988 to replant and manage the village common land, argues that women can motivate women better, and that there should be more female members in FPCs. She herself is a key member in the local FPC and feels her presence in the committee has enhanced her status in the community.[115]

The experience of other NGOs is mixed. PEDO began by setting up all-women groups to regenerate wastelands in parts of Rajasthan, but found that this generated a great deal of hostility and suspicion among the village men. This led PEDO to change its policy and constitute groups of both men and women, but with ambiguous results. An evaluating team noted that

> joint meetings of men and women, while successful in reducing male hostility and
> securing their cooperation, tended to diminish free expression and articulation by
> women. The need to create a separate forum for women, in which they could

express their views and concerns uninhibited by the presence of men, was strongly felt.[116]

They found a way out by starting women's savings groups from the money earned through the sale of surplus grass from the protected land. This also provided a rationale for holding separate women's meetings without antagonizing the men.[117] In other words, the solution accommodated existing gender relations rather than challenging them, although over time it may well empower the women to do just that.

On Gendered Responses and Environmental Action

The experiences of environmental action described in this essay offer further support for the feminist environmental approach to understanding environmental action. We note that rural men too have actively responded to severe deforestation and the degradation of village commons by seeking to contain and reverse these processes. This can be traced to the threat to their livelihood systems and dependence on common property resources for supplementary income and/or for small timber for house repairs and agricultural tools, which are mainly men's responsibility. Women's responses are linked more to the availability of fuel, fodder, and nontimber products, for which they are more directly responsible, and the depletion of which has meant undertaking ever-lengthening journeys. In other words, there is clearly a link between the gender division of labor and the gendered nature of the responses.

The women I interviewed from some Gujarat villages where VIKSAT is working were unambiguous about this:

Q: On what issues do men and women differ in forest protection committee meetings?
A: Men can afford to wait for a while because their main concern is timber. But women need fuelwood daily.

However, whether these concerns get translated into *effective* action is dependent on whether women's rights in common property resources are explicitly recognized, on the influence women command in the community, and on their access to public decision-making forums. A case study of autonomous forest-management initiatives in three districts of Orissa highlights both the gendered impulse for forest protection and the unequal distribution of power that has enabled male interests to supersede women's interests. Commenting on the factors that led to the formation of all-male initiatives in the region, the study notes:

> In most of the cases protection efforts started only when the forest had degraded and communities faced shortage of small timber for construction of houses and agri-

cultural implements. Although there was a scarcity of fuelwood, it hardly served as an initiating factor.[118]

Clearly women's concerns, even if pressing, do not automatically translate into environmental action by women themselves or by the community. For poor women to move from being the main victims of environmental degradation to being effective agents of environmental regeneration is not likely to be an easy one, although, as noted, a gender-progressive NGO or separate women's associations can make an important difference. Sarin and Sharma's observation of women's participation in the regeneration of VCs in Rajasthan also underlines this point:

> There is nothing "automatic" in the extent of women's active participation in the development of village common lands, no matter how acute their hardship of searching for fuel and fodder. Even in the villages where women took the initiative and played a leadership role, this was preceded by enabling them to interact with other women's groups through *melas,* visits, training programmes and awareness generation camps. Continuous interaction with PEDO's women staff has been another crucial input for facilitating women's genuine participation.[119]

The considerable regional and community variation in women's status is also likely to impinge on women's ability to undertake environmental action. In particular, there are significant differences across regions and between social classes and communities (tribal/nontribal, Hindus/Muslims, upper-caste/lower-caste Hindus, hill dwellers/plains dwellers) in the emphasis on female seclusion and segregation, and hence in the constraints on women's mobility, freedom to participate in public meetings, ability to speak out in mixed gatherings of men and women, and so on. We would therefore expect regional, community, and class differences in women's ability to organize collectively. Female seclusion practices among Hindus, for instance, are strongest in north India and virtually nonexistent in south and northeast India; within north India they are strongest among the upper-caste groups located in the plains, and little practiced among upper castes in the hills or among lower-caste and tribal communities anywhere.[120] Seclusion practices among Muslims, although not identical to those for Hindus, show a similar regional and community variation. Manifest less in the practice of veiling (which is not widespread) and more in the gender segregation of public space (e.g., women being discouraged to spend time in spaces where men congregate, as in the marketplace), such practices severely restrict women's free interaction in public forums.[121]

Of course the social construction of appropriate female behavior (the emphasis on soft speech, deference to male elders, etc.) operates in some degree everywhere, even in the absence of overt strictures, including in the hill and tribal communities we have largely been discussing. But since women in such communities are not explicitly restricted, and because women play a visible and substantial role in the economy in all parts of the country, this tends to reduce the importance of the regional dimension. The effect of this dimension on women's ability to undertake collective action is likely to be more significant for upper-caste Hindus and for Muslims. For instance, we would expect it to be much more difficult for upper-caste Hindu women in the northwestern plains of India to participate than those from south India, for the reasons noted. And it would be important to map these regional and community differences for understanding women's responses onto the environmental crisis and the possibilities of their acting collectively in their own interests, as an increasing number of nontribal or non-hill communities get involved in forest and VC management.

SUMMARY COMMENTS

The colonial and immediate post-independence period in India saw a notable shift in property rights over forests and VCs, from substantial community control and management to increasing State and individual control and management. This had particularly adverse consequences for poor rural households, and especially for women in such households, because of their greater and everyday dependence on these resources for basic necessities. More recently, however, we are seeing small but important reversals toward a reestablishment of greater community control over those resources through the emergence of numerous forest management groups, some initiated by the state under the JFM program, others initiated by villagers, and yet others by NGOs.

But unlike the old systems of communal property management where all villagers, including women, had some form of use rights by virtue of being members of the village community, under the new formalized system of control rights are dependent more directly on formal membership of the emergent community institutions, from which women are often excluded. In other words, membership rather than citizenship is the defining criteria for access to these protected commons.

I have argued here that women's exclusion would have serious negative consequences not just for gender equity, but also for the efficient functioning and long-term sustainability of these initiatives, and for women's empowerment. Concerns of equity, efficiency, and empowerment therefore underline the need for women's greater participation.

Although women recognize the importance of participating in these initiatives, a range of factors obstruct them, including membership rules, social barriers stemming from cultural constructions of gender roles, responsibilities and expected behavior, logistical barriers relating to the timing and length of organizational meetings, predominance of men in forest departments, and male bias in the attitudes of those promoting these initiatives, such as Forest Department personnel, village leaders, and sometimes even the intermediary NGOs. In other words, there is a gap between women's interest in environmental action and their ability to claim equal space within such action.

At the same time, the fact that in several regions women have formed their own informal associations for forest protection, and in some cases their formal participation has also increased over time, suggests that these barriers are not insurmountable. Among factors that can enhance women's *formal* participation in the emergent community institutions, the most significant appears to be the presence of a gender-progressive NGO, and especially a women's association. Involving women at the inception of the initiative and the presence of a critical mass of women are also important for their effective and sustained participation in mixed forums.

Finally, the emergence of these varied institutional arrangements highlights the problematic nature of the ecofeminist argument that women simply by virtue of being women have a particular stake in environmental protection that is seldom shared by men. It also highlights how having a stake is not a sufficient condition for effective action, an issue that the ecofeminist debate largely neglects and which the discussion around women's agency seldom addresses. From the examples given, both women and men whose livelihoods are threatened by the degradation of forests and VCs are found to be interested in protection and regeneration, but from different concerns, related to their respective responsibilities and dependence on these resources (women being more concerned with fuel, fodder, and nontimber products; men with timber and cash benefits; and women also being more dependent on communal resources due to their limited private property access). Further, for women to translate their concerns into practice and be effective agents of change, they need to overcome social and political barriers and contend with the preexisting advantages that men as a gender (even if not all men as individuals) enjoy in terms of greater access to economic resources and public decision making forums.

In other words, the gender division of labor, property, and power (viz. the feminist environmental perspective) appears to be a better predictor of the environmental action we are observing than is the perspective provided by ecofeminism.

At the same time, the benefits of women's greater participation in environmental action would flow not just to women, but also to the entire household, as well as to the larger community—the latter by enabling a more biodiverse and sustainable regeneration of forests and VCs.

ABBREVIATIONS

FPC: Forest Protection Committee (under JFM)
JFM: Joint Forest Management
NGO: Nongovernmental Organization
VC: Village Commons
VP: *Van Panchayat* (forest council)

ACKNOWLEDGMENTS

This is a substantially revised and reworked version of the paper presented at the conference "Transitions, Environments, and Translations." I thank Joan Scott, Nöel Sturgeon and the participants of the conference for stimulating discussions. I also thank

Jeffrey Campbell for sharing with me his store of case studies, especially on JFM. Some of the material included here was presented by me at a workshop entitled "Humanities and the Environment," held in May 1995 at the Science, Technology, and Society Program of the Massachusetts Institute of Technology, and will be appearing in a different version in a volume on environment and development edited by Kenneth Keniston et al., and in the journal *Development and Change*.

NOTES

1. Detailed in B. Agarwal, "The Gender and Environment Debate: Lessons from India," *Feminist Studies* 18, no. 1 (spring 1992), pp. 119–58.

2. Some ecofeminists suggest that women are not just conceptualized as closer to nature than men, but are in fact closer to nature. Shiva, for instance, sees women as "embedded in nature" (See V. Shiva, *Staying Alive: Women, Ecology and Survival* [London: Zed Books, 1988], pp. 42, 47) and argues that "women and nature are intimately related and their domination and liberation similarly linked" (p. 47). She and some others also suggest that women's closeness with nature can affirm more nurturing and caring values both between humans and between human and nonhuman nature. Shiva traces this closeness both to biology and to historical and cultural factors; some others (e.g., A.K. Salleh, "Deeper than Deep Ecology: The Eco-Feminist Connection," *Environmental Ethics* 16 [winter 1984], pp. 339–45) place primary emphasis on women's biology.

3. Ecofeminism, as noted, has a number of strands, but the arguments highlighted above are fairly characteristic. See, e.g., Y. King, "Feminism and the Revolt," *Heresies* 13 (1981), pp. 12–16; "The Ecology of Feminism and the Feminism of Ecology," in J. Plant, (ed.), *Healing the Wounds: Feminism, Ecology and the Nature/Culture Dualism* (Philadelphia: New Society Publishers, 1989); Salleh, op cit.; C. Merchant, *The Death of Nature: Women, Ecology and the Scientific Revolution* (San Francisco: Harper and Row, 1980), S. Griffin, *Women and Nature: The Roaring Within Her* (New York: Harper and Row, 1978); and various articles in J. Plant, (ed.), *Healing the Wounds: Feminism, Ecology and the Nature/Culture Dualism* (Philadelphia: New Society Publishers, 1989); and I. Diamond and G. Orenstein (eds.), *Reweaving the World: The Emergence of Ecofeminism* (San Francisco: Sierra Club Books, 1990). For further discussions on some of the central arguments on which ecofeminists agree, see also J. K. Warren and J. Cheney, "Ecological Feminism and Ecosystem Ecology," *Hypatia* 6, no. 1 (spring 1991), pp. 179–97; V. Davion, "Is Feminism Feminist?" in K. J. Warren (ed.), *Ecological Feminism* (London and New York: Routledge, 1994); and J. Birkeland, "Ecofeminism: Linking Theory and Practice," in G. Gaard (ed.), *Ecofeminism: Women, Animals, Nature* (Philadelphia: Temple University Press, 1993).

   There has, however, been a tendency among some scholars in recent years to include under the banner of "ecofeminism" virtually any study or movement that deals with women and the environment (see, e.g., G. Gaard and L. Gruen, "Ecofeminism: Toward Global Justice and Planetary Health," *Society and Nature: The International Journal of Political Economy* 2, no. 1 [1993]). I believe this is a misrepresentation insofar as the central strands of ecofeminism, as formulated theoretically, share some basic premises, such as those discussed above, which the largely descriptive literature on women, environment, and development does not share.

4. B. Agarwal, "The Gender and Environment Debate."

5. In specific terms, in my formulation of feminist environmentalism, I suggest that "the link between women and the environment can be seen as structured by a given gender and class (/caste/race) organization of production, reproduction and distribution. Ideological construc-

tions such as of gender, of nature, and of the relationship between the two, may be seen as (interactively) a part of this structuring, but not the whole of it" (Agarwal, "The Gender and Environment Debate," p. 127).

Although there have been a number of critiques of the ecofeminist perspective in recent years, few provide alternative formulations. The critiques include those by Zimmerman, Cheney, Longino, Nanda, Jackson, and Li (see M.E. Zimmerman, "Feminism, Deep Ecology and Environmental Ethics," *Environmental Ethics* 9 [Spring 1987], pp. 21–44; J. Cheyney, "Ecofeminism and Deep Ecology," *Environmental Ethics* 9 [Summer 1987], pp. 115–45; H. Longino, book review, *Environmental Ethics* 3 [Winter 1981], pp. 365–69; M. Nanda, "Is Modern Science a Western, Patriarchal Myth? A Critique of the Populist Orthodoxy," *Social Science Bulletin* 11, nos. 1 and 2 [1991], pp. 32–60; C. Jackson, "Women/Nature or Gender/History? A Critique of Ecofeminist 'Development,'" *The Journal of Peasant Studies* 20, no. 3 [April 1993], pp. 389–419; Huey-li Li, "A Cross-cultural Critique of Ecofeminism," in G. Gaard (ed.), *Ecofeminism: Women, Animals, Nature* [Philadelphia: Temple University Press, 1993]. It is curious, though, that Li ends with a polemical statement that affirms her whole-hearted support of ecofeminism, in contradiction to the strong reasoned criticisms of various aspects of ecofeminism in the body of her paper. Also Li (op. cit.), Birkeland (op. cit.), and several others who have identified particular problems with Western ecofeminism tend to ignore similar problems embedded in some non-Western ecofeminist arguments, most notably in the work of Shiva (op. cit.). For a critique of Shiva, see especially Agarwal, "The Gender and the Environment Debate," and Nanda op. cit.

6. Such inequalities are found, in varying degree, in most cultures. Tribal cultures, although typically more gender equal, are also not immune. The assumption in some ecofeminist writing (e.g., Birkeland, op. cit., and Shiva, op. cit.) that tribal cultures in non-Western societies are gender-equal is therefore questionable, as is the assumption that at some historical point in time when an organic world view of nature is presumed to have prevailed, gender equality also prevailed. In India, for instance, historical information of even a thousand years ago indicates significant gender inequalities.

7. See, e.g., B. Agarwal, *A Field of One's Own: Gender and Land Rights in South Asia* (Cambridge: Cambridge University Press, 1994) for examples of such resistance from across South Asia; also see V. Oldenburg, "Lifestyle as Resistance: The Case of the Courtesans of Lucknow," in D. Haynes and G. Prakash (eds.), *Contesting Power: Resistance and Everyday Social Relations in South Asia* (Delhi: Oxford University Press, 1991); and R. O'Hanlon, "Issues of Widowhood: Gender and Resistance in Colonial Western India" in D. Haynes and B. Prakash (eds.), *Contesting Power: Resistance and Everyday Social Relations in South Asia* (Delhi: Oxford University Press, 1991).

8. Some authors incorrectly conflate passivity and victimhood, and assume that the assertion of agency (absence of passivity) implies the absence of victimhood. See, e.g., M. L. Eduards, "Women's Agency and Collective Action," *Women's Studies International Forum* 17, nos. 2 and 3 (1994) pp. 181–86; Eduards notes that it is possible for all human beings "to be an agent rather than a passive being, a victim."

Again, Oldenburg (op. cit.), in her celebratory depiction of resistance among the courtesans of Lucknow, does not admit either to the victimhood of these women resultant from the larger economic and social structures of male dominance that place them where they are, nor to the limits on their choices given that the patriarchal values they seek to subvert by creating an alternative lifestyle remain intact outside that alternative. Also, as O'Hanlon (op. cit., p. 104) points out, "the mere celebration of what look like autonomous defiances may do grave disservice to those who refuse to conform . . . , in underestimating the actual weight and harsh social cost entailed in contesting authority."

9. The notion of "agency-freedom" put forward by Sen is useful here (see A. L. Sen, "Well-Being, Agency and Freedom: The Dewey Lectures 1984," *The Journal of Philosophy* 82, no. 4, [April 1985], pp. 169–221). He defines it as "what the person is free to do and achieve in pursuit of whatever goals or values he or she regards as important" (p. 203). There can, however, be restrictions on a person's "agency-freedom", including restrictions imposed by social norms and values. Equally, as Sen also points out in "Gender and Cooperative Conflicts," in I. Tinkler (ed.), *Persistent Inequalities: Women and World Development* (New York: Oxford University Press, 1990), pp. 123–49, the exercise of agency by women need not necessarily lead to enhanced well-being. For instance, women may choose to exercise agency to improve the well-being of the family or community, even if it reduces their own well-being. Also see U. Butalia, "Community, State and Gender: On Women's Agency during Partition," *Economic and Political Weekly* 28, no. 17 (April 24, 1993), pp. WS12–WS24, for examples that raise particularly complex questions in this regard.

10. B. Agarwal, "Gender, Resistance and Land: Interlinked Struggles Over Resources and Meanings in South Asia," *The Journal of Peasant Studies* 22, no. 1 (October 1995).

11. See Kerala Forest Research Institute *Studies on the Changing Pattern of Man-Forest Interactions and its Implications for Ecology and Management* (Trivandrum: KFRI, 1980); W. Fernandes and G. Menon, *Tribal Women and Forest Economy: Deforestation, Exploitation and Status Change* (Delhi: Indian Social Institute, 1987); P. Vieges and G. Menon, "Forest Protection Committees of West Bengali: Role and Participation of Women," paper prepared for the International Labour Organization Workshop "Women and Wasteland Development," New Delhi, January 9–11, 1991; and M. Sarin, "Regenerating India's Forest: Reconciling Gender Equity and Joint Forest Management," *IDS Bulletin* 26, no. 1 (1995), pp. 83–91.

12. B. Agarwal, "Under the Cooking Pot: The Political Economy of the Domestic Fuel Crisis in Rural South Asia," *IDS Bulletin* 18, no. 1 (1987), pp. 11–22.

13. S. Kulkarni, "Towards a Social Forestry Policy," *Economic and Political Weekly* 8, no. 6 (February 6, 1983), pp. 191–96.

14. B. Agarwal, "Social Security and the Family: Coping with Seasonality and Calamity in Rural India," *Journal of Peasant Studies* 17, no. 3 (1990), pp. 341–412.

15. Agarwal, *A Field of One's Own.*

16. N. S. Jodha, "Common Property Resources and Rural Poor," *Economic and Political Weekly* 21, no. 27 (July 5, 1986), pp. 1169–81.

17. In India, the term "state" relates to administrative divisions within the country and is not to be confused with "State," used throughout the paper in the political economy sense of the word. Elsewhere in South Asia these administrative divisions are termed provinces.

18. Jodha, op. cit.

19. On the factors underlying the regional variation see especially B. Agarwal, "Women, Poverty and Agricultural Growth in India," *The Journal of Peasant Studies* 13, no. 4 (July 1986), pp. 165–220; B. Miller, *The Endangered Sex: Neglect of Female Children in Rural India* (Ithaca: Cornell University Press, 1981).

20. B. Agarwal, *A Field of One's Own.*

21. Ibid.

22. Ibid.

23. R. Kaur, "Women in Forestry in India," World Bank, Women in Development, Working Paper WPS 714, Washington, D.C., 1991, p. 43. It is not clear whether the northeastern states have been taken into account in Kaur's calculations.

24. Jodha, op. cit.

25. On communal management of forests and VCs, see R. Guha, "Scientific Forestry and Social Change in Uttarakhand," *Economic and Political Weekly* 20, nos. 45–47, (November 1985),

pp. 1939–52; M. Gadgil, "Towards an Ecological History of India," *Economic and Political Weekly* 20, nos. 45–47 (November 1985), pp. 1909–18; and M. Moench, "'Turf' and Forest Management in a Garhwal Hill Village," in Fortmann and Bruce (eds.), *Whose Trees? Proprietary Dimensions of Forestry* (Boulder and London: Westview Press, 1988), pp. 127–36. On firewood gathering practices, see B. Agarwal, *Cold Hearths and Barren Slopes: The Woodfuel Crisis in the Third World* (London: Zed Books, 1986). Firewood for domestic use in rural households was customarily collected in the form of twigs and fallen branches, which did not destroy the trees. And even estimates of just fifteen years ago indicate that 75 percent of fire-wood gathered for domestic use in rural northern India (and 100 percent in some areas) was in this form (Agarwal, "Under the Cooking Pot").

26. See, e.g., D.W. Bromley and M. M. Cernea, "The Management of Common Property Natural Resources," World Bank Discussion Paper No. 57, World Bank, Washington D.C., 1989; J. M. Baland and J. P. Platteau, "Should Common Property Resources be Privatized? A Re-examination of the Tragedy of the Commons," Discussion Paper, Center for Research in Economic Development, Namur University, Belgium, 1994.

27. In the early 1980s, in parts of Gujarat even a four to five hour search yielded little apart from shrubs, weeds, and tree roots, which do not provide adequate cooking energy (D. Nagbrahman and S. Sambrani, "Women's Drudgery in Firewood Collection," *Economic and Political Weekly*, [January 1–8, 1983]).

28. See S. K. Kumar and D. Hotchkiss, "Consequences of Deforestation for Women's Time Allocation, Agricultural Profuction and Nutrition in Hill Areas of Nepal," Research Report 69, International Food Policy Research Institute, Washington, D.C., 1988.

29. M. Howes and M. A. Jabbar, "Rural Fuel Shortages in Bangladesh: The Evidence from Four Villages," Discussion Paper 213, Institute of Development Studies, Sussex, 1986.

30. B. Agarwal, "Social Security and the Family: Coping with Seasonality and Calamity in Rural India," *Journal of Peasant Studies* 17, no. 3 (1990), pp. 341–412.

31. Ibid.

32. B. Agarwal, "Gender, Environment and Poverty Interlinks in Rural India: Regional Variations and Temporal Shifts, 1971–1991," Discussion Paper No. 62, United Nations Research Institute for Social Development, Geneva, 1995.

33. In 1988 there were an estimated 1300 forest protection committees (FPCs) in three districts: Midnapore, Bankura, and Purulia. Even today West Bengal has the largest JFM coverage: an estimated 350,000 ha of forest area is being protected by some 2350 FPCs. See Society for Promotion of Wasteland Development, *Joint Forest Management Update, 1993* (New Delhi: SPWD, 1994).

34. That excludes the Kashmir part of Jammu and Kashmir.

35. Sarin, op. cit.

36. S. Kant, N. M. Singh, and K. K. Singh, "Community-based Forest Management Systems (Case Studies from Orissa)," SIDA, New Delhi; Indian Institute of Forest Management, Bhopal; and ISO/Swedforest, New Delhi, April 1991.

37. Singh and Khare, quoted in Sarin, op. cit.

38. These are also termed Mahila Mangal Dals in some regions.

39. V. Ballabh and K. Singh, "Van (Forest) Panchayats in Uttar Pradesh Hills: A Critical Analysis," Research Paper, Institute for Rural Management, Anand, 1988.

40. Ibid.

41. Personal communication, Chandi Prasad Bhatt, 1995.

42. Among specific case studies that highlight resource scarcity and relative socioeconomic homo-geneity as conducive to successful group action for forest protection are those by Kant, Singh, and Singh, op. cit., for Orissa; and Sarin, op. cit., for Gujarat.

43. AKRSP works on a variety of village development issues, of which forest protection and waste-land regeneration is one, although a major one. In villages under its ambit, therefore, AKRSP has encouraged the formation of Gram Vikas Mandals (village development associations), which cover a wider set of issues than just forest protection. In some villages women's development associations have also been formed in AKRSP areas.

44. For benefits from protection under JFM, see case studies by N.J. Arul and M. Poffenberger, "FPC Case Studies" in R. S. Pathan, N. J. Arul, and M. Poffenberger (eds.), *Forest Protection Committees in Gujarat Joint Management Initiative* (New Delhi: Ford Foundation, 1990); G. Raju, R. Vaghela, and M. S. Raju, *Development of People's Institutions for Management of Forests* (Ahemdabad: VIKSAT, 1993); Society for Promotion of Wasteland Development, op. cit., for Gujarat; Kant, Singh, and Singh, op. cit., for Orissa; and Viegas and Menon op. cit for West Bengal. See also O. Mansingh, "Community Organization and Ecological Restoration: An Analysis of Strategic Options for NGOs in the Central Himalaya, with particular reference to the Community Forestry Programme of the NGO Chirag," MA thesis in Rural Development, AFRAS, University of Sussex, 1991, for the benefits from protection in some *van panchayat* villages of Uttar Pradesh.

45. K. C. Malhotra et al., "Joint Management of Forest Lands in West Bengal: A Case Study of Jamboni Range in Midnapore District," IBRAD, Technical Paper No. 2, 1990, pp. 22–23.

46. S. B. Roy, R. Mukerjee, and M. Chatterjee, "Endogenous Development, Gender Role in Participatory Forest Management," IBRAD, Calcutta, 1992.

47. P. Guhathakurta and K.S. Bhatia, "A Case Study on Gender and Forest Resources in West Bengal," World Bank, Delhi, June 16, 1992.

48. U. Narain, "Women's Involvement in Joint Forest Management: Analyzing the Issues," draft paper, May 6, 1994.

49. Kant, Singh, and Singh, op. cit.; N. Singh and K. Kumar, "Community Initiatives to Protect and Manage Forests in Balangir and Sambalpur Districts," SIDA, New Delhi, 1993.

50. Ballabh and Singh, op. cit.; A. Sharma and A. Sinha, "A Study of the Common Property Resources in the Project Area of the Central Himalaya Rural Action Group," mimeo, Indian Institute of Forest Management, Bhopal, Madhya Pradesh, 1993.

51. For Orissa, see S. Pati, R. Panda, and A. Rai, "Comparative Assessment of Forest Protection by Communities," paper presented at the Workshop on Joint Forest Management, Bhubaneshwar, Orissa, May 28–29, 1993; Kant, Singh, and Singh, op. cit.; and ISO/Swedforest, "Forests, People and Protection: Case Studies of Voluntary Forest Protection by Communities in Orissa," SIDA, New Delhi, 1993. For Gujarat see Arul and Poffenberger, op. cit. As noted earlier, in some villages tribal women now have part-time employment from mat weaving and leaf-plate making through the raw material they collect from the protected forests (Kant, Singh, and Singh, op. cit.).

52. Arul and Poffenberger, op. cit.

53. See Sarin, op. cit.; Narain, op. cit.; Singh and Kumar, op. cit.; and M. K. Shah, and P. Shah, "Gender, Environment and Livelihood Security: An Alternative Viewpoint from India," *IDS Bulletin* 26, no. 1 (1995), pp. 75–82.

54. Sarin, op. cit.

55. Shah and Shah, op. cit.

56. Ibid., p. 80.

57. Singh and Kumar, op. cit., p. 23.

58. Ibid.

59. Guhathakurata and Bhatia, op. cit.

60. Sarin, op. cit., p. 90.

61. J. Mencher, "Women's Work and Poverty: Women's Contribution to Household Maintenance in Two Regions of South India," in D. Dwyer and J. Bruce (eds.), *A Home Divided: Women and Income Control in the Third World* (Stanford: Stanford University Press, 1989).

62. Sen, "Gender and Cooperative Conflicts"; Agarwal, *A Field of One's Own.*

63. Personal communication, AKRSP project officer, March 1995.

64. Sarin, op. cit.

65. C. Britt, "Out of the Wood? Local Institutions and Community Forest Management in two Central Himalayan Villages," Cornell University, Ithaca, draft monograph, 1993.

66. Ibid., p. 147.

67. Cited in ibid, p. 143.

68. Cited in ibid, p. 147.

69. Cited in ibid, p. 148.

70. M. Sarin and R. Khanna, "Women Organize for Wasteland Development: A Case Study of SARTHI in Gujarat," in A. Singh and N. Burra (eds.), *Women and Wasteland Development in India* (New Delhi: Sage Publications, 1993).

71. Personal communication, AKRSP project officer, March 1995.

72. Agarwal, *A Field of One's Own.*

73. See Agarwal, *A Field of One's Own*; S. Venketeshvaran, *Living on the Edge: Women, Environment and Development* (New Delhi: Friedrich Ebert Stiftung, 1992), and Viegas and Menon, op. cit.

74. Sarin, op. cit.

75. For Gujarat, see S. Ahmed, "The Rhetoric and Reality of Women's Participation in Joint Forest Management: The Case of NGO in Western India," paper prepared for the conference "Women, Poverty and Demographic Change," Oaxaca, Mexico, 1994; for West Bengal, see Guhathakurta and Bhatia, op. cit.; R. Mukerjee and S. B. Roy, "Influence of Social Institutions on Women's Participation in JFM: A Case Study from Sarugarh, North Bengal," Working Paper No. 17, IBRAD, Calcutta, 1993; S. B. Roy, et al., "Profile of Forest Protection Committees at Sarugarh Range, North Bengal," Working Paper No. 16, IBRAD, Calcutta, 1993, and M. Chatterjee, "Women in Joint Forest Management: A Case Study from West Bengal," IBRAD, Calcutta, 1992.

76. Britt, op. cit.

77. Village woman, cited in ibid., p. 148.

78. Village woman, cited in ibid., pp. 146–47.

79. Cited in ibid., pp. 143–44.

80. Cited in ibid., p. 145.

81. Cited in ibid., p. 146.

82. Mukerjee and Roy, op. cit.; Roy et al., op. cit.

83. Narain, op. cit.; Guhathakurta and Bhatia, op. cit.

84. K. Sharma, K. Nautiyal, and B. Pandey, "Women in Struggle: Role and Participation of Women in the Chipko Movement in Uttarakhand Region of Uttar Pradesh," Occasional Monograph, Center for Women's Development Studies, Delhi, 1987, pp. 50–51.

85. S. Bahuguna, "Women's Non-Violent Power in the Chipko Movement," in M. Kishwar and R. Vanita (eds.), *In Search of Answers: Indian Women's Voices in Manushi* (London: Zed Books, 1984); Britt, op. cit.

86. Village woman cited in Britt, op. cit., p. 146.

87. O. Mansingh, "Community Organization and Ecological Restoration: An Analysis of Strategic Options for NGOs in the Central Himalaya, with Particular Reference to the Community Forestry Programme of the NGO Chirag," M.A. thesis in Rural Development, AFRAS, University of Sussex, 1991.

88. Roy, Mukerjee, and Chatterjee, op. cit.

89. Narain, op. cit.

90. Venkateshwaran, op. cit.

91. Guhathakurta and Bhatia, op. cit.

92. Narain, op. cit.

93. Roy et al., op. cit., pp. 15–16.

94. Narain, op. cit.

95. Ibid.

96. Vieges and Menon, op. cit.

97. Mukerjee and Roy, op. cit.

98. N. Adhikari, G. Yadav, S. B. Ray and S. Kumar, "Process Documentation of Women's Involvement in Forest Management at Mahespur, Ranchi," in R. Singh (ed.) *Managing the Village Commons, Proceedings of the National Workshop* (Bhopal: Indian Institute of Forest Management, 1991).

99. N. M. Singh, "Regional Workshop of Forest Department on Joint Forest Management at Keonjhar," in Proceedings of the Workshop, Bhubaneshwar, Orissa, 28–29 May 1993.

100. M. Sarin and C. Sharma, "Women's Involvement in Rehabilitation of Common Lands in Bicchiwara Block of Dungarpur District, Rajasthan," paper prepared for the International Labour Organization Workshop on "Women and Wasteland Development," Delhi, January 1991.

101. A. Singh and N. Burra (eds.), *Women and Wasteland Development in India* (New Delhi: Sage Publications, 1993).

102. Sharma and Sinha, op. cit.

103. Ibid.

104. Viegas and Menon, op. cit., pp. 22–23.

105. This gender divergence in choice of trees in tree-planting schemes is also noted in other parts of India. See R. Brara, "'Commons' Policy as Process: The Case of Rajasthan, 1955–85," *Economic and Political Weekly* 24, no. 40 (October 7, 1989), pp. 2247–54; Sarin and Sharma, op. cit. This can be attributed to gender differences in responsibilities and in dependence on particular categories of trees and forest products.

106. Mukerjee and Roy, op. cit.

107. V. Mazumdar, "Peasant Women Organize for Empowerment: The Bankura Experiment," occasional monograph, Center for Women's Development Studies, Delhi, 1989.

108. Chatterjee, op. cit.

109. Mansingh, op. cit.

110. Ibid., p. 29.

111. Ibid., p. 40n.

112. A. Chandran, "Involvement of Women in the GVM and Forestry Activity: Strategy Paper," xeroxed note circulated at AKRSP meeting in Baruch, Gujarat, March 1995.

113. Britt, op. cit., p. 146.

114. Guhathakurta and Bhatia, op. cit.

115. ISO/Swedforest, "Social Forestry: Case Studies from Orissa," Swedish International Development Agency (SIDA), New Delhi, 1991.

116. Sarin and Sharma, op. cit., p. 20.

117. AKRSP similarly reports from their experience in Gujarat that starting a separate savings scheme for women increased women's attendance in village development association meetings. In this case, however, what the savings scheme did was to enhance women's motivation to attend.

118. ISO/Swedforest, "Forests, People, and Protection," p. 46.

119. Sarin and Sharma, op. cit., p. 39.

120. The link between economic class and seclusion is more complex. Women of richer households are often more restricted, but where they are more educated they are also better able to bypass seclusion norms.

121. For a detailed discussion of regional variations in seclusion practices and more generally in women's participation in public activities, see Agarwal, *A Field of One's Own.*

< 17 >

The Politics of Womanhood in Occupational Inequality

Tsehai Berhane-Selassie

Ideas on the "woman question" and "women's rights" have been imparted to women in rural Ethiopia through the government and other agents who work in development. Because farming has dominated rural economic development activities, accounts of development in Ethiopia have emphasized farmers and excluded other economic and sociopolitical groups such as the potter women who are the topic of this essay.

Potter women in rural Wolayta (south-central Ethiopia) are their community's economic mainstay; they produce and sell pottery individually and control their income autonomously. When these potter women were motivated to assert themselves politically against their men, they made use of the new notion of "women's rights" and at the same time invoked a local, "traditional" sociopolitical system that had, in the past, kept them subordinate to their men and kept their community denigrated and marginalized.[1] It was the resort to "tradition" and not to women's rights that allowed the women to close down a pottery-marketing cooperative that the socialist revolution of 1974 had convinced them to set up. The cooperative had been a piece of a development program, one of the first, put together for just these women. But because only the men had access to literacy and numeracy, the men decided to run the bookkeeping of the cooperative. The women felt their privileges were threatened. On that basis they strategized to maintain their economic power by closing a potential source of institutional power, the cooperative, and going along instead with the demands of the dominant farmers.

Applied anthropologists and development thinkers have been calling for research into "local knowledge" to help them understand such seemingly contradictory sociopolitical processes.[2] While consultants have identified some patterns, development planners appear to make use of their work only at the rhetorical level, promoting "gender-sensitive" planning while proceeding to set up new vocations, work groups, and even institutions that fail to take account of the strategies adopted by groups such as the potters of the Wolayta.[3] These plans are then seen by the potters as irrelevant because they fail to incorporate their work, their institutions, and their lifestyles. Local women's decisions are then often dismissed by planners as a "resort to tradition" that seems to be against the women's self-interest even as these decisions are a potential source of power.

   On the surface, the story of the potter women and the cooperative that I will narrate in this paper may also support the conclusion that women simply resort to the best alternative at their disposal when they come under pressure from their sociopolitical environment. Wolayta traditions impose the category of "despised" on the potter women and on their community as a whole. The dominant group among whom they live, who call themselves *goqa*, designate the sociopolitical subordination of the potters by derogatorily calling them *chinasha* and by evoking a mythical and symbolic history to justify this classification with a logic that resembles that of the nature/culture divide that certain "Western" thinkers claim is a universal way of asserting women's subordination. However, it was by firmly and successfully asserting themselves through these traditional categories that the women claimed their rights as women and brought back into question earlier political and economic experiences that had dispossessed a part of their community. By drawing on aspects of their cultural setting, in which women had a certain kind of centrality and economic autonomy, they managed to manipulate the sociopolitical environment. Their strategy required them to go along with the demands of the *goqa* men while using the "women's rights" line to defy their own men. While this may look double-faced, it can be understood only in the context of the women's experiences in their wider cultural system (which, for example, denigrated *chinasha* while giving the women economic autonomy), taking into account the historical experiences of their community and, of course, how they saw "gender relations" and feminism.

   This essay draws from a wider ethnographic study of the pottery producers of Wolayta in south-central Ethiopia. I am interested in eliciting local perspectives on strategic planning, ideas about what constitutes the "political" in gender relations, and how access to local knowledge helps identify the appropriate "targets" with whom to work in any attempt at a sustainable improvement of women's, and their communities', quality of life. The ethnographic details also provide more evidence for Amadiume's argument that African women's economic history has not always been one of economic oppression. The experience of the potters demonstrates that some traditions have built-in inclusivist systems, which women successfully manipulate to achieve a high level of autonomy. It also suggests that the localized strategies of these women are not merely ways of perpetuating old ideas, nor of expressing a conservative desire for the continuity of local systems. Rather, the strategies are part of the dynamics of change that women at the grassroots level employ to promote their interests in new contexts. What is more, the potters' strategies provide an example of how local people manipulate the forces of development for locally generated goals. Inasmuch as development should involve a two-way flow of communication between "targets" and planners, such responses should be taken seriously and valued. The women's use of both tradition and women's rights refocuses vaguely articulated notions of gender-sensitive planning.

   The case of the potter women and the cooperative also illustrates how superficial gender-sensitive advocacy remains. Advocates of this approach have targeted local women as subjects for "empowerment," ready to "achieve their full potential." But because the gender-sensitive approach has itself not reached its full potential (who is it, after all, who identifies the target in gender-sensitive development?), it has continued to construct those target women in a way that ignores many actual women. In fact, in this sense, the development of rural employment has not progressed since it was articulated by Lourdes Beneria at the beginning of the last decade. The target has remained those producers who work on the land or, more recently in environmental reclamation projects, those who work on the reconstitution of nonfarming communities such that they can accommodate external interventions. Some new groups have emerged that engage in construction and other forms of service-oriented marketable production, but these tend to exist only for the duration of the interests of their initiators. This impact is due to major differences that emerge between local understandings of rural economy and commerce and those of the development industry. Development planners emphasize only farming and animal husbandry in rural areas. Their formal plans address commercial farming, which does diversify the rural economy. But they do not give weight to the existence of rural-based, trade-oriented occupations such as artisanship or pottery.

By contrast, the potter women know that they are an artisan community, a category of rural producers. They are a target group that development planners could usefully address, and around which could develop rural employment, at least for local markets and local economies. But to understand this, some historical background is necessary.

WOLAYTA

By and large, the pottery specialists among the Wolayta are women. They are prominently featured in mythical and historical explanations of the social systems of classification, definition, and prejudice. For more than a century these systems have suffered a barrage of political, economic, and cultural influences aimed at changing the attitudes of the Wolayta and incorporating them into the larger Ethiopian state in its various forms. This incorporation began in 1894. Wolayta—with the rest of Ethiopia—was occupied by the Italians from 1935 to 1940, made a part of the growth-oriented development process in the 1960s, affected by the rise and fall of a socialist government from 1974 to 1991, and, finally, made to participate in the restructuring of the state along ethnic lines that began in 1991. These political pressures have coexisted with traditional relations of gender, particularly in despised or excluded groups. Since the 1870s, Ethiopian governments have been trying to change the status of potters and other artisans, and indeed there have been political changes codified in various laws and decrees that have affected the social position of artisans. But there has been little interaction between the new laws promulgated by the dominant state and the explanatory myths, oral traditions, and dominant thought processes of the Wolayta. The laws have therefore not had much impact on their traditions. This shortfall has precluded fundamental change in their social systems.

The Wolayta number around two million.[4] They belong to the so-called *ensete* culture of south-central Ethiopia,[5] and their language, classified as Omotic,[6] is a lingua franca for several groups in the region. The Wolayta kingdom came into being in the last quarter of the twelfth century and collapsed in an 1894 war of unprecedented carnage. Many Wolayta were carried off into domestic service and eventually made retainers for the army that fought in 1896 at the Battle of Adewa, where for the first time in African history a European invading force was defeated. But not all the Wolayta were scattered, and until 1935 Wolayta retained a quasi-independent status. Its incorporation into the Ethiopian state system remained at the level of the personal relationship between Emperor Menelik II and the last king of Wolayta, Kao Tona, and his family. The emperor acted as godfather to the *kao,* and gave him so high a status that the imperial court had to rise whenever he made his appearance. The *kao* was officially the Emperor's representative. But while Wolayta was exempted from the obligation of billeting troops, the *kao* proceeded to give female Wolayta as slaves to various provincial rulers. The majority of these slaves were reportedly potter women. Even though the distribution of such gifts led to the removal of the *kao* from his new and subordinate position, the slaves remained dislocated from their society.[7]

Wolayta in this period was taxed by the emperor's personal treasury for clothes and cattle, the two resources in which it was richest at the turn of the century. These tax items represented the principal form of reward for men who demonstrated military prowess in the service of the emperor. The increased workload these payments required was carried for the most part by Wolayta women, whose household chores included processing cotton and spinning thread. The tax burden also encumbered the husbands of the potter women, who, in the community's division of labor, were the weavers. The system of tax-in-kind further entrenched the subordination of potters to farmers, who, as the designated taxpayers, considered the potters and weavers as "their" producers.

The potter-farmer relation is not generally seen in gendered terms. Wolayta society traditionally distinguishes between farmers, artisans, and descendants of slaves. Potters in Ethiopia, as elsewhere, are a category of social classification along occupational lines, but their lowly status is justified in Wolayta by their mythical relationship to land, earth, and other natural resources and by a symbolic history—which includes supposed historical events—of the Wolayta political order.[8] As primary groups, farmers are categorically called *goqa* and artisans are called *chinasha*. There is a third category, slaves, and they are called *ayele. Goqa* own land and could give plots of farmland to "their" artisans for use during their lifetime or in perpetuity. *Chinasha* could earn land ownership only by proving themselves as warriors, and therefore only from *goqa* kings, *kao*s. Land ownership, however, was not an automatic right of the *chinasha* warriors, nor did it change their status. *Ayele* and their descendants never had the privilege of land ownership. But changes in category were possible. The loss of land could result if a *goqa* failed to maintain the expected standard of living (for instance, if he borrowed for annual festivals, to repair his hut, or otherwise provide for his family). Being captured in war or entering Wolayta as a refugee were also ways of entering into the *ayele* category. As refugees and war captives were usually state slaves, "owned" by the *kao* as mercenary soldiers, and as they could win their freedom and the right to own land through military prowess, the *ayele* status of most was not permanent. On the other hand, impoverished local people could bond themselves to anyone, including *chinasha,* as domestic slaves, a category in which they and their descendants then remained permanently.[9]

Land ownership has relevance to how Wolayta practice their social categories, but it is not used for defining the relative position of *goqa* and *chinasha.* That position is determined by perceived links between the physical world and the creation (and nature) of human beings. Several concurrent versions of these explanations exist. In one tradition, the *goqa* report that they emerged from the earth. They grow food from the same earth that bore them, and so they are as one with it. They therefore feel challenged by *chinasha* when the latter dig and burn clay to make their pottery. Because, in this definition, *goqa* are defined by a way of treating the earth, other occupations, such as state administrators, can be subsumed within the category *goqa.* Migrants who are mercenaries, refugees, or traders from neighboring communities can also be considered *goqa,* incorporated as long as they are not potters or artisans. The question of who has a closer relationship to the earth or to ownership of land in mythic terms lies behind all stories that narrate social value and historical change. Creation myths about the first fathers of the *chinasha* and the *goqa* claim that the order of seniority was first established at creation by birth order but was permanently reversed soon after. The fathers of those who became *chinasha* and *goqa* were brothers; the *chinasha* ancestor was the elder, but he lost his rights of primogeniture when he ate the carcass of a dead animal, a forbidden (because impure) food. Everyday innuendos about the mannerisms and mysterious powers (such as the evil eye) attributed to the *chinasha* assert a denigrated status that can be traced back to this loss of primogeniture. Marriage between the two groups is strictly forbidden, and the prohibition seems to refer back to the danger of pollution to the *goqa.*

Another creation myth establishes the seniority and primacy of the *goqa* in Wolayta as measured not against *chinasha* but against cattle herders. In this myth, the *goqa* were the first people to emerge from the earth. They brought with them the local staples *ensete* and *boyna,* establishing a firm link between the *goqa,* farming, and the earth. These "first people" then encountered the Aruje, "a people with red cattle," whom they expelled beyond the borders of the expanding Wolayta kingdom. When they reached this border, the Aruje "clapped their hands and disappeared from the face of the earth." According to historical records,[10] these were the borders of Wolayta at the end of the thirteenth century. While this story obviously represents a symbolic history, it is similar to the accounts of other southern Ethiopian peoples.[11] It in effect denies that there was ever any real competition over the ownership of communal land, particularly not from the Aruje cattle-herders, who are still very much in evidence on the northern borders of Wolayta. It also defines these "first" human beings as a distinct people in a cultural rather than physical sense. For while the relations between the *goqa* and the *chinasha* in the first creation myth remain firmly interhuman, the myth of the farmers and cattle-herders asserts that only the *goqa* have relationships with earth and land and therefore that only the *goqa* are human. This allows the Wolayta to avoid the issue of a natural link between *goqa* and Aruje, who "do not even exist," and to excise the Aruje altogether from other explanatory contexts.

There are similar myths in which the *goqa-chinasha* relationship is defined by the conquest of land and the reclassification of society brought about by immigration and a new dynasty of kings. These hold that in former times only a people called the Wolaytamala lived in the land. Divided into several clans, the Wolaytamala were "both *goqa* and *chinasha*." Some time later "Tigre" immigrants came to Wolayta, "bringing with them six other groups from Gojam, Tigre, and other places" in northern Ethiopia. These were the Qesiga (priestly clan), the *chinasha*, the weavers, merchants, and soldiers. The immigrants established trade between Wolayta and the north, and in time became powerful enough to usurp the Wolaytamala king's position. To some extent this story corresponds with written records that show Ethiopian Orthodox Christianity was introduced to the court of a Wolaytamala king, Motolami, around 1270.[12] The oral tradition says that sometime around the beginning of the fourteenth century, a Wolaytamala king was cheated out of his position by a daughter who had married a Tigre immigrant called Mikele. Tales understood as historical anecdotes firmly associate the kings of the new Tigre dynasty with *chinasha*; they say that it was particularly oppressive kings who gave the *chinasha* new importance by inviting them to take part in the conquest and expansion of their kingdom, and by rewarding them with land. But the same tradition suggests that there is a limit beyond which Wolayta society cannot rewrite its history to accommodate the *chinasha*. The reign of the Tigre dynasty ended when one Tigre king designated a politically appointed post for *chinasha* (the post of executioner, with all that bloodletting symbolically implies in terms of purity and danger), and this appointment provoked a rebellion. The relationship between the *chinasha* and the immigrant kings, dangerous to both of them, is immediately negated by their removal and annihilation. Today, except for specific individuals, the Tigre and Qesiga clans are *goqa*.

In traditional stories that express a worldview relating human beings to the earth, it is noteworthy that the *chinasha* are elevated at a moment when political changes rearrange the order of society. It is not surprising, then, that the political fortunes of the *chinasha* are tied to an immigrant group, even though the myth of creation makes them equally as indigenous as the *goqa*. Obviously the *chinasha* are an important category in the social definition of occupational groups. In the myth of primogeniture, the farmers acquire importance only in reversing the natural order of seniority between themselves and the artisans. In the narration of relations with outsiders, the Wolaytamala, who assert their ethnic dominance by emphasizing their cultural and political relations with external or "nonexistent" cattle-herders, have both *goqa* and *chinasha* occupational groups in their midst. In the case of the internal cultural and political relations between the Wolaytamala and the Tigre, on the other hand, delineation between the two groups seems to require threats of symbolic death and dangers that involve the *chinasha*: The newcomers are incorporated into the Wolayta society's political system by creating symbolic associations between themselves and the oppressed group and then by reexternalizing and punishing the *chinasha*. The point of all these stories is clear: Nonexistent cattle-herders and inappropriate *chinasha* are dangers to the political and economic order of the Wolayta.

Indeed, as in other areas of Ethiopia, artisans are considered dangerous to all forms of new life—harvest, calves, kids, children, etc. The artisans' evil eye is supposed to cause harm even to the behavior of people. In historical Wolayta, food items such as dairy products were not sold to artisans because it was thought that this contact might result in a bad effect on the source of the food. Relationships between the dominant groups and the *chinasha* must always be expressed as a permanent state of role-reversal so as to avoid the dangers of the potent power the *chinasha* are assumed by nature to have. Symbolic role-reversal rituals played out by the Tigre kings at times of crisis symbolize this permanent state.

The revolution of 1974 was not the first attempt by an Ethiopian state to directly reach out to these despised groups. A decree intended to emancipate artisan groups was issued in the 1870s. Motivated by the threat of European superiority in weapons technology and the refusal of the British to provide arms for defense against Italian and Mahdist aggression, the decree was aimed at the production of technological innovations, such as guns and gunpowder, and explicitly addressed to blacksmiths and other artisans, which in Wolayta meant the husbands of the potters. But in the end, it was a special corps of soldiers who made gunpowder out of local material.[13] The success of the soldiers have been related to the rewards promised: While they were offered the possibility of winning access to land (the traditional compensation for military prowess), the farmers and the craft producers, in contrast, were promised no rewards. As would be the case for most government initiatives of its kind in Wolayta, the 1870 edict addressed the wrong people. It was written in broad, moralistic terms: Discrimination against artisans must stop because the efforts of all Ethiopians were needed if the country was to compete against the Europeans.[14] But while elsewhere in Ethiopia, the category "artisan" predominantly designated skills such as blacksmithing, tanning, and other men's work, in Wolayta women were the bearers of the identity of the occupational group and their products were household utensils seemingly distant from the government's need for gunpowder and guns. The edict did not quite address the issue of the status of commerce as a lowly occupation left to Arabs, other Muslims, and artisans. Indeed, the denigration of commerce and artifact production was widespread in the region of northeast Africa. The protective aspects of the decree remained only a potential constraint, which potters could evoke if and when they brought formal challenges against individual farmers to promote their personal rather than corporate rights of access to land and other resources. But Wolayta artisans never took full advantage of these legal possibilities, either singly or communally; from their perspective, the difficulties involved in achieving any immediate goals outweighed a vague and distant political purpose.

GENDER ASPECTS

It should be evident that edicts aimed at artisans affected chiefly women in Wolayta. Inasmuch as an occupational group is defined by the work it does for the community's livelihood, the *chinasha* in Wolayta are defined by women's work. Many Ethiopian linguistic groups evoke women's role in their stories of political change and transfer of power, but in Wolayta these stories only demonstrate the linked and confused status of *chinasha* and women. Sometimes the female agents whose interests are most powerfully at stake are *goqa*. On the other hand, in stories about the period in which *chinasha* were given a political position as executioner, women are mentioned only among those who were annihilated by the *goqa*. Symbolic attributes such as invisibility and supernatural powers (the *chinasha*, after all, are still in existence after being annihilated) and danger and pollution are used to describe both women in Wolayta and the *chinasha*.[15] Women of both occupational groups are circumcised, a mutilation that allows men to stereotype and manipulate women. Female infanticide was practiced historically because it was shameful for a man to have daughters. Even nowadays, long after police control has stopped infanticide, the birth of girls is not a cause for celebration. Women's influence politically and in matters of agriculture was also restricted to the household. The only exception was the ritual with which all women celebrate the acquisition of property, especially cattle. The *gima* ritual denigrates enterprise in a ceremony that acknowledges conspicuous consumption. The denigration of the activity of trade castigates the potters' survival through petty trading in pottery and extends a social evaluation to all that women make as part of their household chores. That celebration is also an assertive way of including all women who acquire wealth through trading, for traders are a category of people, who, like the *chinasha* as a whole, did not belong with the dominant farmers. Indeed, the *goqa* conception of *chinasha* blurs the distinction between male and female, deliberately pushing the whole occupational category into a homogenous gender group.

However blurred the categories are in Wolayta, government decrees that tried to address the stigma attached to the *chinasha* did not necessarily stimulate interest on issues of gender relations among the potters. A 1930 decree that restricted women's employment in the army, and thereby their right of access to land, had no direct relevance to the landless potters even though it was the first decree issued about women. (This bill was soon widely challenged and had to be refuted by the government.) A more direct challenge to Wolayta sociopolitical divisions was posed during the period of Italian occupation from 1935 to 1940. The Italians invaded Ethiopia in 1935, reached

Wolayta in early 1937, and, using the knowledge collected by Italian ethnographers before the occupation, tried to win the support of Wolayta men against guerrilla fighters. In addition to removing fief administrators, they tried to pacify lower-class Wolayta by employing the men as foot soldiers, sending them to prepare the area for Italian colonial settlers who in fact never materialized. Potters were employed by colonial settlement programs in the construction of facilities such as administrative offices, exclusive hospitals, and European living quarters. The Italians recruited the men, rather than the women, to prepare handmade bricks that were baked in kilns fueled with firewood from forests on lands that belonged to the old *kao*s. When the Italians left in 1940, a hospital and two administrative offices had been constructed. Some elderly potters around the Ottona hospital see the bricks in those buildings as a monument of their effort because, in their own words, "brick making was innovative." Despite the memory of this challenge to the traditional division of labor, however, neither male involvement in handling clay nor brick making itself survived the occupation period.

Other policies after the occupation did not help the cause of women. The revised constitution of 1956, copied from the French, placed women's issues within the realm of family law. The government of Haile Selassie, resting for more than a decade on the laurels of expelling the Italians, established "modern" institutions of government based on the European model, such as a men-only standing army and other branches, allowing the evolution of an autocratic monarchy and a highly centralized, male-dominated bureaucracy.

The implementation of "modernization" has meant an increasing lack of communication between the central government and the public. Potters work from their homes, and the marketplace is the only public space they share with the wider community. Up until the 1930s, the market was the chief site for the public, oral promulgation of government decrees that could be heard by everybody, including women.[16] Access to decrees was restricted after the war, when the government used other media, such as newspapers and radio, that made the decrees and laws accessible only to the literate or the rich who could afford radio sets. Government policies, from the growth-oriented development process of the 1960s, to the rise and fall of a socialist government from 1974 to 1991 and the restructuring of the state along ethnic lines that began in 1991, were made and promulgated from a distance. As critiques of development have pointed out, "top-down" policies that came from external sources did not reach the people they intended to serve. Innovative brick making and revolutionary challenges to sociopolitical norms could barely make a serious dent in the strong traditions of land tenure, nor in the lifestyle or economic and social status of the potter women when officials of the Ministry of Agriculture, dominant *goqa*, and the men of the potter community saw no reason to relinquish their positions of power over minorities and women, respectively. By 1991, any attempt to promote the specific interests of potters (or even farmers) had been abandoned altogether in favor of reinstating "cultural" (read "traditional") rights. The most recent emphasis on organizing political parties along ethnic lines entrenches the traditions that make a distinction between farmers, artisans, and descendants of slaves.

TWO CASE STUDIES: SHENTO POTTERY COLLECTIVE AND THE WADU

I will offer two examples of government-sponsored development programs that affected the potters: the pottery-marketing cooperative of the 1980s, which potter women closed down when they were kept out of its management; and the Wolayta Agricultural Development Unit (WADU), an economically oriented development program of the 1960s that marginalized the potter communities, displaced some potters from their occupation and their society altogether, and in the process inculcated the notion that men are the senior partners in development. Both programs illustrate the pressures exerted to change gender relations. The narrative of the marketing cooperative is an example of direct, hands-on involvement by women, while WADU illustrates the ways in which the outside status of those who were involved in planning the program from a distance ultimately left the grassroots workers who implemented the programs resentful.

The marketing cooperative was one of the politically motivated changes that resulted from the socialist revolution in 1974. The cooperative was also the last in a series of programs that potter women recall in narratives of their collective experiences of "government," as they label all external sources of influence. While they later attributed their decision to close it down to a women's rights argument, the events are better understood in the context of their historical, political, and economic experiences.

As in many parts of rural Ethiopia, the rigidly hierarchical social system of classification and the prejudice held by the dominant farmers have meant prohibiting potters from having rights of access to land except those that accrue to the patron-client relationship. Because men of the potter community cannot farm for profit, women's production and marketing of pottery are their principal means of economic support. When, in 1974, potter women in Shento (and elsewhere in Wolayta) took advantage of the socialist revolution to assert their rights of free access to land abundant with clay, it was the first time such a claim about the direct relevance of land use had been made in remembered history.

Wolayta is currently administered from Soddo. Located 365 kilometers south of the Ethiopian capital, Addis Ababa, Soddo is at the southern foothills of Mount Damota, while Shento, about twenty kilometers to the north, is in the northern foothills, about eight kilometers off the main road going from Addis Ababa to Arba Minch, the regional administrative center. The mountain features in Wolayta history and in everyday usage as a traditional site of risk taking: "He who does not know how to move dies still wishing to see the top of Mount Damota," as the saying goes. The mountain is said to have been owned by the former Wolayta royal family, and the potters' settlements, scattered all around the foothills, are said to date from the days when they were placed there by members of that family. In historical times, potters settled in close proximity to one another within a wider settlement of farmers. Currently, judging from fieldwork conducted in 1989–90, farmers mix with the potters only at places of worship (such as the church) and at the weekly market held in Shento every Thursday afternoon.

In the 1980s, the potters developed their own compact villages. The settlement pattern in that decade came about as a result of the revolutionary government's program to reshape the former rural pattern of scattered hamlets into compact villages. The purpose was allegedly the better provision of government services such as health, education, and agricultural inputs, but it was persistently rumored that the real motivation behind the program lay in the government's desire to have tighter control over revenue and militias for its wars in northern Ethiopia. The English word villagization has been coined (and accepted in development circles in Ethiopia) to describe the formation of those new settlements.

The villagization program was executed by the government's political cadres, who also doubled as extension workers of the Ministry of Agriculture sent out to organize the "peasants." These young men and women, known as development agents (DAs), had a secondary-school education and some college training in appropriate areas such as agriculture and water technologies. The ministry also had a Rural Women's Agricultural Development (RWAD) section, whose women workers had taken special courses in such "modern" systems—principally vegetable gardening, primary health care, family planning, and nutrition—as were deemed essential for imparting "modern" ideas to rural women. After the revolution, they were also trained to have a working knowledge of Marxism and (later) Leninism. Extension programs had been operational in places such as Shento since the 1960s, and most of the workers were already experienced in working with rural people, so they were able to pass on their newly acquired knowledge of Marxism-Leninism. In their view, and in that of the ministry for which they worked, the goals of the new ideology and those of the rural "peasant" population were identical: the alleviation of poverty and ignorance and the creation of equality.

During the revolution, the RWAD unit had at least one woman worker for each peasants association (PA), and this was equivalent to the number of DAs working with (male) farmers. The male DAs around Shento were responsible to the RWAD women. The role of the DAs was to mediate between the Ministry of Agriculture and the farmers on issues of crop production and animal husbandry. The RWAD women were responsible for introducing rural women to "modern" systems. They also organized grassroots women's associations, and taught about emancipation and the "women question." The differences between men and women were seen to be personal and physical rather than cultural and political. Individual men were criticized for the manner in which they related to women around them, and unfortunately this generated a lot of jokes and images of insincerity about gender issues. Men alone continued to be acknowledged as heads of household, entitled to receive land for farming and construction. In polygamous rural Wolayta, the combination of a perceived insincerity about women's emancipation and the designation of men as landowners created a problem that remained unresolved for many years. Because the revolutionary ideology failed to appreciate local realities, its enthusiastic teaching ended up creating inequality between men and women. But it also gave women new arguments, which the potters then used to justify their actions.

When I did my second round of fieldwork in Wolayta (1989–93), I made friends with a RWAD agent who had been working there since 1983 and who was at the time also coordinating the work of the male extension workers for the area. We explored Shento together. According to my informants, she was the first female extension worker to visit the potter women in their homes, even though there had been other RWAD women in the area since the sixties. All the agents, especially the women, worked under difficult conditions. It was not until 1990 that mopeds were provided for the male extension workers by the Food and Agricultural Organization (FAO). Because RWAD women had the additional problem of budgeting for appropriate "teaching tools," they received no mopeds and had to hitchhike or walk long distances to villages in which they felt comfortable and welcome. In their view this did not include the potters' villages. All of them used such difficulties as an excuse for not working with the potters, and this neglect fed into the pervasive prejudice against potters and their marginalization.

The exceptional concentration of potters living in the village of Shento was a new phenomenon, and one that the most hardened DAs considered "scary." My friend, who herself belonged to a family of local farmers and who was willing to talk at length about these views for my benefit, opened my eyes further to the biases held by farmers against potters. Of course I had known about the prejudice from my home background, too (although I belong neither to potters nor to the wider Wolayta linguistic group), and also from my research in the region between 1973 and 1975, but, being a city woman, I found notions such as those attributing an "evil eye" to other people too remote for me to take seriously. In the constantly changing urban setting where I grew up, the attribute was a temporary accusation leveled against any stranger (that is, anyone of unknown social origin) who came into the neighborhood. Strangers come and go all the time, and those who grow up in urban areas do not develop that intense fear of being victimized by the supposed power of artisans. Potters who move away from their immediate community to settle elsewhere permanently, and who do other work, shed that attribute over time. Neighbors would not have real grounds to attribute the "evil eye" to them. Nonetheless, I have met urban extension workers and development agents who expressed fear and even disgust at the thought of venturing into potters' villages except to visit the market, and even then only if one has to buy pottery from the potters' corner.

When the revolutionary government implemented its villagization program, DAs were required to persuade rural people to dismantle their homes and move to new sites in order to qualify for the right of access to land proclaimed as theirs by the 1976 socialist land reform decree and other services promised by the government. Other requirements included joining mass organizations such as women's, youth, and peasant associations. These organizations served as the lowest level of the political structure of the socialist state, following the Soviet model. Groups such as farmers' producers' cooperatives and grain-marketing cooperatives were also part of the socialist plan for increased productivity and development. The government strategy was to "sensitize" rural society to the need for rebelling against perceived feudal landlords and other such political forces, and enforced redistribution was explained as a part of social progress. In addition to access to land, development (*lemat*, literally "fertility" but broadly meaning a growth-oriented economic system of production) was the ultimate reward the revolution offered. It took a while to persuade farmers to abandon their homesteads and relinquish *their* land to others, particularly to potters. The last participants of the villagization program, including those in Shento, were not fully organized until 1986.

Some potters remained in their old homesteads. Locally recruited agents, who were of course from *goqa* (farmer) families, offered the explanation that they "were not aware that villagers existed in those places" or that the agents "were afraid to go to their villages because of their [the potters'] evil eye." In Gurmu Wayde, in the Western foothills of Mount Damota, the potters were never villagized. For example, in 1991 one *goqa* woman, irritated by our constant attention to the *chinasha*, explained that a return to the old system was in order: "It is against the law of nature. The *chinasha* have no land except for what I allow them to use," she shouted, challenging all of us who were sitting near a source from which some potters were drawing water. The potter women simply laughed and said that she and other *goqa* "need them anyway," and that the worst that would happen was that they would have to pay her for the clay they required from her land. During the years of the revolution the potter women had taken advantage of the emancipatory decree that allowed them to stop paying for the clay. To assert her privilege, the landowner took the villagers (and us, because we "were trampling around on her land") to the local court.

Where DAs executing the villagization programs had been bold enough to approach the potters, they separated them from the farmers, placing them in the most remote and broken parts of the plateau areas selected for settlement. When asked to explain this choice of site, the potters repeated the reason they were given, saying that "firing pottery is a hazardous affair that exposes the whole village to the dangers of fire." The farmers and the DAs explained the segregation in terms of the unclean eating habits and "evil eye" of the *chinasha*. Although the potters continued to practice their craft production in these desolate villages, they complained of the poor quality of land they were given to farm.

The exclusion of potters was also practiced in the formation of the mass organizations of women, youth, and peasants. Everybody was expected to become a member of one of these groups, according to their age, sex, and occupation. Stories abound on the subject of what happened to potters' membership: "They could not be members of the peasants association because they could not afford the basic periodic membership fees, and they could not be elected to leadership positions because they were too busy or, in the case of the women, also too shy." When forming the women's associations, the

RWAD agents were prone to accept the farmer women's opinion that the potter women were "too poor to participate." In fact, potter women had more access to cash than did farmer women. Another possible element at work was a vague religious divide. Most literate Wolayta, including the locally recruited RWAD agents and DAs, came from farmer families and belonged to fundamentalist Protestant churches, which refer to their members as "Christian." These protestants perceive those who belong to the indigenous Ethiopian Orthodox Church, among whom are the potters, as "non-Christian but Orthodox," and therefore as backward.

The peasants association at Shento was an exception in that it was formed by a local potter community whose men joined the farmers' producers' cooperative after asserting their rights to the land. The establishment of the Shento pottery marketing cooperative was made possible by that exception. The cooperative was organized at Shento in 1983, only one year after most of the other mass associations in Wolayta. It was the initiative of a very enterprising and enthusiastic DA who reportedly had had a lot of experience working with the World Bank–supported Wolayta Agricultural Development Unit (WADU), a massive agricultural development program that had been operational in the area since the sixties. He was reputed to have developed a good rapport with the farmers and other rural people. His aim was the introduction of "appropriate technology," such as spinning wheels and potter's wheels. His choice of Shento was obviously calculated to benefit from its situation along a trade route that passes through the territories of several linguistic groups. Traders come from all directions to buy products for which the market is noted, among which are fruits and pottery. Shento pottery is particularly well known for the large brewing and storage jars made by local specialists. Working in cooperation with the Soddo-based rural technology development center, the DA acquired a potter's wheel in 1982 and trained some female extension workers and a male member of the rural potter community in Shento. The potter's wheel was quite a novelty; it had been only briefly introduced in the rural parts of northern Ethiopia during the early nineteenth century but had since disappeared. The DA's choice to train a male potter was explained as the result of the ministry's directive that only literate people could learn new technologies; in the potters' community that could only be a man. But it would not be surprising if his choice had also been based on sheer ignorance about the division of labor. Ironically, the wife of the literate man trained on the potter's wheel is considered the most skilled of the potters'; from childhood she had been making brewing and storage jars and other special utensils, and yet she was never trained on the potter's wheel.

As noted above, the local farmers involved in implementing both the cooperative and villagization programs in Shento were the men and women of the potter community. The Revolutionary Ethiopian Women's Association (REWA), established at the national level in 1976 to coordinate rural and urban women's mass associations, failed to reach the potters elsewhere, but local REWA officers articulated and imparted the notion of the "women question" to the women in Shento. The potter women of Shento who attended revolutionary meetings between 1976 and 1988 passed the word around, especially in the villagized community, because they thought the cooperative—which the community controlled—would be a practical area in which to test out these new ideas. It served as a venue of political participation for potter women, an organization in which to test their potential. In speaking of that time, former female peasants association office holders proudly recall that the first action they took was to secure appropriate sites for the cooperative and the peasants association. Both were close to a large source of high-quality clay and to the market. The traditional role of women, to make and sell pottery, found a public meaning and collective space recognized by the political structure. It should be noted that participation in the peasants association was possible for only the richest, most acclaimed, and perhaps "feminized" but independent women in the traditional sociopolitical system. In this new context, the women refused to cooperate with the men of the association, evoking a women's rights argument in their refusal to learn the use of a potter's wheel from a man. Despite women's involvement in the cooperative, the attempt to introduce technology failed because of the initial mistake of training a man rather than a woman whose occupation was already pottery making.

Two years into the collective program, the agent who took the initiative was dismissed from his position for political reasons: The military government at the time was removing members of political parties that rivaled them, and setting up instead a single party, the Workers Party of Ethiopia (WPE). The local man who trained on the wheel remained attached to the ministry as a wage earner and, after trying unsuccessfully to carry out his duty, safely locked the wheel away in the cooperative store. The women explained his failure later by saying that it was hilarious for a man to train them to make pottery when he himself worked on the potter's wheel only because the ministry paid him a monthly wage. Outside of that forced context, and beyond the usual routines tradition allowed to potters' husbands, the would-be teacher never touched clay.

Further difficulties for the survival of the cooperative were generated when, at about the same time that the resourceful DA was removed, an administrative overhaul prohibited women from participating in decision-making meetings at levels above the peasant associations. By 1983, the REWA head office passed down a message that restricted mass women's organizations to providing support for the peasant associations. In Wolayta this was reportedly justified by the claim that women's involvement in politics, "of which they knew nothing," was making them incompetent in both homemaking and agriculture. While the earlier movement had tried to involve women in state politics, the new direction of REWA was to provide services that "sensitized" the women to their new duties in the Workers Party of Ethiopia. These included cleaning springs, which the potters agreed was in their interest, but also activities such as fund raising for the war effort when, as they complained, they had no say in who among the youth could join the militia. The new directive meant that the Shento pottery producers could no longer participate in making decisions about matters of access to land and other crucial political activities.

Nonetheless, the women in Shento continued to run the cooperative shop, contributing a set quota of their products and generating collective income. By 1987, however, the men in the peasants association accused the women of incompetent bookkeeping, and a year later they took over the administration of the shop. The women reacted by withdrawing their support from the cooperative. Most flatly refused to contribute the quota of pottery required of them, but all kept an eye on their free rights of access to clay. The problem of the cooperative intensified in 1989–90 when a general rejection of the socialist system swept the country. The cooperative shop, which was by that time fully controlled and run by the men, failed to attract any contributions even from the wives of those working in the shop. Most of the women in the village were angered by the men's unsupportive public attitudes. The primary-school teacher who took over the cooperative's bookkeeping, for instance, was very keen to hide information about his wife's pottery work "because it would affect his professional life," as he put it to us.

At the same time, the former landowners began to demand minimum contributions. The potter women immediately made arrangements to make cash payments once a week for access to clay, even though they were not legally obliged to do so. However, they avoided taking clay on the arranged day of the week, a fact the farmers laughed off halfheartedly. Sometimes the women went further afield to collect clay because they claimed other landowners were charging lower prices. They also continued to collect clay from areas where landlords were not watching or were not confident enough to reassert their rights. When asked if it would not be easier to support the cooperative and so be able to assert their right to free access, the women firmly replied that they did not understand why they should sell their pottery through the men in the cooperative shop when they could go on selling directly in the market themselves. According to tradition, men engaged in selling pottery only when women let them do so, either because they could not go themselves or because the pottery was too heavy to carry. Selling pottery, like making it, was women's work, and as long as they had been running the cooperative, as they did long after they had ceased participating in the local revolutionary political decision-making body, participating in it was a continuation of that traditional part of their role.

By 1991 the socialist government had lost control, and the political participation of the potters' husbands in the peasant association (and at higher district levels) was relinquished to the *goqa*, who claimed to support the new government even though it declared a free-market economy while remaining strictly uncommitted with regard to rural land rights. As in most parts of rural Ethiopia, Wolayta owners asserted their claims to their former land holdings, villagers returned to their old homestead sites, potter women reestablished their tradition of firing pottery in the back of their huts at their leisure, and the cooperative was formally disbanded. The last time I was there, in 1993, the potter's wheel was still locked in the storeroom as government property, the potters' would-be teacher was still trying to reassert his position as a wage earner in the ministry of the new government, and the primary-school teacher was working out what to do with the small amount of money the cooperative had made. That money, like the potter's wheel and the wage position, was too exposed to the vagaries of state political changes. The return of the old order, which gives the upper hand to the farmers, reestablishes the localized position of the potters with its problematic place for women. The economic structure that survived the reversals, or persisted through them, was the making and marketing of pottery at Shento. As ever, on Thursdays the market starts at 4 P.M. and stops six hours later, when the potter women return home with their income and torches to light their way, chatting with their husbands and with each other.

In hindsight, it seems clear that the cooperative was threatened less by the reversals of national and local politics than by the gender reversals the men attempted to bring about. The money and effort potters had invested in it would not have been wasted had the men not interfered in the cooperative idea. As a compound and store, the cooperative would have continued to allow the women to maintain their own space and to protect their wares and themselves from the vagaries of nature. Had the women allowed the cooperative to continue by going along with men's control of their income, they would have made themselves totally invisible, segregated away from the marketplace at Shento. At the moment, they at least still practice their occupation, controlling the income from their own product.

What the women lost in closing the cooperative was the capacity to sustain a change of direction toward other possibilities. Traditionally, potter women work individually and therefore reject the possibility of working with one another. Their only collective activity is the sharing of the market space. Had the extension of that practice into the shared space of the cooperative been allowed to continue, it would have opened them to further changes in their work habits, changes from which the potter community as a whole would have benefited. It might have led, for instance, to the sharing of kilns that would allow for glazing. The development that gave men the right to take over the cooperative is at the root of this lost opportunity. The developmental potential of collective pottery making would allow potters to enhance their incomes and positions by becoming competitive in the market, where their production and marketing of utensils is currently being challenged by imported goods—wares made of plastic, aluminum, and glass—that claim to be more durable and more prestigious. It would also allow them to resist other developmental pressures that force the men to become farmers and deprive the women of their inherited skills and occupations and thus of their economic power and centrality.

One of the more enigmatic developments of the revolutionary period was the elevated status of pottery in some parts of the country. The development of pottery was part of a plan to increase overall productivity with small-scale technology for income generation by those who could not fit in the land-focused production scheme. This led to, among other things, the establishment of a substantial workshop that specialized in the production of appropriate technology, the Handicrafts and Small-Scale Industries Development Agency (HASIDA), based in Awasa. HASIDA produced small kilns, fuel-saving hearths, mud technology for rural house construction, and other items such as plaster molds. The possibilities for what the center could produce and for how the tools could be used were wide-ranging, but they were scarcely deployed. The kilns, for instance, were used only at two sites: a potters' cooperative in west-central Ethiopia, close to the capital, and another in the capital itself.[17] Inside Wolayta, the kiln was used at a Soddo-based urban women's income-generating project run by a Catholic convent. There were potters close by in Gurmu Wayde and also in the more immediate vicinity of the Ottona hospital, about a kilometer from the project site. Yet none of the women who took part in this project were from the potter community. To explain this, the foreign nun who initiated the project said that she had had to comply with the demands of the women in her workshop "to keep out those from the potter community." The prejudice was pervasive. In 1991, a government plan was in the offing for the construction of a modern ceramics (glazed and mold-produced pottery) production industry. Needless to say, however, attempts to draw attention to the existence of rural potters and the need for developing their industry by diversifying their products and "upgrading" their skills had a cold reception. Unlike the Shento example, the acceptance of the notion of women's rights at the national level, which resulted in the creation of RWAD and REWA, did not correspond with the sociological reality.

The continuing exclusion of potters, which ultimately obliged the women in Shento to close down the pottery-marketing cooperative and to reject the potter's wheel, is very much rooted in the perception, prevalent since the sixties, that rural development empowers men by intensifying agricultural production, thus promoting their work and increasing their income. For women, this means that they must often take on new work, rather than continue with the work they had already initiated, for "income generation." During the revolution, women of the Shento pottery community realized that their work enabled them to join in political decision making. But they also experienced some of the ways in which development was a source of power for men that eventually gave them access to the desired and prestigious occupation of farming through literacy and numeracy training.

In Wolayta the perception that development meant economic empowerment for men was deliberately inculcated in the sixties by a fundamental economic change that targeted the whole region but radically altered the lives of only the potters. The program that brought about this change was set in motion when two "progressive" provincial governors attracted a World Bank development project called the Wolayta Agricultural Development Unit (WADU). One of only two regional, integrated rural development programs in the whole country, WADU subjected the whole of Wolayta to the cultivation of commercial export crops such as coffee and cereals. While funding

WADU, the World Bank also provided the Ministry of Agriculture with financial support for setting up extension programs that brought the DAs and RWAD workers to the farmers, making Wolayta one of the earliest regions to receive this help.

Because WADU was export-oriented, its leaders took on a more global perspective. This new horizon gave them new ideas about what rural women should be doing for development. Its impact was felt in every part of Wolayta society despite the reluctance of RWAD agents, the only "government" people who were closely related to rural people, to walk into neighborhoods occupied by potters. By insisting on commercial crop production, WADU substantially reduced production of the drought-resistant staple *ensete*, and this subsequently made Wolayta susceptible to famine. It also meant that less food was available to potters who normally bought food from farmers. In addition, WADU cleared valuable forest cover from the low-lying areas of Aballa, around Lake Abaya in the south, so as to maximize the amount of farmland. With support from the "progressive" governor, WADU then proceeded to settle "landless potters" in the clearing and invited Protestant missionaries from World Vision to help encourage the potters to abandon their traditional craft production because it was "backward and a source of denigration." Today these former potters are struggling to survive as Christian farmers in an ecologically precarious environment. If they are to continue to farm the land, they will require heavy capital investment from external sources for necessities such as fertilizer. Throughout Wolayta the commodification of land encouraged by WADU changed the tenure system, dispossessing local farmers and potters of their traditional abodes and, as in the instance of the settlement at Aballa, dislocating others from their traditional occupations altogether.

All this commercial activity, coupled with the buying and selling of land, provoked an outward migration of people from the area. Biographical narratives showed that in the sixties, Wolayta men began to work as seasonal migrant laborers in the Rift Valley sugar plantations to the northeast of their homeland and in the cotton-growing areas of the Gibe Valley, south of Lake Aballa. Many of these migrant laborers intermarried, mostly with Amhara and Oromo, and settled in major cities such as Nazareth, Awasa, Jimma, and Addis Ababa. They added to the dispersion of people of Wolayta descent into many regions of northern, western and southern Ethiopia. Next to the Gurage, who live to the north of them, the Wolayta probably now form the largest group of southern people to be found outside their home area. Constant trade and cultural communication between dispersed relatives brought new ideas that challenged the sociopolitical norms of the relationships between the dominant farmers and the minority potters and artisans all over the country.

Through education, migrant labor, and commerce, Wolayta men (among them a few from potters' families), and a few women from farmers' families, have made space for themselves in the Ethiopian "modern" sector. Those from the potters' community, however, do not volunteer information about their background; When they return home, they recognize their own relatives only selectively and hide from their spouses their ties to pottery production for fear of being rejected. Such reaction is common among other potters all throughout Ethiopia: While it is possible to move out of the occupation by moving elsewhere, it is not easy to remove the stigma attached to the occupation in local settings where farmers dominate. Despite the economic pressures that stimulated the outward migration, much acclaimed at the time, the sociocultural pressure to keep potters in their place only grew stronger as the gap between rich and poor grew wider than before. By the mid-seventies the few who profited, notably descendants of the former *kao* and those who had bought land to cultivate coffee, had grown so rich that the government targeted them for expulsion and "liquidation." Information about this painfully dramatic event was offered by fervent cadres who used it as an argument in favor of the land reform decree and other such requirements of the revolutionary period. Groups who had been feeling oppressed were most convinced about the changes.[18] Thus, although WADU was primarily an economic program, it was also reportedly seen as a political force. Its legacy has been unequal access to education and other benefits, along with differential treatment by various government agents. For example, the failure of the RWAD extension workers to reach out to the potters left the latter with a legacy of resentment, a sense of being left out that was irrespective of the relevance of their programs.

CONCLUSION: POTTERS AND CONTEMPORARY DEVELOPMENT POLITICS

In Ethiopia, and in Wolayta in particular, trying to change rural people's own conception of work and its place in their community's economy means, first and foremost, challenging the general perception that agriculture is the only viable rural lifestyle. Because policy makers are reluctant to acknowledge this, their call for the creation of rural, off-farm employment continues to render hollow their solution to the problems of the shortage of arable land, the diversification of the rural economy, and changes in old attitudes toward craft producers. Targeting women in development, an attempt that has survived several changes in government since the sixties, has been bedeviled by the lack of economic and political efforts in areas that affect women's work and status. In the case of potters, any effort to challenge the control of the farmers would necessarily mean resisting local sociopolitical classifications and the traditional understanding of the right of access to land and other resources. It would also mean a recognition of the fact that pottery represents a market-oriented area of rural work and labor, one predominantly run by women, and this would require a subversion of the cultural prejudice that deliberately buries the importance of market-oriented production in the interests of health, identity, and land control.

The current political structure continues to support RWAD by making them an independent unit of the Ministry of Agriculture, which entitles them to their own budget. It has not empowered them, however, to face up to rural prejudice and to overcome the problems of lost potential for change and the discouraged creativity of potter women who have been left economically stranded. The financial resources RWAD would require to take on these issues simply are not there. Moreover, the current emphasis on commercial crop production is taking Wolayta back to the WADU days of the sixties, entrenching an unnecessary competition over land for food production. The new emphasis on ethnicity has also meant restrictions on the mobility of migrant laborers sojourning among neighboring communities. The RWAD units have no power to resist the likes of the landowner *goqa* who confronted the potters in Gurmu Wayde. Farmers whose lands are being switched to commercial crops lack the alternative outlets they had thirty years ago, and new "progressive" administrators would have to find settlements for the potters whom they dispossess, like those who had to be placed in the clearings in Aballa. The RWAD units are far from identifying and defining the specific initiatives and problems of potter women—that is, if they are at all interested in them as a potential sector of rural development.

The activities of RWAD and other development initiatives in Wolayta have had an influence similar to the changes in the political system detailed above. In the cultural exchanges that take place between women representing the Ministry of Agriculture, international development agencies, and local oganizations, the sociopolitical situation of potters has begun to look somewhat entrenched. The case of former potters in Aballa, for instance, seems to illustrate that being born into the occupation does not entail a status similar to caste. The reason for this appears to be that social categories lose their meaning outside their local context. Wolayta potter women do not pass on their identity to their children; they only teach their daughters to make pottery, the occupation against which the rest of the wider society defines itself. That this traditional meaning does not necessarily travel outside that society is illustrated by the case of urban-made decorative ceramics, which people consider fashionable and buy in exhibition halls. Pottery making has also been introduced to urban schoolchildren as ordinary work not subject to prejudice. The position of these "ceramic artists" is reminiscent of the traditional toleration of potters who move out of their community to engage in other occupations. Indeed, the admiration and high status conferred on those artists suggests that the prejudice is targeted at the context in which potters live and work, rather than the women or the pottery production itself. This in turn suggests that the power relations that define the lives of the men and women involved in the pottery-making occupation might be changed even within Wolayta if appropriate pressure was allowed to develop. But these are the issues that RWAD has not taken up.

If it is to the development process that one looks for an influence capable of initiating political and social change, the rivalry over resources such as cash and education takes on a new significance. We must see that the invisibility of potters in the rest of Ethiopia, reflected in current development projects in the potters' immediate community, is the result of a political process. Development, in the potters' case, would mean access to clay, fuel and provisions that would allow them to diversify and upgrade their production. These changes would require expensive resources and complex and time-consuming programs. While the potential for developing a rural cottage industry is enormous and therefore worthwhile, breaking into the circuit of policy makers has been impossible. Even when they support the development of large-scale industrial ceramics and brick making, policy makers appear to be strongly influenced, or perhaps sheltered, by the sociopolitical relationships that define the potters. In my experience, the estimate that there are ten thousand potters among the two million Wolayta—and the possibility of the existence of even higher numbers among other groups elsewhere in the country—is dismissed as imaginary by a government that then uses the low numbers of the potters as a basis for refusing to allocate appropriate resources that would allow the emergence of a rural ceramics industry. Even researchers who claim to know the rural areas underestimate these numbers and thereby contribute to making potters invisible in the modern sector. The prejudice against potters, who are found in all linguistic groups all over Ethiopia, by those in the so-called modern sector is as complex as that among the Wolayta traditions outlined above. Leaders avoid challenging the dominant rural farmers. Like the DAs working on the ground, they say that they are too afraid of the supposedly potent power of potters to go and determine the actual number of potters living in the rural areas. The leaders in development programs, as in state structures, are mostly male, and despite the rhetoric of the last two decades, their attitudes toward women's interests and work are still very unclear. These political issues of gender relations in contemporary "development" planning should not be caught in the debate between capital-intensive versus labor-focused planning; the vicitimization of women potters and the failure of the expansion of the local economy should suffice to offset these econometric arguments.

The women of Shento potters' village were able to fit the pottery-marketing cooperative into their work scheme because they accepted it as part of their "women's rights," a way of articulation that was imparted to them through the REWA and, after a fashion, the RWAD workers. If planners had empowered the women to maintain their control of its management, for instance by targeting the women for literacy and numeracy training, then the potters themselves would have been instrumental in changing men's attitude toward them and the attitude of farmers toward potters as a whole. Part of the rural prejudice against potters emanates from their dependence on farmers for land, and in the "modern" context (starting with WADU) on their husbands for certain relationships. Removing that perpetual dependence is what removed the structural links of power between potters and farmers during the revolution (and earlier, in the case of the potters settled at Aballa). The change deprived the farmers of their means of control over those potters, although at Aballa it also took away the potters' own identity as pottery producers and sellers. In the Shento example, the potter women who debated with the men in the cooperative forced the men to admit their centrality by referring to the "rights of women," and the men recognized in this their own arguments for asserting minorities' rights of access to land. But in order to be heard the women also had to use the argument of their traditional rights to control their income, and even go further to arrange with the farmers for access to clay in the old manner. The development planners who work in the RWAD section, who fought and earned the right for their unit's independence by using also the "rights of women" argument also, would need to realize the full meaning of their emancipatory arguments by supporting those potters who promote their own initiative in the rural setting. Planning for women's "development" through community effort would encourage only the dominant farmers. Encouraging potter women themselves to promote their own production process would help identify the areas of work they would consider for community work. That was at the heart of the success of the pottery-marketing cooperative while it lasted. Ways of sharing scarce and expensive facilities such as kilns and glazing materials would have been designed by the potters, but their strategizing capacity would have to be acknowledged.

As long as rural development continues to involve the creation of new "target" groups, the exisiting cooperation with Western feminism, which obliged the potters to accept the arguments of "women's rights" and utilize it for their strategizing purposes, will deteriorate. Women such as the potters of Shento will fall victim to the powerful pressure of the free-market economy, which reorganizes land tenure and thereby changes the relations of gender to the detriment of women. Such pressures brought about inappropriate changes in gender relations among potters and also brought competition to their pottery marketing, thereby threatening their economic autonomy. To avoid this pitfall, the differences between the potters' localized perception of women's rights and that of the planners' should be negotiated on equal terms between the two.

NOTES

1. Donald Levine, *Greater Ethiopia* (Chicago: University of Chicago Press, 1969), p. 39; Tsehai Berhane-Selassie, "Gender and Occupational Potters in Wolayta: Imposed Femininity and Mysterious Survival in Ethiopia," in T. Berhane-Selassie, ed., *Gender Issues in Ethiopia* (Addis Ababa: Addis Ababa University, 1991), p. 15.

2. Ifi Amadiume, *Male Daughters, Female Husbands: Gender and Sex in an African Society* (New York: Zed Books, 1987), pp. 13–17; Henrietta Moore, *Feminism and Anthropology* (Cambridge, UK: Polity Press, 1988), pp. 186–187; John van Willigen, *Applied Anthropology: An Introduction,* revised ed. (Westport, CT: Bergin and Garvey, 1993), p. 77.

3. Lourdes Beneria, "Conceptualizing the Labour Force: The Underestimation of Women's Economic Activities," in N. Nelson (ed.), *African Women in the Development Process* (London: Frank Cass, 1981), pp. 10–28; Lourdes Beneria, *Women and Development: The Sexual Division of Labor in Rural Societies* (Praeger, 1982), p. xvii; Margaret Snyder and Mary Tadesse, *African Women and Development: A History* (Witwatersrand: Witwatersrand University Press and Zed Books, 1995), pp. 27–35.

4. In the absence of a sustained census, the political context of giving prominence to "cultural groups" or inflating the number of minorities has become a difficult game. Various figures are produced by researchers, the government, and the local political groups, who argue over "academic," "development," and "self-definitive" assertions, respectively. The number given here is based on a survey I conducted over the period 1991–1993.

5. Werner Lange, *History of the Southern Bonga* (1982), p. 261.

6. Ernesta Cerulli, "Peoples of South-West Ethiopia and its Borderlands," *Ethnographic Survey of Africa* (London: International African Institute, 1956), pp. 56, 102, 103, 107, *and passim.*

7. Tsehai Berhane-Selassie, "Menelik II: Conquest and Consolidation of the Southern Provinces,"

Addis Ababa University, 1969; Tsehai Berhane-Selassie, "The Question of Wolamo and Damot," *Journal of Ethiopian Studies*, (1975).

8. Cerulli, op. cit., p. 56; William Shack, *The Central Ethiopians: Amhara, Tigrina, and Related Peoples* (London: International African Institute, 1974), p. 138.

9. Jacques Bureau, *Wolayta* [in Amharic] unpublished manuscript, n.d.; Afewerk Gebre-Selassie, *Ye Wolayta Tarik* [in Amharic], unpublished manuscript, n.d.

10. Berhane-Selassie, "The Question of Wolamo and Damot."

11. Lange, op. cit., p. 36.

12. Berhane-Selassie, "The Question of Wolamo and Damot."

13. Berhane-Selassie, "Menelik II."

14. Mahetem-Selassie, Zekre Neger (Amharic "Records"), Addis Ababa, 1942 EC.

15. Berhane-Selassie, "Gender and Occupational Potters in Wolayta," pp. 15–30.

16. Mahetem-Selassie, Zekre Neger (Amharic "Records"), Addis Ababa, 1942 EC.

17. Abera Feyissa, "Case Study on the Traditional Potting of the Association of the Association of the Ambro Road Potters in Addis Ababa," senior essay in sociology, Addis Ababa University, 1985, pp. 26–27; R. Hakemulder, *Potters: A Study of Two Villages in Ethiopia* (ECA/ILO/SIDA, 1980).

18. M. Ottaway, "Land Reform in Ethiopia, 1974–1977," *African Studies Review* 20, no. 3 (December 1977), p. 79.

The Politics of Environmentalism

< 18 >

Transitions as Translations

Anna Lowenhaupt Tsing

Environmentalism and feminism face the same challenge: How do we build alliances that do not squash diversity? To do so, we must appreciate the heterogeneity of global coalitions as well as the tentativeness of both linkages and constituent elements. To the extent that social movements define their struggles in relation to histories of ideas, we must retool those histories to allow ourselves to imagine complex global encounters. This means reworking the histories of feminist and environmental theory. We need frameworks that show how multicultural alliances do not filter, misuse, or distort original truths, but rather spark the creative contingencies in which all theory is built.

To move beyond conventional intellectual histories of feminism and environmentalism—which show only a single lineage of thought—to show their integration of culturally heterogeneous resources, it is useful to think of the ideas that inspire these movements as shaped in continuous processes of "translation." We are used to thinking of translation as the process by which a book is made available, with its original meanings intact, to a new set of readers. When we think of the appearance of books such as *Our Bodies, Ourselves* or *Our Common Future* in multiple languages around the world, we think of feminism and environmentalism as spreading with them, fully formed.[1] However, recent cultural theorists have argued that "translation" better refers to a necessarily faithless appropriation, a rewriting of a text in which new meanings are always forged by the interaction of languages. It seems useful to think about such faithless translations as necessary to making *any* meaning: Meaning arises from the slippages and supplements of the confrontation. Any meaningful discourse is already the product of multiple translations. The originary and culturally definitive status of any text is, in this sense, the product of translations that blur and reset cultural lines; the text gains its appearance as the product of a single linguistic lineage as an aspect of this translation project. In this sense of the term *translation*, there are no originals, but only a heterogeneous continuum of translations, a continual process of rewriting in which meaning—as well as claims of originality and purity—are made.[2]

One of the problems we face in writing this history of translations is the common scholarly understanding of both feminism and environmentalism as intrinsically Western. Each, it is said, has developed from the history of Western thought; each expresses Western insights that are now spreading to other countries and cultures. In order to write the new histories I want to see, we must cultivate a critical distance from this story. Of course, certain ideas and resources for both environmentalism and feminism do come out of Europe and North America; we need only think about funding, conference siting, publishing, training—and certainly many basic frameworks and assumptions. Yet perhaps we can acknowledge the power of this flow without identifying it as the only history we know. For, despite the obvious appeal of the West-to-the-rest formulation for both observers of modernization and critics of Western imperialism, it obscures a great deal. Indeed, it is a repetitive story of the constitutive distinction between the West and its Others: the distinction between the site of history, the West, and the site of cultural difference, the non-West. Within this story, the historical formulation of insight and action always happens in the West, while its cultural barriers and transformations necessarily arise in its spread elsewhere. As powerful as this story has been in *creating* Western histories and non-Western cultures, it has not frozen the world in its image. Yet we must redefine history and culture to glimpse the interactions and developments this story has obscured.

This essay suggests three methodological shifts in which such redefinitions might begin. First, instead of tracing a Western history of social thought, we can trace the moves in which lists of Western thinkers appear to be History. Second, instead of following Western originals across non-Western cultural transformations, we can follow the narrative contests through which foci of cultural difference are identified. Third, instead of debating the truth of Western-defined universals, we can debate the politics of their strategic and rhetorical use across the globe. Through these procedures, we can glimpse the heterogeneous encounters, interactions, and developments in which particular discursive resources, including those of feminism and environmentalism, are forged.

In this essay, I use these three analytic moments to intervene in conventional histories of environmentalism to suggest a richer tapestry. Although I won't do it here, I believe these moments would be similarly useful in retelling the history of feminism. We need to ask questions such as the following: How have accounts of the role of theory in the U.S. women's movement drawn attention *away* from the theoretical insights U.S. feminists gained in the 1960s and 1970s from Algerian debates about the politics of the female body, from the Chinese land reform movement's use of female personal narratives, or from Black Power–derived theories of counterhegemonic beauty and pride? That is, how is feminist theory actively and continually created, against much evidence, as a Western thing? Similarly, how do we create the units of Otherness that fuel feminist debates, such that, for example, U.S. minority novels and postcolonial scholarship appear to be describing equivalent kinds of "Other cultures"? Or, third, given feminists' exclusion from the strategic universalisms of post-Communism, is it useful for us to continue to see the Eurocentric universal as a generative logic rather than as a performative strategy?

The idea of translation serves as a focus. European philosophers have used this notion to point to the internal instability of Western culture by showing its necessary indeterminacy.[3] Philosophers of colonial discourse extended the discussion by showing the construction of Western culture at its South Asian colonial borders.[4] They showed how the process of translation is always involved with power. Colonial translations reify cultural differences as markers and explanations of status inequality. At the same time, they open spaces of indeterminacy in which new, unexpected cultural forms arise. Moving beyond South Asia, we might ask about the processes in which particular times and places, such as the South Asian colonial era or the European Enlightenment, become foci for translation technologies that produce historically significant histories. To rewrite histories of Western ideas and movements, the concept of translation triples our attention: How are sites of cultural formation identified? How do their translations reify cultural difference? How do they produce fluid and surprising polymorphisms?

In working with these three questions, I am inspired by a number of recent histories of environmentalism that take processes of cultural interaction seriously. In the next sections, I lean heavily on Richard Grove's spellbinding histories of colonial conservation[5] and Margaret Keck's exciting analysis of the role of narrative in the formation of Brazilian environmental politics.[6] My goal here is to put their work, and that of other environmental historians, into a conversation that allows us to explore the nature of global encounters. I ask what it might mean to see the history of environmentalism as a continuous process of translation.

ONE: THE MAKING OF WESTERN ORIGINS

Let me begin with a protracted scene of rewriting. It is the sixteenth century and the Portuguese are in Goa. A Jewish-Portuguese physician, trained, like other Europeans at the time, in Arab theories of medicine, decides to make his medical science more empirically accurate by tapping sources of local knowledge. Malayali doctors teach him their classification of pharmaceutical plants, which he publishes to great acclaim in Europe. After the Portuguese are kicked out of the area, a Dutchman is inspired to repeat the process. This time Ezhava of the toddy-tapper caste provides the plants and knowledge for publication. Finally, the great classifier Linnaeus reads these books in Leiden in the eighteenth century and unself-consciously adopts South Indian botanical classification into his universalist botanical logic.[7]

Where is *Western* knowledge in this story? Certainly Linnaeus, reimagined as a European original, is central to every history of Western concepts of nature. Yet as historian Richard Grove—who provides the rich account[8] from which I have taken this story—points out, there is not even a confrontation between the West and its Other here; if anything, one might say it traces encounters between Arab and Hindu theories of medical botany. The Europeans are only publicists. In contrast to a later colonial era, it is hard to argue that the Europeans had the power in this period to bracket and contain Indian knowledge through their publicity. Furthermore, these encounters linked individuals, none of whom could claim to represent their high cultures. The Jewish-Portuguese doctor gathered low-caste, non-Brahminical knowledge, already marginal in its homeland. Such encounters among marginals should give intellectual historians pause.

This story of Portuguese and Dutch translations is striking mainly as it ruffles conventions in which the history of ideas about the environment is imagined as a chain of Western ideas. Many accounts begin with the Greeks; U.S. scholars unselfconsciously take this history through England and into the United States for its full flowering. Perhaps the normalization of this story can be appreciated most quickly in looking at the striking schematic diagrams that illustrate environmental history texts. Thus, for example, one important and respected environmental historian, Roderick Nash, offers the following visual schema for explaining the development of environmental ethics:[9] Figure 1 shows the world-historical evolution of ethics from respect for the self to respect for the universe, with various stages in between. Expanding ethical concern leads to environmentalism. Figure 2 shows how this ethical growth process has operated in expanding ideas of rights. Nash attributes the idea of natural rights to Greek and Roman philosophers. The Magna Carta expands the notion, and from there it moves to the Declaration of Independence. After this, the evolution of ethics naturally occurs in

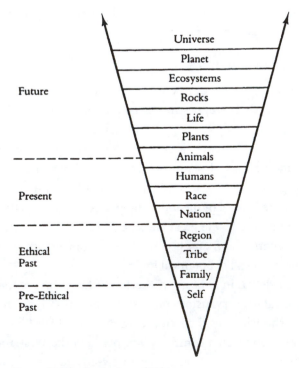

Figure 1 The Evolution of Ethics

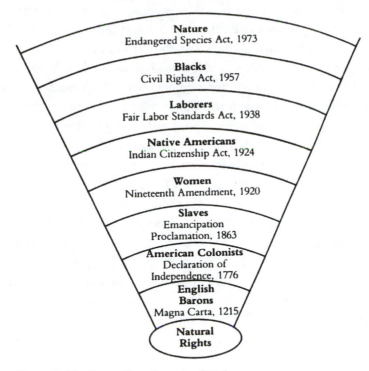

Figure 2 The Expanding Concept of Rights

the United States, culminating in the Endangered Species Act—that is, full-fledged environmentalism.

The naturalized nationalism of the diagrams is especially obvious because they take us from idea to idea and act to act. Most environmental historians instead take us from one great thinker to the next, humanizing the story by showing history as a family tree.[10] It is the genealogical convention that makes these histories seem to work; of course, we know, sons learn from their fathers. Moreover, the unspoken assumption is that we are reading the line of legitimate births. Not all those touched by the father are legitimate heirs; heirs must also themselves be an origin point of knowledge, influence, and further legitimacies. It is this convention, indeed, that limits the lines mainly to men of European origin; it is very difficult for non-Europeans, as well as women, to appear as origin points. Feminists have had some success in getting a white woman or two inserted into canons of Western thought. Yet we might still define the West as that imaginary location in which a thinker's local concerns, by reason of his gender, race, and national origin, can be interpreted as a world-historical origin point.

One of many ways in which this conflation of local concerns and world origins can be made is through a confusion, enabled by living in a powerful country, between nation-making and world-making. I would like to illustrate this in an interpretation of the turn-of-the-century U.S. conservation movement, which is conventionally seen as the starting point of environmentalism, the moment when ideas about nature were turned into an activist program.[11] This was an exciting time, in which men and women concerned about nature in the United States were able to formulate an agenda for parks and reserves: Yosemite, Yellowstone, Big Basin, the Catskills. The charismatic leadership of John Muir sparked a holy crusade, and his inspired descriptions of nature are appropriately revisited by contemporary environmentalists. I don't mean to take away the movement's significance. But what if we reinterpreted it as origin-making translation?

I suggest that the national parks movement was made possible by a nativist rewriting of colonial conservation theory. Most environmentalist histories obscure the earlier nineteenth-century presence of conservation by tracing the lineage through Thoreau, a nature writer but not a conservationist; thus it appears that the late nineteenth-century parks movement, and Muir, invented conservation. Yet in the nineteenth century, there was plenty of thinking going on about conservation; however, most of it was "elsewhere"—in the European colonial periphery.[12] Conservation was the appropriate management of other people's natural resources. What the U.S. parks movement did was turn conservation to native uses; nature protection became appropriate for one's own people, and, indeed, essential to their individual and collective self-development.

One suggestive fragment involves John Muir's interest in the writings of Alexander von Humboldt, the German traveler, naturalist, and romantic thinker whose writings on the severe environmental consequences of European deforestation in Latin America, according to the historian Grove,[13] did a great deal to spread ideas of conservation from one European periphery to others. Muir originally planned to follow Humboldt's route in Latin America, to see the grandeur and vulnerability of nature as Humboldt saw it, but health and financial limitations shifted his itinerary instead to the closer-to-home California landscape.[14] There Muir entered a part of the United States that had only recently been Mexican territory and that was still ridding itself of Native Americans to create safe and culturally cleansed territory for white settlement. Military teams from the East surveyed the natural resources in a rather colonial atmosphere.[15] Muir himself did not have much of an investment in national identity, but those around him were passionate about making a U.S. continent. Furthermore, the spectacular appearance of American nature had long been a point of nationalist pride; if Europe had culture, U.S. creoles proclaimed, the New World had nature to match. In this context, Muir's construction of the landscape as a temple of spiritual renewal could create a national mission among the newly native white Americans.

Environmental historian William Cronon argues that the idea of wilderness that inspired the parks movement involved the superimposition of two frameworks: the Romantic sublime, in which mountains were awesome signs of God, and the frontier story, in which the U.S. character was forged in wild places.[16] By the turn of the century, the frontier was already an object of nostalgia and simulation, and, Cronon says, frontier nostalgia "domesticated" the sublime by making it appear that wild places needed protection, not just awe. One could move from this to argue that frontier nostalgia nationalized the sublime, and that this national sublime brewed the fervor of the nativist sentiments that transformed conservation from a colonial management program into a nationwide social movement. Outdoorsmen, American philosophers, scientists, and women's garden clubs joined the parks movement to renew personal and national identity. Furthermore, the tensions between millenarian passion and disciplinary planning that arose within this nativist translation of colonial conservation have been with the environmental movement ever since.[17]

The 1960s U.S. revival of John Muir and the parks movement rewrote millenarian nativism through a new set of concerns: the image of the blue-green globe floating in outer space; the remaining strands of post–World War II internationalism; fears of global population growth and industry out of control; and suburban white reifications of nature. The new native conservationist was not just a white American but a global citizen, and the planet Earth was his or her home.[18] Here in the making was another point of origin, an insight that denied its own translations to offer itself as a text that could be translated around the world. Yet from the first, the authorial status of the global conservationist was challenged; the globe is not a homogeneous place, some said, and no authorial heir, however inspired, has the right to write everyone into his book. To explore the forms of difference that were marshalled in these challenges, I turn to my next framework.

TWO: SETTING LINES OF DIFFERENCE

The success of the notion of Western origins has meant that few have argued successfully that we can ignore the West. Instead, challenges to frameworks established as Western usually involve assertions of difference that, by necessity, recapitulate aspects of the frameworks they challenge in order to refuse other aspects. It is as if those of us who are not legitimate heirs have needed to prove that we are really descended in the same line in order to show that we have been wrongly disinherited. This is the aspect of creating cultural difference that has been analyzed so brilliantly by colonial discourse theorists. The British colonized India in part by creating forms of Indian difference and Indian agency that recapitulated Britain's supremacy.[19]

Yet there is another aspect of this process that has been less closely analyzed. Those excluded by the discourse of the West develop claims about difference and identity in dialogue with each other. Sometimes subordinate groups learn from each other's strategies. Other times, groups compete for the right to call what counts as Other to the West, that is, for a position of privileged Otherness: wife, not servant. The exclusive focus on contests between the West and its Other—a focus shared by scholars and activists—obscures these interactions. Yet these Other-to-Other translations shape what counts as difference; they make and transform theory that crosses and blurs the West-Other divide.

The negotiation of Otherness creates foci of significant cultural production in some of the same ways as the creation of Western origins: A local concern must come to stand for an inclusive field. To explore this process, one might think of "setting lines of difference" as referring not to the placing of boundaries on a map, but to the setting of lines for fishing or trapping, which aggregate moving resources.

Another scene of rewriting: In 1991, Anil Agarwal and Sunita Narain rewrite the World Resources Institute report on global climate change from the Centre for Science and the Environment in New Delhi. The World Resources Institute is an environmentalist think tank in Washington, D.C. It has just released a report arguing that all the countries of the world should take responsibility for reducing the emissions of carbon dioxide, methane, and CFCs, gases that lead to the greenhouse effect.[20] Agarwal and Narain are particularly upset that WRI has lumped industrialized and developing countries together in this responsibility. Indeed, India and China are among the top five emitters in WRI's chart. (WRI's calculation, as reproduced in Agarwal and Narain, is shown in figure 3.) Agarwal and Narain recalculate the chart, using the same figures but arguing that countries should have a per capita share of the world's greenhouse gas emission quota. In their calculations, developing countries, with the exception of Brazil, have a long way to go before they exceed their per capita share of the carbon sinks of the earth. (Their recalculations are shown as figure 4.) They argue, too, that we must differentiate between the "luxury emissions" of rich countries, caused by overconsumption of fossil fuels, and the "subsistence emissions" of poor countries, caused by among other things, agriculture and cattle raising. "Those who talk about global warming should

Figure 3

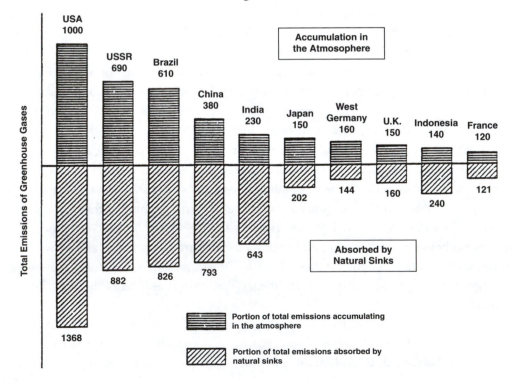

Figure 4 Permissible Emissions vs Total Emissions of Carbon Dioxide of Select Countries on the Basis of Population (in million tons of carbon equivalent)

(as calculated by CSE)

a) Industrialized Countries

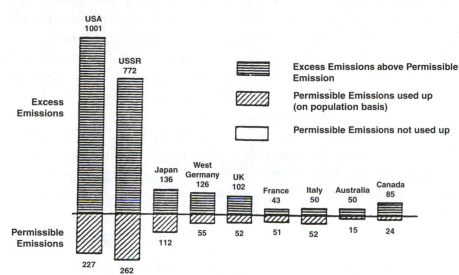

b) Developing Countries

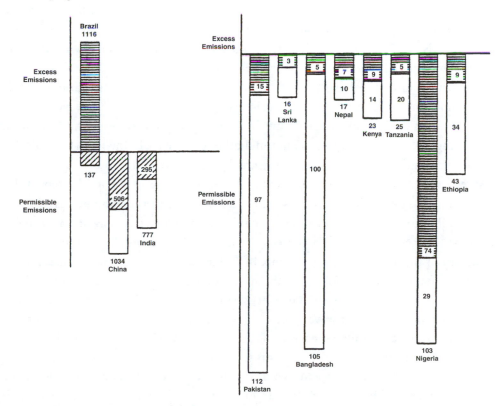

< 261 >

concentrate on what ought to be done at home," they write.[21] This home is not the generalized planet Earth.

Agarwal and Narain are part of a cohort of Indian scholars and activists who have argued that there are currently two environmentalisms in the world: a Northern environmentalism of the rich countries, which attempts to manage global resources for the benefit of Northern nature lovers and consumers; and a Southern environmentalism of the poor countries, which builds from grassroots awareness of the dangers of misusing natural resources and aims for social equity in resource management.[22] Northern environmentalists have disguised the colonial nature of their agenda by calling it global. The anticolonial heritage in South Asia allows scholars and activists to identify and reject this imposition and to build their own social ecology programs. This has been a strong and effective claim. Even global management experts in North America and Europe increasingly acknowledge the separate and legitimate interests of Southern environmentalists.[23] The Agarwal and Narain reinterpretation of World Resource Institute figures, which I just described, is well-read and cited.

In the report, Southern environmentalism is strategically depicted as a matter of *national* interest. Nations are effective units of difference with which to contest the hegemony of the West to the extent that some forum of international interchange facilitates a contest among nations. United Nations environmentalism has had this effect, strengthening the importance of national identities in environmental debates. However, Agarwal and Narain are perfectly aware of the inadequacy of the nation-state as a bulwark of environmentalist struggle. They criticize the Indian government's efforts. Elsewhere, Agarwal articulately takes apart the nation as an environmentalist unit. Great rifts divide urban elites and peasants, forest users and pastoralists, women and men. Transnational markets and capital flows make national boundaries irrelevant in delineating loci of economic responsibility.

Yet the calculation by national units in the report does reveal something key to the building of Southern environmentalism. Rather despite itself, the report reveals divisions within the South. In almost every graph, every developing country except one is shown with a reasonable environmental record. That one is Brazil. The report does note, in some detail, that the figures used to calculate Brazil's greenhouse gas emissions are badly chosen, in that they show a record year of deforestation as ordinary. Yet the report chooses generally to use those bad figures, and as a result, Brazil sticks out from the rest of the South like a sore thumb. In looking at this exception, it makes sense to argue that the Indian version of Southern environmentalism is not just an objection to the North, but also a translation of a Brazilian objection. Indians and Brazilians have vied for control of the narrative space of Southern difference. At the radical end of environmental debates, Indians have won, but the record shows traces of the contest. Indeed, the history of this dialogue, this set of translations, has shaped the concept of Southern environmentalism and its bureaucratic corollary, "sustainable development."

My understanding of Brazil's role in this history is drawn from a paper written by political scientist Margaret Keck.[24] She tells the story as follows: In 1972, Brazil was booming; it was at the height of its "economic miracle." Brazil was an obvious leader of the developing countries. When global environmentalism was brought to an assemblage of national leaders at the United Nations Conference on the Human Environment in Stockholm, the Brazilian representatives would have none of it. "Smoke is a sign of progress," they said.[25] The environmentalism of the time was full of discussion of limits to growth, and Brazil's sense of power was all about growth. Images of heroic endeavor and great enterprise formed national ideology, and, furthermore, these were focused on developing the Amazon. Meanwhile, international environmentalists expressed their concern about Brazilian schemes to place colonists in the Amazon; tropical deforestation began to make its way onto the global agenda. The success of Brazil as a developing nation, however, as well as the support it received from other government representatives (including those of India) amplified the Brazilian government position as *the* Southern agenda. The confrontation between environmentalism and development entered worldwide environmental debate, and for the next decade it was commonplace for even the most dedicated environmentalists to say that Third World countries could not afford environmentalism.

The Brazilian government's rejection of environmentalism—and its staking of its international leadership on this rejection—has had sharp consequences for environmental organizing in Brazil. Political scientist Kathryn Hochstetler has argued that rubber-tappers and indigenous people working against Amazon deforestation have been unable to present themselves as real Brazilians; cut off from national resources, both symbolic and material, they have formed alliances with foreigners, and these alliances reconfirm the subversiveness of environmentalism.[26] Urban environmentalists, meanwhile, avoid discussion of the Amazon in order to hold on to their ability to speak within the story of the nation. Yet internationally, the impact of the Brazilian position has changed. By the late 1980s, the Brazilian economy was a mess. The trans-Amazon highway was impassable. The same government rhetoric of development no longer carried across national lines.[27]

In the political space that Brazilian objections opened but could no longer fill, Indian radicals stepped in to translate "development versus environmentalism" into "two competing environmentalisms." In this translation, development is still a defining feature of the South, but it is equity- rather than progress-oriented. Not an opponent of environmentalism, equity-oriented development is a *version* of environmentalism. The challenge to the North is not a nation-building agenda but an alliance of grassroots protests. This Indian claim, unlike that of Brazilian leaders, is not nationalist, but anticolonial. It depends on an analysis of knowledge as domination. Western development programs, like global environmentalism, are shown to impose dominating agendas on Third World peoples. The movement must build not on these colonial knowledges, but on the history of resistance of the people who faced them. It is the unifying spirit of these tactics that allows activists to move beyond a particular village to the world, connecting the Chipko movement and the Bhopal tragedy, the rural and the urban, forests and industry. One can see the elements of the Brazilian agenda: poverty, participation, resistance to imperial rule. But they have been rewritten into a new framework. Certainly, not all Indians agree about this; I am describing a particular social-justice-oriented strain of environmentalism. And not all "Southern environmentalists" agree. But this is a powerful framework. It has shaped new meanings for the South, and it has not stopped there. As "social ecology," it offers a new network of globalism to replace colonial theories.[28]

One might say this Southern agenda has been becoming the most successful socially oriented environmentalism, except for a hot contender: environmentalism as a leading edge of global civil society. In contrast to social ecologists working for social and economic equity, civil society environmentalists build their message on *political* equality. Since political equality in the 1990s is understood as concomitant to the spread of markets, it becomes identified with acceptance of social and economic inequity in the name of democracy. Political equality is to be built through universal human rights, including the right to be rich. In linking local movements, the demand for political equality replaces the tactical attention of social ecology with the formal universals of human rights. How this is done is the subject of my next section.

THREE: STRATEGIC UNIVERSALISMS

Europe in the second half of the 1980s was a hotbed of environmentalist organizing. Many commentators place the success of the environmentalist takeoff on the Chernobyl accident. Chernobyl reminded Europeans of the breadth of environmental disaster. It also was interpreted as speaking to two powerful political goals. First, the spread of radiation pointed to the importance of transnational cooperation in working for the environment. Second, Soviet mismanagement and coverups were thought to show the environmental bankruptcy of socialism and the need for democracy to achieve environmental reform.

The late 1980s were marked by European environmental organizing on both these political fronts. Through the European Commission and other international organizations, Western Europeans worked together to pass new environmental regulations; environmentalism came to seem a defining feature of the new transnational Europe.[29] At the same time, environmental activism tied to calls for democracy, citizen participation, and the free availability of information which blossomed in Eastern Europe and the Soviet Union.[30] Environmentalism, with its ability to tap a huge reservoir of public concern, seemed "the cradle for the democratic movement"[31] throughout the Communist bloc. Environmental groups also worked together across the East-West divide, and thus environmentalism appeared not just transnational, but also beyond ideology, marking out the birthplace of an emergent post-Communism. "Environment knows no regime," wrote one activist.[32] Rising environmental activism coincided with, and perhaps helped along, the fall of Communism, and it was easy to argue that environmentalism was the bearer of new chances for democracy and global cooperation.

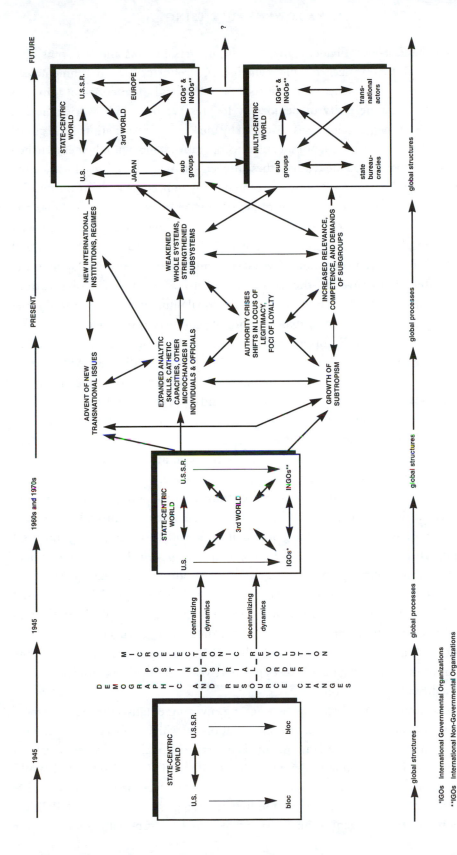

< 265 >

*IGOs   International Governmental Organizations

**IGOs   International Non-Governmental Organizations

Figure 5

Without the East-West divide, many thought, universal truths and freedoms once blocked by socialist intransigence could reemerge. One could look to environmentalism to unite the message of science, as a universal principle, and the message of universal human rights in the necessity of democracy to preserve the whole world's health. Furthermore, environmentalism was advanced by the kinds of transnational and global organizations that could make ignorant and uncooperative states, with their entrenched local cultures of power, see the truth of these universals. Again, diagrams illustrate the dramatic changes imagined as the world seemed ready to become a post-Communist, global place. Figure 5, from an analysis of global environmental politics,[33] shows one imagined timeline. On the left side, the past, the world is ruled by the U.S. and Soviet blocs; on the right, in the present and future, global citizens' groups, with "increased relevance, competence, and demands" have taken command of a new public sphere. The diagram offers a picture of the commitment to a future of globalization. Environmentalism forms the key to this imagined global future in which universal social and natural principles, without the blockage of state conflicts, reveal themselves.

It turned out that the European environmentalist high tide was short-lived. In Eastern Europe and the former Soviet Union, environmentalism disintegrated as attention turned to growth and national representation.[34] In Western Europe, the impetus of building East-West communication was lost. In hindsight, environmentalists' calls for universal human rights and an emergent global culture seem tied to the contingencies of a very particular time and place. It was desire for the reunification of Europe that made the struggle for democracy and scientific freedom appear as an expression of Enlightenment universals and the herald of a global culture.

Yet it is a heady formulation, and it has continued, in a floating, decontextualized form, to instruct environmentalist theory and politics. Many environmentalists are convinced that they serve an emergent global culture devoted to recognizing universal social and natural truths. When people are convinced of such things, they can help make them happen, although not always under the conditions they expect. My argument here is that global environmental universalism has been picked up and used strategically around the world. Just as in Europe, it is shaped and deployed in the service of specific goals. In the process of working for those goals, environmentalists form local systems of alliance, and the kinds of alliances they form determine the use they make of universalisms and global-futures perspectives. Universalisms, ironically, are a flexible medium for translation.

The commitment to universals spreads among environmentalists through an emergent transnational organization of communication in which translation takes new forms. Over the last two decades, international and transnational environmental groups have sprung up like mushrooms after a rain. These are the IGOs, INGOs, or plain old nongovernmental organizations (NGOs) shown on charts like the one I presented.[35] Furthermore, new kinds of linkages and influence strategies have developed. Political scientists point to two organizational forms that have been especially important for

environmentalism. First, governments listen to the advice of transnational communities of experts, who, because they share the common and highly prestigious rhetoric of
science, can form strategic transnational alliances with each other and, upon occasion,
tell convincingly consensual stories about the environmental consequences of policy.[36]
Second, activists form "transnational issue networks" to pursue specific objectives, such
as the protection of sea mammals or rainforests.[37] Transnational issue networks require
no epistemological agreement; they gain their effectiveness through drawing activists
with very different stories to tell into alliances to pursue overlapping goals. These are
alliances not just between activist peers of different countries or philosophies, but also
between national elites and concerned actors from other social strata, such as those
called "grassroots movements" because of their non-elite status. These latter alliances
in particular formulate national, regional, and local agendas in which assumptions
about global communication and universal rights are only one of many competing
frameworks. In these contexts of cultural negotiation, then, universals and globalisms
become strategic and are put to use.

Another scene: In 1995, a U.S. office of an international human rights organization
hosts an informal meeting of visiting representatives of Southern non-governmental
organizations. I attend, together with more than a half-dozen Indonesian environmentalists, who make up one of the larger national caucuses attending.[38] The talk turns
to whether New York and Washington should be setting the agenda for international
human rights. Two articulate South Asian men object to Northern Eurocentrism;
Northerners do not understand economic violence and focus only on political violence,
they complain. Human rights initiatives are already culturally specific; they need to be
culturally aware.

One by one, the Indonesians disagree. It is clear that they have not planned their line
on this; each struggles through a difficult personal story trying to explain why he wants
a stronger statement of universal human rights coming from New York and Washington. As the momentum grows, their statements get more powerful: Their ability to
speak to each other, to figure out what to do, and to organize would not survive without the openings made by universal human rights. Censorship in Indonesia, they argue,
stops one from thinking past it; but a strong articulation with universalism offers a
window of opportunity. It is an awkward moment because the lie of universalism's
global reach has already been exposed. The Indonesians are aware that in trying to
include themselves in Northern universals, they are speaking in contradictions. And yet
it is precisely in those contradictions that they place their ability to work as activists.[39]

Indonesian environmentalists engage with Northern-dominated universalisms of
democracy and human rights to work simultaneously at international and national
levels. On the one hand, their testimony both reaches out and unsettles these universals,
as enunciated in the North. On the other hand, it helps them argue about the role of the
state in Indonesian society. Since 1967, a military-dominated regime has made public
political debate difficult. Many national environmentalists are part of an urban pro-

fessional class whose members would like to see more possibilities for public participation. They draw eagerly on the European precedent: In an anti-Communist regime,
the notion that environmentalism is a post-Communist alternative to ideological politics allows them to survive. Advocacy of the universal claims of science and democracy
shows their activism to be the advancement of reason. This is fertile ground for environmentalism as the universalist expansion of civil society. Yet the national specificity
of Indonesian struggles can be seen from the pun that makes the Indonesian term for
civil society so popular among urban professionals: The *civil* in *civil society* is translit-
erated directly as *masyarakat sipil* (*masyarakat,* "society," *sipil,* "civil"); but sipil also
means "civilian," that is, opposed to military rule.[40] The pun is a subversive national
undercurrent within technical, rational, and globalized discussion.

Yet collaborations are always more varied and colorful than any one set of subversive
undercurrents might allow. There are many parties clamoring to be heard, and the outcome of their interchanges is uncertain. Indonesian national activists have to worry not
only about how to operate in a Northern-dominated globe and under national authoritarian rule, but also how to speak with and for the masses of people who are not
national activists. If the first two are facilitated by their entry into transnational issue
networks, this same entry sometimes makes the latter even more difficult. There is no
Indonesia-wide practice of individual citizen participation that might allow the civil
society concept to travel outside the big cities. Villages tend to be conceptualized as
political collectivities, not associations of free individuals. The alliance that occurs, then,
between national activists and villagers juxtaposes the individualist, citizen-driven environmentalism of transnational space and a social ecology theory of village collectives.
Social ecology and civil society environmentalism are forced together in this collaboration. In juxtaposition, without mixing, each makes it possible for the other to speak.
State repression blocks the voices of village advocates if they are not funneled through
urban civil society; urban elites have no national message without their collaboration
with village advocates.

In working within such local-global contradictions, new theories and forms of
activism emerge. The multiplicity of the activists' challenge hones and directs their
problematic but passionate use of universals. This is not a strategy to be used to speak
to villagers; instead it is directed toward international audiences in the hope of protecting a space activists and villagers share: the space that one could imagine, but has
never yet been protected by the haloed circles of democracy, universal human rights,
and global environmental concerns. In imagining this hardly imaginable space of (crim-
inalized) village custom and (censored) urban freedom, Indonesian national activists
use translated European and North American models in attempts to translate
Indonesian cultural and political priorities back into international conversations. They
take on global environmentalism, liberally citing internationally circulated texts such as
Our Common Future and Al Gore's *Earth in the Balance.*[41] By making themselves a part
of global environmentalism, Indonesian environmentalists argue for a bigger global-

ness; they use globalist texts to argue that global networks must pay attention to their own global wisdom.

A final scene: Indonesian feminist Julia Suryakusuma speaks to the Friends of the Earth Seminar sponsored by the Indonesian Environmental Forum in Jakarta in October 1993.[42] She opens her paper with a line that seemed sure to presage a resounding anticolonial or antiessentialist attack: "There is a myth," she says, "that women are close to nature; indeed, that they are a part of nature." Yet almost immediately she appears to change course completely: "This myth offers an alternative paradigm to the mal- (or male) development that has led to . . . political and environmental degradation."[43] What are universal myths good for? They are good, it seems, for arguing with other universal myths. Strategic ecofeminism, she suggests, brings Indonesian environmentalists into transnational networks with a critical, feminist, and social ecologist eye. If one is going to argue about global culture, why not use translated global texts as tools?

"Both feminism and environmentalism have universal concerns which cross-cut national boundaries," writes Suryakusuma.[44] What those concerns are, and how we might define and position their "universality," is very much debated. Clearly it will not do to see them as geographically homogeneous, socially uniform, or historically already decided. If we are to work with "universal" concerns, it must be in recognition of their shifting, devious, and much-fought-over multiplicity. Yet as we argue our way into alliances, there is a useful point to be heard from Suryakusuma's deployment of a "myth." As long as we cannot get outside the notion of a single theoretical lineage, it does us little good to judge its truth or falsity. To build forms of feminism and environmentalism that encourage diverse coalitions, we need to appreciate the continuous and diverse translations that allow us to work with, rather than exclude, each other. The histories we need are not segregated cultural lines but lumpy and contestable aggregations.

NOTES

This paper owes its approach, its insights, and its concerns to the discussions of the seminar on feminism and environmentalism at the Institute for Advanced Study organized by Joan Scott. I am also most grateful to the American Association of University Women, and to the National Endowment for the Humanities for offering me the time to work on these issues. A number of individuals have read or discussed the paper with me; Bina Agarwal, Yaakov Garb, Debra Keates, Margaret Keck, Michael Ross, Joan Scott, and Noël Sturgeon were each helpful and generous. The errors are of course my own.

1. These are just two examples of widely disseminated books that have helped encourage feminist and environmentalist organizing, respectively; (Boston Women's Health Book Collective, *Our Bodies, Ourselves.* 2d. ed. [New York: Simon and Shuster, 1976]; World Commission on Environment and Development, *Our Common Future* [Oxford: Oxford University Press, 1987]).
2. This paragraph draws on my reading of the following, among others: Walter Benjamin, "The Task of the Translator," in Hannah Arendt (ed.), *Illuminations*, trans. Harry Zohn (New York:

Schocken Books, 1969), pp. 69–82; Homi Bhabha, *The Location of Culture* (London: Routledge, 1994); Judith Butler, "Kantians in Every Culture?" *Boston Review* 19, no. 5 (1994); Paul De Man "Conclusions: Walter Benjamin's 'The Task of the Translator,'" in *The Resistance to Theory* (Minneapolis: University of Minnesota Press, 1986), pp. 73–105; Jacques Derrida, "Des Tours de Babel," trans. Joseph Graham, in Joseph Graham (ed.), *Difference in Translation* (Ithaca, New York: Cornell University Press, 1985), pp. 165–207; Gyan Prakash, "Science 'Gone Native' in Colonial India," *Representations* 40 (fall 1992), pp. 153–78; Tejaswini Niranjana, *Siting Translation: History, Post-Structuralism, and the Colonial Context* (Berkeley: University of California Press, 1992).

3. See, for example, Derrida op. cit.; Benjamin op. cit.

4. See, for example, Bhabha op. cit.; Niranjana, op. cit.

5. Richard Grove, *Green Imperialism: Colonial Expansion, Tropical Island Edens and the Origin of Environmentalism, 1600–1860* (Cambridge: Cambridge University Press, 1995).

6. Margaret Keck, "International Politics in the Amazon," paper presented at the conference on Environmental Conflicts and Movements, Five College Program on Peace and Security, Amherst, Massachusetts, 1995.

7. This paragraph is gleaned from information in Chapter 2, "Indigenous Knowledge and the Significance of South-West India for Portuguese and Dutch Constructions of Tropical Nature," in Grove, op. cit.

8. Ibid.

9. Roderick Nash, *The Rights of Nature: A History of Environmental Ethics* (Madison: University of Wisconsin Press, 1989), pp. 5, 7.

10. See, for example, Donald Worster, *Nature's Economy: A History of Ecological Ideas*, second edition. (Cambridge: Cambridge University Press, 1994).

11. This is a well-studied period, and it is difficult to choose which literature to cite. The following books offer good introductions to environmental concerns of this time: Stephen Fox, *The American Conservation Movement: John Muir and His Legacy* (Madison: University of Wisconsin Press, 1985); Michael Smith, *Pacific Visions: California Scientists and the Environment, 1850–1915* (New Haven: Yale University Press, 1987); Philip Shabecoff, *A Fierce Green Fire: The American Environmental Movement* (New York: Hill and Wang, 1993); Worster op. cit.

12. Grove, op. cit.

13. Ibid.

14. Fox, op. cit., pp. 47–53.

15. Smith, op. cit.

16. William Cronon, "The Trouble with Wilderness: or, Getting Back to the Wrong Nature," in William Cronon (ed.), *Uncommon Ground: Toward Reinventing Nature* (New York: W. W. Norton and Company, 1995), pp. 69–90.

17. Most environmental historians describe two wings of the U.S. conservation movement forming at the turn of the century: the preservationists, led by John Muir, and the conservationists, led by Theodore Roosevelt's chief of forestry Gifford Pinchot (see, for example, Smith, op. cit.). The conventional view is that the Muir-Pinchot split has led to two separate lineages of contemporary environmentalism, in the United States and across the world. Yet environmentalist traditions are much older. The Muir-Pinchot disagreement, I would argue, is only one moment in this heterogeneous formation. Furthermore, the tension between millenarianism and disciplinary planning has frustrated and enabled U.S. environmentalists who identify with each wing of the split, thus suggesting that nativized colonial conservation was important to each.

18. See, for example, Wolfgang Sacks (ed.), *Global Ecology: A New Arena of Political Conflict* (London: Zed Press, 1993); op. cit.; Alexander Wilson *The Culture of Nature: North American*

Landscape from Disney to the Exxon Valdez (Oxford: Basil Blackwell, 1992).

19. See, for example, Bhabha, op. cit.

20. The respective sources are as follows: Anil Agarwal and Sunita Narain, *Global Warming in an Unequal World: A Case of Environmental Colonialism* (New Delhi: Centre for Science and Environment, 1991); World Resources Institute, *World Resources 1990–91. A Guide to the Global Environment* (New York: Oxford University Press, 1990), pp. 11–31, 345–56.

21. Agarwal and Narain, op. cit., p. 25.

22. See, for example, Ramachandra Guha (ed.), *Social Ecology* (Delhi: Oxford University Press, 1994); Vandana Shiva, *Staying Alive* (London: Zed Press, 1989).

23. Peter Haas reviews "global environmental governance" conventions as organized around this North-South divide in his "Global Environmental Governance," paper prepared for the Commission on Global Governance, Geneva, and presented at the 1995 conference "Environmental Conflicts and Movements," Five College Program on Peace and Security, Amherst, Massachusetts, 1994. In recognizing the separate interests of Southern environmentalists, it seems telling that international reports also lace their reports with references to the unrecognized environmental dangers of national industrial objectives, particularly those of India, but also of other countries associated with Southern demands.

24. Margaret Keck, "International Politics in the Amazon," paper presented at the conference "Environmental Conflicts and Movements," Five College Program on Peace and Security, Amherst, Massachusetts, 1995.

25. This vivid quotation was recalled to me by Anil Agarwal, "An Indian Environmentalist's Credo," in Ramachandra Guha (ed.), *Social Ecology* (Delhi: Oxford University Press, 1994), p. 349. He tells another version of the Brazil-India story of Southern environmentalism in his article, a version that stresses India's collaboration in the Brazil-led developmentalism of the 1970s as well as Indian leadership in the anti-developmental movements of the 1980s and 1990s. His explanation of the change points both to an increasing radicalization, through which it became clear that development was not ending poverty, and an increasing obviousness of environmental degradation, which could no longer be ignored.

26. Kathryn Hochstetler, "The Evolution of the Brazilian Environmental Movement and Its Political Roles," in C. Vilas, K. Roberts-Hite, and M. Segarra (eds.), *Rethinking Participation in Latin America* (forthcoming).

27. Keck, op. cit.

28. A stimulating conversation with political scientist Itty Abraham reminded me that a more comprehensive account of the development of radical Indian environmentalism would have to pay much more attention to the key role of feminism in making the connection between environmentalism and social justice concerns. First, feminist organizing in India has stressed the importance of Southern social justice concerns in rethinking Northern-led international social movements; the kinds of Southern organizing created by feminsts have been important in facilitating other Indian-led Southern movements. Second, the organizing work of charismatic ecofeminist Vandana Shiva (see, for example, Shiva op. cit.) has itself stimulated important international effects.

29. See, for example, Sheldon Kamieniecki (ed.), *Environmental Politics in the International Arena: Movements, Parties, Organizations, and Policy* (Albany: State University of New York Press, 1993); Haas, op. cit.

30. See, for example, Barbara Jancar-Webster, "Eastern Europe and the Former Soviet Union," in Kamieniecki (ed.), pp. 199–221; Barbara Jancar, "The Environmental Attractor in the Former USSR: Ecology and Regional Change," in Ronnie Lipshutz and Ken Conca (eds.), *The State and Social Power in Global Environmental Politics* (New York: Columbia University Press, 1993), pp. 158–84.

31. Jancar-Webster, op. cit., p. 217.

32. Jancar, op. cit., p. 173.

33. James Rosenau, "Environmental Changes in a Turbulent World," in Ronnie Lipschutz and Ken Conca (eds.), *The State and Social Power in Global Environmental Politics* (New York: Columbia University Press, 1993), p. 74.

34. I am grateful to women's studies scholar Svetlana Kupryashkina for drawing the importance of the disintegration of environmental organizing in Eastern Europe to my attention.

35. For Rosenau, IGOs are "international governmental organizations" and INGOs are "international non-governmental organizations" (see Rosenau, op. cit., p. 74). Other political commentators also discuss GONGOs, "government-organized non-governmental organizations," and QUANGOs, "quasi non-governmental organizations."

36. See, for example, Peter Haas (ed.), "Knowledge, Power, and International Policy Coordination," special issue of *International Organization* 46 (winter 1992). Haas' work is associated with the approach he labels with the term "epistemic community," and the thesis that scientists are able to cooperate across national affiliations because they share common assumptions about causes and effects. Such theses of "epistemic cooperation" have been much debated; a number of authors have usefully drawn attention to contests among experts and the politically charged formation of knowledge (see, for example, Karen Litfin, *Ozone Discourses: Science and Politics in Environmental Cooperation* [New York: Columbia University Press, 1994]). These challenges are important. Yet Haas' approach has been useful to draw special attention to the presence of scientists, scientific networking, and the rhetoric of science at the center of the political process generated around environmental issues.

37. Margaret Keck and Kathryn Sikkink, "Transnational Issue Networks in International Politics."

38. I do not include organizational and personal names, or exact dates and places, to protect the privacy of those who attended this informal meeting.

39. Judith Butler usefully argues that censorship can produce a "performative contradiction" involving "the emergence of the unspeakable within the domain of the speakable" (Judith Butler, "Vocabularies of the Censor," paper presented at the conference on "Discourses of Power: History, Identity, and Reparation." Center for Cultural Studies, University of California, Santa Cruz, 1996, p. 19). Her argument about the workings of this kind of contradiction at the edge of universalism seems extremely relevant to my analysis here: "The universal begins to become articulated precisely through challenges to its existing formulation, and this challenge emerges from those who are not covered by it, who have no entitlement to occupy the place of the 'who,' but who, nevertheless, demand that the universal as such ought to be inclusive of them" (ibid.).

40. My appreciation of this pun draws from conversations with anthropologist Robert Hefner.

41. Respectively: World Commission on Environment and Development (Oxford: Oxford University Press, 1987); (New York: Penguin, 1993).

42. The papers from this seminar have been published in H. P. Arimbi, (ed.) *Seminar on the Human Dimensions of Environmentally Sound Development, Jakarta, October 14, 1993* (Jakarta: Wahana Linkungan Hidup Indonesia—Friends of the Earth Indonesia), p. 52.

43. Julia Suryakusuma, "Ecofeminism and 'Sustainable Development,'" in as H. P. Arimbi, 1994.

44. Ibid., p. 58.

< 19 >

Lost in Translation

Toward a Feminist Account of Chipko[1]

Yaakov Garb

I want to begin my discussion of the Chipko movement's resistance to deforestation in the Garhwal Himalayas with a story about one of the saplings that the Marquis of Northampton planted just north of London in 1840. The tree, a horse chestnut, was planted on an area of open space, previously used for grazing, as part of the decorative vegetation for an estate he was developing. In the Garhwal foothills of north India during this same period, the relation of villagers to their forests was beginning to change. In addition to some subsistence agriculture and cash crops, these villages had traditionally relied on local forests for grazing and for a range of products that were both used and sold. In the decades following the start of British rule in 1815, however, their access to these forests and thus the sources of their livelihood were increasingly constrained by deforestation and state regulation of forest access. This process intensified after the Indian Mutiny of 1857, when massive cutting provided sleepers and fuel for the railroad expansion that would strengthen the hold of empire, and forestry codes increasingly regulated this newly relevant resource. Very often, additional restrictions on forest access and other state-imposed hardships (such as taxes or corvée labor) prompted a variety of protests that were at times quite fierce. Restrictions on village access to forests was further curtailed after independence in 1947, as the Indian state encouraged commercial forestry on behalf of the national interest and in opposition to the "destructive exploitation" carried out by locals. The 1962 Indo-China war shut down the trans-Himalayan trade on which local villagers relied and accelerated development in the area, especially of roads, hydroelectric projects, and mining. Since this construction scarcely benefited locals, and involved clearing large tracts of forest and making others accessible to commercial logging, it further impoverished households and communities, and village men increasingly sought work in the plains to the south. A series of floods and landslides in the late 1960s and early 1970s, the continued degradation of opportunities for livelihood, and an increasing disillusionment with the helpfulness of local and state authorities heightened discontent.

Beginning in the 1970s, a series of protests began under the banner of a new movement called Chipko. Using this name, Garhwali villagers and students protested at the annual Forest Department auctions where trees were sold to outside contractors, and at the forest sites where trees marked for felling by contractors were to be cut. Chipko representatives also negotiated with Forest Department Officers and administrators. These protests stopped felling in several instances, and prompted a variety of concessions from the Forest Department and the state. These included bans on certain kinds of felling plus a tightening of national-level regulation of any local forest uses.[2]

But before discussing Chipko further, let me return to the marquis's sapling, which by the 1970s stood a hundred feet tall on St. Paul's Place in the north London suburb of Islington. Over the course of this decade, Chipko had become an internationally known icon of Third World environmental activism, and the chestnut had became the focus of a thirteen-year local legal tussle. An accountant who had bought a house on St. Paul's Place complained to the local council that the tree was damaging the perimeter wall of his premises, and should be removed. While some of his neighbors had no objections to cutting the tree, which tempted children to scale their walls looking for chestnuts for playing conkers, others objected. The chestnut was, in the words of a reporter for the *Telegraph*, "magnificent. Tall and upright, with an expansive canopy of leaves and white blooms in season, it creates a kind of portal which half-obscures the grassy area behind, and lends an illusion of quiet, rural mystery." In addition to providing illusion and conkers, the tree apparently had also long served as a meeting place and "a sheltered spot for evening trysts."

The Islington Council thought it important to keep the horse chestnut, since it was one of the few old trees still remaining in a borough that had the least green space of any in the country. It offered to trim the tree and put a lintel over it, as well as rebuild the wall and maintain it in perpetuity. When the accountant refused, many residents "took up the cudgels," supported and encouraged by the local chapter of Friends of the Earth and other environmental groups. Our stories converge in March 1989, at which point Chipko had won both the Right Livelihood Prize (also known as the "alternative Nobel") and the Magsaysay Award (which some have called "Asia's Nobel"), and years of legal battle had culminated in the London Court of Appeals ordering the reluctant Islington Council to carry out a prior lower court order to "abate the nuisance of the tree." As soon as the campaigners heard about this ruling, they organized day-long shifts at the tree, intending to make felling impossible without injuring them.

I want to leave you with an image of the drama around the chestnut on the day the Islington Council workers arrived to chop it down. A local Friends of the Earth member had orchestrated a protest with children painting and drawing around the tree. There was also a man with a snake around his neck and a group of women playing piccolos to the tree, while many people sat around singing and talking. Most relevant for the topic of this essay—the complex globe-spanning construction and translations of local environmentalisms—was a telephone call received by a member of the staff of the Prince of Wales's office at Buckingham Palace. It was from an activist in the Hackney tree group who had spent several previous nights sleeping in the tree to prevent a surprise night-time attack by chainsaws to carry out the high court's order. Speaking on a portable phone from a string hammock twenty feet above the ground, the man, who identified himself as David Chipko, wanted to talk with Prince Charles about the importance of sparing the tree.

In order to ensure at least one question afterward, I'd like to leave you, like Mr. Chipko, hanging, and consider the relevance of this episode to the transitions and translations that are the subject of both the conference from which this volume stems and of my essay. This great arc from the Himalayan foothills to north London, this self-definition through borrowing, is, I would propose, the rule rather than the exception in the formation of environmentalisms. Chipko itself is built in just this manner. A staple of Chipko's storytelling, for example, is the tale of Amrita Devi, which appears in the movement's pamphlets, village meetings, and news conferences.[3] Amrita Devi was a member of the Bishnoi sect in Rajasthan, which has upheld its founder's 1485 prohibition against cutting green trees, sometimes at the cost of their lives. In 1731, these stories tell us, Amrita Devi protected a tree marked for felling for a new palace for the Maharaja of Jodhpur by hugging it. After she was dismembered by the tree cutters' axes, people from eighty-three surrounding villages rallied in protection of the trees, and over three hundred of them were similarly killed, inspiring a change of heart in the maharaja.[4]

I want to make several points about such borrowings. First, they are made as local political interventions in often surprising ways. When the Chipko movement places itself directly in the lineage of Amrita Devi and retroactively calls the Bishnois "Chipko,"[5] a Hindi term for cleaving or hugging first used in this way in 1972,[6] it bridges the cultural distance between Rajasthan in the early eighteenth century, and Uttar Pradesh in the late twentieth for a purpose. The story has been used, quite explicitly, to establish Chipko's efforts as reflecting an ecological consciousness that is indigenous and precolonial, part of a unified continent-spanning Hindu culture, and embodied in the feminine.[7] Similarly, when Mr. Chipko identifies himself, quite literally, with what he sees to be a distant peasant movement protesting deforestation on a Himalayan scale, he is implicitly declaring that his action is not just about a single tree in Islington, nor only about the indulgences of wealthy north Londoners, but about preserving a livable environment as part of a unified movement to save the earth.

Second, as stories travel and are articulated to new purposes, some facts fall away and new ones accrete. When an attorney for the Natural Resources Defense Council uses the image of Chipko in an op-ed piece for the *Los Angeles Times*, he does so to castigate Earth First's monkey-wrench-throwing activities in Western forests and elsewhere, and he explicitly presents Chipko as a form of environmental protest that is nonviolent and property-respecting, and thus suitable for democratic countries such as India and the United States. It would not serve his purposes to highlight the continuity of Chipko's protests with those of earlier peasant protest movements, whose central protest strategy at times was the frequent burning of the British (and later the Indian state's) resented monoculture forests;[8] such movements also resorted on occasion to beating up or branding a forest officer, and sending him packing tied wrong way round on a donkey. Though widely iconized in the West, Chipko's tree-hugging strategy is part of a broader picture that doesn't figure in the attorney's account. It was devised at a meeting of a local workers' cooperative as a way not so much of preventing the felling of trees, but of protesting the preferential allocation of tree resin supplies to distant and highly capitalized factories rather than cooperatively run local ones; tree hugging was arrived at as an alternative to lying in front of the transport trucks or burning down idle resin depots. While always there as a threatened action, tree hugging was first actually used only after five years of protest activity and seldom since.[9] More frequently used tactics in the repertoire of Chipko and the movements it has inspired elsewhere in India are different forms of mild sabotage, such as the uprooting of teak and eucalyptus saplings planted on commercial forestry plantations.[10]

My final points about translation can be more brief, since they are well illustrated by Anna Tsing's essay. These borrowings of bits and pieces of other people's lives are not one-way affairs, but feed back and alter their originating contexts in concrete and often unexpected ways. Chipko's fame as a certain kind of movement has altered the local political scene, since some of the organizations initially comprising Chipko were funded by a string of prizes and others not; some leaders were treated more circumspectly by government authorities than others were. Meanwhile back in Rajasthan, five years after Chipko's appropriation of Amrita Devi's story, her martyrdom was celebrated for the first time in her home village—two and a half centuries after the event, and with state support.[11]

Fourth, rather than seeing translations as occurring between existing spheres or movements, we should see these translations as one of the main ways in which such spheres and movements are constituted and constantly remade. A social movement such as Chipko can be seen as a dense layering of such enabling translations. For example, consider the ways in which Sunderlal Bahuguna, one of Chipko's leaders, has allowed movement participants to understand their actions in (partially) familiar terms and allowed people outside the movement to understand Chipko in terms they can relate to. He has posed both his authority as a leader and Chipko's goals within several powerful frameworks: the *dhandak,* a local form of customary rebellion in the face of a breach of moral economy, and a technique that dates back many hundreds of years; Gandhian understandings of village self-reliance and asceticism in the face of outside corruption; the kind of neopopulism and Hindu revivalism that is growing within India; and various strands of "Western" environmental thought. Each such articulation changes both "origin" and "destination": Gandhianism and Hinduism have been stretched to include the environment in new ways, and Western environmentalism is changed by now including something called Chipko within its imagination.

The density of the kind of translations that can be noted in the previous examples demands that we think of the formation of environmentalisms as an intricately multi-lateral rather than diffusionist process, and it calls for a more sophisticated and politi-cized understanding of how "local" and "global" get defined. Without forgetting the structurally tilted playing field between north London and north India, we should attend to ways in which Islington chestnut defenders are as much a local instance of "Chipkoism" as Chipko is of "environmentalism."

With this general introduction to Chipko's translations in mind, I want to focus now on feminist translations of Chipko in the West. What are my stakes here? Descriptions of Chipko's women are probably the West's best-known image of women's environ-mental activism, both in the popular mind and in more academic circles. So it is impor-tant that our translations of their lives empower the Chipko women, empower women in the West, and deepen a feminist environmental analysis. Such an analysis, in my mind, tells us about how gender relations affect environmental interactions, and how environmental interactions affect women's lives, with an eye toward changing social relations in a way that halts both environmental destruction and the subordination of women. While some of the more common stories about women and Chipko in the West have been significant interventions in Western environmental discourse, impor-tant things have gotten lost in translation. Something always drops out, of course, but what has dropped out of these stories are precisely aspects of the Garhwali situation that are most relevant for a feminist environmental analysis.

The writing of Bina Agarwal, whose essay is included in this volume, has provided an extremely important element of such an analysis. She has demonstrated very con-vincingly the heightened vulnerability of poor rural women in India to the degrada-tion, privatization, and statization of common resources such as forests, and she has helped us understand this vulnerability as an important factor in the constituency and motivations for women's participation in movements such as Chipko.[12] I want to focus, however, on a second feminist account by Vandana Shiva, which offers a history and portrait of Chipko as part of its larger critique of the masculinism of Western devel-opment, science, and economics. I will address this account because it has until rela-tively recently set the tone of feminist treatments of Chipko, which range from uncritical embrace to rejection of its essentialist underpinnings. In particular, it both provides a source for and is typical of the kinds of stories that have circulated about Chipko in the Western media over the last decade and helped frame Chipko as a "women's"[13] or even a "feminist" movement.[14] I want to see what Shiva's feminist read-ing of Chipko has accomplished, and what it has left undone.

Let me give an example of a fairly typical iconic rendition of Chipko. It is from an essay by a Canadian activist explaining where she gets the courage for her work. She writes:

> Last night, I read an account of Chipko women in India, the women who circled the
> trees. The government sent in soldiers to shoot them but the soldiers lost their

nerve. So they sent in army elephants to trample them. The women walked to the elephants and caressed them, stroking their trunks and legs, crooning to them. The elephants knelt and refused to budge.[15]

Several things are clear from this and many similar citations of Chipko. One is that they are powerfully enabling myths, and we would not want to undermine their potential for liberation. Another is that the actual details surrounding a social movement in the Himalayan foothills seems irrelevant for the purposes to which these stories are put; neither elephants nor soldiers, for instance, appear in the dozen or so historical accounts of Chipko I have read, and Chipko's social context and motivations for protest have dropped away. A third is what seems to be the most invariant feature of Chipko stories in the West: an emphasis on the image of tree hugging as a tactic of nonviolent environmental protest, women's concern for nature and their defiance of authority in nature's name.

Now, we could think of such stories as simply manifestations of the imaginary that happen to use Chipko's name and not be too exacting about their fidelity to some originating context, which is a mirage anyway. I want to argue, however, that for all its potential, this Chipko icon—if it is to be used for feminist purposes—must be supplemented with other elements and stand alongside other icons. And I want to claim that the most promising place to look for material with which to do this is in the particular social and historical circumstances from which Chipko emerged. What is going on *around* the women hugging trees or what is taking place *instead of* the caressing of elephants is important for the struggles of Garhwali women, for the struggles of environmentalists in the West, and for the ongoing task of creating a gender-sensitive analysis of environmental issues and protest. To illustrate these claims, I want to focus on Shiva's account, specifically the section "The Women of Chipko," in her best-known book, *Staying Alive: Women, Ecology, and Development* (1989). In its commitment to women, this account left out complexities critical for a feminist analysis.

Shiva's use of Chipko must be located within her attempt to change prevailing understandings of development, human ecology, and environmental protest. The forestry and agricultural practices of the British, and later of a production-bent modernizing Indian state, were largely blind not only to the needs and priorities of people, especially marginal people, who had long depended on India's landscapes, but also to subtle local ecological knowledges they had developed, and finely tuned and sustainable local environmental practices. While this knowledge and these practices were by no means exclusive to women, a gendered division of labor located many of them in the realm of women, which only added to their marginalization in masculinized colonization and development efforts.

Over the years, Shiva has developed a form of ecofeminism that aims to rectify these conjoined marginalizations—of women, of their subsistence activities, and of nature— by placing women and a valorized conception of the reproduction of everyday life at the heart of her analysis of environmental degradation. Women's daily activities, she claims, depend on and therefore work to maintain intact ecological systems, and are paramount considerations in any account of human ecology and environmental conservation and politics. Western science, which de-animates nature-as-resource; economics, which is blind to women's productive and reproductive activities; and development, which destroys subsistence livelihood and nature for commodity production, all override what she calls the "feminine, the conserving, the ecological principle."[16] Women, subsistence, nature, the indigenous, the local, the traditional, the Hindu, the harmonious, and the just are tied together in Shiva's work in an extremely tight systematicity whose essentialism has been criticized.

Shiva's portrayal of Chipko is a way for her to both illustrate and achieve the political reclamation of marginalized people, activities, and knowledges in the face of destructive effects of development and market forces. To represent women as active defenders of these excluded realms, Shiva must also work against a long tradition of women's invisibility in accounts of social movements, and environmental movements in particular. To do so, she had to implicitly take a stand against modes of thinking about protest that have prevailed in social movement theory, labor history, and the history of peasant rebellions, and in which the political actors—indeed political action itself—are masculine.[17] The authors of these accounts usually animated their narratives with categories that marginalized domains in which women spent much of their time, and they defined the activities of those few women who did appear in male spheres as not political. They also seldom attended to ways in which idioms and motivations for protest were gendered.

To give a sense of the biases Shiva was working against, let me mention Ramachandra Guha's 1989 book *The Unquiet Woods: Ecological Change and Peasant Resistance in the Himalaya,* the most extensive scholarly treatment of the movement to date. Guha's central move is to locate Chipko as the most recent form of peasant resistance to a long history of state incursion into their access to forests. Though he notes in passing that nineteenth-century visitors were struck by the degree to which women were involved in all spheres of production in this region, his detailed account of over a century of resistance to state curtailment of this production does not consider gender at all. Despite having been written after Shiva's interpretations of Chipko were well known, Guha's book doesn't tell us whether these new restrictions on forest access differentially affected men and women, if and how women were involved in protest, or whether the notion of a "moral economy"—one of his main analytic tools—is gendered. This bias carries over into his account of Chipko, whose continuity with these earlier protests is the main point of his book. For Guha, Sunderlal Bahuguna, Chandi Prasad Bhatt, and the Marxist-influenced USV (Uttarakh Sangharsh Vahini) constitute the movement's leadership, and women are on the whole adjuncts to the story who occasionally get pulled into protest activity and reproduce daily life so that men are free for political struggle.

Shiva, however, in trying to counter the kinds of biases exemplified by Guha's book, has overcompensated. To make women and their activities visible, Shiva has told a highly selective story about Chipko—as do all the other accounts of Chipko, scholarly or otherwise. But, perhaps out of fear of undermining her claims that environmental destruction and protection are *intrinsically* women's issues, she has hampered the political ends she was trying to achieve. She provides, for example, an account of Chipko leadership that places women at the center of the story as unambiguously strong political actors, while marginalizing the role of men, and thus obscures male political dominance in the Chipko movement and in Garhwali villages. And her coupling of the local, the feminine, the nonmarket, and the natural is so tight and ahistorical that it leaves little space for recognition of the historical specificity of their alignment in the Garhwal, or for imagination of situations in which the linkages are different. Let me focus only on the first issue here, her account of Chipko's leadership.

Shiva's genealogy of the movement begins with Amrita Devi as a leader of those who died in the Bishnoi protest and then lists nine of the "many" women who made Chipko possible, framing the movement's men as "their students and followers." She gives an extended account of the first two women, Mira Behn and Sarala Behn, early students of Gandhi, casting them as students of the region's ecology. Inspired by the lore of local elders, these women recognized the importance of mixed forests and understood the link between deforestation and flooding. Sunderlal Bahuguna is introduced as a student of Mira Behn and the husband of one of Sarala Behn's students, Bimla Behn, who married Bahuguna only on the condition that he settle with her in a remote village in order to awaken the surrounding hill people by living with them. "Sunderlal Bahuguna," says Shiva, "in turn, drew in other activists like Ghanshyam Raturi, Chandi Prasad Bhatt and Dhoom Singh Negi to lend support to a movement generated by women's power. As he often says, "'We are the runners and messengers—the real leaders are the women.'"

Here Shiva is highlighting a network of women's influence and leadership that is almost entirely missing from other accounts of Chipko. But what is the relation of this network to the overwhelmingly masculine structures of power and authority described in conventional accounts, and how does this relationship affect women's goals? Take, for example, the activities of Sunderlal Bahuguna, whom Shiva portrays as "a messenger of Chipko's women leaders." Within the Garhwal, throughout India, and internationally, Bahuguna is often seen as Chipko's leader. And if it is not him, then it is Negi or Bhatt—I could fill pages listing the awards, prizes, and important media acknowledgments of these men's leadership roles in Chipko. Bahuguna's biography is a string of activities that are barely open to Garhwali women: He joined Gandhi's independence movement at the age of thirteen, and went on to become a general secretary of the Tehri branch of the Congress Party. He worked with rural reconstruction and the untouchables for many years prior to his marriage to Bimla Behn and his move from party politics to rural residence in the hills. In the hill villages he became a minor logging contractor and a central figure in efforts for village self-sufficiency. Later through his petitions, organizing, lobbying, protest fasts, several treks across the region in extended *padayatras*, participation on forest ecology committees, lecturing, articles, and reports on Chipko and the region's ecology for both Indian and international audiences, he became regarded by many as the movement's leader.

Between the masculinism of most accounts and Shiva's overcompensatory emphasis on women's role, we seem to lack the information for a good account of the gender politics behind Chipko. In Shiva's book, for example, Mira and Sarala Behn lay the groundwork for a network of Chipko's strong women leaders, such as Bimla Bahuguna, while men such as Sunderlal Bahuguna appear as their messengers. In Guha's book, Sarala Behn is mentioned in a single line as working alongside Bhatt,[18] and Bimla Bahuguna appears once as Sunderlal Bahuguna's wife, who along with other "ladies" supplemented the men's organizing.[19] But the way in which Chipko allows these two very different portraits is one point at which a study of its gender politics can begin: in the hinge between the two accounts, the senses in which they are both "right." Shiva points to a sphere of ecological concerns and a kind of leadership that are central to the movement's emergence. Guha highlights men's domination of the public sphere, in which important forms of power are wielded. But we need models that show us not only why women are more likely to be concerned about environmental destruction in some situations, but also how this concern can be expressed or stymied in the actual worlds in which women are excluded from many of the institutions of power. This political context should not be backgrounded in our images of Chipko: The local politics of gender are often critical for understanding the organization of environmental politics, not only in the Garhwal, but also in the West, where, for example, most environmental movements are still dominated by men.[20]

This is why we need icons and accounts of Chipko that point us not simply to women's original empathy with the natural world, but accurately to the particular circumstances in which this concern arises and is fought for. In the case of the Garhwal, these circumstances include the fact that restrictions on forest access have resulted in almost half the male population migrating seasonally or semipermanently to find paid work in the southern plains, while women perform most of the narrowed range of agricultural and forest-related tasks that remain. In Chamoli district, for instance, traditions are such that those men who don't migrate out for work remain minimally involved in subsistence. They repair dwellings and spend two or three days a year ploughing, an activity taboo for women. Otherwise they pass their time marketing and in the religious, cultural, and political affairs of the villages. While only men own and inherit land and animals, women plant, weed, harvest, and transport crops; they also tend animals, process and cook food, collect water, firewood, and fodder, and rear children. These circumstances do give women a greater stake in, and knowledge of, the local, as well as the linkages between the environment and well-being. But they also mean that environmental attempts to preserve traditional ways of life run the risk of perpetuating traditional forms of domination as well. And they mean that concerns for environmental preservation are not only sometimes opposed to those of a male population whose incentive structure is quite different: such concerns are also located within a social system in which, despite any symbolic valorization of the feminine, men have the power, the authority, and simply the time for the activities that help them express their preferences.

How would the kinds of stories I want to hear differ from Shiva's? A few examples: Shiva describes Bahuguna's famous marches in the hills as his opportunity to "[listen] to the quiet voices of the women." But we can gather from other sources that these hikes are more complex affairs. During the winter and monsoon seasons of his most extensive and famous march of 1982–83, for example, he participated in the NGO forum of a United Nations conference in Nairobi and a United Nations hearing on the environment in London, met with foresters and ecologists in England, Switzerland, and Austria, lectured and attended conferences throughout India, spoke to university and environmental groups around Europe, including the Green Parties of seven countries, and received personal acknowledgment for his work from Prime Minister Indira Gandhi. Given this, rather than accepting Bahuguna's self-assessment of his role as mere messenger of Chipko's women leaders at face value, as Shiva does, I would prefer a critical and perhaps humorous evaluation of it. Surely it presents a wonderful opportunity not only to reflect on the complexities of translation I discussed earlier, but also to investigate Chipko's gender politics a bit more deeply.

In Bahuguna's case, this statement is more than lip service, but still far from accurate. Perhaps it is Bahuguna's way of acknowledging the invisible but large role of women. If so, why doesn't Shiva talk about that invisibility and how it can be overcome, rather than collude in the overestimation of women's power? Or perhaps it is Bahuguna's way of encouraging women to occupy a more active role. Why, then, repeat this mildly patronizing untruth, rather than using it to initiate a discussion of the barriers to women's fuller participation? Or perhaps Bahuguna is pointing to a different kind of sphere in which women do have a form of "leadership." But are we to be satisfied with this gendered division of political labor in which women's will is massive but dormant? Perhaps Bahuguna, who is exquisitely attuned to the predilections of his Western audiences, has framed his role in this way to heighten support for a movement that appears to be (proto)feminist, or in which the preservation of nature and the feminine appear conflated. But—in the long run—will Western feminists or Garhwali women benefit from this masking of subordination in the service of a marketable feminist utopia?

A feminist account of Chipko would be strengthened, not undermined, by details Shiva decides not to tell us. Other accounts of the famous encounter at Reni forest, for example, tell us that women participated decisively in Chipko here for the first time because a Forest Department ploy had lured the village men away on one pretext and the protest leader Bhatt on another, leaving only women in the village. One tells us that these women initially asked the woodcutters to finish their lunch in the forest and then come back to the village to wait for the village men to return, and that only after they were pushed around and insulted did they voice their case and force the loggers to retreat. Shiva's account of this incident, however, doesn't mention any contingency behind the women's involvement, which immediately takes the form of self-confident defiance: the women commanding the woodcutters not to touch the trees. Her interpretation was crafted to be inspirational, but what are its costs? Shiva has excised not only an indication of the traditions of feminine deference that women must overturn (or harness) in their efforts, but also an opportunity for suggesting how identity and strength can be shaped *through* participation in collective actions, not only brought to them ready-made. These are just a few of the many chips littering the floor around the Chipko icon that Shiva has sculpted, and from which a better gender-sensitive account of environmental action might be made.

NOTES

1. In writing this essay, I have benefited from discussions with Haripriya Rangan, Anna Tsing, Debra Keates, Minakshi Menon, and the Gender and Environment reading group at the Institute for Advanced Study (1995).
2. In 1975, legislation replaced the forest contracting system with a State Forest Development Corporation that would be responsible for harvesting and maintaining forests; in 1976, a Tree Protection Act required households to obtain permission from Forest Department officials before felling trees on their own land; a 1980 act made it impossible for state governments to transfer any forest area to nonforest uses without a national Ministry of Environment approval, and in the same year a fifteen-year ban on green felling above 1,000 meters was instituted to allow for forest regeneration. For details, see Haripriya Rangan, Ph.D. dissertation, UCLA, pp. 267–68.
3. Thomas Weber, *Hugging the Trees: The Story of the Chipko Movement*. (New York: Viking Penguin, 1988), p. 91. For an extensive version, see Richard St. Barbe Baker, *The Chipko Message*, pamphlet published by the Chipko Information Center (1987).
4. Weber, op. cit., pp. 91–94.
5. St. Barbe Baker, op. cit.
6. According to J. Bandyopadhyay and Vandana Shiva, the first use was by the Chipko poet Ghanshyam Raturi. *Seminar*, (Aug. 1987), p. 42.
7. This Chipko-Bishnoi link and renewal of interest in Amrita Devi's action are probably related to Hindu revivalist trends. The Bishnois themselves, with state support, began commemorating the martyrdom in Amrita Devi's village for the first time in 1978 (Weber, op. cit., p. 93).
8. Ramachandra Guha, *The Unquiet Woods: Ecological Change and Peasant Resistance in the Himalaya* (Berkeley: University of California Press, 1990), esp. pp. 120–25.
9. Weber, op. cit., p. 53.
10. On the removal of taps in chir pines, see Manisha Aryal, "Axing Chipko," *Himal* 7(1), (1994), pp. 8–23. On the disruption of water supplies see the essay by Sunderlal Bahuguna, "The Women in Chipko," *Manushi* 6 (1980). On the notorious (alleged) burning by Chipko protesters of the Nainital Club building where forest auctions were being held see Pandurang Hegde, "Chipko and Appiko: How the People Save the Tress" (London: The Invictas Press, for the Society of Friends in Britain, Ireland, 1988), p. 20.
11. Weber, op. cit., p. 93.
12. See also Bina Agarwal, "The Gender and Environment Debate: Lessons from India," *Feminist Studies* 18, no. 1 (1992), pp. 119–58.
13. Joan Kuyek, "What is an Organizer?" *Canadian Dimension* 27, no. 3 (May 1993), p. 21.

14. Vandana Shiva, "Development as New Project of Western Patriarchy," in Irene Diamond and Gloria Orenstein (eds.), *Reweaving the World: The Emergence of Ecofeminism* (San Francisco: Sierra Club Books, 1990), p. 191.

15. See, for example, Joan W. Scott, "Women in *The Making of the English Working Class*," in *Gender and The Politics of History* (New York: Columbia University Press, 1988), pp. 68–90.

16. Guha, op. cit., p. 156.

17. Ibid.

18. Of the representatives nominated by the German Green party in recent elections, for example, only 28 percent were women.

19. See Shobita Jain. "Women and People's Ecological Movements: A Case Study of Women's Role in the Chipko Movement in Uttar Pradesh," *Economic and Political Weekly*, (Oct. 13, 1984), pp. 1789–94.

20. The details of his trip appear in Weber, op. cit., pp. 103–11.

< 20 >

Strategic Environmentalisms

Noël Sturgeon

It's clear that in a volume focused on contemporary feminism in a international frame, "transitions" and "translations" should be central ideas. But the concept of "environment," particularly understood as referring to environmentalisms, is much less transparent. The links between environmentalisms and contemporary feminisms are not as easily assumed. Why should the environment be a central focus in a conference such as this one, and at this particular moment of historical transition?

The essays in this section don't address this question directly. Rather, Anna Tsing and Yaakov Garb authors interrogate the meanings of environmentalism (and, to a lesser extent, feminism) with a view to constructing coalition politics across national, cultural, racial, and gender differences. The essays also contain several assumptions about *how* to establish linkages between environmentalism and feminism, even if they do not explicitly address *why* we should promote such a linkage. But first I want to highlight the politically useful analytic tools these authors provide by drawing out some similarities, specifying some details, and then identifying a source of disagreement between the papers.

CENTRAL SIMILARITIES

Both Tsing and Garb use the notion of "translation" to argue for a more nuanced understanding of the current trend toward globalization in environmentalist constructions of discursive practice. Their notion of translation refuses the idea of copies of originals and offers instead a description of a heretical, multivocal, and multidirectional process of meaning-making in which influences abound but cannot be predicted or contained. Both demonstrate immediately that with this notion they can construct histories of environmentalism that counter three common and problematic narratives about the rise of contemporary environmental movements within transnational public domains. These might be called, as Garb and Tsing artfully phrase it, the narratives of "the-West-to-the-rest," "the-West-is-best," and (implied in their formulations) "the-West-is-worst." By attacking such assumptions, they also usefully attack the notion that the West is a whole, underlining the fact that "the West" contains within it Others who continually contest its hegemony and who have structured its discursive practices through political resistance.

SPECIFIC TOOLS

Each of these papers provides us with specific tools for constructing historical narratives about environmental movements that account for their multiple origins and that bring into view their ongoing contests for meaning.

Yaakov Garb's wonderful story of the London horse chestnut points to the creative impulses in the practice of "self-definition through borrowing" that pervades environmentalism and indeed, arguably, all social movements. In this story, and in his careful and subtle working through of the various constructions and deployments of a moveable referent called "Chipko," Garb provides us with an example of how we can substitute the tempting game of debunking with a sense of the validity of multiple, even competing, stories. Such a practice, Garb argues, provides us with three kinds of questions that help us understand social movement practices.

First, Garb shows us how to look for the local purposes of such impure borrowings and creative redefinitions. The English "David Chipko" constructs for himself a lineage that situates his cause as part of a global movement; the attorney for the Natural Resources Defense Council conflates Chipko with only one of its strategies in order to redefine nonviolent civil disobedience away from property destruction in the United States; a Canadian activist uncritically accepts a story of girls caressing elephants because the image of peaceful feminine defiance in the protection of nature persuades her to overcome her fears about women taking political action. Second, Garb reminds us that these borrowings and narrative discontinuities are not "simply stories" but discursive practices with structural results: Western deployments of one or another "Chipko" affect Indian lives just as differing Indian versions of Chipko produce versions of Western environmentalism. Finally, Garb shows us that these competing versions of Chipko are also traces of historical shifts in what might (with some trepidation) be called world-historical social movement configurations. For example, what may have been called at one historical moment a "peasant movement" is now called an "environmental movement." Recognizing these narrative shifts as articulations of particular political conjunctures rather than as right or wrong versions of a simple story suggests a critical perspective on the recent growth of "global environmentalism," one that recognizes both its local and global effects, its multiple origins, its circulation of influences, and its potential to foster both oppositional and nonoppositional impulses, often in the same moment.

Anna Tsing's effort to conceptualize "a heterogeneous continuum of translations, a continual process of rewriting in which meaning—as well as claims of originality and purity—are made" also offers us three analytical methods for producing multilayered, multidirectional historical narratives of globalized social movements. The first method is the identification of a narrative pattern through which a particular lineage of Western thinkers is canonized as History itself. Tsing interrogates the genealogical process that imagines Greece, and then England, and then the United States as the privileged origin not only of environmentalism, but also of knowledge about "nature." She also points out how the degradation and conflation of race, gender, labor, and nature have been as crucial to the construction of these knowledges not only as "Western," but also as projects of the production of white, masculinist national identities.

Refusing the "repetitive story of the constitutive distinction between the West and its Others" allows Tsing to make her second analytic move: examining Other-to-Other contests over meaning. Without denying that these contests may not challenge, indeed may sometimes reinscribe, the dominance of the West, she shows the strength of these debates in shaping international environmentalist discourse. The convincing example of India's reconstruction of the "development vs. environment" debate into the "Northern environmentalism vs. Southern environmentalism" debate demonstrates the necessity of paying attention to horizontal as well as vertical tensions. Like Garb, she sees the need to trace the articulation of these debates to global political conjunctures, while keeping the complexity and dynamism of those conjunctures in view.

Finally, Tsing argues that it is the strategic and rhetorical *uses,* rather than the *truth,* of Western-defined universals that must be debated. She argues that under conditions in which global environmentalism, supported by putatively universal social and natural truths, functions as the dream of a common future, "universalisms, ironically, are a flexible medium for translation." As mechanisms for transnational communication, decision making, and cultural negotiation are built on the promise of global environmentalism, they can also serve as horizontal conduits for localized alliances. Such transnational mechanisms need not work in a single direction (a point Garb also makes); they can be used for the instruction of dominant cultures by marginalized cultures, and they are one means by which these latter cultures influence transnational political processes. As an example of the strategic use of universalisms, Tsing offers the story of Julia Suryakusuma, who argues that the myth that women are closer to nature is a global essentialism useful for arguing with other global essentialisms. Tsing calls Suryakusuma's formulation "strategic ecofeminism."

STRATEGIC DIFFERENCES

Tsing's interesting construction, "strategic ecofeminism," returns us to Garb's paper. While Tsing sees possibilities in "strategic ecofeminism," which she understands as a strategic universalism, Garb warns us against it. While Garb's argument about the local uses of redefinition, borrowing, and retelling brings him to define Vandana Shiva's version of Chipko as strategic, ultimately he rejects the usefulness of her story for the women she champions. It is not simply that he feels her story is untrue, but rather that its unwillingness to admit to the lack of power of women in the Garhwal is not feminist: It does not serve to empower those women but to elide the sources of their continued inequality.

I want to stress that in what follows I am interested not in defending Shiva's story, but in drawing out the implications of Tsing's argument for strategic universalisms as it develops from her notion of multidirectional translation as signifying a constant process of reinterpretation. Without denying the importance of Garb's critique of Shiva, it seems to me that if we take seriously the notion of translation offered by these two papers, we are also invited to look at the ways Shiva's version of Chipko, when translated globally through the processes Garb and Tsing identify here, may not always everywhere have the same problematic effects within local contexts. The essentialist story of Chipko as primarily a women's movement protecting a sustainable nonmarket way of life that Shiva promotes still proves to be useful to David Chipko, to the NRDC lawyer, and to the unnamed Canadian woman activist. One could even argue that in the latter case, the same story that proves not to be feminist in its results for the women of the Garhwal is feminist in its results for the Canadian activist in that it authorizes her own political action. Now, that Shiva's story may do this at the cost of misrepresenting the realities of women's lives in the Garhwal is not a minor problem, especially if it serves to reinforce the dangerous ethnocentrism of Western environmentalism (or Western feminism) that both papers are interested in destabilizing. Yet if these Westernized rewritings are impure but at the same time unpredictable in their effects, then so is Shiva's "original" unsatisfying story. Can we predict the results for the women of the Garhwal as they come to be seen internationally as the leaders of an important grassroots movement? Garb describes how Chipko's popularity leads to "women from hill communities being asked to speak to an audience of urban feminists in a New Delhi auditorium." And it is interesting that while he mentions that "the Hindu card in Chipko's deck is becoming increasingly valuable" in the present political climate in India, he sees only Bahuguna using this card strategically, not Shiva. What are the political consequences of Shiva's tying what she calls "the Hindu feminine principle" to the leadership of women in environmental movements, bringing together presently powerful concepts in national and international politics to promote women's leadership within a process of producing a "global environmentalism" marked by its reliance on masculinist authority? How was Shiva, along with others, able to link her specific representations of Chipko to other grassroots movements transnationally, such as Wangari Matthai's Kenyan Greenbelt movement? What political effects has that had, on, for instance, the feminist intervention into the United Nations Conference on Economic Development at Rio de Janeiro in 1992 and the construction of the kind of "gender-progressive" NGOs that Agarwal has argued are crucial to supporting women's leadership in grassroots environmental movements?

Again, my point is not to defend Shiva's story or to assert simply that there may be possible positive outcomes of its deployment, but rather to raise the complex questions of reception and influence. If we are going to promote the use of global essentialisms strategically, then we had better know how to judge when they are useful and when they are not, and to whom. Given the permeability of translations as Garb and Tsing conceptualize them, and the multidirectional possibilities of such discursive conduits, it's possible, even probable, that a story such as Shiva's is at once both empowering and disempowering to different groups of women, depending upon their location. This would be true even if Shiva's story were more feminist in the way Garb wishes it to be. The notion of translation developed in these two essays does much to point us in creative directions in order to analyze the circulation of influences and discourses, the ever-changing contests constrained differentially by local and global conditions. But they also leave us with some crucial questions.

If constructing better histories is a useful tool for judging the political effectiveness of the deployment of strategic universalisms, we must know more precisely how they are better. Are they more faithful histories? And, if so, faithful to what? Does this notion of translation take adequate account of the power relations that structure communication, as well as the resources that permit the construction of influential narratives? How do we actually move from the rearticulation of historical narratives to more inclusive, more effective, radical political coalitions across transnational and other boundaries? And finally, why is recounting of better histories the way both authors have chosen to address the connection between environmentalism and feminism?

I said at the beginning that these essays only implicitly address this connection. To make these authors' assumptions about this connection explicit, and to touch briefly on why such a connection should be made, I want to look carefully at Tsing's formulation, "strategic ecofeminism." Obviously, it is a play on Gayatri Spivak's "strategic essentialism." But here "ecofeminism" (or the notion that there is some political relation between environmentalism and feminism) stands in for "essentialism," implying that the only connection possible between the two movements is an essentialist one. Garb, in offering Shiva as his intersection between environmentalism and feminism, makes a similar move. And because I know that both of these authors do not necessarily believe that such a connection must be based on essentialist foundations, I want to examine why such slippage occurs here. I submit that it is because a conception of ecofeminism as necessarily essentialist is tied deeply to white Western feminist preoccupations, some of which Tsing specifically challenges elsewhere in her paper. This is not to say that there aren't ecofeminists who are essentialists; certainly there are, as well as many who are antiessentialist. This is also not to say that non-Western feminists haven't been involved in critiquing the essentialism of some ecofeminists; they have. The critical reception of Shiva is a case in point.[1]

The difficulty for white Western feminists in conceiving of an antiessentialist connection between environmentalism and feminism has been particularly acute for three reasons. First, because the wilderness/conservation motif dominant in U.S. environmentalism is, as Tsing rightly points out, about the construction of a white, male, colonizing, national identity. Connecting feminism to *that* conception of environmentalism has not seemed promising. Thus stories that construct a different environmentalism, a more social ecology, like the "Southern environmentalism" Tsing describes, or the U.S. environmental justice movement, are positive developments for imagining a nonessentialist ecofeminism, and they need to be better known by feminist scholars. Second, the now traditional and deeply embedded feminist critique of how "nature" has been used as an ideological underpinning for racism, classism, sexism, heterosexism, and colonialism makes any effort to connect "women" and "nature" dubious to many feminists. But given the growing importance of environmentalism to global and local power formations that these authors identify, as well as the relevance of environmental conditions to women's material situations and their social and political status, developing connections between the environmental and feminist movements (not between "women" and "nature") is not a luxury, and certainly not a misguided project. What is "reproductive freedom," to cite only one example, for women in the Marshall Islands or women in Tomsk, but an environmental issue? Given the present political salience of environmentalism, and especially given its present interpenetration with development discourse, if we don't want essentialist and sexist connections made between "women" and "nature," then we need to take responsibility for constructing antiessentialist, feminist connections between environmentalism and feminism, as Bina Agarwal has done so well. Third, the critique of essentialism, while necessary and useful, can become an obstacle in some ways to developing political coalitions and understanding social movements. Because social movements often rely upon (one hopes momentary) constructions of essentialist notions of identity and power, they become easy targets in an atmosphere of hegemonic antiessentialism in academic Western feminism. Without giving up the necessity of critiquing essentialism in our scholarship, we need to pay attention to the exigencies of political action when evaluating the discourse of movements. This is why it is important to develop political tools for analyzing translations as these authors suggest—to ask, as Tsing does, whether it is useful for us to continue to "see the Eurocentric universal as a generative logic rather than as a performative strategy." The critique of essentialism in Western feminism was initiated, after all, by U.S. feminists of color and non-Western feminists. But those interlocutors did not just call the problem "essentialism"; they more often called it "racism" or "ethnocentrism." Too often, a critique of essentialism has substituted for a critique of power, without asking whether certain kinds of universalisms are creating the conditions for radical political action. After all, antiessentialist narratives can foster racism and imperialism too, especially if they silence a straightforward confrontation of differences. The point, to paraphrase a paraphrase, is not just to change theories, but to create theories of and for change. Understanding all discourses as operating within strategic political contexts, and understanding those contexts as in a continual state of translation, may give us the ability to make choices about which discourses hold out the most promise for a radical politics at a given conjuncture.

What is left is the need to provide criteria for evaluating the use of "strategic universalisms." Let me close by suggesting that, as Kirstie McClure has suggested, the word *strategic* can be deployed in two senses: It can be used to justify a particular course of action, or to draw together or bind disparate elements. I think that we should support "strategic universalisms" only when they have the latter effect, given that *at the same time* the organizational conditions created allow for democratic, participatory debate that can destabilize the very universalisms that create collectivities. Examples of this kind of internal contestation abound in social movement history; indeed, such "divisive" debate is often credited with the decline of particular movements. Further, "inside" a given movement, the strategic, contingent character of a universalizing or essentializing rhetoric is often abundantly apparent. Garb and Tsing's theoretical framework cautions us against evaluating translations on the basis of "originals" or even in functionalist ways in terms of the effects of particular stories on singular local arenas. At the same time, we shouldn't ignore the operative power relations that shape these discourses, and we need to think carefully about our criteria for supporting "contingent foundations."[2] "Better histories" of the kind offered us here by Garb and Tsing are one of our most useful, but not our only, tools in this effort.

NOTES

1. Bina Agarwal, "The Gender and Environment Debate: Lessons from India," *Feminist Studies* 18, no. 1 (spring 1992), pp. 119–58.
2. Judith Butler, "Contingent Foundations: Feminism and the Question of 'Postmodernism,'" in Judith Butler and Joan W. Scott (eds.), *Feminists Theorize the Political* (New York: Routledge, 1992), pp. 3–21.

< part three >

Race and Difference

< 21 >

When the Margin Is the Center

African-American Feminism(s) and "Difference"

Evelynn M. Hammonds

In March 1995, the magazine *Emerge*, which bills itself as "Black America's News-magazine," published a lead article entitled "Is Feminism Too White?" The provocative title prominently displayed on the front cover had a different headline inside: "A Feminist Vision: Black Women Challenge the Community to Examine Issues of Gender, Race and Class." Despite the shift in title, it was clear that the article intended to address the question posed on the cover. The introductory comments to the interview with four African-American feminists noted that "for many African-Americans, feminism is a dirty word."[1] The interviewer reported on a recent national survey of African-Americans conducted by the University of Chicago, which found that 29 percent believed "Black feminists just divide the Black community." When asked to explain why so many Black women find the term *feminist* offensive, lawyer Kimberlé Crenshaw responded, "I think we do have to acknowledge that one of the reasons Black women are so reluctant is [that] feminism is always associated with White women."[2] Crenshaw went on to note that Black feminism differed from White feminism because "from a White perspective, the only issue that they are trying to politicize is gender. . . . For Black feminism, it is impossible to reduce the range of injuries and harm to just gender. You have to simultaneously talk and politicize the ways in which race, along with gender, along with class, contribute to the problem." But scholar/educator Beverly Guy-Sheftall was not in total agreement with Crenshaw. For her, "feminism is not White. Feminism is something that Black women have attempted to define and have been eloquent about since the 1870s." For Guy-Sheftall, the issue for Black women is to "claim that movement and talk about the ways in which we have actually been more revolutionary and more progressive around gender issues than White women have. But as long as we give it up to them, then we won't be as much in touch with our own history."[3] In the final interview, tenant organizer Monifa Akinwole argued that the term *womanist* should be used by Black women who supported a feminist agenda because this term reflected a "self-defining movement" and helped Black women to "identify with something that we've created and named."[4] The exchange among these women foregrounds the most persistent and conflicted questions concerning the possibilities for coalition among White and Black women in this so-called second wave of the U.S. women's movement: Is feminism White? What is Black feminism? Are the needs of Black women who want to address issues of gender, race, and class within Black communities better served by the use of the term *womanist*? Is the move from Black feminism to womanism just one of semantics, or does it reflect and articulate a different understanding of community, gender relations, power, sexuality, history, and heritage within African-American communities? Does Black feminism attend to differences among Black women?

I want to begin to address these questions by examining the construction, articulations, and representations of Black feminism in the United States over the last two decades. To do this, I will examine a tradition of Black feminism as it was defined in the text of the Combahee River Collective statement in 1977. I will then look at the redefinitions, reframings, and rearticulations of this Black feminism at three historical moments, marked by three national conferences. As the conference at which this volume originated demonstrated, the conference has become one of the most important sites of the articulation and enactment of feminism in the United States. But in the genealogy of feminism I am attempting to construct, conferences are curiously unexamined sites of the late twentieth-century women's movement.

The conference is at once a discursive field, a pedagogic apparatus, and a site of cultural reproduction.[5] It is a site generally marginal to the centers of power in American society, yet much of what feminists say and do is mediated through this vehicle. The deconstruction of the opposition between the private and public is implicit in all feminist activity and explicit in some. The conference is a site where the public/private hierarchy is often reversed. These once strange gatherings now consist of a familiar array of objects: panels, keynote addresses, workshops, performances, dances, poetry readings, film showings, cocktail receptions, banquets, book exhibits, plenary sessions, networking meetings, and the ubiquitous "open mike" sessions. The classificatory schema of registration forms produces participants identified not only by name, but also by institutional or organizational affiliation, profession, and in some cases by ethnicity and race. One could argue that conferences have accrued a status once awarded to public demonstrations, e.g., the various marches on Washington for civil rights, women's rights, gay rights, and so forth. Conferences serve several functions. They are now part and parcel of the professionalization process for academics in women's studies, while at the same time they provide a site of both connection and contestation between these academics—the so-called academic feminists—and the so-called feminist activists. Given that conferences are usually held in academic settings, as is the case in the instances I will discuss, the format of their presentations reflects some of the hierarchical structures of the academy. For this reason, activists have often argued that these structures reflect a particular configuration of power relations. This suggests that conferences are sites that both reveal and produce the theory/practice divide so often discussed in feminist studies and the women's movement. The acknowledgment of the inequalities of the conference structure is often made manifest in moments when the structure is challenged.

Moments of rupture, even explosion, are a common feature of feminist conferences. These moments can be productive, opening up a public space for discussion or resolution of difficult issues, and they can be divisive, making collective discussion almost impossible. I want to examine moments of rupture in some notable feminists' conferences in order to examine Black feminism and the question of difference. I argue that these are productive sites to examine this particular question because these moments are when particular conceptions of White feminism and Black feminism are articulated and the oppositional character of Black feminism defined. I have chosen to call this a genealogy of Black feminism because I am interested in chronicling the discontinuities in the discursive field that conferences represent in order to understand how the historical and cultural phenomenon called Black feminism has been shaped in such sites.[6]

For this discussion, I have chosen three conferences: the 1979 Barnard College conference in celebration of the thirtieth anniversary of the publication of Simone de Beauvoir's *The Second Sex*; the 1981 National Women's Studies Association (NWSA) third annual meeting; "Women Respond to Racism," held in Storrs, Connecticut; and the January 1994 conference "Black Women in the Academy: Defending Our Name, 1894–1994," held at the Massachusetts Institute of Technology (MIT), in Cambridge, Massachusetts. These are idiosyncratic choices, and I have made no attempt to be comprehensive.

One of the problems in using conferences as study sites is the kind of documentation available about them. While I am sure each of my selections would figure as an important moment in the contemporary women's movement, different histories of this period would locate these particular conferences along different axes than those I will describe. This disparity would in part be due to the paucity of published proceedings of these meetings. Oral histories abound, though no two stories agree about the importance or significance of any given meeting or event within a meeting. As a result, any historical study of feminist conferences must confront the "struggle of memory against forgetting" and the partiality of all reconstructions.[7] There is a great deal of written commentary about the Barnard conference, and it has achieved a particular status in various histories of contemporary feminism. As for the NWSA conference at Storrs, I was able to obtain only one published report on it, written by Chela Sandoval. Saidiya Hartman's review of the MIT conference, along with commentary from other sources, serves as my text about that meeting. And while I want to interrogate these conferences in order to examine a very specific question, I must first acknowledge that, except for the Barnard conference, I was involved in the others as a participant, a student, and most recently as an organizer.

THE COMBAHEE RIVER COLLECTIVE STATEMENT

In 1977, three African-American women—Barbara Smith, Beverly Smith, and Demita Frazier, who constituted the Boston-based Black feminist group known as the Combahee River Collective—wrote a statement first published in Zillah Eisenstein's anthology *Capitalist Patriarchy and the Case for Socialist Feminism*. As a result of its publication in Eisenstein's book, the Combahee River Collective statement became one of the most widely read discussions of Black feminism. The feminist newspaper *Off Our Backs* reprinted it, and hundreds of copies of the newspaper version were distributed. It was subsequently reprinted in three anthologies, *All the Women Are White, All the Blacks are Men, But Some of Us Are Brave; This Bridge Called My Back;* and *Home Girls: A Black Feminist Anthology*. These anthologies became staples on the reading lists of women's studies courses throughout the country. In 1985, the statement was again published, this time as a pamphlet by Kitchen Table Women of Color Press, and distributed at the United Nations conference in Nairobi, Kenya, that year.[8] It continues to be widely anthologized.

As recounted by the Combahee collective, Black feminism emerged in response to the failure of a racist White women's movement and a sexist Black nationalist movement to address the concerns of Black women. Although from the outset they identify separate movements of women—a White women's movement and a Black women's movement—they do claim feminism for themselves. Feminism is defined as the "political analysis and practice that we women use to struggle against our oppression." Black feminism, however, is based on an awareness of the specific history of Black women, "who had a shared awareness of how their sexual identity combined with their racial identity to make their whole life situation and the focus of their political struggles unique."[9] The Black feminists of the Combahee River Collective were committed to struggling against racial, sexual, heterosexual, class, and economic oppression. They saw their task as the development of an integrated analysis and practice that accounted for the ways in which these major systems of oppression interlock. By articulating the simultaneity of oppressions under which Black women suffer, they felt that Black feminism had moved beyond White feminism in addressing the complexity of women's lives. This perhaps is the single defining criterion for Black feminist theory and praxis: the articulation of the ways in which race, gender, class, and sexuality intersect in the lives of Black women. In their terms, Black feminism, unlike White feminism, was inclusive of all women, and was therefore "the logical political movement to combat the manifold and simultaneous oppressions that all women of color face." Many critics have pointed out the problems in the Combahee statement.[10] Race is not interrogated, and the statement, while it claimed to disavow biological determinism, did not fully explicate race as a social construct. The authors therefore seem to imply that only African-American women could be Black feminists—thus establishing a biological prerequisite for race, gender, and class consciousness.

BARNARD, *SECOND SEX* CONFERENCE

In the fall of 1979, a major conference was convened in New York City in honor of the thirtieth anniversary of the publication of Simone de Beauvoir's classic book *The Second Sex*. This meeting is often cited in many histories of contemporary feminism as the moment when women of color made a sharp and strenuous critique of feminism.[11] Indeed, Audre Lorde, Black lesbian feminist poet and activist, made some very critical remarks about the structure of the conference and the minimal participation of Black women, Third World women, and lesbians. Lorde appeared on the only panel that presented input from Black feminists and lesbians. In her remarks, published later under the title "The Master's Tools Will Never Dismantle the Master's House,"[12] Lorde lamented the marginalization of Black women at the conference, demonstrated by the last-minute invitations to the only two who were asked to participate.

Lorde proceeded to publicly address the issue of racism in the women's movement, but in so doing she made a significant change in the language of her challenge to White women by speaking to the problem of "difference" in feminist theory. Lorde spoke of the exclusion of poor, Black, and lesbian women from the conference and the fact that the experiences of these women had not been included in the analyses being presented by White women. Beginning with the premise of Black feminism that racism, sexism, and homophobia are inseparable, Lorde argued that the problem White women were avoiding was the problem of difference between women. "If White American feminist theory need not deal with the differences between us, and the resulting differences in our oppressions," she argued, "then how do you deal with the fact that the women who clean your house and tend your children while you attend conferences on feminist theory are, for the most part, poor women and women of color? What is the theory behind racist feminism?"[13]

Lorde's remarks marked the moment of rupture in subsequent histories of this conference. According to some reports, her presentation disrupted much of the stated work of the conference and forced White feminists to confront both their explicitly racist practices and the fragmentation inherent in the not-so-innocent category of "women." As Christina Crosby's analysis of this event rightly points out, Lorde's intervention made it clear that "difference" had become the project for feminism and for feminist theory. Feminism was pluralized by race, class, ethnicity, and sexuality.[14]

This was the moment when the nonunity of feminism was recognized by White women or, perhaps more importantly, by a particular group of White women. Lorde's remarks had also indicated the problem of difference for feminist practice generally. What is often overlooked is that Lorde's identification of herself as a Black feminist in and of itself already marked the fragmentation of feminism and the women's movement. Before this conference, White women appear not to have recognized that Black women had already identified the need for a separate movement, nor that feminism was already marked by difference. Black women had been involved in the women's move-

ment since its inception. While it was clear that the Combahee River Collective statement—and other publications by Black women before and contemporaneous with it—
began with the formulation that feminism was not a unitary object,[15] it appears that the
articulation by Black women of a Black feminism had been read (up to this point) as a
political difference between White and Black women, not as a problem for feminist
theory. Thus, some writers have argued that this is the moment when difference became
a problem for feminist theory or, rather, the moment when Black women were recognized through Lorde as speaking "feminism"—that is, speaking "theory"—rather than
simply demonstrating that Black women were different from White women.

But Lorde was also arguing that feminist theory had to attend to the ways in which
Black and White women's lives are connected. She argued for the articulation of a feminist theory that would reflect on the relational nature of different women's lives or, as
historian Elsa Barkley Brown has put it, "White women and women of color not only
live different lives, but White women live the lives they do in large part because women
of color live the ones they do."[16] Lorde pointed out that both White and Black women's
lives were shaped by race and that this was not only a matter for theory but one for feminist politics as well. While this suggests a synthesis of theory and practice to me, this
moment also signified a theory/practice divide in feminism that persists, and which
would be expressed again and again in explosive conference moments.

Lorde's intervention at the *Second Sex* conference was a crucial moment for Black feminism. Two points should be made here. First, the Combahee River Collective statement
was published at the moment when the collective itself had dissolved. Ironically, it dissolved at the point when its ideas and formulations began to have their widest audience,
when the document began to stand in many arenas as the defining statement of Black
feminism. The irony that the group that so eloquently articulated the importance of difference along the lines of race, class, sexuality, and politics in Black feminism was itself
overcome by such differences and divisions has largely been ignored in accounts of contemporary feminism. In the face of these conflicts, the collective reformulated itself as a
study group that would identify and disseminate the writings of Black feminists, while
individual members continued their work on various projects related to Black women.
But while these women recognized that certain differences had undermined their efforts
to work collectively with differently located Black women, they could not see that this
failure might have something to do with the same problem of difference that Lorde identified for White feminism. In other words, they did not see that the problem of difference
was also the problem of Black feminism. They could not see that they had not adequately
theorized Black feminism. Instead, they had assumed that the "shared experiences" of
Black women would overcome differences between and among Black women. No one
asked if Black women (however defined) did indeed experience racism, sexism, classism,
and homophobia in the same way. And if they did not experience their "intersectional-
ity" in the same way, what would this mean for the project of Black feminism? These were
questions that the Combahee River Collective could not answer.

The second point is that Lorde's comments at the *Second Sex* conference set the stage for a performance that would be enacted time and time again. Conferences became sites where Black women repeatedly found themselves demanding accountability from White women on the issue of race in ways that were often perceived as disruptive and divisive by White women. I want to question the impact of this gesture on the representation of Black feminism. Did the challenge to White women to deal with racism serve to re-inscribe feminism as White, especially in the absence of discussion about Black feminism and difference? Here I am asking not about the demand for accountability itself, but about the form that the demand took. In what ways was Black feminism shaped by Black feminists making this demand at conferences where they were in the minority? How often did the public nature of the scene lure people into using the occasion to posture, to take advantage of the moment in ways that sometimes opened up discussion of racial difference but also foreclosed discussion of difference within Black communities? As Hortense Spillers puts it, "The very public nature of the address goes far to hamper incisiveness: microphones, which amplify one's words, often spontaneous and improvised on the spot, define the exchange as ritualistic display—an occasion to posture; against the background of an auditory, which, in its silences, sends up its own demands, not at all answerable in the moment, the participants have 'face' to save, to preserve, and from that point of view, the public forum tends toward the conservative instinct."[17] Did Black women, in performing the role of Other to White women in such settings, lose sight (as well as voice) of the need to interrogate their own theorizing and practices with respect to difference? I would give a qualified answer of yes to these queries.

THE NATIONAL WOMEN'S STUDIES CONFERENCE, 1981

In June 1981 the National Women's Studies Association held its third annual meeting in Storrs, Connecticut. The conference was entitled "Women Respond to Racism." The NWSA had by this time become one of the leading organizations in the women's movement. Eighteen hundred women had attended its 1980 meeting, and 1,300 gathered for the 1981 meeting. The report of the conference that I will use for my discussion is "Feminism and Racism: A Report on the 1981 National Women's Studies Association Conference," written by Chela Sandoval.[18] Sandoval was a representative of the National Third World Women's Alliance, which was formed by women of color who had attended the meeting. The conference had a very unique format. Each morning all the participants were asked to attend one of two available consciousness-raising sessions. One session was slated for all the women of color in attendance, while the other was intended for White women, who were asked to choose from a list that signified their diversity: "White/immigrant," "White/upper-class," "White/working-class," etc. The women of color were immediately suspicious of a conference structure that homogenized them into a single group. To them, this categorization reflected the way in which women of color were positioned in the dominant culture, the women's movement, and the conference itself. Left with no alternative, the three hundred women in this group formed their own conference within a conference. There they began to interrogate not only the women's movement, but also their own separate ethnic liberation movements and the very idea of a unified movement of women of color.

The first question that the group took up was central: How would they name the sisterhood they ostensibly shared as women of color? The group could reach no consensus about whether the term "women of color" (with its emphasis on skin color as a marker of distance or proximity to any center of power) or "Third World" (which underlined the similarity between the oppression of certain groups of racially marked women in the United States and that of women living in Third World countries) better represented their common and particular interests or provided a basis for political solidarity. In the end, despite the ambiguity, both terms were used interchangeably.

The women of color moved on to try to use the morning consciousness-raising sessions at the conference to articulate their commonalities. They finally concluded that what they had was a "shared understanding of the workings of power in the U.S."[19] They agreed that "social relations in the U.S. are overlaid by a dialectic of interlinking patterns, patterns which relegate women of color to the crucial category against which all other categories are provided their particular meanings and privileges." To their credit, they recognized the danger inherent in their formulation, namely that any "unity" of women of color under this rubric could be used to erase the many differences between them. They claimed, however, that a simple unity for feminists of color was not their goal. Unity for women of color, they asserted, would not reinscribe the false unity of the White women's movement. It was instead posited as a tactical strategy to destabilize the web of power that had produced the very categories and attendant social relations that were so problematic for women of color. The women argued for a new definition of community based on the strength of their diversities. The differences between them were figured not as idiosyncratic and personal, but as a rich source of tactical and strategic responses to power. While these developments seemed promising, however, the group rejoined the White women at the conference to share their work before this model could be further articulated.

Sandoval claims that a small joint working group of White women and women of color formed a coalition to prepare a set of resolutions that were to be presented to the larger group. However, these resolutions reflected little of the work produced by the women of color. Instead, the coalition presented resolutions to the conference that focused solely on the failures of the conference structure and the failure of the White participants to "directly address racism." There was no mention of the theoretical work that the women of color group had done. When these resolutions were presented, the conference exploded over the issue of racism. Women of color called for a restructuring of the organization that they characterized as racist, while White women reacted with the claim that the issue of racism was "worn to the bone." By the end of the conference, Sandoval wrote, "the division between Third World and White women had become intensified and cemented with antagonism. It was an ironic ending to a move-ment conference on racism."[20]

A group of women of color left this meeting and formed a new organization, the National Third World Women's Alliance. The "logic of separatism" resisted at the beginning of the conference was welcomed by these same women at its end. The Storrs conference had consequences felt by the NWSA for several years following this meet-ing. The organization's inability to effectively address racism both in its internal struc-ture and at its annual meetings became more and more apparent, and the organization was forced to shut down its operations for a time. But the organization of Third World women was short-lived as well.

The NWSA conference is yet another moment when a promising attempt to theorize difference by women of color was subverted when, in trying to build a coalition with White women, "theorizing difference" became "confronting racism." "Confronting racism" rehomogenized the new political subjectivity that women of color had defined based on a reconceptualization of the differences among them. In insisting on a dis-cussion of "racism" rather than difference, the White women replayed racist logic and ended the potential for coalition. The common project of making a "healthier" femi-nism, to use Sandoval's word, which is one that encompasses difference rather than suppresses it, was undermined. The women of color at this meeting seemed to be aware that "creating a new heroine, a political unity of third world women," could produce new "enemies," i.e., White feminists and the "White women's movement."[21] However, in moving to confront the racism of White women they also reinscribed feminism and this feminist organization as "White." Many of the anecdotal reports of this meeting confirm that the conference broke down in the midst of the explosion over racism, and it became impossible for participants to articulate a common project. The successful negotiation of difference among and between women of color at this conference is often forgotten.

"BLACK WOMEN IN THE ACADEMY: DEFENDING OUR NAME, 1894–1994," MASSACHUSETTS INSTITUTE OF TECHNOLOGY

In January 1994 over two thousand women, the majority African-American, gathered at MIT. This was the largest gathering of African-American women academics in his-tory. It was designed to examine the status of African-American women in the academy. My co-organizer and I put out a call for papers that addressed three broad areas: the current situation of Black women in the academy at every rank; the relationship of Black women's studies to other academic disciplines, most notably women's studies and African-American and ethnic studies; and the role of Black women scholars in the world outside of the academy. The response to the call for papers was extraordinary—proposals came in from a broad range of disciplines and from a wide variety of insti-tutions. With the help of our steering committee, we tried to devise a format for the conference that would allow for the broadest exposure of the diverse proposals we received. There are many things that could be mentioned about this meeting, but in this essay I want to focus on a few points that I think are pertinent to my discussion.

Feminism, even Black feminism, was not the banner under which we convened this conference. While there were many Black women at this conference who identified themselves as feminists in their scholarly writing and in their political work (in which group I include myself), and though there was a panel by the editors and writers of an anthology entitled *Theorizing Black Feminisms* and other panel presentations on feminist pedagogy and theory, I would acknowledge that there was little discussion in the plenary sessions that directly addressed the question of feminism.[22] What was foregrounded was our coming together as Black women academics under the rubric of sisterhood and community. Difference appeared as an unspoken anxiety—would we, as this nascent collectivity of African-American women, be able to speak of our differences at the moment when the desire and pleasure of coming together was so palpable? Could we even speak of what underlay our anxieties when, as Saidiya Hartman noted, "for these embattled Black women academics, the hunger for recognition and a public hearing was so ravenous it was devastating. This coupled with an avid and enduring want of community was almost unbearable, precisely because it was so painful, long lived and impossible."[23]

But the anxieties that bubbled beneath the conference surface were plainly revealed in the question-and-answer sessions at the end of each plenary session. Few questions were put to the speakers about the content of their talks. Instead, these sessions became the time when women came forward to speak about their lives. Many tears were shed as women came to the microphone to ask the speaker and the assembled to acknowledge years of unspoken pain and isolation. It was these moments of confession/witnessing that became the potential explosion points for this meeting, because it was in these moments that our differences of class, color, ethnicity, and sexuality were articulated to the collectivity.

For many Black women present at this meeting, the years of confronting racism in the women's movement had taken their toll. This was work few of the survivors of these earlier confrontations wanted to continue. The MIT meeting presented an opportunity to do the work that had been constantly shunted aside when those confrontations occurred, i.e., the development of a feminist theory and praxis that would attend to the differences among African-American women as well as those among all women of color. Yet in many respects we had no ground upon which to begin. Many of us held our breath during the question-and-answer sessions as we waited for the speaker who would directly confront our inattention to our differences; we could not breathe because few of us had any idea of what we would answer if the question was raised. Many in this meeting had developed sophisticated analyses of our location and positionality in the dominant discourses of the Western world; we had made visible the crisis of representation that had rendered African-American women invisible/hypervisible in art and culture, both popular and high; some had become gifted archeologists, skilled at uncovering the lost texts of our foremothers; many had been participants in international, national, and local political organizations that addressed the economic and health concerns of Black women. Yet even with this knowledge of our selves and our histories we could not risk undoing our collectivity, even though we understood the dangerous ground of sameness upon which it was based.

Was our inability to take this risk a function of the structure of the plenary sessions or of the conference itself? Is it possible or a function fair to expect that these Black women could interrogate the basis of their collectivity at the very moment of its making? The demand for this interrogation, though unspoken in the plenaries, came from those of us who espoused feminism.[24] Should the organizers have been more cognizant of the political implications of this meeting and made the confrontation with our differences the focus of the gathering? Is it possible to do this at a conference when the meanings of the political affiliations/identities of the participants (Black feminist, womanist, and the newest addition to the list, Afrofemcentrist) had not been fully defined but were surely contested? Black feminist, womanist, and Afrofemcentrist are all identities in opposition: to White feminism, to Black (male) nationalism, and to Black (male) Afrocentrism.[25] What are their meanings or utility for differently located Black women? And what of women who identify with none of the above? If a simple appeal to a common identity had failed us at the moment when we celebrated and witnessed our strength, then on what terms were our community and politics to be based?

The MIT conference was not designed to explicitly discuss feminism, but I suggest that the avoidance of the term had to do in part with the stigma attached to feminism, as evidenced by the new categories that African-American women use to identify themselves: womanist and Afrofemcentrist. These terms emerged in a context in which many Black women felt that Black feminism was too much in reaction to White feminism and too inattentive to the concerns of class. Yet these new names depend upon the very same notion of common identity that is a source of problems for Black and White feminism(s). Nor do these terms provide an analysis of political economy or power, or offer new ways to form a basis for political actions.

I view the MIT conference as a watershed moment for Black feminism and for the development of a politics of difference. In a meeting where the confrontation with racism was moved to the margins, the problems of difference and of politics for Black feminists were more starkly revealed. The extraordinary tension and power in the plenary sessions were the result of the boundaries between public and private space being shattered. And in those potentially explosive moments I wondered if we could submit all dominations—including that of our own practices of silencing in the name of sisterhood—to critique, and therefore to structural, political, and personal redress. Once Black women give up our traditional role of harmonizing the interests of White feminists and Black men, the question becomes what kind of politics to espouse. A new politics of difference depends on our reconfiguring the field of representation, and on creating a new context for cultural and political activity as we reconstitute the ground of difference.[26] As Black women across the United States continue to meet in the aftermath of the MIT conference, this meeting, rather than signaling failure, must be seen as a new beginning for the interrogation of "Black women's process of feminist struggle and coming-to-consciousness."[27] If community is not only a referential sign, but also a call or appeal, then "the call of community aims at a response, a calling back."[28] This call potentially initiates a "conversation, prompts exchanges in writing, disseminates, desires the proliferation of discourse."[29] We can see the proliferation of networks and conferences following the MIT meeting as opportunities to develop new articulations of community. But still I must ask: What kinds of structures support the interrogation of sisterhood and community that allow Black women to come together, and which do not? Can the ephemeral space of the conference be a structure with roots deep enough to sustain serious political activity? What kind of community is the community we create in the space of a conference? I question whether the conference format of papers, panels, and plenaries as presently constituted as a space, wherein the messy multiplicity of lived experience—and the power relations within which those lived experiences are played out—can be negotiated to make it a primary space for effective political work.

If not in conferences, then the question is, Where can this kind of positive work be done? In the end, contemporary feminism's reliance on conferences may reflect other, broader organizational weaknesses that need to be addressed. Defining new organizational forms is a project that needs to be undertaken. And beyond that, the question is, What kind of work does feminism do for us? Obviously, different groups of women can come together under names other than "feminism." And certainly at this juncture, feminism shares the problem of all political movements—that is, "having to respond locally to the unlocalized (economic) forces that determine the political, and consequently finding a means and space to address those forces."[30] Yet if feminism(s) have a future, it will be because they are premised upon a commitment to a relentless interrogation of their claims about difference and the way difference structures communities.

NOTES

1. Lori S. Robinson, "A Feminist Vision: Black Women Challenge the Community to Examine Issues of Gender, Race and Class" *Emerge* (March 1995), pp. 20–23.
2. Ibid., p. 22.
3. Ibid.
4. Ibid.
5. Here I am paraphrasing Jane Gallop, in her essay "The Institutionalization of Feminist Criticism," in S. Gubar and J. Kamholtz (eds.), *English Inside and Out: The Places of Literary Criticism* (New York: Routledge, 1993), p. 63. Newspapers and book reviews have also on occasion published articles caricaturing feminist conferences as places where "political correctness" is the norm and non-vegetarian or perfume-wearing women are policed. Rarely do such reports include substantive analysis of the content of presentations.
6. The term *genealogy* is of course taken from Foucault as he described it in "Truth and Power," in

Power/Knowledge: Selected Interviews and Other Writings, 1972–1977, ed. Colin Gordon, trans. Gordon et al. (New York: Pantheon Books, 1980). I am also indebted to the discussion of this concept by Nancy Fraser in her essay "Foucault on Modern Power: Empirical Insights and Normative Confusions," in *Unruly Practices: Power, Discourse and Gender in Contemporary Social Theory* (Minneapolis: University of Minnesota Press, 1989).

7. Here I am not privileging written materials over oral but rather I am concerned with the multiple locations of historical knowledge about conferences and what is repressed and revealed within those locations. The quotation is from Milan Kundera as cited in David William Cohen, *The Combing of History* (Chicago: University of Chicago Press, 1994), p. xiii.

8. For the publishing history of the statements, see the foreward by Barbara Smith in the pamphlet version published by Kitchen Table Press: Combahee River Collective, *The Combahee River Collective Statement* (New York: Kitchen Table/Women of Color Press, 1986).

9. Ibid., p. 10.

10. See the critique of the Combahee statement in Chapter 2 of Patricia Hill Collins, *Black Feminist Thought: Knowledge, Consciousness, and the Politics of Empowerment* (Cambridge, MA: Unwin Hyman, 1990).

11. Christina Crosby, "Dealing with Differences," in J. Butler and J. W. Scott (eds.), *Feminists Theorize the Political* (New York: Routledge, 1992), p. 131.

12. Audre Lorde, "The Master's Tools Will Never Dismantle the Master's House," in *Sister Outsider* (Trumansburg, NY: Crossing Press, 1984), pp. 110–113.

13. Ibid., p. 112.

14. Ibid., Crosby, op. cit., p. 131.

15. I am thinking here of publications such as Toni Cade Bambara's edited volume *The Black Woman* (New York: Signet, 1970), where contributors addressed the problem of racism in the white women's movement.

16. Elsa Barkley Brown, "'What Has Happened Here': The Politics of Difference in Women's History and Feminist Politics," *Feminist Studies* 18, no. 2 (summer 1992), p. 298.

17. Hortense Spillers, "The Crisis of the Negro Intellectual: A Post-Date," *boundary 2* (fall 1994), p. 104.

18. Chela Sandoval, "Feminism and Racism: A Report on the 1981 National Women's Studies Association Conference," in G. Anzaldúa (ed.), *Making Face, Making Soul* (San Francisco: Aunt Lute, 1990), pp. 55–71.

19. Ibid., p. 63.

20. Ibid., p. 70.

21. Ibid.

22. I want to be clear here that the plenary sessions did not result in a discussion of the issue related to the development of a critical consciousness about the structural nature of the racial and sexual oppression of Black women in order to explore the implications of Black feminism. This conference should not be singled out, however, on this issue. See, for example, the discussion by Leslie Hill-Davidson of the conference "Black Women's Leadership: Challenges and Strategies," a symposium held at the University of North Carolina, Chapel Hill, in the spring of 1986. Addressing a tension similar to my own in this commentary, Hill-Davidson reflects on her ambivalence about the gathering. She wrote, "Yet, even as I basked in the celebration of Black women, I was aware of some contradictions and omissions. There was an intellectual breadth that made Black women visible, but not the conceptual depth that such a gathering might afford. . . . Black women there were clearly responding to woman-identified issues, but they did not acknowledge the structural connections these issues have to sexist oppression, nor did they apply the critical— that is, analytical—consciousness with which they would

have associated racial issues with racist oppression. In other words I had the impression that Black women in attendance . . . were willing to embrace the personal significance of feminist issues yet were reluctant to connect those issues to what the white women's movement has named sexist oppression." (*Signs* 12, no. 2 [1987], p. 382).

23. Saidiya Hartman, "The Territory Between Us: A Report on 'Black Women in the Academy: Defending Our Name: 1894–1994'" *Callaloo* 17, no. 2 (summer 1994), p. 407. See also Mary-Christine Phillip, "Black Women Academics Meet, Send Message to Clinton," *Black Issues in Higher Education* Feb. 10, 1994, pp. 13–17.

24. Recently, prominent Black feminist critic bell hooks wrote that she did not attend the MIT conference because she rejected its political and intellectual premises, claiming that it "embraced a rhetoric of positionality and victimhood without problematizing this stance." She went on, "Although I longed to be among a gathering of Black women from various disciplines, I knew that I would not have been welcomed by those participants who wanted more than anything to have the conference superficially project a unitary vision of Black women in the academy. There was nothing in the prefatory statement that acknowledged diversity of opinion or political affiliations. The demand for a unitary vision leads to the exclusion of voices. . . . Black women in the academy, who are busy defending their name, may not be at all interested in engaging in rigorous intellectual discussion and debate" (bell hooks, *Killing Rage: Ending Racism* [New York: Henry Holt, 1995], pp. 231–232). I consider these remarks to be a misreading of the conference call and purpose. Unfortunately, since hooks did not attend the meeting, she did not hear my opening remarks addressing precisely this point. My remarks to the assembled were as follows: "It is precisely the political and material consequences of our work here which calls us to explore not only our common circumstances, but also to pay more careful attention to differences among us. Though we have much to celebrate and much to affirm about each other's work, let us not forget that we cannot create a community of Black women scholars without confronting our differences; we cannot create community by effacing the schisms created by differences of class, educational privilege, or sexual preference. Doing so does not have to divide us, and it is my hope that over the course of the next three days we can begin the difficult but necessary work of exploring and interrogating the kind of community of Black women scholars we want to create, and sustain, as we go forward with our work and our teaching into the next century." I consider this essay to be a crucial next step in the process of defining and interrogating Black feminism as well.

25. The terms *Black feminism, womanism,* and *Afrofemcentrism* are to some extent very loosely defined. Many writers and scholars draw upon the work of sociologist Patricia Hill Collins for definitions of Black feminism: "specialized knowledge created by African-American women which clarifies a standpoint of and for Black women,"—where Black feminist scholars articulate "the taken-for-granted knowledge shared by African-American women as a group." (Collins, op. cit., pp. 22–23.) *Womanism* was coined by Alice Walker, who argued that she rejected Black feminism because it didn't fit. She argued that she wanted a word that indicated that Black women had a different history and tradition from those of White women (see interview in *Essence* magazine, vol. 122, 1989). Art historian Frieda High Tesfagiorgis coined *Afrofemcentrism* as a reference to art by and about Black women that connects to the African diaspora (Tesfiagiorgis, *Sage* 4 [spring 1987], pp. 25–32). One writer argues that Afrofemcentrism is "more original than reactionary as it centers rather than marginalizes the Black female experience"—unlike Black feminism, which, it was argued, had overlooked the concerns of lower-class women. See Sharon L. Jones, "Reading Herstory: An Afrofemcentric Theory of Art," in *The Womanist* 1, no. 1 (summer 1994). Other articles in this journal also favor the use of *womanist* over *Black feminist*.

26. I am influenced here by Gina Dent's essay "Black Pleasure, Black Joy: An Introduction," in M. Wallace and G. Dent (eds.), *Black Popular Culture* (Seattle: Bay Press, 1992), p. 7.

27. Ibid., Hill-Davidson, op. cit., p. 383. I cite this conference as a new beginning because as a result of this gathering, Black women have been meeting across the country to continue the discussions begun at MIT. For example, the University of North Carolina sponsored a three-day meeting in 1995, "Black Women in the Academy, the North Carolina Experience: Naming Ourselves: Embracing Self-Definition and Empowerment," to address the needs of African-American women faculty, administrators, and graduate students in higher education institutions across the state. In addition, professional groups of Black women have also met to discuss themes of power and community, e.g., the June 1995 meeting of African-American women lawyers, "African-American Women and the Law: Exerting Our Power—Reclaiming Our Communities."

28. See Linda Singer, "Recalling a Community at Loose Ends," in the Miami Theory Collective (eds.), *Community At Loose Ends* (Minneapolis: University of Minnesota Press, 1991), p. 125.

29. Ibid.

30. Valerie Wagner, "In the Name of Feminism," in Diane Elam and Robin Wiegman, *Feminism Beside Itself* (New York: Routledge, 1995), p. 127.

< 22 >

Women in South Africa's Transition to Democracy

Jacklyn Cock

Contemporary South Africa raises important questions regarding both the limits and the possibilities of feminist struggle. In the past, the exploitative nature of relations between white and black women meant that South Africa presented a challenge to any notion of "sisterhood." In this essay, I will argue that the South African transition to democracy includes an inspirational example of women's unity.

This unity was brought about not by a recognition of common interests or a shared experience that transcended the divisions of race, ideology, ethnicity, and class, but by a shared sense of exclusion from the negotiation process that marked South Africa's transition from authoritarian rule. That shared sense of exclusion was the generative force behind the formation of the Women's National Coalition (WNC), an alliance of almost a hundred different organizations of women, formed to identify and codify women's needs and aspirations in a "Women's Charter." These needs were not known in advance or "given," but instead were formulated during the two-year-long process of mobilization and charter construction. The common ground of identity was involvement in the charter campaign rather than the status of "feminist" or "woman."

The question at the center of the essay then, is how to explain the emergence of this document that was—in both content and process—revolutionary and transformative. The question is intriguing, given not only the nature of the relations between black and white women under apartheid, but also the fact that feminism was a contaminated ideology in the South African context. It was understood to mean women organizing separately and antagonistically to men and was widely viewed as divisive, as alien, as rooted in the European Enlightenment, and as elitist because of the demands made in its name by white middle-class South African women concerned with extending their own privileges.

THE WOMEN'S CHARTER

The charter, adopted in principle at a national convention convened by the WNC in February 1994, and presented to Parliament in August of that year, is a unique document in that it emerged from a sustained process of cooperation between women's organizations from all across the political and social spectrum.

The charter represented the work of the WNC, the founding of which was a watershed in the history of women's struggles in South Africa. The WNC was formed in April 1992, when some seventy women's organizations came together to identify women's needs, priorities, and aspirations. This information became the basis of a Women's Charter whose demands were intended to influence the constitution-making process. It represented an extraordinary convergence of women across geographical, age, racial, class, religious, ideological, and political lines. The affiliated organizations ranged from political parties to occupational and religious groups, service and special-interest groups, and community organizations. They included women's *stokvels* (savings clubs); organizations of women hawkers, beauticians, and taxi drivers; and political organizations such as the women's sections of the National Party and the right-wing Transvaal Agricultural Union, the Pan-Africanist Congress, the Inkatha Freedom Party, and the African National Congress. With representatives from all the major political parties, the WNC represented a broader grouping than the negotiating forum. Such a show of political unity was unprecedented in the history of South Africa.[1]

The WNC chose to focus on concrete issues and practical campaigns rather than theoretical debate. After lengthy and elaborate consultation, five issues were singled out: women's legal status, women and land, women and violence, women and health, and women and work. Affirmative action and the political representation of women were identified as the major themes running through these five foci. In addition to campaign work, the research process involved focus groups, questionnaires, chain letters, community report cards, tribunals, and in-depth interviews that reached approximately a million women. An attempt was made to connect with different categories of women as defined by demographic mapping. However, certain categories of women, such as white Afrikaans-speaking working-class women, were underrepresented in the research process.

The charter attempted to straddle a recognition of diversity and an appeal to uniformity in its basic statement: "We recognise the diversity of our experience and recognise also the commonalities of our subordination as women." As a statement of women's aspirations, it was a loose document, similar to the Bill of Rights; it represents a broad vision of an alternative society. It was also a political document, one that could be adopted by Parliament and which could serve both as a directive for negotiators when they write the country's final constitution and as a guide for the formation of the courts, policy, and legislation. Its transformative tone was expressed in a comprehensive program: "We require society to be reorganized, and its institutions to be restructured to take cognisance of all women. . . . We hereby set out a program for equality in all spheres of public and private life, including the law and the administration of justice; the economy; education and training; development infrastructure and the environment; social services; political and civil life; family life and partnerships; custom, culture and religion; violence against women; health and the media."

In the interest of this transformative vision, the program was rooted in the principle of equality, again defined broadly: "We recognise that the achievement of social, economic, political, and legal equality is indivisible." Some articles imply significant social changes to benefit all South Africans irrespective of gender, and strong positions on controversial issues were avoided in the name of a commitment to working by consensus.[2] The acknowledgment of difference was linked to an acute tactical sense. Evidence for this is the fact that potentially divisive issues such as lesbianism and abortion were not confronted directly. In place of a strong statement on abortion, Article 11, on health, stated, "Women have the right to control over their bodies, which includes the right to make reproductive decisions."[3] While the research report includes comments about white women's exploitation of black women as domestic servants, the charter discusses employment in uncontroversial terms stressing equal access to employment and training. The charter was silent on gay rights, although a Charter of Lesbian Rights had been submitted to the WNC by the Gay and Lesbian Organization of the Witwatersrand (GLOW). The Charter was also silent on crucial issues such as the military, the arms industry, international relations, and foreign policy. Only one group of women in the Western Transvaal had referred to the military, in the demand for the integration of military formations in a peacekeeping force.

Consensus, however, did not mean simplification. The range and unconventional nature of the "women's issues" identified in the campaign and research activities of the WNC can be illustrated by some of the comments documented in the research process:

There are 22,000 people living here [Port Alfred township].... There are no jobs. There is only domestic work at Christmas and it takes a long time to walk to work in the whites' houses.... The only other job is harvesting chicory. The farmer comes to fetch us and pays us five rand [$1 U.S. = R3.60] a bag but it takes a day and sometimes more than a day to fill a bag." [Black woman from an Eastern Cape Township]

Our main problems are no jobs and no houses.... I live in the squatter settlement.... Our houses are very bad. They are made out of mud, sticks, zinc, tin, plastic, and anything. There is only one tap per street and sometimes long queues. It used to be worse when the water was often only a trickle. [Black woman from an Eastern Cape township]

I live in a well-developed neighbourhood, but there is no social interaction. Nobody helps or is interested in anyone else. Due to the fact that it is a good neighborhood, robberies, theft—especially car theft—is rife. People live behind closed doors with alarms and burglar bars. [White woman living in a well-serviced suburban area]

At one focus group discussion in a remote rural area, the priority issues were identified as polygamy, unemployment, the rights of unmarried mothers and widowed women to own land, electrification, and health and telephone services. A black rural woman maintained that "our worst problem is the soil erosion." However, soil erosion was not accepted by the February 1994 conference as a "women's issue" because it was not "gender-specific." Instead, the charter maintained that "protection of natural resources shall take into account the needs of women." Emphasis on the inclusion of women in development programs that considered accessible, safe water and sanitation, and access to land, as basic needs represented one important way that the charter expanded on the conventional discourse of "women's issues."

Because its interests proved to be in this kind of expansion, there was no precise theorization of "women's issues" during the WNC process. As one woman put it: "Our goal is to begin putting women's issues on the agenda in all political organizations, in religious organizations, in sport, in media, in the law, in education—in all respects of society."[4] The conventional understanding of "women's issues" as child care, maternity leave, sexual harassment, and so on proved far too narrow. It left untouched too many institutions that structured access to power and resources in ways that penalized women. The narrow focus of more-traditional "women's issues" also seemed to imply that it was possible to separate out one's multiple identities and arrange them in a hierarchical order, so that at different times one promotes the interests of women, of the working class, of traditional culture, of citizens, etc. This separation is highly problematic and may be one reason for what Riley calls "the unwillingness of many to call themselves feminists" when the label "women" seems inadequate and "it is neither possible nor desirable to live solidly inside any sexed designation."[5] Instead, the WNC seemed to work with a "gender lens" that recognized gender as a significant social relation that structures social experience and shapes the social world. This implies that all experience is gendered and that soil erosion becomes a gender-specific issue when the sexual division of labor allocates to women the main responsibility for agricultural work.

Overall, the charter shifted somewhat uneasily between a focus on "women" and "gender relations" on the one hand, and a "gender lens" on the other. There was an unresolvable tension between the emphasis on a single social identity—that of women—and women's multiple but always gendered identities as wage worker, trade union member, student, citizen, Christian, black. The strategy of the WNC was to serve as common ground. The needs that were codified in the charter were not fixed or given at the outset; they were generated, articulated, and circulated within a process of organizational development. In the WNC, women found a new collective identity. The coalition attempted to develop a political practice that incorporated and built supportive coalitions based on difference. This notion of "coalition politics" avoided political fragmentation or the superimposition of a false universalism onto the women's movement. It allowed for both autonomous organization and coordinated programs. This is not to suggest that there were no tensions within the WNC. The central challenge it faced was keeping difference from degenerating into division. South Africa is an exceptionally diverse society, one that has not been homogenized by such social forces as public education, mass media, or universal military service. The practical difficulties involved in identifying women's needs and priorities were immense, particularly in view of the fact that 65 percent of rural women cannot read or write. Further difficulties arose because customary law forces many rural women into a subservience to men that they accept.[6]

The WNC process was not free of deep animosities and antagonisms between personalities and between groups, as Letsebe and Ginwala describe: "Tensions, anxiety, suspicion, uncertainty are common features of beginning phases in organizations. Members test each other and the organization for acceptance as they locate themselves in the organization. This was a feature of the coalition at the beginning, both within its leadership structure ... among the participating organizations and within regions. ... The issues of race, class, organizational affiliation, expertise had to be carefully managed in terms of who would be doing what. There were accusations and counter-accusations from all quarters for excluding this or the other organization, for being too middle class, being too black, or too white, for favouring one political party or the other."[7] A suspicion of "ANC dominance" led the Nationalist Party representative to threaten to resign from the Steering Committee shortly before the February 1994 national conference at which the Women's Charter was to be presented, while some ANC women felt that the WNC was dominated by white middle-class women in general, and the National Party in particular. There were controversies over the WNC's mandate, ideological differences, and structural problems such as the fact that the members of the central decision-making body, the Working Committee, were chosen as individuals rather than as representatives of their organizations. At one point in 1993, the co-conveners resigned because "there was no clear role for them." There were also some tensions along racial lines. At one point one of the co-conveners complained that black women were not being sufficently involved in the research process. At another point, the research manager reported feeling "at times that I was being hidden away, perhaps as a white embarrassment."

The time frame for the work of the WNC had to be extended at several points. Initially formed for a year, its existence has now been indefinitely extended. Through the charter campaign South African women have made impressive gains—albeit largely at the level of representation. Since 1990, there has been a reconfiguration of the discourse on gender and a dramatic increase in the number of women in Parliament. So how does one explain the extraordinary coherence that the Women's Charter embodied and the success it has obtained?

TOWARDS AN EXPLANATION OF THE CHARTER CAMPAIGN OF THE WNC

It is possible to point to a number of social forces that helped to initiate and sustain the charter campaign. First was the context of the South African transition to democracy. The transition period of 1990–1994 was marked by a mobilization of energy, a definite upsurge of what Denise Riley has termed a "combative will among women" (see note 5). The charter campaign of the WNC was the organizational expression of this will that coincided with other fundamental changes. "Race" had been *the* "foundationalist concept" in South African history. In the transition, it no longer had a fixed or stable meaning. This destabilization of what had been the central organizing principle of our society for more than three hundred years had wide reverberations; all social relations were unsettled, and there were no longer any preconceived, pre-given identities. We had the strong sense that this was a charged political moment. As Nadine Gordimer said publicly, "Progressive forces in our country are pledged to one of the most extraordinary events in world social history: the complete reversal of everything that, for centuries, has ordered the lives of all our people."

The decisive moment in the transition was the first democratic, nonracial election in April 1994. Voters elected a constituent assembly that would both complete a new constitution and serve as the nation's first democratically elected parliament. The interim constitution provided the foundation of a new political community that celebrated difference and diversity but not mindless, ahistorical pluralism. This document claimed to provide "a historic bridge between the past of a deeply divided society characterized by strife, conflict, untold suffering, and injustice, and a future founded on the recognition of human rights, democracy, and peaceful co-existence and development opportunities for all South Africans, irrespective of color, race, class, belief, or sex." The constitution, and South Africa's transition in general, were the products of negotiations and mass struggle—in the form of "rolling mass action," which included strikes, demonstrations, and marches—which intensified after the removal of restrictions on the prodemocracy forces in 1990.

Because the contribution of black women to this "negotiated revolution" had been well documented—it was principally their rent and consumer boycotts that gave resistance its mass character—it was ironic that the role of women was then subjected to a double exclusion in the theoretical literature on the transition. Women were an invisible social category, and their organized struggles were ignored.[8] Examples of this are found in the works of theorists such as Guillermo O'Donnell, Philippe Schmitter,[9] and Adam Przeworski.[10] They emphasized the role of "elite-pacting" between the reformers in the ruling regime and the moderates in the opposition, when in fact liberalization was a response to mass protest. Underestimating the role of social movements and collective struggles was a crucial weakness in transition theory,[11] as it involved a galvanizing effect on women's political action. During this period, women from across the political spectrum came to the realization that they were excluded from the negotiations that were at the center of the transition process. Women's exclusion took two forms: They were initially excluded within the main political parties (for example, there was not a single woman on the ANC Negotiations Commission), and they were excluded within the multiparty negotiations. This exclusion was an important source of organizational coherence for an extremely heterogeneous grouping, as Letsebe and

Ginwala point out: "It was unthinkable that women coming from such diverse back-grounds—different racial groups, different political affiliations—could hold together. . . . What seems to have held the women together was the fervent need to ensure that they were not marginalised out of the political process and have decisions about their future taken by men."[12] At the same time, there was also a strong sense of the importance of the WNC project and a deep fear of what failure and the disintegration of the WNC would mean. Fortunately, the courage and commitment of a handful of quite remarkable women, including several who had returned to South Africa from exile after the unbanning of opposition organizations in 1990, sustained the coherence of the charter campaign. Among these were women who had been exposed to feminist ide-ologies in the North and who had introduced feminist concepts into their political prac-tice. The WNC, especially in its early stage, relied a good deal on one woman in particular: "Frene Ginwala is widely credited with being the major architect of the WNC initiative and her vision is acknowledged as powerfully instrumental in galvanising sup-port for it from across traditional enemy lines."[13] Gevisser says that Ginwala "must be credited for setting in place a women's movement in SA [South Africa], with the estab-lishment of the WNC."[14] Ginwala had been head of the political desk in the ANC office in London for many years, and her access to ANC leadership and position as head of the ANC's Research Department gave her an added authority. In that, she is like many of the women active in the WNC who brought valuable organizational competencies to it from their experiences in the national liberation struggle in exile, the United Democratic Front, or Black Consciousness formations.

From the outset, these women recognized that the political work of the WNC had to be grounded in the diversity of South African women's experiences, and its issues had to be confronted in separate women's organizations anchored in the specific material conditions and lived experience of their members.

The threat of marginalization experienced early in the transition period may have contributed to a heightened sense of the need for autonomous organizations. But iron-ically, this emphasis on autonomy was another of the forces that sustained the charter campaign. It evolved into a commitment to the principle of inclusivity. "The cardinal and espoused principles that guided the coalition were those of inclusivity and party political non-alignment."[15] Inclusivity was the central principle of the infrastructure set up by the participating organizations to run the campaign. "This in practice meant bal-ancing expertise, experience, organisational affiliation, racial group, and affirmative action. It was not the easiest thing to do."[16] This effort was sustained by a genuine open-ness to the diverse social experience of women of different classes, races, ages, and polit-ical loyalties. Their goals and aspirations were to be discovered rather than assumed; the charter was to be a space for women to articulate their own needs and agendas; strate-gies for improving women's lives were to be constructed within particular organizations on the basis of actual experiences.

All the organizations involved agreed on the need to strengthen women's rights, but the content of those rights differed widely according to different cultures, ideologies, and experiences. It was generally recognized that while all women may have a shared interest in issues such as sexual harassment, violence against women, and discrimination in employment, there are issues specific to black women such as homelessness, polygamy, and customary law generally.[17] For many rural women, the demand for "one husband, one wife" appeared to have more mobilizing force that the "one person, one vote" demand of Western feminism. Consequently, the WNC did not attempt to frame "women's issues" in any *a priori* way. Instead, the energy was directed at locating the largest possible number of women and tapping their interests in an open, exploratory, and nondirective process. While there was some "sisterhood" rhetoric, there was also a genuine acknowledgment of different women's diverse fears and needs. The multiple concrete social realities of women from different cultures and ideologies, women at different stages of the life cycle, and women with different sexual preferences were unequivocally accepted. The charter campaign of the WNC provided the collective identity to frame these needs, rather than a totalizing discourse articulated around the definition of "feminist" or "woman." It became a hybrid organization containing elements that took up the question of difference as well as strands of liberal feminism's emphasis on rights, political representation, and individual personalities. To sustain this hybridity, it relied on practices developed from the principle of inclusivity: for example, its decisions were based on broad consensus rather than voting.

This inclusivity mirrored the South African understanding of the need for reconciliation, whose spirit is institutionalized in the Government of National Unity (GNU). The heavy emphasis on national reconciliation in contemporary South Africa is intended to mute historical antagonisms and is linked to a policy of nonracialism.[18] The African National Congress (now the majority party in the GNU) had long espoused the concept of nonracialism. It did not ignore the salience of race as a social construct, nor deny racial inequalities; indeed, the liberation struggle was directed precisely against such inequalities and the coercion that maintained them. "Nonracialism" asserted a common South African citizenship irrespective of race or ethnicity. ANC nationalism always included a notion of the democratization of both the state and civil society that would encourage the creation of a nonracial democracy.

Nonracialism is antiessentialist; both race and ethnicity are understood to be historically constituted and socially constructed. The commitment to nonracialism was in part a reaction to the unprecedented manipulations of the apartheid state. Whites played a far more important role in the struggle against apartheid than in other African liberation movements. They made distinctive contributions in student politics, the trade unions, the ANC, and the South African Communist Party. The internationalism of the South African Communist Party (SACP) strengthened this nonracial tradition. In fact, the concept was first used by the SACP in the 1920s and was later introduced to the black nationalist politics of the ANC. That racism and capitalism were widely understood to be the twin pillars of apartheid could explain why South Africa is the only country in the world with a growing Communist Party.

But nonracialism is counterbalanced by the widespread acceptance of another principle—that of redress. Redress has two practical implications: a commitment to affirmative action so as to correct the historic injustices of apartheid, and a commitment to black leadership. As one parliamentarian put it: "Nonracialism is important but Africans must lead.... There is a deep suspicion of white domination and control" (ANC woman parliamentarian). Both the coordinators of the NWC were black women, as was the coordinator of the Research Supervisory Group. Writing of the need to establish a "mass-based women's movement in SA," Nozizwe Madlala maintained that such a movement "would be strengthened by the participation of women from the more privileged classes, provided there is a clear understanding that leadership should be drawn from the disadvantaged themselves."[19]

The notion of redress also suggests why there is political support for nonsexism when it is understood in the national context and not for feminism. The majority party has a tradition of support for women's rights. As John Saul has written, "The struggle for women's rights does seem to find much of its strongest resonance, at least for the moment, inside the ANC."[20] The ANC's most famous document, the Freedom Charter, clearly states the importance of equality for women.[21] The outcome of struggles by women within the ANC itself is evident in "On the Emancipation of Women in South Africa," a statement released by the ANC's National Executive Committee in May 1990: "The experience of other societies has shown that the emancipation of women is not a by-product of a struggle for democracy. It has to be addressed in its own right within our organization, the mass democratic movement and in society as a whole. The prevalence of patriarchal attitudes in South African society permeates our own organizations, especially at decision making levels, and the lack of a strong mass women's organization has been to the detriment of our struggle." This statement provided an important political base and ideological impetus to the struggles for women's rights. In addition, the ANC Women's League mobilized considerable energies in the fight for women's rights, although until recently it had tended to subsume these rights in a broader commitment to the nationalist struggle. Women's struggle has been taken forward in the name of an inclusive nationalism. However, unlike contemporary Poland, to take one example, gender inequalities do not have a low level of salience in social consciousness in South Africa. Women here are acutely aware of their subordinate position as a secondary labor force and of their political underrepresentation. The question is how to explain why the awareness of gender inequalities is not framed theoretically or organizationally in terms of "feminism."

FEMINISM IN SOUTH AFRICA

It is important to understand the WNC in the specific context of South African feminism. The origins of modern feminism lie in eighteenth-century claims that women are political subjects, claims that were articulated in the struggle for the right to vote. Two centuries later in South Africa, the issue of enfranchisement triggered what could be described as a postmodern feminist movement. But, as I've said, the WNC did not present itself as a feminist organization. Instead, it illustrated what Riley has called the "strategic willingness to clap one's feminist hand over one's theoretical mouth and just get on with 'women' where necessary."[22] As Riley suggests, one does not always need "the conviction of unifying experience to ground a rallying cry."[23] Because the NWC did not claim to be a feminist organization, the "political massing" remained a loose arrangement that allowed diverse women to assert different understandings and aspirations. It did not style itself a feminist organization and therefore did not feel obligated to homogenize women's experiences and corral their needs into a set of precise demands. It incorporated women from different races, cultures, religions, classes, and ideologies but did not attempt to create a new, shared definition of the "women of South Africa." It provided a platform for the formulation of gender-specific demands by women who generally did not accept the label of feminism. And perhaps because it did operate outside of the false unity imposed by a notion of "sisterhood," disagreement came more easily. The presumption of a shared oppression and a united set of interests might have discouraged tolerence of difference and rendered those conflicts more destructive.

In the North the acknowledgment of these differences has sometimes been interpreted as the subversion of the feminist project. Denise Riley's rephrasing of a new Sojourner Truth plea, "Ain't I a fluctuating identity," should, in the South African context, read, "Ain't I a contested terrain," with an equally "catastrophic loss of grace in the wording."[24] Riley views feminism as the site of that contestation, but this is not appropriate to a situation in which feminism is taken to be an alien ideology, contaminated by its origins in Western Europe and diluted by the idea of a liberal struggle for equal rights.

In South Africa, gender inequalities have been generally understood as epiphenomena, effects of the inequalities created and maintained by the apartheid state, whose influence was so pervasive that it could extend even to prescriptions about legitimate sexual partners. As Watson has written of Poland, "the all-encompassing nature of the political decisions of the State means that there is no area of social life which does not carry a political connotation."[25] Similarly, the sweep of apartheid totalitarianism made the personal political. Thus, one of the pivotal insights of Western feminism—the division between "public" and "private" spheres—had a different meaning in a society where the state penetrated every aspect of private life. Opposition to totalitarianism, whether in the form of state socialism in Poland, as Watson has shown, or the form of the apartheid state in South Africa, is a source of gender unity.

Many other social tensions that have triggered a "feminist consciousness" in women of the North are absent in South Africa. As Ruth Mompati of the ANC has said, debates about how to free women from the kitchen sink have little meaning for women who lack a kitchen or access to clean water and nutritious food for their households. For many women in South Africa—especially the nine million women living in the rural areas—life is a daily struggle for physical survival. Similarly, the strains experienced by women as mothers and workers were understood to devolve from the apartheid state rather than from patriarchal relations within the household or the workplace. The racial character of the apartheid state has obscured its gendered nature. Whereas women in the North have identified the family as a site of women's oppression, black women in South Africa have attempted to protect the family from the encroachments of the state, and they point to the weakening of black family life as one of the most grievous crimes of apartheid.

The feminist issue of reproductive rights might appear to be clear-cut in a society where there are an estimated 300,000 illegal abortions a year. But the problem goes beyond traditional male resistance. "Population control" is widely viewed as an expression of white racism. The hostility to abortion found in a sample group of health workers in Soweto has been linked to the notion that motherhood is an affirmation of womanhood.[26] However, there is no common experience of motherhood that could be invoked as forming a bond among all women. Motherhood has been a central theme of women's political organization in South Africa throughout this century;[27] appeals to women from within both African and Afrikaner nationalist discourses were directed at women as wives and mothers, and in South Africa these were animating rather than pacifying ideologies.

No historical feminist tradition exists in South Africa, no proud connection to the struggles of feminist forbearers whose efforts created important new points of access to power and resources. The suffrage movement in South Africa, which achieved the vote for white women in 1930, was profoundly racist in that it ignored three quarters of South African women.[28]

Indeed, before 1990, the majority of South African women with access to feminist literature who claimed the political identity were often living privileged lives, financed by their husbands and serviced by the black women they employed as domestic servants. There was a tendency for these women who claimed a feminist identity to generalize from their own experiences and to emphasize their own needs in a set of "feminist demands." This means that the feminist voice heard until recently in South Africa was that of an elitist feminism, more concerned with extending the power and privilege of middle-class women than with a total social transformation that would eliminate the source of their privilege. More concerned with making room at the top for a few already privileged women, it fitted very well with the "reform-repression" strategy to which the apartheid state was committed in the 1980s, which utilized all available resources to change South Africa in ways that enabled those in power to remain in power. It deepened existing divisions by privileging some groups and deflected demands for total change.

Consequently, feminism in South Africa is widely viewed as divisive, reactionary, or inappropriate; as a "poison" that spreads infection, as Alexandra Kollontai would put it; concerned with "exotic" and distant issues such as sexual preference. For many, the term *feminist* is stigmatized because of its association with lesbianism. For instance, the well-known author and activist Dr. Ellen Khuzwayo said she did not see herself as a feminist "because there are connotations I don't agree with—like lesbianism."[29] Feminism was seen as "irrelevant" to the needs of blacks in South Africa.[30] An ANC woman told the 1985 Nairobi Women's Conference, "It would be suicide for us to adopt feminist ideas. Our enemy is the system, and we cannot exhaust our energies on women's issues." The feminist movement was dismissed as an "indulgence of bored, rich, white Americans."[31]

This attitude is, however, changing. A small number of enormously influential black South African women now describe themselves as feminists. ANC Member of Parliament and ex-guerrilla Tenjiwe Mtinto is an example. Dr. Mamphela Ramphele has written that, after her banishment, her exposure to "feminist literature" was one of the factors that "contributed to my growth into the person I am now."[32] Some, like Hendricks and Lewis, speak of an emerging "Black feminism" or "new feminism" in South Africa. According to them, black feminism "eloquently identifies its target as white or mainstream feminism, but tends to rely on an essentialist position, arguing that black women automatically have insight into their experiences by virtue of their socioeconomic, cultural, and/or biological heritage."[33] This essentialism, reminiscent of the romanticism of "womanism," which celebrates the spirtuality and creativity of black women, is a perverse and hostile form of feminism whose prime target is other women.[34] If "new feminism" takes this essentialist form, it is in part because the dominant discourse on feminism in South Africa is based on dated conceptions of Western, modernist feminism.

The WNC, in contrast, provided a concrete expression of some of the themes of poststructuralist feminism, such as the continual insistence on difference, the refusal to naturalize the category of "women" or to assume a common female oppression, the refusal to essentialize "culture" or "race," the recognition of the importance of context in framing multiple and fluid identities that are sites of contest and negotiation, and the refusal to naturalize social and economic processes. Because the Women's National Coalition demonstrates an insistence on difference that "undercuts the tendency to absolutist and ... essentialist categories,"[35] it suggests that women do not need an orthodox, narrow ideology to organize together so as to advance their interests. It fostered the "recognition of differences and ambiguities without sacrificing the search for a broader, richer, more complex and multilayered feminist solidarity, the sort of solidarity which is essential for overcoming the oppression of women in its endless variety and monotonous similarity."[36] In South Africa, this means that white middle-class women can no longer constitute their experience as universal. Instead, differences of ideology, age, religion, income, race, ethnicity, geography, and sexual preference among women are acknowledged by the WNC. This change represented a loosening of the notion that "a celebration of women en masse was the only permissible strategy." An oppressively singular Western, modernist feminism has thus been unraveled.

The label *feminist* was "much less important than creating coalitions based on the practices that different women use in various locations to counter the scattered hegemonies that affect their lives."[38] The WNC was part of a wider political project whose aim was to transform all social relations that involved subordination. It thus represented "the pursuit of feminist goals and aims within the context of a wider articulation of demands," and "those goals and aims should consist in the transformation of all the discourses, practices, and social relations where the category 'woman' is constructed in a way that implies subordination."[39] One of its main achievements has been cited as the victory for "equality" in the debate on the status of traditional or customary law—a debate that assumed major importance in the negotiation process.[40] In its objectives, its antiessentialism, it's refusal to conceptualize "women" as a homogeneous category confronting patriarchy as a monolithic structure, and its acknowledgment of the multiplicity of women's subordination, the WNC might better be called a feminist, democratic project.

The WNC represented a form of "emancipatory politics" with a difference. Since emancipatory politics is concerned above all with overcoming exploitative, unequal, or oppressive social relations, its main orientation tends to be "away from" rather than "toward." In other words, the "actual nature of emancipation is given little flesh."[41] The WNC, on the contrary, while focusing on the emancipation of women from oppression, attempted to formulate a broad vision for the goals in the Women's Charter. Viewed as liberation from the dogmatic imperatives of tradition and religion, women's emancipation was part of the dynamic impetus of modernity, and the WNC was part of a clash between modernity and traditionalism.

CONSEQUENCES OF THE CHARTER CAMPAIGN OF THE WNC

In the period of transition between 1990 and 1994 there was an increasing demand that women should participate in the negotiation teams that were to draw up the new constitution. The emphasis on participation was taken up by the WNC as an emphasis on form rather than specific content; that is, on the question of representation rather than issues or policy development. The achievements of the WNC have been largely at the level of representation in two senses: the actual representation of women in the state, and the changed representation of women in the discourse on gender.

The first step for the WNC was to achieve representation in the negotiation process. The ANC entered negotiations about the new political order as a liberation movement rather than as a political party. It was visibly disorganized and unprepared for its new role, and it was subject to the destabilizing activities of the security forces of the apartheid state. It was therefore extremely difficult for women to mobilize effectively for representation in the negotiation process. However, the WNC was able to gain some ground: It was accepted that women should make up at least half of each of the delegations at the negotiation forum, that women should be included in the planning committees, that a gender-equality clause should be inserted in the interim constitution, and that gender equality should prevail over customary law. Women's campaigns established a Gender Advisory Committee and a Sub-Council on the Status of Women to prepare for the participation of women in the electoral process. The Sub-Council was one of the six that were set up to manage the transition until the April election.

Women's participation in all these negotiation forums was not easy. Dubbed by some of their male colleagues as "the broomstick brigade," many of these women often felt undermined by male contempt:

> When they went into the negotiation process [women faced walls] within delegations, within the media, within their families and organizations; they experienced many hostilities and obstacles. The culture had already been established and women were not part of that. [Baleka Kgotsile—Secretary-General of the ANC Women's League]

> I didn't envisage the tough battle that lay ahead or the barriers that would have to be hurdled if the women [in the multiparty-negotiating council] were to achieve their aims. Many of us had little formal preparation for the task ahead and took a while to find our feet. During this first phase, the gender oppression directed towards some of the women delegates was quite awesome. Unbelievably, one male delegate would get up and walk out every time the female counterpart spoke. [Martheanne Finnemore, Regional Chairperson of the Democratic Party Eastern Cape.][42]

But even in the face of these difficulties, an agreement was reached. In 1993, the ANC adopted a gender quota system—one-third representation of women—in their election lists. This represented a significant shift. A proposal for a quota of women in the national leadership of the ANC had been put forward by the ANC Women's League at a 1991 conference but was defeated. South Africa is only the second country in Africa (after Tanzania) to have a mandatory proportion of women candidates, even though it has been found that the best predictor of women's representation is this party-list proportional representation.[43] As one white feminist activist put it, "The one-third quota of women in parliament is an amazing achievement. . . . It will mean a totally different parliament. These women will take up 'women's issues' and give a woman's perspective on all issues."

Of course, the increased representation of women did not guarantee that the content of politics would change. "Getting more women elected may be a necessary but is certainly not a sufficient condition."[44] It is possible that a focus on women's representation is compatible with authoritarian parties and practices. For example, numerous white right-wing women's organizations were concerned not with feminism but with incor-porating women into the struggle to preserve or extend apartheid. These right-wing organizations were best exemplified by the Conservative Party, the official opposition to the Nationalist Party in government, and the Afrikaner Weerstandbeweging (AWB) [Afrikaners' Resistance Movement]. While the AWB explicitly maintains that women are subordinate to men (it is, for example, official policy that no woman shall be in charge of men), the Conservative Party had a constitution that dictated that one of the two deputy chairmen of the party must be a woman, and that 30 percent of the people involved in all decision-making structures must be women. This arrangement predates the ANC's quota by at least four years. But while the content of reform may still seem up in the air, the drive for representation has increased women's participation in the public sphere. Unlike the situation in Zambia, where women remain seriously under-represented in government, the outcome of the WNC activities was a new presence for women within the postapartheid state.

While the Government of National Unity contained an incongruous and potentially discordant blend of the old and the new (past defenders of apartheid, Communists, Inkatha supporters suspected of forming an alliance of convenience with elements of the apartheid regime's security forces, and ANC members), what was indisputably different in this mix was the number of women. Prior to this government, South African women had been largely excluded from political decision making.[45] There was only 1 woman in the National Party cabinet, and 8 women among 308 members of Parliament. The African National Congress had only 1 woman on its 26-person National Working Committee, and 12 on its 90-person National Executive Committee. But in the Government of National Unity, South Africa moved from 141st place to 7th place on the list of countries with women in Parliament. South African women are now better rep-resented than their British and American counterparts; the Americans are just at the global average of 10 percent. South Africa now has 106 women in Parliament, a woman speaker (Dr. Frene Ginwala), 2 women cabinet ministers (out of 30), 3 women deputy ministers, and a woman minister of Security in the Pretoria, Witwatersrand, Verceniging (PWV) regional government. Of 90 senators, 16 are women. Many of these women were active in the WNC—women such as Dene Smuts (the only woman from the Democratic Party, which has 7 seats). There are 10 women MPs from the Inkatha Freedom Party (out of a total of 43 seats); 10 Nationalist Party women (out of a party total of 82 seats); and 84 ANC women (out of the party's total of 252 seats).

These women parliamentarians often seem forced to choose between identifying with their party and being accountable to other women. This is in part because of the way "women's issues" are framed. Take two examples:

> I'm going to Parliament to raise the issues of the working class and sometimes I have problems with this notion of sisterhood. I'd vote for a Chris Hani [assassinated

Commmunist Party leader] before I'd vote for a bourgeois woman any day. [Tenjiwe Mtintso]

The controversy over customary law put Stella Sigcau, an ANC member but a traditional leaders' delegate, in a difficult position: "I had to make a choice.... At that point I had to say that I was first a woman and then a traditional leader."[47]

Differences between women parliamentarians are already emerging. A split occurred around the issue of whether women's participation should change the institution of Parliament. The ANC Women's League delivered a memorandum on International Women's Day demanding that Parliament be transformed into a "woman friendly place." In concrete terms, the memorandum demanded child-care facilities, maternity leave, and adequate cloakroom and toilet facilities for women. But Helen Suzman, for years the only woman in Parliament, described these demands as unrealistic and unnecessary: "For many years, I was able to confront 164 men in Parliament without demanding special privileges."[48] She agreed that women with small children might struggle to meet both parental and parliamentary responsibilities but said, "If women want to enter the political arena, they must realise that it's a big, tough world out there." The Democratic Party's Dene Smuts dismissed the demands of the ANC Women's League as a political ploy "to make the papers and impress the voters." She said, "Our capacity for competence has been established by a generation of pioneers who didn't have the luxury of being able to demand a woman-friendly world."[49] Several women parliamentarians report that their new role has generated domestic tensions.

This is a sophisticated migratory system and is not good for the family that we are trying to rebuild.... There is a negative attitude from men because women earn more and are in positions of decision making and have more power. Some men feel threatened and are suspicious. [MamLydia, ANC M.P.]

But much of the debate between parliamentarians has been focused on gender issues that also gained a new prominence during the transition period between 1990 and 1994. The charter campaign of the WNC inserted women's issues into organizational debates and so raised the general level of awareness about them. It distributed materials on problems such as AIDS, rape, and abortion. The organization made great efforts to reach women throughout the country, particularly poor and illiterate women in the rural areas. By engaging in activities that clearly went beyond a debate that in Zambia, through the women's lobby, "primarily involved the more articulate and more privileged members of society,"[50] women's rights in South Africa have now acquired a legitimacy that it will be very difficult to dislodge. As Frene Ginwala put it: "We've created a climate in which sexism is unacceptable." Or as one white feminist activist told me:

"There's a completely different atmosphere, lots of television and radio talk shows about women's rights and a new attention to issues like the inferior stautus accorded to women by customary law, and to sexism in the workplace." This "different atmosphere" is recent:

> If you raised women's issues three years ago, you were accused of being divisive and detracting from the political struggle against apartheid. Now the importance of those issues is a given.[51]

> Three years ago, women's rights were not on any political agenda in the country. Today there isn't a political group that excludes them. In that sense we have succceeded quite spectacularly.[52]

The altered nature of gender discourse is illustrated by a public meeting in Cape Town on March 20, 1994, at which Nelson Mandela appealed to men to do their share of domestic work—"washing, cooking, and ironing"—on alternative weeks with their wives. President Mandela's speech at the opening of Parliament strongly endorsed the emancipation of women:

> It is vitally important that all structures of government, including the President himself, should understand this fully: that freedom cannnot be achieved unless women have been emancipated from all forms of oppression. All of us must take this on board that the Reconstruction and Development Program's objectives will not have been realised unless we see in visible and practical terms that the condition of women has radically changed for the better and that they have been empowered to intervene in all aspects of life as equals. In addition to the establishment of the statutory gender commission provided for in the constitution, the government will, together with women's representatives, look at the establishment of organs of government to ensure that all levels of the public sector integrate the central issue of the emancipation of women in their programs and daily activities.[53]

Some members of the ANC parliamentary women's caucus objected to his treatment of women "as a separate social category, similar to that of youth." They organized a delegation to present arguments to Mandela to the effect that a gender lens should be threaded through the transformation process. After their push for representation, the WNC asked that new policies and programs be scrutinized through a gender lens so that their implications for women would be taken into account. The Reconstruction and Development Program (RDP), accepted as policy by the Government of National Unity, makes evident that this demand has been heard. The RDP states, for example, that "every woman must have the right to choose whether or not to have an early termination of pregnancy according to her own beliefs. Reproductive rights must include education, counseling, and confidentiality." Throughout the document, "women and the youth" are frequently targeted as social categories that have borne "the brunt of the injustices of apartheid." Other government initiatives manifest similar attentions. There is a bill of rights that guarantees women equality before the law. The right to equality and freedom from discrimination on the grounds of gender is specifically entrenched in the interim constitution, even for women subject to customary law. These specifications are not ends in themselves, and women will have to "engage in political and legal struggle to give meaning to the constitution in ways that will further their interests and rights," as one WNC activist noted.

The first legal struggle has been about the issue of customary law. Govender claims that this was "the most successful issue around which women campaigned and lobbied."[54] Success was marked by the decision that the new South African Bill of Rights would override customary law. Millions of African women married under customary law may therefore use the new constitutional framework to demand greater equality within the household. This decision did not come without debate in the Negotiations Council. The traditional leaders stated strongly that customary law should be recognized in South Africa. They maintained that the demand that the equality clause in the Bill of Rights override discrimination based on culture and custom was "a Western attack on an African way of life." Chief Nonkonyana asserted that "we respect Western culture, and we have respect for Westernised people, but they must respect our traditional African culture," a culture that, it was felt, had to be salvaged from the assaults of apartheid and colonialism. Chief Nonkonyana insisted that South Africans "should promote our own cultures that were diluted by the system of apartheid." Emotions ran high; during the debate, one chief was overheard in the corridors to describe the women who were speaking in the negotiations as "prostitutes."

The first draft versions of the Bill of Rights did make provision for customary law to have equal status with clauses guaranteeing gender equality, but a WNC delegation petitioned the council. In a briefing paper, the WNC argued that the effect of the recommendations of the traditional leaders would be "that two states will be established in the new South Africa: the democratic South African state and an 'invisible' traditional state. The former will be subject to the constitution and the bill of rights, and its citizens will have resort to the bill of rights to challenge discrimination. In the latter, rural communities (and particularly rural women) will be isolated in a traditional state with no resort to the full rights of citizenship. Like the apartheid state, we will be creating two classes of citizens." The WNC then organized an information and mobilization drive intended to reach rural women who traveled great distances to demonstrate outside of the site of the negotiations in Johannesburg. These women argued that customary laws restricted women's rights. They referred to practices such as polygamy and *lobola,* and to customary laws that prevent women from owning land, from inheriting their husband's property, or from having a say in community decision-making bodies, which are limited to men. They also objected to traditional customary practices such as the ritual washing of the chief's feet.

Other women's organizations also protested about the customary law clause in the Bill of Rights. The ANC Commission for the Emancipation of Women argued that a bill of rights is intended to protect the rights of individuals but would in this case be used to protect an institution, namely customary law. They further argued that this clause would reinforce the apartheid-thinking that said Africans were "different" and outside the reach of "Western" human rights. They pointed out that an essentializing "culture" could be a substitution for "race" in a discourse of exclusion. Even with the reinforcement of these submissions, the eventual ruling—that customary law is subject to equality—is widely attributed to the efforts of the WNC.

Not all of the WNC's struggles have been legal and constitutional. The charter campaign of the WNC was also intended to strengthen women's organizations, to deepen their understanding, to get women to support each other, to learn from each other, to share experiences, and to mobilize them into action. The campaign hoped to build a strong women's movement in South Africa. Some think it has achieved these aims: Ivy Matsepe-Cassaburi says that "the Women's Charter has empowered women to engage in the process of change: it is a product for the nation." And Brigitte Mabandla says that while "there is no critical mass of feminists in the ANC to push the women's agenda . . . the WNC has given us a voice."

This aspect of the WNC's work cannot be reduced to a set of measurable outputs, but learning was palpable in workshops where white women found themselves for the first time subject to the authority of a black person who had been elected to chair a discussion. The atmosphere of mutual support definitely enabled many women to speak out in meetings, particularly illiterate rural women whose experience was given an explicit authority in many of the campaigns. Indeed, one of the most forceful of the WNC affiliates was the Rural Women's Movement, a network of forty-five rural women's groups in the Transvaal region of South Africa. They emerged in 1990 as part of the resistance of black rural communities to forced removals and to the loss of their South African citizenship when the government attempted to incorporate them into Bantustans, or racial "homelands." Under the leadership of Lydia Kompe, the confidence of rural woman was immensely strengthened. Their strength was then added to the WNC: "The rural women's movement feels very positive about the WNC. It has given them a voice and connected them to urban women," (said one rural women's activist).

The coconveners of the WNC claim that "we have achieved the objective of ensuring effective equality for women. We can speak today of a gender sensitive constitution."[55] However, some women's rights activists assert that women's struggles have only just begun, that there have not yet been any improvements in material conditions in access to housing, land, jobs, and child care. Others maintain that the achievements of the charter campaign of the WNC are shallow and that there is no widespread understanding of sexism in South African society; that recent gains are limited to middle-class women; that there is a wide gap between rhetoric and what women experience in their day-to-day relationships with men. And because the notion of a "women's movement" implies a national framework, two of our foremost women's activists do not see the WNC as even an embryonic or incipient form of "women's movement." First Mabandla: "There is no national women's movement in South Africa and therefore no strategic plan for advancing women's interests. The WNC provides a temporary mechanism for lobbying for women's rights. There is a need for a strong women's movement if women are to be taken seriously."[56] Then Horn: "What we loosely call the women's movement is not an organized formation with structures able to make decisions about its direction. It is an organic mass made up of many women's organisations—within which has evolved a broad thrust of struggle for women's rights in South Africa. The broadest formation that exists is the WNC. While the WNC represents an extremely wide cross-section of SA's women, it does not have the common purpose that enables it to campaign effectively. On the other hand, the individual organisations that are able to mount campaigns tend to represent narrow groupings among women."[57]

The crucial question will be whether the charter campaign of the WNC can sustain the momentum of revolutionary change of which it was part, as well as the delicate calibration between the celebration of difference and the need for solidarity among women. The danger is that the drive for democratic empowerment and socioeconomic transformation will be derailed and diluted.[58] Earlier, this essay hinted at a feminist critique of the transition theorists such as O'Donnell and Schmitter. They correctly observe that authoritarians often opt for liberalization in the hope of averting the demand for democracy. There is a justified and widespread fear that if this formula is applied in South Africa, the future will see a limited "deracialization" rather than a transformation. (Or a limited "degenderization," which would involve more blacks and more women within the prevailing political order.) The fear is that, just as the concept of black empowerment may be shriveled and reduced to the creation of a black business class, the concept of the empowerment of women will be reduced to the creation of a few women politicians. It is in this context that it is crucially important to assert an indigenous feminism with transformative promise and potential.

CONCLUSION

This essay has attempted to analyze the charter campaign of the WNC as an inspirational display of women's unity and has pointed to some of its consequences. Overall, it is clear that during the transition period beween 1990 and 1994, women activists succeeded in creating the possibility of full citizenship and a gendered democracy in South Africa. This involved creating explicitly gendered institutions by ensuring the presence of women in the decision-making structures of the new democratic state and mechanisms for the consideration of the impact of new policies on gender relations. Now that we have achieved a pluralist political system, universal franchise, and a legitimate state, the consolidation of democracy depends on the transformation of economic and social relations. This consolidation requires specific policies to redress gender inequality. The challenge for feminist activists in South Africa will be to address the concerns of women "in the historicized particularity of their relationship to multiple patriarchies as well as to international economic hegemonies."[59] As feminists, we can "begin to map these scattered hegemonies and link diverse local practices to formulate a transnational set of solidarities."[60]

NOTES

1. The organizations differed widely in every way, including regional scope and size. One Afrikaner women's organization claimed a membership of 32,000, while the South Africa Black Business and Professional Women's Network had only about fifty members. Some organizations such as the Methodist Women's *manyanos* have regular and frequent meetings, others meet only twice or so a year. Some groups have organizational rather than individual membership.

2. Some examples of this are: "There shall be accessible and affordable legal services"; "All definitions of economic activity (such as those used in the national accounts) must be expanded to specific informal sector and subsistence activities and must include all forms of unpaid labor"; "Health and safety standards must be ensured in both the formal and informal sectors of the economy"; "Adequate, accessible, and safe water supplies and sanitation must be made available to all communities, especially in rural areas and informal settlements"; "Electricity or other appropriate sources of energy must be extended to all communities as a matter of priority"; "All governmental institutions, including traditional institutions and non-governmental organisations shall be restructured in accordance with the principles of equality and democracy."

3. The present situation in South Africa is that abortion is illegal except under special circumstances such as severe deformity of the fetus or pregnancy due to rape or incest. The question of whether a woman has the right to terminate her pregnancy was left open by all the major political parties except the ANC. The ANC's draft health policy released in January 1994 proposed the legalization of abortion on demand but suggested there should be further consultation on the issue. The law is currently under review.

4. WNC campaign manager, Pregs Govender, "WNC Campaign Report," March 1994, p. 1.

5. D. Riley, "Am I that Name?" *Feminism and the Category of "Women" in History* (London: Macmillan, 1988), p. 112.

6. For example, at the 1993 annual general meeting of a large church organization that was addressed by WNC workers, a debate ensued on the position of women in the Bible. Several leaders emphasized that "as women we can't get involved in politics. We can't demand things . . . our job is to pray."

7. A. Letsebe and F. Ginwala, "Convenors Report to the National Conference of the Women's National Coalition," 25–27 February, 1994, pp. 3–4.

8. Much of the mainstream "transitions" literature is gender blind. For example, in the writings of Przeworski, "women" appear only in a footnote as "three young ladies" trying to choose between different flavors of ice cream. See A. Przeworski, *Democracy and the Market: Political and Economic Reforms in Eastern Europe and Latin America* (Cambridge: Cambridge University Press, 1991), p. 17.

9. G. O'Donnell and P. Schmitter, *Transitions from Authoritarian Rule: Tentative Conclusions about Uncertain Democracies* (Baltimore: Johns Hopkins University Press, 1986).

10. A. Przeworski, *Democracy and the Market: Political and Economic Reforms in Eastern Europe and Latin America* (Cambridge: Cambridge University Press, 1991).

11. G. Adler and E. Webster, "Challenging Transition Theory: The Labour Movement, Radical Reform and Transition to Democracy in South Africa," *Politics and Society* 23, no. 1 (March 1995), pp. 75–106.

12. Letsebe and Ginwala, op. cit.

13. "Profile: Frene Ginwala," *Negotiation News*, no. 16 (June 15, 1994), p. 2.

14. M. Gevisser, "Crossing the Line," unpublished manuscript, 1994, p. 4.

15. Letsebe and Ginwala, op. cit., p. 1.

16. Ibid., p. 3.

17. A trend that contributed to the formation and coherence of the charter campaign of the WNC was rising rates of violence against women and the worst known rape statistics in the world. It is estimated that one out of every two South African women has suffered or will suffer the trauma of rape, and that one out of every four South African girls will have been subjected to sexual abuse by the age of sixteen. This pattern affects black women most seriously and must be related to rising levels of social disintegration in South Africa's black townships. It is a trend that was used very effectively by the WNC during its campaigning. In fact, "the most succcessful focus in terms of participation and creating public awareness was the focus on violence against women" (Govender, op. cit., p. 9).

18. This spirit is obviously crucial in explaining the different outcomes of the WNC and other African initiatives such as the Women's Lobby in Zambia which claimed a similar nonpartisan identity but operated in a climate intolerant of dissent. The emphasis that leaders such as Nelson Mandela have placed on reconciliation has created an atmosphere that helped the WNC to achieve an extraordinary level of tolerance.

19. N. Madlala, "Building a Women's Movement," unpublished manuscript, 1994, p. 7.

20. J. Saul, *Recolonization and Resistance: Southern Africa in the 1990s* (Toronto: Between the Lines, 1993), p. 129.

21. This document begins, "Every man and woman should have the right to vote and stand as a candidate for all bodies which make the laws." The 1988 constitutional guidelines took the spirit of the Freedom Charter further and committed the ANC to actively address the inequalities between men and women both in the home and in society at large.

22. Riley, op. cit., p. 113.

23. Ibid., p. 100.

24. Ibid., p. 1.

25. P. Watson, "Gender Relations, Education and Social Change in Poland," *Gender and Education*, vol. 4, nos. 1/2, (1992), p. 138.

26. C. Walker, "Conceptualising Motherhood in Twentieth Century South Africa." Paper presented at the African Studies Association annual meeting, Boston, December 4–7, 1993.

27. Walker, op. cit.

28. Despite this, the following news item appeared in April 1994: "Champagne corks popped on Government Avenue, Cape Town when 50 Democratic Party women toasted the suffragettes and a new generation of female liberal democratics. DP MP Dene Smuts proposed the toast to commemorate the day—60 years ago—that South African women obtained the vote and the right to stand for election to public office" (*The Star*, April 4, 1994).

29. *The Star* December 13, 1990. bell hooks is "often told by black people that all feminists are lesbians." (b. hooks, *Talking Back, Thinking Feminist, Thinking Black* (Boston: South End Press, 1989), p. 180.

30. M. Ramphele, "Dynamics of Gender Within Black Consciousness Organizations," in B. Pityana et al. (eds.), *Bounds of Possibility: The Legacy of Steve Biko and Black Consciousness* (Cape Town: David Philip, 1992), p. 223.

31. Ibid., p. 221.

32. Ibid., p. 223.
33. C. Hendricks and D. Lewis, "Voices from the Margins," *Agenda* 20 (1994), p. 66.
34. It has been claimed that there is growing support for feminism in Africa. Throughout the continent women are demanding to be heard, organizing, questioning men's rights over them, throwing into doubt customary practices through which they are controlled, being difficult." This has been related to Africa's "new advocacy of feminism." See C. Baylies and J. Bujra, "Challenging Gender Inequalities," *Review of African Political Economy* no. 56, (1993) p. 5.
35. J. Scott, "Deconstructing Equality Versus Difference, or, The Uses of Poststructuralist Theory for Feminism," *Feminist Studies*, 14, no. 1 (1988), p. 47.
36. N. Fraser and L. Nicholson 1990, "Social Criticism Without Philosophy: An Encounter Between Feminism and Postmodernism," in (ed.) L. Nicholson, *Feminism/Postmodernism* (London: Routledge, 1990) cited by J. Parpart in "Postmodernism: Can it Contribute to Gender and Development Theory and Practice?" unpublished paper, 1992, p. 4.
37. D. Riley, "A Short History of Some Preoccupations," in J. Butler and J. Scott (eds.), *Feminists Theorize the Political* (New York: Routledge, 1992), p. 121.
38. I. Grewal and C. Kaplan (eds.), *Scattered Hegemonies: Postmodernity and Transnational Feminist Practice* (Minneapolis: University of Minnesota Press, 1994), p. 18.
39. C. Mouffe, "Feminism and Radical Politics," in J. Butler and J. Scott (eds.), *Feminist Theorize the Political* (New York: Routledge, 1992), p. 382.
40. The term "customary law" refers to customs and traditions that have historically regulated social relations in indigenous communities in matters such as the paying of brideprice, *lobola*, or a dowry, practices surrounding marriage, birth, and death, and so on.
41. A. Giddens, *Modernity and Self Identity* (London: Polity Press, 1991).
42. See M. Finnemore, "Negotiating Power," *Agenda* 20 (1994), p. 20.
43. See A. Gouws, "Women, Civil Society and Citizenship: A Reaction to Schreiner," in (eds.) N. Rhoodi and I. Liebenberg, *Democratic Nation Building in South Africa* (Pretoria: Human Sciences Research Council Publishers, 1994), pp. 315–324; A. Phillips, *Engendering Democracy* (London: Polity Press, 1991).
44. Phillips, op. cit., p. 70.
45. This is not an unusual pattern in liberal democracies. Liberal democracy "makes its neat equations between democracy and representation, democracy and universal suffrage, but asks us to consider as irrelevant the composition of our elected asssemblies. The resulting pattern has been firmly skewed in the direction of white middle-class men, with the under-representation of women only the starkest (because they are half the population) among a range of excluded groups" (Phillips, op. cit., p. 61).
46. Women's presence in the state is not limited to Parliament. The interim constitution provides for the establishment of a Gender Commission. This could assist with the formulation of policy, assess the impact on women of all government programs, liase with the women's movement, ensure the participation of women at all levels of government, and monitor the implications for women of all legislation.
47. Cited by Gevisser, op. cit., p. 5.
48. *Democracy in Action* 8, no. 2 (April 15, 1994), p. 12.
49. Ibid.
50. B. Liatto-Katundu, "The Women's Lobby and Gender Relations in Zambia," *Review of African Political Economy*, 56 (1993), p. 79.
51. M. Ramphele, cited by J. Battersby, "South African Women close Ranks to Press for Equality," *The Ford Foundation Report*, fall 1993, p. 4.
52. Dene Smuts, Democratic Party M.P., cited by Battersby, op. cit., p. 8.
53. *The Star*, May 25, 1994

54. Govender, op. cit.
55. Letsebe and Ginwala, op. cit., p. 5.
56. B. Mabandla, "Choices for South African Women," *Agenda* 20 (1994), p. 28.
57. P. Horn, "Women at the Crossroads," Work in Progress Supplement. (April/May 1994), p. 2.
58. At a June 1994 meeting the leadership of the WNC decided that the organization should continue; that there was a need for work to popularise the charter and monitor progress; that without the WNC there would be no single women's grouping in civil socety to ensure that women's issues and persectives are acknowledged and incorporated into policy. The WNC is to facilitate an affiliate-based campaign in which affiliates will have the freedom to select and highlight the clauses of the Women's Charter they support. However, the WNC currently appears to be weak and bewildered. This is largely due to a leadership crisis; at the February 1994 meeting, it was decided that individuals who hold public office are barred from taking official positions within the coalition. Many of the women active in the charter campaign have been drawn into state structures and are struggling to negotiate new identities in a changed political environment.
59. Grewal and Kaplan, op. cit., p. 1.
60. Ibid., p. 19.

< 23 >

Whither Feminism?

Mamphela Ramphele

I speak as one whose career and life experience have been shaped by political criticism within the Black Conciousness Movement (BCM) in the 1970s, and within feminist consciousness. These two streams of consciousness occurred at different times but coalesced into a life force more than a decade ago, which translated into greater understanding of power relations as intertwined—the everyday in the public and private sphere and how that shapes the long-term quality of social relations that transcend categories and yet take them into account. Such an understanding is crucial to transitional politics toward greater equity within a democratic framework. It is this perspective that I bring to my reading of Evelynn Hammonds's and Jacklyn Cock's papers.

Evelynn Hammonds's "When the Margin Is the Center: African-American Feminisms and 'Difference'" focuses on three areas of analysis: (1) Historical rivalry between white and black feminism at conferences; (2) inability of feminists, even black feminists, to deal with difference; (3) black feminists defining their role as harmonizers between themselves and white feminists, on the one hand, and black males on the other. The paper raised a question that is fundamental to this conference, viz: What kind of politics of difference should one espouse to make sense of feminism today? Two propositions are presented but are not fully explored: (1) reconfiguring the field of representation; (2) creating a new context for cultural and political activity to reconstitute the ground of difference.

Critical questions which remain are: (1) Is exposing a new politics of difference sufficient to take feminism forward? (2) What about a new theory of difference as a prerequisite to a new politics? (3) Are the silences of black feminists about the differences amongst themselves not an indicator of a lack of, or inadequate theoretical grounding in, the politics of power and their dynamic interplay? (4) What of the silences and defensiveness of black feminists with respect to black male abuses of power in both the private and public spheres? Is that not an indicator of an inadequate theoretical understanding of the relationship between race, class, gender, age, and other social constructs, and their differential impact on people who are differently located in society? (5) How can *womanism* be a better term, or a more inclusive one than *feminism*?

My experience over the last few months working with women parliamentarians in South Africa has been that they are seeking an understanding of both masculinity and femininity. They realize that it takes two to tango—both men and women define gender politics. The problem cannot be adequately addressed by focusing only on understanding women. They would like to understand what makes the men in their everyday lives act the way they do: husbands, boyfriends, brothers, sons, party colleagues. They also want to understand the role they as women have played, and continue to play, to reinforce the form of masculinity which is celebrated by patriarchy.

Jacklyn Cock's "Women in the South African Transition to Democracy" offers a very lucid historical account of origins, rationale, limitations, and tensions within the Women's National Coalition (WNC) and its achievements. The major theme of the analysis is the recognition by the WNC of its plurality, the complexities of women as a category, and the acceptance of a nontotalizing vision of what minimum demands women should make on the process of transition to ensure constitutional provisions for equality before the law and in particular the protection of human rights in the Bill of Rights to challenge or supersede customary law, which binds rural women in perpetual servitude. The essay analyzes some of the tensions within the WNC along lines of race, class, and sexual orientation but shows how managing diversity through a minimalist program ensured success in the end.

The paper also gives an interesting account of the quota system in the African National Congress (ANC) and its impact on other parties. The ANC's support for women's rights has been ambiguous, in my view. It has attempted to "normalize" women as mothers, wives, and sisters in common, hence their exclusion from negotiations—the ultimate embodiment of the public sphere where men from different parties contested power and forged a settlement. But the ANC was forced by the pressure of the ANC Women's League, which was bolstered by the WNC, to make concessions to the representation of women in Parliament.

Unlike Hammonds's account of African-American women's struggles and the silences around black male abuses of power and of women, South African women seem to have taken the extraordinary step of confronting not only racism, but also sexism masquerading as "cultural difference."

Jackie raises an interesting question about the feminist critique of O'Donnell and Schmitter's analysis of transitions from authoritarian rule which focuses on "elite pacts" that by definition exclude women. The debates about "black empowerment" and affirmative action in South Africa raise serious questions about what emancipation is "toward," i.e., what the vision of the new South Africa is or ought to be. Black men would quite comfortably define themselves as the embodiment of "black" and thus the legitimate recipients of "empowerment." The WNC challenged that assumption, and women in South Africa continue to challenge male dominance—black or white.

CRITIQUE OF BOTH PAPERS AND "FEMINIST POLITICS" IN GENERAL

The conference theme was "Transitions, Environments, Translations: The Meanings of Feminism in Contemporary Politics." If the theme is to be taken seriously, then we need to examine the extent to which each one of the key words was incorporated in the deliberations and in the presentations at the conference.

In the light of the above, I wish to suggest that we take seriously both Jackie Cock's and Evelynn Hammonds's propositions that we need a new theory and politics of difference by mapping the scattered hegemonies and linking local practices to formulate a transnational set of solidarities.

But we need to go further than simply doing so as "feminists" to the exclusion of other forms of "solidarities," which are likely to take up the questions of gender power relations within the realities of social relationships across the diversity of environments. Transnational solidarities of feminists must seek alliances with others to become effective agents of transformation of global politics.

I would like to make the following propositions:

1. We need to define a vision of gender equity that recognizes the diversity of its meanings across the globe. Equality between men and women or even between women in different circumstances may be iniquitous. We need to problematize equality and develop an equity framework that enables us and our various societies to address the needs of people—men and women in an equitable way, bearing in mind—the differential impact of race, class, age, and other constraints on power relations.

2. We can no longer ignore the oppression of men by patriarchy, in the same way that in South Africa one could not ignore the oppression of whites by apartheid. The violence embedded in the definition of "manhood" across cultures is at the heart of the violence of patriarchy, both mentally, emotionally, and physically, e.g., male initiation rites, military conscription, and socialization, all of which deny the feminine in men. It may be important to listen to men who are sensitive to issues of gender equity in this regard: "The wounds that men endure, and the psychic scar tissue that results from living with the expectation of being a battlefield sacrifice, is every bit as horrible as the suffering women bear from the fear and the reality of rape. Rise a hundred miles above this planet and look at history from an Olympian perspective and you must conclude that when human beings organize their political lives around a war system men bear as much pain as women. Our bodies are violated, we are regularly slaughtered and mutilated, and if we survive battle we bear the burden of blood-guilt. When we accept the war system, men and women alike tacitly agree to sanction the violation of the flesh—the rape of women by men who have been conditioned to be 'warriors,' and the gang rape of men by the brutality of war. Until women are willing to weep for and accept equal responsibility for the systematic violence done to the male body and spirit by the war system it is not likely that men will lose enough of their guilt and regain enough of their sensitivity to weep and accept responsibility for women who are raped and made to suffer the indignity of economic inequality."[1] How feminists respond to this plea is crucial to

the future. It is not enough for us as women to offer a disclaimer about our conspiracy of silence around war—both private and public—which our husbands, brothers, sons, and other men have to submit to in the name of higher ideals, e.g., the liberation struggle in South Africa or the disciplining of Saddam Hussein in Iraq by United States Marines. Our silence in the war talk that distinguishes "the men" from "the mice" is as culpable as the noise of the war talk itself. The role—passive or active—that women play in this definition of what it is to be a "man" is crucial. We need to theorize this and understand anew what Carolyn Heilbrun meant when she said that "men need women to be unambiguously women for them to be real men."[2] To what extent is women's role as "harmonizer" part of the culture of silence doing violence to young boys who are desperately searching for a new masculinity? The corollary is true about young women—to what extent have feminists given their own daughters mixed messages about what it means to be a woman?

3. We need to articulate a vision of transition from authoritarian rule that offers a different approach to human relations and social power structures than those informed by patriarchal ones. Simply joining cabinets, Parliament, or the military in the name of equality is not going to lead to transformation of these structures of power. We need to infuse a new ethics and morality into the institutional cultures of these structures and insist on the centrality of people in all public and private affairs.

Replacing men with women in positions of power through affirmative action programs is not enough for a transformative politics. We need a new approach that humanizes social relations. We need to develop an equity framework for social relations that promotes development of human potential of all, and a change in the institutional culture to promote a more human-centered development process. In the same way that essentializing, totalizing views of race, class, age, and sexual orientation are not helpful, so too focusing only on "feminists" is unlikely to translate into transformative policies.

I have a sense from the two essays I have been asked to discuss, as well as from listening to other panel discussions, that there is more of a focus on "the meanings of feminism" in this conference than on other key words. Jackie's paper succeeds in discussing these meanings in "contemporary politics" and raises, but does not analyze, "transitions" and the "translations" of South African feminism in the "environments" in which women find themselves. What are the implications of the kind of meanings South African women have developed of feminism for the new South Africa beyond parliamentary quotas, political party lists, and gender commissions?

The history of feminism in the United States is instructive in this regard. A sophisticated feminist critique and consciousness is not enough to transform social relations. The record of women's advances in the United States is impressive in some ways, but not in others. For example, how have the numerous and excellent women's studies programs in the United States contributed to, or failed to contribute to, the transformation of the academy from its male-dominated cultural orientation and practices, which are oppressive of the Other: youth, blacks, and women? What have been the areas of success and failure? What factors have promoted transformative politics in major institutions, and how replicable are these to other institutions?

It seems to me that to deal with them adequately we need to look beyond feminist theory and policy and examine the theories of power and the impact of the definition of "gender" and gender policies and power relations in general. The problematic of gender politics involves both men and women, and this requires a theoretical framework that goes beyond just understanding "women" in their various configurations as defined by race, age, class, sexual orientation, and geographical location.

The insistence of some women on defining themselves as mothers, wives, party political activists, workers, or family people is an indicator of their embracing their environments as they present themselves to them in reality. It is a reality that any feminist movement interested in transition from authoritarian patriarchal rule should take serious account of it, instead of dismissing it as antifeminism and right-wing rhetoric.

If we are to make headway toward transcending the limitations of feminism in the past, we have to confront the unanswered questions posed above.

NOTES

1. Sam Keen, *Fire in the Belly—On Being a Man* (New York: Bantam Books, 1991).
2. Carolyn Heilbrun, *Writing a Woman's Life* (Toronto: Penguin, 1988).

< part four >

Women's Studies/Gender Studies

< 24 >

Defamiliarizing Practices

The Scene of Feminist Pedagogy

Zakia Pathak

I

A feminist pedagogy is committed to knowledge that is ontologically constituted. To be in the world, for women, is to be constituted both by the fiction of woman formulated in the *longue durée* of history, linked to desire and the unconscious, and by cultural discourses circulating in the immediate historical moment that produce women. Agency occurs in the interrogation of the fiction by contestations of, and negotiations with, the culturally encoded feminine.

It is a truism that post-independence India is in a state of transition. Transition is perhaps a category in a classical historiography and can be identified only by hindsight. Contemporaneously, however, it can be figured in the interrogation within discourses of what is understood as tradition. In the discourse of pedagogy, the traditional model, retained as a trace in the cultural memory, was oriented to the needs of a society that was hierarchically structured by the caste system. The modern demand for education is determined by the compulsions of a democratizing state and the market.

In the traditional model, knowledge was grounded in the being of the producers and receivers. Scriptural knowledge was the highest form of knowledge, imparted by the Brahmins to caste members. Education thus equipped Brahmin students for their functions as priests of the community. This knowledge was later expanded to include subjects such as grammar and rhetoric, but it continued to be imparted at the temple or in institutions attached to the temple. The association of formal education with a holy place may be behind the popular perception today of the university as a site of high culture. The other two castes were responsible for technical and professional education. The Kshatriyas, the warrior caste, imparted knowledge of weapons and warfare to their fellow caste members, and the Vaishyas, the trader caste, knowledge of trading practices to theirs. Women and Sudras, the lower castes, were kept outside the pale. Pedagogic authority was inscribed within this structure. A Brahmin would, at his wedding, pray for both sons and pupils.[1]

In the environment in which the university functions today, the certainties of the

Cartesian subject have been destabilized; there is controversy and tension over the object of knowledge, the producers, and the receivers. The postcolonial Indian state took over the agendas of the socialist and welfare states, aiming to retain its centrality in the planned economy as well as in the launching and sustaining of the civil society. In a democratizing and secularizing drive, it has opened up institutions of learning to a variety of populations: tribals, the lower and intermediate backward castes, rural and urban poor, women, the disabled, and others. The process has been—and continues to be—attended by tension and strife. Civil society is uncomfortable with state intervention. In 1990, the then government of India fell on the issue of quotas for backward castes in admissions to the university and in selection for government jobs.

The market economy contributes to these tensions. Rising unemployment, perceived as resulting from the liberalization instituted by the New Economic Policy of 1991, with its emphasis on mechanization and technological change, has led to fierce competition for jobs. The loosening of the fit between profession and caste is the result of job scarcity, and it is also the cause of civil tension.

As a result of these political and market changes, the pedagogic authority and practices deriving from the traditional model have been destabilized. Teachers are not always equipped to handle the proliferating courses of study. The importance of good grades necessitated by the competition for jobs has led to the standardization of examination practice, mass cheating, and demands for reevaluation of grades, often ensured by violent measures that have landed teachers and students in courts of law. Rising consumerism and the greed for money have nudged the humanities out of favor, displaced by lucrative disciplines such as medicine and the law. The models for today's students are those who enjoy power and/or wealth: the politician, the industrialist, the bureaucrat, the business executive in a multinational firm, the successful lawyer, and doctor. If there are any academic figures among these, it is the nonresident academic making what is here considered a "pile" in the universities of the West.

Within the university, the teacher is undervalued in relation to the research scholar. Promotional opportunities are linked to research degrees in mechanical fashion. In undergraduate colleges, for instance, teachers have to handle a variety of courses, and these may be only tangentially related to the areas of their expertise. So undervalued is teaching that teachers who return from long periods of research leave tend to feel sorry for themselves since the intellectual level of their students is far below that of the exalted company they were used to keeping. Rewards for effective teaching are absent, given the resistance to official evaluation of teaching performance, in which teachers are complicit for reasons one need not go far to seek.

The classroom is not a powered space. It cannot be, when attendance is virtually optional and the option widely exercised by students. The latter often find themselves in courses of study not of their choosing due to the limited number of seats in the course desired, higher eligibility requirements than they possess, their opinion that the course of study is useless for employment purposes, or because the teaching is outdated or insufficiently informed. Teaching itself is rendered irrelevant for the average student by the standardized assessment procedures; the availability in the market of guidebooks that churn out standard answers to predictable questions meets their need. Teachers often respond to the situation—or get away with it?—by dictating their own answers to questions; the student obliges by taking these down and may then throw them away. Departures from such standard pedagogic practices are rare. Lectures seldom give way to a classroom discussion that interrogates received knowledge.

The official programs of the university, many conceived for reasons other than academic, do little in their implementation to improve matters. The new education policy introduced by the government of India in the late 1980s unproblematically defines the character of pedagogic practice as the imparting of knowledge. Among the seven objectives of teaching it lists are: "imparting knowledge: lectures," "imparting knowledge: tutorials," and "imparting knowledge: preceptorials." The orientation course for new teachers, organized under the new policy, does not fulfill the expectations generated by the title. According to two "fresh" teachers who attended it, it is only an attempt "to bureaucratise academia, mass producing perfectly oriented, perfectly programmed teachers, their creativity stifled, their critical faculties cauterised."[2] The national eligibility test for students who have qualified at the postgraduate level and wish to enter the teaching profession has been found to be equally inadequate and frustrating. Examining in the humanities cannot be confined to objective procedures. For instance, in the case of English teachers, multiple answers were presented to the question on *hamartia*, of which only one is to be ticked off as the "correct" one. Is *hamartia* a flaw in character? an error of judgment? and so on. These are interpretations of a category in Greek tragedy that have enjoyed currency in literary criticism in different historical periods. It is not surprizing that the student who was ranked first in the postgraduate examination in English literature failed the eligibility test and was smug about her failure.

The pedagogic subject, then, in a travesty of the Cartesian model, unproblematically transmits/receives a text commodified for the market, delivered by mechanized teaching practices, and guaranteed to sell by objective assessment procedures.

II

To expect a feminist pedagogy to function effectively in this environment would be like looking for meaning in the theater of the absurd were it not for a core of students who are intelligent, inquiring, and ready to work. They arouse a dogged determination in the teacher, leavened with a crusading zeal. Some departments in Delhi University—sociology, political science, history—have been successful in introducing a gender perspective in one form or another at the postgraduate level. The Department of English has very recently accommodated the demands of a feminist lobby by conceding a small space for feminist theory, among other theories that comprise half a 100-mark paper at the final year of the undergraduate level. The new course is expected to come into effect shortly.

This is not to say that a feminist pedagogy has been waiting in the wings for a call. Feminist readings of literary texts have been proceeding apace; under the imprimatur of the metropolitan academy they exude respectability. In recent years, however, there is a noticeably growing resistance to feminist readings. The academy, for one, is not exactly hospitable to feminism. It is the project of the academy, determined by its liberal ideology, to articulate a variety of theoretical positions. The theorist in academia is the ironist. A feminist pedagogy, on the other hand, is politically committed and may achieve its insights by a blindness to other epistemological positions. It is also the case that feminist positions taken in classroom discussion are sometimes too naive to command respect. What passes for a feminist pedagogy in many departments of literature is unaware or uncritical of its asumptions, undertheorized.

For a feminist practice to be effective, the feminist teacher must take a position in a tradition of feminist theory in order to articulate disparate experiences and contradictions that arise from our being. Sexual-difference theory may appeal to many teachers and students inasmuch as it engages with the notion of the "real woman," always a potent fiction in the conduct of our lives. But a feminist-standpoint epistemology that is committed to recuperating the female subject and to prioritizing it is resisted as being narcissistic narrative. Gender theory escapes this charge. The gendering process is seen as inevitable to the social ordering and as affecting both sexes. Its feminist potential is not on that account weakened; it remains in the act of making visible the hierarchical ordering of gender. Discourse theory, and the employing of gender as an analytic, is likely to get a response. It is concerned with the structures of statements, beliefs, and practices that are historically and institutionally specific, such as class, religion, and language; it addresses wider questions and escapes the charge of being narcissistic narrative because it engages with the engendering of discourse, interlocuted oppressions experienced in quotidian reality, and the resistance of women to oppression.

The growing hostility to feminist theory may be countered by allowing feminism to speak from the margins of classroom discussion. This is not a politically retrogressive suggestion. It is arguable that such marginalized, informal learning has a greater likelihood of being retained by the student than learning that is officially accountable to syllabi and examinations. Formal learning tends to lose its hold on the ontological base in the process of commodification.

The feminist as literature teacher carries a double burden: the hostility to theory and the marginalization of literature. A major strategy for empowerment is to show sensitivity to the student's prospects in the job market by making available canonized readings of the texts in the metropolitan academy. Western critics are held to be epistemologically privileged in the analysis of their own texts. This strategy forges a relationship between teacher and student and therefore an authority for the feminist teacher that enables her to return to the literary-critical project of inserting the text into contemporary feminist politics.

The project of inserting the text into contemporary feminist politics is bedeviled by the traditional perception of the academy as a site of high culture and of knowledge as free from the contamination of political determinations. This perception may motivate teachers who are active in protest movements outside the classroom to insulate their teaching from the different perceptions gained from their political involvement. On the other hand, there are feminist scholars who give brilliant feminist expositions of literary texts but who are perceived to live their lives unexceptionally within the injunctions of the culturally encoded feminine. Neither of these two kinds of practitioners serves either the community or the academy. The former confines herself to liberal humanist readings of the text in the classroom, and she is unable to effectively counter males outside the classroom who cite cases of women oppressing women, because her exposure to feminist theory is minimal. The latter kind of practitioner reduces her feminism to "simply another way of talking about books."[3]

III

I narrate a story. It will describe the context in which a feminist pedagogy must locate itself.

In 1989, the government of India lowered the voting age to eighteen. This brought a sizeable number of students into the electorate. It gave the students' union of our college (Miranda House, Delhi University), itself an elected body, a feeling of involvement in national politics and a sense of power. The presence of the three major parties on the campus has always been compelling, however indirectly they may exercise influence; teachers' and students' unions are both aligned with one or another of the parties and may receive financial and other kinds of assistance from them in conducting their own electoral campaigns within the campus. The general elections of 1991 were imminent. The president of the students' union and her supporters in the executive were sympathizers of the ruling party of the day. As part of the annual cultural festival of the college, scheduled as usual in the winter, and in that year before the general elections, the president extended an invitation to the candidate of the ruling party who was contesting the elections from the constituency in which our college is located.

The Department of English, alert to the political implications of the invitation, eventually decided to intervene and have the invitation canceled. To provide a platform to the candidate of a single political party, they believed, vitiated the liberal commitment of the academy, which dictated impartiality and conditions conducive to objective assessment of the contesting candidates. An emergency meeting of the Staff Council was requisitioned. It became clear in the course of the meeting that a number of teachers from the other departments were also opposed to the invitation. It was canceled by the principal. This infuriated the president, and she reacted violently, using intemperate language and damaging college property in expressing her rage. Later that night she interrupted dinner at the college hostel with similar behavior. For three days running, developments in the college made the media. Newspapers carried reports of the clandestine support given to the President by some workers of the ruling party who stationed themselves outside the college and abetted her in her rampaging. The students split over her behavior, with the hostel union demanding disciplinary action against her. The groupings prevailing till then, teachers versus students, dissolved.

Hostelers in our college are a privileged group. Their superior academic performance at the school-leaving level, due in no small measure to their proficiency in the English language, which is privileged as the medium of instruction and examinations, gives them a decided edge in admission to the hostel, seats there being limited. Class is implicated in academic merit; it dissolved the prevailing configuration of interests. In the new groupings, teachers from the Department of English by and large supported the honors students, and teachers of the Department of Hindi were with the president and her supporters, largely from the pass (general) courses of study. Honors students are more at home in English than the pass course students. Language is now recognized as a site where people become aware of their class differences and fight them out. English is the language of power in India, of a neocolonial elite. It functioned as a consolidating force across the line of official authority and the students. In the tensions that followed, demands were made that the negotiations be conducted in Hindi.

The following day, the principal convened a special meeting of the general body of the students' union to assess the consensus on the president's behavior. The president was then suspended. She and her supporters immediately went on a hunger strike in the foyer of the college, demanding that the suspension order be withdrawn. Her choice of the form of protest is significant. Women can adopt the hunger strike and remain within the norm of passive behavior and exertion of moral influence that defines woman. It was given legitimacy by Mahatma Gandhi who claimed to have been inspired by women's use of it in domestic politics. The immediate response of the honors students to the strike was one of dismay; strikes of any kind are perceived by sections of the professional middle classes as a form of violence against constituted authority in which they are implicated. Male students from elite colleges are equally reluctant to strike. After day-long deliberations, however, they decided to go on a counter-hunger strike, demanding that the suspension order remain. The counterstrike represented a gendered intervention in class determination and was received by the president and her group with equal dismay. It dispersed the silent moral appeal conferred by Gandhian tradition on the hunger strike and—by extension—on the cause it supports. It leveled the playing field. This was clearly an impasse for the president. It cannot be comfortable for union politics to have students against you and teachers on your side.

Tension was now at fever pitch, and the principal intensified negotiations with teachers and students to end the impasse. By afternoon of the next day, the President's stand became conciliatory; the change was believed to be motivated by a direction from the ruling party, which was uneasy with the adverse publicity in the newspapers and the impact it might have on the electoral fortunes of their candidate in the constituency. Late that night, a compromise was reached. The president apologized unconditionally for her behavior, the suspension order was withdrawn, and both strikes were called off. The president walked up to the opposing group and extended a plea for restoring student unity. It was an astute move. She asked them to join her in the students' union slogan: "Long live the students' union!" They did.

Every narration is a narrativization. Every context is a text. How can one read this text in the interests of a feminist pedagogy?

First, in an all-women environment, such as that of a women's college, it is easier to act out ambition and aggression; the male gaze is lodged in the feminine norm, but in the absence of the physical presence of men, is less coercive in pushing women into stereotypical postures dictated by the fiction of the "real woman."

Second, relations outside the classroom inevitably reproduce themselves inside it. A constant reflexivity must attend the production of the subject if students are not to be alienated; positions must be understood as political and provisional. Were we, as teachers, purely positioned by academic discourse? It is true that we were motivated to ensure conditions for a rational electoral choice by students, but it is equally a fact that many of us were opposed to the ruling party and resented its dominance on the campus. Did we displace our resentment onto academic discourse? Was the president enraged because she read our intervention as political but camouflaged by our impeccable liberal credentials? Did it checkmate her alibi, as we perceived it, the cultural festival? The multiple and shifting positioning makes any simple moral judgment unsustainable.

Third, all discourse is engendered, but gender is experienced as oppressive at the intersection of discourses, where it sets up resistances. Realpolitik legitimates aggressive protest, even violence if necessary. Class discourse where the feminine is implicated forbids it. The president found herself isolated because of her violent behavior. The choice of the hunger strike was a negotiation. Again, realpolitik pushes the subject into partisan positions, and constructs a shifting subject as diseased. Academic discourse demands rationality and neutrality in the authorities, and constructs a shifting subjectivity as emotion-driven, as feminine. The ironic stance negotiates a relation with both. Irony is not the paralysis of political will; it is the stance of the intellectual who does not make grand statements and is open to other vocabularies. Irony creates confusion in order to say something that exceeds logic.[4] It is the belief that the individual is unified that suspends her continually on the brink of political involvement. To understand the subject as produced is to prepare it to act from a position of partial truth. Partial truths and provisional positions are the conditions for political participation. In politics we simplify to achieve our end.

Fourth, the university is in and of the world. The pedagogic space is traversed by discourses, and discourses are social. If the feminist pedagogue is committed to a knowledge that is ontologically based, then the literary text must be inserted into feminist politics. And the insertion of a Western literary text into the Indian social text needs a legitimating theory.

IV

To insert the Western literary text into contemporary feminist politics needs theoretical legitimation and direction. Theme criticism that was pressed into service on this account does not satisfy because it represses difference. The dominance of the universalizing imperative that directed theme criticism until recently may have derived its legitimacy from the hegemonizing ideology of "English," where the suppression of difference between colonizer and colonized was to work in the interests of continued imperial domination. Today we need a theory that will recognize difference without constructing the Other in hostility.

Defamiliarizing theory meets that need. It enables us to foreground our cultural practices as the object to be understood. This is felt as urgent for a nation emergent from colonial domination, in transition toward a cultural identity that is not homogenizing. But we need, as women, to perceive those practices as constructed, to denaturalize the patriarchal meanings invested in them. Identity is established in difference. Kurt Wolff speaks of the sociological project as introducing us to a world we do not know, or telling us—shocking us with—the truths about the world we know.[5] Defamiliarizing theory brings both worlds into one problematic; by and through the world we do not know, we come to the truths about the world we thought we knew.

And we can recognize our culture without cultural arrogance or cultural cringing (felicitous Australian idioms).

I would like to present two instances by way of a possible classroom practice to suggest how defamiliarization works. In the first instance, I record how the reception of Shakespearean plays in the Indian classroom can defamiliarize the injunction against the use of bawdy language by women. In the second, I examine how a novel by Thomas Hardy can defamiliarize judicial verdicts in cases of custodial rape in India, and the activist response to them.

The bawdy language in the comic scenes of Shakespearean plays can present problems in the Indian classroom. It is incomprehensible to most students. At a seminar held in Delhi a few years ago, teachers discussed how the problem might be tackled. A literal translation of the bawdy language into an Indian language does not get the bawdiness across; a male teacher reported how he had to resort to free translations. A female teacher[6] reported finding that her women students resisted the translation of bawdiness even by a young woman teacher in an all-women class. In Shakespearean plays, bawdiness is relegated to the subplot and spoken by the lower citizenry. But this teacher discovered that the resistance of her students to bawdiness had nothing to do with the notion of the feminine as it governs the speech of a lady. Their resistance did not issue from moral prudery. These same students enjoyed the bawdy songs in Hindi films that were then attracting public ire. Several letters to the editor in the daily newspapers indicted the Film Censor Board for not doing its job. The students were not affected by the controversy; they had often been heard to sing these songs with gusto. In their perception, however, the university classroom was an altogether different place, a site of high culture and chaste speech. Sex must not be talked about in the classroom. "How can we tell our parents that this is what we talk about in class?" they told her.

On the other hand, bawdiness is freely allowed in social, secular gatherings of women at the wedding ceremony. We do not have an equivalent of the locker-room humor of the West or the convention of the stag party on the eve of the Christian wedding. Instead, at these gatherings of women in many states of north India, traditional bawdy songs are sung. (Today, some men may also be present.) The bride to be, a virgin, is also present, and the songs are an initiation for her. In Bihar, on the occasion of the last meal before the wedding (after which the bridegroom's party leaves with the bride), the women of the bride's family hurl choice abuse at the bridegroom's party, who until then have lorded it over them as the male's family, and especially at the father-in-law, the supreme figure of authority.[7]

The carnivalesque may ultimately function conservatively, but the point pertinent here is the ritual recognition of the need for release of emotions in uninhibited speech; it concedes the fictionality of the sign of Woman as naturally chaste in speech. To fictionalize women as emotional, and then to deny them the expressive speech allowed to the rational male, does not make sense even in patriarchal logic. Speech practices in our cultures are seen to be discursively determined; that chaste speech essentially describes a lady is a notion imported from the West. Norms are engendered within discourses and permit contradictory practices.

References to sexual practices are *de rigueur* in the discourse of marriage. In Karnataka, elders give ritual advice to the bride to ensure a happy marriage, exorting her to take several guises as required by the situation: to be like a mother when her husband comes home hungry, like a courtesan when he comes to her bed. Though, as previously mentioned, in Shakespearean plays bawdiness is confined to the lower citizenry and to the subplot, in the Karnataka case the ritual advice is given by the elders of the family and in the Sanskrit language, the same language in which the holy rites are performed.

In my second instance, I show how defamiliarizing theory works by inserting Thomas Hardy's novel *Tess of the D'Ubervilles* into the Indian social text comprised of judicial verdicts in cases of custodial rape. I choose Hardy not only because he is a canonized writer and as such has been in English literature syllabi in India for decades. More important for us at this historical stage of transition is the fact that his novels mark the transition in England from a rural economy to an industrialized one. I choose him because he is a male writer, and so more useful for a feminist practice that privileges gender theory. I choose *Tess* because the novel focuses on the issue of character and consent in sexual intercourse.

Tess gives a new perspective on the "fallen woman." Such characters are seen "as deviating from the . . . womanly ideal without moving into the unwomanly category. Hence the preoccupations of males—both narrators and characters—with establishing a reading for them; and hence the contradiction in these readings."[8] The novel puts the fact of Tess's intercourse with Alec D'Uberville into the discourse of sexuality as it is spoken by two cultures, the bourgeois and the rural folk, which are oppositionally constructed. This opposition is problematized in later revisions; the peasants, for instance, begin to murmur of an element of coercion in the rape/seduction, which is at odds with the unfettered sexuality of the rural mores in Hardy's representation. Again, as has been noticed, nature is sometimes presented within a Romantic world view, at other times within a Christian one. Nevertheless, the opposition of nature and culture remains to organize the formal elements in the novel: the plot is punitive, Tess is hanged; the narrative stance constantly interrogates its logic.

The centrality of the rape/seduction issue interpellates the text of judicial verdicts in India in cases of custodial rape. These hinge on the determination of the victim's character as moral or immoral, which will then determine the issue as rape or seduction. Rape within the family seldom makes it to the law court because the ideology of the family silences the victim. By concentrating on rape in custody, activists remove the act of sexual intercourse from the discourse of sexuality and place it in that of authority. The state is the guarantor of civil liberties; the raping by policemen of the women in their custody is an abuse of constituted authority. Removing rape from the discourse of sexuality is more likely to get some justice for the victim.

To place the intercourse in the discourse of authority also wins for the victim the sympathy of the males in the community who have themselves been oppressed by these authorities in other ways. It is noted that the victim is not ostracized when she is raped in custody; the question of her consent is displaced from the center of the narrative.[9]

In the decentering of sexual discourse, the pitfalls of the characterological debate are bypassed. The law is governed by the conception of history as linear, and the classic conception of character that accompanies it; when the fact of intercourse is placed in sexual discourse, it becomes the beginning of a realistic narrative that constructs the victim as "lewd" and "lascivious," and therefore the author of her destiny. The conception of character as unified and freely willing, even when dislodged by legal amendments (in 1983, Section II–4 of the Indian Penal Act and Section 376 of the Indian Penal Code were amended) turns on the issue of reliable testimony to prevent justice to the victim. In the case of the 25 year-old judgment acknowledges that "it will not help the defence merely to show that the woman was of easy virtue," but it goes on to say that "it must be conceded that immoral character would still not be an absolutely irrelevant circumstance. It may render her story itself as incredible, it may take away the probative force (evidential value) of the story, told as it is by a woman of no scruples or morals."[10] "Experienced women," (a term that occurs in legal judgments) may have difficulty in proving even the fact that sexual intercourse occurred; that Hardy decided to give Tess an illegitimate child removes intercourse from the area of speculation or female imaginings.

Women's organizations and women in civil rights groups have denounced judgments exonerating the rapist as issuing from "male bias" and "sexist blindness." They were well aware that in these very same cases, male judges in the lower courts had sentenced the rapists. This essentialization of the male character may have been provoked by the essentialization of Woman as corrupt. So deeply is this internalized that social workers first have to deal with the traumatized victim before civil rights activists can begin their work. One such group, Samvad, based in Bangalore, reports that a victim of sexual molestation broke her silence of days with two words, continuously repeated; "Forgive me."

In the light of the sophisticated strategy of discursive displacement described above, this essentialization of the male sex can be seen as a strategy to organize and articulate resistance. But the danger is that cries of sexist blindness begin to function as the "common sense" of feminist discourse and alienate sympathizers of both sexes.

In Hardy's novel, the two moral positions within the discourse of sexuality, organized formally through plot and narrative stance, are not resolved. The hanging of Tess is closure; it does not resolve the controversy as to whether justice has been done in her case. This controversy is transposed into legal discourse as the controversy of formal and substantive law.

Formal justice keeps within the expectations generated by the social norms governing the community. Formal injustice results when the truths of popular morality are disregarded to the disadvantage of those who act according to them. The task of the judge is to administer these laws impartially and consistently. Substantive justice involves having just laws. The law is an arm of the state; judicial verdicts must be assessed within the ideology of the state as a protector of customary rights or as a force for social change. The judicial activism we are witnessing today is widely perceived as necessary because the state has abdicated its welfare responsibility.

Defamiliarization is dependent on the concept of alienation, which distances the viewer from the literary work so as to disrupt the automatized response to it and denaturalize its meaning. The Western literary text is a position the Indian reader occupies, and it distances her from the Indian social text. It is not a position of cultural cringe but a recognition that identity is established in difference.

V

An essay by Peter Widdowson also uses defamiliarization, also on *Tess*. For Widdowson, defamiliarization comes about in "moments of vision." "Vision" is at once a literal seeing and a metaphysical revelation. "Moments," in a metaphor he takes from physics, are both the stopped moment in the temporal and a vision always in motion, swinging around a pivot that in this case is the subtitle: "A pure woman." For Hardy, "vision in this binary sense ('double vision'?) is a way of 'defamiliarizing,' of 'making strange' the naturalized world of conceptualized reality, of 'seeing things as they really are.' . . . It is subversive in many ways. Hardy was not just 'doing defamiliarizing' by chance—as an automatic and unwilled reflex of his (unconscious) and protomodernist mind. On the contrary, he was thinking about it throughout his writing life."[11]

In my use of it, defamiliarization has little to do with the epiphanic and much to do

with semiotics. I have described the novel as interpellating the text of the judicial verdicts, but this process is motivated by the perceived equivalence of signs and the relations
between them. In both my texts, *Tess* and the judical verdicts, source text and target, there
is the invariant core: the vulnerable woman (Tess is in Alec's employ; the custodially
raped women are laborers or tribals or migrants, all highly vulnerable groups); the jour-
ney at night where the unaccompanied woman cannot choose her companion; the
rape/seduction; the trial, the verdict. There is also an equivalence of effect: the disruption
of conventional meanings and naturalized notions. As such, the defamiliarization process
belongs in translation studies.[12] It is now accepted that there can be no correct translation, since words have different associative fields and sentential meaning is therefore
indeterminate. Also, translation is determined by the purpose of the translator. What
translators seek to achieve is equivalence in the transposition of signs and the equivalence
of effect. Translations are dynamic; the values attached to signs are culture-specific. In my
reading, the differences in the values attached to the sign system place one text in the discourse of sexuality, the other in the discourse of authority.

The novel as visionary. The novel as semiotic. What are the associative fields of these
words between East and West?

The question put to the participants in the conference session in which this essay was
first presented was: How do non-Western feminists use feminist theory to teach, do
research, etc.? Naming is often a game of power; "Arabic" numerals continue to be so
described even though it is known that the Arabs took them from India. The drive to
establish national identities for theories continues in the face of the problematizing of
the terms: East and West. The struggle of Indian comparative literature theorists to
establish an Indian literary theory and history is instructive. Both the conservatives and
the moderns among them go back to Sanskrit aesthetic theory and seek to make it the
ground for the contemporary. The conservatives freeze the past and universalize its
literary categories. Terms such as *author, reader,* and *text* are not problematized. Homogenization is rife. References abound to "the Indian author/reader" and "the national
psyche." Aesthetic categories are absolutized. "Poetic beauty" transcends caste and class;
situations are essentially the same; a "congruent association of words, phrases and
images" ensures universal appeal. After Bharata and Abhinava Gupta (first century and
tenth and eleventh century A.D.) there can only be "a continuous development," "not
different contending theories but only stages of development." The violence that has
greeted plays and novels and short stories in the last decade alone must falsify such a
theory. The moderns, on the other hand, attempt a radical reading of the aesthetic categories but come up in the end with findings—the "suggestibility of the text," the "indeterminacy of meaning"—so like the Western theories as to make the whole project an
exercise in cultural arrogance or an example of cultural insecurity.[13]

It would be more profitable to consider why certain "Western" theories have appeal
at certain historical moments. In a period of transition, when tradition is at once valued

and contested, we need a theory that will problematize it. As women, we urgently need a theory that will help us understand our "fickleness" and valorize local struggles and small resistances. Given these needs, poststructuralist theory must necessarily appeal. As feminists, teaching English literature to Indian students and seeking to make it relevant, we need defamiliarization theory. This is not cultural cringing. We are suspicious of sexual difference theory because we fear that it may reinstall the old patriarchal stereotypes. We distance ourselves from a radical feminism that gives primacy to the body and to sexual freedom because we consider other problems to be more urgent: the right of women to work and to equal pay; the right not to be sexually harassed in the workplace; the right to an equitable distribution of domestic responsibilities. We notice that a radical feminism that prioritizes the body alienates many women and throws back the feminist struggle into the binary opposition of East and West.

Who's "we"? The subject produced by this conference's statement of purpose that describes feminism as Western in origin and universalist (read "Western"?) in theory?

But what is feminism? Any attempt to confine it within a semantic horizon is difficult at best.[14] If feminism is a consciousness, can an act be feminist if those who perform it are not conscious of that aspect of the act? A number of illiterate women got together in a village of Andhra Pradesh a couple of years ago to force the closing down of an *arrack* (liquor) bottling plant in order to ensure that their husbands came home on payday, pay packet intact. If feminism is a movement, what political meaning attaches to resistance within the home? The history of the hunger strike is instructive. Gandhi took it from Indian women. Martin Luther King, Jr. took it from Gandhi. Is feminism a theory? Women have theorized their experience in genres not counted as theory.

Proverbs and aphorisms are a genre that raises these basic questions of reading. They are described as representing the pith of experience. But whose experience? Oral texts cannot be tied down to an authorship. As utterances, they take their meaning from enunciative positions. As uttered by men, they construct a descriptive and normative reality. "A woman is a cipher; joined to the figure one, she is ten" (Bengal). "A woman is always on the road" (Kerala). "Women and cows need to be taken care of" (Uttar Pradesh). When uttered by women, they carry a different illocutionary and perlocutionary force, and they are often charged with a bitterness that signifies recognition of an oppressive practice and resistance to it. Declarative form and intent come together only in utterances from positions of power. Even a saint, if she is a woman, uses the interrogative form. A Bhakti woman saint from Karnataka asks in the fourteenth century, "When a man loves a woman she is his chattel; what, then, when a woman loves a man?"[15]

Interrogation has always been a favored pedagogic practice, East and West. A feminist pedagogy deploys and employs it—in the Socratic mode of simulated ignorance in order to lead, and as a radical practice in order to bewilder, to lead astray.

ACKNOWLEDGMENTS

I am grateful to Professor Joan Scott for the opportunity to attend the conference at which this volume originated and for the varied "experience" it has given me.

I am grateful to Professor Scott and her group of scholars at the Institute of Advanced Studies, Princeton, 1994–95, for their critique of my paper as it was presented to the conference, especially to Rosi Braidotti, Anna Tsing, Debra Keates, and Yakov Garb. I trust this essay will not embarrass them. Back home, Sharada Nair was always on call and generously forthcoming with discriminating comments and helpful suggestions; my grateful thanks. Saswati Sengupta made reading material available; sterling service to a retired academic.

To the British Library at Delhi and particularly to Naaz Dalal and Prema Subramaniam for unfailing library assistance over twenty-three years of pedagogical practice, belated but sincere acknowledgment. To the Nehru Memorial Museum and Library for reading facilities, thanks.

Owing to Shankar Pathak for all kinds of encouragement from fractious discussion to smooth domestic takeovers, a debt that cannot be written of/off.

NOTES

1. Sukumari Bhattarji, "Motherhood in Ancient India," *Economic and Political Weekly*, 42/43, p. 50.
2. Nivedita Menon and Saswati Sengupta, "Attending an Orientation Course," *Social Text* (1989).
3. K.K. Ruthven in Paula Treichler, "Teaching Feminist Theory," in Cary Nelson (ed.), *Theory in the Classroom* (Urbana and Chicago: University of Illinois, 1986), p. 88.
4. Richard Rorty, "Introduction," in S. Seidman and D. Wagner, (eds.), *Postmodernism and Social Theory* (London: Basil Blackwell, 1989), pp. 92–93.
5. Kurt Wolff, "Sociology?" in W. Outhwaite and M. Mulkay (eds.), *Social Theory and Social Criticism* (London: Basil Blackwell, 1989), p. 13.
6. Smita Mitra, Indaprastha College for Women, Delhi.
7. I am thankful to Dr. Anand Prakash, Hansraj College, Delhi for sharing his experiences with me.
8. Patricia Ingam, *Thomas Hardy*, Feminist Reading Series. (London and New York: Harvester Wheatsheaf, 1989), p. 68.
9. I thank Ramya Srinivasan, English teacher and civil rights activist, for a helpful discussion on the stand of the Peoples Union for Democratic Rights.
10. "Custodial Rape: A Report on the Aftermath," People's Union for Democratic Rights, New Delhi (December 1994), p. 14.
11. Peter Widdowson, "Postmodernising Tess," in Charles Pettit (ed.), *New Perspectives on Thomas Hardy* (MacMillan, St. Martin's Press, 1994), pp. 90–91.
12. Amiya Dev and Sisir Kumar Das (eds.), *Comparative Literature, Theory and Practice* (Delhi: Allied Publishers, 1988), have a section entitled "Literary Theory, Literary History, and Translation," containing essays in which these terms are used.
13. Susan Bassnett-Mcguire, *Translation Studies* (London and New York: Routledge, 1994), pp. 26–29.
14. Rosalind Delmar, "What Is Feminism?" in Juliet Mitchell and Ann Oakley (eds.), *What Is Feminism*, (Oxford: Basil Blackwell, 1986), chapter 1.
15. I am thankful to Shankar Pathak for this item.

< 25 >

Uneasy Transitions

Women's Studies in the European Union[1]

Rosi Braidotti

This paper is a reflection on the current state of the interaction between specialists in European women's studies and their North American colleagues. I will start by situating the women's studies debate within a larger context of transatlantic intellectual transactions, emphasizing two new factors: on the one hand, the role of the European Union, and on the other, the ongoing campaign against "political correctness" in contemporary American politics. After presenting as a case study a brief outline of cooperation in women's studies within the European Union, I will address more specifically the question of feminist multicultural practices and their function in contemporary exchanges between women's studies in the European Union and the United States.

The urgency I feel about these issues is due to the distance I perceive at this moment between American and European political climates in general and feminist debates in particular. As Michael Sprinker put it in his analysis of contemporary American politics, the neoconservatism and the right-wing backlash of the 1990s have undone the links that critical intellectuals in the United States had established with their European counterparts in the 1960s.[2] Cornel West shares this analysis and remarks that in the United States after McCarthyism, left-wing intellectuals turned to Europe to find a critical tradition and appropriated the Marxist theories of the day, thus inaugurating the phenomenon of "traveling theories" that was to have such an impact on later events.[3] Since then, the drift between Europe and the United States has grown so large that Cornel West now has called for a new alliance between different kinds of critical intellectuals.

Pursuing this analysis further, Jeffrey Williams points out that the rejection of the latest "traveling theories" imported into the United States from Europe, namely deconstruction and poststructuralism, is one of the main aspects of the "culture wars" currently being waged by the right in the United States.[4] In his analysis, what is at stake in this campaign of rejection of European-made theories is, first of all, a turn away from the 1960s legacy of civil rights, women's rights, and social welfare. Second, it marks a rejection of the 1960s flair for theory per se in favor of a generalized appeal to pragmatism, often expressed in terms of "realism." The latter is an expression of the general anti-intellectualism that is dominant in the 1990s. What is at stake in these media campaigns is the future of liberal education as a whole, and of progressive social thinkers. The campaign against "political correctness" plays a central role in this conservative onslaught, which is especially aimed at women's and black studies and other progressive educational programs.

What emerges from these analyses is a situation in which the areas that are especially targeted for termination in the new Right-wing political climate in the United States are the "Gang of Four," constituted by feminists, Marxists, multiculturalists, and cultural theorists, all of whom are accused of betraying the national cultural heritage, because theirs are "traveling theories" coming from Europe and more especially from French poststructuralist philosophy and deconstruction. This reading of European thought by the American conservatives in turn situates women's studies courses at the heart of a backlash the effects of which—I will argue—are felt on both sides of the Atlantic. It is because I am extremely worried about the terms in which this debate is being constructed and more specifically about the misconstruction of European women's studies within this debate, that I am writing this essay.

One of the reasons why this misconstruction is so effective has to do with the American media's misinformation about the range of cultural and political effects of the European Union. Adopting a catastrophe-prone style of reporting about European affairs, the U.S. press has not sufficiently covered the course of events linked to European unification and more especially their effects on education and culture. I think that, as a consequence of this lack of updated information, real divergences have emerged on the two sides of the Atlantic between their respective understandings, definitions and expectations about "Europe," as evidenced by the increasing use of the adjective *Eurocentric* as a pejorative term in both general and feminist debates in the United States. Rather than giving in to easy polemics, I wish to stress the need to problematize and to historicize the question of what, if anything, constitutes European—as opposed to American—identity at this particular moment of our respective and collective histories.

I would like to raise this question because I do not see the grounds for identities of any sort as fixed, God-given, or essential foundations—be it of the biological, psychic, or historical kinds of essentialism. On the contrary, I see them as being constructed in the very gesture that posits them as the anchoring point for certain kinds of social and discursive practices. Consequently, the question I would like to put on the table in terms of European or American cultural identity is not the essentialist one—What is it?—but rather the critical genealogical one, namely, How is it constructed? By Whom? Under which conditions? For which aims and for whose profit? The political issue at stake is: Who is entitled to claim this legacy, speak on its behalf, and turn it into a policy-making tool?

There is also another added factor, however, which has to do with feminist politics. Feminism has based its political and discursive practices on the notion of "the politics of location." This term, inaugurated by Adrienne Rich, stresses the need for feminists to think of and devise political practice from a lucid analysis of their specific spatiotemporal locations.[5] It results in embodied and embedded perspectives, which aim at making one accountable for one's inscription in a set of power relations, in opposition to abstract and falsely universalistic practices. Feminists inspired by Foucault have enlarged this practice in terms of "technologies of the self" and also as "microphysics of power"; others prefer to analyze them in terms of differences of class, race, age, sexual preference, and other structural variables that result in what Donna Haraway calls "situated knowledges."[6] In all these cases, and more forcefully in poststructuralist feminism, "situated" practices have become a central criterion in feminist knowledge claims.[7]

Not only is the situated approach an important contribution to the analysis of theoretical and political practice after the decline of Marxism, but it also translates into simpler ideas—for instance, that in intellectual debates a little less abstraction would be welcome indeed.

All of this is of the greatest importance in situating the debate about European women's studies within the framework of the European Union. To explain this, I need to go briefly into what I would define as the paradox of European identity.

Following the insight of poststructuralist feminism, I would suggest that Europeans, i.e., people who have been situated in this particular geopolitical location for some time and identify with and feel accountable for its history, are not very gifted in the art of situated knowledges. Quite on the contrary, Europeans have perfected a trick that consists of turning themselves into the center of the universe. The corollary of this obsession with being at the center is that, in the European mind-set, one's location acquires the greatest abstraction, while the rest of the world becomes one huge periphery. Neither the political left nor the feminist movement is an exception. How much time and energy has been spent speculating about, for instance, the terrible status of women in other lands and other cultures, as if the status quo in the here and now of European daily practice were so incredibly perfect? Yet women of color, such as Chandra Mohanty, have warned us very strongly against the ethnocentric habit that consists of constructing the "third world woman" as an object of oppression that requires support or "solidarity."[8] It is against this flight into universalistic abstraction that feminists have proposed situated perspectives and applied the politics of location.

What I would like to suggest next is that the project of the European Union has a lot to do with the rejection of the disembedded and disembodied ways of thinking that European culture has perfected. Far from being the triumphant assumption of a sovereign identity, being a European in the sense of the European Union is the sobering experience of taking stock of this specific geopolitical and historical location and finally putting to rest the universalistic pretensions that historically have made Europe into the site of nationalism, colonialism, and fascism. In other words, I would like to suggest that the European Union is about accountability and situated perspectives, which is the opposite of ethnocentrism.

Daniel Cohn-Bendit, former leader of the May 1968 student movement in Paris and now a Euro-Parliament member especially active in the field of antiracism, recently stated that if Europeans want to make their unification work, they really must start from the assumption that Europe is indeed the place where they live and that they must take responsibility for it.[9] Claiming anything else would be a repetition of that flight into abstraction for which European culture is (in)famous: at best, it may procure them the benefits of escapism; at worst, the luxury of guilt. It is important to start from where one is at.

What I mean is that postmodernity as a specific historical location requires that intellectuals think through the simultaneity of potentially contradictory effects. Facing up to these contradictions is the historical responsibility of early twenty-first century transatlantic thinkers who are committed to thinking alongside their world and not to pretending that it does not exist or hoping that maybe it will go away and leave them alone in the contemplation of their Olympian thoughts. One of the significant elements of this historicity that I would like to emphasize is that the entire project of the European Union rests on the premise of the historical decline of the European nation-states. At the end of the Second World War, as Adenauer, de Gasperi, and de Gaulle laid the foundation of the European Union, they were attempting not only to reconstruct the European economy, with hefty support from the United States, but also to prevent more intra-European "world" wars.

Which is not to deny that the single most important purpose of the EU has been economic, but rather that its economic program has been devised as a response to a situation—the transnational economy—that has spelled the death of nation-states as principles of economic organization. Just consider the simple fact that the fastest-growing economies in the world today are not Western; they lie instead quite away from the historically sanctified binary relationship United States–Europe, in Asia and the Pacific Rim.

This results in a process that Cornel West calls "the decentering of Europe," that is to say, its economic and social decline, which can only be understood in terms of the emergence of postcolonial subjects. One immediate effect of the global economy for Europe is the multicultural mix that has occurred in the last thirty years. In turn, this has laid to rest another important cultural myth: namely that European culture is homogeneous, that is to say, invariably white and predominantly Christian. Of course, when one looks at European societies at any one point in time, one will find abundant evidence to the contrary: Successive waves of migrations from the East and the South make mockery of any claim to ethnic or cultural homogeneity, while the persistent presence of Jewish and, more recently, Muslim citizens challenges the priority of Christianity. Nonetheless, the myth of cultural homogeneity has been, and remains, crucial to the making of European nationalism.

Postmodernity explodes all these myths and calls for the kind of political intervention that takes into account transnational economic factors and the evident historical decline of national bases as a principle of organization not only of the economy and of organized politics, but also of political opposition.

In this context, the project of the European Union is an attempt at a response to the decline of European nation-states. The project developed from the ruins of postwar Europe as a bastion against Soviet-style Communism and turned into a positive solution to the never-ending problems of European nationalism. The EU carries with it the seeds of antinationalism, and as such it spreads beyond the economic dimension to encompass culture and education as well. Significantly, however, the integration of these areas was much slower and met with more resistance than the economic realm, because it challenges more directly European identity and is therefore more "difficult" and potentially more divisive. As Stuart Hall put it, the great resistance against European union, as well as the American suspicion of it, is a defensive response to a process of effectively dismantling European nation-states.[10] The short-range effect of this within Europe is to unleash cultural and political nostalgia, in a wave of nationalistic paranoia and xenophobic fears, which is the form taken by contemporary European cultural racism.

Just how difficult the process of European cultural integration is can be demonstrated by some elements of contemporary politics, such as the paralysis into which the European political left seems to have sunk, unable to renew its role in the age of the global economy. This results in some significant paradoxes: on the Continent the opposition to the European Union is led, on the one hand, by the authoritarian right, especially Jean-Marie Le Pen and his cronies, and, on the other hand, by the nostalgic left, which seems to miss terribly the topological foundations for working-class solidarity. The "internationalist" tradition of the organized left is of no assistance at the time of the transnational economy. Speaking as a left-wing intellectual, I must say that the political left is as unable as most other political forces at the moment to react with energy and vision to the historical evidence that is the increasing irrelevance of Eurocentric modes of practice and thought to today's world. The left's traditional empathy with the Third World and especially with Third-World socialism reproduces— albeit unwillingly—the center-periphery relationship and seems unable to subvert it. In such a context, more lucidity is needed along with a renewed sense of political strategy, both of which would profit immensely from feminist insights and practice.[11]

In conclusion, "European identity" today is a contested zone, where issues of entitlement and access, of exclusion and participation, are crucial. "Europe" today means a site of possible political resistance against nationalism, xenophobia, and racism, which accompany the process of European unification.[12]

To return to the question of "traveling theories," I would like to add that the main thinkers of the poststructuralist generation—the very same authors whom the Right uses in its attacks on liberal education in the United States, especially Deleuze, Lyotard, Derrida, Kristeva, and Cixous—argue quite firmly that postmodernity has to do with the shift of geopolitical power away from the North Atlantic. In their philosophical standpoint, this shift gets theorized in terms of the decline of Eurocentered systems of thought, which is often rendered through the death metaphor: "the decline of Western humanism."

They all tend to point out one interesting fact about this shift of geopolitical power relations that makes their discourse about the end of Western European hegemony radically different from the fascist and right-wing nostalgic discourse about the "decline of the West" at the beginning of this century: namely that what makes the Western philosophical culture so perniciously effective is that it has been announcing its own death for over a hundred years.[13] Since the apocalyptic trinity of modernity—Marx, Nietzsche, and Freud—the West has been thinking through the historical inevitability and the logical possibility of its own decline, so much so that the state of "crisis" has become the modus vivendi of Western philosophers: They thrive on it and write endlessly about it, to the point that if the crisis did not exist, they would have to invent it in order to justify their existence.

In her analysis of the Paul de Man case, Barbara Johnson comments lucidly on this paradox, which in some way captures the complexity of poststructuralist philosophy as a whole.[14] It is the paradox of a philosophical thought that serenely contemplates the necessity of its own death, apparently subverting its own foundations, while at the same time turning this non-foundationalist gesture into the very raison d'être for Western philosophy. Simultaneously undermining and underscoring his authority in a mode of ironical self-reflection which is also and without possible contradiction narcissistic self-deprecation, the Western philosopher turns this paradox into a quasi-universal posture.

Reread in a poststructuralist frame, this paradox results in the glorification of the aporic and its edification into a dominant mode of discourse that itemizes the "death of the subject" as the central concern.[15] Consequently, I think nobody, let alone critical thinkers, should take the notion of the "crisis" of the West naively or at face value. This state of prolonged and self-agonizing crisis may simply be the form Western post-modernity has chosen to perpetuate itself.

Gayatri Spivak makes the point succintly when she argues that

> given the international division of labor of the imperialist countries, it is quite appropriate that the best critique of the European ethico-politico-social universals, those regulative concepts, should come from the North Atlantic. But what is ironically appropriate in postcoloniality is that this critique finds its best staging outside of the North Atlantic in the undoing of imperialism.[16]

Spivak then goes on to argue that there are forces at work in the North Atlantic region that aim at rewriting universalism as "solidarity," thus reasserting the historical advantage of the center of the empire, in spite of evident signs of economic and cultural decline.[17]

In confronting these complexities, feminists and critical intellectuals are bound to come up with different accounts, which are contingent upon different locations. Confronted with the inevitable diversity of positions and genealogies, instead of panicking or fearing relativism it would be better to turn differences into objects of discursive exchange. Differences should not be homogenized into a falsely unified and self-congratulatory understanding of either European or American identity. In other words—to paraphrase Foucault—attention must be paid to the paradox of exclusion and affirmation, of power and truth, which lies at the heart of the quest for identity, especially in the European context and in issues related to the great transatlantic disconnection.[18]

EUROPEAN WOMEN'S STUDIES

The issues raised above weigh rather heavily upon contemporary exchanges in women's studies across the Atlantic and contribute to the lack of information that I have already denounced. In this section, I will provide a counterreading of European feminist practice, based on the experience of inter-university European cooperation in this field. I hope both to expose the inadequacy of the way in which European feminism is constructed in ongoing American political debates and also to provide alternative information aimed at highlighting the positive role played by the European Union in the development of women's studies.

Women's studies developed across Europe in a manner that is both similar and strikingly different from the North American model, following the variety of academic and cultural traditions in the different countries. Although the need to set up women's studies programs emerged from grassroots and students' demand in the 1970s, this field developed into more than the academic wing of the women's movement. As a whole, it grew into a dynamic field of study that aims at the transformation of education and university curricula in such a way as to reflect and further the social changes in the status of women. This diversity does complicate the issue of European cooperation, because it means that women from countries with strong, institutionalized women's studies programs work together with women from universities where women's studies still has a marginal position. Experience shows that it is both possible and desirable to learn from each other.

European cooperation in women's studies involves women and men from diverse national, cultural, and disciplinary backgrounds; speaking different languages; having different expectations about university education; and working with a variety of intellectual and political perspectives. Surveying the programs in this subject area, one cannot help being impressed by the quality and quantity of the work done by teachers and students despite, or maybe because of, these differences.

The discussion as to what a distinctly European perspective on women's studies could be has been at the center of many of these debates. Only Northern European universities have opted for visible and autonomous programs and departments, for both teaching and research purposes. This is due, on the one hand, to the absence in Europe of anything comparable to the private foundations that have played such an important role in the development of women's studies in the United States.[19] On the other hand, it is also related to the enormous influence of the conventional disciplines and of disciplinary distinctions in the European university system, which is traditionally resistant to interdisciplinarity. Countries in southern Europe have been both culturally and intellectually more resistant to assimilating North American methods and teaching material. Considering the structure of universities in these countries, the question of the creation of specific institutional positions for women's studies has also proved quite controversial. In France, Italy, or Spain there are practically no specific women's studies positions, though first-class work on women's studies is done by academics in positions that are "integrated" in existing departments, and also by feminist groups outside the institutions.

Thus the vast majority of women's studies programs on the Continent are of the "integrated" rather than the "autonomous" kind. What they tend to be integrated into is often departments of American literature or American studies, especially in Southern and Eastern European countries. This results in the paradoxical situation of disembedding these programs from their immediate national context, which in turn means that, for instance in the humanities, the programs that cater to national literatures or cultures simply ignore the feminist input, all too happy to delegate it to the reassuring foreignness of the Americans. Although the situation is better in the social sciences, this pattern of development remains both widespread and problematic.

In an attempt to respect the variety of institutional settings and feminist cultural traditions, the European Inter-University Network of Women's Studies in the EU works at the moment with a rather open definition of women's studies. A sort of consensus has emerged that what is needed in Europe is a coalition between three areas of teaching and research: women's studies, feminist studies, and gender studies.

The different names express different political and epistemological positions; relying on Sandra Harding's system of classification,[20] I would say that "women's studies" relies on "standpoint feminism," privileging the view from below in acccordance with materialist epistemology. It also rests on an unproblematized notion of women's "experience" as the foundation for feminist knowledge claims. It is by far the most widespread epistemological and institutional structure across the European Union.

"Gender studies" is a compromise term, borrowed from English-language discussions about the social construction between the sexes. More scientific-sounding than its alternatives, gender studies enjoys institutional support, especially in Eastern Europe, where it fulfills the more radical function of setting sexual politics on the academic agenda.

Not surprisingly, "feminist studies" is the least represented position, which tends to gravitate around postmodern theories and deconstruction and work on the critique of identity with a rather radical feminist agenda. By comparison to the United States, this position is absolutely a minority one in European Union women's studies.

In spite of their different names, they all challenge male domination of the academic disciplines, and they all provide methodological and theoretical tools to study the visible and invisible power mechanisms that influence women's access to responsibility in social, economic, political, intellectual, and cultural life. They all aim at revealing the full reality of women's lives, which has been hidden because men were the predominant subjects and objects of knowledge. They all attempt to improve the position of women in society.[21]

Women's studies is a field of scientific and pedagogic activity devoted to improving the status of women and to finding forms of representation of women's experiences that are dignified and empowering and which faithfully reflect the range of women's contributions to cultural, economic, social, and scientific development. Women's studies is a critical project insofar as it examines how science perpetuates forms of discrimination and even of exclusion, but it is also a creative field in that it opens up alternative spaces to women's self-representation and intellectual self-determination.

Because of the diversity of cultures and political traditions involved, the experience of setting up women's studies in a European perspective has proved to be a delicate exercise in cross-cultural analysis and comparison.[22] One thing that is already clear to all concerned is that the idea of "Europe" that feminists have in mind is far more critical of ethnocentrism and nationalism than the official guidelines from the European Commission would suggest. Most European feminists have taken their distance from the legacy of European nationalism and are deeply concerned by the rebirth of xenophobia, racism, and anti-Semitism on the Continent. Moreover, without turning their back on our historical heritage, many have also voiced pertinent criticism of the increasing isolationism and protectionism fostered by the idea of a "United" Europe.[23]

In fact, it is important to stress that although, as citizens of the EU, feminists do their best to participate in the creation of a shared cultural space that may contribute to lessening intra-European infighting and economic competition, they are also perfectly well aware of the limitations and the dangers of a unified Europe. More specifically, feminists are worried about European racism and ethnocentrism and the exclusionary policies that are currently standard practice in European immigration and asylum laws, and which are becoming ever more restrictive. In this respect, a multicultural, antiracist approach to the making of European women's studies seems essential at this difficult moment of European history. This is one of the points where European women's studies has a lot to learn from the United States, whose reflection on race and ethnicity is much more advanced.

The aim of European multicultural feminists is that these concerns can be put to the task of contributing actively to the construction of a genuine European community spirit, where sexism, racism, and other forms of exclusion will be targeted for elimination. As Helma Lutz put it, the EU today needs to put an end to the specific European habit that consists in self-edification into an ethnocentric center.[24] Lutz explores especially the condition of immigrants in the EU today as a significant case of peripheral existence within the alleged center of this community. In other words, women's studies is not only education for women, it is the reeducation of a whole culture, to help it move away from discriminatory practices, so that it can give the best of itself to the development of a renewed sense of a common European house.[25]

Whether integrated or autonomous, however, most women's studies departments in Europe share some common features. First, they all depend to a very large degree on under- or unpaid female academic labor: Subsidies for the setting up of women's studies curricula are uneven and insufficient at the best of times. If there is one point of consensus, therefore, it is the need for more resources at all levels.

Secondly, most of these programs are heavily dependent on teaching material and manuals produced in the United States or written in English. There is an enormous lack of introductory material written from a local European perspective and drawing on local feminist viewpoints and traditions,[26] especially in Southern and Eastern Europe. In cases when such material exists, it is written in languages that are not accessible to an international audience and often presents huge translation problems and translation costs. Although new initiatives, such as *Nora: The Nordic Women's Studies Journal* and *The European Journal of Women's Studies* are great steps forward, the situation remains critical. On the Continent at the moment there is not one publisher, nor even a coalition of publishers, who are willing or have the capacity to monitor and develop the feminist intellectual production in a trans-European manner.[27] All this simply increases the collective dependence on American material and publications.

Noting in fact that both the terminology and most of the existing teaching material in this field is of North American origin and consequently is available only in English, European women's studies scholars have been faced with a double task. On the one hand, they have had to struggle to get this new field of study accepted in their respective countries and institutions; on the other hand, they have had to develop their own instruments for teaching and research. I have often mentioned the specific difficulties associated with the translation of the term *gender,* as well as the distinction between *sex* and *gender,* into most Romance, Nordic, and other European languages.[28] Having become a compulsory term of reference in international feminist discussions, *gender* nonetheless plays nowadays a crucial role as a "traveling theory," i.e., an object of discursive exchange and of multiple (mis)translations across many feminist cultures worldwide, which is best discussed in a historicized and embedded manner.

In this context, the support that women's studies academics have been able to gather from the Commission of the European Union has been and remains crucial. Whereas countries in which this field is underdeveloped have benefited from both the financial and moral support of the European Union, well-endowed programs in other countries have experienced European Union support as a form of international recognition and therefore of scientific legitimation. In both cases, the impact of the Commission's stamp of approval is enormous.

One should note, as a point of introduction, that the Maastricht treaty places great emphasis on the need to coordinate a Europe-wide system of education, to train a highly flexible but extremely educated workforce, and to set up a system of qualifications that would be recognized across the borders of the EU. The main aim of the "European dimension in education" is to bring the member states to implement comparable standards of training and thus help reduce unemployment. A related aim, however, which is sanctioned by the Charter of Workers' Rights and upheld by the European Trade Unions' Council, is to defend the principle of social security and help combat exclusion so as to sponsor an equitable idea of European citizenship.[29] It should come as no surprise, therefore, that a great deal of the European cooperation programs in this field are supported by the Commission of the European Union in Brussels.

First and foremost among these exchange programs are the interuniversity exchanges, a scheme—called Erasmus—set up by the commission in order to promote student and staff mobility and cooperation between higher education institutions within the member states of the EU. The scheme was extended from 1987 to 1995 and is being continued under the new scheme—called Socrates—of the commission.[30] All the interuniversity exchanges were extended in 1992 to include members of the European Free Trade Association (EFTA) countries, that is to say, Austria (which, however, joined the European Union on January 1, 1995), Finland, Iceland, Liechtenstein, Norway, Sweden, and Switzerland.

These exchanges allow students to follow courses in women's studies at the host university, to work on the preparation of their thesis, or to do practicals. Acquiring cross-cultural experience on the academic level as well as on the personal level was one of the main programmatic goals for students. The students receive funds for travel and living expenses and are granted academic recognition at the home university for the work they do abroad.

The largest of these networks—NOI♀SE[31]—decided to intensify its efforts to develop a common European program of study to develop a joint curriculum in interdisciplinary and multicultural women's studies for all the partner universities of this network.[32] This curriculum is currently being taught as a summer school. The central topic of the proposed European multicultural curriculum is the intersection of race, ethnicity, and gender and the issue of ethnic specificity and cultural differences. This reflects the concern for cultural diversity, antiracism, and a multicultural perspective, which are central to understanding the field of women's studies in Europe.

Emphasis is placed on practical, political issues of curriculum development, such as outlining how each feminist academic tries to integrate the ethnicity issue in her work and how "white" and "black" women's, organizations can cooperate, or how second generation immigrant women feel about feminist values and ideas. It is meant to raise the consciousness of the many Erasmus students and teachers, to make them aware of the problems with, and possible obstacles, to "pan-European feminism." The participant will be confronted with the multiple faces of Europe in the process of unification.

The feeling is strong among European women's studies academics that this field can only be genuinely "European" if it addresses rigorously issues of ethnic identity, multiculturalism, and antiracism. The issues of cultural and gender identity are intimately interlinked and cannot be easily separated. I would even like to go so far as to suggest that no perspective in women's studies can be considered truly "European" unless it addresses the need to produce non-exclusionary and non-ethnocentric models of knowledge and education. The fostering of a European consciousness can only profit from the enlarged definition of knowledge, which women's studies implies and enacts.

In this respect, many women's studies scholars feel very strongly that they need to strengthen and broaden the antiracist European dimension of their work. More international exchanges are needed in order to develop an in-depth understanding of the cultural diversity of women's studies traditions and practices in the European community today. Moreover, for this work toward a common and yet diversified definition to succeed, discussions are needed in a comparative framework with women from the EFTA countries, from Eastern and Central Europe, from the United States, and from Asia and Africa. On the issue of multiculturalism and the intersection of gender with ethnicity, an attempt has been made to establish institutional contacts with U.S. universities within a newly established scheme of transatlantic exchanges.[33]

FOR MULTIPLE MULTICULTURALISMS

In this concluding section, I would like to return to the complexities of the ways in which terms such as *eurocentrism* and *multiculturalism* are currently being used as objects of discursive exchange between the United States and Europe.

First of all, one needs to take note of the impact of "traveling theories." Cornel West argues that when U.S. intellectuals in quest of a critical tradition turned to Europe, they not only appropriated, but also invented, the phenomenon of "traveling theories" at a time when postwar Europe "was trying to understand its decline in terms of difference as it had been decentered by the colonized peoples."[34] This coincidence between postcolonialism and poststructuralist philosophies is precisely one of the reasons why West approves of poststructuralism. He argues that the advantage of deconstruction is that it can provide new openings, but the risk is one of extreme skepticism and a difficulty in seeing the interrelatedness of different forms of power. The undeniable convergence between the discourse of the "crisis" of the West within poststructuralism and the postcolonial deconstruction of imperial whiteness is not sufficient—though it is a necessary condition—for a political alliance between them. At the very least, it lays the grounds for the possibility of such an alliance.

Secondly, as I argued earlier, in a context of political conservatism in the United States, the campaign against feminism is often disguised as generalized anti-intellectualism; the latter is attributed, in the right-wing anti-political-correctness attacks, to European brands of feminism, especially French. There seems to be a general wisdom among most feminists in the United States that Continental feminist practices, symbolized by "French feminist theories" and "the French postmodern stuff," have done a great deal to alienate the more pragmatic-minded American feminists from their "theoretically sophisticated" European counterparts. This has resulted in a backlash against these theories in the United States and the consequent dismissal of the whole of European feminism.

To complicate matters even further, one must keep in mind that the European non-feminist press tends to believe the American sources quite literally. This means that most newspaper reports throughout Europe cover the phenomenon of political correctness known as "P.C."—as if it were an authentic manifestation of some perverse turn in American feminism. As a matter of fact, nothing could be further from the truth, given that, as Barbara Johnson put it,

> political correctness is the name chosen by critics of multiculturalism to attack the ways in which the movement to eliminate racism, sexism, and xenophobia has attempted to implement the right to equal access to education.[35]

A great deal of this discussion seems to be predicated not so much on an attentive reading of the structures and the agenda of European women's studies, but rather on a side issue, namely the politics of postmodernism in the American academy. The first wave of feminist "traveling theories," which exported to the United States postmodernism, deconstruction, and sexual difference in the seventies, met in fact with an institutional practice of academic co-optation that often purged them of their radical politics. Cornel West is not the only one who stresses the importance of assessing the American reception of deconstruction, which has become associated with an ahistorical and depoliticized formalism in which every text can be turned against itself, undermining its own foundations and thus precipitating itself into a vacuous rhetoric.

In fact, the American reception of these "traveling theories" failed to question the aims of this appropriation. This silence causes great problems. In Europe, postmodernism was perceived to be an answer to the decline of modernism, Marxism, and post-Marxist ideology, and it represented an attempt to redefine leftist politics, or, as Frederic Jameson put it, a chance for the left to reinvent itself. In attempting to explain the form taken by the American reception of these European theories, one important element has to be the fear of the political impact of deconstruction. Butler and Scott speak explicitly of the fear of loss of cognitive mastery as one of the central factors in the right's campaign against radical theories, exemplified by deconstruction.[36] This highlights the extent to which these campaigns are merely the expression of cultural privileges and vested interests that poststructuralism attempts to debunk in the ironical mode I already commented on.

Moreover, it is well known that the leading figures of European postmodernism shun this term, yet in the United States find themselves exemplars of it. One also needs to keep in mind that the critiques proposed by Deleuze, Derrida, and others, which may appear as dominant from an American academic perspective, are far from being so from a European standpoint. These theories have always been perceived as politically radical and have met with a great deal of oppositon as a consequence. Last but not least, let us add to this that the theoretical opposition to these thinkers also translates into institutional opposition: Neither Derrida nor Irigaray, nor any of the leading figures of this theoretical generation, achieved his desired institutional success.[37] The same thinkers who are perceived as cult figures in the American context are rather marginal to European institutional and academic life. They are even more so—much to my regret, I should add—to women's studies programs in the European Union.

I would like to suggest that all the above needs to be analyzed in terms of a commodification of feminist intellectuals, especially in the academy: a convenient division of labor that predates the postmodernism debate. I do think that a serious case of dissonance has emerged between Europe and the United States on the issue of the political utility of poststructuralism and deconstruction, and especially of their feminist theories.

Moreover, as Cornel West put it, to set up a meaningful conversation between multicuturalism and Eurocentrism, monolithic definitions of either must be rejected so as to do justice to historicized and embedded genealogies. The question then becomes:

> What do we mean by Eurocentrism? Which particular European nation do you have in mind? Which classes of Europeans do you have in mind?[38]

And again, even more forcefully:

> If one is talking about critiques of racism, critiques of patriarchy, critiques of homophobia, then simply call it that. Eurocentrism is not identical with racism. So, you deny the John Browns of the world. You deny the anti-racist movement in the heart of Europe. Eurocentrism is not the same as male supremacists. Why? Because every culture we know has been patriarchal in such an ugly way and that you deny the anti-patriarchal movements in the heart of Europe. And the same is so with homophobia. *Demystify the categories in order to stay tuned to the complexity of the realities.*[39]

Cornel West's call for demystification and subtlety can be taken as a plea for what Joan Scott has defended in terms of "the practice of theory," defined as reading critically

> the categories that organize and explain our existence, but figuring out how they work to produce their effects. This figuring out is done by readings that map relations of power and the operations of knowledge and difference that sustain them.[40]

In other words, what I would like to expose is the construction of European feminist theories, in a neo-Eurocentric manner, within a broader scheme of commodification of

European thought by the American academy. Speaking as an eyewitness to the marketing of French theories by Americans and as someone who has been critical of the commodification of French feminism from the very start, I feel entitled to restate my case.[41] I have to agree with Cornel West that a distinction has to be made between the American construction of a commodified rendition of European theories as a gesture that reproduces colonial European hegemony and the actual decentering of Europe that these same theories are actually proposing when read in an embedded contemporary European location. To judge, one simply has to take a look at a survey of European women's studies courses and at the programs of European cooperation in women's studies.

As a whole, European women's studies programs do not suffer from the same hiatus between theory and practice as their American counterparts. Moreover this divorce between theory and practice increases the communication problems between American and European women's studies communities. These problems become especially difficult on issues related to multiculturalism, race, and ethnicity, where the Eurocentric legacy in the United States projects a negative shadow upon possible cooperation with feminists who happen to be nonethnocentric Europeans. Speaking as someone who is both a postmodernist feminist theorist, a women's studies professor, and a critic of ethnocentrism, I would want to critique most strongly this set of mutual misconstructions and plead for more respect of the complexities involved.

In conclusion, I would also like to propose that the time is ripe for a transverse alliance along the women's studies front, across the United States/Europe divide. The question is how European feminists' deconstruction of their Eurocentric tradition from a situated and accountable perspective can be a point of theoretical and political alliance with U.S. feminists. Among other things, it could help unmask the commodification of "traveling theories" from Europe in American academic circles. This commodification results in, among other things, a disembedding of the European theorists and gives them a universal pretension that clashes with their explicit political commitment to decentering Europe. It also feeds into the "culture wars" raging in the United States right now, which are targeting women's studies for termination.[42] In this respect, the project of confronting multiple and diverse forms of multiculturalism, in the quest for diversity, could achieve the aim of both demystification and a flair for the complexity due to respective locations.

NOTES

1. I am very indebted to the 1994–95 members of the School of Social Science at the Institute for Advanced Study in Princeton, especially Evelynn Hammonds and Anna Tsing. Special thanks are also due to Joan Scott for her unfailing support and shrewd criticism. In Utrecht, Gloria Wekker's and Anneke Smelik's criticism of earlier drafts proved crucial.
2. Michael Sprinker, "The War Against Theory," in Jeffrey Williams (ed.), *PC Wars: Politics and Theory in the Academy* (New York: Routledge, 1995), pp. 149–71; the citation is on p. 156.

3. Cornel West, *Prophetic Thought in Postmodern Times* (Monroe, ME: Common Courage Press, 1994).

4. Jeffrey Williams, "Introduction," in Jeffrey Williams (ed.), *PC Wars: Politics and Theory in the Academy* (New York: Routledge, 1995), pp. 1–10.

5. Adrienne Rich, "The Politics of Location," in *Bread, Blood and Poetry* (London: Virago, 1987).

6. Donna Haraway, "Situated Knowledges," in *Simians, Cyborgs, and Women* (London: Free Association Books, 1990).

7. For an impressive historical overview of the notion of "politics of location," see Karen Caplan and Inderpal Grewal, *Scattered Hegemonies* (Minneapolis: University of Minnesota Press, 1994).

8. Chandra Mohanty, "Under Western Eyes: Feminist Scholarship and Colonial Discourse," *Boundary* 23 (1984) pp. 333–58.

9. Daniel Cohn-Bendit, "Transit discussion," *Newsletter of the Institute for Human Sciences* 50 (June–August 1995), pp. 1–4.

10. Stuart Hall, "'Race,' Ethnicity, Nation: The Fateful/Fatal Triangle," the W.E.B. Du Bois Lectures, Harvard University, April 25–27, 1994.

11. As argued by Anthony Giddens in *Beyond Left and Right: The Future of Radical Politics* (Cambridge: Polity Press, 1994).

12. Rosi Braidotti and Judith Butler, "Feminism by Any Other Name," *differences*, (summer-fall 1994), pp. 27–61.

13. See especially Massimo Cacciari, *Geo-filosofia dell'Europa* (Milan: Adelphi, 1994).

14. Barbara Johnson, "Double Mourning and the Public Sphere," in *The Wake of Deconstruction* (Cambridge: Blackwell's, 1994).

15. Rosi Braidotti, *Patterns of Dissonance*, (New York: Routledge, 1991).

16. Gayatri Spivak, "French Feminism Revisited: Ethics and Politics," in Judith Butler and Joan Scott (eds.), *Feminists Theorize the Political* (New York: Routledge, 1992), p. 57.

17. This remark is explicitly aimed at Richard Rorty's notion of "solidarity."

18. I am borrowing this expression from Domna Stanton, "Language and Revolution: The Franco-American Dis-Connection," in Hester Eisenstein and Alice Jardine (eds.), *The Future of Difference* (Boston: G.K. Hall, 1980), pp. 73–87.

19. Special praise must be given to the Ford Foundation, whose activities are exemplary. Of special importance are the reports that Ford publishes regularly about women's studies, for example Catharine Stimpson, *Women's Studies in the United States* (1986), and Beverly Guy-Sheftall, *Women's Studies. A Retrospective* (1995).

20. I am relying here on the classification of feminist epistemology provided by Sandra Harding in, for instance, *Whose Science, Whose Knowledge* (Milton Keynes: Open University Press, 1991).

21. For this definition I am indebted to Jalna Hanmer et al.: *Women's Studies and European Integration. Report to the Equal Opportunities Unit, DGV, European Commission*, April 1994.

22. For a detailed account of the experience attempted in Utrecht, please see the special issue "Women's Studies at the University of Utrecht," of *Women's Studies International Forum* 16, no. 4 (1993), edited by Rosi Braidotti. See also the special issue "Women's Studies in Europe," *Women's Studies Quarterly* 20, nos. 3 and 4 (1992), edited by Angelika Köster-Lossack and Tobe Levin.

23. See in this respect, R. Braidotti and C. Franken, "United States of Europe or United Colours of Benetton?," *differences* 2, no. 3 (1990), pp. 109–21.

24. Helma Lutz, "Obstacles to Equal Opportunities in Society by Immigrant Women, with Particular Reference to the Netherlands, the United Kingdom, Germany, and the Nordic

Countries," paper presented at the meeting of the Joint Specialist Group on Migration, Cultural Diversity and Equality of Women and Men, Strasbourg, October 1994.

25. See also the very important report *Confronting the Fortress: Black and Migrant Women in the European Community*, a report to the European Women's Lobby, produced by the European Forum of Left Feminists and Others, September 1993.

26. A notable exception is the excellent volume edited by R. Buikema and A. Smelik, *Women's Studies in Culture. A Feminist Introduction* (London: Zed Books, 1995; Amsterdam, Coutinho, 1994).

27. Special schemes devoted to the development of cultural programs with the former Soviet-block countries have been available at the Commission of the European community for years, especially the Tempus program. They have not shown, however, a great deal of support for feminist issues and concerns. In an attempt to improve the situation, the Council of Europe (located in Strasbourg) set up the European Network for Women's Studies, which was also heavily subsidized by the Dutch government. ENWS did extremely important work in developing ties to higher education institutions in Eastern Europe. Of special relevance is the report of the workshop "Establishing Gender Studies in Central and Eastern European Countries," held in Wassenaar, the Netherlands, in November 1992; the report was published by the Council of Europe.

28. See, for instance, the chapter "Theories of gender, or: 'Language is a Virus,'" in Rosi Braidotti, *Nomadic Subjects* (New York: Columbia University Press, 1995).

29. For an interesting summary of the EU policy on this matter, see Donald MacLeod, "Learning to be Europeans," *The Guardian Weekly*, October 23, 1994, p. 22.

30. As coordinator of the NOI♀SE Network and with the assistance of Christine Rammrath and Ellen de Dreu, I chaired the Area Evaluation of Women's Studies in Europe for the Education Division of the Commission (DGXXII) in the academic year 1994–95. This evaluation officially concluded the Erasmus phase, with a detailed analysis of achievements and shortcomings of each Erasmus network, a detailed national report from each member country of the European Union, and a concluding conference held at the University of Coimbra, Portugal, in June 1995. After such a positive evaluation, the commission agreed to fund the creation of a European Thematic Network in the Area of Women's Studies, which is officially due to start in January 1997.

31. For a fuller introduction to the NOI♀SE network, which is coordinated at Utrecht University see Rosi Braidotti, Esther Captan, and Christine Rammrath, "Introduction: A Noisy Tale," *Women's Studies Quarterly* 374 (1994), pp. 209–14.

32. Which to date are: Antwerp (Belgium); Bielefeld (Germany); Bologna (Italy); Dublin (Ireland); Madrid (Spain); Odense (Denmark); Paris (France); Thessaloniki (Greece); Turku (Finland); Utrecht (the Netherlands); York (United Kingdom).

33. This scheme is jointly sponsored by the Division of Education (DGXXII) of the European Commission and by the International Education Office (FIPSI) in Washington, D.C. A consortium of U.S. and European universities, led respectively by Rutgers and Utrecht, submitted an application in 1996. At the time of writing, the outcome is yet unknown.

34. West, op. cit., p. 137.

35. Johnson, op. cit., p. 23.

36. Judith Butler and Joan W. Scott, in Judith Butler and Joan Scott (eds.), "Introduction," *Feminists Theorize the Political* (New York: Routledge, 1992), pp. xiii–xvii.

37. Derrida was refused chairs at the University of Nanterre, at the Sorbonne, and at the College de France; Irigaray never held a teaching position since she was sacked by Lacan in 1974; Deleuze, Lyotard, and Cixous went on teaching at Vincennes/Saint Denis, which is a university whose degrees are not officially recognized by the French education ministry and is conse-

quently very marginal to the whole French system. Most of them hold regular jobs in well-
endowed, mostly West Coast, universities in the United States.

38. West, op. cit., p. 5.

39. Ibid., p. 20.

40. Joan Scott, "The Rhetoric of Crisis in Higher Education," in Michael Bérubé and Cary Nelson
(eds.), *Higher Education Under Fire* (New York: Routledge, 1995), pp. 293–304; the citation is
on p. 302.

41. See, in this respect, the very critical review I coauthored with Jane Weinstock of the anthology
New French Feminisms, "Herstory as recourse," *Hecate* 2 (1980); reprinted in *Camera Obscura*
7, 1981.

42. I am thankful to Susan Foster, Sue-Ellen Case, and Susan Jeffords for helping me with this formulation at the conference "Women, Sexuality, and Violence," held at the Annenberg Center,
University of Pennsylvania, March 28–April 2, 1995.

< 26 >

On the Threshold of the Classroom

Dilemmas for Post-Soviet Russian Feminism

Anastasia Posadskaya-Vanderbeck

As I listened to these the conference's many descriptions of identity—of what a feminist is and of what "I am"—I was reminded that one of the roles of the conference was to bridge different constituencies. The session I participated in was the session about bringing feminism into the curriculum, into the sphere of education. In thinking about what to say, I have asked myself why among all the activities that our feminist community in Russia has been trying to do—contribute to the independent women's movement, conduct independent feminist research, and influence the government—the educational part seems to be the most difficult. Finding a theory of feminist education seems to be a step that requires a lot of careful thought because the consequences, positive or negative, could be very crucial for the whole agenda of feminism in Russia.

Two years ago I wrote an article for the Fifth International Interdisciplinary Congress on Women (held in Costa Rica, in February 1993). It was called "Women's Studies in Russia: Prospects for a Feminist Agenda," and a report on the conference was published in *Women's Studies Quarterly* in a special edition devoted to the world view of women's studies.[1] The article gave a brief overview of the development of feminist analysis in studies of economics, politics, legal reform, and mass media, as well as of the development of feminist methodology in social research. Speaking about the impact of women's studies in education, I concluded that "there is practically no integration of women's studies into the sphere of elementary, secondary, and higher education."[2] My main concern at that time was how to maintain a feminist agenda in women's studies with only a few feminist scholars and an emerging independent women's movement. The answer I gave was that in the current situation, the project to develop women's studies was not and could not be confined to the university, and that to be an effective feminist in academia one had also to be a part of a women's movement. At that time I took for granted that everyone agreed about what it meant to be a feminist and to develop feminist research: to be a scholar and an activist at the same time. My concern was, however, about the difficulty—which many feminists in Russia face—of combining research and public activity: to mainstream academics, we are not "pure scholars";

for the women's movement—sometimes—we are too elitist, too academic. Whatever the challenges of building a positive environment for feminism, we strongly believed that only an explicitly political agenda would maintain the feminist content of women's studies.

I think it is important to explore a bit more why it is only now that the feminist community in Russia can speak in practical terms about translating knowledge, research, and practices into the sphere of education. On January 24–25, 1996, the Moscow Center for Gender Studies sponsored the conference "Gender Studies in Russia: Issues of Cooperation and Prospects for Development," which brought together eighty researchers, teachers and activists working on gender studies from fifteen cities in Russia and Ukraine.[3] It was the first such conference in Russia to focus on teaching gender studies. The meeting was historically significant because it initiated a dialogue among previously isolated women's studies educators. The participants in the conference exchanged their views on ways of developing women's studies/gender studies/feminist studies in Russia as a new discipline, what experiences already exist, and what lessons should be learned. For the first time we raised the issue of the language we use; we discussed the pros and cons of Western "imported" concepts and our relations to the newly established, state-approved "feminology" studies.[4] Extensive discussions were devoted to the issues of what to teach, how to teach, where to teach, whom to teach, and how to teach teachers so that feminism will not be lost. A special plenary session addressed the relationship between women's studies and the women's movement.

Why did we not have this focused conversation on teaching feminism right away, in 1988, 1990, or 1993? Let me give here my very subjective answer to this question. We are speaking about years that were revolutionary and hence required immediate political action. That is why we were writing manifestos and declarations, organizing independent women's forums rather then developing curricula and syllabi and offering courses on feminism in universities. Perestroika was happening without women, and it was an immediate political mission of post-Soviet Russian feminism to claim that "democracy without women is no democracy." Politics, not education, was the entry point for feminism.

Before teaching feminism—in order to teach feminism—we had to do feminism. We first had to create Russian women's experiences in contributing to and challenging the processes of democratization in order to be able to learn from and teach about those experiences.

Our agenda during the first period of transformation in Russia, from 1986 to the attempted coup in August 1991, was very much focused on a critique of *perestroika's* project of sending women home.[5] Our critique after 1991 was focused on the lack of a gender dimension in the democraticization project when the concept "women go home" was implicitly endorsed by the new politicians and by all political parties ranging from democrats to all sorts of "nationalists" or "patriots." We tried to bring about an understanding that women should be subjects, not objects, in the transformation of

Russian society. At all times we were working against the current because the language of equality was hardly popular at the time.[6]

Why do we suppose that today we are ready for a crucial move to feminist education? Let me just briefly enumerate the main changes, which, I believe, constitute a new environment for this transition of Russian feminism into educational practice:

1. Over the past few years we have managed to create a number of supportive places to do feminism, from the academy to grassroots networks.

2. A variety of new feminist discourses have been initiated and brought into different locations, from feminist networks and an alternative press to the national mass media and the Duma (the Russian parliament). Among them are gender equality, gender analysis, women and/in politics, violence against women, reproductive rights, and women and privatization.

3. A growing body of Russian-based and internationally informed gender research has been developed in the country.

4. More than twenty gender research and/or teaching programs and courses have been operating or offered both inside and outside the academy.

5. The independent women's movement has been developed into several stable networks of organizations, which coordinate their activities that maintaining and valuing their differences.

6. Over the last four years the independent women's movement has conducted more then forty conferences, seminars, and workshops devoted to different local and national issues relating to the position of women and the movement's development.

7. The "women go home" approach is no longer agreed upon "by default" among Russian politicians.

8. Several government documents have been issued recently, that the women's movement can use in order to claim national resources for different women's programs, including women's studies.[7]

9. There is an explicit demand from the women's movement for feminist educational programs.

10. A number of feminist periodicals have been published and distributed through the independent women's movement networks (*You and We, All People are Sisters, Vestnik of the Independent Women's Forum, Bulletin of the Moscow Center for Gender Studies, FEMINF, Transfiguration*).

11. The independent women's movement conducted several successful advocacy campaigns in the Duma and at the local level. It promoted in the Duma a draft law on reproductive rights in the Russian Federation, instead of a previously considered draft law on family planning. It initiated a campaign against the discriminatory draft law on maternity, paternity, and childhood, providing the political groundwork that resulted in inclusion of an article on equal rights and

equal opportunities for women and men in all spheres of social life to the new constitution of Russian Federation. It is currently campaigning for a nonsexist labor code.

12. A growing collection of classic Western feminist literature has been translated into Russian, which creates a possibility for its broad reading "with Russian feminist eyes" and for cultural translation into Russian social context.[8]

Of course, feminism in Russia has an open agenda. We owe our women and our society a number of vitally important discourses, such as feminist perspectives on nationalism and racism in Russia, the issues of war and peace, gender and the formation of a new class society, the role of international and national capital in the hardships of transition, and a feminist analysis of the activities of the Woman's Party in the Duma. However, I strongly believe that feminist education in Russia has today a solid experiential foundation.

The feminist community in Russia also has been discussing the issue of who will be the students: undergraduate or graduate students, teachers of social sciences and humanities who are willing to integrate women's perspectives into their courses, or activists from the women's movement? Shall we go to universities? To grassroots organizations? The answer has been prepared by the history of the new Russian feminism. We need a variety of courses, for different audiences; sites for teaching should be both at universities and in the movement. We also realize that there is a danger in imposing feminism as a new ideology, if we develop only *one* textbook, even if it is approved by the feminist community. In order to keep a diversity of women's voices we need feminist education to promote its diversity. We should not believe that we already know what feminism and feminisms in Russia are; we have the task of developing the Russian meanings of this notion in our everyday challenges and in our contradictory practices of research, action, and teaching.

In reference to the title of this volume, *Transitions, Environments, Translations,* I would like to bring up several more points. *Transition,* for Russian women, is a transition from being organized from above to being self-organizing, from being positioned by the State or a party, to self-positioning. This is a transition from the society in which possibilities for women's education and women's work outside the home were taken for granted, to a society where the women's movement should secure those values by putting them on the political agenda.

As for *translation,* let me refer to some examples of what I call the "cultural translation," or the contextualization, of Western feminist frames. I think that the integration of the word *gender* (we pronounce it with hard g and r) into the Russian language was very important. It helped us to deal with instrumental approaches to women's and men's roles based on the essentialist notion of the "sexes' natural predestination."[9] Speaking of my own experience, I want to say that, quite remarkably, it was my Marxist education that helped me to accept the concept of gender; it is very Marxist from a methodological point of view. Actually, we deal here with another kind of transition—from the Soviet type of Marxism to its new reading, because it takes time to disentangle Marxism from socialist reality and from the way it was interpreted in our Soviet textbooks.

We also adopted the concept of *equal opportunities* for women and men, which helped us to bring back the notion of "women's liberation" without mentioning the concept of "equality," which had a strong negative connotation of imposed sameness in our postsocialist context. The equal opportunity approach gives us a concept that insists on a kind of equality that presupposes differences. We have to take account of the differences between women so as to distinguish our understanding of gender equality from the one employed by the socialist state, which said, "You are equal," and then explained away inequalities on the basis of the "natural predestination" of women. The new democratic parties argued a reverse logic but achieved similar ends: they would say, "Women are different, so let us completely remove the question of equality from our agenda." We should say that we need both equality and difference. And to explain this we try to use the concept of equal opportunity.

To understand what feminism is about in our country in terms of feminist practice, or "doing feminism," it is important to emphasize *independence* and to try to understand why we always attempt to enhance this concept.[10] We wish to be independent from the state and/or any other political organizations which claim to speak on behalf of women, something which has been a regular practice in Soviet and contemporary times. During the socialist era, both women and politicians got used to the idea that an independent women's voice did not and could not exist in this country. That is why from the very beginning we emphasized the grassroots and self-organized character of our movement. But this approach has its problems, namely the extreme difficulty of association building given the slow, very refined technique that is necessary. This is very different from the way associations are built from the top down, a practice we have long experienced. I would like to illustrate this point by a brief history of the gradual development of the Independent Women's Forum as an example of a new collective feminist identity.

In the summer of 1990, an attempt was made to set up a coalition of independent women's organizations. The declaration was mostly prepared within the Center for Gender Studies, and it was enthusiastically received by a group of seventy women invited to read it. Even now it is used by a number of local women's organizations around Russia.[11] This declaration is known as NeZhDI Manifesto ("Ne ZhDI," or "Do Not Wait," is a Russian acronym for the Independent Women's Democratic Initiative).[12] It was the first time that we used the slogan of our movement: "Democracy without women is no democracy." However, the coalition did not take on real organizational life. I think that one of the reasons for this was the fact that the coalition invited only a limited number of women's organizations to join, and its decisions were made without real participation by others. New women's groups did not want to join somebody else's initiative; they wanted to participate in the process from the very beginning. However, we did succeed in suggesting a feminist agenda that was different from the feminist agenda imposed under socialism, and I think that we did try to develop a more holistic feminist agenda.

The mandate of the Independent Women's Forum is much more substantial than the initial declaration. It was suggested by a group of different grassroots feminist organizations that made a decision to convene the first Independent Women's Forum in Dubna. The first forum, held in 1991 with more than two hundred participants from all over the USSR, had the same slogan: "Democracy without women is no democracy." For the first time in the history of the Soviet state, the final document of the Forum declared that there was discrimination against women in all spheres of social life under socialism and during the time of perestroika.[13] But the problem of organization building surfaced: The contradiction between the attempt to construct an organization and the fear that this organization would monopolize women's voice was very explicit during the first Independent Women's Forum. As a result, the first Independent Women's Forum established the structure of a network, a form of flexible, nonhierarchical ties or connections between individual women and emerging women's groups. At the second Independent Women's Forum in Dubna, at the end of 1992, the different women's groups were already much less afraid of establishing a single organization because we felt that we had had some experience working together, and that this was the type of alliance we needed, one that is not imposed on us.

I want to keep this historical part fairly short, but I should say that I do not want to smooth over this history to say: "Oh, what a beautiful organization we have now." No, to build any kind of institution and to contribute to creating a space for independent women's voices is always painful at a personal level, as many women who already have some experience of trying to do this know. It's not always the work that brings you happiness. But still I feel that we are trying to use this unique chance to reconstruct the forms in which women's voices can be heard in our country, and we all feel that this may be our only chance. If we do not contribute, we are doomed to fail in our attempt to build another kind of society in Russia. We always say that it is vital for us to be together, and at the same time we always say: "Yes, but I'm different, our organization is different." If the choice is to have a "strong" organization or to have a nonhierarchical, flexible structure open to differences and to a diversity of women's voices, we tend to choose the second. We work within this dialogue and this dialectic, between the contradiction of being different and yet having a common goal. But this is not a theoretical discourse for us, or not simply a theoretical discourse; this is a practice of our everyday life, our feminist practice.

Speaking about politics as an entry point for feminism in Russia, I think we also have some lessons to learn. These lessons are about the question of why on some occasions the state could be very receptive to the language of women's equality. For example, in 1993, President Yeltsin issued an order that contained many progressive measures aimed at helping women meet the challenges of the market economy.[14] Unfortunately, this order was a typical paper document; it paid lip service to Russian women but allocated no funds for implementation. From this we drew an important lesson: The state can support the language of emancipation when the women's movement is weak and can't require accountability. There were also other signs of official usage of feminism with similar implications, and they warned us of the need to assess each and every use of the language of equality by state decision makers. The most recent example is the statement of the government of Russia in January 1996, "On a Concept of the Improvement of Position of Women in the Russian Federation," which was made as a follow-up to the Beijing conference on women.[15] Again, we have many good words, actually sometimes direct co-optation of feminist language, but no real resources as well as no mechanisms of accountability—discourse without action. Who is using whom here? Are women using politics, or is politics using women?

Let me cite another recent example of how what looks like a "soft entry point" may in fact be a trap. In December 1994, the prime minister of Russia, Victor Cherno-myrdin, addressed a national conference of women called by state officials with a view toward the Beijing world conference on women. He admitted the existence of discrimination against women in Russian society, and we were amazed. However, very soon we realized the reason for this admission: President Yeltsin wanted to assure himself of women's support, at least at this conference, on the eve of the war against Chechnya. In fact, at this conference a resolution was offered asking the women of Chechnya to oppose their leaders' opposition to Russian rule. Some of us said that this question was not appropriate at a conference about discrimination, that Chechnya was about power, and that if it takes presidents—both Russian and Chechen—to talk to one another in order to prevent war, they must talk regardless of their ambitions. Our group at the conference, the Independent Women's Forum, and those in the audience who didn't support the resolution wrote our own letter to President Yeltsin and Prime Minister Chernomyrdin. It is important to mention here that representatives of the Woman's Party in the Duma at the conference unanimously supported the official resolution. There was a small group of the Independent Women's Forum that refused to be used to legitimate the political decisions of the central government. The war began anyway, but still we believed that it was important not to allow women's voices to be manipulated, even if we were promised important concessions in exchange.

Coming back to feminist education, let us consider where the entry points for women's studies existed and why we were very cautious about immediate "entering." In 1992, I was invited to speak to the minister of higher education in Russia, who had just come back from a UNESCO conference and was intrigued by the idea of women's studies. "If most Western universities have these programs," he said, "why shouldn't we?" He suggested the establishment of a National Institute for Gender Studies following the model of the Moscow Center for Gender Studies. The main task for the institute would be the development of a national curriculum for women's studies, to be widely introduced into the system of higher education in Russia. After initial excitement, my colleagues at the Moscow Center for Gender Studies concluded that the center could not take on this task. Why did we decide not to use this opportunity? We had several related reasons. First, we were concerned that the development of women's studies at schools, in the absence of any broad support from the new women's movement (support that had occurred in the West), could easily turn these programs into tools of central government manipulation. In the absence of the national women's agenda proposed by women themselves, women's studies could be only the realization of a bureaucratic state agenda, resulting in the inevitable discrediting of this initiative. The interest of the minister of higher education was superficial and casual. The institute was supposed to produce "state-approved curricula on feminism." However, we did not, and do not, believe in the state way of "disciplining feminism." We believe that it is our task to keep the dialogues and diversity open to many different women's voices. In addition, we could easily find ourselves trapped by a situation in which funds for the new project could be held up for any arbitrary reason. New ministers would be appointed who had not participated in the UNESCO conference and who would cut the budget; there would always be reasons why the budget should be cut. We risked losing our place in the Academy of Sciences, which, in Russia, is not an educational institution but an independent research institution. If we lost this place, we might not be able to find another roof under which we could continue our work. And finally, maybe most important, we realized that there was a lack of feminist research in contemporary Russia that conceptualized (from a feminist point of view) the experiences of women in our country. Without such research there was no basis for the solidification of a positive environment for women's studies in the academy and in the society.

However dispiriting it may seem, this situation helped us formulate a strategy for the promotion of women's studies in the schools, one we call "go slow." Maybe this doesn't sound very exciting. We emphasize the need to develop a Russian-based body of research, conducted under the auspices of the Academy of Sciences, that can be the core of women's studies educational programs. In other words, we cannot just import Western feminism, even if we like it, to understand Russian society, but rather we must develop the meaning of Russian feminisms while understanding the Russian experience of gendered social interactions. Why is this important? It seems to me that it is crucial for building a women's constituency in Russia, that will be able to contribute independently and actively to social change. This constituency will then be able to evaluate short-term and long-term consequences of recent developments in Russian society for women. Feminism should not be foreign, because if foreign it will be vulnerable to rejection. I also think that the analysis of gender under socialism and during the transition could be an important contribution to the development of a global feminist perspective. The socialist past gave us lessons that feminists in Russia and in the world should not forget. Even the best and most emancipatory agenda is doomed to fail if it is imposed from the top and/or from the outside. The demand for a new agenda should come from civil society, and the labor necessary to the fulfillment of the new emancipatory agenda is the labor which makes civil society possible.

I foresee that the move of Russian feminism to education will open new ventures for environments, translations, and transitions. One of the ventures is to increase the visibility of Russian women's experiences in the context of international women's studies and international women's activities. Translations are not only about translating feminism from English into Russian, Ukrainian, Hungarian, or Polish, but also about translation from Ukrainian, Polish, Hungarian, and Russian into English and other languages. I am sure that global feminism has a lot more to understand from the experiences of the postsocialist countries. And this is, I think, one task of feminists in Russia: to contribute to feminism and to speak about it from a global perspective.

NOTES

1. A. Posadskaya, "Women's Studies in Russia: Prospects for a Feminist Agenda," in *Women's Studies Quarterly* 3 and 4 (fall/winter 1994), pp. 157–71.
2. Ibid., p. 158.
3. A. Posadskaya-Vanderbeck and D. Schultz, "Assessments of Need for and State of Gender Studies in Russia," report to the Shaler Adams Foundation, 1996.
4. "Feminology" chairs have recently opened in several Russian universities, mostly under the initiative of women former professors of Marxism-Leninism. The term "feminology studies" is used in order to distinguish from both too-radical feminist "gender studies" and not-academic-enough "women's studies." At the January 24–25, 1996 conference "Gender Studies in Russia: Issues of Cooperation and Prospects for Development," several representatives of "feminology" studies from Ivanovo and Moscow participated. The conference acknowledged the importance of finding ways of cooperation between "gender studies" and "feminology studies" wherever possible.
5. N. Zakharova, A. Posadskaya, and N. Rimashevskaya, "How We Decide the Woman's Question," in *Communist* 4 (1989). Or in French: "Comment Nous Resolvons la Question des Femmes" in *Sociétés Contemporaines* 2 (1990).
6. These issues are addressed by Russian feminist scholars in Anastasi Posadskaya et al. (eds.), *Women in Russia: A New Era in Russia's Feminism*, trans. Kate Clark (London: Verso, 1994).
7. President Yeltsin's order of April 1993 "On the Urgent Measures for the Advancement of Women's Status in Russia"; the statement of the government of Russia of January 1996, "On a Concept of the Improvement of the Position of Women in the Russian Federation."
8. Miriam Schneir (ed.), *Feminism: The Essential Historical Writings*, Russian edition introduced by O. Voronina (Moscow: Progress, 1994); Betty Friedan, *The Feminine Mystique*, Russian edition introduced by O. Voronina. (Moscow: Progress, 1994). The Russian version of *Our Bodies, Ourselves* was published by Progress in 1995 under the title *You and Your Body*, which is an example of how feminism can be "lost" in insensitive translation.
9. A. Posadskaya, "Changes in Gender Discourses and Policies in the Former Soviet Union," in V. Moghadam (ed.), *Democratic Reform and the Position of Women in Transitional Economies* (Oxford: Clarendon Press, 1993).
10. "From Problems to Strategy": Materials of the Second Independent Women's Forum (Moscow and Hilversum: Moscow Center for Gender Studies and Foundation for Women's Activities Promotions, 1993). In English and Russian.
11. We know about NeZhDI local women's organizations in Kemerovo, Tomsk, Voronezh, Petrozavodsk, Novozybkov, and Naberezhnye and Chelny.

12. "'Democracy Without Women Is No Democracy': A Founding Document," *Feminist Review* 39 (1992), pp. 127–33.

13. *Materials of the First Independent Women's Forum.* (Moscow: Institute for Socio-Economic Studies of Population, 1991). In Russian.

14. See note 7.

15. See note 7.

< 27 >

The Limits of Research

Women's Studies in Ukraine

Svetlana V. Kupryashkina

> When given wings, fly!
> —Lesya Ukrainka, 1901

The word *studies,* when translated into Ukrainian, is a homonym for the word *studio,* meaning an artist's work space. When a group of enthusiastic Kiev scholars were going through the registration process to obtain legal status for the first Ukrainian Center for Women's Studies, the most commonly asked question was: "Where will this place be where women can come and draw pictures?" This reflects both the novelty of the field and the inapplicability of the term "women's studies" within current discourse, as well as the confusion people experience when they encounter it. As a result, the picture that can be drawn of the emergence of women's studies as a discipline, a research field, or even a simple notion is still somewhat erudite. Many details of this picture are still missing. For example: Who embodies feminist ideas? What could be considered an academic base for their development? Whose needs and interests might such an approach articulate? How are the existing curricula to be influenced? And, finally, is this novel approach in any way generated by or connected to any of the existing women's movements?

The field of feminist research in post-Communist countries and in particular in Ukraine, has itself been inadequately researched. It is therefore possible that any assessment of its current status may suffer from eclecticism, as references must be drawn from several different sources and levels of the production of feminist knowledge. There is work being done on this topic both inside the region and outside the region, and different working groups often retain their own theoretical frameworks. Another hazard in attempting such a study would be to limit it to the author's personal experience, however diverse and well grounded, still has its limitations. My intention here, therefore, will be to offer a sketch rather than a complete picture of the possibilities for the development of feminist research in Ukraine, with implications for other republics of the former USSR, and to outline the limits of such research.

The present paper will discuss, first, the lack of feminist presence in Ukraine; second, the appropriation and subsequent discreditation of the socialist feminist agenda for propaganda purposes, such as the recent attempts by women's blocs and women's parties to use feminist rhetoric; third, Western feminist input and its effect, especially as it has added to the confusion about Sovietology-Kremlinology research on women in the USSR; and finally the rationale for developing women's studies in the academy: Are there any perspectives? What are the dangers of appropriating new paradigms? Will there be divisive theoretical splits, a Slavophile feminism versus pro-Western feminism? Will women's studies become a search for national roots? What about the lack of a tradition of feminist interpretation of empirical knowledge?

My general hypothesis is this: The lack of a common discourse between feminists in the East and the West poses serious obstacles to the development of women's studies in Ukraine and makes it difficult for those feminist scholars to join the international feminist community and to influence its ideas.

WHY WOMEN'S STUDIES?

The development of women's studies in post-Communist countries has by and large been generated by two types of change. General structural changes have taken place in the academy that have opened it up to both Western research and funding. These outside sources make it possible to develop independent research initiatives inside and outside the academy. But what motivates this outreach to the West is the deteriorating status of women in the newly established democratic states, the concurrent rise of nationalism with its specific gender politics, and the loss of many legal rights and benefits that the previous system guaranteed. While changes in the academy served as a prerequisite for introducing a new discipline, social changes determined the basis for the development of a feminist agenda. Now, after almost five years of intensive growth, there are women's studies institutions in almost all twenty-four Eastern European and newly independent states. They are situated inside and outside the academy and vary in size, in the issues they address, and in the degree of visibility they attain locally and in the West.

The most characteristic feature of the development of women's studies was, and remains, their efforts to be autonomous. The distance they aim for reflects the lack of recognition accorded them by the more mainstream disciplines in the humanities and the social sciences, but also the wish neither to be caught up in the methodological crisis of those sciences nor to be described in their terms. Under such conditions, feminist research presents a unique vision of changes in society and poses a serious challenge to policy planners and other agents of social change.

Because of its close ties with emerging women's movements and with regional policymakers who demand "scientific explanation" of problems that affect women, feminist research in ex-Communist countries is often a direct response to current issues. Many scholars are directly involved in the activities of women's groups and organizations.

Women's studies is a constantly changing and developing field of knowledge, as more and more issues begin to be realized and understood as issues of feminist concern, and as more and more feminist tools are acquired by scholars and activists. Eastern European feminism cannot always refrain from becoming a simple translation of feminist knowledge from the West. As we mentioned above, there are differences in the production of feminist knowledge in the East and in the West. It remains to be seen what will be the most commonly accepted version of feminism in Ukrainian discourse, and if it is an abridged version of white middle-class American feminism, we must ask why this is so. But if there is a distinctly Eastern European version of feminist studies, then it is important that it be recognized and encouraged as part of a broader feminist discourse, particularly now that Ukraine is a region where women's status is currently being redefined and women's roles in society reversed and sacrificed to the promotion of quasi-capitalist systems.

WOMEN'S STUDIES: HOW?

It is very important to determine, even before elaborating a curriculum for women's studies, whether we can arrive at a mutually agreed-upon understanding of the Communist and post-Communist historical context, and how it affected the lives of women. Currently, no clear consensus on this exists among researchers, as the ideology of the discourse was established before, and remains superior to, its methodology. That is to say, Ukrainian feminists arrived on the scene when most of the issues concerning the position of women in their region had been well established within the framework of the critique of how the "women's question" was solved by Communist countries. Much of Western scholarship falls within the paradigm, which, following the definition of Nora Jung, a Hungarian feminist scholar, has two tendencies: (1) a "focus on failure," in which authors fundamentally opposed to socialism postulate that Communist governments failed to emancipate women despite their commitment to formal equality; and (2) "credit for achievements," in which authors acknowledge that state socialism did to a certain extent promote the emancipation of women.[1] During the decades in which there was no dialogue between scholars in Communist countries and Western feminist scholars, Western-produced research on women in Communist countries started to deviate from feminist analysis and shifted to Sovietology or to other areas of Slavic studies. This shift of focus is not surprising given the heavy ideological component of any such relevant research. Women's position in Communist countries has always been one of the primary political issues in the description and evaluation of Communist societies, and was viewed as such both in the West and in the East.

Therefore, it could not remain long within the realm of scholarship alone. It was this kind of focus that was subsequently adapted by the corresponding research in Ukraine. And at the same time, the broader feminist scholarly community in the West did not scrutinize these developments or was discouraged from, scrutinizing them.

After the political changes in 1991, socialism became increasingly discredited. In the academy, erasing everything associated with Marxist-Leninist analysis was a matter of honor. But in this general housecleaning were also erased pages from the history of nineteenth-century Russian liberalism, which was thought to be somehow associated with Communism but which had in fact produced one of the few manifestos for equality between the sexes: the *Chto Dyelat?* ("What Is to Be Done?") of Nicolai Chernyshevsky.[2] The vacuum in the social sciences and humanities created by this rejection began to be filled either by previously forbidden disciplines such as anthropology, Freudism and neo-Freudism, and modern philosophy or by semiscientific, so-called nontraditional forms of knowledge, often with a religious or occult content. It is this second option that draws response from women, especially those who are living in frustration and misery. In Kiev, one lecture by a visiting Western feminist was held next door to a lecture entitled "Woman in Cosmogonic Processes," which drew large crowds. It is in this very contested environment that contemporary Ukrainian feminists are trying to throw some light on women's, and other societal, issues.

Because there is no well-established place for feminism in Ukrainian society and scholarship, the term requires no accountability either substantively or theoretically. At the same time, those carrying out traditional sociological research and demographic studies on women continue to ally themselves with policy planners who have less than liberal family-planning intentions. Under such conditions, many feminist groups and scholars, worried about current conditions in their countries, were more concerned to cultivate Western connections than to ensure a climate for feminism at home. They did not manage to maintain themselves as a fully visible and recognizable group. Now that the democratic situation is deteriorating and social disparities continue to grow, some elements of the language of "women's issues" have been appropriated by leaders of numerous women's groups with a strong populist, often neo-Communist, agenda. The ease with which candidates, some of them women, in the Ukrainian elections manipulated issues such as discrimination against women and unemployment, mixing them freely with the loss of benefits while introducing the "protection of women and children" as a major plank of their electoral programs, reflects the potential these issues have either for consolidating or for disrupting society. It also demonstrates how the lack of feminist presence in general political debates allows reactionary forces to exploit women's issues for their own use.

In a similar manner, the terms "women's studies" or "courses on feminism" do not always mean the same thing in all places. Some institutions in Ukraine and also in Russia, such as Russian Humanitarian University in Moscow and Slavic University in Kiev, are trying to introduce an old-fashioned model of "higher women's courses" (*bestuzhevsky vyshye zhenskie kursy*, analogous with the "higher women's courses" held in Kiev and Kharkov at the end of the previous century), which aimed at "restoring old traditions in women's education, creating conditions in which to form women as personalities according to the social and cultural peculiarities of their sex, so as to prepare women to be social workers, etc." The justification for such projects often points to the increasing number of women involved in prostitution, crime, and drug use, as well as concern over the "loss of the desire for motherhood in women" and the decreasing birthrate in the region. Another common location is the newly established private universities, often endowed by Western funds, which try to conform to their "Westernized" image by including feminism as part of the philosophical or sociological curriculum.

We must probably conclude that the academy of science in general, and institutions of higher learning in particular, are seriously limited in their ability to incorporate women's studies, first because of the unreformed character of education itself in those institutions and the lack of adequate accompanying disciplines, and second because of the growing commercial pressure that results in the creation of strict hierarchies of university and college departments, ranked according to established disciplinary standards.

WOMEN'S STUDIES: THE CASE OF UKRAINE

There is a long history of community organizing by women in prerevolutionary Ukraine, and then in western Ukraine before 1939. There was also a tradition of Ukrainian liberalism beginning in the mid-nineteenth century. In that period, all progressive intellectuals worked for Ukrainian national emancipation from the Russian tzarist regime. Women were relatively visible in intellectual and public spheres, a tradition that began in the 1870s with figures such as Lesya Ukrainka, Marko Vovchok, and Olga Kobylanska, and continues into the first decades of the twentieth century with women such as Milena Rudnytska and Olga Kobrynska, and even into the next generation of intellectuals in the 1930s and 1940s whose tragic fate it was to be torn between the battle against Bolshevism and collaboration with the Nazis in their struggle for independence.[3] Generally speaking, the individual rights and freedoms of a woman were considered only within the framework of the national cause and mattered only when they coincided with that cause.

Organizations such as the Ukrainian Society of Women in Higher Education had a certain impact on the country's intellectual life, and their representation at the International Federation of University Women enhanced the status of Ukrainian women in general. While many of them did not insist on the term *feminism* as a description, the issues they addressed were genuine women's issues.[4] Unfortunately, in another twist of history, Soviet historiography carefully erased all records from this period, along with many other names and organizations labeled "nationalist."

In intellectual circles of a newly independent Ukraine, feminist ideas have recently started to circulate due to greater liberties in foreign travel and access to previously censored literature. More women academics have taken advantage of opportunities to attend international conferences on women and feminism, to gather and discuss various ideas, and to try to adapt them to the Ukrainian reality. This is how the feminist seminar at the Institute of Literature of the Ukrainian Academy of Sciences, headed by Solomea Pavlychko, was organized. Women active in public life also began to write. The first collection of essays in feminist literary critique of Ukrainian literature appeared in the journal *Slovo I Tchas* ("Word and Time").[5] The Ukrainian Center for Women's Studies was opened as a public organization of women scholars "to enhance the position of women in Ukrainian society, promote research on women, and disseminate feminist ideas." It has a small library of feminist literature and publishes a bilingual newsletter.

In 1992, two Western scholars with Fulbright fellowships brought women's studies courses to Kiev University. Dianne Farrell, from Moorhead University, in Minnesota, taught a course on the history of women in Europe in the Department of Mass Communication and Journalism, and Martha Bohachevsky-Chomiak, from Georgetown University, in Washington, D.C., came to teach in the Department of History. Since the appearance of such novel disciplines was unprecedented in Ukraine, both found it difficult to fit into the standard university curricula, which naturally did not contain women's studies or women's history. The audience was very receptive to their ideas, but some students did not hide the fact that they had enrolled because they wanted to hear lectures delivered in English or learn more about America. In addition, the courses were not offered for credit and thus did not require an adequate level of commitment from the students. Because these are the predominant conditions in which women's studies courses are taught in Ukraine, many Fulbright fellows (and many who come with other sources of funding) do not feel at ease with the Ukrainian educational system, which is only now beginning to be restructured.[6]

The experience of these two American scholars in academic positions in Kiev reminded us how incongruous most of these approaches were within our system of education. It also reminded us of the difficulty we have had in choosing terms: Women who develop research on women inside or outside academic institutions try to replace the term "women's studies" or "feminism" with "gender research" because they think it is more neutral. There is a need to know how women's studies programs were integrated into the curricula of Western universities, but the fact that most of the literature is available only in English considerably limits the number of people able to study the program. Language, therefore, must be considered another factor that limits development of women's studies in Ukraine. This is a difficulty that will persist until feminist knowledge is produced in adequate amounts in local languages.

For these and other reasons, the future of women's studies most probably lies outside of the institutes of conventional learning. The critical breakthrough may be achieved by the creation of women's libraries and women's information and resource centers that are free from academic requirements, where women academics still will be able to teach and work with women in a systematic and less controlled manner. Many of them exist but are poorly funded. Because access and enrollment in such programs will be based on individual commitment and voluntary activities, they will inevitably bring about a more positive response to the issues of women and so generate feminist consciousness in a productive manner.

NOTES

1. N. Jung, "East European Women With Western Eyes" in *Stirring It: Women's Studies and Feminist Practice* (London: Francis and Taylor, 1994).

2. Nicolai Chernyshevsky, *What Is to Be Done? Tales About New People* (London: Virago Press, 1982).

3. Lesya Ukrainka (the literary pseudonym of Larysa Kosach, 1871–1913) is the most famous Ukrainian poet and playwright. Her name, along with that of Taras Shevchenko, serves as a symbol of the Ukrainian nation.

4. One of the best references for this historic period may be found in the book by Martha Bohachevskv-Chomiak, *Feminists Despite Themselves: Women in Ukrainian Community Life, 1884–1939* (Edmonton, Alberta: University of Alberta, Canadian Institute for Ukrainian Studies, 1986).

5. Solomea Pavlychko gives a vivid description of her turn to feminism in *Letters from Kiev* (New York: St. Martin's Press, 1992), which is also a wonderful diary of the events in Ukraine of that time. She also talks about the change of attitudes it brought to her within academia.

6. The humanities were the field most strongly affected by ideologization during Soviet times. An entirely new discourse has to be created, both for research and instruction. Martha Bohachevsky's impressions of Ukrainian educational system, the treatment of women in academia, and her experience of work with Ukrainian students are widely presented in her publications, such as "Rediscovering the Humanities in the Ukraine," *Humanities: The Magazine of the National Endowment for the Humanities* 15, no. 3 (1994).

< 28 >

Feminisms in an Islamic Republic

Afsaneh Najmabadi

Is it possible to imagine optimistically a future for feminism in Iran? Recent intellectual and cultural developments and the remarkable blooming of women's creative productions in Iran over the past decade make this query less fanciful than it may appear at first. Sixteen years after the 1979 Islamic revolution in Iran, not only have women not disappeared, they have an unmistakably active presence in public life. For a secular feminist, it is very tempting to claim that Iranian women have achieved all this despite the Islamic Republic and even against Islam as the dominant discourse in the country.[1] Indeed, for some women it has been this deep existential sense of proving themselves against all odds that has become the creative energy of their productions. Yet it is not only oppositional reactive energy that accounts for this creative outpouring. The rise of the Islamic movement in the 1970s in Iran signified the emergence of a new political sociability and the dominance of a new discourse, within which Woman, standing for culture, occupied a central position. In this paradigm, the imperialist domination of Muslim societies was seen to have been achieved not through military or economic supremacy, as earlier generations of nationalists and socialists had argued, but through the undermining of religion and culture, and that undermining was achieved through women. Woman became bearer of the burden of cultural destruction.[2] This centrality of gender to the construction of an Islamic political discourse turned what had been marginal, postponed, and illegitimate into something central, immediate, and authentic. The "women question" acquired urgency, not only for the discontented, but even more so for the supporters of the new order and for women and men who had power. In particular, women in sympathy with and as supporters of the Islamic Republic were placed in a position to take responsibility for its misogyny: to deny it, to justify it, to challenge it, to oppose it, but not to ignore it. Moreover, the Islamic Republic's claim that its kind of polity is the ideal solution for all societal problems has put it in a continuous contestation with feminism as far as women's issues are concerned. It exists under the pressure of outdoing feminism.[3]

Whereas during the reign of the Pahlavis women's activism and feminism had been scripted by the opposition, secular or Islamic, as a discredited venture in the service of the state or as foreign colonial importation, both have now become authentic, ironically opening new possibilities for growth of all kinds of feminisms—including secular. New configurations of Islam, revolution, and feminism are now emerging. A number of women's organizations and institutes and a variety of women's journals now published in Iran attest to the significance of these reconfigurations. The three journals, *Zan-i rūz*, *Farzaneh*, and *Zanān*, which I will discuss in the rest of this paper, are interconnected by genealogical affiliation and current ideological self-definition.

Zan-i rūz ["Today's Woman"] is part of an important publishing conglomerate that goes back to the time of the shah. Benefiting from the financial, human, and political resources of that institution, it was taken over in the postrevolutionary period by a group of Islamic women activists who turned it into a successful platform from which to mount a campaign against some of the worst onslaughts against women's positions in the early postrevolutionary years and for improving women's rights in the new Republic within an Islamic framework.[4]

Farzaneh [The Wise Woman] is a more recent venture. It was launched in the fall of 1993 as a "Journal of Women's Studies and Research" under the editorship of Mahboobe Ommi and as a publication of the Center for Women's Studies and Research, headed by Moneer Gorgi, the sole woman representative in the 1979 Assembly of Experts that drafted the Islamic Republic's constitution. In the English editorial of its first issue, Mahboobe Ommi argues that

> in every corner of the globe Women's Studies is presently a well recognized necessity and an essential component of social, cultural and economic development. Women's Studies emerges as an important area of academic research not only as a solution to women's issues themselves but as a key to many socio-economic predicaments.[5]

At the same time, the editorial firmly distances itself from feminism:

> Encountering women's issues with a biased inclination towards women as a particular social strata has proven to be inefficient. Feminism, now branched and divided according to various tendencies, seems to face a serious crisis as a natural consequence of the course it has embraced. Instead of isolating women's issues from the mainstream of human life and societies, and dealing with her from a prejudiced, woman-centered, woman-oriented viewpoint, feminism could have chosen to consider the woman in the context of her natural identity and role, to lay emphasis on the rapidly disintegrating family and her central part in that institution, and finally to balance her dynamic relationship with her society both male and female.[6]

To appreciate the tension in this editorial, which goes from arguing for the necessity of a women's studies center and journal, on the one hand, to rejecting the woman-centeredness of feminism because it was potentially subversive, on the other, we need to look at an earlier point of tension introduced by Ommi in the Islamic discourse on feminism. Two years earlier, Ommi had authored a series of mildly polemical articles in *Zan-i rūz*.[7] Unlike common dismissals of feminism as a sign of the "social deviation of Western women" and their "Weststruck" counterparts in the "non-West," a common tactic of both Islamic and secular political thought in Iran, Ommi's rhetoric in these articles centered on accepting the historical validity and positive contributions of feminism for the West. It defined feminism "as a set of philosophical, economic, political, and social solutions which enables the women's liberation movement to emancipate women from the injustices arising from discriminations between men and women."[8] At the same time, it emphasized that "feminist thinking is only compatible with the intellectual climate of the West," where misogynous religious and secular thought produced it as a reaction against beliefs, laws, and practices that treated women as inferior to men.[9] Ommi's line of argument, by abandoning Islamic universalism—that is, by accepting that in other times and places, other solutions to problems of social injustice had validity—produced tensions that the author seemed unwilling to resolve. Throughout the articles she raised a number of significant questions and left them unanswered. For instance, after pointing out that it was necessary to deal with issues raised by feminism now that "feminism has some supporters in Iran and there are even attempts afoot to Islamicize it," she asked rhetorically, if not unambiguously, "but is an Islamic feminism indeed a realizable/unavoidable matter?"[10] An answer implicit in the rhetoric of Ommi's articles would be that since Islam did not share the misogynous concepts of Christianity and Judaism, there did not seem to be any grounds for feminism in an Islamic country. Yet it is significant that despite the author's promise to deal with this question in the final installment of the articles, she never took it up. One can conjecture that this might very well have been a time of disputes and uncertainties for her as the editorial in the first issue of the new journal registered an important shift of perspective. In the earlier essays, the differences between the "West" and "us" had been emphatically constructed so as to exclude the desirability of feminism by limiting the grounds for feminism to the West. In the editorial the same differences were now largely employed to convince a presumably skeptical reader of the necessity of developing local, nationally sensitive research and solutions to an unproblematically evident and accepted "womens' question" in Iran. Nonetheless, feminism in the pages of *Farzaneh* continues to be projected as the unacceptable boundary not to be crossed, demarcating the borders of the new journal's identity. In a critical review of a book, for instance, the book is criticized for "mixing valuable historical research with feminist proclamations," for being "influenced by extremist feminist writings," and for offering solutions that are "translations of feminist literature."[11]

It is within this discursive map that the emergence of the journal *Zanān* (edited by a former editor of *Zan-i rūz*) marks an important watershed. In its three years of publication, the journal has embarked on a project of thorough and radical interpretations of Islamic sources concerned with women's rights. Although there is a history of interpretive attempts within Islam to deal with questions posed by modern transformations of Islamic societies, including the "woman question," which date from the mid-nineteenth century, *Zanān*'s interpretive venture is novel in a number of ways which promise to make their overall interpretive strategies productive of cultural change and social power for women.

The predominant method of reformist interpretation of women's issues has been the use of more woman-friendly sources from an already existing set of authoritative exegetical texts. This confined the reinterpretive attempts within a highly misogynist canon, producing an endless array of contradictory positions for reformers. With rare exceptions, *Zanān*'s authors do not use this technique. They engage in direct interpretations. It is this assertive move to take charge of the canon and reinterpret it thoroughly from a woman's perspective that has brought the fire of the more traditional Islamic advocates upon them. Muzhgān Kīānī Sābit, a critic of the journal, states categorically: "All laws of the Islamic Republic of Iran are derived from Ja'farī [Shī'ī] rules and jurisprudence. . . . Therefore, any criticism of the Islamic laws weakens the faith and belief and religion of Islam."[12] Further, she argues that "what constitutes the majority or consensus opinion of the clergy . . . is impossible to revise or oppose. Opposing these laws constitutes opposition to the holy law-maker, that is, God Almighty."[13] Despite such threatening warnings, the journal continues to engage in reinterpretation and defends it as a right not only for every Muslim, but even for non-Muslims. Such a radical expansion of the domain of interpretation is further insisted upon when another author suggests that not only does Islam need to be reinterpreted and new laws deduced according to the needs of the time—which is a well-established ground for reformist currents in Islam—but that such revisions should be also carried out in the light of "contemporary schools of philosophy and thought."[14] This level of openness to influences from "the outside," so to speak, contrasts with the usual hostility toward all that is branded as foreign to Islam, an attitude obsessively cultivated by most ideologues of the government and Islamic leaders of the country.

Whereas dominant Islamic discourses on women—misogynist or reformist—have grounded their case for differences of rights in differences between women and men in creation, writers of *Zanān* interrogate these accepted connections between differences-in-creation and social responsibilities and rights of women.[15] They argue for equality of rights of women with men. Insisting on the distinction between equality and sameness, Zuhrah Zāhidī, in an artide entitled "Rehabilitating Eve," notes in passing some of the physical and temperamental differences attributed to men and women, asking: "But do such differences . . . mean privileging one over the other? Difference does not mean superiority. It just means difference. When we talk of equality, we mean equality of rights of human beings. Discrimination on any basis, whether racial, gender or class, is counter to this concept of equality."[16]

This move, similar to and informed by discussions of the social construction of gender differences, has enabled these writers to draw vastly different conclusions about gender relations in an Islamic society.

Instead of beginning with creation as a narrative of the origins of women's rights and responsibilities, they place the individual woman, in her contemporary social concreteness, and her needs and choices at the center of their arguments. The introduction of each individual woman's choice and autonomy into an Islamic discourse is one of the significant innovations of *Zanān*. Various authors in this journal carry this notion into their reinterpretations of Islamic sources, a move that opens up a new discursive space for conversations between secular and Islamic feminisms in Iran.

In a series of articles, the journal took up controversial issues such as whether women could become judges, exercise power of interpretation, and become ruler/jurisprudent. Needless to say, their answers to these queries were affirmative. Men and women are considered equal in their ability, as well as their obligation, to pursue and seek knowledge, to take up any profession, to implement justice, to seek spiritual perfection, and to reward and punish; they are also equal in their obligation toward social improvement. These moves toward describing women as equal with men are subsequently expanded to the possibility that women could hold such positions as membership in the Council of Guardians (which checks all legislation passed by the parliament to ensure it does not contravene Islamic precepts), commander of the armed forces, and ruler/jurisprudent, the highest position of political power in the new Iranian state, first occupied by Ayatollah Khomeini and since his death by Ayatollah Khāminah'ī.[17]

While the writers of *Zanān* use the familiar reformist historicizing or contextualizing arguments in order to delimit the effective field of Qur'anic verses to particular times, places, and circumstances, and while they have also introduced some new interpretive strategies, perhaps what is even more notable is that they carry out these interpretative ventures in a different social space. They appear in the printed pages of a women's journal in a public space rather than the private chambers of a religious scholar. They speak as "public intellectuals" rather than as private teachers. Their audience is other women (and men) as citizens, rather than theological students and other clerical commentators. They write not in order to command the believers into obedience, but, as they put it, in order "to awaken women" so that they would proclaim their rights.[18] This new public space for interpretation of canonical theological texts is in part produced as an unintended consequence of Khomeini's doctrine of the rulership of jurisprudence, which became encoded into the new Iranian constitution. Where the jurisprudent is granted the power of political rule and the constitution is said to be derived from canonical texts, every citizen, by virtue of the rights of citizenship, becomes entitled to take charge of these texts and to exercise the power of interpretation. That women interpreters have now positioned themselves as public commentators on these texts promises that any future democratization of politics might not remain an exclusively masculine preoccupation. *Zanān*'s approach thus produces a radical decentering of the clergy from the domain of interpretation by placing woman as interpreter, and her needs as grounds for interpretation, at the center of their revisionist efforts.

Zanān has displayed a very different attitude toward feminism. More often than not, Iranian women's response (secular or Islamic) to attacks against feminism has been one of gender conservatism and Westophobia: that is, to distance themselves from any identification with feminism on the grounds that it is threatening and Western. *Zanān*, on the contrary, has built itself in affiliation with feminism. It freely translates from Western feminist journals and writers (including Gilman, de Beauvoir, Woolf, and Faludi) whatever it judges useful to its readership. It has begun, in its own work, to weave new textual connections between Muslim women and Western feminism. It has also endeavored to overcome the current state of suspicion and hostility between women who reside in Iran and those who, in the aftermath of the 1979 revolution, either left or were forced to emigrate. The dominant Islamic writings continue to mark Iranian women abroad as corrupt "escapees" of the old regime, monarchists, and leftists—in a word, as culturally inauthentic, morally corrupt, and politically alien. Secular women who continue to reside in Iran consider their counterparts abroad to be women who have chosen the easier option of exile instead of the hardships of staying and struggling inside and who are therefore cut off from and ignorant of the realities of daily oppression experienced by those inside. For their part, most secular Iranian women abroad consider those inside as either supporters of the regime, or as those who have subsequently compromised themselves in order to survive, or as silent victims that need a voice outside. *Zanān*'s approach opens up the possibility of productive cooperation between Iranian women across the borders of their current residences.

Finally, *Zanān* has broken down the dichotomy between secular and Islamic women in Iran itself. Not only are its pages open to the contributions of well-known secular and non-Muslim women, but it has also embraced and made its own the tradition of secular women writers and poets of the previous decades, constructing a combined geneology for Iranian feminism. It is precisely this gesture that is deemed dangerous by critics of the journal. Bādāmchīān, advisor on social issues to the head of the judiciary, in a letter to the editor, reprimands her for forgetting that "the martyrs of Revolution ... shed their blood so that ... true Islam will survive ... and colonialists would no longer be able to introduce corrupt and loose women ... as symbols of free and progressive women."[19] Another critic similarly takes the journal to task: Does the journal not know "what a deep chasm separates today's responsible Iranian woman from the woman of yesterday who was favored by a monarchical society?"; "Do the people in charge of *Zanān* deny the fundamental and principal differences between women of our society today and women of prerevolutionary society that they seek to use the well-known feminist ideas of the time of the monarchy?"[20]

The alarming tone of these attacks against *Zanān* speaks to an ideological panic.

What is perceived as threatening is the reversal of an important historical trend within which the West and the East, modernism and Islam, feminism and cultural authenticity, have been constructed as exclusionary categories, forcing Iranian women to choose between claims to a cultural self and those to a feminist self.[21] What has proved so useful to ideologues of the Islamic Republic, however, has been anything but empowering to Iranian women. It has become almost a self-evident truth to consider Iranian (and Middle Eastern) feminism as born, originated, and formed under the ideological influence, if not the colonial tutelage, of the West. In response, there has been a rejection of the "Western-oriented" feminism of the "elite" and/or a search for a more culturally authentic genealogy for women's rights, thereby authorizing one tendency against another. But Iranian women who raised their voices for women's rights, from the late nineteenth century onward, did not constitute themselves in these late-twentieth century categories. They made rhetorical use of any available position to invent a female-friendly discourse. When pointing to "advances of women in other countries" (and these other countries included not only Europe and the United States, but in Iranian writings also China, India, Japan, and the Ottoman Empire), they were not "the blind imitators" and "inauthentic apers of the West" they were made out to be by the later ideologues. When taking advantage of the widespread acceptability of the "new sciences" as the alchemy of the civilizing progress to argue for the education of women, they used modernist and Islamic justifications to inscribe and constitute their new selves as literate citizens. Though there were contestatory positions on these issues, they were not consolidated as incompatible and contradictory positions, one negating the other. In the early years of the constitutional regime in Iran—that is, in the first two decades of the twentieth century, and in the pages of the constitutionalist press and the early women's journals of the 1910s and 1920s, there were a wide spectrum of positions coexisting and arguing with each other on issues related to women. While the anticonstitutionalist forces grounded their political opposition in their interpretations of Islamic precepts—for instance, arguing that new schools for girls were an example of the abrogation of the laws of God—advocates of the new schools also drew from the same sources, using, for instance, prophetic narratives as arguments for female education. In other words, clerical voices were not allowed to monopolize Islamic truth. The rift between traditionalist and modernist women, though an important part of the modernist and counter modernist discourses on women from the mid-nineteenth century became consolidated into negating categories during the Pahlavi period. This change resulted largely from particular sets of state policies initiated by Rizā Shāh, and the reaction of the clerical establishment to those policies in which both sides demarcated mutually hostile territories. Twice, once in the 1930s and once again in the 1950s and 1960s, the Pahlavi state closed off all possibilities for independent women's initiatives and took over the "women question" as a domain of state policy. In response, in each period, the clerical faction opposed to any changes in women's social conditions constructed women's liberation as state policy that was un-Islamic, illegitimate, and corrupt. Thus the modernist state and the Shi'ite clergy constructed each others' domains of authority and produced Islam and feminism as mutually exclusive, so much so that many of us continue to find the category of Islamic feminism difficult to imagine, and a feminist Muslim an impossible identity.[22]

The emergence of *Zanān* as a vocal women's position is a radical break from this past. By opening up the domain of interpretation to nonbelievers and non-Muslims, by insisting on the equality of women and men in all areas, by disconnecting "natural or created differences" between women and men from the cultural and social constructions of gender, *Zanān* has opened up a new space for dialogue between Islamic women activists and secular feminists that begins to reverse a sixty-year-old rift in which each treated the other as antagonist.

This move also has the possibility of reaching across yet another divide: that between women of the Muslim majority in Iran and women of other denominations. The interpretive strategies in which the authors of *Zanān* engage have precedents in Jewish and Christian feminist rereadings of Biblical and Midrashic sources. These alternative feminist traditions could build a new space for dialogue among women of these communities with Muslim and secular women in Iran.[23]

What will come about from these new possibilities is, of course, not predictable. It will in part depend on how secular feminism relates to and takes part in these remappings, whether it reacts to it defensively or engages with it constructively. In Iran there are already signs of cooperation and a new recognition that the old exclusionary categories need be abandoned. Secular feminists, non-Muslim authors, and Islamic feminists contribute to the pages of *Zanān* with no worry about crossing the old boundaries. Outside the country, however, the reception of the emergence of an Islamic feminism has been marked by a great deal of anxiety, if not outright hostility. Fears among many secular Iranian feminists that the Islamic appropriation of feminism will further reduce their already precarious space continue to project these spaces as mutually exclusive of one another, rather than envision a reconfiguration of a political and cultural space in which women of different outlooks can have a common stake in its production.

Zanān has begun to construct an Iranian feminism that does not draw its identity from counterposition of an Islamic/traditional/authentic geneaology versus a secular/modern/Westernized one. By inventing new visions and revisions of Islam and simultaneously constituting itself as the "greening hands" of secular feminism, it has audaciously confused our comforting categories of "Islamic" and "secular." By echoing Woolf, Gilman, de Beauvoir, and Faludi while speaking at once Qur'ānic verses, Zoroastrian texts, and Sufi writings, it has made West and East speak in a new combined tongue. Iranian secular feminism needs a similar boldness of vision and generosity of imagination to redefine itself.

NOTES

1. For some recent secular feminist perspectives on women in post-revolutionary Iran, see Haideh Moghissi, *Populism and Feminism in Iran* (London: Macmillan, 1994); Mahnaz Afkhami, "Women in Post-Revolutionary Iran: A Feminist Perspective," in Mahnaz Afkhami and Erika Friedl, (eds.), *In the Eye of the Storm: Women in Post-Revolutionary Iran* (London: I. B. Tauris, 1994), pp. 5–18; and Valentine M. Moghadam (ed.), *Gender and National Identity: Women and Politics in Muslim Societies* (London: Zed Books, 1994), particularly chapter 6, pp. 110–47, "Modernity, Islamization, and Women in Iran," by Nayereh Tohidi.

2. For a fuller discussion, see Afsaneh Najmabadi, "Power, Morality, and the New Muslim Womanhood," in Myron Weiner and Ali Banuazizi (eds.), *The Politics of Social Transformation in Afghanistan, Iran, and Pakistan* (Syracuse: Syracuse University Press, 1994), pp. 366–389.

3. Headlines from the government-supported English-language journal *Mahjubah: The Islamic Magazine for Women*, published in Tehran by the Islamic Thought Foundation, provide an expression of such contested claims: "Zimbabwe Women in Uphill Fight for Equality" (*Mahjubah* 13, no. 12 [December 1994], p. 25) reports that "of ten state-appointed governors who run the country's eight provinces, only one is a woman." (Never mind that there are none in Iran!) Other headlines from 1994 issues of this journal include: "Sexual Harassment at the United Nations" and "Combatting Sexual Harassment at Work," no. 4 (April 1994), pp. 5 and 6 respectively; "Violence Against Women," no. 5 (May 1994), pp. 23–24; "Discrimination Against Woman Persists Despite Progress," no. 6 (June 1994), p. 29; "Women and Development in the EROPA Conference," no. 7 (July 1994), p. 20; "Female Genital Mutilation in Southern Nigeria," no. 8 (August 1994), p. 27.

4. See Manijeh Saba, "Tahlîlî az dîbâchah'hâ-yi *Zan-i rūz* dar dawrah-i ba'd az inqilāb," *Nimeye Digar* 1, no. 14 (spring 1991), pp. 8–34.

5. Mahboobe Ommi, "Women's Studies: The Indispensible Cultural Factor," *Farzaneh* 1, no. 1 (fall 1993), pp. 1–4; quote from p. 3.

6. Ibid., p. 2.

7. Mahboobe Ommi, "Fiminîzm az āghāz tā'kunūn," *Zan-i rūz*, part 1, no. 1342 (December 14, 1991), pp. 10–11 and 58; part 2, no. 1344 (January 4, 1992), pp. 12–13; part 3, no. 1345 (January 11, 1992), pp. 24–25; part 4, no. 1346 (January 18, 1992): 32–33; and part 5, no. 1347 (January 25, 1992), pp. 28–29.

8. Ommi, "Fiminīzm," part 1, p. 11.

9. Ommi, "Fiminīzm," part 5, pp. 28–29.

10. Ommi, "Fiminīzm," part 1, p. 11.

11. Sa'īd 'Uryān, "Dar sāyah" (review of *Shinākht-i huvīyat-i zan-i Irānī dar gustarah-'i pīsh'tārīkh va tārīkh* [Tehran: Rawshangaran, 1992]) by Shahla Lahiji and Mihrangiz Kar, *Farzaneh* 1, no. 2/3 (winter-spring 1994), pp. 305–12; quotes from pages 306, 307, and 308 respectively. The usage of *feminism* for marking off political boundaries of acceptability is not limited to Islamic currents. Here is an example of a socialist paper's similar usage: "The Iranian women's movement in exile suffers from dispersion, passivity, and the penetration of feminist influences. We should struggle for the formation of independent women's movements geared towards concrete goals and programs, devoid of feminist tendencies" (*Payām-i kārgar* 81 [March 1991], as quoted by Moghissi, op. cit., p. 187).

12. Muzhgān Kîānî Sābit, "Naqd-i sukhanrānī-yi Khānum Mihrangīz Kār," *Zanān* 2, no. 14 (October-November 1993), pp. 42–49. Quote from p. 42.

13. Ibid., p. 44.

14. Zaynab al-Sādāt Karmānshāhī, "Jāygāh-i zan dar fiqh-i kayfarī-yi Islām," *Zanān*: part I, 2, no. 13 (September 1993), pp. 56–60; part II, 1, no. 15 (December 1993–January 1994), pp. 52–55; part III, 3, no. 16 (February–March 1994), pp. 38–44. Quote from part I, p. 56.

15. The differences between reformist and misogynist uses of the differences-in-creation argument are of course important, despite their common ground. Whereas misogynist positions use these differences-in-creation to argue for superiority of men over women, the reformist positions argue that in God's view, superiority arises only from superior piety and religiosity. Gender differences should thus not be used for giving more social worth to men compared to women. They should be taken as value-neutral differences. For a critical review of these positions, see pp. 41–51 of Nahid Yeganeh, "Women's Struggles in the Islamic Republic of Iran," in Azar Tabari and Nahid Yeganeh (eds.), *In the Shadow of Islam: The Women's Movement in Iran* (London: Zed Press, 1982).

16. Zuhrah Zāhidī, "I'ādah-'i haysīyat-i Havvā," *Zanān* 3, no. 16 (February-March 1994), pp. 2–6; quote from p. 4.

17. For a detailed discussion of these issues as explicated in the pages of *Zanān*, see the expanded version of this essay that appears in *Islam, Gender and Social Change: A Reconstituted Tradition*, edited by John Esposito and Yvonne Haddad (Oxford University Press, 1996).

18. Zaynab al-Sādāt Kirmānshāhī prefaces her article on the criminal code in these words, "This essay is a critical discussion in order to help legislators to revise laws; it is not meant as a discussion pertaining to religious opinions [fatwa] and innovations [bid'at]." ("Jāygāh-i zan dar fiqh-i kayfarī-yi Islām," part I, p. 56.)

19. Asadallāh Bādāmchīān, "Bidūn-i sharh . . . ," *Zanān* 3, no. 19 (August–September 1994), pp. 9–11. Quote is from p. 11.

20. Nāsir Haqjū, "In qāfilah tā bah hashr lang ast," *Kayhān-i havā'ī* 1113 (28 December 1994), p. 8.

21. For an eloquent presentation of dilemmas and difficulties of claiming a feminist room of one's own, faced by an Iranian secular feminist, positioned in the crossfire of Iranian socialist antifeminism, Islamicism, anti-Orientalist ethnocentrism, and Western feminist cultural relativism, see the introduction, pp. 1–20, in Moghissi, op. cit.

22. It is not accidental that the centralization of the state and of the clerical hierarchy occurred as twin social processes in these two crucial periods and around importantly gendered themes, in the first around women's veil, in the second around women's vote. See Michael Fischer, *Iran: From Religious Dispute to Revolution* (Cambridge, MA: Harvard University Press, 1980), especially pp. 108–23, "The Religious Establishment and the Expanding State."

23. Perhaps the single most difficult divide to cross would be recognition of the Baha'i nd Babi traditions, both denied status of religious minorities in the Iranian constitution, banned and persecuted. It is unlikely that the journal could risk embracing Qurrat al-'Ayn, the female leader of the Babis. On Qurrat al-'Ayn, see Farzaneh Milani, *Veils and Words: The Emerging Voices of Iranian Women Writers* (Syracuse: Syracuse University Press, 1992), pp. 77–99, and Abbas Amanat, *Resurrection and Renewal: The Making of the Babi Movement in Iran, 1844–1850* (Ithaca: Cornell University Press, 1989), pp. 295–331.

< 29 >

Comparative Perspectives

Alice Kessler-Harris

In the subtext of this rich array of papers lies a crucial message about women's studies: all the authors agree that everywhere the field holds the key to the transformative potential of the current women's movement, capturing its hopes and possibilities as well as its tensions. A shared set of assumptions about the relationship between how women think and what they can do guides their discussions. Rooted in the sense that the production of knowledge about gender has been shaped by historical circumstance and appropriated to affirm and perpetuate inequality, women's studies practitioners share a commitment to demystifying the intellectual and political limits on women's lives. To intervene in that reciprocally confirming process, practitioners of women's studies believe, is necessary to diffuse the use of sexual difference as a weapon in the ongoing battle for power. Broadly conceived as the project of educating women and men to explore the history and uses of gender relations, women's studies forwards the search for gender equity through the creation and dissemination of knowledge. It seeks to do this in the context of academic and political activism framing new knowledge with theoretical and explanatory content that enhances understanting of how equity might be achieved.

But a shared project does not necessarily imply shared stategies, and questions about how to breathe content into women's studies lie at the heart of these papers. What is the relationship between feminism and women's studies? Are academic women's studies most effectively rooted in the soil of women's movements? Is the university the right place for women's studies? What about freestanding research centers? Or journals that can spread ideas more freely than institutional structures? What is the effect of these decisions on how women think about their past and future? For these authors, issues of location provide the boundaries within which the field operates and the opportunities it presents. As each author takes on the task of describing and analyzing the meaning and purposes of women's studies, she reformulates the meaning of the field and measures its possibilities for achieving gender equity in the context of particular cultures and traditions. The result is at first disconcerting: an apparent fragmentation and disruption of the larger effort. But a second look reveals the crucial importance of location as the fulcrum that enables conversation among the authors as well as between them and the denizens of Western feminist thought against which they align themselves.

In its literal and tiered meanings, but even more in its symbolic uses, location serves to warn scholars of women's studies to identify and problematize their own positions. Among these scholars it also announces the interdependence of new ideas on inevitably diverse contexts. Location sometimes identifies an intellectual environment within which knowledge is produced and that informs and sometimes circumscribes the thinking of women's studies theorists, as for example, in the notion of "Western feminist thought." It often distinguishes a geographical arena with a particular set of economic constraints and gendered social expectations. It shapes intersecting spatial patterns between religion and politics, for example. In these papers, it frequently defines social contexts (such as communities of poverty, or sex-segregated educational institutions) within which the idea of women's studies is received, reshaped, and created anew.

The resulting differences in perspective, and sometimes passionate disagreements, are swathed in efforts to reconcile the commitment to affirming distinct situations with the effort to achieve a common meaning for feminism. So, for example, the authors raise fundamental questions about the relationship of indigenous to Western feminist theory, about appropriate structures for housing women's studies in different cultural and geographical contexts, and about how to create a "feminist" women's studies. Answers to these questions demand the most intimate knowledge of gender and national politics as well as familial and economic structures. They require theoretically sophisticated positions on pedagogical and practical issues. The structural and theoretical problems with which these authors grapple constitute a rich demonstration of the complexities of thinking about multiple forms of "women's studies" within the situational contexts in which it is conceived.

Some simple illustrations will make the case. Permeating the papers is a lengthy debate over efforts to acknowledge the importance of Western feminist thought, on the one hand, and a sense of its limits, on the other. Rejected as universally applicable, Western feminist theory serves nevertheless as counterpoint and touchstone to reveal the particularities of other theoretical models. The phrase "Western feminism" sometimes serves as a code word for the form of neocolonialism that substitutes the imposition of ideas for that of economic and political power. At the same time, it points up the centrality of theory in capturing information exchange. For example, the authors of these papers puzzle over how the international feminist community can function as a source of inspiration to women who operate in particular cultural contexts without promulgating resistance to the imposition of foreign ideas. Writing about Ukraine, Svetlana Kupryashkina is most eloquent in making this point, arguing that in the post-1990 effort to wipe out socialist thought, some key achievements in the emancipation of women were repressed. She fears that distorted perspectives on women's condition, coming from ultimately from both Eastern and Western feminists, may have discredited feminist thought for the long term. Russian Anastasia Posadskaya-Vanderbeck concurs in the importance of developing a national constituency of women who can both contribute to changing women's lives and and evaluate the consequences of change: "We cannot just import Western feminism, even if we like it, to understand Russian society, but rather we must develop the meaning of Russian feminisms." (p. 380).

But the problem is less one of accepting Western feminism or not than of coping with the mechanisms of change that feminist thought of all kinds introduces. Afsaneh Najmabadi suggests that this was the issue boldly faced by the Iranian women who founded the journal *Zanān* and other women's journals. Their successful search for a "culturally authentic genaeology for women's rights" relied on the use of Islamic rhetoric and justification, which they refused to set up in opposition to Western models. In Najmabadi's view, women's reliance on familiar language and tradition created and nurtured an oppositional culture that could survive within a repressive Islamic regime. Yet Western feminism was not irrelevant to Iranian women. It provided them with illustrations of structures and strategies within which they could debate interpretations of women's positions.

In opposition as well as in inspiration, "Western feminism" remains a problematic concept containing a range of meanings within it. Rosi Braidotti interrogates some of these meanings as they emerge in the sometimes negative impact that American interpretations of European feminist thought have had on American academic practice as well as theory. In her view, the dominant theoretical component of what we call Western feminism has been a somewhat abused French feminist theory. As this theory has crossed international borders within Europe, it has become enmeshed in, even partially become a product of, new constructions of European unity and identity. These efforts to make use of feminist theory to enhance the project of supranational unity have masked the tendencies of American feminism to focus on multiculturalism and diversity. The resulting disservice, from which Americans are only beginning to disentangle themselves, also serves non-Western states with strongly rooted cultural traditions poorly as well.

The Western model of the apparently benign state seems to attract as much distrust among women in non-Western countries as Western theory, particularly with respect to how the state functions in relation to universities—the main vehicle for constructing and disseminating women's studies the world over. Western feminism and the U.S. model, which locates women's studies (research and teaching) within universities, casts a deep shadow over the possibilities elsewhere. For all the disagreements that beset advocates of women's studies in the United States, the field appears from abroad to have benefited from its association with academia. The university has offered financial support, physical space, access to good minds, and a degree of legitimacy. All of these have contributed to the rapid expansion of women's studies, lending it an aura that extends beyond national borders. But the university may have subverted the goals of women's studies as much as it has sustained them. Arguably, it has enabled women's studies to engage in the antiracist and transformative mission of the multicultural agenda and to participate in efforts to evaluate the sensibilities within that an oppositional consciousness can emerge. But these have come at a cost which is evident on several fronts. Women's studies remains only loosely connected to its original roots in women's organizations, and most observers would argue that the enterprise is now committed more completely to transforming institutions than to changing society. Those who see the university as a restrictive site for women's studies comment on its enforced adherence to academic hierarchy in place of democratic participation; its financially and structurally imposed constraints on feminist pegagogy; the constraints it imposes on scholars' efforts to move beyond the reification of Western thought; the limits traditional disciplinary organization imposes on scholarly imagination; and the isolation of intellectuals from activist influences and connections.

These positive and negative effects are enhanced in the thought of non-Westerners by the close connection between most national states and their university systems. With the Soviet experience in mind, Posadskaya-Vanderbeck and Kupryashkina challenge the possibility for independent thought and action in educational and research environments that are in any sense dependent on the state. So painful has been the Russian state's insistence on representing the voice of women in the past, Posadskaya argues, that feminists should shy away from allowing it any role in their work. State officials may articulate the language of equality, but women cannot hold them accountable for their promises. Posadskaya-Vanderbeck's mistrust extends to the institutions the state regulates and controls. Faced with the choice of merging an independent gender studies center with a university and garnering state support, she and her colleagues refused the invitation. Despite the temptations of financial security and of developing a national curriculum for women's studies, she and her colleagues were skeptical. "We were concerned that the development of women's studies at schools in the absence of any broad support from the new women's movement . . . could easily turn these programs into tools of central government manipulation." In the abence of women's input, she suggests, "women's studies could only be the realization of a bureaucratic state agenda" (p. 380).

It is not always clear where the sites of greatest freedom for women lie. In contrast to the United States and much of Europe, where women's claims to knowledge were initially sustained by independent women's movements, those claims seem to emerge more diffusely in religious states such as Iran. Najmabadi validates the journalistic strategies of Iranian women as being among the few paths open to them that are both consistent with their traditions and tolerated by an otherwise restrictive state. But she suggests that Iranian women may also find havens inside the university, where women are solicited to contribute to debates around cultural change and policy decisions on women's issues. In an atmosphere in which women are encouraged to express a public voice, women may be less inhibited by the twin pressures of Islamic clerics who are simultaneously government officials. Najmabadi notes approvingly the process of initiating university-based women's studies programs as vehicles for consolidating women's voices and making them more powerful.

A similar effort to articulate new visions among women occurs in India, according the report of Zakia Pathak. There, however, a secular political environment imposes pressure and foments questions about how women's voices are to be heard. Pathak describes the protests of Indian women students who were prevented from inviting to campus the representative of a particular political party. When the young women, instead of observing the time-honored technique of passive resistance or the sexually validated route of silent protest, responded with destructive rampages and a hunger strike, sympathy for their cause plummeted. The incident serves to alert Pathak to the importance of a pedagogy that acknowledges tradition and yet draws on a variety of feminisms to illustrate the emergence of new ways of thinking about women. For her, the great danger to Indian women's studies lies in a stifling pedagogic uniformity that threatens to subvert the political consciousness of students and teachers alike. Her message is not entirely pessimistic. A feminist pedagogy, she proposes, would permit the adoption of an ironic stance—a stance that would enable the interrogation of traditional values in the interests of creating a feminist politics. But she cautions us that there is danger in irony. Like an uninformed pedagogy, it can readily "abort an oppositional consciousness." Pathak describes the struggles within an Indian women's college to reconcile efforts to construct a feminist pedagogy that has an explicit political component with refusal to allow support for a particular political party.

These challenges might give American feminists pause as to the constraints that universities impose on their own capacity to think freely. Braidotti cautions women's studies practitioners to beware of how they are caught in the vortex around "political correctness." She might have illustrated her point with the growing numbers of "antifeminist feminists" who, in the name of resisting efforts to categorize women's studies along with Marxism, cultural studies, and multiculturalism as simply another politically correct program, seek to place it in more disciplinary contexts. Kupryashkina, too, suspects the traditional biases of institutions of higher learning. The "unreformed character of education" and "the growing commercial pressure that results in the creation of strict hierarchies of university and college departments," she argues, limit their ability to house women's studies.

It is not merely incidental, then, that the search for a viable location for women's studies takes place in a variety of geographical and intellectual locations that profoundly affect the conception of women, the practice of women's studies, and the policies that seem desirable. Braidotti's faith in the capacity of Western and non-Western women to successfully create a usable theory, Kupryashkina's decision to opt for community-based women's studies supported by women's organizations, and Pathak's willingness to create a theory that interrogates the intersections between Indian activism and Western literature are all products of different cultural traditions and institutional locations. Indeed, the question of where to constitute the search for knowledge is among those over which the authors disagree most vehemently, raising questions about the relationship between the construction of theory and the structures within which it is produced, regulated, and disseminated.

If these papers do not provide any answers, they do offer a rich array of material illustrating the wide range of solutions to some fundamental political questions that have stymied Western women's studies and encouraged efforts to reach beyond its current borders. On the theoretical front, they demonstrate how attention to the multiple meanings of feminism provides access to a conversation about its shared sources and goals. These papers alert us to the importance of naming feminist research and clarifying its uses as part of the continuum of research and also in opposition to it. They diffuse the notion that the field is still concerned with old problems of binary oppositions such as women's studies/gender studies or West/East divisions thus moving forward the arena of debate to more complex relational questions. Second, these papers problematize narrower forms of university-based women's studies as sources of social change, particularly as they query the university's ability to move beyond disciplinary boundaries. All of the authors speak to the importance of recognizing women's particular economic positions and cultural traditions in identifying appropriate venues for exploring change, and they juxtapose these against histories of the state and of party politics. Though the relationship between the location of women's studies and policies toward women are not explicitly interrogated here, the implication of these papers is that they too require formulating within the multiple and layered contexts of nations and cultures. Third, and finally, in raising questions about the location of women's studies, its practice and practitioners, these papers speak to a complicated and diverse array of mechanisms for the appropriation of cultural meaning. Their surprisingly different approaches evoke possibilities for constituting the culture of gender as a central focus of inquiry. Together, they suggest the fundamental political importance of addressing issues of what kinds of teaching/learning situations can most effectively enable the development of knowledge about women in radically different contexts.

Contributors

Bina Agarwal is professor of economics at the Institute of Economic Growth, University of Delhi. She has written extensively on environmental issues, technological change, poverty and inequality, and women's status, especially from a political economy and gender perspective. Her latest book is *A Field of One's Own: Gender and Land Rights in South Asia* (New York: Cambridge University Press, 1994).

Tsehai Berhane-Selassie is a visiting assistant professor at Tufts University. She has written on women and development in Ethiopia with special attention to women's economic and military roles in African societies.

Rosi Braidotti holds the chair of women's studies at the University of Utrecht. She is the author of many works on feminism and feminist theory and is the organizer of the Erasmus network for a Europe-wide graduate curriculum in women's studies. Most recently she is a coauthor of *Women, the Environment and Sustainable Development: Towards a Theoretical Synthesis* (London: Zed Books, 1994).

Lin Chun teaches at the London School of Economics and is the author of *The British New Left*. She returns to China frequently and recently visited a number of places undergoing profound changes, including the collective farm she was assigned to during the Cultural Revolution. She is now at work on a book on political emancipation in China, with a special interest in the experience of women.

Jacklyn Cock is professor of sociology at the University of the Witwatersrand. She has written extensively on gender, environmentalism, and militarization issues in South Africa. She is the author of *Maids and Madams: A Study in the Politics of Exploitation* (Johannesburg: Ravan Press, 1980; London: The Women's Press, 1989); *Colonels and Cadres: Gender and Militarisation in South Africa* (Cape Town: Oxford University Press, 1991); and coeditor of *Society at War: The Militarisation of South Africa* (New York: St. Martin's Press, 1989), and *Going Green: People, Politics, and the Environment in South Africa* (Cape Town: Oxford University Press, 1991).

Krassimira Daskalova teaches history at Sofia University in the Center for Theory and History of Culture in Bulgaria. She has written on the history of the book and on aspects of women's history in nineteenth- and twentieth-century Bulgaria. She has recently finished research on women, gender, and transition in Bulgaria.

Myra Marx Ferree is professor of sociology and women's studies at the University of Connecticut. She has published numerous articles on German feminism, including most recently: "Making Equality: The Women's Affairs Officers in the Federal Republic of Germany" in Dorothy Stetson and Amy Mazur (eds.), *Comparative State Feminism* (Beverly Hills: Sage, 1995); "After the Wall: Explaining the Status of Women in the Former GDR," in *Sociological Focus* (1995); "'The Time of Chaos Was the Best': Mobilization and Demobilization of the East German Women's Movement" in *Gender and Society* (1994). She is currently working on a large collaborative project analyzing abortion discourse in German and American newspapers from 1962 to 1994.

Malgorzata Fuszara teaches at the Institute of Applied Social Sciences and is head of the Center for Socio-Legal Studies on the Situation of Women in Warsaw. Widely published in Polish, English, and German on law and gender, she is now working on abortion rights, feminism, and the construction of the public sphere in Poland.

Milica Antić Gaber is a research assistant at the Faculty of Arts, Sociology Department, University of Ljubljana. She is currently involved in work on women and politics, with a special interest in strategies to promote women in politics. She has published several papers and articles in Slovene and English journals and books; the last was on women and elections in Slovenia.

Susan Gal is professor of anthropology at the University of Chicago. She is the author of a book on linguistic change in Austria. Her current work focuses on language ideology as well as the poetics and performance of political rhetoric in socialist and postsocialist societies. She is also co-editor of a forthcoming book on women, gender and the transition in Eastern Europe.

Yaakov Garb, a member of the Program on Science and Technology at the Massachusetts Institute of Technology, works on environmental issues from the perspective of cultural history. He has published articles on political ecology, ecofeminism, and conceptions of the "whole earth."

Evelynn M. Hammonds is an associate professor of the history of science in the Program in Science, Technology, and Society, Massachusetts Institute of Technology. She is working on a study of the representation of African-American women in AIDS narratives.

Hana Havelková is assistant professor at the Institute of Humanities, Charles University, in Prague. She lectures on social theory and gender and feminist theories. She has edited *Human Rights, Woman and Society* (Prague: ESVLP, 1992); a gender issue of the Czech Sociological Review (1995); and *Is There a Central European Model of Marriage and Family?* (Prague: Divadelní ústav, 1995). Her most recent article is "Ignored but Assumed: Family and Gender Between the Private and Public Realms," (in the English issue of the Sociological Review, Prague [forthcoming]. She is a board member of the International Association of Women Philosophers and the Gender Studies Foundation in Prague. She speaks from her research and writing on private and public subjectivity and citizenship for women in the Communist and post-Communist period.

Cora Kaplan is Professor of English at the University of Southampton, England. Her work on contemporary feminism includes *Sea Changes: Essays on Culture and Feminism* (London: Verso, 1986). She is completing a book on the rise of racial thinking in Victorian Britain.

Debra Keates is finishing a dissertation in the Humanities Center at the Johns Hopkins University.

Alice Kessler-Harris is professor of history at Rutgers University. She directed the women's studies program there from 1990 to 1995. Her publications include *Out to Work: A History of Wage-Earning Women in the United States*; *A Woman's Wage: Historical Meanings and Social Consequences*; and *Protecting Women: Labor Legislation in Europe, Australia and the United States, 1880–1920*, which she coedited with Ulla Wikander and Jane Lewis.

Djurdja Knezevic has degrees in history and archeology from the University of Philosophy in Zagreb, where she is currently the coordinator of the Women's Infoteka (the Women's Information and Documentation Center). She has recently published "'We' vs. 'I' in Feminism: The Problem of Political Identity in Croatia," in *Travelling through European Feminism* (Utrecht, 1993), "Women from the Former Yugoslavia: Three Years After," in *Dokumentation* (1994), and "Violence Against Women in the former Yugoslavia: Tools of the Nationalist Mobilization or a Starting Point for Feminist Self-organizing," in *Beitrage zur Feministischen Theorie und Praxis* 37 (1994).

Svetlana V. Kupryashkina is Director of the Ukrainian Center for Women's Studies. A linguist who has translated Western feminist writings, she has lectured widely in Britain, the United States, and Europe on women in the former USSR. She explores the difficulties and possibilities of interpreting and appropriating Western feminist ideas in the Ukrainian and Russian contexts.

Sabine Lang is a research and teaching associate in political science at the University of Leipzig, Germany. She has previously worked as director of communications for the Berlin Ministry for Labor Affairs and Women. Her publications include articles on the development of the public sphere as well as on feminist politics and the women's movement in Germany.

Eva Maleck-Lewy studied at Humboldt University in East Berlin and received her Ph.D. at Lomonossow State University in Moscow. She is currently a lecturer at several German universities and is also at work on a research project about women's political participation and the East German women's movement. She is one of the cofounders of the East German Independent Women's Association (UFV). She has published numerous articles, coedited four books, more recently with Virginia Penrose, *Gefährtinnen der Macht* (1995). She is the author of *Und wenn ich nun schwanger bin? Frauen zwishen Selbstbestimmung and Bevormundung* (Berlin: 1994).

Afsaneh Najmabadi teaches women's studies at Barnard College. Trained first as a physicist in Iran and then as a sociologist, Najmabadi is now working on a book about women and nation building in Iranian history. She has also written on current feminist movements in Iran and their relation to the Islamic regime.

Zakia Pathak taught English literature at Miranda House, University of Delhi. She has practiced and written about the pedagogical implications of feminist theory.

Andrea Petö is an assistant professor at the Central European University, Department of History, Budapest, teaching courses on comparative social history and women's history. She publishes on Hungarian women's employment and women's movements in transitions from a Central European perspective.

Anastasia Posadskaya-Vanderbeck is founding director of the Moscow Center for Gender Studies. She has a Ph.D. in economics from the Russian Academy of Sciences, Institute of Economics (1989). She was a member of the organizing committee of the first, and cochair of the second, Independent Women's Forums in 1991 and 1992. She was a member of the Commission on the Issues of Women, Family and Demography, established by President Yeltsin (1993–1995). She is currently at work on an oral history project in collaboration with Barbara Engel, "A Revolution of Her Own: Retrieving the Voices of Old Women in Russia."

Mamphela Ramphele was deputy vice chancellor and is now Vice Chancellor of the University of Cape Town. In that position she is responsible for promoting gender and racial equality among students and staff. Trained first as a physician and then as an anthropologist, she is coauthor of *Uprooting Poverty: The South African Challenge*;

author of *A Bed Called Home* (a book on migrant labor hostels); and coeditor of *Bounds of Possibility*, a study of the legacy of Steve Biko.

Renata Salecl, a philosopher and sociologist, is a researcher at the Institute of Criminology at the Faculty of Law, Ljubljana, Slovenia. She also teaches at the New School of Social Research and Cardozo School of Law, both in New York. Her publications include *The Spoils of Freedom: Psychoanalysis and Feminism After the Fall of Socialism* (Routledge, 1994), *Politik des Phantasmas* (Turia und Kant, 1994), *Die Shatten der Liebe* (Turia and Kant, 1996), and *Love and Gaze as Love Object* (coedited with Slavoj Žižek; Duke, 1996).

Joan Wallach Scott is professor of social science at the Institute for Advanced Study. The author of *Gender and the Politics of History* and a coeditor, with Judith Butler, of *Feminists Theorize the Political,* her most recent book is *Only Paradoxes to Offer: French Feminists and the Rights of Man.*

Svetlana Slapsak is senior lecturer of Balkanology, women's studies, and modern Greek, Department of Sociology of Culture, University of Ljubljana. A 1992 PEN Award winner, she is currently working on the gendered languages of ethnicity and nationalism.

Ann Snitow teaches literature and gender studies at Eugene Lang College and the Graduate Faculty of the New School for Social Research. A feminist organizer in the United States since 1969, she has written widely about women's writing and women's movements and, since 1990, has worked on feminist issues in East-Central Europe and the former Soviet Union as one of the founders of the Network of East-West Women.

Noël Sturgeon teaches in the Women's Studies Department at Washington State University. Her book *Ecofeminist Natures: Race, Gender and Transnational Environmental Politics* will be published by Routledge in 1997.

Anna Lowenhaupt Tsing is professor of anthropology at the University of California, Santa Cruz. Tsing is the author of the much acclaimed *In the Realm of the Diamond Queen: Marginality in an Out-of-the-Way Place.* She is working on a project that examines the local, national and international conflicts around the exploitation of rainforests in Indonesia.

Peggy Watson is at the Faculty of Social and Political Sciences, University of Cambridge, United Kingdom. She has contributed chapters on gender, feminism, and the democratization of Eastern Europe to a number of recent collected volumes. These include: "The Rise of Masculinism in Eastern Europe," in M. Threlfall (ed.), *Mapping* *the Women's Movement* (London: Verso, 1996); "Marriage and Mortality in Eastern Europe" in C. Hertzman et al. (eds.), *Environmental and Non-Environmental Determinants of the East-West Life Expectancy Gap in Europe* (Boston: Kluwer, 1996), and "(Anti)Feminism After Communism" in A. Oakley and J. Mitchell (eds.), *The Backlash Against Feminism* (Harmondsworth: Penguin, 1997). Her book *Civil Society and the Mobilization of Difference in Eastern Europe* is to be published by Polity Press.